School of American Research
Advanced Seminar Series

DOUGLAS W. SCHWARTZ, GENERAL EDITOR

SCHOOL OF AMERICAN RESEARCH
ADVANCED SEMINAR SERIES

Late
Lowland
Maya
Civilization

Georges and Florence Dapples
are gratefully acknowledged
for their thoughtful interest
in the programs of the
School of American Research.

Late Lowland
Maya Civilization
CLASSIC TO POSTCLASSIC

edited by Jeremy A. Sabloff
and E. Wyllys Andrews V

A SCHOOL OF AMERICAN RESEARCH BOOK
University of New Mexico Press   •   Albuquerque

Library of Congress Cataloging-in-Publication Data
Main entry under title:

Late Lowland Maya civilization.

(School of American Research advanced seminar series)
"A School of American Research book."
Bibliography: p.
Includes index.
1. Mayas—Antiquities—Addresses, essays, lectures. 2. Indians
of Central America—Antiquities—Addresses, essays, lectures.
3. Indians of Mexico—Antiquities—Addresses, essays, lectures.
4. Central America—Antiquities—Addresses, essays, lectures.
5. Mexico—Antiquities—Addresses, essays, lectures.
I. Sabloff, Jeremy A. II. Andrews, E. Wyllys (Edward
Wyllys) III. Series.
F1435.L38   1985   972.8'01   85-16513
ISBN 0-8263-0836-8

*To the archaeologists
of the Carnegie Institution of Washington,
who led the way*

PREFACE

The Advanced Seminar entitled "After the Fall: New Perspectives on the Postclassic Period in the Maya Lowlands" was held at the School of American Research in Santa Fe, New Mexico, October 18–22, 1982. The participants (with their institutional affiliations at the time of the seminar) included Jeremy A. Sabloff (University of New Mexico) and E. Wyllys Andrews V (Middle American Research Institute, Tulane University), co-chairmen; Anthony P. Andrews (New College of the University of South Florida); Joseph W. Ball (San Diego State University); Arlen F. Chase (University of Pennsylvania); Diane Z. Chase (University of Pennsylvania); David A. Freidel (Southern Methodist University); Arthur G. Miller (University Museum, University of Pennsylvania); David M. Pendergast (Royal Ontario Museum); Prudence M. Rice (University of Florida); Fernando Robles C. (Centro Regional Sureste, Instituto Nacional de Antropología e Historia); and Gordon R. Willey (Peabody Museum, Harvard University). Willey and Freidel wrote their papers approximately a year before the seminar, in order to provide the participants with general overviews of some of the problems to be talked about in Santa Fe. The other participants circulated their papers from one to four months before the seminar. All the participants had the opportunity to revise their papers after the very lively, provocative, and intellectually stimulating discussions. Gordon Willey agreed not to change his paper, so that it could stand as a yardstick against which many of the new ideas presented at the seminar could be measured. Charles Lincoln (Harvard University) and Don Rice (University of Chicago) also were invited to contribute papers to this volume (Lincoln's was circulated several months before the seminar). The editors of this volume prepared their contributions, the introductory and summary chapters, after reviewing the revised papers in the spring and summer of 1983. Final revisions to all the papers were made by the summer of 1984.

The idea for this Advanced Seminar was originally suggested by Douglas W. Schwartz to Sabloff in 1979. Sabloff enlisted the collaboration of Andrews V, and we then began to plan the Seminar. By the end of 1979, we submitted a formal proposal for an Advanced Seminar to the School of American Research, and this proposal was subsequently approved. In the proposal we argued:

[Post-A.D. 800] studies have, until recent years, been the "poor relative" of lowland Maya archaeological research. With most attention focusing on the Classic Period, the Postclassic was generally relegated to a relatively minor role in Maya development, particularly as regards the time after the decline of Chichen Itza. This neglect was coupled with favored treatment of sites in the southern lowlands at the expense of the northern portion of the Yucatan Peninsula.

Fortunately, the past decade has seen the redress of this imbalance. Beginning with the major Mayapan and Dzibilchaltun Projects of the 1950s and 1960s and culminating in a host of projects in the 1970s, Postclassic research has entered a boom time. Recent fieldwork in Yucatan, Campeche, Quintana Roo, Belize, and the Central Peten has uncovered information which is significantly changing the traditional views of Maya archaeology. Moreover, archaeologists are coming to realize that Postclassic materials are quite relevant to many important theoretical questions of current concern in American archaeology. With many of the recent Postclassic projects now completed or nearing completion, the time is ripe to bring together many of the scholars involved in the Postclassic "renaissance" to consolidate new knowledge, programmatically examine future directions for research, and discuss appropriate methodologies and research strategies which might be utilized in such research. Given the School's sponsorship of the "origins," "settlement," and "collapse" Advanced Seminars, it would be fitting indeed for the School to complete the cycle by hosting the "Postclassic" Seminar.

With the recent growth of interest in Terminal Classic/Postclassic research, we had the good fortune of having a large number of potential contributors upon whom we could have called to participate in this volume. We chose a group of scholars whose research, we believed, was having or could have a significant impact on previously held conceptions of the post–A.D. 800 era in the Maya Lowlands. We were particularly interested in including those archaeologists who could focus attention on what had traditionally been seen as the Classic-Postclassic transition and its immediate aftermath since we felt that much of the new research in the Lowlands held greatest implication for older, entrenched models of this time period. Under the constraints of the limited number of people who can participate in an Advanced Seminar and the general page limits of an Advanced Seminar volume, we were forced to be highly selective. Clearly, there are many scholars who might have made important contributions to the volume who are not represented in these pages. We also actively tried to include additional archaeologists from Mexico in this volume, but despite our efforts, only Fernando Robles from the Centro Regional Sureste (I.N.A.H.) was able to contribute. Finally, we also invited a couple of scholars whose synthetic abilities we greatly respect.

As always, the support of Douglas W. Schwartz and his staff and Jane Barbarousse and her staff at the Seminar House was simply superb. We also wish to take this opportunity to thank Doug Schwartz for going out of his way to support the four Advanced Seminars (so far!) on the ancient Maya and to recognize the important role he has played in facilitating the advance of Maya studies. We hope that the significant ideas put forth in this volume will have as productive an impact on the field of Maya archaeology as did the three previous Maya archaeology volumes in this series. Finally, we deeply appreciate the critical help of Wendy Ashmore and Jane Kepp in the preparation of this volume.

Jeremy A. Sabloff

E. Wyllys Andrews V

Contents

PART ONE
Background

1
Introduction

JEREMY A. SABLOFF

University of New Mexico

E. WYLLYS ANDREWS V

Middle American Research Institute, Tulane University

Archaeologists' understanding of pre-Columbian cultural development in the Maya lowlands is just beginning to come into its own. A variety of new fieldwork, research interests, and analyses have begun to bring about wholesale changes in the ways in which scholars view the growth of ancient Maya civilization. This is an exciting time in Maya archaeology, although currently there is much uncertainty about how all the new pieces of knowledge about the Maya will fit together. Such uncertainty is particularly evident in regard to the post–A.D. 800 era in Maya development. Long neglected by Maya archaeologists relative to the great attention placed on the Classic Period, problems in Postclassic archaeology are now being attacked from a number of directions. As a result, the papers in this volume are, of necessity, quite diverse. In addition, they raise a host of culture-historical and processual questions and problems that, owing to our relative lack of control of basic chronological data, are simply unanswerable.

Given the penchant of Mayanists to argue endlessly about currently unanswerable questions, the Advanced Seminar participants might justifiably have succumbed to the temptation of surrendering themselves to such fruitless yet immensely enjoyable debate. Fortunately, we often were able to rise above such squabbling and focus discussion on the immediate implications of recent research. Many times, in fact, the tenor of the conversations, which we believe is clearly reflected in the written papers, was directed at identifying important questions about the Classic-Postclassic transition and subsequent developments and at looking for feasible ways to examine and test these questions now and in future research.

Although the chapters that follow vary widely in content, geographic and chronological emphasis, and opinion, certain themes appear again and again. Several of the most significant themes are critically addressed in our concluding chapter to this volume. As a way of introducing readers to the diversity of ideas represented herein, it seems worthwhile to comment on the three sections (consisting of eleven chapters) that make up the bulk of the book. It should be stressed that these comments represent our personal views and not necessarily those of the participants.

As will become clear in the chapters that follow, authors have different ways of labeling the centuries that came at the end of the Classic Period and immediately followed it (about A.D. 800–1250). What one contributor calls the Terminal Classic is for another the Early Postclassic and for another the Terminal Classic and Early Postclassic. The choice for each author was determined by the area and the problems with which he or she was trying to come to grips, and we were unable to agree on a standard terminology for the period. This problem lies at the very heart of our study. Another issue often not explicitly dealt with is the use of terms that equate, in a sort of shorthand fashion— not, we hope, in confusion—data categories with each other and possibly with ethnic groups. An example is the rather broad use of such terms as "Toltec" and "Puuc" to denote ceramic units, architectural styles, and peoples.

The Overview section consists of four papers by Gordon Willey, Fernando Robles and Anthony Andrews, Arlen Chase, and Charles Lincoln. Willey presents what might be termed a traditional view of the Postclassic, Robles and Andrews paint a new and strikingly different picture of the northern Maya area in the Classic and Postclassic periods, and Chase and Lincoln offer controversial arguments for a new Postclassic chronology and a new perspective on Chichen Itza, respectively.

Gordon Willey's essay provides a clear, concise synthesis of current published data on the Classic-Postclassic transition and the Postclassic Period. Willey graciously consented not to revise his paper significantly

4

after the seminar so that his overview could stand as a benchmark against which the new interpretations might be compared. The traditional view as presented by Willey is built on a chronological framework that emphasizes successive cultural climaxes from the Late Classic in the Southern Lowlands to the Terminal Classic in the Puuc region to the Early Postclassic at Chichen Itza. Furthermore, a significant cultural gap is postulated following the "collapse" of Classic Maya civilization in the Southern Lowlands. As the other participants argue throughout the rest of this volume, these traditional "givens" are no longer tenable in light of the data gleaned from recent research. As the seminar participants quickly realized, however, these older perspectives have become so ingrained in our thinking and so color our interpretations that it is harder to break away from them than we might have thought (witness the bias inherent in the Classic/Postclassic terminology and how this terminology unconsciously affects our thinking). These perspectives have in effect become assumptions, and it is usually harder to change them than to try to accommodate divergent data to these perspectives. Nevertheless, although the participants often disagreed as to the nature of such changes, they unanimously agreed that some changes are necessary and that the time to make these changes is now.

Several particular revisions came to the fore in the seminar and are discussed at length in our concluding chapter. First, there appear to have been two distinct architectural/artistic climaxes in Late Classic–Terminal Classic–Early Postclassic times: one in the Southern Lowlands between A.D. 600 and 800 and another in the Northern Lowlands between A.D. 800 and 1100. Moreover, the latter climax apparently occurred about the same time at the Puuc region sites and at Chichen Itza. Second, strong cultural continuities seem to exist between these two climaxes, and the significant disjunction occurs not with the "collapse" of Classic Maya civilization but with the demise of Chichen Itza as a major political center.

It should be stressed that we would not argue that the traditional view is wrong and the newer views propounded in this volume right. Rather, expanding research in the Northern Lowlands and in relatively late sites suggests that the relationship of Classic to Postclassic in the Maya Lowlands was much more complex than heretofore postulated.

Most summary articles and general books on the ancient Maya in recent years have concentrated on sites, events, and problems in the

Southern Lowlands. The Northern Lowlands receive either very limited coverage or a treatment that omits consideration of much of the recent literature and is therefore somewhat out of date. The first half of the chapter by Robles and Andrews provides an antidote for this malady. They describe in some detail the major projects and publications of the past ten or fifteen years, especially the more recent ones. A great part of this work has been done by the vastly expanded Centro Regional Sureste of the Instituto Nacional de Antropología e Historia, directed from 1973 to 1982 by Norberto González Crespo.

The second half of Robles and Andrews's paper draws on this recent research, especially on the data from Coba and the East Coast, to create a picture of late northern prehistory that differs substantially from earlier reconstructions. They suggest that the northern Maya area was divided into major spheres from the Formative Period until the Spanish conquest: one centered in the west and central part of the peninsula, with a number of important centers that changed through time and that controlled large, often competing polities; and the other dominated by one massive site, Coba, throughout the Classic Period and into the Postclassic.

Toward the end of the Classic Period they see the beginning of social and political disintegration in the Northern Lowlands, caused primarily by increasing demographic pressure, without the possibility for technological advances in food production that seem to have been important in the South. The entrance of the Itza, a foreign elite, was in a sense the culmination of many years of external pressure. Upon entering the peninsula, they established control over Chichen Itza, much of the northern coast, and the preexisting trade networks. The military skill of this group enabled them to impose a tribute system, perhaps including human labor, that hastened the downfall of other large sites in the West. Their sphere, however, never included Coba, which for some two hundred years was able to withstand pressure from the West. Its eventual collapse in about A.D. 1100 may have been caused in part by Itza control of circumpeninsular trading routes and sites along the coastal frontiers.

In the East, Robles and Andrews note, no one Late Postclassic site in the province of Ecab seems to have been significantly larger than the rest and, they suggest, this reflects a political decentralization in marked contrast to the western consolidation of power at Mayapan. To this extent, then, they interpret the Late Postclassic in the northern

Maya area as a drastic restructuring of earlier political and economic systems.

Few Mayanists today espouse a correlation of the Maya and Christian calendars at 11.3.0.0.0; the large majority prefers instead the Goodman-Martínez-Thompson solution, which places the arrival of the Spaniards shortly after 11.16.0.0.0 in the Maya Long Count. No other correlation today commands wide support.

Arlen Chase makes a vigorous appeal in his chapter for the later correlation at 11.3.0.0.0, marshaling evidence of several kinds from archaeology and ethnohistorical sources. Following Kirchhoff and Kubler, he argues that more than one calendar was in operation in the Northern Lowlands during the Postclassic. One, he believes, is presented in the Chilam Balams of Tizimin and Mani and in the first part of the Chumayel, while a second, the calendar of the Itza, is found in the latter part of the Chumayel. He suggests that there was a "series of differing regional calendars, possibly referable to a single katun." If this is true, the application of astronomical data to the correlation problem becomes exceedingly more difficult.

The evidence from radiocarbon dating tends to support an 11.16.0.0.0 correlation, and some dates, especially in the north, have been used to argue for a solution at 12.9.0.0.0. Chase contends that radiocarbon dating is still extremely unreliable and that we should be wary of accepting C-14 dates, most of which support an 11.16.0.0.0 correlation, at face value. He notes that an overlap of Puuc and Toltec in northern Yucatan would make it far easier to accommodate late Maya prehistory in a period shortened by 256 years, as the 11.3.0.0.0 solution requires. He then turns to events in the Postclassic Peten and in northern Belize and suggests that this shortened span is also adequate to provide the frame for what we can see happening there. Although he does not discuss Nohmul in this paper, the work of Hammond (1974, 1985) at the site, amplified by the Chases' research, provides some of the strongest evidence yet for the overlap of Terminal Classic and Toltec ceramics and architecture in the Southern Lowlands.

Finally, Chase returns to the ethnohistoric sources to present a reconstruction of Postclassic events for both the Northern and Southern Lowlands that is consistent with an 11.3.0.0.0 correlation. He argues that most archaeologists ill-advisedly ignore these chronicles, relying instead wholly on archaeological data. It is indeed true that many shy away from too strong a reliance on them, believing that they contain too many contradictions to allow multiple historical reconstructions of Postclassic events.

Charles Lincoln's chapter is directly concerned with the archaeological sequence at Chichen Itza and with the problem of an overlap between Toltec Chichen Itza and the Puuc architectural style at that site and at sites in the Puuc region. As the emphasis placed on this issue in the concluding chapter to this volume shows, the seminar participants consider this to be one of the most burning matters in late Maya prehistory. In his article Lincoln confronts the archaeological evidence at Chichen Itza itself, especially the ceramic data.

He argues that the sequential dating of Puuc and Chichen Itza, widely accepted for some fifty years, is wrong and that the features we recognize as Toltec in architecture, ceramics, and sculpture should be seen as regional variations totally overlapping in time with Puuc architecture, sculpture, and ceramics. Lincoln's position with regard to this overlap is more extreme than that of most, though by no means all, of the seminar participants. The original Chichen Itza excavations by Carnegie and INAH were not designed to establish a chronological sequence, and the core of Lincoln's argument is that since we do not have ceramic stratigraphy at Chichen Itza that runs from levels with Puuc pottery up into levels with Toltec pottery any more than we have architectural superposition of Toltec over Puuc, we have no firm evidence that Toltec architecture is not contemporary with Puuc or Maya architecture there. He points out that no pure levels of Puuc pottery were ever found at Chichen Itza.

To support his views, Lincoln suggests several reinterpretations of ceramic data from this period. He argues that Silho Orange, a Toltec-period diagnostic, was contemporary with Balancan and Altar Orange and with Chablekal Gray, all Puuc ceramic groups. The presence of Tohil Plumbate at certain sites and not at others, he thinks, results from varying trade patterns. And he believes that Puuc and Chichen Slate, Puuc and Chichen Red, and Puuc and Chichen Unslipped are so similar to each other that they are best viewed as almost indistinguishable regional variants.

Lincoln mentions other evidence favoring the contemporaneity of Puuc and Toltec: the fact that the very best (and probably latest) architecture is found in both Puuc and Toltec buildings; the linking of the Toltec center of Chichen Itza to predominantly Maya, or Puuc, groups by causeways; and the occurrence of both Puuc and Toltec structures around the same plazas at that site.

Arthur Miller writes about the east coast of Quintana Roo, especially the sites of Tancah and Tulum, where he has recorded murals and undertaken limited excavations. His chapter deals primarily with changes in Postclassic architecture and murals and with the potential events these changes may indicate. Miller sees two major Acalan-Chontal, or Putun, intrusions into this area in the Postclassic Period. The first occurred at about A.D. 770 and is linked with a new mural style similar to that found in the Temple of the Warriors at Chichen Itza and in Central Mexico, and also with Cehpech sphere ceramics and possibly Puuc veneer architecture. Placement of the mural style and the inception of the Early Postclassic at A.D. 770 will probably be too early for some. The second "entrada," by Chontal-Nahua, Miller places at A.D. 1400. It, too, brought a new mural style, closely related to the Mixteca-Puebla, and such architectural traits as 3-in-1 buildings, negatively battered walls, and miniature shrines. He believes both intrusions were responsible for demographic peaks in the area. The visual oppositions of the post–1400 murals reflect, he suggests, the "tension" of the political situation caused by the Chontal usurpation of power from the native Maya rulers. The location of late sites, such as Tulum, on the coast, in contrast to the inland locations of many earlier sites, suggests a contrast between indigenous, agricultural Mayas and late-arriving Chontal, interested in coastal trade. Miller argues against trade, however, as the cause of fundamental political changes in the East Coast Postclassic, preferring instead "brute force combined with skillful manipulation of political alliances." His comparison of the Putun with the Vikings of Scandinavia is interesting but speculative, for we know next to nothing about the Putun and their effect on the polities of Yucatan.

The overall picture in the Maya Lowlands between about A.D. 800 and 1000 must encompass the collapse of the Classic order. By A.D. 1000 most of the big cities, even in the north, had fallen into decline. But, as David Pendergast warns, we must be wary of viewing the Postclassic as a time of decadence everywhere or of assuming that all Lowlands regions and sites suffered the same fate or shared similar experiences in these years.

The large site of Lamanai, in northern Belize, where Pendergast has been working for several years, seems not to have suffered a severe decline in the Postclassic, unlike other Classic sites in that region, such as Altun Ha. Pendergast describes the period from A.D. 850 to 925 as "vibrant" at Lamanai, noting that neither the ceramics nor the architecture shows a clear break at the beginning or the end of the Terminal Classic. He suggests that the Terminal Classic ends at about A.D. 1200. During the early Terminal Classic the first ball court was built, a large Classic temple was maintained, residential construction was heavy, and a huge platform of about 10,000 square meters was constructed, perhaps over the course of 100 years. A series of four late Terminal Classic structures, one of which was colonnaded, marks a departure from the Classic tradition.

Rebuilding of ceremonial structures continued through at least the early fifteenth century; two platforms of this late period bear uncarved stelae. Deep middens accumulating around the bases of the ceremonial structures attest, Pendergast believes, to a large resident population. The late pottery resembles that of Mayapan in many ways, but it seems to appear earlier at Lamanai, before A.D. 1140, than at the northern site, perhaps suggesting a southern origin for part of this complex. Silho Orange is indirectly, but probably firmly, associated with a cluster of C-14 dates averaging A.D. 1140. This is one of the most reliable dates we have for that ceramic type.

Heavy occupation continued throughout the Postclassic until about 1570 and the arrival of the Spanish, who built a church and maintained it until 1640, after which it was occupied by squatters. Pendergast notes that the artifacts left from post–1640 middens are indistinguishable from pre-Hispanic materials, a finding he calls "both instructive and unsettling."

Pendergast ends by stressing the diversity of the Postclassic in different areas. He urges that we not create one model for the Postclassic as a whole, because no single model will be applicable in all regions of the Lowlands.

The ninth through eighteenth centuries A.D. have traditionally been written off by Maya archaeologists as a time when relatively little of significance occurred in the Peten. Except for isolated studies by scholars such as William Bullard (1970) and George Cowgill (1963), this cultural backwater has been treated with benign neglect. In recent years, however, archaeologists in the Peten have begun to give this period more attention, in keeping with the heightened interest in the

Postclassic Period throughout the Lowlands. Two of the leaders in this new trend have been Prudence Rice and Don Rice.

Based on her study of ceramics, Prudence Rice argues that the two tenets of the traditional view of the Peten Postclassic, significant cultural discontinuity and isolation from the rest of the Lowlands after the Classic collapse, are no longer viable. On the basis of recent research in the Peten lakes region, she postulates strong Terminal Classic–Early Postclassic continuities and important Postclassic interchange between the lakes region and the Northern Lowlands, Belize, the East Coast, and the Guatemalan Highlands (particularly with Topoxte). She suggests that although ceramic production was regionalized, there still were widespread contacts throughout the Lowlands, which led to stylistic similarities among pots produced at different, sometimes distant sites.

Don Rice's chapter, focusing on settlement patterns and architecture, is a nice complement to Prudence Rice's ceramic chapter. He summarizes and discusses the implications of the data from the nearly 2,000 structures that were mapped by the Central Peten Historical Ecology Project. Although the data indicate a significant reorganization of population during the Terminal Classic and Postclassic periods, Don Rice argues that there still is evidence of strong locational continuities in the settlement as well as clear indication of foreign, non-Peten Maya influences. He relates these influences to comparable ones in Terminal Classic times at the site of Seibal on the Río Pasión.

Nevertheless, it must be admitted that the Rices' data are still much too scanty for them to understand the nature of the apparent widespread contacts among Postclassic sites or the kinds of political or economic ties that linked the various sites of the Peten lakes region, or those sites and other Lowland sites. Their studies are a beginning, albeit a very important one, toward understanding the often-neglected Postclassic occupations in the Central Peten.

The three interpretive essays by Diane Chase, Joseph Ball, and David Freidel present very different views of the Postclassic. In part, these differences are due to their principal geographic foci: northern Belize for Chase, Campeche and Yucatan for Ball, and the entire Lowlands for Freidel. However, the differences also result from the varied ways in which scholars approach and assess the kinds of data available on the Postclassic Period. One general similarity among these essays is worth noting: the authors' use, in varying degrees, of ethnohistoric

11

data. Although lip service is regularly paid to the importance of ethno-history for Maya studies, this significant data base has not been ex-ploited by Maya archaeologists nearly as much or as carefully as it can or should be.

Diane Chase examines several aspects of sociopolitical organization during the Late Postclassic from the perspective of the site of Santa Rita. She considers such questions as social status, spatial organization, and provincial organization from both archaeological and ethnohistoric vantage points and makes several stimulating suggestions about the probability of a continuum of statuses rather than a limited set of statuses and a barrio organization of major centers rather than a con-centric ring pattern.

On a more general level, Chase tackles what we think is one of the most critical tasks facing Maya archaeologists: the linking of the ar-chaeological record with the behaviors that helped produce it (see L. R. Binford 1983 and Sabloff 1983, 1985 for more general discussions). Certainly, Chase's attempt to link architectural and settlement form and function is a useful first step in this regard, but a more rigorous methodology for giving meaning to the archaeological record needs to be worked out to tighten the current practice of shifting back and forth between ethnohistoric evidence and the archaeological record.

Joseph Ball offers several alternate models (what he terms paradigms) for interpreting the Terminal Classic and Postclassic periods in Cam-peche and Yucatan. Although none of the models is fully satisfactory, as Ball readily admits, he does carefully sift through their various strengths and weaknesses. Ball does not test these three models (nor a fourth, which is briefly outlined in a footnote and which may turn out in the long run to be the most viable of all the alternatives), but he does set them forth so that they are readily amenable to future examination. He also issues a fervent plea for the casting off of old assumptions about Postclassic events and a recasting of the foundations and parameters for research on this period. In relation to old assump-tions, we might add that while we agree with Ball that culture-historical and processual studies are complementary, we further believe that the former do not logically precede the latter, since culture history cannot be written without considerable knowledge of culture processes. Clearly, many of the historical problems raised in this volume can only be solved when we acquire better understanding of process.

Finally, David Freidel presents a provocative synthesis of the Classic

12

and Postclassic periods from a politico-economic perspective. He argues that the political economies of Mesoamerica were administered economies which were closely intertwined throughout the area. He further posits the existence of "cartels" during Classic times. He defines a cartel as a "symbiotic economic trade relationship in which there is an actual merging of political economies over distance" and asserts that such cartels were particularly effective means of "ensuring access to markets and resources." He then shows how a cartel model might have great potential explanatory power in relation to the Classic collapse in the south, the florescence in the north, and the later collapse of Chichen Itza. Two of the greatest strengths of this imaginative exercise are, to our minds, its attempt to find a common explanation for the differing cultural developments in both the Southern and the Northern Lowlands (also see Andrews IV 1973) and its effort to link the Maya Lowlands with Mesoamerica-wide trends. Looking at the specifics of Freidel's stimulating synthesis, however, we believe that by and large they will remain in the realm of speculation until Freidel or others suggest the means by which they can be tested and begin to proceed in such a manner.

In the concluding section, we examine in some detail several of the major themes of this volume and the seminar discussions. We believe that the essays gathered here offer the reader a useful introduction to current thought regarding the development of Lowlands Maya civilization "after the fall." They indicate that the culture history of the Lowlands between the collapse of Classic Maya civilization in the south and the coming of the Spanish in the sixteenth century was far more complex than scholars heretofore have admitted. While offering no definitive answers to the many questions raised by recent field research and review of the extant literature, the chapters do point out the manifold problems with traditionally held views of the Postclassic and suggest some potentially productive directions that future research can take in order to move the field forward in coming years.

PART TWO

Overviews

2
The Postclassic of the Maya Lowlands: A Preliminary Overview[1]

GORDON R. WILLEY

Harvard University

This paper was written in the summer months of 1981, and it stands essentially as it was written then. Three members of our Santa Fe symposium group, Arlen F. Chase, Diane Z. Chase, and Prudence M. Rice, have been kind enough to point out to me some errors of fact or emphasis and some omissions of data, and I have benefited from their criticisms by making minor changes in the original text; however, the main theses of the presentation—its chronological and cultural unit organization and its interpretations of the configurations of cultural development through time and space—remain the same. My original assignment, as I understood the wishes of the symposium organizers, was to prepare a preliminary summary of the available data and archaeological interpretations bearing upon the subject of the Lowland Maya Postclassic Period and cultures. This preview was then to be circulated to the other members of the symposium group some time prior to the preparation of their own individual and more specialized papers, using my summary structure as a kind of background frame of reference and, indeed, as a "target," against which to project their own various and several disagreements. Thus, as I have indicated in my introductory remarks, which follow, I was endeavoring to present what might best be described as a "conventional" or "traditional" view of the Lowland

17

Maya Postclassic (and the presumably antecedent Terminal Late Classic). At the time I wrote, I was reasonably convinced of this kind of presentation and interpretation of the data. As a result of my reading of the other symposium papers, together with our week-long discussions at Santa Fe, I would now modify my original views somewhat both as to the timing and as to the nature and quality of events characterizing the Postclassic. For one thing, I would agree with the symposium consensus that there was a considerable chronological overlap (at least a century, if not more) between cultures that have heretofore been considered to belong to the Terminal Classic Period and those traditionally thought of as being Early Postclassic. Most particularly, this applies to the Puuc sites and culture of the Northern Lowlands and what is usually referred to as "Toltec" Chichen Itza.
December 1982. G.R.W.

This paper is a preliminary, general, and brief survey of the archaeology of the Maya Lowlands during what is generally known as the Postclassic Period (A.D. 1000–1520). It was written to provide a point of departure for the more specialized papers that follow; it was also designed to serve as a starting point for the seminar discussions on the subject.

At the risk of being too personal, let me say that it is probably fitting for me to be the one to draw up such a preliminary statement. Along with that of most Maya archaeologists of my generation, my attention has been directed largely to the Preclassic and Classic periods. When I have approached the subject of the Postclassic it has been, so to speak, from "below," from the end of a waning Classic and from the "abyss" of the "collapse." My terms here are selected intentionally to reflect a bias about the Postclassic, and I will confess at the outset that I am still not altogether disabused of this frame of mind. I have, however, endeavored to learn as much as I could about the Postclassic Period Maya of the Lowlands, and this is an attempt at an objective summary and evaluation.

The archaeology of the Postclassic Period in the Maya Lowlands has not been completely ignored. After all, one of the earliest large-scale Maya excavation programs was at Chichen Itza (Morris, Charlot, and Morris 1931; Ruppert 1935); in recent years investigations of a comparable scale have been carried out at Mayapan (Pollock et al. 1962). More recently there has been a spate of work on Postclassic sites and problems, much of which will be referred to further along

18

and which provides many of the basic data for this volume. Nevertheless, as will be apparent to the reader, research on the Lowland Maya Postclassic centuries is only now becoming a major concern, and this book should serve as a stimulus for a continuation of this interest.

My plan is to survey the Maya Lowlands on the three major horizons of the Terminal Classic, the Early Postclassic, and the Late Postclassic. For each time horizon I will proceed by regions, or "zones" as these have been called in a recent cultural-geographical breakdown of the Maya Lowlands (Hammond and Ashmore 1981; see map [Fig. 2.1], reproduced as Figure 2.1 in this chapter). Following this horizontal treatment I will recapitulate, very briefly, by presenting salient points of the main data from a diachronic perspective within each zone. In this data survey emphasis will be upon the presence of sites and upon architecture, monuments, residential units, and general settlement pattern. Such information will be related, especially for relative dating purposes, to ceramics. As I see my task, I am to attempt to draw together, in a preliminary single chapter, the form and substance of the Postclassic occupation (as well as its Terminal Classic immediate antecedents) of the Maya Lowlands.

THE TERMINAL CLASSIC

Any closeup examination of the Postclassic must begin with the antecedent Terminal Classic Period (A.D. 800–1000). These last two centuries of the first millennium A.D. were obviously a time of radical culture change in the Maya Lowlands. They were also a time of change and unrest in much of Mesoamerica. In the Southern Lowlands the ninth century saw the decline and abandonment of the great Maya cities—the so-called collapse. Farther to the north events were somewhat different, but change was also in the making.

Let us begin with the Central Zone (see Fig. 2.1 for zone locations), the heartland of Classic Maya development in the Lowlands. The ninth century corresponds to the Tepeu 3 ceramic phase and horizon in this zone. After A.D. 810 (9.19.0.0.0) major construction and stela dedication virtually ceased at the major sites. (Note to the reader: all Maya dates in this chapter are rendered in Christian calendrical dates following the 11.16.0.0.0 correlation). In addition, there is good settlement evidence for a marked population drop, at least in and around

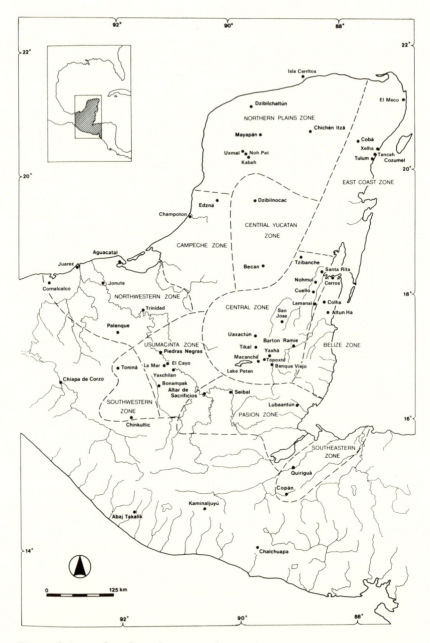

Figure 2.1   Archaeological zones and sites of the Maya Lowlands. Modified from Hammond and Ashmore (1981:Fig. 2.1).

some of the great centers. Thus, Culbert (1973a) estimates that the Tepeu 3 or Eznab population at Tikal was only one-tenth the size of its pre–A.D. 800 maximum. On the other hand, Arlen Chase (1979) states that "the central Peten appears to have been heavily populated during the Terminal Classic Period." Chase may be referring mainly to the Lake Peten-Itza–Tayasal vicinity, but there is some additional support for his views in the surveys Anabel Ford (personal communication) has carried out in the region between Tikal and Yaxha as well as in the Barton Ramie data from the Belize Valley (Willey et al. 1965), where the Spanish Lookout phase subsumes both the Tepeu 2 and 3 horizons and where residential mound occupation may have remained more or less constant for this duration. In an appraisal of the Barton Ramie data (Willey 1973a), with this point in mind, I was unable to come to any definite conclusions about Terminal Classic population density, but, suffice it to say, the problem of Tepeu 3 or ninth-century population estimates for the Central Zone is still with us and is of great importance, for it relates directly to the nature of the "collapse."

The ceramics of the Tepeu 3 horizon in the Central Zone derive from the Maya Peten tradition of Tepeu 1 and 2 and imply a continuity of population (Gifford 1976; Chase 1979; Rice and Rice 1980a). Chase has made the point that the Tepeu 2 and 3 ceramics are often difficult to differentiate. Tepeu 3 contexts have been marked by the presence of foreign fine paste wares, but, as Chase rightly cautions, such wares may occur differently at different Maya sites and cannot be used uniformly as criteria for the Tepeu 3 time horizon.

For a long time the second half of the Terminal Classic Period in the Central Zone, A.D. 900–1000, was poorly known or its occupations not recognized. Prudence Rice (1979) once referred to a hiatus separating the end of Tepeu 3 ceramics from those of the Postclassic Isla phase at Topoxote, but is now inclined to doubt that such a hiatus occurred (personal communication). Moreover, the Rices (1979) have recently made new excavations at Macanche Island, in Lake Macanche, also in the Peten Lake districts, which have established a sequence of ceramic types that appears to span the presumed hiatus. They refer to an unnamed early facet, probably falling in the tenth century, of what they designate as the Early Postclassic Period. This unnamed facet consists of three unslipped types which, they say, would be at home in earlier Tepeu 3 contexts, again suggesting some pop-

21

ulation continuity from Terminal Classic to Early Postclassic. These types are found along with those of later recognized groups, such as those designated as Pozo, Trapeche, and Paxcaman. The early facet complex shows few trade ties to other regions or zones. There is no associated architecture of consequence. A reasonable explanation would be that a "postcollapse" population stayed on in the locality and, perhaps, was joined by immigrants from elsewhere. Arlen Chase's (1979) Lake Peten-Itza data may have a bearing on this Macanche possibility of a Terminal Classic–to–Postclassic continuity. He emphasizes the significance of the dates of the aforementioned Trapeche ceramic group—earlier than and definitely transitional to Paxcaman group ceramics and at least partially contemporaneous with the pottery known as the Augustine group. Augustine ceramics were considered by Bullard (1973) to be the earliest part of the New Town phase at Barton Ramie and, thus, to span the Classic-to-Postclassic transition at that site.

To sum up briefly to this point, there was a clear cessation of large-center architectural and related activity in the Central Zone in the ninth century. There was some continuity of population, although we do not yet know just how large this population was in relation to previous Classic population figures. For the tenth century, evidence is both scant and uncertain, but it would appear there was some minimal continuity of residence, at least.

Moving toward and into the Belize Zone, let us look at some other locations of Terminal Classic activity. At Benque Viejo, the largest ceremonial center in the near vicinity of Barton Ramie, building activity was largely over by A.D. 800 although there was some elite use of the site for another fifty years (see Thompson 1940; Mackie 1961). Whether or not the terminal Benque Viejo IV ceramic phase continued on into the tenth century is unknown. A series of caves in southern and central Belize—Actun Balam (Pendergast 1969), Río Frío Cave E (Pendergast 1970), Actun Polbilche (Pendergast 1974), and the Eduardo Quiroz Cave (Pendergast 1964)—were all used by the Maya at the end of the Classic. Ceramics correlating with Tepeu 3 were found in the first two, while the last two showed both Tepeu 3 horizon and Early Postclassic materials. These finds suggest, perhaps, that religious and ritual activities may have been shifted to caves at a time when the old Classic ceremonial centers were being abandoned (Collea 1981).

Near (but not on) the coast of northern Belize, Altun Ha (Pendergast 1967, 1979), which had been very active in the Early Classic, showed a decline in construction in the Late Classic, continuing into the Terminal Classic; then construction stopped altogether. The cessation here was accompanied by the desecration of earlier tombs and buildings, apparently by a population that continued to live on the site. Some modest construction occurred in the Postclassic, probably both Early and Late. At San José, also in northern Belize but actually in the Central Zone, there is good evidence of Terminal Classic activity (Thompson 1939). This small ceremonial center was occupied from Preclassic times through the Terminal Classic. Its San José IV phase (ca. A.D. 800–900) is on the Tepeu 3 time level, during which there was some construction; construction continues through San José V (ca. A.D. 900–1000). Constructional activity is unusual for the Terminal Classic, especially for its second half. While we have no radiocarbon dating for San José, Thompson's ceramic analyses of the phases would appear to support the chronological placements. Terminal Classic vigor is shown even more strongly at Lamanai. This is a major center, much larger than San José, located somewhat north of the latitude of the latter site and Altun Ha and about equidistant between the two of them (Pendergast 1981a). Two of its major building complexes were initiated in the Terminal Classic, and construction continued on these until well into the Postclassic Period. Located on a large lagoon connected to the Caribbean by the New River, Lamanai was well situated for trade, evidences for which have been found in abundance at the center. Still farther north, the substantial center and occupation area of Colha also give evidence of a vigorous continuity of construction and other elite activities through the Tepeu 3 horizon (Adams and Valdez 1980; Hester, Eaton, and Shafer 1980). At about A.D. 900, however, the Terminal Classic occupation was ended violently, an event visible in the archaeological record in what are interpreted as mass pit-burials of the elite. There is an Early Postclassic occupation at Colha, but it is not accompanied by large-scale building. In far northern Belize, Nohmul, on the Río Hondo, is a major center which was largely constructed in Preclassic and Classic times; some of its structures, however, evidence Late Classic–to–Early Postclassic building continuity and use (Hammond 1974; A. F. and D. Z. Chase, personal communication).

We see, then, that in northern Belize the story is somewhat different.

23

Elite activity continued well into the Terminal Classic Period. Episodes of violence appear to have terminated such activity at some sites; at others, such as Lamanai, the entire Terminal Classic Period seems to have been active, with evidences of continuity into the Early Postclassic.

The Pasión Zone, to the south of the Central and Belize zones, includes the southernmost part of Belize and the Pasión drainage of the Peten. There are some major centers in southern Belize. The one most thoroughly reported upon is Lubaantun (Hammond 1975), and, because of its Tepeu 2–3 occupation, it is also the most germane to our Terminal Classic survey. Hammond places the last major building activity at the site at about A.D. 850; after that the site ceased to exist as a major center. The two largest centers on the Pasión are Altar de Sacrificios and Seibal. Altar, which lies at the confluence of the Chixoy-Salinas-Usumacinta system with the Pasión, has a long history, extending into Tepeu 2–3 times. Its Boca phase is essentially contemporaneous with Tepeu 3 and the earlier half of the Terminal Classic Period.

The Boca phase was not a time of either important building (Smith 1972) or stela dedication at Altar (Graham 1972), although there was a considerable resident population at the site (Adams 1971; Willey 1973b). Altar is situated on what amounts to a small riverine-swamp island. This island was thoroughly surveyed, and, we should point out, our settlement data in support of the above statement derive from the island. About settlement pattern change over time in the lower Pasión Valley (presumably the support area for Altar de Sacrificios), we know much less. The Jimba phase succeeds the Boca at Altar, and its estimated dating is A.D. 900–1000. There was no public building during the phase, although the site continued to be occupied. It has been speculated that the Jimba phase represents the invasion of an alien people (Sabloff and Willey 1967), perhaps Putun or Chontal Maya from the Tabasco Gulf Coast (Willey 1973b). The ceramics of the Jimba phase are fine paste wares, the Terminal Classic Fine Oranges and Fine Grays (Adams 1971). The phase is also marked by the appearance of fine paste figurines that break with the Classic Maya figurine tradition in presenting images that do not depict an obviously Maya physical type. Fine paste wares and figurines, it should be noted, began to appear at Altar during the Boca phase, at which time they were a minor addition to the total ceramic complex. In the Jimba phase, however, virtually all pottery is fine paste. After the close of the Jimba phase (ca. A.D. 1000) Altar de Sacrificios was abandoned.

Seibal had a quite different history from that of Altar de Sacrificios. There is a long sequence of occupation here, but some of the most impressive buildings and stelae date to the Terminal Classic Period (Willey et al. 1975). This latest phase at Seibal is contemporaneous with Tepeu 3. The ceramics are in a Peten ceramic tradition, but the assemblage is heavily laced with Fine Orange/Fine Gray increments. The several stelae that date to the phase—from 10.1.0.0.0 to 10.3.0.0.0—are in the style of portraiture that suggests "foreign," probably Chontal-Putun, influences (Thompson 1970). At about A.D. 930, this major center was abandoned. The extensive settlement pattern surveys made in a 5-kilometer radius around Seibal have not yet been fully analyzed or published (Tourtellot 1970); however, if house mound occupation continued beyond A.D. 930 it would appear to have been of a very minor nature.

The Southeastern Zone is the Motagua-Chamelecón region of Guatemala and western Honduras. The two main sites here are Quirigua, in the Motagua floodplain, and Copan, on a Motagua tributary in the hill-and-valley country toward the South. Quirigua (Jones and Sharer 1980) was a vigorous center in the Late Classic. Major construction was going on as late as 9.19.0.0.0. (A.D. 810) and for a few years thereafter. Subsequently, there is little in the way of a building record and no more stelae dedications. The site, however, continued to be occupied throughout the Terminal Classic and into the Early Postclassic, before being fully abandoned at about A.D. 1250.

Copan also had a brilliant Late Classic development, and the center drew upon large outlying residential populations in the Copan Valley (Willey and Leventhal 1979). Shortly after A.D. 800 it ceased to be an important city. Some Early Postclassic ceramic markers, such as Nicoya polychromes and Plumbate ware, have been found in superficial levels of the main center or in occasional tombs there (Longyear 1952), so it is likely that there was some scattered occupation or use of the main site; nevertheless, it is fair to say that the old Maya Classic culture, and most of the population that went with it, had been dissipated by the beginning of the Terminal Classic Period.

The western part of the Maya Lowlands has been defined in terms of three zones: the Usumacinta, along the middle course of the stream and including the major site of Piedras Negras; the Southwestern Zone, lying to the west, and including Toniná and Chinkultic; and the North-western Zone of the Lower Usumacinta drainage, including Palenque. Piedras Negras, the best-studied site in the Usumacinta Zone, probably erected its last dated monument in 9.18.5.0.0 (A.D. 795) although it is possible that such activity continued for another katun and a half at this center. The Chacalhaaz ceramic phase at Piedras Negras corresponds to the Tepeu 2 horizon and tradition. Subsequently, the short-lived Tamay phase, sherds of which are found superficially in post-architectural levels, breaks clearly with the Peten Tepeu tradition and is represented by fine paste wares. Most of these fine paste wares, however, are not the Fine Orange and Fine Gray seen in the Terminal Classic phases of Altar de Sacrificios or Seibal but, instead, relate to the north, to Tabasco, Campeche, and Yucatan. A few scattered Fine Orange and Fine Gray sherds, which would be at home in the late phases of Altar and Seibal, have been found at Piedras Negras, but it is believed that these postdate Tamay (Rands 1973b). Stela dedication at other Usumacinta Zone sites waned or died at about the same time as at Piedras Negras: Bonampak, 9.18.10.0.0 or A.D. 800, La Mar, 9.18.15.0.0 or A.D. 805, El Cayo, 9.19.0.0.0 or A.D. 810, and Yax-chilan, between 9.19.0.0.0 and 10.0.10.0.0 or between A.D. 810 and 840 (see Rands 1973a for a summation of these datings; also see Pros-kouriakoff 1950, 1960, 1964 and Ruppert, Thompson, and Proskour-iakoff 1955). In sum, the Usumacinta Zone major centers appear to have given up about a century before those of the Pasión drainage.

At Toniná, in the Southwestern Zone, elite activity trailed off more gradually than in the Usumacinta Zone. Becquelin (1979) reports a decline in monument building after A.D. 805; however, some contin-ued to be erected until A.D. 909 (10.4.0.0.0). At that date or shortly after, Toniná suffered a brutal desecration and destruction of monu-ments and sculptures, and the site appears to have been abandoned for a time. There is, however, a scattered Early Postclassic occupation of the site; but in this period the most important center of the Ocosingo Valley was nearby Chamun and not Toniná. At Chinkultic (Ball 1980) there was continuity of elite architecture and stela dedication from the Late Classic into the Terminal Classic in the Yobnajab phase (A.D. 700–900). The late facet of this phase shows Altar Fine Orange and related Fine Gray pottery. The succeeding Tepancuapan phase (A.D. 900–1250?) exhibits ceramic continuity with Yobnajab, with fine paste wares present in its early facet. There is also some constructional continuity into this Early Postclassic Tepancuapan phase.

The Northwestern Zone comprises the lower Usumacinta and environs, including such sites as Palenque, Jonuta, Trinidad, and others, known from the surveys of Rands (1967a, 1967b, 1973b, 1979) and Berlin (1953, 1956). The zone lies largely outside the Peten ceramic traditions; it is, without much question, the original hearth of the fine paste wares, which date here to well back into the Classic Period. These wares inspired the later and better known Altar and Balancan Fine Oranges, which are Tepeu 3 time markers on the Pasión and upper Usumacinta. At Palenque an Early Balunte phase, in which Classic-type construction continues, correlates chronologically with the latter part of Tepeu 2. The ceramics are largely fine paste but do not include Balancan or Altar types. The subsequent Late Balunte phase, in approximately the first half of the ninth century, is the time of constructional decline and cessation. Some Balancan sherds appear at this time. After what may have been a short period of abandonment, there is a reoccupation, which has been dated as Early Postclassic although it may have been confined largely to the end of the Terminal Classic Period (ca. A.D. 900–1000). At Jonuta, Initial Series dates are missing, but Proskouriakoff has placed some sculptures there stylistically in an A.D. 750–810 time range, and these, interestingly, show non–Classic Maya elements (Thompson 1970). The site, however, is best known from the subsequent Jonuta horizon, dated at about 9.19.0.0.0 to 10.5.0.0.0, or A.D. 810 to 928, in effect to the early half of the Terminal Classic. The Jonuta-horizon ceramics are in fine paste wares and include Balancan Fine Orange and related Fine Grays. The end of the horizon is, apparently, coeval with the late reoccupation at Palenque.

The Northwestern Zone must be of particular interest in any consideration of the Terminal Classic Period since it was apparently the homeland of the Chontal or Putun Maya (Thompson 1970), considered by some to have been the instigators of the Classic "collapse" in the Southern Lowlands (see Willey and Shimkin 1973, for a summary of such views). This question is a complex one, and direct Chontal or Putun invasion of the Pasión Valley, via the Usumacinta (see Sabloff and Willey 1967), is not the only possibility, or certainly no more than a part of it. It is reasonably certain that northern and foreign influences began to impinge on the Late Classic cultures of northern Yucatan toward the close of the eighth century A.D., resulting in the synthesis of the Puuc florescence of the Terminal Classic (Ball 1974a); it may have been from this base that foreign invaders moved southward in the Terminal Classic Period to, for example, Seibal (Thompson 1970; Willey 1973b; Ball 1974a; Sabloff 1975).

The Campeche and Central Yucatan zones lie to the northeast of the lower Usumacinta country. Some surveys have been conducted along the Campeche coast, extending from the edge of the Northwestern Zone around Laguna de Términos as far north as the city of Campeche (Eaton 1978; Ball 1978). This reconnaissance indicates major site construction activities through the Terminal Classic and probably into the Early Postclassic. Fine Orange and Fine Gray ceramics, comparable to those of the Jonuta horizon, are present in the ceramic complexes.

The Central Yucatan Zone is known for the Río Bec–Chenes architectural tradition of the Late Classic Period (Potter 1977). The best-known sequence is that established by Ball (1977a) at Becan, where the Río Bec–style buildings date from the Bejuco phase (A.D. 600–750). This phase is followed by a short Chintok phase (A.D. 750–830) during which constructional activity declines and ends. The story at the nearby site of Chicanna is similar; the last structure there dates to the end of Chintok (Eaton 1974b). At both sites, however, there is evidence of an immediately subsequent squatter-type occupation, that of the Xcocom phase (A.D. 830–1100), spanning the Terminal Classic and extending into the Early Postclassic. In Ball's (1974a) opinion, Xcocom ceramics show a synthesis of older resident traditions with new modes brought by an invasion or migration of peoples from the north. This interpretation recalls the foregoing comments about Chontal-Putun infiltrations into northern Yucatan and the subsequent movements of these peoples and cultural traditions to the south during the Terminal Classic. New ceramic types in the Xcocom assemblages include Balancan Fine Orange. An interesting observation in connection with the Xcocom cultures is that while the populations of this phase occupied the old Bejuco and Chintok temples and palaces as residences, they did not continue to maintain and use the extensive system of agricultural terraces that had been an important feature of Late Classic life in the Becan-Chicanna vicinity.

The Northern Plains Zone covers the northwestern and central portions of the Yucatan Peninsula. Here, quite unlike the events of the Maya Lowlands in most of the south, the Terminal Classic Period was a time of vigorous ceremonial-center construction and maintenance. In the local regional chronology this is referred to as the Pure Florescent Period (Andrews IV 1965a; Ball 1974a). At Puuc sites, such as Uxmal, this corresponds to the Cehpech (Smith 1971) ceramic phase. Ball (1974a) has argued, and I think rightly so, that Puuc and Pure Florescent architectural adornment is strongly "Mexicanized" (see also Sharp 1981). He would further link this to the Chontal-Putun incursions into northern Yucatan beginning in the latter part of the eighth century. Ball (1974a) sees the founding of Chichen Itza in A.D. 780–800 as a "first coming" of a Chontal-Putun group known as the Itza. They were responsible for the Pure Florescent or Puuc-style buildings at that site during the Terminal Classic Period. And they are to be distinguished from a "second coming" to Chichen of Itzas, perhaps also Chontal-Putan, who were responsible for the Early Postclassic Toltec phase of the site's history.

The sequence at Dzibilchaltun, in far northern Yucatan (Andrews IV and Andrews V 1980), parallels in part that at Chichen Itza. The Pure Florescent or Terminal Classic Period, which lasts from A.D. 800/830 to 1000, was one of considerable architectural activity, and this in the Puuc style. The ceramics of Copo 2 phase are contemporaneous. They show resident continuity out of the earlier Copo 1 (A.D. 600–800) styles but with the addition of new types, including Fine Oranges, Fine Grays, and Thin Slate Ware. Copo 2 pottery is coeval with, and related to, Smith's (1971) Cehpech complex. Unlike Chichen Itza, Dzibilchaltun has no building activity in the immediately following Modified Florescent or Early Postclassic Period. The site was, however, occupied at this time, and this occupation is referred to as the Zipche 1 ceramic phase, which is coordinate in time with Smith's (1971) Sotuta complex. The period of Zipche 1 (A.D. 1000–1125/50) is, of course, the time of Chichen Itza's great Toltec Early Postclassic growth. In Zipche 2 (A.D. 1125/50–1200) there was a modest building revival at Dzibilchaltun which then continued on into the Late Postclassic.

Ball (1974a) has stated that the Terminal Classic (Pure Florescent) Period in the Northern Plains Zone was a time of prosperity and peace. On the first score there seems to be no argument. As he has said elsewhere, Puuc architecture represents the apogee of Lowland Maya great building construction—perhaps of all Mesoamerican architectural achievement. Cities such as Uxmal, Kabah, Sayil, and Chichen Itza of the Pure Florescent Period are without rivals. On the second score, that of peace, I would be less certain. Webster (1978) has described three smaller Northern Plains places—Chacchob, Cuca, and Dzonot Ake—that are walled, probably for defense, and that appear to date from the Terminal Classic. On a more general interpretive level, it seems at least likely that in a period of growth of populations there would have been increasing rivalry among centers. Moreover, this was also, as has been argued, a period of Chontal-Putun infiltration, which suggests another source of unrest. Finally, if the Terminal Classic in the Northern Plains was brought to an end by the "second coming" of the Itzas at Chichen, an event with very militaristic overtones, we can infer that the political climate of the period may have been a warlike one.

We are left with the remainder of northern Yucatan, the East Coast Zone, which consists largely of the state of Quintana Roo. The zone was well occupied in the Classic Period, with Coba the largest city of that time; however, Coba was abandoned prior to the Terminal Classic. But a number of lesser sites show continued Terminal Classic occupation and building; among them Tancah (Sanders 1960; Miller 1975, 1977b), Xelha (Andrews IV and A. P. Andrews 1975), Calderitas (Sanders 1960), El Diez (Sanders 1960), and others (Parry 1981). Architectural features in some of these sites relate them, in a marginal way, to what was going on in Puuc centers farther to the west. The coastal island of Cozumel enjoyed a marked population increase during the Terminal Classic, accompanied by architectural construction (Freidel 1976; Fogel 1981).

Can these statements about the Maya Lowland Terminal Classic Period, already synoptic to a high degree, be further reduced in any kind of a meaningful summary? I believe some general observations can be made.

First, there is what we have known for a long time: a decline and eventual cessation of elite politico-religious activities in the ninth century A.D. occurred over a large part of the Lowlands. The decline begins to be manifest at about A.D. 800—the beginning of what we have called the Terminal Classic Period. There is some regional and site-to-site variation in the speed of this decline, but complete or near-complete cessation of elite activities occurs by the end of the century. This decline-and-cessation is seen in the Central Zone, the southern and central portions of the Belize Zone, the Pasión Zone, the Southeastern Zone, the Usumacinta Zone, and the Central Yucatan Zone. It is less pronounced in the Southwestern, Northwestern, and Campeche zones.

Second, it appears that the succeeding tenth century, or the last half of the Terminal Classic Period, represents the very nadir of elite activity, and perhaps overall population decline, in those zones where the decline-and-cessation phenomenon was most pronounced. This is true even for Seibal, that rare exception in the Central Zone, where major building and stela activity continued vigorously throughout the ninth century, immediately after which the site was abandoned.

Third, the phenomenon of the ninth century decline and cessation of Classic elite activity did not occur in the Northern Plains Zone, in the East Coast Zone, and at certain sites in the northern part of the Belize Zone. In the north, if anything, some of the most brilliant center construction took place during the Terminal Classic Period.

Fourth, while facts of decline and cessation in elite architectural and stelae dedicatory activities are there for all to see, events in the wider socioeconomic sphere are less clear. How great were population losses? To what extent did large nonelite populations continue to occupy small centers and outlying hinterlands? This old problem in Lowland Maya settlement archaeology is still with us.

Fifth, the "Pure Florescent" of the Northern Lowlands contains within it, as expressed in architectural styles, sculpture, and iconography, as well as in ceramic traditions, "foreign" or "Mexicanoid" elements, suggesting that the continued vigor of the north during the ninth and tenth centuries owed something to "foreign" inspiration. That this inspiration may have come from invaders is a possibility, and such invaders have sometimes been identified as Chontal or Putun Maya; however, it is quite possible that more than a single group of "invaders" was involved. The new or alien influences are seen most clearly in the Northern Plains. They are present in northern Belize but less strong in the East Coast Zone. Presumably, the original homeland of these "foreigners" was the southern Gulf Coast of Mexico, in the Northwestern Zone. Neither here, however, nor in the adjacent

31

Campeche coastal region, do we see architectural expressions like those found in the Northern Plains Pure Florescent sites of the Puuc tradition.

THE EARLY POSTCLASSIC

The foregoing account of the Terminal Classic Period has not only laid a foundation for our consideration of the Early Postclassic but has anticipated it to a degree in referring to some Early Postclassic sites and occupations. As a result, we can move somewhat more swiftly from zone to zone as we cover the Early Postclassic time level. Since any examination of this period must bring us to Chichen Itza, let us change our geographical order and begin at that great site, in the Northern Plains Zone.

The Toltec horizon at Chichen Itza is generally accepted as the beginning of the Postclassic Period, with a round date for its inception of A.D. 1000 (Thompson 1941b). This horizon, and this Early Postclassic rebuilding of the site, has also been referred to by some as a "second Mexicanization" of the city, or as noted in our discussions of the Pure Florescent Period, a "second coming" of the Itza.

The Chichen I Period (A.D. 750–1000) refers to a Puuc-related city of the Pure Florescent Period (Tozzer 1957). The ceramics of the period are in the tradition of the Thin and Medium Slate wares; Balancan and Altar Fine Orange types occur as trade (Brainerd 1958). This is, in effect, the Cehpech (Smith 1971) ceramic complex.

The Chichen II and III periods subsume Tozzer's Toltec-Maya architectural Stages A and B. They extend from A.D. 1000 to 1250, or the Early Postclassic Period. Tozzer's distinctions between Periods II and III are made in terms of specific buildings at the site and architectural styles and features of these buildings, supported to some extent by architectural stratigraphy. For the purposes of our survey the subdivisions within the period are not of great importance. Significant, perhaps, is the fact that these Toltec-Maya buildings were constructed immediately after Period I; there was no destruction, although there was some abandonment, of earlier buildings. There is some continuity in constructional techniques and even architectural styles between the earlier Puuc-related buildings of Period I and the Toltec-Maya buildings of Periods II–III. There are also some innovations: pyramidal temples without plinths, frequent use of columns, larger rooms supported by columns, gallery-patio arrangements making use of columns, and I-shaped, Tula-related ball courts. The ornamental iconography of the Toltec-Maya buildings is heavily Mexican or Toltec. The associated ceramics (Sotuta phase) remain in the slateware tradition, and trade wares include Silho or X-Fine Orange and Tohil Plumbate. Except for trade types, the pottery is distinctly local and not that of Tula proper or Central Mexican Toltec assemblages. Tozzer's Chichen IV Period belongs to the Late Postclassic and pertains to a squatter-type occupation of the site or to its later use as a pilgrimage and sacrificial center.

Attempts to correlate Chichen archaeology with the legendary history of the Books of Chilam Balam (Roys 1933) are a source of considerable controversy (see Thompson 1941b; Tozzer 1957; Roys 1962). Are the Itza to be identified with the Pure Florescent Period founders of the city in A.D. 750–800? Or did they arrive in A.D. 987 and found the Toltec-Maya city on the location of the earlier one? Were the Chontal-Putun involved on both occasions? To what extent were Tula Toltecs a part of the conquest of A.D. 987? Or are the Itza to be identified with a group who first saw Chichen in the twelfth century, probably after its abandonment, and who, from their base at Mayapan, used the earlier city only as a sacred pilgrimage center? As far as the specifics of history go, I am more inclined to accept the last interpretation about the Itza (Geselowitz 1981). In wider archaeological perspective, and in the context of our seminar, I think that the important point is that the Maya of the Northern Plains had long been under Mexican influences, both ideological and commercial, and that these were probably mediated through the Chontal-Putun.

One of the problems and complexities of the Early Postclassic Period in the northern Maya Lowlands is what appears to be a lack of other large sites in the Chichen Maya-Toltec tradition. That is, Chichen Itza is not only a paramount city of the period; it is the only great city. There are, of course, some indications in the archaeological record, as well as in the legendary historical or ethnohistorical record, that former Terminal Classic Period sites, such as the great Puuc center of Uxmal, continued to be occupied and continued to play a part in the political history of the area. But there was no significant building at these places. On the face of it, the power establishment at Chichen Itza would appear thoroughly to have reduced the rest of the northern Yucatan Peninsula to subordinate political status. Perhaps significantly, in connection with coastal trade or with salt production, there are substantial occupations of Early Postclassic date at a number of coastal sites in the Northern Plains and East Coast zones. Eaton (1978) refers to some of these, including Emal and Xcopte, both located on salt lagoons; he notes: "Materials collected from Xcopte suggest occupation by foreigners, possibly those called Itza, who appear to have had control of the salt beds." (Eaton 1978: 64). Other Early Postclassic coastal sites are Vista Alegre and Chiquila, first noted by Sanders (1960), and about which Eaton (1978: 65) says: "Their large structures suggest a relatively rich economy which may have been based more on commerce than on agricultural produce and salt collection. They are not located close to any known salt beds."

In the interior, away from the coasts, there was a continued occupancy at several sites but no notable Early Postclassic construction. The Zipche 1–phase occupation, already mentioned in the discussion of Terminal Classic Dzibilchaltun, would be an example. In the interior of the East Coast Zone, El Diez, Monte Bravo, and Santa María all show Early Postclassic ceramics (Parry 1981). A search of the literature showed little Early Postclassic evidence on Cozumel (Fogel 1981), and Connor (1975) notes a decrease in ceramic remains from the Terminal Classic into Early Postclassic. Freidel (1976) does, however, date one group of structures to the Early Postclassic Period, and Robles (personal communication) says that the period is well represented on the island.

Our Early Postclassic survey of other Lowland Maya zones can move more rapidly. Campeche Zone sites—the Islas Jaina, Piedras, and Uaymil—continued to be used during the period, although it was probably not a time of major construction. To the west and south, in the Northwestern Zone, there is little that can be identified as Early Postclassic, and the same is true for the Usumacinta Zone. In the far Southwestern Zone we have already referred to the establishment of an Early Postclassic center in the Ocosingo Valley following the fall of Tonina; and at Chinkultic there was some ceramic and constructional continuity from the Terminal Classic into the Early Postclassic Tepancuapan phase.

In the Central Yucatan Zone we have mentioned Terminal Classic-to–Early Postclassic ceramic continuity in the Xcocom phase (A.D. 830–1100); but this has been described as "squatter" activity on earlier Río Bec–Chenes centers.

34

The Pasión Zone shows no evidence of elite class activity for the Early Postclassic although Gair Tourtellot (personal communication) reports a scatter of sherds for the period on Seibal's peripheries.

In the Southeastern Zone Copan had no history of consequence in the Early Postclassic. At Quirigua, occupation, as indicated by ceramics, continued after the cessation of most major building and stela dedications, and this occupation lasted through the Early Postclassic. An I-shaped ball court at the site probably dates from this time.

In the northern sites of the Belize Zone there is considerable evidence of Early Postclassic building in contrast to the relative lack of such activity in the rest of the southern Maya Lowlands. Terminal Classic–to–Early Postclassic continuity of ceremonial center construction has already been alluded to at Lamanai and Altun Ha; and to these we can add the sites of Nohmul and Cerros, both Late Preclassic centers, abandoned during the Classic, then rebuilt in the Terminal Classic/Early Postclassic. At Colha there is also some modest Early Postclassic construction, which followed the Terminal Classic destruction of that site. With regard to Early Postclassic ceramics in northern Belize, Arlen and Diane Chase inform me (personal communication) that these relate to Payil Red, a variety of Tulum Red, and so suggest a link to the East Coast.

This brings us back to the Central Zone. Prudence Rice (1979) would place the New Town late facet, at Barton Ramie, in the Early Postclassic. The Barton Ramie data are ceramic and come from house mound occupations. Prudence Rice (personal communication) has called my attention to temple assemblages and large structures at Muralla de León and Zacpeten, in the Peten lake country. While these indicate that some elite activity was going on in some places, neither its volume nor its elaboration is very impressive when compared to Late Classic standards for the Central Zone. The Islas-phase ceramics from the eastern Peten lakes country are seen by Prudence Rice as contemporaneous with New Town pottery. In the western Peten lakes country, the Trapeche and Augustine pottery groups pertain to the Early Postclassic, and both these groups show some continuity, or at least chronological overlap, with Paxcaman- and Topoxte-group wares, both of which continue on through the subsequent Late Postclassic Period (see Chase 1979; P. Rice 1979, Rice and Rice 1979; I am also indebted to the Chases and the Rices for personal communications on these points).

The available archaeological site reports that I consulted in the preparation of this overview offered little information on the presence or absence of Central Zone Early Postclassic public or ceremonial architecture. Bullard's (1970) Topoxte Island report seemed to indicate that all the major building at that site dates as Late Postclassic; however, Prudence Rice has pointed out to me (personal communication) that Bullard's excavations were on the main island only. New settlement and architectural data on the Peten Postclassic as a whole have been presented by Don Rice in the present volume—data not available to me at the time of the writing of this paper. Even in the light of this new information, which I will not attempt to incorporate here, I am still of the opinion that elite architectural activity in the Central Zone in Postclassic times was not impressive.

What generalizations can we make about the Early Postclassic?

First, the establishment of a Toltec-related presence, by whatever means or processes, at Chichen Itza at about A.D. 1000 is the marker event for the inception of the period. Following this, there can be little doubt but that Chichen then became the power center of the northern Maya Lowlands for approximately the next two hundred years.

Second, this Toltec presence at Chichen climaxed a gradual cultural "Mexicanization" of parts of the Maya Lowlands which had begun and continued throughout the preceding Terminal Classic Period. This "Mexicanization" of the Maya is believed to have been mediated through the Chontal or Putun Maya who may or may not have been the group responsible for the Toltec establishment at Chichen. (This generalization is related to, or is essentially the same as, the one made in our Terminal Classic Period summary.)

Third, during the Early Postclassic Period there is a scarcity of major sites and major site activity throughout the Northern Lowlands. It is assumed that this relates to Chichen Itza's dominance. The only exceptions—although these are not major sites in an architectural sense—are several coastal locations which may have served as salt-collecting or fishing stations or trading ports.

Fourth, elsewhere in the Maya Lowlands activity and occupation were spotty during the Early Postclassic Period. There was some continued occupation and public building construction in Belize, at Nohmul and Lamanai, as well as at Colha. Some coastal sites were occupied in the Northwestern Zone; there was some activity in the Southwestern Zone; at Quirigua, in the Southeastern Zone, occupation and limited building continued; little seems to have been going on in the Pasión and Usumacinta zones. In the Central Zone, we have referred to residential site occupations on the upper Belize River and around the Peten lakes. There was also some—but to my mind modest—elite activity in the lake country (see D. S. Rice, this volume).

Fifth, the Early Postclassic Period closes with the dissolution or withdrawal of the Toltec presence, and its power, at Chichen Itza. This occurred sometime during the first half of the thirteenth century.

THE LATE POSTCLASSIC

Mayapan (Pollock et al. 1962) in the Northern Lowlands Zone is the principal Late Postclassic center of the Maya Lowlands. A scattering of Terminal Classic sherds (Cehpech phase) comes from the lowest levels of the site; and an even smaller number of Early Postclassic (Sotuta phase) sherds have been recorded there; but no architectural remains date to either of these periods. Site construction of any scale begins at Mayapan in the brief Hocaba phase (A.D. 1250–1300) and continues in the succeeding Tases phase (A.D. 1300–1450). This Tases-phase ceramic complex represents what has come to be thought of as the Mayapan ceramic horizon (see Smith 1971 for Mayapan pottery analyses).

Ceramic continuity from the Early Postclassic Sotuta phase of Chichen Itza to Late Postclassic Mayapan is minimal. Only one style, Peto Cream Ware, which occurs at Chichen late in the Sotuta phase, is found in the Hocaba phase at Mayapan. It is of interest, however, to note that the Hocaba-phase complex is present at Chichen where it occurs in contexts suggesting a squatter occupation after the abandonment of the Early Postclassic public buildings.

The Tases-phase pottery of Mayapan is characterized by a distinctive Mayapan Red Ware and by unslipped modeled effigy censers. The Tases phase is completely post-Plumbate in time and also postdates the Fine Orange marker-type Silho; however, a few sherds of Matillas Fine Orange (formerly V-Fine Orange) are found as foreign increments in the assemblage.

Mayapan is a walled city of concentrated residential settlement clustered around a ceremonial or civic center. Population for the 4.2 square kilometers found within the wall is estimated at 11,000–12,000 persons, to which might be added another couple of thousand who lived in residential units immediately outside the wall. The form of the wall, with its parapet-like feature, suggests a defensive function (Webster 1976b, 1978). Richard Ebright (1981) has emphasized the discontinuities and dissimilarities between Mayapan and Chichen Itza architecture. The Mayapan dry slab-and-block masonry is in strong contrast to the finished and elegant stucco-and-veneer styles of Early Postclassic Chichen. Shrines and oratories, which are a common feature of Mayapan, are not found at Chichen; and ball courts and sweathouses, well known at Chichen, are missing at Mayapan. The typical Mayapan residential unit has what is known as the "tandem front-back room plan." The front room is open along most of its length, with wooden posts or stone columns supporting the lintel. A low, wide bench lines the rear and the two ends of this front room. The closed rear room, entered by a central doorway, has no benches although sometimes it may have a small altar abutting the center of its back wall. With its use of columns and the presence of an altar or shrine, the residential unit has a generic similarity to the Mayapan shrines and oratories. This house plan and the tradition of Mayapan architecture have no known antecedents (Freidel 1981a). There are, of course, a few well-known continuities between Chichen and Mayapan architecture: the Mayapan central Castillo resembles the building of the same name at Chichen Itza; a serpent-columned temple at Mayapan suggests Chichen's "High Priest's Grave"; and a round Mayapan structure has something of a homologue in the Chichen Itza Caracol. But even in these examples there are differences between the buildings at Chichen and their much cruder Mayapan counterparts.

To return to the questions of archaeology and legendary history that were raised in our comments on Chichen Itza, were both cities built by Itzas? Thompson (1945), Brainerd (1958), and others have believed that they were. Roys (1962) thinks otherwise. In Roys's opinion, the Toltecs erected Chichen and ruled there until they were expelled ca. A.D. 1200. The Itza then occupied the city, as "squatters," early in the thirteenth century—presumably after their expulsion from Chakanputun, an interpretation that would identify the Itza as Putun Maya. The Itza then founded Mayapan in 1263. They did this, however, in conjunction with the Cocom, and the latter gradually rose to prominence in the city's affairs. Richard Ebright sees a confirmation of this legendary historical and ethnohistorical data in the archaeology. The

Hocaba-phase "squatter" occupation of Chichen is to be correlated with the Itza's arrival and short stay at that site early in the thirteenth century. The subsequent Tases phase sees the supremacy of the Cocom element in the city. Mayapan was abandoned sometime in the middle of the fifteenth century in an atmosphere, according to the legendary historical sources, of tribal rivalries and civil war.

Archaeological knowledge of the Late Postclassic in the Northern Plains and East Coast zones is still spotty. In early historic times there was a concentration of population in the northwest interior of the Yucatan Peninsula (Freidel 1981a). This is the general region of Mayapan, and it seems likely that there were other Late Postclassic centers here. At Dzibilchaltun, which is 40 kilometers north of Mayapan, there was a modest-sized resident population during the period. Some public or ceremonial building continued from Early Postclassic times, and hieroglyphic medallion texts in one building appear to date from A.D. 1392 to 1431, contemporary with the Tases-phase occupation at Mayapan. Dzibilchaltun Late Postclassic ceramics, designated as the Chechem phase, include such Mayapan diagnostics as Peto Cream and Mayapan Red. Dzibilchaltun continued to be occupied after the fall of Mayapan and was an active site up until Colonial times (Andrews IV and Andrews V 1980).

Another Late Postclassic population concentration was along the East Coast of Quintana Roo. We have already noted that there were some sites on the coast in Early Postclassic times, but the later period shows an increase in size and numbers of locations. Sanders (1960) surveyed some of these. Beginning at the northeast, there is Vista Alegre, also referred to in the Early Postclassic discussions and a site which appears as a sizable town in early Spanish accounts (see Lothrop 1924). Other sites include Ichpaatun, Xelha, Tulum (see Lothrop 1924), and Tancah, to name only a few. The walled city or town of Tulum is linked closely to Mayapan in its architecture and ceramics. The Late Postclassic also saw population and site increase on Cozumel Island (Sabloff and Rathje 1975b; Sabloff 1977), which has been interpreted as an important link in a Maya coastwide trading system of the period. Such a system was undoubtedly tied to the Mayapan polity, but it also may have enjoyed a kind of semiindependent status as an "international port-of-trade" enclave. The "internationalism" of this system seems further supported by a style of mural painting found at Tulum and as far south as Santa Rita (Gann 1900) in Belize. The style resembles the Mixteca-Puebla codices of the Late Postclassic (Robertson 1970).

A more recently discovered Late Postclassic site concentration has been reported by Harrison (1979, 1981) in the interior of southern Quintana Roo. Harrison refers to this Late Postclassic culture as the Lobil phase, drawing upon a sample of 81 sites. It is characterized by rough stone constructions, in general keeping with the stone masonry styles and techniques of Mayapan. These constructions, in some cases, have been built over earlier, Classic Period elite buildings; in other instances they are ground-level, residential-appearing low platforms. Associated ceramics resemble Tases-phase censers and redwares of Mayapan. Harrison states that his survey seems to indicate that Lobil style architectural remains extend from south-central Campeche, across all of southern Quintana Roo, and into northern Belize in the vicinity of Chetumal Bay. All of this, preliminary and tentative as it may be, implies a sizable Late Postclassic population for a large part of the Maya Lowlands lying well to the south of northern Yucatan.

To continue the Late Postclassic survey toward the south, we have evidence of only squatter-type occupation of the major sites of the Central Yucatan Zone. Becan is an example, where Mayapan-like effigy censers are found occasionally and superficially (Ball 1974b, 1977a). In addition we can refer to the above-mentioned Lobil-phase distribution, which is reported as extending as far west as south-central Campeche (which could be considered within the Central Yucatan Zone). Ball (1978) has stated that the archaeological record along the coast of the Campeche Zone is somewhat disappointing for the Late Postclassic in view of early ethnohistoric accounts about the region. North of Champoton he found very little. There is a ceramic complex at Champoton (Ruz 1969) which dates to the Late Postclassic on the basis of Matillas Fine Orange and Peto Cream sherds; and both Aguacatal (Xicalango) (Ruz 1969; Matheny 1970) and Tixchel (Ruz 1969) are reported to have pottery collections of the period.

This edges us over the coast of the Northwestern Zone, where the site of Juárez, west of the Grijalva Delta, was an impressive politico-religious center with a large residential population (Berlin 1956; Jaeckel 1981). Much more large-scale digging needs to be done in a site like Juárez to reveal its full history and dating; but, even on basis of the information we have at present, there seems little doubt that the Spanish accounts of important towns or cities along this section of the Gulf

Coast do have some archaeological support. Following these accounts, it seems certain that these towns were important coastal trading centers with ties into the system referred to on the east coast of Quintana Roo.

Farther inland in the Northwestern Zone, and on up the Usumacinta River into the Usumacinta Zone, no substantial Late Postclassic occupation is recorded. Still farther, in the Southwestern Zone, the Tepancuapan phase at the Chinkultic site and vicinity, which has been referred to under the Early Postclassic, may extend, on the basis of some ceramic finds, into Late Postclassic times, although this is uncertain (Ball 1980).

Switching back to the east, and to northern Belize, we can consider the Late Postclassic evidences from the site of Santa Rita. The site had an earlier history, was abandoned, and then reoccupied and built over in the Late Postclassic. Constructions of this date, although relatively modest in size, contain the well-known murals which Robertson (1970) has designated as being in a Late Pre-Columbian Mesoamerican "international style." Diane Chase (1981) has also reported upon recent excavations into Late Postclassic platforms at the site. Also in northern Belize, the sites of Aventura, Chowacol, Cerro, El Posito, Nohmul, and several others have Late Postclassic ceramics. A bit farther south, we come to Lamanai which, it will be recalled, showed impressive public construction through the Terminal Classic and into the Early Postclassic. According to Pendergast (1981), there were also some small building projects at the site that date to the Late Postclassic or fourteenth and fifteenth centuries. Late Postclassic identifications rest upon pottery that resembles Mayapan Red ware and Mayapan effigy censers, and they raise a problem since the radiocarbon dates from Lamanai suggest a date of A.D. 1140, or a century or so before such pottery styles appeared at Mayapan. Following upon this carbon dating, Pendergast has suggested that the Mayapan Tases complex, which appears with some suddenness in northern Yucatan, may have had its origins in northern Belize. In southern Belize there is virtually nothing that can be placed as Late Postclassic. The exception is the site of Wild Cane Cay, off the coast, which has been a Late Classic through Late Postclassic occupation. The island also shows occupation up into Colonial times (Rice 1974).

For the Pasión and Southeastern zones there are no substantial Late Postclassic data.

In the Central Zone we have the Late Postclassic sites of the Isla phase from the Peten lakes district. There is a small but clearly elite-style architectural complex on Topoxte Island in Lake Yaxha (Bullard 1970). Measuring about 175 by 100 meters, the complex consists of temple- and palace-type buildings arranged around courtyards. Earlier constructional levels on the island date back to Classic and even Pre-classic times. Late Postclassic buildings have been constructed over earlier Classic ones. There are a number of stelae and altars at the site. The sculptured ones are left from Classic times; but the plain ones (probably once painted and stuccoed) pertain to the Late Post-classic center. The Late Postclassic temples at Topoxte have wide door-ways divided by columns and, in general, resemble the Postclassic architecture of the Northern Plains and East Coast zones. On the matter of relationships, however, Bullard (1970: 276) offers the caution:

In sum, the visible architectural remains of the Isla phase display a number of features which are characteristic of the Postclassic Period. Probably most indicative are the building plans using columns and the stairway "balustrades" with the vertical upper zones, as well as the concentrated settlement pattern and the island location. Certain architectural details—the slot-like basal mold-ings and the absence of medial moldings are two examples cited—appear to be local features on the basis of the little we know about Postclassic Maya architecture. Certainly, the resemblances between the Topoxte buildings and the known Postclassic buildings in Yucatan and Quintana Roo are not of such an order to support a belief that the Isla Phase represents a direct colonization from either of those areas.

The pottery of the Topoxte site is largely of the Topoxte pottery group, although some few sherds of Paxcaman wares are also present (Bullard 1970). There seems to be a geographic division in the lakes district between Topoxte pottery, which is common in the east, and Paxcaman-group pottery, which is characteristic of the western lakes (P. Rice 1979 and personal communication; A. F. Chase 1979; A. F. and D. Z. Chase, personal communication; Rice and Rice 1979). Paxcaman has a somewhat earlier inception than Topoxte, probably having begun in the Early Postclassic; Topoxte beginnings may not go back that far. In the eastern lakes country, at Macanche and Zacpeten, the Trapeche ceramic group, which had Early Postclassic beginnings, also continues into the Late Postclassic (P. Rice, personal communi-cation). While Isla-phase and contemporaneous Late Postclassic Peten ceramic complexes probably have roots in the Peten Tepeu tradition, and in the Tepeu 3 phase of the Terminal Classic, there are, at the same time, elements within the Isla complex, such as the effigy censer forms, that imply contacts with the Northern Lowlands, especially with the Tases horizon of Mayapan.

These ceramic similarities between the Peten lakes Isla phase and the Late Postclassic Northern Lowlands may relate to legendary history and especially to the supposed arrival of the Itza in the Peten at an 8 Ahau katun ending (Thompson 1951). Certainly the Itza were in the lakes region in early historic times.[2] Was their 8 Ahau arrival in A.D. 1201 or 1458? My own guess would be the latter date. The date of 1458, obviously, would be too late for an introduction of Mayapan-derived ceramic traits, which are so definitely associated with the To-poxte ceramic group (Chase and Chase, personal communication). Thus, it seems likely that there were introductions into the Peten lake country from the north, by either diffusion or migration, substantially in advance of a mid-fifteenth-century arrival of the Itza.

Let us conclude this section with some generalizations about the Late Postclassic.

First, the key site of the period is Mayapan, in the Northern Plains Zone. Mayapan retains some "Mexican" elements and some architectural resemblances to Chichen Itza; however, the position taken here is that these resemblances have been overstressed. Mayapan culture is a new synthesis and an essentially Lowland Maya one. Its ceramic complex, especially that of its principal Tases phase, is quite different from that of Early Postclassic Chichen Itza; and it has been suggested that it may have origins in northern Belize.

Second, during the Late Postclassic Period there are many sites along the coast, especially the Quintana Roo coast. This follows a pattern observed in Early Postclassic coastal settlement except that in the later period it is much more pronounced.

Third, elsewhere in the Maya Lowlands there are sites along the Campeche and Northwestern Zone coasts, in the southern interior of the East Coast Zone, in the adjacent Central Yucatan Zone, in northern Belize, and around the Peten lakes in the Central Zone. There is some elite architectural construction associated with some of these Late Postclassic cultures. One has the impression, from architectural similarities and from related ceramic complexes, that a synthesis of a new, widespread Maya Lowland culture may have been in the making.

Fourth, it has been noted by many observers that the Late Postclassic of the Maya Lowlands was heavily oriented toward seacoast trade and traffic. This is expressed in site locations, in the presence of trade materials, and in early historic accounts.

ZONAL RECAPITULATION

The foregoing treatment of three time periods—Terminal Classic, Early Postclassic, and Late Postclassic—has been deliberately "horizontal," or synchronic, in an attempt to emphasize connections among what was going on, or seemed to be going on, at similar times throughout the Maya Lowlands. It might be well to summarize or recapitulate now on the "vertical," or diachronic, dimension and to do this by the zonal subdivisions to which we have been referring.

The Central Zone. The Terminal Classic saw the relatively swift ninth-century abandonment of the major centers. This abandonment is clearly registered in the decline and cessation of elite architectural and intellectual activities. There were either large-scale population losses or drastic population dispersals in many localities; in some places, however, small sites or residential areas continued to be occupied. For the tenth century, or the second half of the period, we have very little information.

The Early Postclassic sees occupation in some localities, especially around the Peten lakes. There was some elite activity, evidenced by temple assemblages and stelae; however, this was on a smaller scale than previous Classic building. In the Late Postclassic we have the integration of the Islas phase, with small ceremonial or civic centers in the lake district.

The Southeastern Zone. There was rapid decline here in the Terminal Classic. Copan ceased to be a center; Quirigua continued as an occupied place into the Early Postclassic although without stelae dedication and with little major building. The record stops after this.

The Pasión Zone. The record is mixed for the Terminal Classic. Altar de Sacrificios declined; Seibal enjoyed a century of elite activity. Subsequently, the record trails off in this period, with no Postclassic occupation of consequence.

The Usumacinta Zone. Terminal Classic decline in this zone was swift and conclusive, occurring early on in the ninth century. There is no Postclassic record.

The Southwestern Zone. Elite activity continued through the ninth century of the Terminal Classic. At Chinkultic, on the southern border of the zone and near the Chiapas highlands, some occupation continued through the period and into the Early Postclassic and, perhaps, Late Postclassic Periods. At other sites in the Ocosingo Valley there was elite building activity in the Postclassic.

The Northwestern Zone. Palenque suffered a ninth-century "collapse." At Jonuta and other sites, a Jonuta Horizon occupation continued well into the Terminal Classic Period, but the record fades after this. There is little in the zone that can be identified to the Early Postclassic. For the Late Postclassic, however, both archaeology and ethnohistory attest to impressive trading centers.

The Campeche Zone. Most information here comes from the coast, where there was major building of sites through the Terminal Classic into the Early Postclassic. The Late Postclassic sees a tapering off of activities and site occupations. In the southeastern interior of the zone there is a substantial Late Postclassic occupation (Lobil phase), with the building over of old Classic sites in a rough masonry style.

The Central Yucatan Zone. Río Bec–Chenes centers were abandoned in the ninth century. Some show evidence of "squatter" occupation throughout the remainder of the Terminal Classic and into the Early Postclassic. There is little direct information on the Late Postclassic, but there is squatter evidence at some sites.

The Belize Zone. Activities in major centers of the southern part of the zone cut off in the ninth century; however, some cave sites may have been used as shrines or sacred places well into the Terminal Classic. In the northern part of the zone some sites show "times of trouble" toward the end of the ninth century; but there are also indications of continued building and activity in centers through the Terminal Classic, into the Early Postclassic, and on into the Late Postclassic. Near the coast there are Late Postclassic sites that appear to have been trading centers.

The Northern Plains Zone. The Terminal Classic Period in the Northern Plains Zone marked an apogee of architectural development and is referred to as the Pure Florescent Period. There were many regional centers of magnificence. While essentially local in inspiration, both the architecture and the art of the period show alien influence of a "Mexican" quality, often associated with the Chontal or Putun Maya. The founding of Toltec-Maya Chichen Itza at about A.D. 1000 coincides with a drastic change in settlement. Most old great centers are reduced to apparent impotence. The only outlying sites in the

Early Postclassic are coastal locations—trading towns, salt works, or fishing stations.

In the Late Postclassic, Chichen Itza is abandoned; the Toltec presence disappears; Mayapan becomes the main city of the Northern Lowlands. There are some other smaller centers in the interior of the Yucatan Peninsula; some others exist on the coast although the northwest peninsular coast seems largely uninhabited. Mayapan dominance or hegemony continues until the mid-fifteenth century. After that, power appears to have decentralized.

The East Coast Zone. The East Coast Zone in the Terminal Classic appears to be somewhat marginal to the Northern Plains, but it, too, participates in the developments of the Pure Florescent era. It also follows suit in the Early Postclassic, being largely denuded of major centers in the interior although there are some important towns along the Quintana Roo coast. In the Late Postclassic there is something of a boom in small trading cities or towns along this coast, including the island of Cozumel. Ceramics and architecture of these several towns are related to Mayapan. Many of these places appear to survive up to the time of the Spanish conquest.

SOME CONCLUDING REMARKS

As I said at the outset, my paper has been an attempt to record, however briefly, the facts of settlement and cultural activity throughout the Maya Lowlands from A.D. 800 until the Spanish entradas. I think I have done this with relative objectivity although, as I also stated, I carry, like all archaeologists, some preconceptions and biases. Let me, in these concluding remarks, offer some observations, more subjective and interpretive than the data survey just recounted.

My experience in Maya archaeology suggests to me that the Lowland Maya lived in a condition of political instability. This was intermittent and recurrent. A waxing and waning of Lowland Maya political orders can be traced back to the upswing of the Late Preclassic, with the founding of the first great centers or cities. During the latter part of the Late Preclassic, or in a time period (0–A.D. 250) sometimes referred to as the "Protoclassic," there may have been the beginnings of a retrenchment, with the abandoning of some centers (Willey 1977). This was followed by an Early Classic resurgence in some places; but, again, there was a notable dropoff in constructional activity and stela dedication during the sixth-century "hiatus" (Willey 1974). In the Late Classic there was an undeniable growth spurt as witnessed by the revival of many centers, the construction of new ones, and a proliferation of stelae dedications—all this accompanied by every indication of overall population increase for the Lowlands. Then came the decline and "collapse" of the Terminal Classic. Finally, in the Postclassic, there is the rise, dominance, and then abandonment of Chichen Itza, the subsequent rise of Mayapan, and finally its desertion prior to the arrival of the Spaniards.

In stating all of this I have tended to generalize, to see surges, declines, and resurgences as area-wide phenomena. Recently, David Freidel (1983a) has questioned some of this synchronization and geographical inclusiveness. It is Freidel's argument that Lowland Maya polities were always in a state of flux, with ephemeral states and chiefdoms struggling side by side, approaching centralization and then backsliding toward local petty autonomies. Without attempting to argue about the validity of wide-scale geographic synchronizations of these phenomena, I think that we are in agreement about the theme of Lowland Maya political instability, and it is a theme to be considered in our evaluations of the Postclassic. If this impression of Lowland Maya political instability is correct, where does the cause lie? Is it in the difficulties encountered in establishing and maintaining centralized control of agricultural production in a tropical lowland setting (Sanders and Price 1968; Sanders 1977, 1981)? Did certain natural resource weaknesses or shortages disadvantage the Maya? And did such factors keep any one Lowland Maya polity from rising and maintaining full statehood dominance over the others? Were the Maya unusually vulnerable to "foreign" penetration, and, if so, why?

The drift of these questions leads us to another observation and set of questions about the importance of foreign or external agents as causative factors in Maya Lowland development and change. Some decades ago it was the fashion to give considerable weight to external influences. More recently, *in situ* forces have been seen as the more important, perhaps righting the balance. But whichever emphasis one prefers, the facts of Lowland Maya involvement with peoples and cultures of other Mesoamerican regions must be given some interpretive consideration in any analysis of either history or process. The "Mexicanization" of the Terminal Classic Period, the establishment of Toltec Chichen, and the trading contacts of the Late Postclassic,

47

all of which we have been reviewing in this overview, have numerous predecessors in the Lowland Maya archaeological record. External contacts go back to the very beginning of this record, with the appearances of the earliest Lowland Maya pottery (Hammond et al. 1979). Later there are suggestions of Olmec relationships to the Maya Lowlands (e.g., Willey 1978: 97–98); and in the Late Preclassic we have ample evidence of ideological contacts between the Chiapas-Guatemalan Highlands and Pacific slopes and the Maya Lowlands (M. D. Coe 1977; Quirarte 1977; Graham 1979). These contacts, revealed in hieroglyphics, iconography, and calendrics, leave the general impression that much of the basic content of elite Maya Lowland culture was assimilated from these "external" sources. Subsequently, in the Classic Period, we know that there was continued communication between major Lowland Maya cities, such as Tikal, and Kaminaljuyu of the Guatemalan Highlands; and this communication network also involved Teotihuacan in Central Mexico. Raw materials and manufactured goods were exchanged as well as ideas. In politics and dynastic matters it is possible that Lowland Maya political centralization and state formation of the Early Classic were stimulated by and linked to the policies of Kaminaljuyu and Teotihuacan. And from here the story can be continued into the "Mexicanoid" and "Veracruzoid" impingements of the Late Classic and Terminal Classic (Proskouriakoff 1951; Sabloff and Willey 1967; Parsons 1969b).

I think we have to view Lowland Maya culture history against the background of these two interrelated conditions—political instability and "foreign" involvements—to understand the events of the Terminal Classic and Postclassic periods. Surely the southern "collapse" of the ninth century must have been related in some way to the amazing florescence of the north at the same time; and both these developments, in my opinion, are rooted in the circumstances of inherent political instability and susceptibility to alien influences. Admittedly, we do not yet understand the processes of these developments. A single explanation, such as military invasion and conquest, seems too simple an answer; and the facts and findings of archaeology do not back it up, although it may have taken place in certain instances. Trading cutoffs and disruptions may be more generally applicable, but they are not altogether satisfactory. If such problems brought about the downfall of the south, what of the north? Why did the cities there flourish at the same time that the south faded? Was it because the Northern Lowlands were bolstered by an actual alien presence—the Putun Maya, who, in turn, had assimilated Mexican ideas and behavior? Had the north, in this manner, through more gradual exposure to "foreign" values and institutions, accommodated or adjusted to them, become immunized against them, as it were, in contrast to the more protected south?

The establishment of Chichen Itza as the great center of the Early Postclassic Period was a climax to the Terminal Classic buildup of Lowland Maya "Mexicanization." Almost certainly, this was a power maneuver involving military force. Whoever or whatever the nature of the contending parties at this time, the event inaugurated a new socioeconomic and politico-religious regime in the Northern Maya Lowlands that was to persist for two centuries, dominating the north and keeping the south in the shadows.

The subsequent Late Postclassic society of the Northern Lowlands was also linked to greater Mesoamerica and to Mexico, although in a different way. It now became a part, more, I think, than it ever had before, of a commercial and trading network, one which had its essential direction from Central Mexico and which was especially mediated through coastal traffic. There was, in a sense, a Maya "resurgence" in the Late Postclassic, but what was its nature? It was not a resurgence along the lines of the Classic achievements—measured in grandeur of architecture, stela dedications, and the hieroglyphic texts speaking of the hallowed and aristocratic lineage ancestors. The times had changed; there were other and different values. Charles Erasmus (1968) argued this some time ago (see also Sharer 1982). Recently, Ronald Nigh (1981: 709) has stated:

We also find annoying the persistence of naive ideas of the "Classic" Maya and their "collapse", a natural result of the fixation on large stone monuments. It is still forgotten that Maya history did not end with the abandonment of such monuments, and that when the Spanish arrived on the scene most of the Maya area was densely populated by a thriving commercial and agricultural society. The Spanish describe the Chontal of Tabasco as dominated by a commercial class who lived in large houses in towns and owned many slaves to work their cacao plantations and drive their long-distance trading canoes. It seems that the abandonment of stone monument construction, as well as variations in agricultural intensity, could more convincingly be explained by analysis of the relations among the slave class, the priests and the merchants, in the context of an evolving pan-American economic system, where the social field conditioned the allocation of labor, resources, and power within Maya society.

I tend to agree with Erasmus's and Nigh's argument in favor of an "upward collapse," in one sense, although I would disagree about the naivete of relying upon stone monuments as an archaeological gauge for sociopolitical integration. There was a Classic Period in the Maya Lowlands, defined very clearly by calendrical dates, big architecture, and carved monuments. It was a reality, but this kind of life faded away, in some places rather rapidly, or was severely modified. In an effort to "make a case for the Postclassic" it is not necessary to deny the record. But what kind of "case" can we make for the Postclassic that will best help us to understand it and to put it in larger Maya and Mesoamerican perspective?

The Postclassic, and particularly the "resurgent" Late Postclassic, has been described as a society representing a set of values built around the wide distribution of consumer goods and the ethos of the wealthy mercantilist and trader (Rathje 1975; Sabloff and Rathje 1975a; Nigh 1981). But in the context of the Maya Lowlands, and particularly within that context as conditioned by its tradition of political instability and vulnerability to alien incursions, what did this mean? Trade and mercantilism, at least when organized on a scale like that of the Meso-american Late Postclassic, are extractive strategies, techniques of imperialism and colonialism that are, in last analysis, imposed by the strong on the weak. The much-vaunted wider distribution of consumer goods is a process that benefits the imperialistic, extractive state, not the society under its commercial jurisdiction. It is in the imperialist state that the goods and benefits may, to a degree, trickle downward in the social strata (Barroll 1980). In the exploited domain only the upper class retains any of this wealth generated by trade. In the present situation I think we can be sure that the Late Postclassic Lowland Maya were not the imperialist power at the head of the trade chain. That power lay first, perhaps, along the Gulf Coast, but eventually in Central Mexico, where all great Mesoamerican power had resided since the Early Classic preeminence of Teotihuacan. In the evolution of the state and of the institutions of trade, there had, indeed, been an "upward collapse"; however, the Toltecs and Aztecs of Central Mexico participated in the "upwardness" while the Lowland Maya enjoyed the "collapse."

Because of this, I regard the Lowland Maya Late Postclassic society as a reduced, shrunken, impoverished version of its former Classic condition, brought to this status by its successive confrontations with the rising Mexican states and empires, culminating with the Aztecs. This reduction is reflected—and here I unashamedly turn to the monuments—in the shoddiness of Mayapan architecture and in the curiously "warped" and dwarf-like temples of Tulum and Cozumel. Situated at the far end of an extractive commercial chain, led by parvenue merchants who were allied with their Mexican exploiters, their former glories were remembered only in legends and prophecies, in the civilized rhetoric of their remnant priestly class who, with aristocratic and intellectual disdain, recounted the comings and goings of their various vulgar conquerors (Brotherston 1979).

NOTES

1. In preparing this paper I am indebted to the students of my Harvard graduate seminar held during the spring of 1981. Our theme was the Lowland Maya Postclassic Period, and the seminar papers and discussions were all addressed to it. Participants were Fred Valdez, Jr., Beth A. Collea, Paul Jaeckel, James Parry, Michael N. Geselowitz, Richard H. Ebright, and Heidy Fogel. Their papers are listed in the bibliography and are on file in the Tozzer Library, Peabody Museum at Harvard University.

2. The location of the Itza in early historic times was at a site referred to as Tayasal (Thompson 1951). There is some dispute as to whether this place was located in or around the Lake Peten-Itza (Jones, Rice, and Rice 1981) or at the location of the Topoxte ruin on that island in Lake Yaxha (Chase 1976).

3

A Review and Synthesis of Recent Postclassic Archaeology in Northern Yucatan[1]

FERNANDO ROBLES CASTELLANOS

Harvard University

ANTHONY P. ANDREWS

New College of the University of South Florida

The Postclassic history of northern Yucatan presents a paradox that has frustrated scholars for decades. It is a time whose records include detailed accounts of people, places, and events, and whose reconstruction promises invaluable insights into the entire panorama of Maya history. Moreover, this wealth of data is bolstered by a wealth of ethnographic continuities recorded in the early colonial period. The Postclassic, then, is a period in which the archaeologist might comfortably begin to feel like an historian. Yet despite this vast array of data, the period remains a puzzle whose assembly has eluded scholars for more than a century.

The irony of Postclassic research lies in the enormous corpus of data which, appearing to hold the answers to all questions, in reality only obfuscates the events and processes of a very complex period. Much of the confusion arises from the incompatibility of the various sources of information: the plentiful historic data, rendered somewhat murky by their semimythical nature, and often distorted by those who recorded the events, simply fail to mesh with the archaeological data. A case in point is the never-ending effort to find a correlation between the Mayan and Christian calendars, a problem whose solution clearly lies in Postclassic research. Differing katun counts and an array of

53

radiometric and excavation data offer a wide spread of possible alignments, and a somewhat perverse challenge to the scholar who wishes
to make a choice. Heightening the irony is the seeming ease with
which we perceive earlier periods of Maya history, whose reconstruction is built upon straightforward archaeological data, aided by an
occasional ethnographic analogy, but unclouded by documentary confusion.

In the following paper we review recent research and present a
reconstruction of the period based on the results of that research. The
scope of our discussion will be limited to the northern third of the
peninsula, which we have demarcated by drawing a line from Jaina
to Tulum (Figure 3.1). The Postclassic Period of northern Yucatan has
traditionally been dated A.D. 1000–1542; however, recent evidence
indicating a substantial chronological overlap between materials of the
Terminal Classic (or Pure Florescent) and Early Postclassic (or Modified Florescent) periods has led us to consider the earlier period as
well. Moreover, an adequate discussion of the Postclassic is impossible
without a consideration of the prior events that shaped the period; thus,
our review and reconstruction begins at the onset of the Terminal
Classic Period, toward the middle of the eighth century.

Our reconstruction of Postclassic northern Yucatan has grown out
of two earlier attempts to analyze new data on the Terminal Classic
and Early Postclassic periods (A. P. Andrews 1978b; Andrews and
Robles C. 1985). Those attempts raised questions that we shall further
explore in this paper. Of particular interest are the factors involved in
the rise and fall of the Itza polity, and the relationship of that polity
to the eastern domain of Coba, which was long assumed to have been
abandoned before the rise of Chichen Itza; recent research has shown
that this was not the case, and Coba is now viewed as a major force
in the events that shaped Postclassic Yucatan (Robles C. 1980). Another
concern of the present volume is the nature of the Yucatecan Postclassic
in the larger context of Maya history: why did the north continue to
flourish after the southern collapse? Were events in the north merely
a delayed response to the decay that was spreading out of the south
(Willey 1982)? Or was the north embarked on a radical new trajectory
(Rathje 1975)? Relevant to these questions is the reversal, in Late
Postclassic times, of an apparent trend toward political and economic
centralization on the peninsula, a trend that began during the Classic
Period, if not earlier. Whether this reversal represents a final disinte-

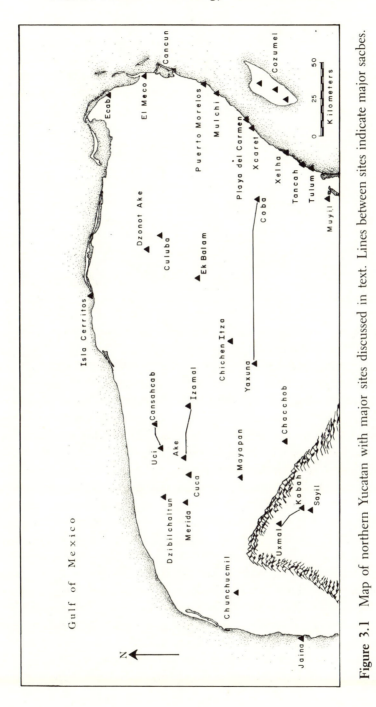

Figure 3.1 Map of northern Yucatan with major sites discussed in text. Lines between sites indicate major sacbes.

gration of Maya culture or a further refinement of its development remains a central issue with important implications for our understanding of the development of civilization in tropical lowland environments. In order to begin to address some of these issues, it is necessary to review the recent research on the Yucatecan Postclassic.

POSTCLASSIC RESEARCH
IN NORTHERN YUCATAN, 1970–1983

Although there are many reviews of the history of recent Maya research, only a few contain significant syntheses of the recent work carried out in Postclassic northern Yucatan (Wauchope 1968; Adams 1969; Gallareta 1979; Barrera Vásquez 1980, 1981; Adams and Hammond 1982). Only one study, by Benavides Castillo (1981c), summarizes some of the research of the last decade.

Fieldwork

The major development in northern Yucatan archaeology during the 1970s was the establishment of the Centro Regional del Sureste, of the Instituto Nacional de Antropología e Historia (CRS-INAH), and the growth of its program of research in anthropology, linguistics, and history under the direction of Norberto González Crespo from 1973 to 1982. The program has emphasized fieldwork in archaeology, and its far-ranging surveys and excavations throughout the peninsula have yielded substantial new data on the Postclassic Period which will be summarized in the following review.

Several foreign institutions also contributed to the research of the period, the most prominent being the Middle American Research Institute of Tulane University (MARI), whose program of research included the completion of various projects in Yucatan (Dzibilchaltun), Campeche (Becan and the Río Bec Area), and Quintana Roo (Xcaret and the Central Coast), as well as the recent excavations at the Formative Period community of Komchen, in northwest Yucatan (conducted jointly with CRS-INAH). Many of the MARI programs, which have been carried out in close cooperation with CRS-INAH, have included substantial work in conservation.

Programs conducted by other foreign institutions include the Harvard University–University of Arizona Cozumel Project, the National

Geographic Society–CRS-INAH Coba Mapping Project (part of the larger ongoing CRS-INAH program of research at that site), the Tancah-Tulum Mural Project, and the Pennsylvania State University Cuca–Chacchob–Dzonot Ake Project. The funding for the majority of these projects came from the National Geographic Society and the National Science Foundation, as well as other sources.

The following review of recent Postclassic research is organized according to the areas and/or sites that have been the primary targets of fieldwork.

Northern Plains. The two most significant recent contributions to the archaeology of the northern plains are the survey of the state of Yucatan, part of a peninsula-wide *Atlas Arqueológico* program conducted by CRS-INAH, and the ongoing program of publication of the work of MARI at Dzibilchaltun.

The survey, conducted by numerous investigators throughout the 1970s, is perhaps the most ambitious surface reconnaissance ever undertaken in the Maya area. The work involved a synthesis of the site and survey reports of the area, the assembly of a massive map and airphoto archive, and intensive ground, water, and air surveys, carried out under the supervision of Silvia Garza T. de González and Edward B. Kurjack (1977, 1980). The first result, published as the *Atlas Arqueológico del Estado de Yucatán*, contains an inventory of more than 1,000 sites, accurately located on 19 sheets at an approximate scale of 1:200,000; each site is cross-indexed by alphabetical name(s), location code, and bibliographic sources. No attempt was made in this publication to include chronological data, though such information is available for many sites in the files of the *Atlas* office at CRS-INAH. The survey is by no means complete, and the less-accessible eastern and southern portions of the state have received relatively little attention; however, a working framework and file system have been established, so that the survey may continue indefinitely. At present, the file is being expanded to include ongoing *Atlas* surveys in Campeche and Quintana Roo.

The final reports of the program of field research at Dzibilchaltun (1957–66) began to appear in the 1970s, adding a major dimension to our understanding of Maya prehistory. The continuous sequence of occupation at Dzibilchaltun from Middle Formative to Early Colonial times has provided a baseline for the cultural chronology of northern Yucatan (Andrews V 1978, 1981); the first reports include the final site map (Stuart et al. 1979; Kurjack 1979a), descriptions and analysis of the excavations and architecture (Kurjack 1974, 1978; Andrews IV and Andrews V 1980; Andrews V 1981; Cottier 1982), and a thorough diachronic study of the settlement patterns and developing urban nature of the community, carried out by Kurjack (1974, 1977, 1978, 1979). Reports on the ceramics, artifacts, and sculpture are in preparation.

During the 1970s, several problem-oriented surveys and limited excavation projects were carried out in the northern plains. The discovery of a number of fortified sites led to work at Cuca, Chacchob, and Dzonot Ake (Kurjack and Andrews V 1978; Webster 1978, 1979), while other projects focused on *sacbe* systems (Maldonado 1979a, 1979b), residential settlement patterns (Baker 1976; Vlcek 1978; Vlcek, Garza T. de González and Kurjack 1978), and diverse aspects of individual sites, such as the culture history of Ake (Maldonado Cárdenas and Repetto-Tio 1981), the discovery of Puuc architecture at the eastern site of Culuba (Andrews V 1979), and conservation work at archaeological sites in the vicinity of Merida (Gallareta and Callaghan 1981; Barrera Rubio 1983a; González Licón 1983). Intensive surveys of the west and north coasts of the peninsula were also carried out during this period, yielding important data on the role of coastal resources and trading patterns in the prehistoric development of the area (Ball and Eaton 1972; Ball 1977b, 1978; A. P. Andrews 1977, 1978a, 1978b, 1980a; Eaton 1978).

The Puuc. Research in the Puuc region over the last 12 years can be broken into three categories: architectural studies, settlement pattern and ecological studies, and reports of work at Uxmal.

The long-awaited publication of H. E. D. Pollock's survey of Puuc architecture (1980) has provided the field with an invaluable body of data that will stand as the main reference source on the subject for decades. Timely follow-ups to Pollock's work are updated analyses by E. Wyllys Andrews V (1979) and George Andrews (1982) of recent data concerning the chronological development and spread of Puuc architecture in northern Yucatan.

Until recently, attempts to visit many well-known Puuc sites were frustrated by the absence of adequate maps of the region. The surveyors of the *Atlas* program also encountered this problem, and mounted a major and successful effort to plot most of the known sites, as well as a fair number of previously unreported ones. These efforts also led to

58

preliminary analyses of the settlement patterns and human geography of the region (Kurjack, Garza T. de González, and Lucas 1979; Garza T. de González and Kurjack 1980; Kurjack and Garza T. de González 1981a, 1981b). More recently, CRS-INAH crews conducting conservation work in the Puuc have published brief reports on several sites, including Yaxche-Xlabpak (Benavides C. and Morales L. 1979), Xkokoh and Nakaskat (Benavides C. and Burgos V. 1982), Sabacche (Barrera Rubio 1982), and San Diego (Barrera Rubio 1983b).

During the 1970s CRS-INAH carried out conservation projects at Uxmal at the temple of the Magician and the Great Pyramid (Sáenz 1972, 1975a), at the ball court (Maldonado Cárdenas 1981b, n.d.), and at several buildings affected by the installation of light and sound equipment (Konieczna and Mayer Guala 1976). In addition to these projects, CRS-INAH embarked on a settlement-pattern study of the environs of Uxmal, which has included the mapping of the site wall, as well the exploration of more than 100 chultunes, or underground cisterns (Barrera Rubio 1980b; González F. 1981). Other contributions of the period include the publication of Morley's 1941 field notes on the Stela Platform (1970) and a detailed architectural analysis of the House of the Governor (Kowalski 1981).

Chichen Itza and Vicinity. The beginning of the period saw the publication of the results of the 1959 INAH-MARI explorations of the cave of Balankanche (Andrews IV 1970), and a preliminary report on the 1967 exploration of the sacred well, in which several institutions took part under the supervision of INAH (Piña Chan 1970; for a popular account, see Ediger 1971). Another major recent contribution to the archaeology of Chichen Itza is John Bolles's exhaustive study of the Monjas Complex (1977), based mainly on fieldwork carried out under the Carnegie program in the 1930s. In the same vein is the ongoing research, by several scholars, on the artifacts and ecofacts recovered by Edward Thompson from the Cenote of Sacrifice; the publication of these studies, supervised by Clemency Coggins, is forthcoming.

During the 1970s most of the fieldwork at Chichen Itza was carried out by CRS-INAH to mitigate the impact of encroaching communal (ejido) lands and the construction of new tourist facilities; with the exception of a few short reports, little information is available on these projects (Barrera Rubio 1976b; Schmidt 1981a; see Márquez de González et al. in the section on ecofacts, below). Other contributions during the period include a study of the Great Ball Court (Cohodas 1974, 1978) and analyses of the phallic cult and cenote of sacrifice rituals (Folan 1972, 1980). Additional research on the murals, inscriptions, and chronology of Chichen Itza is discussed below.

Coba and Vicinity. The single largest project on the peninsula during the 1970s and early 1980s has been the CRS-INAH Coba Project, which began in 1974. Several other institutions, including the National Geographic Society and the Universidad Nacional Autónoma de México, have participated in the project, as have numerous scholars from different countries. The results of the fieldwork to date have appeared in several reports, theses, and dissertations.

The earliest efforts of the project focused on survey and mapping, with special emphasis on the vast *sacbe* network, the largest known in the Maya area (Figure 3.2; González F. 1975; Benavides C. 1976a, 1977, 1980a, 1981d, 1981e; Benavides et al. 1976; Benavides and Robles C. 1976; Robles C. 1977; Folan and Stuart 1977; Peniche Rivero and Folan 1978; Fletcher 1978; Kintz 1978; Cortés de Brasdefer 1981a, 1981c, 1981d; Folan, Kintz, and Fletcher 1983; cf. also Navarrete, Con Uribe, and Martínez Muriel 1979 for an earlier survey of Coba, conducted in 1972). The explorations included a survey of the 19-kilometer *sacbe* leading to Ixil, a distant outpost of the metropolitan area (Robles C. 1976; Folan 1977); this site was also surveyed, and is believed to be an architectural satellite of the main city (Robles C. 1976). In addition to the surveys and settlement pattern studies (discussed below), a fair amount of conservation work has been carried out in the central part of the site (Benavides et al. 1976; Cortés de Brasdefer 1981b).

Another major aspect of the Coba research was the establishment of a ceramic sequence, which revealed a continuous occupation at the site, from Late Formative to Late Postclassic times. This study, based on the analysis of the ceramics from a site-wide test-pitting program (136 test-pits), as well as surface collections (including Ixil) and architectural excavations, provides a preliminary sketch of the growth and decline of the community throughout the sequence (Robles C. 1980).

In addition to the above work, studies have been made of the mural paintings (Fettweis-Vienot 1980, 1981), sacrifice stones, and limestone quarries (Folan 1978a, 1978b). The stelae were also recorded by Eric von Euw, for eventual publication in the *Corpus of Maya Hieroglyphs.*

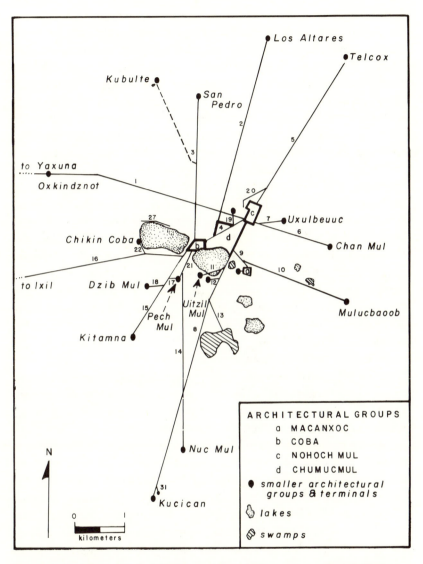

Figure 3.2 Map of Coba, Quintana Roo. Sacbes are numbered. Redrawn from Benavides (1981: Fig. 10), with permission of the author.

The East Coast. Academic interest as well as concern for conservation have prompted research on the East Coast in the last 12 years. The development of the entire area as an international tourist resort has had and continues to have a serious impact on the archaeological remains, and while the construction of new resorts has had the positive effect of creating many opportunities for research, it has also fostered even greater opportunities for looting and destruction. The most convenient way to outline the recent east coast fieldwork is to do so by areas and sites. We will begin at Cabo Catoche and proceed southward.

As we have noted, the early historical record of Yucatan has often confused those attempting interpretive histories. Such was the case regarding the location and history of the important Late Postclassic and Early Colonial port of Ecab, near the northeast corner of the peninsula. In 1976 and 1978, CRS-INAH conducted brief aerial, water, and ground surveys of the northeast corner of the peninsula, locating Ecab and another site of Late Postclassic date, Porvenir. The final reports of these brief surveys contain new maps and an updated history of the region, as well as detailed architectural plans of the large open chapel and curate's residence at Ecab. The pre-Hispanic community, which was also located but not explored in any depth, remains a priority for future research (Benavides C. and Andrews 1979; Benavides C. 1980b, 1981a).

Another prominent Postclassic northeast coast site, El Meco, has been the subject of more intensive work, prompted by conservational needs. Beginning in 1977, CRS-INAH and the Municipality of Cancun sponsored a program of survey, test-pitting, and architectural consolidation at the site, which is believed to have been the mainland port of embarkation for Isla Mujeres in pre-Hispanic times. It is also probable that it was, along with Ecab, an important node in the long-distance trade networks that stretched from the north coast down the east coast, to the Bay of Honduras and the Southern Maya Lowlands (Andrews and Robles C. 1985; Robles C. 1981a; Trejo Alvarado 1981).

The largest east coast project of the period, also spurred by conservation needs, was the 1975–76 Cancun project, which encompassed the archaeology of the entire island. Large-scale excavations and consolidation work were undertaken at the sites of El Rey–Pinturas, San Miguel, and Pok-Ta-Pok (Campo de Golf); many other sites were surveyed. With the exception of one midden, all the sites on the island appear to be exclusively Postclassic in date. The final report on the

Cancun project is in preparation, and several preliminary studies are available (Mayer Guala 1977, 1978, 1981; Vargas Pacheco 1978). This project marked the beginning of a new trend in east coast archaeology, namely, cooperation between CRS-INAH and the organization responsible for the development of the island, in this case, the Fondo Nacional de Turismo (FONATUR), which provided substantial logistical and financial support for the project. Such cooperation between archaeologists and developers, whether organizations or individuals, is now common on most east coast projects.

Playa del Carmen, the Postclassic and Early Colonial port of Xamanha ("north water"), was the site of a preliminary survey by MARI in 1972 and, more recently, of large-scale excavations and conservation by CRS-INAH. An important point of embarkation for the island of Cozumel, Xamanha appears to have served primarily as a trading port and religious sanctuary for pilgrims en route to the island (Andrews IV and Andrews 1975; González de la Mata 1981; González de la Mata and Trejo Alvarado 1981).

The main port of embarkation for Cozumel in pre-Hispanic and colonial times was Pole ("place of trade"?), today Xcaret. Here, a rocky inlet, or *caleta*, provides a protected harbor for seafaring vessels, a feature that is absent at the open beach site of Xamanha, seven kilometers to the north. The study of this site by MARI in 1955 and 1972–73 was accompanied by a survey of the central coast between Playa del Carmen and Tulum (Andrews 1973, 1976; Andrews IV and Andrews 1975). Pole, one of the larger Postclassic sites on the east coast, functioned as a way station for pilgrims on route to the shrine of Ixchel on Cozumel. The preponderance of religious structures at the core of the site underscores its importance as a ceremonial center, and its port facilities and pre-Hispanic name strongly suggest that it was a prominent trading port. While the occupational history of Pole dates back to Late Formative times, the vast majority of the standing architecture and surface ceramics date to the Late Postclassic Period; there is also evidence of a significant Early Colonial occupation, including the remains of an open chapel.

There are many other large Postclassic sites on the central coast, including Paamul, Chakalal, Akumal, Xelha, Tancah, and Tulum, all next to natural harbors. There has been substantial fieldwork during the last decade at the latter three sites.

Xelha ("opening of water"?), also reported historically as Xala, is located next to the largest natural harbor on the east coast and has a long history of occupation, from Late Formative to Early Colonial times. Several investigators explored parts of the site during the 1970s, reporting many new structures, some with murals (Andrews IV and Andrews 1975; Farriss, Miller, and Chase 1975; Benavides C. 1976a; Miller 1982; Mayer 1983c); preliminary explorations of the caves and bottom of the *caleta* yielded small amounts of ceramics and other artifacts (Navarrete 1974; Farriss and Miller 1974; Luna E. 1976). In 1980, CRS-INAH, with the support of the Fideicomisco Caleta de Xelha y del Caribe, began a major program of investigation at the site (Robles C. 1981b; Pérez Álvarez and Robles C. 1981). At present, the site map and the test-pitting program have been completed, and a large number of buildings have been excavated and consolidated. Among the more interesting features uncovered to date are several large complexes of Classic Period architecture, and a Teotihuacan-style mural. The preliminary analysis of the ceramic and settlement pattern data indicates that the predominant occupation occurred during the Classic Period, when the site covered at least two square kilometers; the site continued to be occupied up to the conquest. The survey revealed an internal *sacbe* system, but failed to locate a *sacbe* leading inland toward Coba—a frustrating situation, as it is widely believed by scholars working in the area that Xelha was the main port of Coba, an idea corroborated by architectural and ceramic data.

One of the more specialized projects of the period was the Tancah-Tulum Mural Project, directed by Arthur G. Miller in the early 1970s. This project, which involved the recording of the known murals in the region and the interpretation of their chronological and cultural implications, also included excavations and consolidation at Tancah; the sequential data from the research on the ceramics, architecture, and murals at Tancah has revealed evidence of a continuous occupation from Formative times to the Spanish conquest, and important data on cultural changes during the Postclassic Period (Miller 1973a, 1973b, 1974a, 1974b, 1975, 1977b, 1981, 1982; Miller and Farriss 1979). Barrera Rubio (1976a), Fettweis-Vienot (1976, 1981), and Paxton (1982a, 1982b) carried out further work on the murals at Tancah-Tulum, and CRS-INAH consolidated Str. 12 at Tancah (Benavides C. 1976b).

CRS-INAH conducted fieldwork at Tulum and its surrounding area in 1974 and 1975; this work included surveys, excavations, and architectural consolidation (Velásquez Valadez 1976; Barrera Rubio 1977a, 1977b, 1980c). A large research program, under the direction of Ernesto Vargas, was initiated in 1981.

Cozumel. The 1972–73 Harvard-Arizona Cozumel Project represents the first major attempt to reconstruct the prehistory of the entire island and, in particular, the role of Cozumel in the changing economic patterns of northern Yucatan during the Postclassic Period. Members of the project have published various papers dealing with the research design, theoretical background, and preliminary results of the fieldwork (Sabloff and Rathje 1973, 1975a, 1975b, 1980; Rathje and Sabloff 1973, 1978; Sabloff et al. 1974; Sabloff and Freidel 1975; Sabloff 1977). Several reports are also now available on the analysis of the architecture and settlement patterns of the major Postclassic communities of the island (Leventhal 1974; Gregory 1975; Rathje and Phillips 1975; Freidel 1975, 1976; Freidel and Cliff 1978).

Between 1980 and 1982 CRS-INAH carried out a program of survey, excavation, and consolidation at the site of San Gervasio, the largest pre-Hispanic community on the island (Robles C. 1981c; Sierra Sosa and Robles C. 1981).

Topical Research

Chronology. At the beginning of the 1970s the most widely accepted sequence of cultural development in the Northern Maya Lowlands was that established by Andrews IV (1965a, 1973). Even though Andrews on occasion favored the 12.9.0.0.0 Spinden correlation over the more commonly employed 11.16.0.0.0 Goodman-Martínez-Thompson correlation, his basic relative sequence of periods has withstood the test of time. Nonetheless, new data have indicated the need for several modifications and refinements (Andrews V 1978, 1979; Ball 1979a, 1979b; Andrews IV and Andrews V 1980;).

Today most Maya scholars still favor the GMT correlation, which has been bolstered by several new lines of evidence (Closs 1976; Edmonson 1976; Andrews V 1978; Andrews IV and Andrews V 1980); still, the question is far from being fully resolved, and alternate correlations are being considered by a number of scholars (Ball 1979b, this volume; Lincoln 1982; Kelley 1983; A. Chase, this volume).

The major modification to the traditional sequence proposed by Andrews IV concerns the chronological relationship of the Pure Florescent (or Terminal Classic) and Modified Florescent (or Early Post-classic) periods, which were originally envisioned as sequential, nonoverlapping cultural horizons. In the traditional scheme, the first period saw the development of the Puuc architectural tradition and the related Cehpech ceramic sphere; it was followed by the abandonment of the Puuc cities, around A.D. 1000, and the rise of Chichen Itza, whose architecture incorporated a modified Puuc style, chronologically associated with the ceramics of the Sotuta horizon. The relative dating of this sequence of events was based primarily on ceramic evidence whose stratigraphic relationships had not been well defined.

Several new lines of evidence now suggest that there is considerable chronological overlap between these two periods. Recent excavations at Coba, El Meco, Tancah, and San Gervasio (Cozumel) have revealed that Cehpech ceramics may date to as late as A.D. 1100, or even A.D. 1200 (Ball 1979a; Robles C. 1980, 1981a; Sierra Sosa and Robles C. 1981). New data also suggest that certain diagnostic ceramic types of the Sotuta ceramic sphere predate A.D. 1000. For example, diagnostic Sotuta-phase ceramics from the cave of Balankanche may date to the late ninth or early tenth century (Andrews IV, 1970; Ball, this volume). At Coba, Dzitas Slate Ware ceramics were recovered from sealed deposits beneath the plaza floor of the Nohoch Mul complex; incorporated into this same floor is Stela 20, which bears the date A.D. 780 (9.17.10.0.0; Stuart 1975; Robles C. 1980). The notion of chronological overlap beetween these two ceramic spheres has been further reinforced by several reports of the discovery of Cehpech and Sotuta ceramics in associated contexts at several other sites (cf. Ball 1979a; Robles C. 1980, 1981a; Andrews IV and Andrews V 1980; Lincoln 1982; Chase and Chase 1982).

While most scholars would now agree with the notion of chronological overlap between these two periods, there is no consensus on the extent of the overlap. Critical in determining the degree of overlap are the dating of the diagnostic Silho Fine Orange and Tohil Plumbate ceramics of the Sotuta sphere and the dating of the "Toltec" architecture and monumental art work at Chichen Itza, which has been the subject of some debate. Several recent studies have suggested that the Chichen Itza remains date to Late Classic and/or Terminal Classic times (Cohodas 1974, 1978; Lincoln 1982), but the lack of firmly associated chronological markers has left the issue open. The recent discovery of Itza-style architecture at the site of Nohmul in northern Belize, associated with mixed San José/Cehpech/Sotuta ceramic deposits, argues in favor of a substantial degree of overlap (Chase and Chase 1982; D. Chase 1982b). There is also some uncertainty about the dating of Silho and Plumbate ceramics, traditionally considered diagnostic of the post-A.D. 1000 period; tantalizing bits of evidence raise the possibility that these types may date to as early as A.D. 900 (Ball 1979a; Lincoln 1982; Maldonado Cárdenas n.d.).

Viewed together, the data now available suggest that the Cehpech-sphere remains may date later than A.D. 1100, whereas the Sotuta-sphere ceramics and architecture may have originated sometime prior to A.D. 900; in short, the data favor an overlap of more than 200 years, or 100 or more years in each direction. This overlap, however, may not be uniform across the peninsula: recent excavations in Quintana Roo, for example, suggest a relatively late appearance of Sotuta remains in that area. The implications of this situation will be further discussed below.

Architecture. Many field reports include architectural data that need not be rehearsed here. The last decade saw few detailed analyses of Maya constructions, the principal one being Pollock's (1980) survey of the Puuc, and George Andrews's (1975) study of Maya cities; the latter includes descriptions and plans of Edzna, Uxmal, Kabah, Sayil, Labna, Oxkintok, Dzibilchaltun, Chichen Itza, Mayapan, and Tulum in northern Yucatan. More recently, George Andrews (1982) carried out a detailed analysis of the evolution of the Puuc architectural style. Another regional survey, of the Late Postclassic architecture of the central coast of Quintana Roo, was published by Andrews IV and A. P. Andrews (1975). Extensive reports and analyses of the architecture of many sites on Cozumel Island are also available (Leventhal 1974; Freidel 1975, 1976; Freidel and Cliff 1978).

The final report of the Dzibilchaltun excavations includes an analysis of the development of the architecture at that site, the first sequence to be chronologically secured by stratigraphic excavations (Andrews IV and Andrews V 1980). Other studies, which deal with aspects of style, construction, and chronology, have focused on individual buildings, such as the Palace of the Governor at Uxmal (Kowalski 1981), the Monjas complex (Bolles 1977), and Great Ball Court (Cohodas 1974, 1978) at Chichen Itza.

Another very fertile area of research, and one which we cannot even begin to outline here, has focused on the astronomical alignments of Postclassic architecture. Most of the results of these studies are available in the works written and edited by Anthony Aveni (1975, 1977, 1980; cf. also Lamb 1980).

Settlement Patterns. The *Atlas* survey program represents the single greatest effort to study the settlement patterns of northern Yucatan. To date it has provided a large number of reports and studies on community distribution, analyses of ecological factors affecting settlement patterns, and reconstructions of territorial and political organization (Garza T. de González and Kurjack 1977, 1980, 1981a, 1981b; Vlcek, Garza T. de González, and Kurjack 1978; Kurjack and Garza T. de González 1981a, 1981b; Kurjack 1975).

The most detailed settlement-pattern study carried out to date in Yucatan is that of Dzibilchaltun, which involved a survey and diachronic analysis of 8,500 structures in a 19-square-kilometer area. At its height in the Terminal Classic Period, Dzibilchaltun had an estimated population of 10,000 to 20,000 (Kurjack 1974, 1978, 1979a), and although it qualifies as a fair-sized urban community, it is by no means among the largest in northern Yucatan.

The sites of Tihoo (Merida), Izamal, Uxmal, Chichen Itza, Ek Balam, and Coba were much larger than Dzibilchaltun. Of these, only Coba has been the subject of a large-scale settlement pattern study, which is in progress. The preliminary results attest to a dense population (see Fig. 3.3) spread over an area of at least 70 square kilometers, which places Coba in the ranks of the largest cities of Mesoamerica (Fletcher 1978; Kintz 1978; Garduño Argueta 1979a, 1979b; Folan, Fletcher, and Kintz 1979; Benavides Castillo 1981b, 1981d, 1981e; Cortés de Brasdefer 1981a, 1981c; Gallareta Negrón 1981; Folan et al. 1982; Folan, Kintz, and Fletcher 1983). Settlement studies of other urban sites in northern Yucatan are limited to a few preliminary surveys at Uxmal (Barrera Rubio 1980b), Chunchucmil (Vlcek 1978; Vlcek, Garza T. de González, and Kurjack 1978), Izamal (Lincoln 1980), Chichen Itza (Schmidt 1981a), and the environs of Merida (Gallareta and Callaghan 1981; Baker 1976).

Many of the field projects conducted on the East Coast in the last decade have produced substantial survey data that will be of use to future settlement-pattern research; the reports from these projects, cited above (see section on East Coast), need not be repeated here. The only detailed settlement-pattern study in the area is that of Cozumel

Figure 3.3   Coba: Aerial view of residential area. Courtesy of Antonio Benavides and Edward Kurjack and the Centro Regional del Sureste, I.N.A.H.

(Freidel and Leventhal 1975; Freidel 1976), which is being continued by Robles C. (1981c; Sierra Sosa and Robles C. 1981). Intensive surveys are also under way at Xelha (Pérez Álvarez and Robles C. 1981), Punta Piedra (south of Playa del Carmen; González de la Mata 1982), and Tulum-Tancah. With the exception of a few minor sites and Xelha, where a large Classic Period occupation has been identified, most of the east coast settlements date to the Late Postclassic period.

This was a period of unparalleled growth in the East: more than 100 sites have been located on the Quintana Roo coast and adjoining islands; the term *site*, however, refers to anything from isolated coastal shrines to very large communities, and given the lack of systematic typology, it is difficult to assess the overall nature of the settlement pattern of the area. A further problem in this respect is the determination of boundaries between sites: in many areas of the central coast

69

between Cancun and Tulum, the pattern appears to be one of contiguous "towns" interconnected by residential zones of varying densities; thus, until more detailed surveys are carried out, it will not be possible to determine where one site ends and the next begins. At present, it is possible to point to several areas where the clustering of both monumental and residential remains hints at communities of metropolitan proportions: the Cancun area, the Puerto Morelos–Mulchi area, the Playa del Carmen–Xcaret area, the San Gervasio zone on Cozumel Island, Paamul, Xelha, Muyil (Chunyaxche), and the Tulum-Tancah area. Chiquila, on the far north coast of Quintana Roo, would also fall into this category.

Sacbeob and Canal Systems. The far-ranging survey work of the 1970s has allowed researchers to re-examine the remains of the extensive *sacbe* networks of northern Yucatan, and a closer scrutiny of their context has led to the new interpretations of their functions. Detailed surveys have been made of the *sacbe* system at Coba (Benavides C. 1976a, 1977, 1980a, 1981d; Benavides C. and Robles C. 1976; Folan 1977; Folan, Kintz, and Fletcher 1983) and of the *sacbeob* between Uci-Cansahcab, Ake-Izamal (Maldonado Cárdenas 1979a, 1979b) and Uxmal-Kabah (Garza T. de González and Kurjack 1980). Most of the intersite *sacbeob* appear to have been constructed during the Classic period, and many were undoubtedly maintained and used during the Postclassic; the longest *sacbe*, between Coba and Yaxuna, was apparently not built until Terminal Classic times. While not rejecting the long-held view that *sacbeob* may have been used as "ritual roads," researchers have recently suggested that the *sacbeob* served political and economic functions by connecting political centers with outlying communities and providing conduits between rural production areas and central markets. In this context, then, the *sacbeob* may be viewed as skeletons of large political domains, and such is obviously the case at Coba and Izamal (Kurjack and Andrews V 1976; Benavides C. 1976a, 1977, 1981d; Robles C. 1977). Internal *sacbeob* may have served similar functions, but as Kurjack (1977) has argued, they may also reveal kinship ties between elites in dispersed architectural compounds.

The Yucatec Maya living in coastal areas also utilized canals for transportation. While historical data clearly indicate that many of the coastal canals around the peninsula were opened during the nineteenth century for the exploitation of lumber and dyewood (Millet 1981), there is evidence to suggest that many canals were in use before the conquest (Farriss and Miller 1974; Edwards 1976; Andrews 1977, 1978a, Benavides C. and Andrews 1979). Many of these canals appear to be natural, but there is a strong possibility that a few were opened in pre-Hispanic times.

Ceramic Analysis. Since 1970, two major ceramic sequences for northern Yucatan have been completed: Robert Smith's (1971) study of the ceramics of Mayapan, and Fernando Robles's (1980) analysis of the Coba ceramics. Smith's worked focused primarily on the Late Postclassic pottery of Mayapan, and, to a lesser extent, on small collections from Uxmal, Kabah, and Chichen Itza. The Coba study encompassed materials from Late Formative to Late Postclassic times. Surveys and excavations during the last decade have yielded large collections of Postclassic ceramics from a wide range of sites. Studies include the analyses of ceramics from sites along the coasts of the peninsula (Ball 1978, 1982a) and from Cuca, Chacchob, and Dzonot Ake (Webster 1979); in addition there are preliminary reports on the pottery of Uxmal (Sáenz 1975b), Cozumel (Connor 1975; Bronitsky 1978), Cancun (Mayer Guala 1981), and El Meco (Robles C. 1981a).

While most ceramics studies have focused on chronology, some include discussions of diagnostic tradewares (Ball 1978, 1979a; Robles C. 1980, 1981b). Most wares appear to have been traded within the peninsula during the Postclassic, and only a scattering of sherds can be traced to external sources; one study, however, has revealed the widespread use of volcanic ash temper in Postclassic wares, suggesting a long-distance trade of this material (Simmons and Brem 1979).

Artifact Analysis. Two major studies of northern Yucatan Postclassic artifacts appeared in the 1970s: Tatiana Proskouriakoff's (1974) analysis of the Chichen Itza jades, and David Phillips's (1971a) dissertation on the artifacts of Cozumel. The final report on the artifacts of Dzibilchaltun, which include a substantial Terminal Classic and Postclassic assemblage, has also been completed by Jennifer Taschek (1981; n.d.). In addition to those works, there are several reports on smaller collections from coastal sites: Cozumel (Connor 1975), Tulum (Barrera Rubio 1980c), and various sites along the north and west coasts (Eaton 1978). These collections yielded large quantities of specialized tools whose analysis has provided important data on pre-Hispanic Maya fishing technology (Eaton 1974, 1976; Phillips 1978, 1979b; Barrera Rubio 1980c).

71

Other studies have focused on more specific groups of artifacts, such as metal goods (Bray 1977), ground stone tools (Andrews IV and Rovner 1973; Maldonado Cárdenas 1981a), and obsidian artifacts (Rovner 1978). Trace analyses of obsidian from several sites have aided in the reconstruction of the major Postclassic trade routes between Yucatan and Guatemala (Nelson et al. 1977; Nelson 1980; Nelson, Phillips, and Barrera, 1983).

Ecofact Analysis. Despite the extensive excavations of the last decade, relatively few reports on ecofacts have appeared. The analysis of Postclassic human skeletal remains is limited to reports on the remains from five sites: Dzibilchaltun (Stewart 1974), Chichen Itza (Márquez de González, n.d.; Márquez de González and Harrington 1981; Márquez de González and Schmidt 1981), Cancun (Ramos Rodríguez 1978; Ramos Rodríguez, Vargas Pacheco, and Guillermo Espinosa 1980), Playa del Carmen (Márquez Morfín 1982), and Tancah (Saul 1982).

While several researchers have discussed the role of marine fauna (Lange 1971; Eaton 1978) and various animals (Benavides C. 1975b; Montoliu 1978; Hamblin 1981; Pohl 1981; Pohl and Feldman 1982; Pohl 1983) in Maya subsistence and ritual, only two projects have completed analyses of faunal remains: Dzibilchaltun (Wing and Steadman 1980) and Cozumel (Hamblin and Rea 1979; Hamblin 1980, 1981). There have been, however, several analyses of molluscan remains, which have yielded data on subsistence, trade, and ritual; these include two general studies of the distribution of archaeological mollusca in the Maya Lowlands (Andrews IV 1969; Feldman 1972), as well as analyses of collections from Cozumel (Vokes 1977, 1978), Tulum (Barrera Rubio 1980c), Tancah (Andrews 1982), and El Meco (Andrews, in Andrews and Robles, n.d.).

Art Studies. With few exceptions, most of the art research of the last decade has focused on mural painting. The exceptions are the studies of Puuc mosaic sculpture by Rosemary Sharp (1978, 1981), a survey of cave petroglyphs in the Puuc region conducted by Matthias Strecker (1976a, 1976b, 1979, 1981), and several studies of Puuc sculpture by Karl Mayer (1982a, 1982b, 1983d) and Barrera Rubio (1983b).

Barrera Rubio has published two surveys of Yucatan mural painting (1979, 1980a); most of the murals, which are found in the Puuc, Chichen Itza, or the Coba/East Coast area, date to Terminal Classic or Postclassic times. One major exception, still unpublished, is a Teotihuacan-style mural uncovered in Str. 26 at Xelha (cf. map in Lothrop 1924; Mayer 1983c), which dates to the Early Classic Period. During the last decade, four studies have focused on the paintings of western Yucatan: three have dealt with the analysis of painted capstones from Puuc and Chenes sites (Thompson 1973; Jones 1975; Mayer 1983a); the fourth is Miller's (1977a, 1978) analysis of the paintings in the Upper Temple of the Jaguars at Chichen Itza, based on Adela Breton's renderings. Miller has interpreted these scenes as representing major conquests in the military history of the Itza.

The contrasts between the mural paintings of the Classic and Postclassic periods have long been a subject of interest to Maya scholars, and recent studies have continued to explore the ramifications of this evolution (Robertson 1970; Maldonado Cárdenas 1977; Miller 1982).

Most of the art research of the last decade has focused on the Postclassic murals of the East Coast and Coba, which represent a relatively uniform corpus fitting into what Donald Robertson (1970) has called the International Style of the Postclassic. The largest research effort in this area has been the Tancah-Tulum Mural Project, conducted by Miller, which has involved the careful recording of a large body of paintings as well as a wealth of interpretation (cf. references by Miller in bibliography). Others have also published brief reports on the Tancah-Tulum murals (Barrera Rubio 1976a; Fettweis-Vienot 1976, 1981; Paxton 1982a, 1982b; Mayer 1983b) and the murals of Xelha and Coba (Fettweis-Vienot 1976, 1980, 1981; Mayer 1983c).

Inscription Studies. Few Postclassic inscriptions have been discovered in recent times in northern Yucatan, and the scant studies on the subject have focused on the analysis of specific texts at Uxmal (Morley 1970; Kowalski 1980), Playa del Carmen (Mayer, González de la Mata, and Trejo Alvarado 1979; Hartig 1979), and Chichen Itza (Kelley 1968; Proskouriakoff 1970; Thompson 1977; Davoust 1977, 1980). The work of Kelley and Davoust has resulted in the identification of several of the early rulers at Chichen Itza. These rulers may have been related to one another, but the absence of birth, accession, and death dates has forestalled the reconstruction of a dynastic sequence.

Social Organization. The reconstruction of northern Maya social organization has been a popular subject in the last decade, and the resulting studies include works on kinship (Haviland 1972, 1973; Bastarrachea 1980), social classes and craft specialization (Andrews IV and Rovner 1973; Benavides C. 1976a, 1980c), the priesthood (Barrera Rubio 1973–74), and military organization (Repetto-Tio 1979a, 1979b).

Settlement-pattern studies have provided a wealth of data on social and political organization (see section on settlement patterns, above) that clearly attest to the existence of large political units and urban centers with complex patterns of organization, as well as highly differentiated and often specialized rural settlements. A subject that remains elusive is the nature of the changing political organization of Postclassic Yucatec society, an issue which David Freidel has addressed in recent papers (1981a, 1981b, 1983, this volume), and which we shall discuss later in this chapter.

Economics and Trade. As in other areas of the Maya world, the pre-Hispanic Yucatecan economy was based on local production and external trade. The internal economy was based primarily on agriculture, and despite recent interest in pre-Hispanic Maya agriculture (cf. Harrison and Turner 1978; Vlcek, Garza T. de González, and Kurjack 1978; Schmidt 1981b; Flannery 1982), there are few detailed studies of the variability of cultivated resources in Postclassic northern Yucatan. There is good evidence to suggest that intensified garden and tree cropping (fruit and ramon trees) were an important part of the domestic subsistence economy, but we have no idea how widespread these practices were (Puleston 1968, 1982; Netting 1977; Folan, Fletcher, and Kintz 1979; Marcus 1982; Lambert and Arnason 1982). Ethnohistoric sources note that Yucatan exported a variety of crop goods, from cotton and copal to annatto, but we have no notion of the volume of the production and trade of these goods. Marine resources and domesticated fauna were also important in the internal economy (see references on faunal remains, above), but again we lack a quantitative assessment of the economic role of these products. Studies of the internal trade networks of northern Yucatan (Roys 1943, 1957; Benavides 1975a, 1980d; Piña Chan 1978) highlight all these products, but fail to determine their relative importance.

Scholars have recognized since the sixteenth century that long-distance trade played an important role in the pre-Hispanic economy of northern Yucatan. During the Postclassic Period, Yucatan imported substantial quantities of obsidian, jade, and metal artifacts, as well as a variety of less common articles. In return, Yucatan supplied most of the Maya Lowlands and adjoining areas with salt (Andrews 1978a,

1980b, 1983); it also exported—among other things—slaves, cotton, honey, wax, and copal (Roys 1943; Thompson 1970).

During the last two decades, the study of long-distance trade has been perhaps the most popular issue in Maya archaeology. The literature is extensive, and need not be repeated here: a comprehensive history of Maya trade studies is available elsewhere (Andrews 1980a). Several recent historical reconstructions of northern Yucatan have stressed the role of trade in the major political events of the Postclassic Period, but these studies can, at best, be considered tentative (Ball 1977c; Andrews 1978b; Andrews and Robles, n.d.). Of particular relevance to this issue are the various models that served as a research design for the Cozumel project. Sabloff and Rathje have argued that changes in the economy—changing commercial values, shifts in production and distribution systems, the rise of a new mercantilism—were the underlying factors differentiating Postclassic society from that of previous periods (Sabloff and Rathje 1975a, 1975b). While their arguments have generated a fair amount of debate, their basic notion that developments during the Postclassic were dynamic new adaptations, rather than a continuing decline of older ways, has appealed to many scholars. Just how profoundly these changes affected the core of native Maya society is not clear: while there is undeniable evidence of continuity in many aspects of the life of the commoners, it would seem that the emergence of new elites effected profound changes in the political economy and ideology of the society (Rathje 1975; Freidel 1981a, 1981b, this volume).

POLITICAL AND ECONOMIC PANORAMA AT THE END OF THE CLASSIC PERIOD

The political and socioeconomic changes that took place in the Postclassic Period were clearly responses to many of the events and cultural processes of the Late and Terminal Classic periods. Recent archaeological research suggests that Classic Period northern Yucatan can be divided, primarily on the basis of ceramics and architecture, into at least two major cultural spheres: a Western Sphere, comprising most of the northwestern and north-central Yucatecan plain and Puuc Hills region, and an Eastern Sphere, which encompassed what is today far eastern Yucatan and northern Quintana Roo. While it is not possible

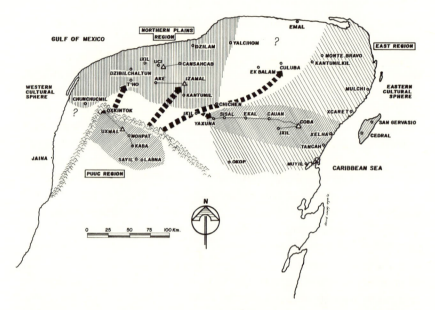

Figure 3.4 Major Terminal Classic Cultural Spheres in Northern Yucatan. The Western Sphere includes the Northern Plains and Puuc Regions; the Eastern Sphere is less well known, but appears to have been dominated by the Coba polity. The blank area in northeastern Yucatan is not well known archaeologically, and is not assigned to either sphere. The arrows indicate the spread of Puuc architecture.

at present to draw a precise boundary between the two spheres, we feel that such a division might run approximately as follows: Lake Chichancanab–Yaxuna–Chemax–Chancenote–Colonia–Yucatan–El Cuyo (Fig. 3.4).

A relatively homogeneous ceramic development from Formative times onward appears to have characterized the Western Sphere; it was accompanied by the development of variant regional architectural styles during the Classic Period (Andrews IV 1965a; Roys and Shook 1966; Lincoln 1980). Toward the middle of the eighth century (the beginning of the Terminal Classic period), a new cultural tradition emerged in the Puuc region of northern Campeche and western Yucatan; its origins can be traced to a mix of indigenous development in northern Yucatan, architectural influence from the Chenes and Río Bec regions, and foreign ceramic and architectural influences from the Gulf Coast and

76

Central Mexican highlands. This tradition eventually spread across the northern plains; in some northern plains sites, such as Dzibilchaltun, Yaxcopoil, Oxkintok, Ake, and Yaxuna, Puuc-style buildings appear, some of them superimposed on or added to earlier structures. Puuc architecture spread as far east as Chichen Itza and Culuba. By the end of the period, it was the dominant cultural force in the Western Sphere.

We can also trace the origins of a distinct Eastern Sphere to Formative times, as the earliest ceramics of northern Quintana Roo are quite different from those of the Western Sphere. During the Early and Late Classic periods, the spread of Peten-style architecture, ceramics, and sculpture into northern Quintana Roo helped mold a local tradition dramatically different from that of the west. Remains of this tradition are found at such sites as Coba, Xelha, Muyil, Okop, San Gervasio (Cozumel), and Kantunilkin.

Recent investigations at Coba have revealed that Peten-style constructions continued to be built well into Terminal Classic times. The ceramics, however, change: Peten-style polychrome wares and vessel forms disappear around A.D. 750 and are replaced by a local slateware tradition related to that of the western Terminal Classic Puuc tradition. Surprisingly, though, there is no evidence of Puuc-style construction anywhere in the Coba region, or for that matter, anywhere in the Eastern Sphere except Yaxuna, which lay at the boundary between the two spheres.

The distinct architectural styles, then, clearly delineate two separate cultural spheres in northern Yucatan during Terminal Classic times. However, we see the relationships between the two spheres most clearly in the light of the differences and similarities in their ceramic assemblages.

Traditionally, the ceramics of Terminal Classic northern Yucatan have been classified collectively as being part of the "Cehpech ceramic sphere" (Smith 1971; Ball 1978, 1979a). However, recent analyses of Terminal Classic ceramics from several sites in northern Quintana Roo have revealed basic differences between eastern and western Cehpech-sphere ceramics (Robles C. 1980). This is particularly evident in the Muna Slate group, which includes the most common diagnostic ceramic type of the Cehpech sphere. While almost identical in consistency, hardness, and surface treatment, the western Muna Slate types are characterized by a grayish slip, whereas in the east they consistently display a brownish slip. The same occurs in the Ticul Thin Slate group. Both groups also exhibit differences in vessel shape in the Eastern and Western cultural spheres, as do the utilitarian ceramics, which also show differences in surface decoration (Figure 3.5). The ash temper composition of eastern and western Cehpech ceramic wares is also different (Simmons and Brem 1979). Finally, certain ceramic groups are exclusive to one or the other cultural sphere, such as the Vista Alegre striated group, which is restricted to the east, and the Balancan Fine Orange and Unslipped Chum groups, which are found only in the West.

The Terminal Classic transition in ceramic assemblages in the east, from Tepeu-like types to Cehpech types, appears to reflect a realignment of the eastern cultural sphere with northwestern Yucatan rather than with the cities of the Southern Lowlands, whose influences had long dominated northern Quintana Roo communities. This shift was the logical outcome of the decline of the communities in the Southern Lowlands, and a manifestation of new trends in the political organization of the Northern Lowlands as well.

While at present it is not possible to define the nature and extent of the political units of the northern Yucatan during the Classic Period, certain lines of evidence suggest that relatively large polities existed at that time. While ceramic and architectural affinities would appear to hint at regional political interdependence, the appearance of long-distance *sacbe* networks provides even stronger indications of territorial organization and political centralization in certain specific areas (Be navides C. 1976a, 1981d; Kurjack and Andrews V 1976; Garza T. de González and Kurjack 1980; see others cited above in the section on *sacbeob*). Once again, the Eastern and Western spheres differ in this respect: while the Western Sphere has several *sacbe* systems that would appear to delineate territorial units of various sizes, the Eastern Sphere has only one, which is the largest of them all, the Coba *sacbe* network. We believe this situation reflects certain fundamental differences in the political and economic organization of the Eastern and Western cultural spheres.

The Western Sphere consists of several ecological zones, the most prominent being the northern plain and the hilly region of the Puuc. When the Spanish arrived in Yucatan in the sixteenth century, they found that the northern plains communities produced basic agricultural foodstuffs, cotton, and salt: the last two were major exports, and eventually became primary items of tribute, along with corn and hu-

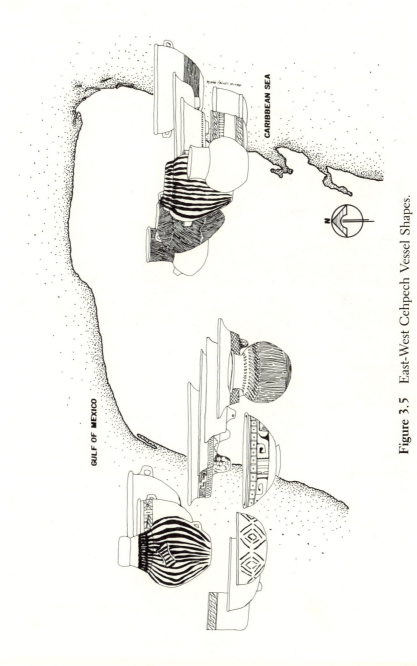

Figure 3.5 East-West Cehpech Vessel Shapes.

Figure 3.6 Possible agricultural terraces near Yaxhom, Puuc region, Yucatan. Courtesy of Peter J. Schmidt and the Centro Regional del Sureste, I.N.A.H.

man labor. Historical sources say little about the Puuc region, which may have been sparsely inhabited in the sixteenth century; during the later Colonial Period, however, this was a major maize producing area (Patch 1977), and we know from geographic and agricultural studies that the soils there are extremely fertile for agricultural production (Kurjack, Garza T. de González, and Lucas 1979; Kurjack and Garza T. de González 1981b). Although soil erosion has long been a problem in the hilly Puuc area, the Maya may have dealt with this problem by using terraces. Several terrace-like features have been recently reported in the vicinity of Yaxhom, approximately ten kilometers southwest of Oxkutzcab; they probably date to Terminal Classic times (Benavides, personal communication; Figure 3.6). If such terrace systems were widespread, the potential architectural production of the Puuc region in pre-Hispanic times would have been enormous.

Viewed globally, then, the Western Sphere would appear to have been not only self-sufficient in basic foodstuffs, but capable of long-distance export of valuable resources, such as salt and cotton. At the time of the conquest, northern Yucatan was also an exporter of honey, wax, copal, and slaves.

The Eastern Sphere has a more homogeneous environment (a flat plain bordered by the Caribbean) and was likely under the control and/or influence of Coba. Unlike northwestern Yucatan, which appears to have been made up of various polities, the Eastern Sphere had only one major polity, which implies a greater degree of political and economic centralization. This greater centralization may have reflected a need to maximize the exploitation of a less varied ecological zone and resource base: while historical documents have little to say of the pre-Hispanic economy of northern Quintana Roo, we can surmise that agriculture and marine resources were the mainstay of the local subsistence economy. Evidence of this centralized control is seen in the *sacbe* network of Coba, whose purpose was apparently to link agricultural satellites to the urban core (Robles C. 1976; Benavides C. 1977). A major question that arises at Coba, then, is what it had to offer beyond its subsistence base. It may have supplied agricultural surpluses to adjoining regions, and it may have cultivated and exported cotton, but, lacking evidence on these points, we can only speculate. How then, did it develop into one of the largest and richest urban centers in the Maya area, with extensive ties to the great cities of the south? The answer would seem to lie in its centralized political and economic organization and its strategic location. Lying between northern Yucatan and the Caribbean trade networks, Coba linked the north to the Bay of Honduras and the rivers that fed into the Southern Maya Lowlands. That it was, from Late Formative times onward, a middleman in the north-south trade is reflected in its strong ceramic ties to Yaxuna, to the west, and to Xelha, on the Caribbean coast. Moreover, it probably controlled the central Quintana Roo coast and, therefore, the north-south movement of sea-borne products, such as salt and obsidian, among other goods.

During the Terminal Classic Period, the city of Coba reached its ultimate size. The Nohoch Mul architectural complex, the largest at Coba, was built at this time, and from it was built the *sacbe* No. 1, which extended 100 kilometers to the west, to Yaxuna. This *sacbe* probably served two purposes: delineating the western boundary of the domain of Coba and reinforcing the commercial ties to the Western Sphere. Furthermore, it is at this time that the eastern Cehpech ceramic tradition develops, displacing the Peten-related wares of previous periods. The appearance of Cehpech-sphere ceramics in the Coba region may reflect an alliance of sorts between the Puuc cities and Coba, but on this matter we can only speculate; the absence of Puuc architectural features and related foreign elements from the Gulf Coast would suggest that the alliance, if it existed, was perhaps limited to commercial ties.

It would appear, then, that northern Yucatan had a highly developed network of regional polities and a complex and well-integrated economy. This economy was also integrated into the larger trading spheres that had long existed between the Northern and Southern Lowlands, and beyond, to the highlands of Guatemala and Central Mexico.

NORTHERN CLASSIC DISINTEGRATION AND THE COMING OF THE ITZA

While in many respects the Terminal Classic Period was one of cultural florescence in northern Yucatan (Andrews IV 1965a), it also gave rise to its own decline. The apparent prosperity of Late and Terminal Classic times brought about an unprecedented growth in population. Data from the Yucatan *Atlas* surveys clearly indicate that the period of highest demographic density in northern Yucatan occurred toward the end of the Terminal Classic Period (Garza T. de González and Kurjack 1980); as noted above, the same holds true for the Coba region in northern Quintana Roo. It is now becoming apparent that this population growth strained the resource base of the north. Unlike the population of the Southern Lowlands, which had a variety of technological options for increasing agricultural productivity (Harrison and Turner 1978), the people of northern Yucatan had few. Although terrace-like features have recently been found in the Puuc, agricultural systems employing such features do not seem to have been very widespread (future fieldwork, however, may prove otherwise). Alternative possibilities, such as heavier reliance on marine resources, intensified gardening, and arboriculture, were also available, but we do not know to what degree they were exploited (see the section on economics, above).

This demographic impasse undoubtedly led to competition over the resource base, and ultimately, to social disintegration and the break-down of the political systems. The recent discovery of fortifications at several Terminal Classic sites in northern Yucatan, such as Cuca, Chacchob, Muna, Ake, Chunchucmil, and even Uxmal, provides evidence of widespread warfare, which was very likely a result of increasing competition over land resources and decreasing political centralization (Kurjack and Andrews V 1976; Webster 1978, 1979; Garza T. de González and Kurjack 1980). The gradual deterioration of the sociopolitical situation of Terminal Classic northern Yucatan was not due solely to internal processes. Yucatan was also affected by events elsewhere in Mesoamerica, and eventually succumbed to intrusions by foreigners.

As we have noted, the Puuc tradition was characterized in part by cultural traits from Central Mexico and the Gulf Coast region; these traits clearly indicate close commercial ties between the Puuc cities and those areas. Moreover, there is good evidence that these commercial ties preceded the deployment of foreign military groups—often referred to in the recent literature as Gulf Coast Putun or Chontal Maya—along the west and north coasts of the peninsula (Andrews 1978b). These military groups may also have eventually penetrated the heart of the Puuc region (Roys 1966; Ball 1974a; Andrews and Robles C. 1985).

The entry (or entries) of foreign groups into Yucatan was part of a much larger deployment of outside groups in the Maya area during Terminal Classic times. These groups moved down into the Usumacinta basin around the middle of the ninth century, establishing outposts at Altar de Sacrificios, at Seibal, and possibly at the more distant site of Salinas de los Nueve Cerros, where they would have gained control over the largest salt source in the Southern Lowlands (Sabloff and Willey 1967; Thompson 1970; Sabloff 1971; Andrews 1983: 127). These "conquests" would have given the Maya-Chontal control over the Usumacinta River basin, the main artery of communication between the Southern Maya Lowlands and the rest of Mesoamerica. Moreover, it is possible that these groups crossed the base of the peninsula; Thompson (1970) suggests that the people who had established themselves at Seibal had also reached Ucanal, on the headwaters of the Belize River. From such a position, they could easily have reached the Caribbean and the east coast trade route between northern Yucatan and the Bay of Honduras.

The events that followed in northern Yucatan are well known: the foreign groups, now known as the Itza, moved inland, and established their capital at Chichen Itza. Exactly when this happened is not clear; most scholars agree that the various entradas occurred in the tenth century. The major Itza campaign is believed to have been recounted, in legendary fashion, in the Hunac Ceel epic the Chilam Balam de Chumayel. According to this chronicle, the Itza disembarked at Pole (Xcaret), proceeded across northern Yucatan into the Puuc heartland, and eventually arrived at Cetelac (Yaxuna). That this was a campaign of conquest may be corroborated by mural evidence from Chichen Itza: the "red hills" in the battle scene in the Temple of the Tigers are strongly reminiscent of the terrain and soil of the Puuc hills, and the picture may well record the Itza subjugation of this area (for an alternative interpretation, cf. Miller 1977a). It is worth noting that the first part of the Itza itinerary outlines the northern border of the domain of Coba, a fact which suggests that there was one polity the Itza were not able to penetrate. Elsewhere, it would appear, they met little resistance.

What happened at Cetelac is unclear. We know only that the Itza and the ruler of Cetelac had some differences, for the account notes, somewhat euphemistically, that "they agreed in their opinions." It further records that the ruler of Cetelac subsequently agreed to pay tribute to the Itza, who then settled at nearby Chichen Itza (Roys 1933).

It is surprising that the Postclassic chronicles of northern Yucatan fail to make more than an occasional passing reference to Coba, which was obviously the largest polity encountered by the Itza when they arrived in Yucatan. We suspect that the Itza encountered massive resistance at Cetelac, which was the western outpost of the domain of Coba; the ensuing standoff would have enabled the Itza to consolidate their control over western and northeastern Yucatan, but not over the eastern Coba polity. We believe, then, that the early Postclassic history of northern Yucatan was transmitted to posterity by Itza historians, who purposely garbled the events at Cetelac.

The total absence of Silho Fine Orange and Tohil Plumbate ceramic groups at Coba and Yaxuna—good indicators of Itza presence elsewhere in the north—adds support to the notion that the Itza were unable to enter the domain of Coba. Moreover, the continuity of eastern Cehpech ceramics at Coba well into the twelfth century suggests a certain degree of isolation.

The present data, then, suggest that two competing polities emerged in northern Yucatan around A.D. 900/1000. While it is clear that the two polities represent a continuation of the traditional east-west dichotomy of the Yucatec Maya, the boundaries between the two have yet to be mapped. On the basis of the known distribution of diagnostic ceramic types of the Sotuta sphere (Silho and Tohil groups), we can surmise that the Itza controlled the territory spreading from Tabasco and western Campeche across northern Yucatan to the northeast coast of Quintana Roo, at least as far south as El Meco, opposite Isla Mujeres. Recent investigations have also uncovered significant quantities of Silho ceramics and a few sherds of Tohil Plumbate at San Gervasio, on Cozumel Island (Connor 1975; Robles C. 1981c; Sierra Sosa and Robles C. 1981); furthermore, San Gervasio exhibits a number of architectural features, and other characteristics in the layout of the core of the site, that have strong parallels at Chichen Itza (Robles C. 1981c). These data lead us to believe that Cozumel either was in the Chichen sphere, or was closely allied through commercial ties (Figure 3.7).

The nature of the Itza presence on the East Coast is at present poorly understood. The diagnostic Sotuta-sphere ceramics from El Meco and San Gervasio were stratigraphically associated with Peto Cream Ware, a diagnostic ceramic that has been dated to ca. A.D. 1100–1300 (Andrews V 1978). At El Meco, these ceramics were found mixed with Cehpech materials; at San Gervasio, they were found above stratigraphic layers containing pure Cehpech deposits. This would suggest that the Itza presence on the East Coast was relatively late, occurring at least 100 years after their arrival at Chichen Itza. On the central coast opposite Cozumel, diagnostic Sotuta ceramic types are rare (a few diagnostic sherds have been found at Xelha, but it is not clear whether these represent an Itza occupation, or were the result of sporadic trade contacts); this pattern may indicate that this coast was under the control of the domain of Coba and thus not open to the Itza. Farther south, however, in the Belize Cays and at Aventuras and Nohmul, Sotuta-sphere diagnostic ceramics have been reported (Hammond 1976; Chase and Chase 1982; P. Schmidt and J. Ball, personal communication). This is not at all surprising, since the Itza are known

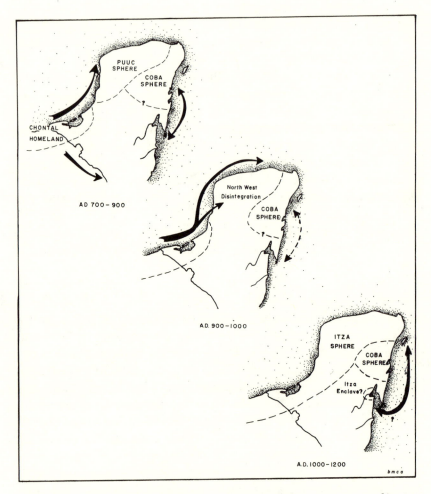

Figure 3.7 Major political spheres and major trade, migration and/or invasion routes of Terminal Classic and Early Postclassic Yucatan, ca. A.D. 700–1200.

to have traded heavily in the Bay of Honduras and Central America. Even if they did not control the central east coast, they could easily have sailed around it from their base in Cozumel (David Freidel, personal communication).

CHICHEN ITZA AND
THE NEW MASTERS OF THE OLD ORDER

Chichen Itza was an eminently logical choice for the seat of the powerful new elite who came to control northwestern Yucatan. Chichen Itza is located in the center of the northern part of the peninsula, almost equidistant from the east and west coasts, and a mere 70 kilometers from the north coast. It is also situated between the two major cultural spheres that had dominated northern Yucatan for more than 10 centuries, and near the community of Cetelac, the "gateway" between the two spheres. Thus, the Itza were in an ideal position to regulate the flow of trade between northwestern Yucatan and the eastern domain of Coba.

The territory under the direct control of Chichen Itza was most likely the same domain that had been ruled by Izamal during the Classic Period. In fact, it would appear that the Itza inherited the bulk of their ceramic tradition from that region: two of the major ceramic groups associated with the Sotuta sphere—the Dzitas and Sisal groups— evolved in the northern plains area during the Classic Period before the arrival of the Itza (Maldonado Cárdenas, personal communication; see also Robles C. 1980). The Itza, then, appropriated a large and wealthy territory, filling a political vacuum left by the decline of Izamal, which they may have also conquered and reduced to tributary status (Roys 1933: 178–81).

The success of the Itza was undoubtedly a result of a combination of factors, the most salient ones being the weakened sociopolitical situation in the Western Sphere, the control of the coasts and related trade networks by Gulf Coast merchant groups, and the military skills of the group (or groups) who finally invaded northern Yucatan. They consolidated their position by setting up a tributary system (or appropriating the tribute of earlier states) and channeling the wealth of the land into their capital (Roys 1933: 197).

As we have noted elsewhere (Andrews 1978b; Andrews and Robles C., 1985), the control of the coasts was an important factor in the rise

87

Figure 3.8 Aerial view of Isla Cerritos, north coast of Yucatan; the artificial harbor wall and remains of sacbe between the island and mainland are indicated by arrows.

of the Itza state, for it provided them with a military and economic base that gave them powerful leverage over the interior. Once in power, they consolidated their hold on the coast by establishing a string of ports that stretched from Campeche to Cozumel; their main port may have been at Isla Cerritos, on the north coast at the mouth of the Rio Lagartos estuary, 70 kilometers north of Chichen Itza (Figure 3.8).

That Chichen Itza became one of the wealthiest cities of Meso-america is well documented: few sites in the New World have yielded comparable quantities of rich trade goods, many of which came from lands thousands of kilometers distant. The full extent of the site is still not known, but it is clearly one of the largest in the Maya area, covering at least 25 square kilometers (P. Schmidt, personal communication). Given its tremendous growth over a relatively short span of time, it is most probable that Chichen became a demographic vortex, absorbing substantial quantities of immigrants from the Yucatecan countryside. This growth was paralleled by the decline of population centers elsewhere across northern Yucatan, which suggests that the Itza tribute included human labor along with agricultural produce.

While internal resources may have sustained the Itza capital, its grandeur was ultimately based on its external connections and trade. The Itza control of the Yucatecan salt beds was undoubtedly critical, giving them access to the wider trade networks of Middle America, for distant lands depended on Yucatan for this vital resource (Andrews 1978b, 1980, 1983). It is also quite probable that the Itza controlled the export of other Yucatecan goods, particularly cotton cloth, which they would have acquired through their tributary system, much as the Spaniards did later, in the sixteenth century.

Many see in the rise of Chichen Itza the emergence of a new order that introduced elements of Mesoamerican high culture to a provincial region. In fact, the coming of the Itza only marked the culmination of a gradual buildup of Mexican influence that began in the Classic Period (Andrews IV 1973; Sharp 1978). The tangible contribution of the Itza to the culture of northern Yucatan was minimal: a handful of architectural and sculptural features, and two new ceramic wares (Fine Orange and Plumbate). Local slatewares and utilitarian wares constituted the majority of the ceramics employed by the Itza, and their architecture was a modified version of the style developed in the Puuc region. On a higher plane, they introduced a few new deities to the regional pantheon, but there is little evidence of fundamental changes in the ideology of the populace (cf. Freidel 1981b). Nor is there evidence that the Itza attempted to give new direction to the existing socioeconomic system. Changes in this area were under way, but they had begun long before the Itza arrived. The only innovations brought about by the Itza were in the realm of the elite superstructure; the social and cultural base remained unchanged.

In the Itza takeover of northern Yucatan one sees, then, a small elite appropriating the resources of a ravaged land and channeling a substantial portion of them into their own capital and foreign trade. Eventually, this process drained the countryside of its human and agricultural resources, a pattern that can be traced in the gradual decline and abandonment of communities throughout northwestern Yucatan. The most visible victims were the Puuc cities, which faded out of existence during this period. Even though it remained independent of Chichen Itza, Coba, too, ultimately declined as the Itza circled its domain and cut off its trade routes to the northwest and south. The extent of the depopulation of Coba is quite apparent in the archaeological record: the data from the test-pitting program indicate that the sites at the terminals of the *sacbe* system were abandoned around A.D. 1100. A smaller population, however, continued to inhabit the immediate area around the lakes, in the core of the ancient city (Robles C. 1980).

Approximately one century or less after the decline of the Puuc and Coba, the Itza capital also collapsed. The chronicles that survive attribute this event to a widespread uprising of native Yucatec Maya against the Itza oppressors. While such an event probably took place, it was most likely the outcome of a gradual weakening of the Itza political and economic organization, which was ultimately nothing more than an exploitative apparatus draining the resources of an older system that had been declining before the Itza arrived. Viewed in retrospect, the Itza were little more than entrepreneurs attempting to revitalize a dying system; they offered few innovations, and only delayed the inevitable process of decay. They did not, then, introduce a new order; they merely became, for a brief period, the masters of the old order.

THE LATE POSTCLASSIC: ATTEMPTS TO FORGE A NEW ORDER

After the fall of Chichen Itza and the older Classic Period cities of northern Yucatan, Maya society underwent a series of changes that might best be viewed as a search for a new order. As many scholars have noted, this was a period of fundamental changes in the social, economic, political, and ideological fabric of Maya life. In brief, scholars have proposed that this was an age of materialism, secularization, social mobility, and militarism (Thompson 1970; Sabloff and Rathje 1975a, 1975b; Rathje 1975; Freidel 1981a). While there is undeniable evidence of such trends, we do not see them as characteristics exclusive to the Postclassic Period: these features originate in the Classic Period, and are simply molded into new forms by the circumstances of changing times. The basic difference between the Late Postclassic Period and earlier times lies in the attempts to restructure the organizational base of the old order; such efforts took diverging paths in western and eastern Yucatan, a result, no doubt, of the different characteristics of the two spheres.

90

The traditional reconstruction of Late Postclassic history places the beginning of the period around A.D. 1200, when the Itza are over-thrown and Chichen Itza is destroyed. There follows a hazy period, of apparent disorganization, in which different groups were undoubt-edly jockeying for power; it culminated with the rise of a new political capital at Mayapan, around A.D. 1250. Scholars believe that Mayapan controlled a large part of northern Yucatan for approximately 200 years, and then also collapsed, in A.D. 1441. Afterward, political power dispersed; northern Yucatan broke up into 16 independent provinces with differing types of government, which survived until the arrival of the Spanish in the early sixteenth century (Roys 1957).

The above reconstruction tends to overemphasize the sequence of development from a monolithic Mayapan to smaller political units, creating the impression that the provinces did not emerge as indepen-dent entities until after A.D. 1441. We do not believe this was the case: it is more likely that most of the provinces were well-defined political units long before the advent of Mayapan. Roys, whose research led to the identification of these provinces, clearly indicates that while many of them formed part of the joint government of Mayapan, others remained outside the sphere of Mayapan control. Ecab, for example, was undoubtedly an independent political province throughout the Late Postclassic Period (Benavides C. and Andrews 1979; Robles C. 1981a). As we have noted, then, the political development of northern Yucatan is best understood in the light of the previously defined eastern and western cultural spheres, for they continued to function as a base upon which were built the foundations of the new political structures (Fig. 3.9).

In the Western Sphere, the rise of Mayapan represents an attempt to forge a new state which would rekindle the power and grandeur of Chichen Itza. In undertaking this task, the rulers of Mayapan "repro-duced" many of the features of the Itza capital, incorporating Itza deities in their pantheon and attempting to lay claim to the territorial domain of Chichen.

This was obviously an effort to continue the old order, but the ingredients were quite different. Chichen Itza was the seat of a very powerful group or groups of foreigners who had substantial mercantile and military power when they arrived in Yucatan; they were not com-promised by local alliances nor committed to the native culture or ideology. The elites who made up the Confederation of Mayapan were

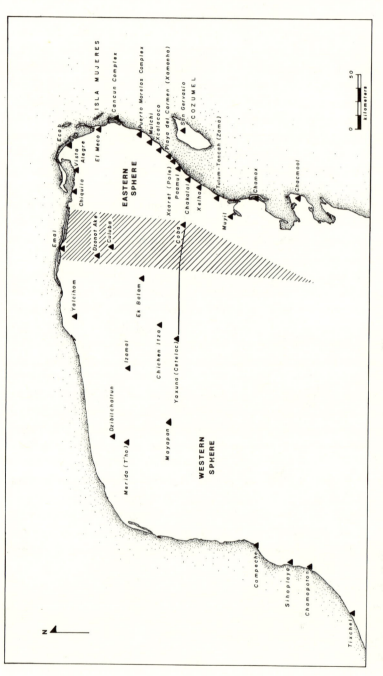
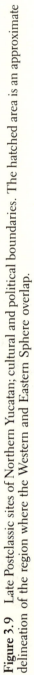

Figure 3.9 Late Postclassic sites of Northern Yucatan; cultural and political boundaries. The hatched area is an approximate delineation of the region where the Western and Eastern Sphere overlap.

representatives of different provinces whose goal was the revitalization of the old order under a single government; while the drive for reunification may have been strong, it was undoubtedly limited by conflicting interests, which may be the basic reason Mayapan never emerged as a Pan-Yucatecan state.

According to Roys (1957, 1962), the League of Mayapan incorporated the provinces that occupied most of the Western Sphere: Ah Canul, Chakan, Cehpech, Hocaba, Mani, Ah Kin Chel, Sotuta, and Cochuah. It is possible that Cupul and Tases may have been part of the league, but the evidence is equivocal. Canpech and Chanputun, which may have been part of, or allied to, the Itza sphere, were not in the orbit of Mayapan. Chikinchel, which lay on the border between the Eastern and Western spheres, was also independent of Mayapan. Ecab, the largest independent province, incorporated most of the older domain of Coba and northern Quintana Roo. Cozumel Island, which may have been an Itza outpost during the previous period, appears also to have been an independent enclave during the Late Postclassic Period; it was very closely aligned with the coastal communities of Ecab, but also retained ties with Mayapan, a situation well documented by substantial historic and archaeological evidence (Roys 1957, 1962, 1966; Leventhal 1974; Freidel 1976, 1981a; Robles C. 1981c).

All in all, Late Postclassic northern Yucatan appears to have been divided into a Western Sphere, dominated by the League of Mayapan, and an Eastern Sphere, dominated by the loosely allied cities of Ecab and Cozumel. This division is evident in the archaeological record, particularly in the architecture and ceramics.

While east and west share a great number of architectural traits during the Late Postclassic, there are substantial differences between the construction style of Mayapan and that of the East Coast: one need only compare the relevant reports by Proskouriakoff (1962) and A. L. Smith (1962) on Mayapan, and those by Lothrop (1924), Sanders (1955, 1960), Leventhal (1974), Andrews IV and Andrews (1975), and Freidel (1976, 1981a) on the east coast and Cozumel.

As in Terminal Classic and Early Postclassic times, there are marked differences between the ceramics of east and west. Several ceramic types and/or varieties are dominant in one or the other sphere: Payil Red and Palmul Incised, both of the Payil group of Tulum redwares and the Cancun variety of Mama Red, are primarily eastern, while the red Mama-Panaba group types and the Buff Polbox group types are predominantly western. The surface treatment, paste, and temper of certain utilitarian ceramics also differ: jars of the Nabula group are plain in the east (Nabula unslipped type) and striated in the west (Yacman striated type); they also exhibit different paste color, temper composition, and vessel shape (see Fig. 3.10; Robles C. 1980, 1981a).

While there are prominent cultural differences between Mayapan and Ecab/Cozumel, the boundary between their respective spheres is not so clearly drawn. In fact, it would appear that there is a transitional zone between the two spheres. The provinces of Cupul, Chikinchel, and Tases are a case in point, as it is not clear to which sphere they belong. According to Roys, Cupul and Tases may have been allied to Mayapan, but Chikinchel appears to have been independent. The available archaeological data, which are scant, indicate that Chikinchel may have been an independent province influenced by both spheres. Late Postclassic ceramics from the Chikinchel coast consist of mixed assemblages of eastern and western wares (Ball 1978; Andrews, field notes); preliminary analysis of the ceramics from Dzonot Ake also suggests a mix of east and west (Webster 1979); next to nothing is known of the Postclassic architecture of the province.

Coba lies farther south along this transitional zone and exhibits a similar mix of east and west: during the Late Postclassic Period, the predominant ceramics are those of the west, while the architecture, sculpture, and mural painting are, beyond question, typical of the East Coast. Thus, it would appear that Coba's domination of the Eastern Sphere faded as the east coast communities rose to prominence and became the new centers of power.

The region comprising the northeast corner of Yucatan and east coast of Quintana Roo (i.e., the provinces of Ecab and Chikinchel) was, without a doubt, one of the most densely inhabited regions of the Maya Lowlands during the Late Postclassic Period. The only comparable region, to judge from historic sources and archaeological data, was the Chontalpa region of Tabasco and Chiapas, and the adjoining area of southwestern Campeche. It is not surprising, then, that these regions, which were in close contact through the trade networks, were the most prominent centers of political power when the Spanish arrived.

Despite extensive research on the East Coast during the last decade, many questions remain unanswered. The most intriguing problem concerns the nature of the sociopolitical organization of the region.

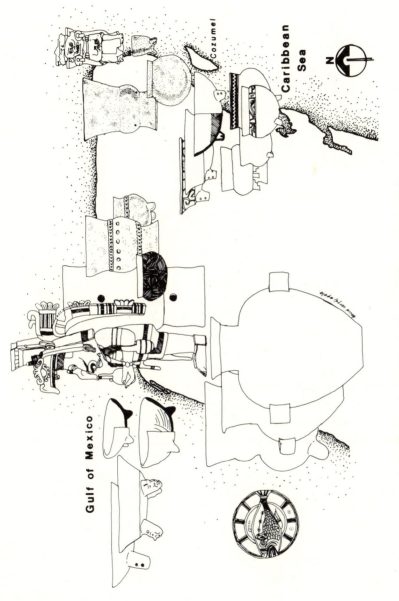

Figure 3.10 East-West Late Postclassic Vessel Shapes.

Certain communities, such as Muyil, Tancah-Tulum, and Ecab, may have reached urban proportions, but there is little evidence, as yet, to suggest that any of them was the political center of a major territory. While the walled fortress of Tulum would certainly appear to be the seat of a powerful elite, all the available ceramic, architectural, and mural evidence suggests that Tulum was a very late settlement, established within the larger and older community of Tancah (Miller 1977b, 1982). At almost all the heavily excavated sites on the East Coast, a large percentage of the architecture is associated with Peto Cream Ware ceramics, indicating that these communities predate A.D. 1300 (Robles C. 1981a, 1981c); at Tulum, the few Peto Cream Ware sherds that have been found come from levels well beneath any of the architectural foundations of the standing buildings, or from nonarchitectural contexts (Sanders 1960; Barrera Rubio 1977a; E. Vargas, personal communication).

In sum, there is no concrete evidence that the province of Ecab was dominated by any single community during the Late Postclassic Period. In fact, while the communities of the region were closely knit culturally—through elites who shared kin ties and mercantile relationships—Ecab appears to have been a politically acephalous province (Roys 1957). From Ecab to Muyil, then, the Late Postclassic communities flourished in a politically decentralized world that did not interfere with entrepreneurial activities.

We believe that the basic difference between east and west in Late Postclassic times, and the ultimate reason for the collapse of Mayapan and the continued resurgence of Ecab, lies in their different responses to the collapse of the Classic order, which led to quite distinct social and political structures. The new rulers of Mayapan attempted to perpetuate the old order, which had revolved around a strong centralized state apparatus; their new style of government, however, was inconsistent with such a state. Izamal and Chichen undoubtedly had virtually monolithic governments, whereas authority at Mayapan was shared by a group of provinces with a variety of conflicting interests; moreover, several of the provinces that made up the confederation had strong central governments under the leadership of powerful *halach uinicob* who were often at odds with the Cocom rulers of Mayapan. Unable to resolve this internal factionalism, Mayapan never consolidated its power over the north, and eventually collapsed (Roys 1957, 1962).

The communities of Ecab, on the other hand, evolved gradually out of the political vacuum left by the demise of Coba. They did not have an immediate prior megastate, such as that of the Chikinchel, to emulate, nor did they feel that they had to "revitalize" the ancient polity of Coba. These circumstances enabled them to develop along a new trajectory, without the concerns of establishing a centralized state and erecting massive monuments to enhance and promote its grandeur. As Thompson, Sabloff, Rathje, Freidel, and several others have argued, their markedly different priorities suggest the development of a world view radically different from that of previous periods. In this sense, then, they may have truly reached the threshold of a new order.

This new order, however, may have been developing while clouds gathered on the horizon. The growing power of the Aztec empire in the west was beginning to be felt in northern Yucatan, and tantalizing bits of historic and archaeological evidence suggest that links were being forged between the Yucatec and the Nahuatl. It has been documented that Aztec merchants had established a strong presence at Xicalango in southwestern Campeche, and at Zinacantan and Soconusco in Chiapas; their trading expeditions may have reached as far as Panama. Just how far they or their allies had advanced into the peninsula remains unclear, but the very late appearance of scattered Central Mexican cultural elements in Yucatan, and of rather unusual fortified sites at Tulum and Ichpaatun, certainly hints that the peninsula was being drawn into the mainstream of foreign developments. These events were unfolding at a very fast pace, and we have only fragments of evidence in the archaeological record. Whatever was happening, it was cut short by the Spanish, whose arrival marked the beginning of yet another order.

NOTE

1. A substantial body of the data presented here is the result of the research conducted during the last decade by members of the Centro Regional del Sureste, of the Instituto Nacional de Anthropología e Historia, under the direction of Norberto González C. It is unfortunate that Norberto was unable to participate in the seminar, for his guidance and criticism over the last few years have been instrumental in advancing our knowledge of Yucatecan archaeology. We are also indebted to the members of the CRS-INAH team for their support and assistance in our own recent research. Special acknowl-

edgment is due to Rubén Maldonado Cárdenas for sharing unpublished data from his recent work at Uci, Cansahcab, and Ucanha. Robles acknowledges the administrative support of Febronio Díaz Figueroa, director of Fideicaribe, during the preparation of this paper. We also thank Antonio Benavides, Edward Kurjack, and Peter Schmidt for allowing us to reproduce the illustrations in Figs. 3.2, 3.3, and 3.6, and David Cortés and Barbara Andrews for drafting Figs. 3.1, 3.4, 3.7, 3.8 and 3.9. This paper has benefited from the substantive and editorial comments of several people, including Barbara Andrews, E. W. Andrews V, Wendy Ashmore, Antonio Benavides, Arlen and Diane Chase, Jane Kepp, Edward Kurjack, and Peter Schmidt.

4

Time Depth or Vacuum: The 11.3.0.0.0 Correlation and the Lowland Maya Postclassic

ARLEN F. CHASE

University of Central Florida

Although research in the Maya area has been increasingly concerned with the spatial, rather than temporal, distribution of Maya remains, the correlation of independent regional chronologies throughout the Maya Lowlands is still confused for the later part of Maya prehistory. Several reasons may be cited for the disparate picture that currently exists for the Postclassic era: the distinct change of gears that this time period represents from the Classic Period; the repeated intrusion into the Lowland area by groups of foreigners (and, presumably, the introduction of associated artifactual assemblages) as represented in the limited ethnohistorical references available; and, most important, the conceptual limitations of the existing archaeological paradigm in which researchers often associate differences in archaeological remains, particularly pottery, with temporal change prior to evaluating evidence for the presence of spatial and/or cultural factors.

The differentiation of spatial and temporal dimensions is a difficult task, especially for the Postclassic era. Unlike Classic Period buildings, which often engulf and encompass each other (thus providing a clear temporal sequence), Postclassic remains are often spatially distinct, unstratified constructions; thus, the problem of distinguishing temporal change from variation within a single time period is not easily solved. In addition to the general lack of stratigraphy, the problems of separating time and space in the Postclassic Period are exacerbated by problematic radiocarbon dates. Because of these difficulties, schemata for correlating different ceramic complexes and regional sequences during the Postclassic Period have proliferated, perhaps most notably in Ball's (1974, 1979a) work on the possible relationships between the ceramic complexes of northern Yucatan.

The work of Ball (1974a, 1979a, 1979b, 1985a) in northern Yucatan and of D. Chase (1981, 1982a, 1985) and myself (1983, 1985) in northern Belize and central Peten points to serious problems in the present conceptualization of the Terminal Classic–Early Postclassic Period in particular and of the Postclassic Maya Lowlands in general. It is suggested here that these recent efforts to correlate and understand regional sequences for the era point to the need for a Maya-European calendric correlation different from the current 11.16.0.0.0 bulwark. Probably some version of the 11.3.0.0.0 correlation is called for. Unlike earlier attempts to bind the Maya and European calendars together, however, this does not assume that there ever was any one-to-one day correlation, but rather a series of differing regional calendars, possibly referable to a single katun.

Both recently excavated data and the native documents, especially the Books of Chilam Balam, indicate that an 11.3.0.0.0 correlation may be profitably utilized for interpreting Lowland Maya Postclassic history. That some version of an 11.3.0.0.0 correlation is applicable to the Maya area finds support not only in recent information from the Yucatecan and Peten areas, but also in advances that have been made in the anthropological understanding of archaeological remains since the original arguments for this correlation of Maya and European calendars (Lehmann 1910; Escalona Ramos 1940; Thompson 1941a, 1950). Much like a paper once written by Thompson (1941: i–ii), this statement has been written in order "to outline tentative solutions which conform to information now on hand, with the purpose not of supplying final answers but of stimulating interest in these problems." However, given current information on the Maya, this paper argues that the 11.3.0.0.0 correlation is a logical solution to certain of the above mentioned problems now being encountered in cross-regional syntheses of Lowland Maya Postclassic archaeology.[1]

Any correlation of the Maya and European calendars must deal with an array of widely scattered and conflicting data. To be accepted by the modern archaeologist, a correlation must coherently "fit" or account for the various kinds of archaeological information available from the Maya area: radiocarbon dates; calendrical, hieroglyphic, and astronomical peculiarities; the extant archaeology; and the existing ethnohistory. Before each of these bodies of information is tackled, however, an explanation of the Maya calendrical system and its various correlations with the European calendar is necessary.

THE MAYA CALENDAR AND ITS CORRELATION WITH THE EUROPEAN CALENDAR

The Maya calendric system was based upon the juxtaposition of two counts: (1) a 260-day ritual count comprised of the coincidence of 13 day numbers (possibly deities) with 20 named days; and (2) a 365-day vague year count formed by 18 months of 20 days each with the addition of 5 ceremonial unnamed days at the end of the year (see Satterthwaite 1965 for more detail). Within this system of recording time a particular day only recurred every 52 years; these 52-year periods are known as "calendar rounds." During the Classic Period, calendar-round periods were utilized in conjunction with a system of linearly recording time, known as the "Long Count"; the Long Count registered the absolute passing of time in a vigesimal system from a fixed starting point in the distant past. Long Count dates are currently transcribed in a specific way with the completed number of each of the baktuns (20 katuns or 144,000 days or roughly a 400-year period), katuns (20 tuns or 7,200 days or roughly a 20-year period), tuns (18 uinals or 360 days or approximately a year), uinals (20 kins or 20 days), and kins (days) followed by a period. For example, 10.3.0.0.0 1 Ahau 3 Yaxkin implies a Long Count date of 10 baktuns, 3 katuns, 0 tuns, 0 uinals, and 0 kins correlating with a calendar-round date of 1 Ahau 3 Yaxkin. Thus, during the Classic Period a calendar-round date was fixed in place by its associated Long Count date.

With the onset of the Postclassic Period, however, the Long Count system of recording time fell into disuse. Although the 52-year calendar round continued to be utilized, it was no longer placed in relation to an absolute scale of linear time. During the Postclassic Period, the Long Count was replaced by a truncated recording system that combined calendar-round and katun information into a single notation. This "Short Count" recorded only the day on which a particular katun (or 20-year period) ended; because all katuns ended on the day Ahau, this notation always consisted of this day in combination with one of the thirteen primary numbers (in the Maya system, these were not recorded in standard numerical order, but rather proceeded cyclically as follows: 13, 11, 9, 7, 5, 3, 1, 12, 10, 8, 6, 4, 2, 13, . . .). In the Short Count, no uinal information was recorded; rather, the Ahau date represented an entire katun. Thus, each named Ahau date in the Short Count recurred only after 256 years. Although events were recorded in relation to the specific named katun in which they occurred, they were not placed within a time-distance count of depth greater than 13 katuns, or roughly 256 years.

Most of the possible Maya correlations are based on the fact that a Katun 13 Ahau ("The Katun of Conquest") shifted to a Katun 11 Ahau during the first half of the sixteenth century. The last known Katun 13 Ahau date that can be correlated with a Long Count date is the calendar-round date 13 Ahau 18 Cumku, which is associated with a 9.17.0.0.0 date in the Classic Maya Long Count; therefore, a Katun 13 Ahau in the Short Count system could be related to any 256-year period that occurred after this Long Count date. In Long Count notation, these periods of time fall at 10.10.0.0.0, 11.3.0.0.0, 11.16.0.0.0, 12.9.0.0.0, and 13.2.0.0.0. In fact, each of these dates has been mentioned as a possible correlation point with the sixteenth-century European calendar (10.10—Vaillant 1935; Thompson 1935: 70–72; 11.3—Vaillant 1935; Thompson 1935: 72–73, 1941; Andrews IV 1940; Escalona Ramos 1940; Wauchope 1947, 1948, 1954; 11.16—Goodman 1905; Spinden 1924, 1928, 1930; Martínez Hernández 1926; Thompson 1927, 1935: 73–78; Beyer 1934; 12.9—Morley 1910; Thompson 1935: 78–80; 13.2—Long 1931; Thompson 1935: 80; see also L. Roys 1933). An additional possible correlation, the 11.10.0.0.0 (Kriegauer), was noted as a possibility by Andrews IV (1940) and Lothrop (1952); recently Kelley (1983) has suggested an 11.5.0.0.0 correlation. Although the 11.16.0.0.0 correlation has been generally accepted and presently dominates Maya archaeological thought, the following sections demonstrate both the need to reassess the current correlation problem and the value of an 11.3.0.0.0 correlation.

RADIOCARBON DATING: WHY 11.3.0.0.0?

Few scientific techniques or methods have had as much effect on archaeology as the development and implementation of carbon-14 dating. One area on which radiocarbon dating has had both a methodological and a conceptual impact is the testing of the validity of possible Maya calendrical correlations with the European calendar; in fact, support for different correlations paralleled the development and refinement of the dating technique and the dates that it yielded. Since the inception of radiocarbon dating, Maya researchers have adhered to the method, first arguing for Spinden's 12.9.0.0.0 correlation (Andrews IV 1965a) based on the early datings, and then arguing for Goodman, Thompson, and Martínez's 11.16.0.0.0 correlation, with Satterthwaite and Ralph's (1960) article based on later datings.

The early 1950s radiocarbon support of the 12.9.0.0.0 correlation (Kulp, Feely, and Tryon 1951; Libby 1954) seemingly forced many researchers who had been considering the 11.3.0.0.0 correlation to seek "refuge" in a middle ground 11.16.0.0.0 correlation. Satterthwaite (1956) found it necessary to remind the early 12.9 supporters that the 11.16 correlation (let alone an 11.3 correlation) was still a viable option. Deevey, Gralenski, and Hoffren (1959) noted that "the difference between the two correlations, 260 years, is small, corresponding to about 3 percent difference in net C-14 content, and methodologic errors of this order of magnitude are inherent in any radiocarbon measurement," concluding that "the question of the Maya-Christian correlation" was "still an open one."

The Tikal excavations produced over 100 radiocarbon dates and supported an 11.16.0.0.0 correlation in 1960, overturning an earlier backing of the 12.9.0.0.0 correlation being argued for in the Yucatan (Andrews IV 1965a). Andrews V (1972, 1978: 381; Andrews IV and Andrews V 1980: 281–85) subsequently attempted to bring the Yucatecan sequence and its associated radiocarbon dates into line with an 11.16.0.0.0 correlation as opposed to a 12.9.0.0.0 correlation, but in all his attempts concluded that "radiocarbon determinations from the Maya area will not solve the correlation problem for us."

Presently the 11.16.0.0.0 paradigm dominates Maya dating. One of the last stalwarts for an alternative correlation, Robert Wauchope, adopted the 11.16.0.0.0 correlation in 1975 even though he had earlier noted (1954: 20) that it afforded him "considerable difficulty to try to reconcile post-Classic sequence with the 11.16.0.0.0 correlation." Before the advent of radiocarbon dating, Wauchope forcefully demonstrated (1947) that the ethnohistory of the Maya Highlands, when combined with the known archaeology, implied the need for an

103

11.3.0.0.0 correlation. Even earlier, Thompson (1941a, 1942) and Vaillant (1935) had also argued for an 11.3.0.0.0 correlation based on archaeological and ethnohistoric associations. Although Wauchope eventually opted for the "most widely accepted GMT correlation," his discussion (1975: 66) of the correlation question in terms of Zacualpa is still not convincing and only serves to bring out the possible application of *either* the 11.3.0.0.0 or the 11.16.0.0.0 correlation at that site.

Mayanists have long been aware of the difficulty in dating their material because of the problems of half-life, sigma, average death rate, postsample error, placement history, contamination, and various other statistical, chemical, and archaeological problems (Stuckenrath, Coe, and Ralph 1966: 372–74; Stuckenrath 1977; Andrews IV and Andrews V 1980: 285). In many instances, even an awareness of these factors has not helped them to obtain successful dating (for example, see Adams 1971: 143–52). The 1960 dates utilized by Satterthwaite and Ralph (1960) to uphold an 11.16.0.0.0 correlation may now be questioned simply by recalibrating them; they no longer fall into perfect harmony with the 11.16.0.0.0 correlation.

An example of methodological problems in radiocarbon dating causing problems in interpretation can be found in Ball's (1974) reconstruction of the Early Postclassic Period of the Yucatan Peninsula. Using the understanding then current of radiocarbon dates from Balankanche Cave, Ball postulated two "Itza" invasions in the Yucatan peninsula. The first he placed (1974a: 91–92) anywhere from A.D. 750 to 900 and associated with the Balankanche material; the second he placed around A.D. 980, basing this idea on other known archaeological material. However, a recalibration of the radiocarbon dates from Balankanche, based on new advances in the technique (MASCA recalibration tables), places these dates from A.D. 940 to 950; the new dates tend to meld Ball's two invasions into one and serve to illustrate the difficulty in basing culture history and, indirectly, dating paradigms on a method that is still being refined. As radiocarbon dating becomes both more precise and possibly more accurate, future recalibrations of the Balakanche dates will undoubtedly alter the current picture.

The present paper, like those of Deevey, Gralenski, and Hoffren (1959) and Satterthwaite (1956) before it, argues that the Maya correlation question is far from settled. Given the role that radiocarbon dating has played in the debate over the correlation, supporters of the current 11.16.0.0.0 paradigm must be reminded that there are methodological problems in the radiocarbon dating technique (Ogden 1977; Pardi and Marcus 1977; Stuckenrath 1977) which could yet shift the paradigm forward another 260 years.

CALENDRICAL CONSIDERATIONS

Much has been written on the astronomical and calendrical capabilities of the Maya, and these skills must be considered in effecting any correlation. The use of Maya astronomy and calendrics as evidence in support of one correlation rather than another requires examination of ethnohistoric references to the coincidence of the Maya and European calendars in addition to a consideration of the basic workings of the calendar. Most scholars have sought to use this combination of calendrics and ethnohistoric statements to argue for a precise correlation of a specific day in the European calendar with a specific katun ending in the Maya Short Count. While many would suggest that a precise day-to-day correlation of the European and Maya calendars is possible given calendric, astronomical, and ethnohistorical information, the evidence presented below indicates not only that such a search for a single correlation is inappropriate, but also that the European calendar may best be placed in a general association to the 11.3.0.0.0 correlation.

In past dealings with the correlation question the majority of researchers have been in search of a single day-to-day correlation that could then be compared with astronomical information. This paper does not purport to espouse any particular day-to-day correlation, but rather suggests that some general version or several versions of an 11.3.0.0.0 correlation may plausibly be applied to the Postclassic Period in the Maya Lowlands. It is in fact proposed, following the Books of Chilam Balam and in accordance with the research of Kirchoff (1950) and Kubler (1976), that more than one calendar was in operation in the Postclassic Lowlands at any point in time and that a search for a single day-to-day correlation equivalent will prove fruitless. This would accord well with other evidence from Mesoamerica, for data from highland Mexico also suggest the use of several calendars (Nicholson 1975: 491). The use of multiple calendars in the Maya Lowlands during the Postclassic Period would not be surprising given the regional differences in its organization (see D. Chase, this volume).

105

One secure ethnohistoric reference pertaining to calendrics and the correlation question comes from the central Peten, where Villagutierre (1933) stated that Fuensalida and Orbita noted that A.D. 1618 occurred in a Katun 3 Ahau. While this observation brackets Katun 3 Ahau to a 40-year period ranging from A.D. 1598 to 1638, it provides little other information, for it is not clear that the Itza calendar of the central Peten can definitely be associated with one from northern Yucatan. Earlier, Landa (Tozzer 1941: 168) had noted that "the Spaniards finally arrived at the city of Merida in the year of the birth of our Lord, 1541, which was precisely in the first year of the era of Buluc Ahau"; this statement has repeatedly been contested by various Mayanists (see Tozzer 1941: n.279), although the implied Katun 13 Ahau/Katun 11 Ahau shift in A.D. 1540 accords with other known evidence (see below).

Although Thompson is widely considered to have found the "correct" correlation when he suggested an 11.16.0.0.0/A.D. 1539 correlation (1935), he unfortunately formulated his correlation without taking serious enough account of the native history reflected in the Books of Chilam Balam. These books contain important calendric information on a postcontact horizon. While probably the most important sources from the ethnohistorian's standpoint, they have often been summarily dismissed by many Maya archaeologists.

Morley and Spinden place great reliance on the various statements on the correlation to be found in the Chilam Balam of Chumayel, Mani, and Tizimin, but in this summary these statements are discarded as original material, being used only as confirmatory evidence. (Thompson 1935: 57)

Thompson also sought to show that a Katun 13 Ahau ended in the fall of 1539; basing his belief on page 66 of the Chronicle of Oxcutzcab, as discussed by Morley (1920), he commented (1935: 59): "Although this page can not be classed as original material, its value is greater than that of the various books of Chilam Balam." Thompson's selective use of ethnohistory appears to have introduced a source of bias into his commonly accepted 11.16.0.0.0 correlation, for Morley's (1920: 494) reasoning in favor of a 1539 13 Ahau date, followed by Thompson, may have been incorrect. Page 66 of the Chronicle of Oxkutzcab, compiled by the Xiu family of Yucatan between 1608 and 1817, was supposedly written in 1685. Morley (1920: 472, 497) believed this page to have been transcribed from a codex, but it is not at all clear why, as it deals only with postconquest events. More important, its year

106

bearers (the numbered days that begin the Maya year) are consistently off by a year from those in other native documents (Satterthwaite 1971: 30). It would appear that the early attempts at a Maya-Christian correlation prematurely dismissed data that were difficult to reconcile with a single day-to-day correlation.

The search for a "single" correlation is evident in Closs's (1976) attempt to show that Ponce de León reached the Yucatan in 1513 (Tio 1972) and, thus, that Thompson's 11.16.0.0.0/A.D. 1539 correlation is valid. Closs (1976: 194) believes that the appearance of Ponce de León corresponds with the first mention of the Spaniards in the Books of Chilam Balam (Tizimin) in Tun 13 of Katun 2 Ahau. He interprets the linkage of these two events as proving an 11.16.0.0.0 correlation, ignoring the probability that Spaniards had reached the peninsula at an earlier date. Brinton (1882: 132) argued that Pinzón had reached the peninsula in A.D. 1506 (although this argument has been largely dismissed; see Rubio Mane 1957) and that Aguilar and Guerrero had been shipwrecked on the coast in A.D. 1511; these latter two individuals were widely known to the Protohistoric Maya. This evidence of early Spanish presence suggests that the Tizimin reference may not relate to Ponce de León. Even if Ponce de León had arrived in mid-July, as Closs says (1976: 194), the Maya year was then in the process of changing; the Tun 13 of Katun 2 Ahau that would be assigned to the 1513 Ponce de León landing by the Tizimin chronicle may actually be one tun too late (i.e., it may have occurred in Tun 12). In any case, the positioning of this tun not only agrees with an 11.16.0.0.0 correlation, as argued by Closs, but could coincide with any correlation, especially if no single day-to-day correlation (or Ahau equation) exists.

While much research has been expended on the search for a specific day equivalency between the Maya and European calendric systems, the Maya correlation question can be approached from several other avenues dealing with Maya glyphs and calendrical data. Glyphic data on at least one historic personage suggest the plausibility of an 11.3.0.0.0 correlation. An important potential connection may be made between the hieroglyphic texts at Chichen Itza and the katun records in the Books of Chilam Balam; this linkage is such as to argue for an 11.3.0.0.0 correlation if only a single person is involved. Kelley (1967: 263–64) has provided a convincing argument that a person named Kakupacal may be associated with Chichen Itza sometime after 10.2.0.0.0. This name reappears in the Books of Chilam Balam and corresponds nicely with the noted abandonment of Chichen Itza in a Katun 1 Ahau (see below). The name Kakupacal also reappears in the seventh tun of Katun 8 Ahau as being the person who conquered Chakanputun. Providing that the date 10.2.0.0.0, ascribed by Kelley (1968: 164) to Kakupacal, is his birth date and that the second reference is to the same person (and not a son), he would have been approximately 87 years old at the time of this conquest under an 11.3.0.0.0 correlation. Any other correlation would mandate that the Kakupacal of the hieroglyphs and the Kakupacal of the Chilam Balams be different individuals.

Other calendrical data also suggest the validity of an 11.3.0.0.0 correlation. Edmonson (1976) argues that a "reform" in the year bearers of the Maya calendar "proves" the validity of the 11.16.0.0.0 correlation. Although there may have been a calendar reform, such a reform would not verify either the 11.16 or the 12.9 correlation, but could possibly verify an 11.3 correlation. Edmonson (1976: 713) concludes that "it was the Tikal calendar that was in use in Yucatan at the beginning of 1539" and notes the existence of a two-day difference between the Tikal and colonial Mayapan calendars. It is suggested here that this difference may be due to a baktun-cycle change of year bearers and that this cyclical change may be seen as coincidentally adding further evidence in favor of an 11.3.0.0.0 correlation based on the mandated number of changes.

> In early Classic times in Tikal (8.12.0.0.0; A.D. 277) the yearbearers were Ik, Manik, Eb, and Caban (Morley 1947: 301). By 9.12.0.0.0 (A.D. 672) in Campeche a new set had been installed: Akbal, Lamat, Ben, and Etz'nab (Thompson 1960: 304). In the colonial calendar of 16th century Mayapan (11.16.0.0.0; A.D. 1539) the yearbearers were Kan, Muluc, Ix, and Cauac. By the 18th century in Valladolid (12.6.0.0.0; A.D. 1756) they had changed again to Imix, Cimi, Chuen, and Cib (Roys n.d.). (Edmonson 1976: 713)

There are only four possible combinations of year bearers, all represented in Edmonson's summary. The days missing from the above list are Chicchan, Oc, Men, and Ahau, but these four days could not have served as year bearers since the first day of the Maya year "was counted by its *last* day, which was *always* Ahau" (Edmonson 1976: 713; my emphasis). Knowing that there were shifts in the sets of year bearers, it is logical to assume, in accord with the nature of the Maya calendar, that such shifts were cyclical. Based on the known temporal occurrence of the four possible groupings of year bearers, it may be suggested that the year bearer sets changed in a regular cycle every baktun—perhaps at the end of the twelfth katun of each baktun, to judge from the above-mentioned Classic Period evidence. A diagram of this cyclical phenomenon (Table 4.1) shows how the cycle would have carried into the eighteenth century and would have been continuous under an 11.3.0.0.0 correlation. The cyclical nature of the shift from the Tikal to the Campeche to the colonial Mayapan calendar in fact indicates a continuity that is impossible in any correlation other than the 11.3.0.0.0; specifically, the 11.16.0.0.0 introduces too much time into the calendrical record to allow for such a cyclical shift.

While a cyclical shift is in accord with Maya calendrics, a day-to-day equivalency between the Maya and European calendars does not appear to be possible. The Books of Chilam Balam, discussed below, indicate the use of at least two calendars during the Maya Postclassic Period. This would indicate that the search for an Ahau Equation (or single day-to-day correlation between Maya and European calendars; see Satterthwaite 1965), thought to be so important in effecting any correlation, is in fact meaningless, for even though there is calendric continuity from the Classic to Postclassic, the existence of more than one calendar precludes distinguishing which are continuous with their Classic counterparts. The differing versions of the Maya calendar are, therefore, only "accurate" in a general sense and are not precise on a day-to-day level. Because several Postclassic calendars seem to have

Table 4.1

Christian Year	Bactun Beginning In Maya Long Count	Year Bearers	Location Of Use
A.D. 520	8.12.0.0.0	Ik, Manik, Eb, Caban	Tikal
A.D. 920	9.12.0.0.0	Akbal, Lamat, Ben, Etz'nab	Campeche
A.D. 1320	10.12.0.0.0	Kan, Muluc, Ix, Cauac	Colonial Mayapan
A.D. 1720	11.12.0.0.0	Imix, Cimi, Chuen, Cib	Yucatan

Table 4.1: Diagram using a rough equation in which A.D. 1540 equals 11.3.0.0.0, showing the cyclical change of year bearers through Maya history, assuming that year bearers changed in the twelfth katun of each baktun.

existed, because these appear to vary within a limited frame, and because no day-to-day precision can be attributed to them over time, arguments over the applicability of astronomical data to a single Maya calendar are fairly pointless. Even if there was only one Postclassic calendar, the associated astronomical data are much disputed. For instance, the 11.3.0.0.0 day-to-day correlation put forth by Escalona Ramos (1940) used the Ahau equation 678,108, making 11.3.0.0.0 13 Ahau 13 Pax equal March 11, 1543. Thompson (1950: 308) disputed Escalona Ramos's Ahau equation, stating: "Although I have not been averse to an 11.3.0.0.0 correlation, I can see little to recommend this particular version of it." He argued that the Escalona Ramos day count did not correlate well with the Dresden Codex in terms of the heliacal rising of Venus after inferior conjunction and also claimed (1950: 308) that Ramos's "lunar data are about nine days out" if he accepts Landa. Satterthwaite (Satterthwaite and Coe 1968; Christopher Jones, personal communication), however, argued that the Ramos 11.3.0.0.0 correlation was more accurate in terms of moon ages than either the 12.9.0.0.0 or the 11.16.0.0.0 correlation and saw Escalona Ramos's (1940) day count as only off by one-third of a day. Disagreements like these become meaningless if one accepts the calendric disuniformity of the Postclassic Maya.

ARCHAEOLOGY

In a discussion of Maya archaeology and the 11.3.0.0.0 correlation, one invariably turns to the ceramicist for interpretations. Ceramic support for an 11.3.0.0.0 correlation has been noted by Vaillant (1935) and Wauchope (1948). Even Thompson (1950: 306) remarked in his discussion of Chichen Itza that "perhaps this ceramic and architectural frame can be garbed in the 11.3.0.0.0 correlation." In his work dealing with the coast of Campeche, Ruz Lhuillier (1969: 215–52) was also suspicious of the 11.16 correlation and added that the "door is open" for the 11.3 correlation; he did, however, cast doubt on this latter correlation (1969: 252) in view of his reading of the Books of Chilam Balam.

Many arguments in favor of an 11.16.0.0.0 correlation have been based on the limited temporal occurrences of ceramic complexes and horizon markers. Recent archaeological work has led to a re-evaluation of much of this temporal framework. Newly recovered data have increased the temporal and spatial understanding of former horizon markers such as Plumbate and Fine Orange. The spatial relationships between ceramic complexes have also undergone critical rethinking. Ball's (1971a: 30–35) discussion of the overlap among Cehpech, Sotuta, and Hocaba in northern Yucatan more than ever suggests the probable validity of an 11.3 correlation because of the time compression involved.

Thompson (1941b: 109), who designed much of the temporal frame now utilized for interpreting the Maya, invalidated an 11.3.0.0.0 correlation in his reading of the Chilam Balam to indicate that "under such a correlation plumbate would coincide with the Old Empire." Plumbate is one of the most important horizon markers for the early part of the Postclassic Period; Shepard (1948: 1) has noted that "its associations indicate a relatively short period of manufacture, estimated at between 150 and 250 years." Radiocarbon dates on material associated with Plumbate place it in existence at A.D. 1400 in the Highlands (Bilbao date TBN-315-2). In addition, though, Plumbate is known from the "Old Empire" sites of Quirigua and Copan. "At Quirigua it is found on a Terminal Classic level in Group B as well as in the Central Acropolis" (Jones, Ashmore, and Sharer n.d.: 38). Although Thompson did not believe it possible, Plumbate seems to coincide with the end of the Maya Classic Period; the ware apparently extends at least through the middle of the Postclassic Period. Thus, one of the early objections to an 11.3.0.0.0 correlation—that Plumbate would coincide with the end of the Maya Classic Period—has proven untenable.

R. E. Smith (1958, 1971: 20–21) and Brainerd (1941, 1953) have dealt extensively with Fine Orange Ware, whose various types are important horizon markers for the Terminal Classic through Late Postclassic periods. There is some question, however, whether spatial or cultural differences have become temporal differences under the rigidification of the type concept for this particular ware. Brainerd (1953) demonstrated that X-Fine Orange must be contemporaneous with the Mazapan–Chichimec–Monte Alban IIIc–Aztec I horizons as defined by Vaillant (1938). Although the strict associations are not spelled out, it may be more than coincidence that the sites listed by Brainerd (1953: 181) as containing heavy amounts of X-Fine Orange are also noted as generally having a heavy Late Postclassic component. In attempting to sort out this possible temporal inconsistency, Smith (1958: 151) defined five kinds of Fine Orange—X (Silho), Y (Altar), Z (Balancan),

V (Matillas), U (Cunduacan); he ended up, however, calling the Isla de Sacrificios material "problematical," since Brainerd (1953: 151) had noted a large proportion of X-Fine Orange in obviously late contexts. While such an occurrence would not be unexpected under an 11.3.0.0.0 framework, it cannot be accepted under an 11.16.0.0.0 correlation. Smith (1958: 160) noted that "there are a number of fine orange specimens difficult to place within the 5 known fine orange types," indicating that the phenomenon of "intergrading," noted by Sharer and Chase (1976) for Barton Ramie's Paxcaman type, may exist. In his later work, Smith (1971: 19–20) indirectly addressed this problem by specifically noting the complementarity of U and V Fine Orange, especially as witnessed in their mutual exclusivity in forms and decorative techniques. Recent investigation has indicated that X, Y, and Z Fine Orange wares may be generally grouped together (Ball 1977a: 45–46) as may the V and U categories of Fine Orange wares (J. Ball, personal communication). As tradewares, these two groupings may in turn be associated with the Terminal Classic and Late Postclassic periods; what, if any, Fine Orange occurs between these two temporal limits is presently undefined. It may be posited that X, Y, and Z Fine Orange are directly ancestral to V and U Fine Orange, which indirectly lends credence to an 11.3.0.0.0 correlation.

At present, the archaeological understanding of the Postclassic Period in the Northern Lowlands is clouded; the key site in clearing the present mists, especially as they now envelop the ceramic sequence for this area, is Chichen Itza. Work done in the 1930s at Chichen Itza emphasized the architectural complexes (Morris, Charlot, and Morris 1931; Ruppert 1935, 1952; Bolles 1977); the ceramics and artifacts were virtually ignored except for brief treatments by Brainerd (1958), Stromsvik (1937), Smith (1971), and Bolles (1977). While the position of Chichen Itza in Mesoamerican history has long been considered important, especially for the Maya Postclassic, the site has largely been placed in time by means of various interpretations of the Books of Chilam Balam, with little use being made of its extant archaeology. While more data have been published on Mayapan (Pollock et al. 1962; Smith 1971) than on Chichen Itza, Mayapan's inception, like that of Chichen Itza, is not securely placed in time. In part these gaps were due to the then-current argument over dating schemes going on in the Northern Lowlands (Andrews IV 1965a) and in part to preconceptions about the native histories, although ethnohistoric references

112

were interpreted to place Mayapan's abandonment at about A.D. 1440 (Pollock et al. 1962). The final Cozumel Project Report may be able to suggest answers to some of the temporal and spatial questions in the Yucatecan area; the publications now available (Rathje and Sabloff 1973; Sabloff et al. 1974; Rathje 1975; Sabloff and Freidel 1975; Sabloff and Rathje 1975a, 1975b) do not attempt to answer such questions. Connor (1975: 129), however, notes that there is a scarcity of sherds representing the Modified Florescent on Cozumel, but that a quantity of Pure Florescent material does exist on the island; as Ball (1979a) has posited that each of these bodies of ceramic material represents two spatial spheres, this distribution is particularly interesting at Cozumel and may be viewed as possible supporting evidence for one of Ball's alternative temporal frameworks.

Smith (1971) produced the most definitive statement on Postclassic pottery in the Northern Lowlands. His analysis of the temporal limits of the Mayapan ceramics, specifically at the complex and group levels, however, appears to have been largely based on the commonly accepted interpretations pertaining to the Books of Chilam Balam (which followed an 11.16.0.0.0 correlation) and not strictly on archaeological data. He appears to have overlooked the concept of "sloping ceramic horizons," which would indicate contemporaneous variability among pottery, and its applicability to Postclassic Yucatan; assuming that sloping horizons existed, Smith's earlier two ceramic complexes, termed Cehpech and Hocaba, could easily be encompassed within a single phase (as suggested by Ball 1979a). Tschopik (1950: 217) had already demonstrated for Protohistoric Peru that "class-linked ceramic styles should receive serious consideration in the reconstruction of . . . prehistory," and, later, Morris (1972: 394–95) illustrated the contemporaneous existence of two completely different ceramic complexes in the same area of Peru because of political exigencies. Although this is apparently the same phenomenon that existed in the Yucatan during Postclassic times, individual and/or current interpretations of Yucatecan ethnohistory have been allowed to dominate the archaeology.

Among the first scholars to attempt to remodel the framework of Maya archaeology, Joseph Ball has been especially innovative in conceptualizing temporal and spatial problems that had previously been delicately ignored. Especially noteworthy is his reworked presentation of the northern Yucatec data (Ball 1979a, 1979b), containing interpretations that seriously counter the previous linear arrangement presented both by himself (1974a) and by Smith (1971). His application of "sloping ceramic horizons" to the problems he encountered in the generally accepted linear arrangement of the archaeology of northern Yucatan (Andrews IV 1965; Smith 1971) succeeded in at least partially solving a tricky chronological problem.

Ball's research also raises a more important question. If one accepts the probability that Cehpech and Sotuta were overlapping, if not co-eval, and that Hocaba may also have overlapped with the other complexes, then one is forced to reanalyze the temporal frame in which these complexes are being placed. The postulated overlap would, in effect, shrink the time heretofore allotted for these complexes. The question is, How much of a vacuum is there and what does this shrinkage do to the present conceptualization of the Maya Postclassic Period? An acceptance of such overlap may, I suggest, minimally dictate the consideration of alternative Maya-European correlations. The archaeology, when interpreted in terms of the known ethnohistory, would, I believe, support a version of an 11.3.0.0.0 correlation (see Table 4.2).

Looking at specific examples of temporal frames provided for specific areas, sites, and ceramic groups under an 11.16.0.0.0 as opposed to an 11.3.0.0.0 correlation (Table 4.2), it is clear that an 11.3.0.0.0 correlation fits well with the currently defined archaeological situation. The span provided for Puuc architecture and associated events is roughly the same under either correlation (280 years in 11.6; 240 years in 11.3). The span provided for the florescence of Chichen Itza is considerably shortened, from 340 years under the 11.6 correlation to 260 years (or less) under the 11.3 correlation. That Chichen Itza's florescence can be dated to the Maya Terminal Classic Period (at least to 10.2.0.0.0 in the Long Count) is indicated by hieroglyphic associations with "Toltec" architecture (see Lincoln, this volume) and by events farther south (see Chase and Chase 1982). The culmination of the site would be dated by katun records to about 10.19 under an 11.6 correlation and to circa 10.8 under an 11.3 correlation. While it is clear that Chichen is reoccupied during the Late Postclassic Period, it is also clear that most of the site is clearly Terminal Classic in date; thus, a 10.19 end date is improbably late. Under either correlation, the span provided for the existence of Mayapan is relatively consistent (240 years in 11.6 and 220 years in 11.3). Ceramics make perhaps the best case for an 11.3 correlation. The span provided by an 11.16

Table 4.2

11.16 Correlation

MAYA	A.D.					
11.16	1539				·	
11.15	1520				·	
11.14	1500				·	
11.13	1480				·	
11.12	1461				·	
11.11	1441		x		·	
11.10	1421		x		·	
11.9	1401		M		·	T
11.8	1382		A		·	U
11.7	1362		Y		·	L
11.6	1342		A		·	U
11.5	1323		P		·	M
11.4	1303		A		·	·
11.3	1283		N		·	R
11.2	1263		x		P	E
11.1	1244		x		E	D
11.0	1224		x		T	W
10.19	1204	x	x	·	O	A
10.18	1185		x	·	·	R
10.17	1165		x	·	C	E
10.16	1145		x	·	R	·
10.15	1125		x	·	E	·
10.14	1106		C	P	A	·
10.13	1086		H	L	M	·
10.12	1066		I	U	·	·
10.11	1047	x	C	M	·	·
10.10	1027	x	H	B	·	
10.9	1007	x	E	A	·	
10.8	987	x	N	T	·	
10.7	968	P	x	E	·	
10.6	948	U	x	·	·	
10.5	928	U	x	·		
10.4	909	C	x	·		
10.3	889	x	x	·		
10.2	869	x	x	·		
10.1	849	x		·		
10.0	830	x		·		
9.19	810	x		·		
9.18	790	x				
9.17	771	x				
9.16	751					
9.15	731					

11.3 Correlation

MAYA	A.D.						
11.3	1540						·
11.2	1520						·
11.1	1501					T	
11.0	1481					U	
10.19	1461			x		L	
10.18	1442			M		U	
10.17	1422			A		M	
10.16	1402			Y		·	
10.15	1382			A		R	
10.14	1363			P		E	
10.13	1343			A	·	D	
10.12	1323		x	N	P	W	
10.11	1304		C	x	E	A	
10.10	1284		H	x	T	R	
10.9	1264		I	x	O	E	
10.8	1244	x	C	x	·	·	·
10.7	1225	x	H		·	·	·
10.6	1205	x	E		P		·
10.5	1185	x	N		L		
10.4	1166	x	x		U		
10.3	1146	P	x		M		
10.2	1126	U	x		B		
10.1	1106	U	x		A		
10.0	1087	C	x		T		
9.19	1067	x	x		E		
9.18	1047	x					
9.17	1028	x					
9.16	1008	x					
9.15	988						

Table 4.2: Archaeological Data and the 11.16 and 11.3 correlations as viewed from the Northern Lowlands. Data from the Southern Lowlands, with a 10.3 "collapse," only have a tangential effect on the correlation question, whereas data from the

continuously occupied Northern Lowlands are crucial for arguing either correlation. This figure assumes substantial overlap between the Cehpech, Sotuta, and Hocaba ceramic complexes in the Northern Lowlands; the spreads for the 11.16 correlation are derived from Ball 1979a (especially Fig. 17); the spreads for an 11.3 correlation are derived from archaeological and other data presented in this paper. A brief definition of the significance of each of the categories in the figure follows:

PUUC. The span provided for Puuc architecture and associated events is roughly the same under either correlation (280 years in 11.16; 240 years in 11.3).

CHICHEN. The span provided for the florescence of Chichen Itza is considerably shortened from 340 years under the 11.16 correlation to 260 years (or less) under the 11.3 correlation. That Chichen can be dated to 10.2 is suggested by hieroglyphic association with "Toltec" architecture (see Lincoln this volume) and by events further south (see Chase and Chase 1982); its culmination is dated by katun records to circa 10.19 under an 11.16 correlation and to circa 10.8 under an 11.3 correlation.

MAYAPAN. The span provided for Mayapan is relatively constant under either correlation (240 years in 11.16; 220 years in 11.3).

PLUMBATE. The span provided by an 11.6 correlation for plumbate is minimally 400 years in length given the extant archaeological data; this span is shortened to no more than 180 years under an 11.3 correlation.

PETO CREAM WARE. Peto Cream Ware exhibits a span of approximately 360 years under an 11.16 correlation; this span is shortened to approximately 120 years under an 11.3 correlation.

TULUM RED WARE. Based on archaeological data, Tulum Red Ware would be in existence for approximately 600 years under an 11.16 correlation; this span would be shortened to approximately 340 years under an 11.3 correlation.

---

correlation for plumbate, a supposed "horizon marker," is at least 400 years according to the extant archaeological data; this span is shortened to no more than 180 years under an 11.3 correlation. Peto Cream Ware exhibits a span of approximately 360 years under an 11.6 correlation; this span is shortened to approximately 120 years under an 11.3 correlation. Under either correlation, Tulum Red Ware, as currently defined in the literature for the eastern littoral of the Maya region, is enigmatic. Based on archaeological data, Tulum Red Ware would be in existence for approximately 600 years under an 11.6 correlation; this span would be shortened to approximately 340 years under an 11.3 correlation.

The crucial time frame for judging the validity of the 11.3.0.0.0 correlation is that period of time between the Terminal Classic and Late Postclassic periods. It is important to be able to define both how much time elapsed and what continuities exist between these two archaeologically defined limits. However, the exact end of the Classic

Period, the exact beginning of the Postclassic Period, and the mechanisms involved in this transition form one of the murky lagoons of Maya prehistory. Not only has this transition been difficult to document archaeologically given the extant data, terminology has also obscured the nature of this ill-defined time period. It has been called both Terminal Classic (Coe and Broman 1958: 40, 48) and Postclassic at Tikal (W. Coe 1965a, 1965b, 1967), one term remanding the problem solely to the Classic Period while the other places it squarely in the later period. Smith and Gifford (1965: 525) have referred to this period both as the "protopostclassic" and as a "transition" era, reflecting a similar conceptual problem. Others (D. Chase 1982a; Chase and Chase 1982; Miller 1982) now refer to this time as the Terminal Classic–Early Postclassic, thus emphasizing the overlap between the two periods. There is an obvious problem in defining the relationship between the Terminal Classic and the Late Postclassic, for it is difficult to determine if an Early Postclassic and Middle Postclassic exist and whether they lead directly into a Late Postclassic. The whole problem is compounded when one considers the regionalization that characterizes this era.

While what may be termed the Terminal Classic–Early Postclassic problem was first analyzed from the standpoint of northern Yucatan (Andrews V 1979; Ball 1979a, 1979b), archaeological evidence (presented below) can also be mustered from both northern Belize and central Peten in support of an alternative, and temporally compressed, interpretation of the transition from the Terminal Classic to the Late Postclassic periods. By association, additional support is given to an 11.3.0.0.0 correlation.

The Central Peten

The Tayasal-Paxcaman Zone (Figure 4.1) was extensively investigated by a University of Pennsylvania Project in 1971 and 1977 (A. Chase 1979, 1983, 1985). This research, geared toward defining the Postclassic Period in the Central Peten, succeeded in generating many data that go far toward achieving the research goal. The general Postclassic sequence for the region may be presented under either an 11.16 or an 11.3 correlation, as either could fit the data. As now understood, the sequence for Tayasal varies from the rest of the Late Classic material for the Peten (Imix-Eznab at Tikal; Tepeu 2–3 at Uaxactun) during

117

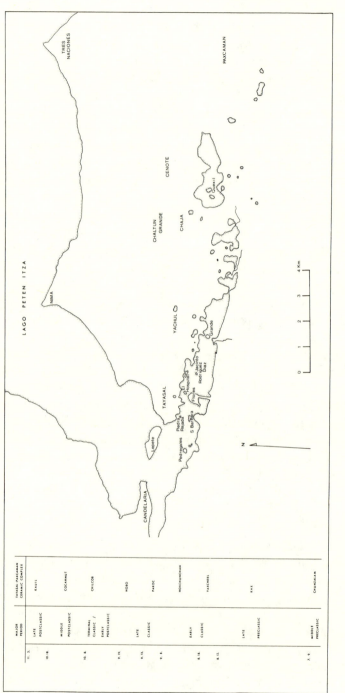

Figure 4.1 The Tayasal-Paxcaman zone and its archaeological sequence.

the Terminal Classic Period (late facet Hobo) with the continuation of the Tepeu Ceramic Sphere in the area in addition to the establishment of regionalized ceramics (Simaron Group). The Fine Orange wares prominent at Seibal (Sabloff 1973, 1975: 189–213) and Altar (Adams 1971: 26–30, 45–52, 1973) do not make a prominent appearance in this region. Settlement patterns appear to follow the traditional Classic pattern, revolving about the site center.

The late facet of Hobo is either immediately followed by Early Postclassic Chilcob or interdigitates with these Postclassic materials. Evidence from Tayasal could show that Augustine materials were in use during the late facet of Hobo and that late-facet Hobo and Chilcob could be compressed into a single phase. The epicentral part of Tayasal definitely includes construction efforts that date to the Chilcob era and seem to be continuous with earlier efforts. A burial pattern ascribable to the Chilcob phase uses bowls of Late Classic form and design, thus possibly also indicating interdigitation (rather than the use of heirlooms). I have argued that there was a general replacement of Hobo ceramic forms with those of Chilcob (A. Chase 1983) and that the Chilcob phase is generally one of innovation and experimentation.

By the end of Chilcob, Augustine ceramics had generally been replaced by Trapeche Pink ceramics, which appeared briefly (A. Chase 1979), and the experimental Tanche Red group. While both the Trapeche and Tanche ceramic groups probably overlapped with Augustine pottery, they also form clear ancestral types for Paxcaman Red pottery, which is predominant in the later history of the central Peten. Trapeche is similar in many respects to slateware (as is much of the fireclouding found on early facet Chilcob Augustine Red). Both the Trapeche and the Tanche ceramic groups contain unusual forms that are not generally replicated in the later Paxcaman material. Tohil Plumbate also appears in the Tayasal sequence by this time; besides the relative abundance of Plumbate at Tayasal as compared to other sites in the Peten, the ware is present in many scattered locales at Tayasal and contrasts with the more limited appearance of Fine Orange. The settlement pattern also changes by the end of Chilcob to a heavy emphasis on the lakeshore, with little exploitation of the higher hinterland for settlement.

The Cocahmut phase represents the later Postclassic history of the central Peten and is characterized by the Paxcaman Red ceramic group. Perhaps the only temporal distinction evident in these redwares is the

119

diminution in size of tripod plates over time. Some large-scale construction ascribed to this time period was undertaken at Tayasal on the bluff immediately above Lake Peten in the form of a small structure in epicentral Tayasal and one or more large platforms supporting one or more structures in the eastern part of Tayasal. In general, however, most of the construction was confined to smaller house-platforms near the lakeshore. Incision characterizes pottery from the earlier part of the phase. Censerware includes hourglass and human effigy censers, but both these forms are generally rare and do not occur as abundantly as they do to the north.

The latest phase recognizable at Tayasal has been called Kauil, and two facets have been defined for it. The earlier facet sees the continuation of Paxcaman Red, but with the introduction of a red-on-paste mode of decoration and an associated introduction of Topoxte Red. While the Topoxte Red material appears to be associated with a more compact settlement pattern and Yucatec-style "temple assemblage" groups in the eastern part of the Peten (Topoxte—Johnson 1985; Rice and Rice 1985; Macanche—Rice and Rice 1979, 1981; Salpeten—Rice and Rice 1980b), this settlement pattern is not replicated in the Tayasal-Paxcaman Zone.

By the end of the Kauil phase, the former snail-paste Paxcaman Red pottery is replaced by a hard granular paste which is often black in color both in redwares and plainwares (Chilo Unslipped). Two caches recovered on the Tayasal mainland point to the continuance of this practice into the Protohistoric Period. The distribution of Historic Period materials in the region accords with the lakeshore pattern established much earlier, indicating a continuity in settlement pattern from the Postclassic to the Historic Period for the Lake Peten region.

The Tayasal sequence may readily be adapted to an 11.3 correlation; such a framework in fact allows for a better interpretation of the culture history of the Southern Lowlands following the collapse. Under an 11.3 correlation, the Terminal Classic Hobo would interdigitate with the Early Postclassic Chilcob and date from about A.D. 1050 to 1250. With or without the 11.3 correlation, an intrusive group appears to have entered the Lake Peten area at this time (A. Chase 1983, 1985). Although foreign groups also appeared in the Usumacinta drainage on the same temporal level (Adams 1971, 1973; Sabloff 1973), the distribution of Fine Orange wares versus Plumbate ware in the Peten would indicate that these two groups were distinct. The exclusivity of

120

these ceramics may, in fact, be taken to indicate the existence of differing trade, or possibly warfare, patterns at or following the end of the Classic order. Two major changes may be ascribed to the new group in the central Peten: the introduction of Augustine Red and the introduction of what would appear to be different organizational principles, which eventually led to a settlement pattern different from that found in the Classic Period (A. Chase 1983). Trickle ware and a Chichen-style stela at Flores may indicate that this new group had ties, remote or otherwise, to the eastern lowlands of northern Yucatan (A. Chase 1985).

The use of the 11.3 correlation obviates the need for an Early Postclassic, and the subsequent history of the Peten may be ascribed to Middle Postclassic and later times. The 11.3 correlation eliminates a 260-year period, needed under an 11.16 correlation, during which an almost unchanging ceramic tradition must be postulated to have existed. This Middle Postclassic Period would therefore see the logical development of the Cocahmut phase out of Hobo-Chilcob and the introduction of new elements, probably from Topoxte, into the Lake Peten sequence during the fifteenth century A.D. Considered in this light, the 11.3 correlation provides adequate time for all the known events in the Postclassic Peten.

Northern Belize

Perhaps even more than that of the central Peten, the archaeology of northern Belize (Figure 4.2) fits an 11.3 better than an 11.16 framework. The probability that the Terminal Classic—Early Postclassic led directly into the Late Postclassic was first alluded to by Hammond (1974; see also Heighway et al. 1975: 71), although Hammond (1977: 57–58) later retracted most of his original statement. D. Chase (1982a, 1982b) has attempted to define the Postclassic Period in northern Belize on the basis of her work at Nohmul and Santa Rita Corozal. When her data are combined with those from Lamanai (Pendergast 1981a, 1981b, 1981c, this volume), the complexity of the Postclassic in northern Belize emerges.

The site of Santa Rita Corozal has been identified by D. Chase (1981, 1982a, 1985, this volume) as the regional capital for the province of Chetumal; the archaeological remains from this site may be roughly positioned in time as bracketing the final part of the Postclassic

121

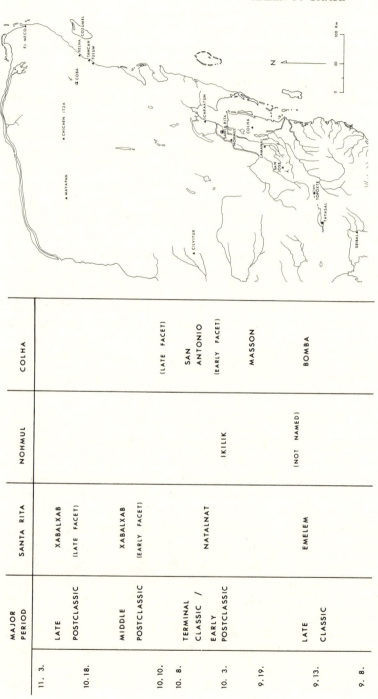

MAJOR PERIOD		SANTA RITA	NOHMUL	COLHA
11. 3.	LATE POSTCLASSIC	XABALXAB (LATE FACET)		(LATE FACET)
10. 18.	MIDDLE POSTCLASSIC	XABALXAB (EARLY FACET)		SAN ANTONIO
10. 10.	TERMINAL CLASSIC / EARLY POSTCLASSIC	NATALNAT		(EARLY FACET)
10. 8.				
10. 3.			IKILIK	MASSON
9. 19.	LATE CLASSIC	EMELEM	(NOT NAMED)	
9. 13.				BOMBA
9. 8.				

Figure 4.2 Northern Belize and defined Classic and Postclassic sequences from Nohmul, Santa Rita, and Colha.

Period in northern Belize. Pendergast (1975, 1977, 1981a, 1982d) has further defined the terminus of the Belize Protohistoric with his work on the Historic Period church at Lamanai. Both sites show evidence of having used effigy censers, which suggests some relation to the Northern Lowland sequence since these censers were common during the Late Postclassic in northern Yucatan (Smith 1971).

While the end of the Postclassic in northern Belize can be bracketed at Santa Rita Corozal and Lamanai and while the Late Postclassic can be adequately defined, at least for Santa Rita Corozal, the question of how to define the Terminal Classic–Early Postclassic looms even larger in northern Belize than in the central Peten. Pring (1975, 1976a, 1976b: 43–45) has examined the ceramics of various sites in northern Belize and has noted the existence of at least two spatially overlapping ceramic complexes for both Classic and Terminal Classic sites. Subsequent research at Nohmul (A. Chase and D. Chase 1981; D. Chase 1982a, 1982b; D. Chase and A. Chase 1982), Colha (Hester 1979; Hester, Eaton, and Shafer 1980), and possibly Lamanai (Pendergast 1977, 1981a, 1981b, 1981c) has supported Pring's original supposition. The work in the Nohmul area has been even more informative; it may indicate the existence of class-linked ceramics at that site for the Terminal Classic Period, especially when the site core Ikilik ceramic complex (D. Chase 1982b) is compared to the data recovered outside the site center (Robert Fry, personal communication, and observation). Thus, data from northern Belize indicate that recognizable spatial distinctions are clearly at work during the Terminal Classic–Early Postclassic Period.

Perhaps even more than ceramics, other archaeological data suggest the dynamic character of the Terminal Classic Period at both Colha and Nohmul; these data incidentally reaffirm the distinct possibility of confusing time and space in the archaeological record during this transition era. The Colha Classic Period sequence is viewed as coming to a dramatically violent end with the beheading of the local elite (Hester, Eaton, and Shafer 1980: 5–6). The termination of the Nohmul Classic Period sees the intrusion of a nonlocal architectural complex into the site center and the melding of local and nonlocal ceramics into a single complex (Chase and Chase 1982). Paradoxically, the data available from Lamanai suggest a gradual development out of the Classic into the Postclassic Period (Pendergast 1981a: 43).

A consideration of the Terminal Classic–Early Postclassic Period at three sites in northern Belize therefore reveals three different situations. Lamanai's gradual ceramic and architectural development out of the Classic into the Postclassic has led Pendergast (1981a: 48–49) to suggest that northern Belize ceramics were the forerunners of some northern Yucatec ceramic traditions. The violent end of the Classic order and traditions at Colha is followed by an Early Postclassic redware tradition that is clearly ancestral, if not equivalent, to Paybono Red and the Tulum redware tradition. Nohmul's situation is most similar to that of Seibal, where a foreign elite may have usurped power (Sabloff and Willey 1967; Chase and Chase 1982).

Three different ceramic traditions may, therefore, be tentatively ascribed to northern Belize during the Terminal Classic–Early Postclassic era. While the sequences at Nohmul and Colha do not extend to the Late Postclassic, the Lamanai sequence leads directly into the Late Postclassic. At Santa Rita Corozal (D. Chase 1982a), ceramics of the Tulum Red tradition, common at Colha, are found only infrequently in mound fills; more commonly found in these fills, however, are ceramics relating to the Ikilik ceramic complex at Nohmul (D. Chase 1982b). The Santa Rita Corozal sequence indicates that Late Postclassic pottery followed directly after Ikilik-related ceramics. The northern Belize data, therefore, effectively indicate the realities of the Terminal Classic–Early Postclassic compression mandated by an 11.3.0.0.0 correlation.

ETHNOHISTORY:
THE BOOKS OF CHILAM BALAM

According to Brinton (1882: 69), "Chilan [sic] Balam . . . is not a proper name, but a title, and in ancient times designated the priest who announced the will of the gods and explained the sacred oracles." Morley (1911: 197) noted that a total of sixteen Books of Chilam Balam were in existence, each one distinguishable from the others by its identification with a specific town; of these books only three—those of Mani, Tizimin, and Chumayel—contain accounts of ancient chronologies. In fact, these three Books of Chilam Balam are the only ones that have been dealt with and translated in any detail in the published literature.[2] Besides ancient chronology, preconquest history, and postconquest history, the Chilam Balams also concern themselves with astrology-prophecy and medicine. These books are most likely Hispanicized Maya transcriptions of the "ancient" glyphic codices of the Maya, of which three are known. The importance of the katun rounds, or *u kahlay katunob*, found in the Books of Mani, Tizimin, and Chumayel is that they can be used in establishing the Maya-European correlation as well as in possibly correlating the katun record with the Classic Maya "Initial Series," or Long Count, record of time. The katun rounds, in fact, appear to be extremely accurate records of Postclassic Maya history.

The first account of the Books of Chilam Balam and the history they contained was presented by Stephens (1843), where Pío Pérez argues that the Maya had 24-year katuns. Valentini's doctoral dissertation, on the "Katunes of Maya History" (1880: 97), disagrees with Pérez, stating that the katuns were arranged in periods of 20 years. Valentini's argument for the 20-year katun was immediately challenged in a series of articles by Brinton (1881, 1882) and Thomas (1881a, 1881b, 1882, 1886). Morley (1920) and Spinden (1924) were the first to show that the 20-year katun argument was correct. Articles by Weitzel (1930, 1931a, 1931b), Teeple (1930), Thompson (1932, 1950), and Jakeman (1947) continued the argument over the validity of the chronologies given in the books.

The *u kahlay katunob* appear to be closely related to ancient glyphic counterparts. Brinton (1882: 70) stated that the Book of Chilam Balam of Mani "was undoubtedly composed not later than 1595, as is proved by internal evidence." Morley (1920: 469) believed that these three books "were *copied* by native Maya, perhaps directly from Maya historical codices, which have since been either lost or destroyed." This supposition may, in fact, be demonstrated by Roys's translation (1967: 155–61), for he noted the existence of extra numbers in one of the chronicles and inserted the word *katun* into the translation as being the understood word; however, he could not ascertain a reason for starting the implied "new count," as the original katuns were in correct order. If *fold* is the understood word in the Roys translation, the inconsistencies he noted disappear and the form of the ancient prophetic book of Chumayel can be reconstructed as shown in Table 4.3. It would appear that the Maya scribe kept the Katun Count in correct order and read horizontally even though his European training had taught him to read page by page (fold by fold); thus, he read "11, 9, 7, 5, . . ." instead of "11, 1, 4, 9, . . ." To resolve this inconsistency, he noted every time he changed a page and thus noted on which page

125

Table 4.3

FOLD 1	FOLD 2	FOLD 3	FOLD 4	FOLD 5
KATUN 11 AHAU	KATUN 9 AHAU	KATUN 7 AHAU	KATUN 5 AHAU	KATUN 3 AHAU
KATUN 1 AHAU	KATUN 12 AHAU	KATUN 10 AHAU	KATUN 8 AHAU	KATUN 6 AHAU
KATUN 4 AHAU	KATUN 2 AHAU	KATUN 13 AHAU	MISSING	MISSING

Table 4.3: Reconstructed Maya codex from which part of the Book of Chilam Balam of Chumayel was copied (of which the illustration on Chumayel Page 84c might be a garbled copy). It is suggested that the Maya scribe kept the Katun Count in correct order and read horizontally even though his European training had taught him to read page by page (fold by fold); thus, he read "11, 9, 7, 5, . . ." instead of "11, 1, 4, 9, . . ." To resolve this inconsistency, he noted every time he changed a page and thus noted on which page a given katun was recorded, allowing a reconstruction of the codical format of the manuscript he was copying.

a given katun was recorded, allowing a reconstruction of the codical format of the manuscript he was copying (as shown in Table 4.3).

The *u kahlay katunob* of the Book of Chilam Balam of Tizimin resembles closely its counterpart from Mani; Morley (1920: 469) felt that this chronicle "must have been copied from the original . . . probably at the same time." Brinton (1882: 136–37) pointed out several internal problems with the Tizimin *u kahlay katunob*: (1) the insertion of extra katuns, (2) the possible mistranscription of part of the series, and (3) the possible repetition of certain katuns. Both Brinton (1882: 152) and Morley (1920: 473) believed that the Book of Chilam Balam of Chumayel and its three *u kahlay katunob* were translated by Juan Josef Hoil in 1782, as his name and that date occur on page 81 of the manuscript, which was photographed by Gordon (1913) in 1911. Roys (1960: 8), however, noted that "its language suggests the seventeenth century more than the eighteenth, and it contains no reference to a twenty-four year katun."

Much of the current argument over various correlations rests indirectly on data gathered from the Books of Chilam Balam. Besides the information contained directly in the histories, other information related to the books has also been utilized. This has sometimes presented paradoxical situations in which clearly stated material is rejected out of hand in favor of secondary interpretations concerning the documents. In fact, investigation shows that the current 11.16.0.0.0 correlation is based upon data that have been incorrectly derived from the books. Brinton (1882: 83) stated that "all the native writers agree, and I think, in spite of the contrary statement of Bishop Landa, that we may look upon it as beyond doubt that the last day of the 11th Katun was July 15th, 1541." The writers do *not* agree; only Nakuk Pech (in Brinton 1882) states this. Morley (1920: 468) placed most of his confidence in *The Chronicle of Chacxulubchen*, a translation of which occurs only in Brinton (1882). This chronicle was believed to have been written by Nakuk Pech in 1562; Morley argued that Pech received training in the Maya priesthood *before* the Spanish conquest. Because Nakuk Pech evinced accuracy in the European calendar, Morley (1920: 468) stated that this "gives to any statement he may make about his own calendar the highest degree of reliability"; Morley also noted, however, that "the original Pech manuscript has disappeared" and that a "duplicate chronicle by Ah Naum Pech . . . which . . . is practically a word-for-word transcription of the Nakuk Pech chronicle, with only the name of the author changed" was used. However, Nakuk Pech is credited with noting that a katun was 24 years in length, a concept Roys (1960: 7) has pointed out as originating sometime in the seventeenth century. Doubt may therefore be cast on the supposed early date of this chronicle. However, many of the basic tenets of the current 11.16.0.0.0 correlation rest directly on the Nakuk Pech material.

An examination of the Books of Chilam Balam in fact reveals that two different calendrical correlations may be obtained directly from them. Landa (Tozzer 1941), discredited above by Brinton, stated that 1541 was the first year of Katun 11 Ahau. This agrees with internal data in some of the Books of Chilam Balam and allows the establishment of one possible calendar, here called the T-M-CI (Tizimin–Mani–Chumayel I) correlation (first year of 11 Ahau began in July 1540 and ended in July 1541). This correlation may or may not concur with the Oxcutzcab correlation. A second calendar may be established from data in the Chumayel III or "Itza" chronicle based on internal dating consistencies (first year of 11 Ahau began in July 1535 and ended in July 1536). These two Yucatec calendars are graphically illustrated in Table 4.4.

Table 4.4

YEAR	EVENT	ITZA (CH. III) CALENDAR	TIZIMIN-MANI-CH. I CALENDAR
1535			
1536	Death of Alpuhla	1st Year of 11 Ahau	14th Year of 13 Ahau
1540			
1541	Spaniards Arrive	7th Year of 11 Ahau	1st Year of 11 Ahau
1542			
1562	Toral Dies	6th Year of 9 Ahau	9 Ahau
1579	Landa Dies	7 Ahau	7 Ahau

Table 4.4: Chronological data from the Books of Chilam Balam indicating the existence of two different "Maya" calendars prior to the colonization of the Yucatan Peninsula by Spaniards.

The establishment of these two calendars probably accounts for much of the confusion over the attempts to set the European dates found in the chronicles into a single correlation, for it is clear that different calendric systems were being used at the same time in northern Yucatan. It is proposed here that the T-M-CI calendar had the change from Katun 13 Ahau to Katun 11 Ahau occurring on July 15–16, 1540; Landa (Tozzer 1941: 168) appears to be following this calendar. The Itza calendar changed from a Katun 13 Ahau to a Katun 11 Ahau on July 15–16, 1535, for, as Brinton (1881: 721) pointed out,

The Maya year did not begin January 1 as does ours, *but July 16,* at or about the time of the transit of the sun by the zenith in the latitude of Merida. Hence the Maya chronicler identified the 6th year from the end of the Ahau with 1536, because the greater part and the latter part of that Ahau was actually in A.D. 1536. In point of fact, Chief Ahpula, whoever he was, died Sept. 11, 1535, O.S.

In summary, the Books of Chilam Balam can be used to demonstrate the probable existence of at least two calendars from northern Yucatan. This effectively dismisses any search for a "single" correlation. If no single day-to-day correlation exists between the European and Maya calendars, then many of the astronomical arguments and attendant baggage that accompany the 11.16.0.0.0 correlation are not relevant to effecting a correlation. Therefore the archaeological and ethnohis-

128

torical data must answer the correlation question. These archaeological data may be utilized to indicate that some version of an 11.3.0.0.0 correlation is the correct one; the ethnohistoric data contained in the katun records of the Chilam Balam also indicate the potential validity of an 11.3.0.0.0 correlation.

The 11.3 Correlation, The Books, and Lowland Culture History

Having briefly reviewed both the Books of Chilam Balam and some of the early arguments over their chronology, we can now offer a synthesis of the history recorded in the various documents according to an 11.3 correlation. Presented in Tables 4.5–4.9, this arrangement differs from that given by Brinton (1882: 87–88) and Morley (1920: 503), upon which the currently accepted paradigm is based. Just as the codices were read in a different order from that dictated by a Western perspective, so were the Books of Chilam Balam. They do *not* consist of a linear arrangement of katuns, but rather deal with the specific katun histories for certain places, people, or events—histories which were not meant to be placed in a strictly linear, diachronic arrangement as Brinton (1882) and Morley (1920) did. Accordingly, the interpretation for the katun history presented in Tables 4.5–4.9 follows that presented in the various books, but assumes a basically cyclical-linkage reading of events linked to specific places and covering a period of about two katun rounds. The dating of the events described is based on internal consistencies in the documents.

It appears to me, in conclusion, that the chronicles from The Books of Chilan [*sic*] Balam have much to recommend them as reliable sources for the reconstruction of Maya history. When these records fail to agree, which is the exception rather than the rule, it has been shown that in some cases, at least, disagreement may have arisen from errors in copying or translation, for which the original texts themselves cannot be held responsible. Again it has been shown that in age, authorship, subject matter, and general agreement, these native chronicles are such that they constitute their own best guarantee of truthfulness. In view of these facts and one other, that they are almost the only native sources left to us for the recovery of the main events of Maya history, we are justified in accepting them for what they purport to be: The Maya Chronicles. (Morley 1911: 204–5)

In order to understand the histories recorded in the Books of Chilam Balam, it is necessary to understand who or what the Itza were, es-

Table 4.5 The Book of Chilam Balam of Mani and its eight narrated events adapted to an 11.3.0.0.0 correlation.

BOOK OF CHILAM BALAM OF MANI

LONG COUNT	AHAU	(1)	(2)	(3)	(4)	(5)	(6)	(7)	(8)
9.12.0.0.0	10								
9.13	8	Nonoual left by Tutulxiu							
9.14	6								
9.15.0.0.0	4								
9.16	2								
9.17	13	Holon Chantepeuh arrives in Chacnouitan	Ahmekat Tutulxiu arrives at Chacnouitan	Ziyan-caan or Bakhalal discovered and ruled; Chichen discovered	Chanputun seized and ruled by Itza				
9.18	11								
9.19	9			Chichen Itza ruled					
10.0.0.0.0	7								
10.1	5								
10.2	3								
10.3	1								
10.4	12			Chichen abandoned for Chanputun where Itza were					
10.5.0.0.0	10								
10.6	8				Chanputun abandoned				
10.7	6								
10.8	4				Chanputun lost; houses established a second time				
10.9	2								
10.10.0.0.0	13					Ahcuitok Tutulxiu founds Uxmal; Uxmal in league with Chichen and Mayapan			
10.11	11								
10.12	9								
10.13	7								
10.14	5						(8 Ahau) Chac-Xib-Chac driven from Chichen; Hunac Ceel?		
10.15.0.0.0	3								
10.16	1								
10.17	12								
10.18	10								
10.19	8								Mayapan depopulated
11.0.0.0.0	6								
11.1	4								
11.2	2							?	
11.3	13							Itza invade land; Mayapan depopulated	Spaniards first passed Ahpula died pestilence
11.4	11								
11.5.0.0.0	9								

Table 4.6: The Book of Chilam Balam of Tizimin and its nine written events adapted to an 11.3.0.0.0 correlation.

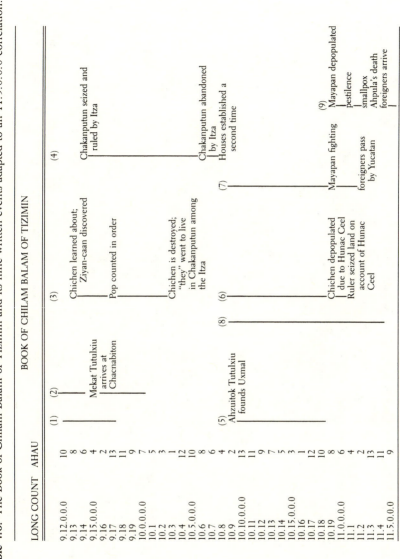

BOOK OF CHILAM BALAM OF TIZIMIN

LONG COUNT	AHAU
9.12.0.0.0	10
9.13	8
9.14	6
9.15.0.0.0	4
9.16	2
9.17	13
9.18	11
9.19	9
10.0.0.0.0	7
10.1	5
10.2	3
10.3	1
10.4	12
10.5.0.0.0	10
10.6	8
10.7	6
10.8	4
10.9	2
10.10.0.0.0	13
10.11	11
10.12	9
10.13	7
10.14	5
10.15.0.0.0	3
10.16	1
10.17	12
10.18	10
10.19	8
11.0.0.0.0	6
11.1	4
11.2	2
11.3	13
11.4	11
11.5.0.0.0	9

Events:

(1)

(2) Mekat Tutulxiu arrives at Chacnabiton

(3) Chichen learned about; Ziyan-caan discovered / Pop counted in order / Chichen is destroyed; "they" went to live in Chakanputun among the Itza

(4) Chakanputun seized and ruled by Itza / Chakanputun abandoned by Itza / Houses established a second time

(5) Ahzuitok Tutulxiu founds Uxmal

(6) Chichen depopulated due to Hunac Ceel / Ruler seized land on account of Hunac Ceel

(7) Mayapan fighting / foreigners pass by Yucatan

(8)

(9) Mayapan depopulated / pestilence / smallpox / Ahpula's death / foreigners arrive

Table 4.7 Books of Chilam Balam of Chumayel: I and II—adapted to an 11.3.0.0.0 correlation.

LONG COUNT	AHAU	THE BOOKS OF CHILAM BALAM OF CHUMAYEL: I AND II		
		I	(2)	II
9.13.0.0.0	8			
9.14	6	(1) Chichen discovered		
9.15.0.0.0	4		Chakanputtun seized by Itza	Birth of Pauahs; descent of rulers; Chichen found; the four divisions
9.16	2			
9.17	13	Mat counted in order		
9.18	11			
9.19	9			
10.0.0.0.0	7			
10.1	5			
10.2	3			
10.3	1			
10.4	12			
10.5.0.0.0	10	Chichen abandoned for Chakanputtun (3)	Chakanputtun abandoned by Itza	
10.6	8			"Remainder of Itza" arrive and rule Chakanputtun; Little Descent of the four divisions
10.7	6			
10.8	4			
10.9	2			Mayapan founded
10.10.0.0.0	13			
10.11	11			
10.12	9			
10.13	7			
10.14	5			Hunac Ceel?
10.15.0.0.0	3			
10.16	1			
10.17	12			
10.18	10			
10.19	8	Ichpaa Mayapan fighting	Itza abandon homes again due to Hunac Ceel	town abandoned
11.0.0.0.0	6	pestilence	Ichpaa Mayapan seized by Itza due to Hunac Ceel	ceased to be called Maya
11.1	4	smallpox		souls cry out
11.2	2	Napot Xiu died		
11.3	13	arrival of men		
11.4	11	Christianity began		Maya men called Christians
11.5.0.0.0	9			

Table 4.8 The Book of Chilam Balam of Chumayel: III—adapted to an 11.3.0.0.0 correlation.

LONG COUNT	AHAU	THE BOOK OF CHILAM BALAM OF CHUMAYEL: III (THE "ITZA" KATUNS)
9.11.0.0.0	12	
9.12	10	
9.13	8	
9.14	6	people of Conil dispersed
9.15.0.0.0	4	
9.16	2	
9.17	13	
9.18	11	
9.19	9	
10.0.0.0.0	7	"Foreigners Without Skirts" arrived, but did not depopulate the land
10.1	5	
10.2	3	
10.3	1	Tancah Mayapan was depopulated
10.4	12	
10.5.0.0.0	10	
10.6	8	"Remainder of the Itza" founded "their" town and establish Zaclactun
10.7	6	Mayapan; Chakanputun perished due to Kakupacal and Tec Uilu
10.8	4	
10.9	2	
10.10.0.0.0	13	
10.11	11	
10.12	9	
10.13	7	
10.14	5	town of the ruler of Izamal destroyed by Hunac Ceel
10.15.0.0.0	3	
10.16	1	"Remainder of the Itza" driven out of Chichen and Chichen is depopulated
10.17	12	stone taken at Otzmal
10.18	10	stone taken at Zizal
10.19	8	stone taken at Kancaba
11.0.0.0.0	6	stone taken at Hunacthi
11.1	4	stone taken at Atikuh; pestilence occurred
11.2	2	stone taken at Chacalna
11.3	13	stone taken at Euan
11.4	11	stone taken at Colox-peten; Napot Xiu dies; Spaniards first arrive
11.5.0.0.0	9	no stone taken; Toral arrives

Table 4.9 Synopsis of Yucatecan history contained in the Books of Chilam Balam adapted to an 11.3.0.0.0 correlation.

LONG COUNT	AHAU				
9.10.0.0.0	1				
9.11	12				
9.12	10	Chacnouitan	Chichen Itza	Chakanputun	Ziyan-caan / Bakhalal
9.13	8	Holon Chantepeuh	Chichen discovered	seized by Itza	
9.14	6	leaves		and ruled	discovered and ruled
9.15.0.0.0	4				GREAT DESCENT
9.16	2	Ahmekat Tutulxiu			
9.17	13	Holon Chantepeuh			POP COUNTED IN ORDER
9.18	11	arrive	Chichen ruled		
9.19	9				
10.0.0.0.0	7				
10.1	5	Chacnouitan left			
10.2	3				
10.3	1		Chichen abandoned		(CLASSIC MAYA COLLAPSE)
10.4	12		by Xiu for Itza		
10.5.0.0.0	10		Chakanputun		
10.6	8		Chichen occupied	abandoned by	
10.7	6		by Ytza	Itza	
10.8	4			seized by Ytza	Uxmal	LITTLE DESCENT
10.9	2			and ruled	founded by	Mayapan
10.10.0.0.0	13				Xiu	founded
10.11	11		Tribute to Chichen			(by Itza?)
10.12	9					
10.13	7					
10.14	5		Hunac Ceel episode			
10.15.0.0.0	3					
10.16	1		Ytza driven out of			
10.17	12		Chichen			
10.18	10				end ?	
10.9	8		Conquered by Mayapan			destroyed ?
11.0.0.0.0	6					
11.1	4		Land seized			
11.2	2					
11.3.0.0.0	13					SPANIARDS ARRIVE
11.4	11					
11.5.0.0.0	9					

(rightmost column, vertical text: LEAGUE OF MAYAPAN)

pecially in view of their importance to Postclassic Maya history and, indirectly, to the correlation question. Jakeman (1945, 1946) and Thompson (1946) were the first to debate this sore point in Maya archaeology. It is believed that these Itza migrated from the Yucatan to the Peten of Guatemala around A.D. 1450 (see A. Chase 1976, 1982 for amplification). The Books of Chilam Balam, however, use the term *Itza* to refer only to "foreigners" to northern Yucatan, as Jakeman (1945, 1946) points out. The term *Itza* may have been either applied to or adopted by *any* foreign group who arrived in the Yucatan Peninsula. The Chilam Balam of Chumayel (Roys 1967; Brinton 1882), in fact, makes a distinction between the "native" historical katuns and those of the Itza, which are recorded in a separate chronicle. As the

Books of Chilam Balam appear to concern themselves only with the Terminal Classic and Postclassic periods, it should be possible to correlate the histories in these documents with extant archaeological data from the Northern Lowlands. This interpretation counters Scholes and Roys's (1968: 74) assertion that the "Yucatecan historical tradition . . . probably does not go back to the advent of certain foreign invaders, who were the bearers of a Mexican culture and who established themselves in the country as a new ruling caste."

Four groups of people are described in the books: the Tutulxiu, the Maya, the Itza, and the "Remainder of the Itza." The preface to Chumayel III equates the Maya with the Itza. A people called Ah Conil, also mentioned as being the original inhabitants of the land, may represent yet another group of "Maya." The Books of Chilam Balam refer to two intrusions into the "Maya" area, referring to them as the Great and Little descents. As interpreted here the Great Descent occurred around 9.14.0.0.0 (ca A.D. 970) and affected the lower Yucatecan area while the Little Descent occurred around 10.7.0.0.0 (ca. A.D. 1230) and affected the northern Yucatecan area.

The Great Descent involved only four areas: Chacnouitan, Chichen Itza, Chakanputun, and Bakhalal or Ziyan-caan. Chacnouitan is not readily identifiable, although it may have been far to the south as Valentini (1880) placed it. It is proposed here that Chacnouitan may have been associated with the archaeological site of Seibal, since the dating for an intrusion at the site as noted in the monuments (Graham 1973) agrees with the statements in the chronicles under an 11.3 framework. Additionally, Seibal is noted as having "Puuc"-type architecture (Willey and Smith 1967) which is consistent with the Tutulxiu being present. One division of the Tutulxiu remain at Chacnouitan until about 10.1.0.0.0, when other foreigners are reported as arriving; this again accords well with the archaeological interpretations of data from Seibal (Sabloff 1973) and Altar de Sacrificios (Adams 1971).

Chichen Itza and Bakhalal are identifiable. The Tutulxiu were the rulers of Ziyan-caan and/or Bakhalal by 9.14.0.0.0 and of Chichen by 9.16.0.0.0. Chakanputun may or may not have been located in the area of present-day Champoton. Chakanputun was seized from the Ah Conil by the "Itza," who may have been one of the four Tutulxiu divisions, at approximately 9.13.0.0.0. Chichen ("Tancah Mayapan") is recorded as having been destroyed around 10.3.0.0.0, possibly by the "Ytza," and then abandoned by the Tutulxiu, who went to Chakanputun to live among the Itza. In 10.6.0.0.0 a group often confused with the Itza and referred to by Roys as the "remainder of the Itza," here called "Ytza" (as opposed to "Itza"), drove both the Tutulxiu and the Itza out of Chakanputun under the leadership of Kakupacal and Tec-Uilu. This may be the event depicted in the murals of the Temple of the Warriors at Chichen Itza (Miller 1979), for, as Willey (1979: 215) points out, these paintings "show what appear to be Putun warriors attacking other Putun peoples." The Ytza were associated with Tan-Xuluc-Mul and Ppoole and were also noted as having established "Zaclatun Mayapan"; until 10.16.0.0.0 the Ytza were associated with Chichen. It may be that the Ytza were equivalent to the group often referred to as "Toltec"; the abandonment of Chichen Itza by the Tutulxiu in the early part of Katun 8 Ahau corresponds well to the historical material provided by Vaillant (1938), in which a Toltec invasion led by Quetzalcoatl was presumed to have conquered Chichen Itza in A.D. 1191 (Spinden 1924: 55).

The Little Descent took place in 10.7.0.0.0, when the "houses" were established a second time. Ahcuitok Tutulxiu was recorded as "founding" or "establishing his lineage at" Uxmal in 10.8.0.0.0, while "Ichpaa Mayapan" was "founded" in 10.9.0.0.0, probably by the Itza. The relationships evident between Cehpech and Hocaba ceramic spheres may mirror the close ties between the Tutulxiu and Itza in Chakanputun. The Sotuta ceramic sphere may be viewed as being that of the Ytza. The League of Mayapan was also established with the Little Descent.

Circa 10.13.0.0.0 Hunac Ceel, the ruler of Mayapan, destroyed the town of the ruler of Izamal, Kinich Kakmoo, as well as Pophol Chan. The Mani manuscript's account of this episode, even if confused, is correct in terms of its chronology of this event. It is possible that the Tizimin and Chumayel manuscripts were copied in part from the garbled Mani manuscript. The Itza chronicles, however, indicated that the Ytza under Chac-Xib-Chac were driven out of Chichen in 10.6.0.0.0. The Tutulxiu rule of Uxmal ended at approximately 10.18.0.0.0. Ichpaa Mayapan was destroyed in or around 10.19.0.0.0, possibly in retaliation for the treatment of Ulmil and his "Itza" men on the east coast of Yucatan. Although the Mani chronicle reported the destruction of Mayapan by the "Itza," Brinton (1882: 131) argued that "the Itzas seized the territory in and around Mayapan, but they were not the ones who destroyed the city. This was the work of Ahuitzilzul, foreign mountaineers." It is interesting to note that the Itza chronicle contains no reference to the destruction of Mayapan.

Roys (1962: 80–81) associates the fall of Mayapan with the Aztec ruler Montezuma, thus linking Mayapan with the Valley of Mexico lineage chronology worked out by Vaillant (1938). Montezuma I's reign, given as A.D. 1440–69, correlates well with the Maya Katun 8 Ahau in which Mayapan was depopulated. It also explains the heavy presence of Nahua names at Mayapan indicated in the Mani chronicle, for an unpopular alliance with the Mexicans was supposed to have been made at Mayapan. According to Brinton (1882: 129), Landa and Herrera noted that Aztec warriors were in fact invited to Mayapan. It may be that the Postclassic sites of the east coast of Yucatan, such as Tulum and Xcaret, whose general architectural plan differs from that of Mayapan and Chichen Itza, represent areas ceded to the Aztecs by the League of Mayapan. This is also the probable location of the ruler of Ulmil Ichpaa and his "Itza" men. In fact, the downfall of Mayapan may be directly linked to its attempt to redominate this area in the Hunac Ceel episode and the retaliation from central Mexico in the form of the Ahuitzilzul.

Much of the above picture would be clarified by better understanding of the archaeological record in northern Yucatan. While it is possible that certain temporally distant events have been linked in the Books of Chilam Balam, the general outline presented above is quite plausible within an 11.3.0.0.0 framework. The ancestral identity of the Itza, however, remains an open question.

The Books of Chilam Balam and Postclassic Maya Prehistory

The Books of Chilam Balam provide overlapping histories of several centers. While they are useful in supporting the 11.3 correlation, they may also be interpreted (following Table 4.5–4.9), especially when combined with the extant archaeological data, as presenting a series of local histories dealing with areas important in the regulation of trans-Yucatecan trade routes. The Great Descent may well have been concerned with establishing control over a trade route through the Southern Lowlands, thus indirectly or directly resulting in the Classic Maya Collapse. The Tutulxiu were reported to have first established themselves at Chacnouitan and Bakhalal/Ziyan-caan, while the Itza had dominion over Chakanputun. Relationships between the Itza and Tutulxiu appear always to have been quite amiable and may have been based on economic as well as political alliance. The location of the Itza and Tutulxiu in Chakanputun and Bakhalal/Ziyan-caan indicate the probable existence of a band of control across the basal portion of the Yucatan Peninsula. If Chacnouitan was Seibal, its position in the Peten would have been ideal for gaining control of an Usumacinta trade system.

The Little Descent appears to have been preceded by an attempted usurpation of the southern routes by the Ytza. This attempt may have resulted in a reorganization of the newly adopted Southern Lowland trade routes and a possible relocation of them through the northern portion of the peninsula. Both land and sea routes may have been involved. Terminal Classic–Early Postclassic Nohmul may be viewed as a southern outpost of the Ytza resulting from an early attempt at consolidating their ascendancy on the basal riverine trade route. While the Ytza, by means of an outpost at Nohmul, may have gained control of the Hondo drainage, they were apparently stymied on the New River drainage as attested by the continuous sequence at Lamanai. The Bakhalal area is not mentioned in the chronicles after the Great Descent. Ytza control of Chichen Itza and Chakanputun probably circumvented the Southern Lowlands by shifting the routes northward. Such a northern route may have formed a major economic basis for the League of Mayapan and would have been operative until approximately 10.15.0.0.0, when Chichen Itza was overcome by Mayapan.

With the destruction (abandonment) of Chichen Itza, Mayapan acceded to its brief period of total dominance in Yucatan. It may be hypothesized that Mayapan was in league with the peoples of Tabasco and/or central Mexico, possibly the Aztec, and that Nahua-related peoples were responsible, at least in part, for the east coast architecture. It is possible that there was at least partial Mexican control of the trans-Yucatecan trade routes and salt resources. Some group of central-Mexican-related peoples may have previously moved to fill the east coast void caused by the failure of the Ytza to dislodge an indigenous northern Belize tradition and a prospering central Peten tradition. Colha would date the existence or founding of the east coast Tulum tradition to the "Early Postclassic," indirectly indicating, based on the extant archaeological data and shared ceramics, that Tulum may have also been established by this period.

It was evidently not until the later part of the "Late Postclassic" that northern Belize was enveloped by the Yucatecan cocoon. Santa Rita, Chetumal's regional capital, may at this time either have supplanted or rivaled Lamanai as a local capital and continued into the Historic era. In the Peten, Topoxte may represent the post-Mayapan legendary Itza outpost, for the site has late-Yucatec-related ceramics, architecture, and layout.

CONCLUSION

Revised conceptions concerning the dating of and relationships among sites, archaeological complexes, and horizon markers indicate that Lowland Maya Postclassic history can be successfully subsumed by an 11.3.0.0.0 correlation. When spatially overlapping events are not forced into a sequential order, both the archaeology and the ethnohistory permit the use of such a framework. Still troublesome, however, to an 11.3.0.0.0 correlation are the extant radiocarbon dates from the Maya area. However, general methodological problems in the dating technique and the recent recalibrations indicate that future modifications may not preclude such a framework. In light of the general disuniformity of the dates, perhaps less emphasis should be placed on their utility in solving the correlation problem.

The establishment of two protohistoric calendric systems is most significant for its implications for the Maya-Christian correlation. The existence of two calendars in which the same katun change differed by five years implies that no day-to-day correlation exists. Other Postclassic calendars that changed katuns at different times probably also existed; which one, if any, of these calendars was directly descended from the Classic Maya Long Count is impossible to determine. The search for a single Ahau equation is, therefore, meaningless for the Postclassic Period. However, the cyclical, ordered, and continuous shift in year bearers, seemingly every baktun, strongly supports an 11.3.0.0.0 correlation.

In summary, an 11.3.0.0.0 correlation is not only applicable to the prehistory of the Southern Maya Lowlands, but may be interpreted as uniting extant archaeology and ethnohistory into a conceptual whole. The problems involved in radiocarbon dating and calendrical considerations do not preclude such a correlation, and the archaeology and ethnohistory may be viewed as being more supportive of such a framework than of the one presently in use. The problems of interrelating the various areal sequences of the Maya area are now being overcome through increased consideration of spatial phenomena and the application of sloping ceramic horizons and interaction spheres. Temporal concepts as well as spatial concepts, however, need to be seriously reconsidered for the region. I venture to prophesy that such review and future archaeological studies will both vindicate some version of an 11.3.0.0.0 correlation and establish it as the dominant paradigm for the Southern Maya Lowlands.

NOTES

1. An earlier version of this paper was first written in 1976 and circulated in 1977; it has been substantially reworked since then. Many of the substantial changes wrought in earlier versions were due to the editorial comments of Christopher Jones, Robert J. Sharer, Jane Kepp, and the editors of this volume. I owe much inspiration over the years to many hours of productive discussions with Joseph Ball and Diane Z. Chase. Diane Z. Chase has also graciously read and helped revise this manuscript innumerable times. Any errors of interpretation, however, are solely the responsibility of the author.

2. E. W. Andrews V (personal communication) has noted that Edmonson would see only twelve books of Chilam Balam, that parts of Kaua and Tusik were translated by Barrera, and that M. Hires has translated the Chilam Balam of Chan Kan.

The Chronology of Chichen Itza: A Review of the Literature[1]

CHARLES E. LINCOLN

Harvard University

During the Terminal Classic–Early Postclassic transitional period, Chichen Itza emerged as one of the primary centers of Mesoamerican civilization. It was surely the most magnificent site of its time in all Mexico in terms of art and architecture. Within the regional context of the Northern Maya Lowlands, only Coba, Izamal, Tihoo (Mérida), and Uxmal rival Chichen Itza in area and architectural volume. While Chichen Itza may well be the most famous archaeological city in the New World, even the skeletal chronology of settlement and construction activity remains poorly understood (see Schmidt 1981a). Most scholars agree that Toltec Chichen belongs either in the Terminal Classic or Early Postclassic Period of the Maya Lowlands sequence. The problems of relative dating within the period of A.D. 800–1200 (9.19.0.0.0–11.0.0.0.0[2] in the Maya Long Count) and cultural continuity or discontinuity with the Classic Maya culture(s) of the Southern and Northern lowlands, however, remain controversial (see especially discussions in Andrews V 1979; Ball 1979a, 1979b; Andrews IV and Andrews V 1980; Chase and Chase 1982; Andrews V and Sabloff, this volume).

Our current understanding of the Terminal Classic–Early Postclassic Period(s) in northern Yucatan traces its origins to two distinct sources:

the very earliest descriptive and classificatory work on Maya ceramics and chronology by George C. Vaillant (1927: especially pp. 335–67) ["dirt archaeology"] and Alfred M. Tozzer's identification and interpretation of Maya and Toltec figures in the architectural sculpture and painting of Chichen Itza (1930, 1957) [art history and iconography]. The present paper will critically examine both perspectives on the archaeological chronology of Chichen Itza and Yucatan more broadly. The author has attempted to achieve a new formulation of the culture history of Chichen Itza rather than propose another modification of the traditional understandings derived ultimately either from Vaillant's stratigraphic or Tozzer's stylistic work or both. It should be noted that the earliest scholars, such as Morley (1913) and Seler (1909) did not assume the existence of any chronological or spatial divisions within Chichen Itza such as those hypothesized by later authors. The author of this paper believes that ceramic stratigraphy will ultimately prove the key to unraveling the sequence of development at Chichen Itza, but it is this perspective which rests for the moment on the weaker data base.

Vaillant's historic study established the precedence of ceramic analysis in assessing cultural succession throughout the Maya area[3] and eventually all of Mesoamerica (Vaillant 1927, 1935). At Chichen Itza, Vaillant carried out stratigraphic excavations in the Temple of the Initial Series/House of the Phalli (5C) group. While his field methodology and published descriptions left much to be desired, Vaillant's pioneering attempt to relate architectural and ceramic stratigraphy remains the only one of its kind ever completed at the site[4] (Ruppert 1952: Appendix I). As a result, later writers, such as Tozzer, Brainerd, and Andrews IV, have modified Vaillant's sequence more in detail than in basic structure. Vaillant proposed a "period of Great Period [Late Classic Maya] influence," a "period of Toltec trade," and a "Decadent Period" (1927: 365).

The gaps in our knowledge, and hence the controversy surrounding Chichen Itza, owe their existence largely to the nature of previous work at the site. The Carnegie Institution of Washington (CIW) Chichen Itza project, under the direction of Sylvanus G. Morley from 1923 to 1937, concentrated on architectural excavation and restoration aimed at revealing to the public the great and unique monuments of art and engineering. It was in the Southern Maya Lowlands (i.e., at Uaxactun), where abundant Initial Series or Long Count dates in architectural contexts offered the apparent opportunity for an "absolute" time scale, that the CIW focused its trailblazing research on archaeological stratigraphy and chronology. Mexico's National Institute of Anthropology and History (INAH) has continued to focus its work at Chichen Itza on goals with a more public than academic orientation. In the postwar era, Carnegie scholars did attempt to develop a regional sequence for northern Yucatan, but the controversy that still surrounds the details of the chronology suggests that their work was not totally successful.

The previous investigations at Chichen Itza did, however, bring into clear focus the pivotal position at which the site stands in the culture history of Mesoamerica. The architectural sculpture, bas-reliefs, and murals for which Chichen Itza is famous seemingly attest a unique blend of Maya and Mexican cultural traits and stylistic elements. For the past 55 years (since Tozzer's landmark paper, published in 1930), this distinctive complex, called "Toltec-Maya," has been interpreted as evincing an intense interaction between the peoples and ideologies of Highland Mexico and those of the Maya Lowlands comparable to no other case of pre-Hispanic acculturation in Mesoamerica.

While the terms *Mexican, Toltec,* and *Toltec-Maya* do not satisfactorily describe the distinctiveness of the art and architecture at Chichen Itza, there is as yet no other name that adequately conveys the cosmopolitan but very original character of this site. Tozzer coined the phrase *Toltec-Maya,* and even though including the word *Maya* as part of the label more accurately reflects the basic heritage of Chichen Itza, Proskouriakoff rejected the term in reference to the figural sculpture of the site (1950: 1), preferring to simply use *Toltec.* As Kubler has argued, the ties linking Chichen Itza and Tula, Hidalgo, do not cover anywhere near the complete range of sculptural forms and styles found at the former site (1975: 185–215). The corpus of monuments at Tula seems more like a stylistically inferior subset of those at Chichen Itza, so *Toltec* seems an inaccurate designation as well. Complete examination of this issue lies outside the scope of the present endeavor, unfortunately.

Alfred M. Tozzer's encyclopedic *Chichen Itza and Its Cenote of Sacrifice: A Comparative Study of Contemporaneous Maya and Toltec* (1957) remains the basic descriptive text on the archaeological and ethnohistoric data pertaining to this great pre-Columbian city. Tozzer formulated what has become the "traditional" reconstruction of the preconquest history and archaeology of Chichen Itza in particular and northern Yucatan in general. He made two basic interpretations, which have only recently come into question. His first proposal was that Chichen Itza as an archaeological site and historical entity comprised two components, one in the Late/Terminal Classic and the other in the Early Postclassic, divided by a break in occupation and urban construction. Tozzer's second premise was that the two periods of history and archaeology at Chichen Itza were characterized by a contrast in the ethnic makeup of the site: the earlier period was exclusively "Yucatan Maya" (1957: 23) and the later was "Toltec" or "Toltec-Maya" (1957: 25–30). The second, Toltec period at Chichen Itza began when invaders from Tula, Hidalgo, Mexico, conquered the Maya and became overlords of Yucatan, taking as their capital the "City of the Sacred Well" (Willard 1926). During the Toltec domination, the Maya remained at Chichen Itza as a major, subordinate population, and portrayals of individuals belonging to the two major ethnic groups appeared in the bas-reliefs and murals throughout the site's era of greatness.

Archaeologists were never entirely comfortable with this basically art-historical reconstruction of events. Subsequent chronological schemes proposed by Brainerd (1958, based primarily on ceramics), Andrews IV (1965a, 1965b, based primarily on architecture), Smith (1971, based on ceramics exclusively), and Andrews IV and Andrews V (1980, based primarily on research at Dzibilchaltun) generally take Tozzer's sequence as a basic assumption. However, all authors emphasize major aspects of cultural continuity from the Late/Terminal to Early Postclassic periods and implicitly or explicitly reject Tozzer's vision of Chichen Itza having been abandoned during an interim separating the Maya and Toltec horizons.

The drift away from Tozzer's position occurred only gradually, but the consensus now emerging is that "Toltec" traits did not appear simultaneously throughout Yucatan, and that the Late/Terminal Classic architecture and ceramics of the Andrews IV Pure Florescent (1965a, 1965b) and of R. E. Smith's Cehpech complex were still being produced when the earliest "Early Postclassic" Modified Florescent architecture and Sotuta Complex ceramics first came into being at Chichen Itza[5] (cf. Andrews V 1979, 1981; Andrews V & Sabloff, this volume). It is noteworthy that aside from art history, Tozzer based his reconstruction in part on interpretations of Maya "history" as found in the native chronicles, especially the Books of Chilam Balam. None of the above-named archaeologists who followed Tozzer have seriously attempted to reconcile either of these intractable sources (art historical or ethnohistorical) with the "dirt archaeology."

OVERVIEW: THE TRADITIONAL ARCHAEOLOGICAL PERSPECTIVE

Brainerd's sequence (see Table 5.1) followed Tozzer in emphasizing, at least terminologically, the idea of a break between the Late Classic Puuc sites (which he substituted for ceramic samples from "Maya Chichen," see below) and Early Postclassic Chichen Itza. Brainerd called the former "Florescent" and the latter "Early Mexican" (1958: 3–4). In fact, these phase names more dramatically accentuate the contrast between Classic and Postclassic than do Tozzer's numbered designations, Chichen I, II, and III.

Andrews IV proposed a new classification which substantively contrasted with Brainerd's, whereby both Uxmal (and the allied Puuc sites) *and* Chichen Itza belong to the "Florescent" period, with the former representing an earlier and "Pure" subphase and the latter a subsequent and "Modified" subphase (1965a, 1965b: Table 4). Andrews's classification rested on the essential technological identity of Pure and Modified Florescent architecture: both use finely cut boot-shaped veneer (nonfunctional) vault stones and equally fine veneer wall stones. The mechanically functional element of Florescent architecture is the concrete-rubble core encased beneath the veneer exteriors; these cores can remain standing even after the finely faced stones have fallen. While recognizing architectural continuity, Andrews IV accepted Tozzer's basic theorem: that the style and iconography of the sculpture and painting at Chichen Itza effectively and completely distinguished it in time and cultural/ethnic affiliations from Uxmal and other Puuc sites (not to mention the rest of the Maya Lowlands).

The characteristic Florescent mosaic-element manner of architectural decoration commonly occurs at both Chichen Itza and Uxmal, in addition to the basic mechanical similarity of the walls and vaults of these two sites. But the presence of uncounted "typical Toltec warrior" (Tozzer 1957: 155) columns at Chichen Itza and of more-or-less-typically Maya royal stelae at Uxmal defines the difference in culture and ethnicity perceived between the greatest centers of the peninsula. The Andrews IV chronological nomenclature clearly improves over its

Table 5.1: Traditional and "Total Overlap" Chronologies for
Late Yucatecan Prehistory Compared

A. M. Tozzer 1957	G. W. Brainerd 1958	E. W. Andrews 1965
Late Postclassic *Chichen* V A.D. 1460–1552* Abandonment	(no name/dates incl. in Late Mexican)	*Decadent Period—2nd* 1440–1540 Post-monumental
Middle Postclassic *Chichen IV* Dissolution A.D. 1280–1450	*Late Mexican* Substage-Mayapan 1280–1450	*Decadent Period—1st* Mayapan-monumental 1250–1440
Early Postclassic *Chichen III:* Toltec-Maya B″ Mexicans regain supremacy Toltec-Maya B′ Maya resurgence A.D. 1150–1260	*Middle Mexican* Substage defined by "Coarse Slate Ware" Dais of the Mercado, perhaps Mercado, built 1180–1280	*Black-on-Cream* Transitional Phase Black-on-cream is the same as "Coarse Slate Ware" 1050–1250 (12.9.0.0.0)* 1120–1250 (11.16.0.0.0)
Chichen II: Toltec-Maya A Initial Period of Toltec domination Cult of Quetzalcoatl/ Kukulcan A.D. 948–1145	*Early Mexican Substage* Medium Slate: Chichen X Fine Orange Plumbate Mexican ceramic affiliations 980–1180	*Florescent Period—2nd* *Phase*, Toltec-Chichen shows architectural continuity with Puuc (1st Phase) 800–1050 (12.9.0.0.0) 1020–1120 (11.16.0.0.0)
Late/Terminal Classic *Chichen I* Maya Chichen hieroglyphic inscriptions and "range structures" are essential defining characteristics A.D. 600–1000	*Florescent Stage* Medium Slate: Puuc Y, Z Fine Orange no Plumbate few or weakly represented Mexican ceramic forms 750–980	*Florescent Period—1st* *Phase:* Puuc-style veneer vaulted architecture, found mainly in Puuc sites but also at Chichen Itza 600–800 (12.9.0.0.0) 900–1020 (11.16.0.0.0)

*All dates are given A.D. and in terms of the 11.16.0.0.0 correlation of Maya and Christian calendars except as noted by reference (under Andrews IV 1965) to the 12.9.0.0.0 correlation.

R. E. Smith 1971	Andrews V 1981	Proposed Sequence with "Total Overlap"**
Chikinchel 1450–1550	(no name/dates included in Chechem)	*Post-Mayapan* 1440–1540
Tases Mayapan 1300–1450	*Chechem* Decadent 1200–1540	*Mayapan* Postclassic 1200/1300–1440

R. E. Smith 1971	Andrews V 1981	Proposed Sequence with "Total Overlap"**
Hocaba Peto Cream Ware: Kukula Group: Xcanchakan Black- on-cream type = "Coarse Slate" 1200–1300 *Sotuta* Chichen Slate Silho Fine Orange Tohil Plumbate The Sotuta Complex is best known from Chichen Itza. 1000–1200	*Zipche 2* Modified Florescent structures at Dzibilchal- tun show influence from Toltec Chichen 1100/1150–1200 *Zipche 1* a rare gap in architectural sequence at Dzibilchal- tun suggestive of de- population 1000–1100/1150	*Gap* can be filled by extending Mayapan backward or Chichen Itza forward, but the evidence is weak either way. The two sites show strong similarities in art styles/iconography, building types, and settle- ment patterns. 1100–1200 at least 1000–1300 at most
Cehpech Puuc Slate Ware Altar, Balancan Fine Orange. The Cehpech Complex is best known from the Puuc sites 800–1000	*Copo 2* Pure Florescent struc- tures at Dzibilchaltun in- cluding palaces or "range structures" and glyphic stelae 830–1000	*Terminal Classic/* Com- bined *"Florescent"* pe- riod, with all elements of Chichen I, Chichen II, and Chichen III (Ceh- pech, Sotuta, and Ho- caba) included. 800–1000/1100

**Compare this "total overlap" sequence with that given by Ball (1971a: Fig. 17) in which the Sotuta complex runs from 866 to 1194, Mayapan (Hocaba and Tases) begins just after 1000, and the Cehpech complex ends around 1150, allowing for regional variations on all of these dates. The revised version of "total overlap" presented and endorsed here emphasizes the poor fit between the data as known and the 11.16.0.0.0 correlation. The Terminal Classic Period is seen as dating from 9.19.0.0.0–10.9.0.0.0 in the Long Count. The last date at Chichen Itza (on a "Toltec warrior" column) is 10.8.10.11.0 on the Temple of the High Priest's Grave. The gap of 100–300 years in the sequence might come before or after the Mayapan period, but there is no archaeological justification for hypothesizing a major disjunction in either the architectural or ceramic sequences in northern Yucatan. This view contrasts with that of Willey (1984: 53) who writes that "the real break in the north came after the fall of Chichen Itza and immediately preceded the Late Postclassic." While it is ceramic and architectural technology which is identical between Pure and Modified Florescent, with differences visible in decoration and organization, it is precisely the decoration and organization which remain the same between Chichen Itza and Mayapan (pottery and buildings) across a technological transition or "decadence." Thus, although a continuity or identity is manifest in different ways, the transformation of the Classic into the Postclassic was probably swift and definitely unbroken or radically discontinuous.

Chase and Chase (1982: 608–11) point to evidence from Nohmul, Belize, which supports the hypothesis that Toltec Chichen (specifically the building types characteristic of Tozzer's Chichen II and Chichen III) might be partially if not completely coeval with the Terminal Classic Tepeu 3 or San Jose V phases in the Southern Maya Lowlands (see also Arlen Chase, this volume). A. Chase has arrived, by different lines of reasoning and evidence, at much the same conclusions about the relative and absolute timing of the Toltec phenomenon at Chichen Itza and its relevance to the correlation question as has the present author. The major contrasts between his position and the one articulated here involve differences of subject matter and methodology. The end points of the two research endeavors are in fact quite congenial.

predecessors in that it more accurately reflects the patterns of cultural history in the Northern Lowlands, but it still holds incontrovertible the traditional assumption that the divergence between the Pure and Modified manifestations of the Florescent was the result of a Toltec or Nahua conquest of or migration into Yucatan, taking Chichen Itza as the capital of a new state, following the end of the Classic Period (Andrews IV 1965a: 315–16).

According to the traditional reconstruction of culture history in the Maya Lowlands, the Toltec or Mexican city at Chichen Itza stands out as the only great center of cultural vitality during the Early Post-classic (ca. 10.6.0.0.0–11.2.0.0.0 or A.D. 950–1250 in the Thompson correlation; Tozzer 1957: 245; Willey 1982: 266). The "cultural processes" seen to be in action at this time involved a kind of rekindling or "hybrid vigor" in the collapsed Maya civilization as a result of the Toltec invasion, thought to have occurred after A.D. 940–60 (Tozzer 1957: 15–16, 25–35). After the conquest of Yucatan, Chichen Itza emerged as an island of unequaled artistic and demographic exuberance amidst the ruins of the collapsed Classic civilization, now mostly emptied of their former population and power (cf. also Kelley 1984). Andrews IV argued that some northern centers such as Dzibilchaltun continued to be occupied during the Modified Florescent, but their populations were small and declined in all areas except Chichen Itza (Andrews IV 1965a: 319–20; Andrews IV and Andrews V 1980: 281). Some scholars even speculated that the Maya were forcibly relocated from all over the peninsula by their foreign conquerors (e.g., Cowgill 1964).

One implicit feature of the traditional chronology, whether articulated by Tozzer, Brainerd, or Andrews IV, was the assumption that any and all cultural variability, whether manifest in architecture, sculpture, or ceramics, expresses either cultural differences due to ethnicity or change through time. "Function" as a determinant of form or decoration was mentioned by Tozzer (1957: 32) and by Thompson (1959: 119), but only in fleeting discussions regarding the predominance of one cult in one temple vs. another cult in a second temple. A second assumption was that the Maya Lowlands constituted a monolithic cultural entity. That is, all periods were assumed to be pan-peninsular, so that the existence at one site of a particular complex not documented at others meant that the two sites could not be contemporary. This assumption essentially stood as a complement to the first. Of the authors of the "linear succession" reconstruction, only Brainerd appears to have entertained the notion that regional variation within one time period could possibly account for the contrast between his Florescent (Andrews's Pure Florescent) and Early Mexican (Modified Florescent) ceramics of the Puuc sites and Chichen Itza, respectively. He regarded the idea as "somewhat farfetched in view of the nearness of sites," and essentially dismissed further consideration of contemporaneity (1958: 44).

However, Andrews V now believes that Robert Smith's (1971) Cehpech (Pure Florescent) and Sotuta (Modified Florescent) ceramic complexes at least partially overlap in time (1979, 1981). An increasing quantity of evidence suggests that ceramic types formerly defined as diagnostic of two distinct and sequential periods (Terminal Classic and Early Postclassic) were in fact "available contemporaneously" as indicated by their occurrence together in such unmistakable contexts as burial lots and caches (Ball 1978: 138, 1979a: 33, also this volume). The greater part of the present paper is devoted to examining the evidence for such temporal equivalence of pottery types and wares (see below).

Coba has provided a different kind of evidence, not of direct association of pottery types so much as apparent proof that the patterns of succession and replacement of ceramic complexes do not follow the same sequence everywhere. At the third and most easterly of the great northern Maya centers (after Uxmal and Chichen Itza) the transition from the Terminal Classic Cehpech ("Oro") complex into a Mayapan-related Middle–to–Late Postclassic ("Seco") complex occurred without an intervening Early Postclassic Sotuta-related phase (Robles C. 1980: 248–52; Robles C. and Andrews 1985). Excavations at Coba also produced contextual and typological indications that the Sotuta Complex of Chichen Itza might have existed at the same time as the local Terminal Classic Oro Complex.

Similarly, new evidence from Uxmal suggests that Sotuta-complex ceramics exist in significant quantity at this site which, according to the traditional linear reconstruction, should have seen a cessation of construction by the beginning of the Early Postclassic (Toltec or Sotuta) Period at Chichen Itza. Unfortunately the stratigraphic relationship of the abundant Sotuta pottery to the Puuc or Cehpech ceramics has yet to be clarified at Uxmal (cf. Saenz 1972, 1975a, 1975b; Konieczna and Mayer 1976; Maldonado Cárdenas, n.d.). The possibility that

Maya Uxmal might turn out to be at least partially contemporaneous with Toltec Chichen Itza should not come as too much of a surprise; Proskouriakoff long ago wrote of the style and costume elements of Stela 14 at Uxmal: "This monument tends to suggest a direct transition from the Classic style in its full flower to the Toltec style at Chichen Itza" (1950: 164; see below).

Further afield, evidence for the chronological overlap of Sotuta-phase diagnostics with Terminal Classic materials has also been reported from San José V contexts at Nohmul in Belize (Chase and Chase 1982). "Yucatec influence" has previously been noted in the local Terminal Classic and Postclassic complexes (Hammond 1974: 183–84). The basic continuity in Maya society documented at Lamanai (see Pendergast, this volume) suggests a pattern of continuous cultural development more like that at Coba, where Chichen-related traits are mostly absent and the Postclassic appears to be "Mayapan-related."

Andrews V and Ball have discussed at length some of the evidence referred to here. Ball (1979a: 30–34, Figure 17, 1979b: 48–51) has provided a particularly broad view and synthesis of the issues involved. He outlines the choice among models of sequential development (traditional), partial overlap (favored by Andrews V and Sabloff, this volume), and total overlap (favored by Ball himself and by the present author). It is Ball who must be credited for first bringing the problem of Terminal Classic/Early Postclassic ceramic chronology into clear focus.

OVERVIEW: THE TRADITIONAL PERSPECTIVE ON ART, ICONOGRAPHY, AND HIEROGLYPHIC WRITING AT CHICHEN ITZA

Despite being a major focus of the present paper, ceramics do not present the only chronological problem at Chichen Itza. Some might question the relevance of pottery and stratigraphy compared to the basic issue of whether Tozzer's interpretive identification of Maya and Toltec figures in the architectural sculpture and painting of Chichen Itza (1930, 1957) is correct. Ceramics obviously hold the key to understanding whether or not two ethnic groups were in fact *living* at Chichen at any given time, and only stratigraphic analysis will determine when that time was, if ever, in relative and absolute terms. Now, however, we will turn to some preoccupying matters of art history and epigraphy.

The presence of hieroglyphic inscriptions constitutes the most basic criterion for identifying buildings of the earlier, supposedly ethnically pure, Maya period at Chichen Itza. While Sylvanus G. Morley entertained the idea that the Maya inscriptions might be contemporaneous with the other glyphs, which he called Nahua, at Chichen and hence provide a key to decipherment or eventuate in the discovery of a Maya-Nahua "Rosetta stone" (1913: 61–91), Tozzer firmly believed that the Chichen Maya inscriptions predated the great preponderance of bas-relief columns, benches, and murals at Chichen Itza, which he ascribed to and made definitive of the periods labeled Toltec-Maya. The logic was beguilingly simple. The hieroglyphic inscriptions at Chichen Itza, while unusual in composition and subject matter, fit the general norms of variation known from other Late/Terminal Classic Maya sites, while the figural sculpture in large part represents individuals and gods who seemed—to Tozzer and many others—ethnically different from the Maya on grounds of costume, facial features, and the activities in which they were involved. Further, Maya glyphs occur on only five monuments (see below) in direct association with sculpture of the Toltec-Chichen mode (Proskouriakoff 1950: 170–71, 1970; Tozzer 1957: 35).

Thus, Tozzer and those who followed him argued that the Toltec came from Mexico to Yucatan, intermingled with the Maya, and formed a new culture called "Toltec-Maya," which developed entirely after the fall of the Classic civilization. No firm stratigraphic proof for this succession of cultures and events has ever been provided, but it is undeniable that in general, Maya and Toltec-Maya glyphs and art/iconography do not appear in the same structures. That the intruders were designated as "Toltec" relates to another argument: that Chichen Itza had specific historical ties with the site of Tula, Hidalgo. Wigberto Jiménez Moreno argued for this linkage on grounds of ethnohistorical as well as archaeological and art historical data (1941). Tula clearly belongs to the Early Postclassic Period in the Central Highlands of Mexico, so the placement of Toltec Chichen in the Early Postclassic of the Maya area seemed quite reasonable. Tozzer and others enthusiastically embraced this argument and elaborated the idea that the artistic connection between Tula and Chichen Itza gave a firm historical anchor for the legends of Kukulcan/Quetzalcoatl.

Problems in tying this interpretation to the archaeological record were always apparent, but few Mesoamericanists wanted to challenge the vast scope of Tozzer's and Jiménez Moreno's scholarship and research in archaeology and ethnohistory.[6] Tozzer's synthesis of these two lines of data led to an elaborate five-phase (with subdivisions) history of Chichen Itza (1957: 20–65). Personal communications from Brainerd, which Tozzer himself cites, reveal that from the beginning archaeologists tried to avoid dealing directly with the complicated sequence of events as Tozzer proposed them. Most archaeologists have, however, accepted the basic dichotomy of Maya vs. Toltec at Chichen Itza.

Tozzer tended to deemphasize the strong similarities between the architecture and ceramics of the Maya and Toltec components of Chichen Itza. Since settlement pattern archaeology was at that time in its infancy, it is not surprising that Tozzer placed no importance on the pattern of distribution of the structures he assigned to two different and sequent periods. He thought it perfectly reasonable that there would be an earlier pure-Maya center and a later hybridized Toltec-Maya capital.

The distribution and layout of architectural monuments and ancient causeways within Chichen Itza do not support such an interpretation. At the level of overall site planning, one can see from the Carnegie map (Ruppert 1952: Figure 151) that the urban core of the largest and most complex (Toltec) architecture is connected to several of the secondary, smaller and less complex (Maya) groups by radial *sacbeob*. While ethnic dominance of one group by another might account for such a pattern, it seems just as likely that the function or social status of groups that differ in size determines relative internal complexity and the content of architectural decoration. At the group or platform-compound level of analysis, it will be seen that Maya- and Toltec-type structures usually stand on a single platform as part of a single set of buildings. These sets represent the intermediate size-class of construction at Chichen Itza, and we refer to them here as "elite" complexes. It is a common pattern for elite compounds to include range structures, temples, gallery-patio structures, and colonnades in varying specific orientations with regard to one another (see Ruppert 1952 for ground plans of 5C1–17, 5D1–4; Lincoln and Anderson, in preparation). All the buildings Tozzer assigned to Maya Chichen are range structures (series of adjoining simple rooms without columns; 1957: 23–24), while the rest of the set belong to either the Chichen II or the Chichen III Toltec period.

In short, Chichen Itza is best interpreted as an integrated whole community, considering both the overall site plan and the organization of individual architectural groups. The settlement pattern and architecture provide no evidence of ethnic heterogeneity at the site. Rather, the picture is one of a highly stratified and internally complex political society that was *probably* ethnically uniform and Maya.

One of the major objections to this conclusion is that Maya hieroglyphic writing is not associated with "Toltec" Chichen. The five major constructions of Toltec Chichen are located on a single central platform (south of the Sacred Cenote and at the north end of the Carnegie map, but centrally located with regard to site extent as known from reconnaissance). These five are the Castillo, the Great Ball Court complex (including the Temple of the Jaguars), the Temple of the Warriors, the Court of the Thousand Columns Colonnade, and the Mercado. Name glyphs occur in all except perhaps the Castillo, but their specific forms resemble Oaxacan or Central Mexican forms more than Classic Maya. Typically Maya hieroglyphs have only been found in association with the Great Ball Court Complex (the so-called altar, see below; Wren and Schmidt 1984). The central or Toltec platform (also called *La Gran Nivelación*) was probably the focus of the largest public sociopolitical and religious ceremonies ever held at Chichen Itza.

Hieroglyphic writing occurs most commonly on the lintels of range structures at Chichen Itza, a seemingly private context at a site where no typical classic Maya public-oriented stelae have been found. By contrast, the Toltec columns, wall panels, and benches occur in temples, the functionally enigmatic gallery-patios, and other types of structures, but usually in public view. Whether on structure exteriors or inside spacious colonnaded rooms, Toltec art seems to have had a potentially wider audience than the Maya glyphs at Chichen Itza, because range structures were almost certainly elite residences.

Thus perhaps social rather than temporal and ethnic differences explain the contrast between Maya and Toltec structures at Chichen Itza. The Maya Chichen inscriptions exhibit a degree of phoneticism intermediate between Late Classic public monuments and the surviving Maya codices (Peter Mathews, personal communication 1984). Phonetic writing may be more common in contexts such as books or residences where a limited, elite audience is addressed rather than in inscriptions that function to communicate and validate the message or royal power to a presumably less literate, wider public. Stelae and similarly displayed texts were probably not directed toward vast illiterate masses but at the middle ranges of Maya society, whose members were perhaps able to understand some elements of the text and iconography. (John Justeson has written the only summary of which I am aware of the evidence for literacy in the Classic Maya area, 1978: 237, 318–34.) In any event, the size and spatial arrangement of most southern Maya sculptures would not appear to suggest a mass audience for royal propaganda.

On the other hand, it has been argued that glyphic phoneticism tends to increase as a percentage of the Maya inscriptions through time, and the Chichen Itza sample comes at the very end of the Classic Period. However, contemporaneous tenth-cycle stelae at Seibal, for example, employ phoneticism primarily in name glyphs, whereas at Chichen Itza phonetic spellings occur in all parts of speech (Peter Mathews, personal communication 1984). Furthermore, the glyphic paintings in the eighth century A.D. cave of Naj Tunich in Guatemala also contain a notably high proportion of phonetic elements when compared with similarly dated texts. This cave almost certainly served as the site of limited-access elite rituals, and its arcane records date 140 years earlier than the Chichen Itza texts (G. Stuart 1981; David Stuart, personal communication 1983).

By contrast, the Toltec monuments at Chichen Itza are almost entirely iconic or pictorial, and what few glyphs occur most closely resemble Highland Mexican, especially Zapotec forms (cf. Proskouriakoff 1970: 171), and seem to function exclusively as individual names. What information the Toltec monuments convey about the political and religious world order, then, can be understood by illiterates. Further, as has often been pointed out, the organization of interior and exterior ceremonial space at Chichen Itza is much better suited to mass participation in rituals than comparable space at most known southern Maya sites (but Yucatec sites such as Izamal and Ake have immense plazas and/or flat, open space atop pyramidal terrace-temples). The availability of such space, in addition to the not-very-subtle iconographic adornments, suggest that direct communication with illiterate masses may have been one of the functions of the major buildings of Toltec Chichen.

154

Hence, one way in which Chichen Itza differs from other Maya sites is that glyphic monuments appear to have a narrower audience and pictorial/iconographic monuments a much broader appeal and aim than is typical for similar vehicles of official propaganda elsewhere in the Maya Lowlands. One might say that the media of communication at Chichen Itza are more specialized, in being distinctly designed for the intended recipients of the information involved. Likewise, the diversity of major structure types at Chichen Itza indicates specialization in the mechanisms for achieving and maintaining social cohesion (Lincoln 1983). The degree of political complexity and social stratification apparent in such specialization exceeds the expectations for any society at lower than the state level of integration.

In sum, the expression of power at Chichen Itza takes two different forms corresponding to two contrasting types of architectural context—one appears to be public and the other private. We assume a public function for the Toltec temples, ball courts, colonnades, and gallery-patio structures, and a private function (probably, but not always necessarily, residential) for the range structures (e.g. the Akab-Tzib, Casa Colorada, Temples of the Three Lintels and Four Lintels, and Las Monjas [a range structure hard to imagine as residential, but where limitations on access to the inscribed lintels seem obvious nonetheless]). Thus, building function and the social status of the intended consumers of the information carved in the glyphic or iconographic panels would serve to explain the difference between the Maya and Toltec modes at Chichen Itza. It should be clear at this point that the terms *Maya* and *Toltec* are used here as labels to designate well-known iconographic and architectural forms. By using such proper names I do not imply acceptance of the traditional position that two ethnic groups were present at Chichen Itza at any time prior to the arrival of the Spaniards.

Proskouriakoff (1950: 169–70), Lothrop (1952: 111–13), and Rands (1954: 281–82) presaged by several decades the chronological overlap model of Chichen Itza as a Terminal Classic Maya site. Proskouriakoff observed that the Toltec-Chichen style consists largely of elements referable to Classic Maya parallels or antecedents. In support of her analysis, Lothrop and Rands observed that while the dramatis personae of the scenes at Chichen Itza on sculptural, painted, or metal media may have Maya *or* Toltec costumes and features, purely Maya iconography composes the frames or borders enclosing the major subject matter in all cases. Lothrop and Rands also proposed that the evidence from Chichen Itza indicates a later correlation of Maya and Christian calendars than that favored by Thompson. They interpreted representational art at Chichen Itza as describing a cultural milieu just as closely tied to the Late/Terminal Classic Maya culture as to that of Tula and the Early Postclassic of Central Mexico. They argued that such a situation in turn suggests a major realignment of Mesoamerican cultural chronologies. Proskouriakoff showed that the Chichen Itza–Toltec style shares many stylistic and organizational elements (as well as Toltec- or transitional-to-Toltec-type figures) with some of the Terminal Classic Puuc monuments of Yucatan and northern Campeche (cf. 1950: 189–90, 197 in the table of monuments). While Proskouriakoff herself clearly believed that the Toltec were an intrusive non-Maya element in Yucatan (1950: 1–2, 170–72), her work and observations on the diversity of styles in the Northern Lowlands in large part laid the foundation for the argument that the style and iconography dominant at Chichen Itza are not so intrusive to northern Yucatan as the traditional view would maintain (Lincoln 1982).

In the realm of art history, strictly defined, Proskouriakoff has long since presented a seemingly irrefutable case for intersite and interregional divergence and provincialism in the sculptural styles of the Late/Terminal Classic in the Northern Maya Lowlands (1950: 154–72). She points out the presence of Toltec traits, as well as elements of style and organization characteristic of Chichen Itza, in the stelae of Oxkintok, Edzna, Kabah, and Uxmal. Her consideration covers the arrangement of scenes in panels (relatively common in the Southern Maya Lowlands of this time horizon as well), specific costume elements and weapons, facial features, and characteristics of pose and gesture. One logical extension of her argument is that if artistic/stylistic heterogeneity is so well developed in Terminal Classic Yucatan, perhaps the so-called Toltec style of Chichen Itza simply represents a more fully developed expression of this diversity. The traditional, Tozzerian model presumes that the northern Maya were culturally and stylistically homogeneous before the invasion from Mexico.

However, each year new discoveries produce highly aberrant or distinctive specimens of Yucatec sculptures from even the smallest sites, such as the lintels of San Diego in the Puuc (Alfredo Barrera Rubio 1983) and the wall panels of Xtelhu near Yaxcaba (E. B. Kurjack personal communication; field observations by the author, 1982–83).

These apparently unique local developments emphasize the hetero-geneity of stylistic Yucatec art and make the idea of intrusion seem both less necessary and less likely as an explanation for the phenom-enon of Chichen Itza.

Among the apparently significant formal similarities between the art of Toltec Chichen Itza and the Puuc sites is the shared presence of (1) dynamic-narrative scenes (2) arranged in panels, (3) sometimes framed by guilloche bands or borders. These occur, for example, on Stelae 9 and 21 at Oxkintok, 3 at Uxmal, and in the Lower Temple of the Jaguars at Chichen Itza as bas-relief murals, to mention only a few cases with all three traits. Proskouriakoff elaborated in particular on the case of the Lower Jaguars bas-reliefs, and their similarity as narrative art to monuments of the Late/Terminal Classic in the south-ern Maya Lowlands:

The presentation of the subject in the Lower Temple of the Jaguars as a narrative is probably due to the fact that it replaces in function the painted mural, of which we have examples at Uaxactun and Bonampak and which are clearly distinguished from the Classic monuments. (Proskouriakoff 1950: 171).

By contrasting the function of the painted and bas-relief murals with the "Classic monuments," Proskouriakoff emphasized the stereotypical Maya stela with one dominant figure, today identified as a royal por-trait. Peter Mathews points out that some Late Classic stelae and numerous lintels at such sites as Yaxchilan, Piedras Negras, and Seibal also depict narrative scenes (personal communication 1984). On the other hand, single figures *are* portrayed on each face of the four-sided "warrior columns" so characteristic of Toltec Chichen Itza. In Meso-america, outside the Maya area, any stone sculpture focused on in-dividuals is extremely rare, and while the poses on the warrior columns at least generally recall those of some Southern Lowland stelae, it seems unlikely that the Toltec Chichen portrayals are rulers. Thus, any connection between the Classic stelae and the warrior columns would be more formal than substantive. It should be noted, however, that there are very few examples of comparable "Toltec warrior col-umns" at Tula, Hidalgo.

Proskouriakoff correctly points to the parallel in *function* between the Bonampak murals and the Chichen Itza bas-reliefs. However, it remains to be seen if this similarity actually reflects parallels in content.

157

The Bonampak murals are also presented in paneled scenes (two or three plus iconographic border above compared with the five panels in the Lower Temple of the Jaguars plus iconographic border below). Further, the costumes of the figures portrayed in the Lower Temple of the Jaguars more strongly resemble those of Late/Terminal Classic Maya sculpture, especially in the area of the Usumacinta drainage, than do most Toltec-style monuments (Proskouriakoff 1950: 171; Tozzer 1957: 25, 167–69, 180–84). Finally, the presence of battle scenes in Room 2 of Bonampak and the Upper Temple of the Jaguars at Chichen Itza (Miller 1977a; Coggins 1984) hints that the details of the two narratives may be similar as well.

If the Upper and Lower jaguar temples are taken as a unit, the dramatic sequence at both Chichen Itza and Bonampak describes the events surrounding a battle or war and an ensuing ceremony involving three rulers and processions of their subordinates (see A. Miller 1977a; M. Miller 1981; D. Kelley 1982, 1983). The specific historical details inferred by various authors do not concern us here, although the present author has strong reservations about all historical interpretations of the Temple of the Jaguars sequence which invoke a Toltec or Putun invasion (see esp. Kelley 1984; Coggins 1984).

Most intriguing is the potential for sociopolitical comparisons between Bonampak and Chichen Itza. While a complete discussion of the possibilities presented by the dramatic-narrative scenes at these two sites lies outside the scope of the present paper, we may take note of some promising leads. The suggestions revolve around parallels in the formal presentation of the iconographies of power, which do differ in apparent content.

To begin with, as noted, three rulers appear to preside over both dramas. They are visually identified at Bonampak by distinctive robes and headdresses, as well as glyphic titles, and at Chichen Itza by oversized name emblems. Hieroglyphic captions name the Bonampak ruler as Chan-Muan, accompanied by a Bird-Jaguar of Yaxchilan, and a certain Ah Balam (Peter Mathews, personal communication 1984; also M. Miller 1981). David Kelley interprets Miller's single protagonist "Captain Serpent" as two individuals, Mixcoatl and Quetzalcoatl, after their emblems of cloud-hook serpent and feathered serpent (A. Miller 1977a: 209; Kelley, 1982, 1983: 205). Kelley infers that Captain Sun Disk is the local ruler of Chichen Itza and that the two Captains Serpent are foreigners (see also Kelley 1984). Kelley's specific identification of Captain Sun Disk will be discussed below. Our present interest is in the possibly significant coincidence that three rulers are portrayed in each of the two narratives.

The conclusions that can be drawn from this are limited by small sample size and the lack of directly associated glyphic data at Chichen Itza. Other Maya murals, such as those at Uaxactun (Smith 1950: Figures 45–47), Mul-Chic and Chacmultun (Barrera Rubio 1980a), and Cacaxtla (Foncerrada de Molina 1980; Kubler 1980), preserve some elements of processional and/or battle scenes reminiscent of Bonampak and Chichen Itza, but the whole plot cannot be reconstructed at these other sites. It would be interesting to examine these other dramatic murals for evidence of further thematic parallels.

Besides the rulers, Peter Mathews has identified certain iconographically subsidiary figures at Bonampak as individuals of secondary political rank by the presence in their name phrases of a glyph read *cahal*. This is interpreted as a title, deriving from the word for "town" or "people," of noble rather than royal status. *Cahal* contrasts with and is clearly inferior to the title of *ahau*, reserved for rulers and their immediate families. At secondary centers, as known from monuments at smaller sites such as La Pasadita, *cahals* appear to be the local, hereditary governors, dependent on *ahaus* at primary political capitals such as Yaxchilan, Piedras Negras, and Bonampak. The relationship of Late Classic *cahals* to *ahaus* is inferred to be the same as that of the Late Postclassic and Contact Period *batabs* to *halach uinics* in northern Yucatan (Roys 1943: 134–41). Many of the individuals arrayed in processions behind the rulers at Bonampak bear the *cahal* title (all of the foregoing, Peter Mathews, personal communication 1984).

The question emerges, if the parallels in form and presentation of the narrative at Bonampak and Chichen Itza indicate participation in the same or closely related traditions of mural art, can we infer that the iconographically secondary figures at the latter site possess an analogous social or political rank to those at the former? The number of persons portrayed in the Lower Temple of the Jaguars is much greater than in Structure 1 at Bonampak. The lowest of five paneled registers at Chichen alone includes 24 individuals in procession compared with 10–14 all told in the Bonampak murals. If the secondary figures at Chichen Itza were interpreted to be *cahals* or *batabs* of politically subordinate centers, the territory controlled by this site might include most of north central Yucatan, a view not inconsistent with the paucity of major Florescent Period centers in that part of the peninsula and with the apparent sociopolitical complexity of the City of the Sacred Well as interpreted archaeologically (see above). It is noteworthy that it is the iconographically less important individuals portrayed in the Lower Temple of the Jaguars who are characteristically named by "non-Maya"-appearing name glyphs. Nominal emblems or icons such as designate the primary or royal figures at Chichen Itza (Serpents and Sun Disk) occur in the Southern Maya Lowlands primarily in contexts where real or mythological ancestry is implied, usually in the upper register of Late and Terminal Classic stelae, such as at Yaxchilan, Ucanal, and Ek Balam (Peter Mathews, personal communication 1983–84; David Stuart, personal communication 1983; archives of the Corpus of Hieroglyphic Inscriptions project, Peabody Museum, Harvard). We must now briefly turn to a consideration of the hieroglyphic inscriptions at Chichen Itza.

Thompson's "new method of deciphering Yucatecan dates" at Chichen Itza (1937), now universally accepted among epigraphers (D. H. Kelley 1982), suggests a relatively rapid sequence of construction for the eleven or so buildings associated with such dates (cf. Thompson 1937: 186). While it is these buildings which have traditionally been considered as definitive of Maya Chichen, David Kelley has made the revolutionary identification of the name which he deciphered as *Kakupacal* (in 1968) in the hieroglyphic inscriptions of Chichen Itza with the iconographic figure called "Captain Sun Disk" by Arthur Miller in the purportedly Toltec murals and bas-reliefs of the Upper and Lower Temples of the Jaguars and the North Temple of the Great Ball Court complex, as well as the East Wing of the Monjas and the Temple of the Wall Panels (Ruppert 1931: Plate 11; Miller 1977a: 209; Kelley 1983: 205, 1983b). While the grounds for this identification are too complex to be discussed in the context of this review, the present author accepts Kelley's argument and believes the interpretation can only be amplified. One must assume at the very least that if Kelley is correct in identifying Kakupacal with Captain Sun Disk, then a strong continuity of historical tradition links the Maya inscriptions and the Toltec figural/iconographic records. Following the interpretation presented above that the contrast between glyphic and iconographic modes of expression/communicaton reflect building functions rather than temporal or ethnic change, the position taken here is that the Sun Disk icons are essentially contemporaneous with the dated hieroglyphic texts spelling the name Kakupacal. The identification of Kakupacal with Captain Sun Disk will become a central issue in any discussion of the relationship between Maya and Toltec elements at Chichen Itza, as will the intriguing historical clues provided by Kelley's and Miller's interpretations of the quasi-historical scenes in the murals and bas-reliefs of the Temple of the Jaguars, although the jury will surely remain out on the specifics of these reconstructions for some time (Miller 1977a; Kelley 1982, 1983; Coggins 1984).

Less dramatic, perhaps, but more archaeologically solid, are five major stone sculptures on which clearly Maya glyphs are carved on the same stone as figures and motifs traditionally defined as Toltec. The cases of direct association are:

(1) Column 4 at the summit of Structure 3C1, the Temple of the High Priest's Grave (shown here in Figure 5.1; see Thompson and Thompson 1938);

(2) the tenoned circular stone from the Caracol (Ruppert 1935: Figures 168–169; Morley 1935; 282–83);

(3) the "sombrero" or altar from the Great Ball Court (Thompson 1937: 189; Wren and Schmidt 1984; Carnegie Institution of Washington Archives, Peabody Museum);

(4) the column from Structure 6E1 in the Hieroglyphic Jambs Group (Proskouriakoff 1970: 461–65);

(5) the west jamb from the superstructure of Structure 5B18, the Castillo of Old Chichen (Proskouriakoff 1970: 461).

Of these sculptures, only one is securely dated.

Column 4 of the High Priest's Grave superstructure bears the date 2 Ahau 18 Mol in a Tun 11 of a Katun 2 Ahau (Thompson 1937: 185–86), placed in the Long Count at 10.8.10.11.0 or A.D. 998 (in the Thompson correlation; A.D. 1214 in Kelley's new correlation, 1982, 1983). The pyramid of Structure 3C1 resembles that of the Castillo in having the same orientation and four radial stairways; the temple superstructures are not identical, however, and that of 3C1 faces east while the Castillo faces north (cf. the map of Chichen Itza in Ruppert 1952: Figure 151). Tozzer ascribed the Toltec warrior figures on the columns of the Temple of the High Priest's Grave to his Chichen IIIB' period, second-to-last in the Toltec sequence at the site (1957: 43). Thompson argued that the unique association of a hieroglyphic date with a "Toltec warrior" figure in fact resulted from the

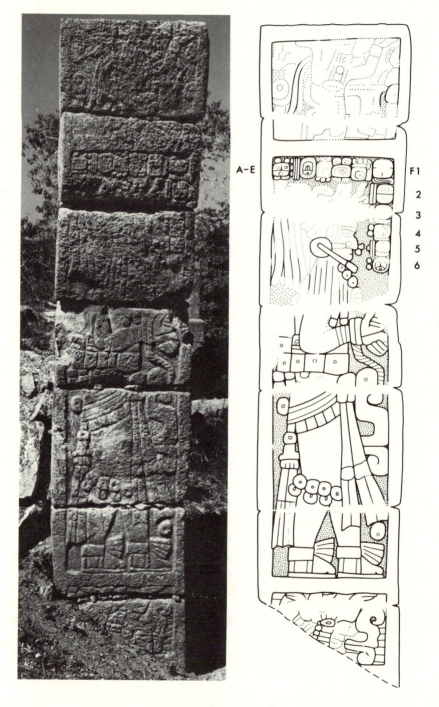

A-E   F1
       2
       3
       4
       5
       6

162

reuse of an older stone (1937: 185, 1938: 59). Tatiana Proskouriakoff disagreed: "The design of the glyphic panel, however, is fully integrated with the figure on the column, and since the inscription spans two blocks and no blocks of such thickness are used in Maya buildings, I fail to see how this view can be justified" (1970: 459). Column 4 is reproduced in Figure 5.1.

Dates have been proposed for the carved circular stone from the Caracol (9.19.10.0.0 8 Ahau 8 Xul??? by Morley 1935: 282) and the unpublished altar stone from the Great Ball Court (11.7.5.3.0 6 Ahau 13 Pax proposed by Enrique Palacios and cited in Thompson 1937: 189), but neither of these dates seems very secure or acceptable as yet. Both these monuments show opposing groups not unlike those of the Great Ball Court benches. Wren and Schmidt (1984) argue in a traditional vein that these facing processions are Maya and Toltec warriors or opposing teams of ball players. There are no dates whatsoever on the 6E1 column or the west jamb of Structure 5B18.

Other structures that exhibit a mixture of Maya and Toltec traits are the Caracol, the Temple of the Hieroglyphic Jambs, and the Temple of the One Lintel. The Caracol is particularly enigmatic because round

---

Figure 5.1 Photograph of Column 4, Temple of the High Priest's Grave, from 1953 negative in the archives of the Carnegie Institution of Washington, now housed in Cambridge, Massachusetts. Drawing by Peter Mathews, Peabody Museum, Harvard University.

This enigmatic "warrior column" from Structure 3C1, which Tozzer considered stylistically late within the Tolte construction sequence at Chichen Itza, is the only known example in which a "Toltec warrior" figure is portrayed on such a column in direct association with a Maya hieroglyphic inscription. On analogy with other Toltec warrior columns, one might expect a name glyph in the position of this text in the panel, but the inscription apparently begins and ends with a calendrical expression. The inscription is eroded, but David H. Kelley accepts J. Eric Thompson's interpretation of the date as 10.8.10.11.0 2 Ahau 18 Mol.

The "warrior's" wrists appear to be bound by rope which trails below the hands. The motif of tied hands commonly occurs at Chichen Itza and is best exemplified by a set of warrior columns in the Northwest Colonnade (Morris, Charlot, and Morris 1931: Plates 93, 94, 96, 97, 99, 100, 102, 103). David Stuart has suggested that numerous individuals portrayed on the so-called warrior columns of Tolte Chichen are in fact engaged in ritual bloodletting or autosacrifice (pers. comm. 1983). The "tied-hands" motif may relate to this complex.

163

structures are thought to be associated with Quetzalcoatl/Kukulcan as Wind God (cf. Pollock 1936), but the discovery of major glyphic inscriptions integrated into its architecture led Tozzer to place the structure either in the Maya period or (like the Lower Temple of the Jaguars) the very earliest years of the Toltec period (1957: 24). I believe that Marvin Cohodas (1982) is correct in arguing that the Caracol makes a visual and iconographic "pair" with the Castillo, presumably reflecting aspects of Quetzalcoatl as Wind God and Sun God. This association may or may not indicate contemporaneity of construction.

The Hieroglyphic Jambs that made Structure 6E3 famous define the entrance to a Chichen III gallery-patio structure (again according to Tozzer's chronology of building types, 1957: 41–44). Recent field inspection of this structure has ruled out the possibility that the wall including the jambs belonged to an earlier (non-gallery-patio) structure as Tozzer had suggested (1957: 35). D. H. Kelley reads the date on the Jambs as 9 Ben 1 Zac, placed at 10.2.15.2.13 in the Long Count (1982: Table 1).

Another case of a Toltec building ground plan associated with a Maya inscription is the Temple of the One Lintel (Structure 7B1), which appears to be a Chichen II or III two-room temple with twin-column entrance (Tozzer 1957: 41). The date on the lintel (presumably set above the interior doorway) is Tun 15 of a Katun 1 Ahau, corresponding to 10.2.15.0.0 (Thompson 1937: 186). While Tozzer minimized the importance of these occurrences of Maya glyphs with Toltec architecture and sculpture (1957: 24–25, 35), it seems that whatever the relative dating or functional interrelationship of the Maya hieroglyphic and Toltec iconographic monuments, the evidence does not support the notion of major historic or ethnic disjunction at Chichen Itza.

CERAMICS AND PUUC/CHICHEN ITZA OVERLAP

The architectural and iconographic distinctiveness of Chichen Itza, then, may reflect a greater level of institutional complexity than existed at other Late–to–Terminal Classic Maya sites. Some variability in cultural materials, however, cannot be explained by reference to larger social phenomena. Ceramics vary in such an independent fashion, conforming only to patterns of vessel function, local preference, or changing trends in decorative style. These patterns or trends may reflect regional as well as diachronic fluctuations in popularity. The position taken here is that Cehpech pottery was produced in the Puuc region at the same time as Sotuta ceramics were manufactured at Chichen Itza, during the period 9.19.0.0.0 to 10.9.0.0.0 or A.D. 800–1000 (Thompson correlation).

This view represents a marked break with traditional thought on ceramic complexes as articulated by Brainerd, who remarked that the notion of synchronic variability in assemblages was "somewhat far-fetched in view of the nearness of sites" (1958: 44). Regional diversity in ceramics has a lengthy history in the Maya Lowlands, and roughly contemporaneous pottery can now be identified as coming from different areas by at least the Late and perhaps the Middle Formative. Few specialists today would see any conceptual or theoretical barriers to interpreting similar but not identical sets of artifacts from different sites as contemporaneous in the absence of stratigraphic or absolute-chronological evidence to the contrary.

In fact, no stratigraphic, radiometric, or hieroglyphic data from Coba, Uxmal, or Chichen Itza clearly support the Cehpech-to-Sotuta succession. Only the still incompletely published information on the Dzibilchaltun ceramic sequence might stand as evidence for the replacement of Pure by Modified Florescent cultural manifestations (Andrews IV and Andrews V 1980: 180–90, 274–75). The question is, Do specific typological cross-ties demonstrate interaction between Chichen Itza and the Uxmal/Puuc Hills area? The present paper will examine in depth the cases of the Fine Orange groups and Puuc and Chichen Slate wares.

The Minority Wares

J. W. Ball's excellent summary of the problem of Northern Lowland Late Classic–to–Early Postclassic chronology (1979a, 1979b) suggests that the traditional definition of Toltec Chichen (Sotuta complex) ceramics actually depends on the presence of two minority-frequency ceramic wares, Silho (X Fine Orange) and Tohil Plumbate. By the "linear succession reconstruction" (Ball 1979a: 32), Uxmal and other Terminal Classic sites lack both these wares completely. As Andrews V stated (1979: 9):

many diagnostics of the Sotuta Complex, such as Plumbate and X Fine Orange, are very widespread during Toltec times and could be expected to

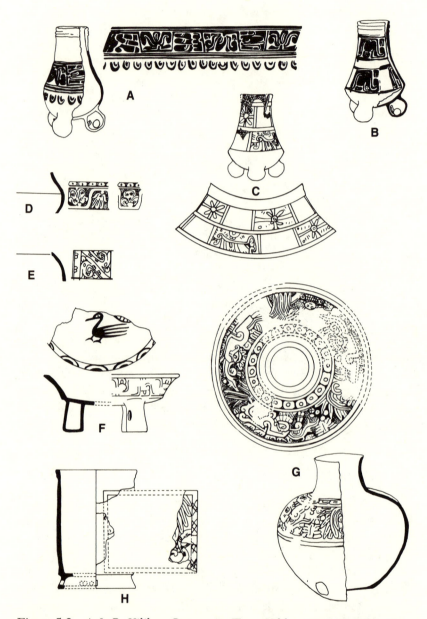

Figure 5.2   A & B: Kilikan Composite Type: Kilikan Variety, Silho Group Fine Orange, from Las Monjas at Chichen Itza. Excavation in the Monjas complex yielded "an unusually large percentage of X Fine Orange (Brainerd 1958:43)." In no phase or context of its construction did this "major pre-

166

Mexican architectural complex at Chichen Itza (Boles 1977: title)" lack Early Mexican substage pottery. It seems clear that Sotuta Complex *ceramics* can and do occur in primary association with buildings assigned by *architectural* style to the Pure Florescent. At Chichen Itza, at least, the evidence contradicts the temporal equation of Pure Florescent or Puuc-style architecture with Cehpech ceramics. The hieroglyphic inscriptions of the Monjas are securely dated to the third katun of the tenth cycle (e.g. 10.2.10.11.7. 8 Manik 15 Uo, Thompson 1937:186), thus placing the Early Mexican/Sotuta pottery in a context apparently earlier than A.D. 900 in the Thompson correlation (cf. Ball 197a, 1979b). (Figures A & B are adapted from Brainerd 1958: Figures 77m, 77p). C: Kilikan Composite type: Kilikan Variety, Silho Group Fine Orange, from Tepeu 3 context at Uaxactun. Robert E. Smith reported several examples of Early Mexican/Sotuta ceramics from Tepeu 3 contexts at Uaxactun, the type site for the southern Lowland "core" sequence. Brainerd coupled the occurrence of Silho (Chichen) Fine Orange with the grater bowls mentioned below (Figure 3F) to foreshadow the present "overlap model" by suggesting some contemporaneity between Tepeu 3 Uaxactun and Early Mexican Chichen Itza (1958:260).

Along with Kilikan Composite: Kilikan Variety, another Silho type, Yalton Black-on-Orange: Yalton Variety, also occurs in Tepeu 3 contexts at Uaxactun (Smith 1955, 2: Figure 55-b-5; Figure C is adapted from Smith 1955, 2: Fig. 43-b-12). D & E: Some typical design motifs on Silho Fine Orange vessels from Las Monjas at Chichen Itza. Designs on Fine Orange pottery of the Silho, Altar, and Balancan groups recall those on the monumental sculpture of Chichen Itza and other Terminal Classic Maya sites in the southern as well as northern Lowlands (cf. Sabloff 1973: 125–126; Figures D & E here are adapted from Brainerd 1958: Figures 77i, 77,l). F: Kilikan Composite: Kilikan Variety dish from Chichen Itza. This vessel resembles that found by Ruben Maldonado Cardenas in the ballcourt at Uxmal. (Figure F is adapted from Smith 1971, 2: Figure 22r). G: Holtun Gouged-Incised: Holtun Variety jar from the Cenote of Sacrifice at Chichen Itza. The designs on Chichen Red Ware appear to imitate Silho Fine Orange in many cases, but also bear direct iconographic relationships to the architectural sculpture of Chichen Itza (Figure G is adapted from Brainerd 1958: Fig. 85a). H: "Fine Orange Ware, Altar Group, Pabellon Modeled-Carved type vase . . . This specimen does not appear to belong certainly to any of the fine-orange groups including Balancan, Altar, or Silho, but to something in between . . . (Smith 1971, 2:40)." This vessel, like those sculptures which directly associate glyphs with Toltec sculpture, epitomizes the patterned integration of Terminal Classic and so-called Early Mexican traits which at the same time suggest and validate the "overlap model" whereby these two sequential periods become one. The incomplete, reconstructed vessel reproduced here as Figure H is from Mayapan (adapted from Smith 1971, 2: Figure 27,l. Thanks due to the Peabody Museum Press of Harvard University, especially Ms. Donna Dickerson, for permission to adapt all the figures copies from Smith's 1971 *Pottery of Mayapan* for inclusion in this volume).

167

appear at most, or perhaps all, major sites in the northern lowlands still occupied during the Toltec period. That they do not appear must have chronological significance.

Andrews's point remains a valid objection to a model of overlap between Cehpech and Sotuta. However, in the case of Silho Fine Orange, the data are at least somewhat equivocal.

Contrary to what is generally believed, the stratigraphic context of Silho (X Fine Orange)[8] in the Maya Lowlands does not clearly indicate a later date than Altar (Y Fine Orange) or Balancan (Z Fine Orange). Moreover, recent compositional analysis places Silho with Chablekal Gray (a Cehpech-complex diagnostic) and suggests that both were manufactured in the lower Usumacinta drainage (Rands and Bishop 1982). There is no evidence from this study to suggest that the two groups (Silho and Chablekal, assigned to two different wares, Fine Orange and Fine Gray) were chronologically distinct (Rands, personal communication 1982). The simplest (but unproven) inference would appear to be that the ceramics traded to northern Yucatan were manufactured at the same time as the other Maya Fine Orange/Fine Gray wares, which were produced at various centers along the Usamacinta during Terminal Classic times (Sabloff et al. 1982).

The traditional sequence defines the Pure Florescent or Cehpech (Terminal Classic) complex largely by the presence of Balancan Fine Orange and the absence of Silho, whose presence in turn largely defines the Modified Florescent or Sotuta (Early Postclassic) complex, found primarily at Chichen Itza (see notes 3, 4, and 5, below). Oddly enough, one may turn to Brainerd and Smith, architects of the traditional chronology, for hints that the Silho and Balancan groups can and do occur together in stratigraphic context. Brainerd felt that the failure to demonstrate the existence of unmixed Florescent strata underlying Early Mexican deposits at Chichen Itza signified flaws in the sequence (1958: 44, 248, 254), but Smith believed that the linear reconstruction remained valid even without such evidence (1971: 170–71).

As the traditional model would predict, excavations at Chichen Itza yielded "the largest collection in existence" (1,053 sherds and 11 whole vessels) of Silho Fine Orange (Brainerd 1958: 57). By contrast, very little Balancan was recovered (1958: 34–45). Brainerd reported certain cases, however, where the contrast between Florescent and Early Mexican deposits at Chichen Itza seemed weak and of little utility for dating structures to one period or another. For example, in trenches excavated near the Akab'dzib, Balancan sherds were found with Tohil Plumbate (the Early Mexican substage diagnostic par excellence); "the deposit is limited to Florescent *and* Early Mexican date by its local wares, with indications of both periods in its tradewares" (1958: 35–36; emphasis mine). A similar case is that of the "Temple of the Three Lintels" (7B3), perhaps the best example of Pure Florescent, Puuc-style architecture at Chichen Itza. If the traditional chronology were correct, the Temple of the Three Lintels would be associated with Balancan group Fine Orange exclusively; Brainerd identified ceramics only of the Silho group (his "Chichen Fine Orange," 1958: 38). The collection from the Temple of the Three Lintels included sherds (especially slate wares) otherwise characteristic of *both* Brainerd's Florescent and Early Mexican complexes. Brainerd saw that a paradox existed here and suggested the sample provided evidence for a Florescent–Early Mexican transition (1958: 40). The traditional authors (Brainerd, Smith, and Andrews IV) assumed that the stylistic change from Maya to Toltec-Maya ceramics, architecture, and sculpture occurred "simultaneously, at the same rate, and from the same stimuli" (as Wendy Ashmore summarized the uniform and unilinear paradigm of northern Maya prehistory). Thus the paradox of finding typologically "later" sherds in an "earlier" building had either to be explained away or ignored.

Likewise the excavations in the Monjas complex "should" (according to traditional chronological interpretations of its architecture) have produced Florescent Balancan Fine Orange. The earlier construction phases of the Monjas epitomizes what is defined as the "Maya" period at Chichen Itza (Tozzer 1957: 23). But "all Monjas pottery collections . . . contain some pottery definitely belonging to the Early Mexican substage," and these same samples provided "one of the best type collections" for the Silho group (Brainerd 1958: 42–43). Brainerd admitted that the lack of Florescent deposits argued against dating the Monjas earlier than the Toltec structures at Chichen Itza. Brainerd even admitted that "the ceramic evidence can be interpreted to allow some overlapping for these [Maya and Toltec-Maya] occupations" (1958: 43–44).

Smith also mentions some instances in which Cehpech diagnostics (e.g., Balancan Fine Orange) are found in Sotuta contexts at Chichen Itza (1971: 260), but more important are his discussions of classification. Hints appear in a number of sources, of which Smith's is the earliest, that the Silho, Balancan, and Altar groups blend together typologically in ways that make rigid chronological distinctions among them difficult or impossible. Smith reports a vessel from Mayapan that cannot be clearly assigned to any one of the three styles, but is instead "something in between" (1971, Volume 2: 40; see Figure 2H of this article). Ball has also discussed the typological, chronological, and geographical blending of the several Fine Orange ceramic groups (1977a: 46).

Ball now agrees that his original (1977a) analysis of the Terminal Classic ceramics at Becan requires some revision (personal communication 1982, and this volume). Excavations did not provide evidence for a subdivision of the local Xcocom complex on the basis of stratigraphic superposition. Ball instead divided the Terminal Classic into early and late facets, defined by the presence or absence of Sotuta diagnostics such as Silho Orange or Tohil Plumbate. He noted that "the categorization of much plain ware as Altar Orange or Silho Orange is based primarily on context and is thus almost totally arbitrary" (1977a: 46–47). In other words, it was Tohil Plumbate whose presence or absence determined whether a given context belonged to the early or late facet of Xcocom. Implicitly, at Becan at least, there is evidence not only that Altar and Balancan Fine Orange chronologically overlap with Silho—the three groups appear to be closely related if not indistinguishable. Xcocom, then, ought not be divided into early and late facets without stratigraphic proof. Thus, in southern Campeche, the diagnostics of the Cehpech and Sotuta complexes apparently occur together and "contemporaneous availability" (Ball 1979a: 33) is indicated. Relatively uncommon "elite" wares such as Tohil Plumbate, Fine Orange, and Thin Slate (type Ticul Thin Slate, another Cehpech diagnostic found in Xcocom contexts at Becan), probably would not occur consistently together in all contexts, even if manufactured and used contemporaneously. Contemporaneity does not imply equality of access or identity of function among classes or types of ceramic wares.

The conclusion that Silho was manufactured at the same time as other Fine Orange groups should not surprise us. R. E. W. Adams reported a Jimba (Terminal Classic)–phase burial at Altar de Sacrificios that contained both Silho and Altar Orange vessels (1971: 106). He cited "generic resemblances between Pabellon [Terminal Classic Modeled-Carved Fine Orange] and the Toltec styles at Tula in Mexico and Chichen Itza" (1973: 146), and he seriously considered the possibility that "Toltec Chichen can be placed as beginning contemporarily with Terminal Classic in the Peten" (1973: 155). Even earlier, thirty years ago Robert E. Smith reported "X Fine Orange" from Tepeu 3 contexts at Uaxactun (1955: 28–30, 194–97). On this find Brainerd commented, in a rather obscure caption to "medium slateware bowls and grater bowls from Chichen Itza," that "Tepeu 3 may be of the same horizon as our early Mexican, since a Chichen Fine Orange bowl comes from the same subphase [i.e., Tepeu 3]" as "one grater bowl of form close to the Chichen Itza specimens" (1958: 260, Fig. 72). On purely typological grounds Smith later reassigned the Uaxactun examples of Silho group Kilikan Composite to the Early Postclassic Sotuta complex (Smith and Gifford 1966: 159).

The recent literature abounds with new discoveries of ceramics diagnostic of Sotuta found in association with those of Cehpech. Ball (1978: 138) and A. P. Andrews (1978b: 81–84; 1980a: 105) first reported data from the northern coast of Yucatan (especially Isla Cerritos) demonstrating the temporal equivalence of Silho Orange and Tohil Plumbate with at least one Cehpech diagnostic: Chablekal Gray. Andrews and Robles C. report that excavations at El Meco have produced massive quantities of such Pure Florescent pottery as Puuc Slate and Ticul Thin Slate in stratigraphic association with Modified Florescent Chichen Slate Ware, Silho Fine Orange, and Peto Cream Ware (personal communication 1982; Robles C. 1981a: 159–62). Research on Cozumel and at numerous sites along the east and northeast coasts of Yucatan has produced similar results (A. P. Andrews personal communication 1982). Although Robles C. reports no Fine Orange pottery from Coba, Puuc and Chichen Slate wares appear to overlap in time there (Robles C. 1980: 248–52, 281–92, 310–12). Scattered reports support a model of chronological overlap, such as that of a looted cache from Calotmul, which included a Silho pyriform vase (similar to a common Plumbate form) with a tripod Puuc Slate bowl, a characteristic Cehpech artifact (Andrews IV and Andrews V 1980: 280; see also Fig. 5.2).

Finally, substantial evidence has now accumulated documenting the presence of Sotuta-complex ceramics at Uxmal. Sáenz (1972, 1975b) has reported ceramics "corresponding to the Early Postclassic" (1972: 37). Konieczna and Mayer (1976: 6–9) also report "great quan-

171

tities" of Chichen Slate as well as Chichen Unslipped Ware (plain and striated) in contexts implying that "it is all contemporaneous with the Puuc-style ceramics, which is to say, it pertains to the Late Classic" (1976: 7; my translation). They also report finding all three groups of Fine Orange (Altar, Balancan, and Silho) at Uxmal (1976: 7). A. P. Andrews comments that the collections of Sáenz and Konieczna and Mayer include pottery identical to Sotuta complex materials from Chichen Itza itself (personal communication 1982). Finally, R. Maldonado Cárdenas (n.d.) has reported a dedicatory cache from the ball court at Uxmal (ball-court rings glyphically dated 10.3.15.16.14, Kelley 1982: Table 1) that included a single Silho-group (Kilikan Composite) tripod bowl sealed beneath a floor in clear, primary architectural context. For questions of chronology, it matters little whether the Sotuta pottery was imported from Chichen Itza or elsewhere, or manufactured at Uxmal. Certain structures at Uxmal that are integral to the layout of the Pure Florescent site were unquestionably constructed or at least significantly remodeled at a time when Sotuta ceramics were in use.

The meaning of the data remains unclear, because of insufficient information on the context, associations, and distributions of various ceramic wares at Uxmal. Probably only one period, the Terminal Classic, is represented. The modes and attributes that define Early Postclassic Sotuta-complex types may have a wider areal distribution than was previously believed, and certain vessel forms or decorative complexes may have a ritual or other specialized significance, thus accounting for intrasite irregularities in the occurrence of Early Postclassic pottery at both Chichen Itza and Uxmal. Another possibility is that the later construction phases of Uxmal indeed pertain to a Sotuta period contemporaneous with major Toltec architecture at Chichen, in which case the total overlap model of ceramic styles would stand refuted. But if future work determines that Uxmal flourished at the same time as Early Postclassic Chichen Itza, Mayanists will still be obliged to rethink completely both the traditional and the more recent schemes for interpreting prehistoric events in Terminal Classic–Early Postclassic northern Yucatan. Whatever the solution to the problem, it now seems irrefutable that major construction at Toltec Chichen Itza chronologically overlapped, partially or totally, equally major construction at Maya Uxmal.

Andrews V noted the virtually complete absence of Tohil Plumbate from Lowland Maya sites dated to the Terminal Classic as part of his argument that the Sotuta complex (and Silho Fine Orange) equated with the Early Postclassic (1979: 9, as quoted above). I have already reviewed evidence that Silho may be contemporaneous with the Altar and Balancan groups during the Terminal Classic. The case of Tohil Plumbate is even less clear. Almost universal agreement places the pan-Mesoamerican Plumbate horizon before A.D. 1200 in absolute time and after 10.4.0.0.0 in the Maya calendar in relative time (Shepard 1948: 103–37; Kelley 1976:32, criterion 1 for accepting or rejecting a correlation of the Maya and Christian calendars). Although Konieczna and Mayer mention Plumbate at Uxmal (1976: 9), they do not specify its provenience or quantity, and virtually no Plumbate has previously been found at the site (Brainerd 1958: 57). Adams reported only two Plumbate sherds at Altar de Sacrificios (1971: Fig. 74), Sabloff noted one at Seibal (1975: 225), and Robles C. found none in massive samples from the local Terminal Classic–Early Postclassic Oro complex at Coba (1980: 310–12).

Robles C. (1980: 312) and Andrews and Robles C. (1985) have proposed that competition or conflict between Chichen Itza and Coba prevented the diffusion of Plumbate and Silho Orange to the latter site. While such an explanation might work for Coba, I doubt that it could account for the more general absence of Plumbate from Terminal Classic Maya sites. In this connection, it is noteworthy that the supposed "late facet" of the Xcocom complex at Becan included more Tohil Plumbate than the Carnegie project found at Chichen Itza. Becan contexts yielded Plumbate in association with Ticul Thin Slate, a Cehpech-complex diagnostic (Ball 1977a: 135–37). "This suggests the existence of different trading patterns with not everyone getting the same items, even when they were geographically close" (Chase and Chase 1982: 611). Conversely, certain sites may have participated in similar exchange networks even though great distances separated them (e.g., Chichen Itza and Becan) and they had little else in common (i.e., there are no examples of "Toltec-Maya" art or architecture at Becan).

All of the foregoing suggests that we may be laboring under certain methodological and analytical handicaps. If pure deposits of Cehpech ceramics exist at Chichen Itza, it seems unlikely that Brainerd, Smith, and numerous other Carnegie Institution archaeologists would have missed them. Brainerd suggested pointedly, however, that Carnegie excavation techniques were not ideally suited to chronology building (1958: 43).

With regard to interpretations, Uxmal and Chichen Itza *might* have been built and occupied at the same time. If they were, it is clear that these cities did not extensively trade or exchange Fine Orange Silho, Balancan, or Tohil Plumbate with each other. Neither Brainerd's nor Smith's assumptions or procedures would have allowed the detection of such interaction if it existed, however, because of their prejudices about what the sequence should be. When considering the slate wares (see below) it becomes especially clear that whatever types or modes occurred predominantly in the Puuc region and not (or less frequently) at Chichen Itza became diagnostic of the Florescent, and whatever was encountered in greater quantity at Chichen Itza than in the Puuc defined Early Mexican. Thus, any trade goods from the Puuc found at Chichen Itza would be ascribed to stratigraphic "mixing" and would be assigned on typological grounds to the earlier period. Only absolute identity of ceramic inventories between Chichen Itza and the Puuc sites could have overridden the conclusions derived from a basic equation of cultural variability with chronological change and the historic assumption (inherited from Tozzer) of a linear temporal succession and replacement.

Constructing chronologies by stylistic seriation with somewhat rigid assumptions about typological change and replacement has created distortions that might not have emerged had more emphasis been placed on the strict interpretation of stratigraphic succession. Brainerd's analysis depended on a less formal classification system than Smith's type-variety method, and as a result, Brainerd was more open to the possibility that the ceramic and stratigraphic data might not be in perfect accord with the assumed chronological sequence. That Brainerd followed Tozzer in defending the correctness of the two-component (Maya and Toltec-Maya) model for Chichen Itza probably bespeaks Tozzer's persuasiveness and prestige more than Brainerd's own misinterpretations of the data. For Smith, the type-variety system mandated certain rules of what a ceramic complex should contain. These rules certainly weighed equally in shaping Smith's analysis, descriptions, and conclusions with the historical model of succession and replacement, which Smith accepted unquestioningly. The case cited above, in which Smith reassigned the Uaxactun examples of Silho Fine Orange from Tepeu 3 to Sotuta without reference to stratigraphic context, is a prime example of this classificatory rigidity. One must hope that the future of Maya ceramic studies will see the type-variety system modified by detailed attribute analyses and the determination of statistical ranges of variability in describing the contents of pottery groups and types.

The Majority Wares

Three "wares" comprise the overwhelming majority of the ceramics recovered at all sites of Cehpech/Sotuta date. First in importance are the "slateware" types (Vaillant 1927: 76; Brainerd's "Medium Slatewares" of the Florescent and Early Mexican substages [1958: 52–53, 55]; Smith's Puuc and Chichen Slate wares [1971: 16, 27–28]). Then there are the Puuc and Chichen Red wares (Brainerd 1958: 53–56; Smith 1971: 15–16, 27); and Puuc and Chichen Unslipped wares (Brainerd 1958: 52, 54–55; Smith 1971: 16–17, 28–29). Brainerd and Smith generally agree in describing the paired Puuc and Chichen Itza counterparts in the three wares as very similar.

It is not certain how meaningful in cultural or chronological terms the contrast between the pottery of the Puuc region and that of Chichen Itza really is, and how close or distant a taxonomic relationship should be inferred. That is, are Puuc and Chichen Slate varieties of the same type, types within a group, or two distinct wares, as Brainerd and Smith defined them? Most archaeologists working in northern Yucatan agree that the "slate wares" are in fact very similar, and that much more typological overlap between Puuc and Chichen Slate exists than the Brainerd and Smith classifications (as opposed to their descriptions) suggest. A simple example is "trickle" decoration, the use of which is an indistinguishable attribute of both Puuc and Chichen Slate wares (see Figure 5.5). Nor can the more complicated modes of rim decoration and design themes be regionally segregated into Puuc and Chichen patterns (see Figures 5.3 and 5.4). On the other hand, studies specifically designed to analyze these interregional ceramic relationships in a precise, quantitative fashion have yet to be carried out. Such data will only derive from future excavations at sites both on the northern plains and in the Puuc area. Chichen Slate has now been reported in stratigraphic association with Puuc Slate from Coba (Robles C. 1980: 248–52), El Meco (Robles C. 1981a: 159–62), elsewhere along the northern and eastern coasts of Yucatan (A. P. Andrews 1980a; personal

175

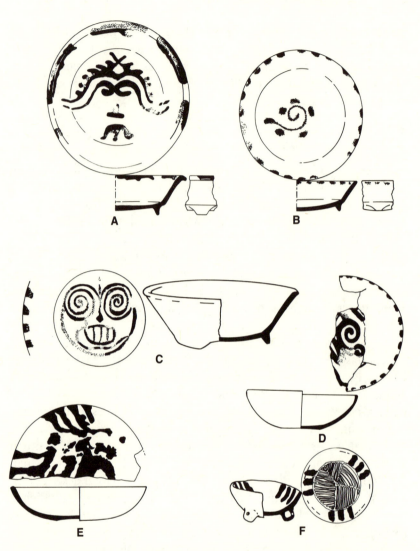

Figure 5.3 A & B: Sacalum Black-on-Slate: Sacalum Variety (Puuc Slate Ware). The bowl forms of Figure 3, A–E, constitute a continuum or "seriation" of vessel shapes. Figure 3A is most common in the Puuc region; Figure 3E is most common at Chichen Itza; the intermediate vessels display attributes found in both regions. The modes of rim ticking or rim bands and interior decoration likewise occur in varying frequencies on the slate wares from all over northern Yucatan. Compare the faces painted on the interior of Figures 3A and 3C with Figure 4B, which is a seriationally "intermediate" design between the other two. While insufficiently detailed stratigraphic stud-

ies are available, it seems as likely that the "seriation" of slate ware forms and decorative motifs could be diagnostic of spatial (intra-regional) as temporal variation. (Figure A is from Labna and B is from Ticul, both are adapted from Brainerd 1958: Figures 62q and 47i respectively). C: This vessel could be classified as either Sacalum Black-on-Slate or Balantun Black-on-Slate (the Chichen Slate Ware equivalent to Sacalum). This vessel is from the Caracol at Chichen Itza. (Figure C is adapted from Brainerd 1958: Figure 67a). D & E: Balantun Black-on-Slate: Balantun Variety (Chichen Slate Ware). This common type of the Sotuta Complex cannot be easily distinguished from its Cehpech counterpart in most modes of shape and decoration. Slip translucency is often considered diagnostic, as are certain forms. Curving vessel walls and lack of leg-supports are considered more characteristic of Chichen Slate bowls than Puuc Slate, but one may question whether there is any stratigraphic proof that this distinction has chronological significance. The rim ticks more often become elongated and curve into elaborte, less formal designs in Balantun Black-on-Slate than in Sacalum Black-on-Slate. (Figures D and E are adapted from Brainerd 1958: Figure 74d and Smith 1971, 2: Figure 13d). F: Balantun Black-on-Slate: Balantun Variety grater bowls from Las Monjas complex. Part of Brainerd's case that Early Mexican Chichen Itza at least partially equated in time with Tepeu 3 Uaxactun rested precariously on grater bowls. "Tepeu 3 . . . may be of the same horizon as our Early Mexican, since a Chichen Fine Orange bowl comes from the same sub-phase (as the Uaxactun grater bowls; Brainerd 1958: 260)." Similar grater bowls occur at Xpuhil, Seibal, and Altar de Sacrificios. Smith illustrates the Uaxactun grater bowls in his classic monograph (1955, 2: Figures 31,f,1-4; Figure F here is adapted from Brainerd 1958: Figure 74,h).

---

communication 1982), from Uxmal (Sáenz 1975a; Konieczna and Mayer 1976), and in fact from Chichen Itza itself (Brainerd 1958: 34–44, especially 43, 55; Smith 1971: 259–60). Brainerd and Smith did not believe that the observed association represented any ancient ceramic complex, but perhaps reflected postdepositional mixing during prehistoric building or reconstruction, or contamination of samples by Carnegie archaeologists (Brainerd 1958: 43). At Balankanche Cave, near Chichen Itza, Thin Slate was found sealed with Chichen Slate and Peto Cream (Andrews IV 1970: 66–68).

The above data, taken together, strongly suggest that the Sotuta and Cehpech ceramic complexes coexisted. But until the typological relationships of Puuc and Chichen Slate have been analyzed, taking ranges of normal variability (as opposed to abstracted "types") into account, the culture-historical significance of stratigraphic co-occurrence will remain conjectural. Future analyses of the range of attribual and

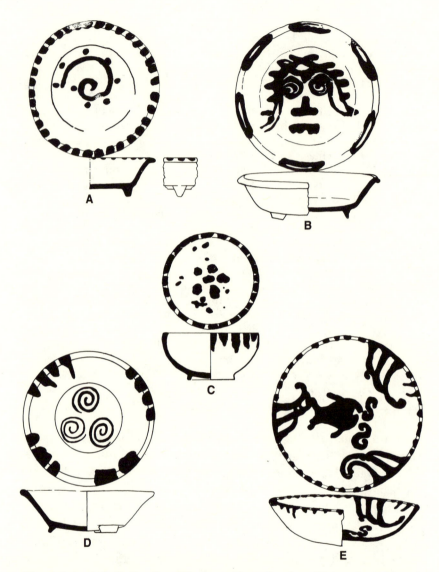

Figure 5.4 A & B: Sacalum Black-on-Slate: Sacalum Variety from Uxmal. These bowls exemplify the "partial overlap" in modes of design between the Puuc and Chichen Slate decorative repetoires. Unbiased samples from new, modern excavations might establish whether or not there are statistically significant differences in the frequency of certain formal or decorative attributes and modes between the Puuc and Chichen Itza regions. No unequivocal case of the presence or absence of certain traits has yet been advanced to distinguish between Pure and Modified Florescent ceramic deposits. (Figures

178

A & B are adapted from Brainerd 1958: Figures 47b & 47c respectively). C & D: Sacalum Black-on-Slate: Sacalum Variety from Mayapan, a well-documented site geographically intermediate between the Puuc and Chichen Itza Sotuta and Cehpech could not be stratigraphically isolated at Mayapan, supposedly owing to later mixing (Smith 1971, 1: 112; 1971,2: Table 24). Figure C is a basin form, common in Chichen Slate, while D is an example of a bowl with leg-supports but slightly curving walls, more similar to the supposedly predominant mode at Chichen Itza (Figures C & D are adapted from Smith 1971,2: Figures 26-b-19 and 26-b-23). *Figure E*: Balantun Black-on-Slate: Balantun Variety from Chichen Itza. The cache context of this "definitive" Early Mexican form in the Monjas suggests a paradox, in that the Monjas has always been considered one of the "definitive" Florescent buildings at Chichen (Brainerd 1959: 260; Figure E is adapted from Brainerd 1958: Figure 74c).

---

modal variations in the slate wares at any given site of the northern Maya Terminal Classic–Early Postclassic may well reveal so great a descriptive overlap between the assemblages at individual sites as to render invalid and irrelevant the simple contrast between two slate wares or two ceramic complexes.

In essence, the problem lies unsolved until further data become available from excavations specifically designed to address the problem. Published analyses are inadequate, as they lack descriptive precision and are contradictory. For example, the definition of Chichen Slate Ware is questionable. The modes and attributes that define this "ware" are only vaguely understood. Brainerd writes: "The primary sorting criteria between Florescent and Early Mexican Medium Slatewares were not those of ware (paste and slip), but of form and decoration" (1958: 55). Smith likewise comments: "The ceramic complex [Cehpech or Sotuta] of a slate sherd having red paste, volcanic ash temper, and no distinguishing decorative features can only be recognized by its shape" (1971: 178). There is, however, significant overlap of decorative techniques and of Chichen Itza and Puuc Slate forms, as both Brainerd (1958: 52–53, 55) and Smith (1971: 153, 177–78) detail. These two authorities do not agree on the criteria for distinguishing Puuc from Chichen Slate Ware. They both nevertheless describe these "wares" as characteristic (if not easily diagnostic) of two distinct and sequential periods, the Terminal Classic Cehpech and the Early Postclassic Sotuta. It is not at all certain that to define "true" Chichen Slate as "opaque white-slipped" (Andrews IV and Andrews V 1980:

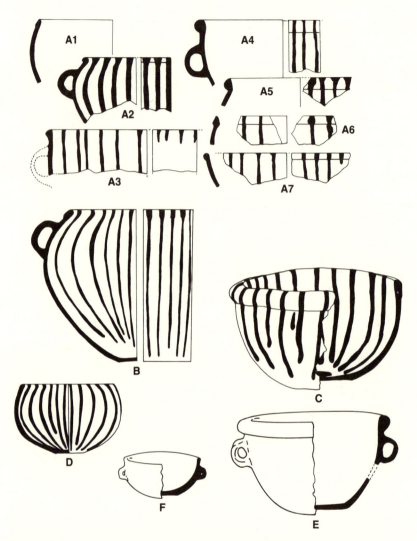

Figure 5.5 A: Such supposedly time-sensitive modes as those of shape and decoration frequently do not aid in the sorting of Chichen from Puuc slate wares. All sherds in Figure 5A come from Chichen Itza, but on varying grounds of paste color and slip translucency or opaqueness, Smith has distinguished both wares in this collection. As noted throughout this paper, neither Brainerd nor Smith produced conclusive stratigraphy at either Chichen or any Puuc site to support the hypothesized replacement of Cehpech by Sotuta. In particular, Smith comments that the forms of 4 and 6 commonly occur in both Chichen and Puuc slate wares. (Figure 5A is adapted in whole from Smith 1971, 2: Figure 16a–g, by permission of the Peabody Museum).

1 is a Dzitas Slate: Dzitas variety undecorated basin, Sotuta Complex. 2 is a Balantun Black-on-Slate: Balantun Variety restricted basin, illustrating the characteristic northern Yucatecan "trickle-on-cream" decoration, with handle and rim forms typical of Chichen Slate. 3 & 5 are Sacalum Black-on Slate, the Puuc Slate equivalent of Balantun. 4 could belong to either category. 6 could likewise be classed as either Chumayel Red-on-Slate (Puuc Slate Muna Group) or Balm Canche Red-on-Slate (Chichen Slate Dzitas Group). Smith identifies this particular sherd as Chumayel. 7 is Sacalum Black-on-Slate. B: Balantun Black-on-Slate: Balantun Variety Basin. This is a very common from at Chichen Itza. (Figure B is adapted from Smith 1971: Figure 15e). C: Sacalum Black-on-Slate: Sacalum Variety from Labna. Restricted bowls or basins appear to be equally common in the Puuc at at Chichen Itza. Likewise, the most common handle appendages and rolled or reinforced rim morphologies appear to be equally common in both areas. (Figure C is adapted from Brainerd 1958: Figure 43a). D: Balantun Black-on-Slate: Balantun Variety from Chichen Itza. Exhibits typical northern Lowland trickle decoration on a restricted basin. Not surprisingly, this simple rim form is equally frequent in the Puuc and Chichen Itza regions. (Figure C is adapted from Smith 1971: Figure 13h). E: Muna Slate: Muna Variety basin from Sabacche. (Figure E is adapted from Brainerd 1958: Figure 43b). F: Dzitas Slate: Dzitas Variety from the Caracol at Chichen Itza. A Sotuta Complex unrestricted basin with appendage handles (compare with Figures C–E). A few illustrations in an article such as this cannot possibly convey the range of variability in the northern Yucatecan collections. The best source for a real picture of the known diversity is Brainerd (1958; Figure F is adapted from Brainerd 1958: Figure 74f).

---

274) adequately portrays the complexities involved (cf. Brainerd 1958: 55; Smith 1971: 177). In fact, the only consistent conclusion one may draw with certainty from the descriptions provided by both authors is that the range of variation in ceramic decorative and formal modes is greater at Chichen Itza: the range of variation is much greater than at any other Maya site studied to date. To summarize: the descriptive contrast between Chichen and Puuc Slate wares is minimal, and the culture-historical meaning of what variation does exist remains unknown.

Although the red and unslipped wares have received less attention than the slate wares, much the same generalizations appear to apply. Differences in decorative norms are minor, and shape modes are argued to be most diagnostic (Brainerd 1958: 52–57; Smith 1971: 173, 177, 181). Both authors agree that the Chichen and Puuc variants of the red and unslipped wares are very similar and difficult to sort with certainty (see also Brainerd 1958: 248, Fig. 68). As noted above, Chichen Unslipped Ware, plain and striated, has been reported from Uxmal (Konieczna and Mayer 1976: 7).

One might reasonably ask how Brainerd and Smith distinguished the Cehpech and Sotuta complexes to begin with, since they are described as so similar typologically. Brainerd saw the problem in analytical methodology most clearly. There was no definite ceramic stratigraphy at Chichen Itza in which Early Mexican pottery overlay Florescent deposits, so "all sherds not fitting into the Puuc repertory and having a light slip color were assumed to be of the Early Mexican substage" (Brainerd 1958: 55).

Brainerd further explained what he saw as the weakness of his approach:

The sorting of Medium Slateware at Chichen Itza suffers, as does all sorting there, from lack of pure deposits of Florescent date. The Puuc collections were substituted for such a standard in the sorting and non-Puuc-like Medium Slateware assumed to be Early Mexican. (1958: 254, Fig. 71)

Smith believed the linear sequence could stand as a sequence even without stratigraphic proof, as he explained in commenting on Brainerd's concern over methodology just quoted:

We have approached the problem somewhat differently. Instead of worrying about not finding pure deposits of Chichen Itza Cehpech pottery, we felt that at a site where the principal part of the visible *architecture* was Sotuta Phase, there must exist refuse dumps containing pottery representative of this cultural phase, unencumbered by earlier or later sherds in any quantity. (1971: 171; emphasis mine)

In sum, the Yucatecan slate wares, red wares, and unslipped wares, like Fine Orange Ware, probably vary due to synchronous regionalism, capricious patterns of exchange, and undetermined functional differences rather than differences in time (Robles C. 1980: 294–316; Chase and Chase 1982: 608–11; Andrews and Robles C. n.d.). Stylistic divergence between the ceramics of different regions of the Northern Maya Lowlands appears at least as early as the Late Formative (Brainerd 1958: 44; Andrews V, personal communication 1981). The construction of regional chronologies has geographic as well as diachronic components and implications (Ball 1977a: 46; Harrison 1980).

182

Brainerd and Smith both assumed that Tozzer (1930, 1957) and J. E. S. Thompson (1945) had already established beyond reasonable doubt that Chichen Itza flourished on a later, completely different, time horizon from the Puuc sites. Robert E. Smith's statement quoted above draws particular interest, because he pointed to "Sotuta Phase" *architecture* as the definitive proof that the predominant, "Toltec" ceramics at Chichen Itza came later than the "Cehpech" cities of the Puuc. Referring to architectural or sculptural complexes by ceramic designations is at best a circular argument for dating one set of remains or another. Further, just as there is no good ceramic stratigraphy to prove that the Toltec period postdates the Maya at Chichen Itza and/ or other sites, neither is there any such architectural stratigraphy.[9]

ARCHITECTURE AND SETTLEMENT PATTERN

Nowhere do we see a veneer-vaulted structure with Pure Florescent or Puuc-style sculpture buried beneath a similarly vaulted structure with Modified-Florescent sculpture. Indeed, given that the figural sculptures of Toltec Chichen and the various Puuc sites blend together (Proskouriakoff 1950: 154–72), sharing specific traits, elements of style, and patterns of composition, it might be difficult to identify or interpret such a case of stratigraphc succession even if one were found (cf. also Kubler 1975: 185–98; Lincoln 1982). More concretely, where a succession of superimposed buildings has been encountered at Chichen Itza, the sequence documented is one of replacement and enlargement of the same architectural types.

The Castillo and Castillo-sub have very similar temple superstructures and decoration, although the Castillo-sub pyramid has only one, northward facing, stairway while the Castillo has four, of which the most important faces north. The Caracol is the last of a sequence of circular structures. The Temple of the Warriors and its enclosed Temple of the Chac Mool have almost identical ground plans, varying only in scale. The Monjas building represents the progressive enlargement of a range structure built on a high plinth. Only in the Group of the Initial Series (5C) or House of the Phalli, where George Vaillant excavated, is there some evidence for the replacement of one structure type by another, probably indicating a change in function. Unfortunately Vaillant's methodology and reporting do not allow a convincing reconstruction of this sequence to be made (Ruppert 1952: Appendix I).

To recapitulate some of the points made earlier in this paper, the key feature of the argument—advanced twenty years ago by E. Wyllys Andrews IV—for including both Puuc and Toltec architecture in the Florescent tradition was the occurrence of the finest veneer-vault and wall masonry in the finest buildings both at Uxmal and related sites *and* at Chichen Itza. While Andrews IV never broke with the traditional model of succession and replacement, his argument now seems like the cornerstone of the "overlap" chronology. Nontechnological aspects of architecture that bear on culture-historical reconstructions include the typology of ground plans and the organization of interior and exterior space at Chichen Itza in contrast to those at other Maya sites (cf. Pollock 1965; Chase and Chase 1982). The diversity in building types at Chichen, as already discussed here, probably indicates comparatively greater social complexity within the city of the "Itza." While building types or ground plans, like any formal criteria, may be chronologically diagnostic, the evidence from recent fieldwork at Chichen Itza strongly suggests that structure types which Tozzer ascribed to his Chichen I, Chichen II, and Chichen III phases (1957: 20–65) occur together in regular and predictable patterns, more indicative of functional integration than chronological dispersal (Lincoln and Anderson, in preparation).

With regard to the issue of Maya and Toltec Chichen, one settlement-pattern datum is most important: in most medium-sized to large architectural groups, structures assigned by typology to the two ethnic groups or Tozzer's three periods consistently occur together, laid out in relation to one another around plazas or on the same platform-terraces. For example, the Monjas, Caracol, and Temple of the Wall panels seem oriented toward one another as in a plaza (in CIW map quadrants 3–4C). The Initial Series/House of the Phalli group (in quadrant 5C) constitutes an even more positive example. Here the House of the Phalli (a typically Maya range structure) and Structure 5C2 (a colonnade with a broad stairway) face each other on the southern and northern flanks, respectively, of a plaza bordered on the east by Structure 5C4 (the Temple of the Initial Series, a Toltec-type temple wherein the original context of the famous hieroglyphic lintel is lost), and 5C11 (a small room with Toltec-style atlantean figures) on the

184

west (see Ruppert 1952). While Vaillant recovered some stratigraphic details regarding the construction and modification of individual structures, there was no positive evidence of the ordering of these particular constructions relative to one another. Vaillant's ceramic collections were lost before Brainerd had the chance to examine them. All buildings in the 5C group stand on the same terrace or substructural platform.

Another such cluster of Maya and Toltec-type buildings sharing the same platform is the complex designated on the Carnegie map as 5D1–5D3. This group includes a range structure (5D2, representing Tozzer's Chichen I), a "typical Toltec temple" (5D1 representing Chichen II), a gallery-patio structure (5D3, Tozzer's Chichen III), and (not shown on the CIW map) an I-shaped ball court, another two-room Toltec temple with twin column entrance, and a colonnade. This specific list of structure types appears to be typical of Chichen Itza. In a group just west of the 5D1–3 platform, identified only by the number 5D4 on the Carnegie map, new, detailed mapping undertaken last year has revealed that the two already located platforms, connected by a *sacbe*, together support two Toltec-type temples, a range structure, a gallery-patio structure, a colonnade, and several smaller altars and less distinctive remains (Lincoln 1983; Lincoln and Anderson, in preparation).

One last example, although not recorded on the Carnegie map, shows that the most impressive architectural compound at Chichen Itza conforms to the pattern associating range structures, Toltec temples, gallery-patios, and colonnades first noted in the smaller groups. Sacbe 6 links the central, Toltec platform (*Gran Nivelación*) at Chichen with what Ruppert called the East Group (1950: 150), a little over a kilometer east of the Court of the Thousand Columns. The East Group is found to include the only "palace type" structure at Chichen Itza with Classic Puuc boot-shaped veneer vault stones. It is also the only such structure known from Chichen with what appear to be two stories of vaulted rooms (the upper story is badly ruined; photo in Schmidt 1981: 62, Figure 6). The platform of the East Group supports a Toltec-style colonnade in addition to the range structure. Thus, if the *gran nivelación* and East Group are taken as a unit, then the site core of Chichen Itza includes a Puuc-style palace along with the colonnades, gallery-patio-type Mercado, Temple of the Warriors, the Great and

Lesser ball courts, as well as altars and other smaller constructions. In short, it appears that the pattern of group composition typical of secondary complexes characterizes the largest, also.

In short, as Chase and Chase (1982) previously indicated, Tozzer's Chichen I, II, and III phases are most likely contemporaneous. We add here that these "phases," as typological entities, may in fact designate functionally complementary subcomplexes of architecture and perhaps iconography as well.

Settlement patterns suggest a few additional points about Maya and Toltec architecture at Chichen Itza. As the report above on the East Group reiterates, the volumetrically dominant core of Chichen Itza on the central or Toltec platform is connected by *sacbeob* to smaller, outlying Maya groups. Another example is the Temple of the Four Lintels, with its extensive hieroglyphic inscriptions and nonveneer vault architecture, which is linked to the *Gran Nivelación* by *Sacbeob* 4 and 7, assuming that these were originally continuous (Ruppert 1952: Figure 151).

From the standpoint of culture history, comparison of settlement patterns shows that Chichen Itza directly and immediately precedes Mayapan. Great continuity or identity in structure types and group layouts can be seen between Chichen Itza and Mayapan in the Carnegie maps of those sites (for Mayapan see Pollock et al. 1962). Colonnaded structures, two-room temples with twin-column entrances, and rooms with interior elevations or "altars" are examples of the unusual "Toltec" patterns that relate these two sites. The complex at Chichen Itza known as "The Group of the Bird Cornice" (5A1–5B1) has a layout indistinguishable from the Mayapan pattern, for example, but with architecture that is technologically Puuc-style veneer or Pure Florescent, typical of Toltec Chichen. Structure types similar to those shared by Chichen Itza and Mayapan also commonly occur in sites along the East Coast of Quintana Roo during the Mayapan-Tulum Postclassic horizon (F. Robles, T. Gallareta, and R. Cobos, personal communications 1983).

Given that the Mayapan Postclassic is traditionally interpreted as a period of Maya cultural resurgence after the Toltec domination at Chichen Itza, it is noteworthy that the continuity in structure typology involves those building plans considered characteristic of Toltec rather than Maya Chichen. If ethnicity were the cause of variation in structure types, one might expect range structures to predominate at Mayapan. If Maya and Toltec-type architecture are in fact primarily distinguished by function, it seems easier to understand that in fact, the fundamental innovations that reshaped Maya politics at Chichen Itza survived after the onset of the "Decadent" Postclassic.

CONCLUSIONS

The traditional proposition that Toltec Chichen Itza temporally followed and culturally replaced Maya Chichen Itza relied on a series of assumptions about the archaeological data in question. It presumed the existence at Chichen of a Maya ceramic complex equivalent in time and typology to that found in the Puuc Hills region of Yucatan. This Maya pottery was then presumed to be associated with Maya architecture, as identified principally by the presence of hieroglyphic inscriptions, the absence of "Toltec" sculpture, and a building ground-plan type that we would now refer to as that of a range structure. Scholars assumed without further investigation that "Maya Chichen Itza" constituted a coherent, internally organized community, as contrasted with another "Toltec" urban layout. Most important of all, Toltec Chichen Itza was viewed as radically different from all other northern and southern Lowland Maya sites. The city was seen to be so different from all others in eastern Mesoamerica as to lead to the twin inferences of invasion and ethnic replacement from another part of Mexico, specifically from Tula, Hidalgo.

The present paper has been aimed at undoing, to a greater or lesser degree, the factual basis for this now classic perspective on Chichen Itza. One large segment was devoted to showing that there is no "Maya Florescent" or Cehpech ceramic complex at Chichen Itza. At least, no such entity has ever been stratigraphically isolated from the dominant "Toltec" or Early Postclassic Sotuta-phase pottery. During the discussion of ceramics, it also became clear that where collections have been adequately curated for later study, as with the Monjas collections examined by Brainerd, Sotuta ceramics are as strongly associated with "Maya Florescent" structures as with those definitive of "Toltec Modified Florescent" Chichen Itza. A task which the present author hopes to undertake in the not-too-distant future is to test different structure types systematically to determine whether any particular ceramic complex can be associated with one structure type or another. Such association might exist to indicate building chronology or building function.

187

The best guess at the present time is that no regular distinctions in ceramic associations will differentiate structure types.

Along similar lines, another major point of this paper is that the correlation of highly phonetic inscriptions with private residences and highly pictorial iconographic messages of power with public places is most consistent with a social and functional interpretation of the contrast between Maya and Toltec at Chichen Itza. While this correlation is logical and explains part of the situation at Chichen, it is also true that five well-documented examples show the direct association of Maya hieroglyphs with Toltec figural or iconographic sculpture in Toltec buildings (the Temple of the High Priest's Grave, the Caracol, the Great Ball Court, Structure 6E1, and the Castillo of Old Chichen). Two other Toltec-type structures, the Temple of the Hieroglyphic Jambs and the Temple of the One Lintel, also bear Maya inscriptions, so that the use of glyphic texts as a criterion for identifying Maya as opposed to Toltec structures is also suspect.

In the realm of settlement pattern analysis, a pattern of integration rather than segregation characterizes the distribution of Maya and Toltec-type structures at Chichen Itza. This interpretation does not seem to support the idea of a two-phase sequence and ethnic replacement. My own recent mapping and reconnaissance work has confirmed this impression derived from examination of the Carnegie Institution map of the site. These new survey data are still being analyzed, however, and more fieldwork will be needed before final and conclusive statements can be made (Lincoln and Anderson, in preparation). Obviously, excavation will finally confirm or invalidate the inferences drawn from surface inspection only.

What this paper has touched on least is Chichen Itza's relations outside the Maya Lowlands. The site has traditionally been tied to Tula, Hidalgo, on grounds of architectural and sculptural similarity. Recently, evidence has been presented that some of the parallels between Chichen Itza and Tula reflect archaeological reconstruction rather than archaeological evidence (Molina Montes 1982). Kubler (1975: 199–201) was the first to point out that Tula, Hidalgo, in fact displays only a fraction of the artistic variety and "cosmopolitan" richness that exists at Chichen Itza. I believe that subsets of the totality of sculptured monuments at Chichen have parallels at many sites in Mexico: at Mitla, Tajin, Xochicalo, Tenochtitlan, and even at Tula.

188

Of these, however, only the Aztec imperial capital of Tenochtitlan is fully comparable in scope and urban character to Chichen Itza.

The question of external connections leads us to the last problem to be considered here, the absolute chronology and placement of Chichen Itza in Mesoamerica. On the one hand, much of this paper has been devoted to arguing that Toltec Chichen Itza is in fact a Terminal Classic Maya site. On the other hand, I believe that, in terms of connections with Central Mexico, Chichen Itza *by any criteria* must be more closely related to Tenochtitlan than to Tula or Teotihuacan. Indeed, a chronology that would shorten the timespan separating Terminal Classic Chichen Itza and the foundation and growth of the Aztec capital seems extremely desirable. It is difficult to envision how this might be accomplished within the confines of the Thompson correlation.

The absolute timing could be reworked in several ways. In the Thompson correlation, Chichen Itza probably dates to between A.D. 800 and 1000. If the Temple of the High Priest's Grave is correctly placed in the Long Count at 10.8.10.11.0, one might argue that the site continued past 1000, perhaps to A.D. 1100. The traditional dates for Mayapan are A.D. 1250–1450. The strong similarities between buildings and settlement patterns at Chichen Itza and Mayapan preclude the insertion of a 100-year gap between them. I regard the close similarity between these two sites, and their cultural-generic and temporal proximity, as incontrovertible facts. Thus, one compromise might be to arrange the chronological column so that Mayapan begins at A.D. 1100. While a 300-year timespan is credible for Chichen Itza, it is not for Mayapan. Even the traditional 250 years allotted for Mayapan seems like a great deal of time for the little evidence available for structural remodeling and superposition of structures. One possibility, more attractive in terms of archaeological relationships between the Classic and Postclassic in Yucatan, would be to end Chichen Itza at A.D. 1050 and run Mayapan thereafter until A.D. 1300 at the latest. This chronology will withstand any criticism except ethnohistory, which fairly positively indicates that Mayapan was abandoned 100 years or so before the conquest.

The traditional solution was to count backward from Mayapan 200 or 250 years, then insert "Early Postclassic" Chichen Itza, and finally reach the Late Classic. One might say that the traditional model of

Northern Lowland prehistory was the only archaeologically possible justification for the Thompson correlation. If one accepts "overlap," the temporal equation of Toltec Chichen Itza with the Terminal Classic period, one must either throw out one of the few consistent and relatively positive statements in all of Maya ethnohistory (see note 6), which is that concerning the comparatively recent date for the fall of Mayapan, or abandon the Thompson correlation.

While either solution is possible, I insist that the relative chronology should read as follows. Puuc architecture began to take its classic or "Pure Florescent" shape sometime around 9.14.0.0.0 or shortly thereafter. Chichen Itza, counted as a single, whole community, taking Maya and Toltec elements together, probably began to emerge just after 9.19.0.0.0. At this time, its nearest neighbors were probably Ek Balam (with an early 10th cycle stela), Izamal, and Ichmul I [see *Atlas* sheets 16Q-d(8, 9, and 12); Garza T. de Gonzalez and Kurjack 1980]. These sites lie at an average distance of 53.7 kilometers from Chichen Itza, essentially typical for the dispersion of Late Classic Maya centers in the Southern Lowlands (Peter Mathews, personal communication 1984). By 10.4.0.0.0, Chichen Itza may well have come to dominate these polities in the north, in addition to centers nearer-by such as Ichmul de Morley and Tzebtun, as well as Isla Cerritos, perhaps, on the north coast near Rio Lagartos [Atlas 16Q-d(3); A. P. Andrews and F. Robles C., personal communications 1983–84].

Chichen Itza may have continued as late as 10.9.0.0.0, because of the date on Column 4 of the High Priest's Grave, but by this time Mayapan was already in existence and expanding its influence. A hundred years later, by 10.14.0.0.0, Chichen Itza had ceased to exist as a major population center and Mayapan was probably just past its peak of greatest development. The major question, to my mind, is whether 10.14.0.0.0 fell in A.D. 1106, as it would according to the Thompson correlation, or between 1322 and 1362, as it would if David H. Kelley's new (1983) correlation, or the more traditionally derived 11.3.0.0.0 correlation were correct.

In any event, at Chichen Itza at least, "overlap" is no longer either an issue or a particularly useful concept to consider. There are *not* two distinctive entities, Maya and Toltec, which may or may not temporally equate or "overlap" in time. The problem worthy of study is to define the nature and causes of architectural and sculptural variabilty at this incredibly diverse or cosmopolitan urban center. Particularly, what social and political structures generated and/or were supported by the numerous architectural/functional components of the volumetrically large "elite ceremonial" platform compounds? Did these social structures also demand a diversity of iconographic modes of communication? It is worthy of mention that the internal dimensions of the art and iconography of Toltec Chichen alone, never mind its integration with Maya Chichen, have never been explored.

Once Chichen Itza can be understood on its own terms, it will become more possible to compare it with other, simpler sociopolitical systems in the Puuc and southern Maya regions. One hopes that future archaeological and art-historical research will proceed without the anthropologically obsolete equation of material-cultural with ethnic variability. Because of the evidence that all Maya and Toltec traits are integrated in a regular and consistent pattern within Chichen Itza, functional hypotheses should take priority in the design of all future investigations.

NOTES

1. Acknowledgments: This article began as the term paper for Gordon R. Willey's Seminar on Middle American Archaeology at Harvard University, fall semester, 1981–82. Dr. Willey has given me much guidance and encouragement throughout.

Discussions with Peter Mathews, codirector of that same graduate seminar, have had an immeasurably beneficial impact on the research and writing of this paper, from its inception to its much revised completion. I naturally hold him responsible for any errors I may have made in the interpretation of glyphs and iconography. Peter Mathews was also kind and generous enough with his time and talent to draw Column 4 of the Temple of the High Priest's Grave especially for inclusion as Figure 5.1.

Edward B. Kurjack, likewise, has had an early and formative role in the evolution of my thinking on the Terminal Classic. It was he who first suggested I tackle the "overlap" issue. His help and guidance in dealing with the literature, and understanding the contradictions inherent in all things, has been invaluable. Kurjack has also been my "expeditionary" adviser, in all matters archaeological and Yucatecan during the past five field seasons (1979–83).

Joseph W. Ball shared a great deal of time and his vast knowledge of Maya ceramics with me during various stimulating and crucial conversations during my research. Fernando Robles Castellanos, too, provided me his own perspectives and clarified many points on the ceramic sequences from Coba and other sites in Quintana Roo. Rubén Maldonado Cárdenas and Anthony P.

Andrews have generously offered me their well-informed points of view, providing useful hints about the nature of the problem in general, as well as unpublished details concerning the presence of Sotuta complex ceramics at Uxmal.

Wendy Ashmore suggested some badly needed clarifications in the text, as did many friends who read the seemingly infinite number of preliminary versions of this paper. Chief among these are Clemency C. Coggins and Patricia K. Anderson. Patricia also prepared the ceramic illustrations (Figures 5.2–5.5).

To my undergraduate adviser at Tulane, E. Wyllys Andrews V, I owe some very special debts. He has never failed to offer corrections, comments, criticisms, mild censorship, and generally great encouragement and guidance to me, since my first course in archaeology. I thank him and Jeremy A. Sabloff for inviting me to submit this paper at the last minute.

2. Correlation: all dates cited within the text are presented in terms of the Thompson or 11.16.0.0.0 correlation, except where alternatives are specifically noted. However, the author strongly believes that serious consideration should be given both to Arlen F. Chase's revival of the Vaillant/Wauchope 11.3.0.0.0 correlation and to David H. Kelley's new 663310 correlation (216 years later than Thompson but about 40 years shy of the 11.3.0.0.0; Kelley 1983).

3. Ceramics take precedence over other lines of evidence because of their universal applicability to every site younger than 2000 B.C. in Mesoamerica. The present paper does not focus on ceramics to the exclusion of hieroglyphic, iconographic, and architectural lines of evidence, but the author believes that the final resolution of the question of chronology at Chichen Itza can only be resolved through stratigraphic analysis of the culture-historical sequence. In particular, an effort must be made to find some positive earlier and later stratigraphic brackets indicating exactly what came before and after the Sotuta Complex. The present best guess might be that a Tepeu 2–related slateware complex (cf. Copo 1 at Dzibilchaltun or Smith's "Motul" phase?) came before, with the Tases complex of Mayapan evolving immediately afterward.

4. Henry B. Roberts's study of Yucatan pottery was never completed. George W. Brainerd later made use of Roberts's incomplete field notes and the collections (whose bags and labels were found in a somewhat decayed condition) reported to have totaled between 100,000 and 300,000 sherds (Brainerd 1958: 5–6). This enormous sample resulted from 15 years of Sylvanus G. Morley's immense Carnegie Institution of Washington Chichen Itza Project but, owing to poor curation, was almost entirely useless.

Brainerd, most unfortunately, never conducted his own excavations at Chichen Itza. R. E. Smith did, during 1954, conduct 19 trenching operations at Chichen Itza, but none of these was conducted with the purpose of relating architectural stratigraphy and ceramic sequence (since Smith took the chronological position of Toltec Chichen as an assumption). Smith's primary aim was to produce samples for typological analysis and description, but what stratigraphy was encountered he considered consistent with the traditional chronology (1971: 5, 9, 259–60).

The first published appearance of Vaillant's sequence is in the CIW Annual Report (Morley 1931). Vaillant himself published a slightly revised version in his 1935 summary.

Numbers such as "5C," "5D1–3," "6E1," and "7B3" refer to the J. O. Kilmartin map of Chichen Itza (published by Karl Ruppert in 1935: Figure 350 and [with revisions] in 1952: Figure 151). At best, the Kilmartin map covers the central third of the total site area of Chichen Itza.

5. One can only bemoan the monstrous terminological confusion here (see Table 5.1). Tozzer defined the earliest phase at Chichen Itza as "Maya" and the later as "Toltec-Maya." His primary concern was to indicate ethnicity as a cultural determinant. Brainerd used the terms "Florescent" and "Early Mexican" to equate with Tozzer's Maya and Toltec-Maya respectively. Brainerd's (1958) phase names implied evolutionary stages of northern Maya culture history while retaining and indeed amplifying the ethnic contrast between the "Maya" Classic and the "Mexican" Postclassic. Andrews IV (1965a, 1965b) partially retained Brainerd's nomenclature but tried to downplay the evolutionary and ethnic implications. Andrews IV also made his phases reflect his concern with architecture more than ceramics, which Brainerd had emphasized, or figural sculpture, which Tozzer had emphasized (1930, 1957). Thus Brainerd's Florescent became "Pure Florescent" and Early Mexican became "Modified Florescent" (emphasizing the continuity in basic architectural technology which Tozzer and Brainerd had not seen as particularly important). Smith (1971), following the practice of the type-variety system, gave the time periods in question ceramic complex labels without cultural evolutionary or ethnic significance. Smith's "Cehpech" equates temporally and substantively with Andrews' Pure Florescent, and "Sotuta" corresponds to modified Florescent. It was impossible to standardize terminology in this paper, one of whose purposes is to examine the intellectual development of our present understanding of the Northern Lowland chronology and to preserve the terminology used in its historical context (when referring to the work of various earlier scholars). To standardize the terminology would be to assume the correctness of one historical interpretation or another, thereby negating the purpose of this paper.

6. Ball (1974a, 1979a, 1979b, and this volume) and A. Chase (this volume) have followed suit in attempting to reconstruct preconquest chronology, applicable to archaeological data of the Terminal Classic–Early Postclassic horizon in Yucatan, based on varying interpretations of the postconquest Spanish and Maya documentary sources, especially the Books of Chilam Balam. I doubt that this procedure will resolve the chronological problems of the archaeological record. J. E. S. Thompson and A. M. Tozzer spent years trying to synthesize archaeological and ethnohistoric data, and new perspectives and changed assumptions seem unlikely to make these documents a more fruitful ground for archaeological reconstruction. The Books of Chilam

Balam are mystic, calendrically oriented mythologies that treat secular history as a kind of epiphenomenon to the great procession of the ordered, regular events mandated or explained by calendric prophesy and the actions of the gods. My interpretation is closer to that of M. S. Edmonson (1978: 9–18, 1982: xvi–xx). Edmonson has interpreted the Chilam Balam of Tizimin as providing meager information on any but the last 100 years or so of preconquest history. As Edmonson suggested (1979), however, the Books of Chilam Balam can and do offer insights into the deeply rooted preconquest Maya social order (e.g., kinship), religious cosmology, and ideology. Beyond the chronicles, it is a pity that archaeologists have not yet begun to exploit other kinds of ethnohistoric data, particularly the archival sources for community organization, social, political, and economic life which have been described for colonial Yucatan (e.g. Roys 1939: P. C. Thompson 1978).

Dates from the hieroglyphic inscriptions, while rarer in the Northern than in the Southern lowlands, nonetheless offer the archaeologist's best guide to both absolute and relative chronology. The only other available dating method is radiocarbon, which has certainly produced less than completely satisfactory results in the Maya area (see A. Chase's chapter in this volume and note 9 below). Carbon-14 techniques, at best, are insufficiently precise to distinguish, for example, between models of "partial" and "total" overlap as discussed with reference to Chichen Itza.

One goal of future research should be to carry forward the work begun by Proskouriakoff (1950) of relating hieroglyphic dates to styles of carving. From a chronology of figural sculpture one might be able to develop a series of independent checks on architectural and even ceramic sequences, especially in the Northern Lowlands where representational art is often integrated into structural decoration in facades, doorways, and on columns or pilasters. This procedure promises more consistent and comparable results than further experimentation with the documents. Sabloff's discussion of the similarities in style and iconography of figural portrayal on Bayal Period Fine Orange ceramics and Terminal Classic stelae at Seibal is an example of the sort of research suggested (1970: 403–4, 1973: 125–26), but should be extended by consideration of the material in question in greater detail.

7. Narrowly defined types of pottery from any given site, period, or complex are likely to be misleading with regard to ranges of variability within any given context or class. No studies have yet been done which describe types *in terms of* ranges of variability and overlap between taxonomic units. Therefore, the reader should consult one or both of the standard sources on the ceramics of Chichen Itza (Brainerd's *Archaeological Ceramics* and Smith's *Pottery of Mayapan*) for a wider range of illustrations than it has been possible to include in this paper (Figures 5.2–5.5, but also see the illustrations in Robles C. and Andrews, this volume).

Of the standard sources, Brainerd (1958) provides a far better range of variation for each pottery type in his illustrations, especially with regard to such attributes as rim form and vessel shape. Brainerd also juxtaposes Chichen

194

and Puuc varieties of the unslipped, red, slate, and fine orange wares in the same illustrations, along with examples of sherds which are "intermediate between Florescent and Early Mexican" (1958: 258, Fig. 73; see also Fig. 48 and p. 196. Most of the relevant illustrations in Brainerd are found in Figures 67–91, pp. 246–99.)

Smith's illustrations (1971: vol. 2) are neither as numerous nor as inclusive of variability within types, but in general, are larger and show more details of surface decoration. The Chichen Itza pottery is shown in Figures 11–23 on pages 20–34. Smith also provides useful comparative Sotuta material from Mayapan (Figure 27). Smith emphasizes less, but also illustrates, cases in which Chichen and Puuc ceramics are difficult to distinguish (e.g., Fig. 16, pp. 28–29).

8. In the case of ceramics, I have standardized to the extent of using Smith's terminology whenever possible. Brainerd's term for both Chichen and Puuc slatewares was "Medium Slateware" of which "Florescent" and "Early Mexican" variants were recognized. Brainerd used "X, Y, and Z Fine Orange" to refer to what Smith called "Silho, Altar, and Balancan Fine Orange," and sometimes it has been more convenient to refer to these by the Brainerd terms. Other terms for "X Fine Orange" (Silho) are "Chichen Fine Orange" (used by Smith 1955) and "Early Mexican Fine Orange" (used by Brainerd 1958). Confusion also arises because in Smith's use of the type-variety hierarchic system of pottery classification "Fine Orange" is a *ware* designation; "Silho Fine Orange" is a *group*; and "Silho Orange" is a *type*. Thus Balancan and Silho belong to Fine Orange Ware, but Balancan Fine Orange is another group and Balancan Orange is a type name only.

Smith and Brainerd both refer to Chichen and Puuc Slate as "wares," but Smith's Chichen Slate Ware consists of only one "group" (Dzitas) and Puuc Slate includes only the Muna group (1971: 16, 28). There are then, within these groups, parallel Chichen and Puuc Plain Slateware, Black-on-Slate, Red-on-Slate, Incised, and Gouged-Incised types and varieties. In accord with descriptions presented in this paper, one may argue that insufficient data have been presented in the literature to warrant the establishment of more than one "Slate Ware" and one slate group for both the Chichen and Puuc pottery assemblages. Each "type" of decorative mode would be retained, according to type-variety rules, and different regional varieties might be established. The difference in paste described for Chichen and Puuc slates is not a difference in ware (technology) but perhaps one of raw materials (clay and tempering), which could be expected to vary regionally or along socioculturally defined lines of differential availability.

9. The need for a dating technique directly relevant to architecture is obvious. Epigraphic dates are too few and not always in primary context within the buildings where found (as in the initial series lintel excavated by E. H. Thompson in Structure 5C4). The six radiocarbon dates available from architectural contexts at Chichen Itza constitute only an additional source of confusion in trying to sort out the chronology of this site. As discussed in the

Excavations at Dzibilchaltun volume (Andrews IV and Andrews V 1980: 281–85), the dates from Chichen Itza tend to support the traditional "linear succession" model (wherein the Modified Florescent Toltec-Maya replace the Pure Florescent Maya), but only according to the Spinden (12.9.0.0.0) correlation! Kelley (1983) has also addressed this problem.

PART THREE

Data

6
From the Maya Margins: Images of Postclassic Politics

ARTHUR G. MILLER

University Museum, University of Pennsylvania

The archaeological record clearly indicates that a fundamental change took place between the Classic and Postclassic periods in the Maya Lowlands. Yet the nature of this change has, in the past, been over-simplified. For example, warfare has been said to have increased during the Postclassic (Morley 1946), but Mayanists are now generally in agreement that warfare was common in the Maya Lowlands during the Classic Period as well. More recently, it has been proposed that the major difference between the Classic and Postclassic periods was the Postclassic growth of long-distance trading networks and the con-comitant rise of a mercantile elite whose power was based on the control of those networks (Rathje 1975; Sabloff and Rathje 1975a, 1975b). Sabloff and Rathje (1975a) suggest that trade was more widespread and that it involved more people at different levels of society during the Postclassic than during the Classic. But long-distance trade in luxury goods was a part of Classic Maya life, too (Jones 1979; Tourtellot and Sabloff 1972). In fact, there does not seem to be sufficient difference in the presence of war and trade between the two periods to account for the changes perceived in the archaeological record.

Just what was involved in the Classic-to-Postclassic change in the Maya Lowlands? I would characterize it as a disruption of Classic

Maya "hypocoherence," resulting from a fundamental shift in political climate and world view, from relative stability insulated by the enduring sociopolitical network that underlies the Southern Maya Lowland Classic Period and its formulation in the Northern Maya Lowlands in the Puuc and at Chichen, to a condition of uncertainty and unrest that is a concomitant of the breakup of that political and social stability. While both warfare and trade existed before and after the Mesoamerican milestone of the "collapse" in the South, their character changed significantly. Warfare no longer was carried on to aggrandize territories and to validate the authority and prestige of long-established rulers. The Postclassic issued in waves of new aggressive entrepreneurs from the margins of the Maya area who were now claiming sovereignty over the territories of once-complacent rulers. These people were still Maya, but they were not the traditional Maya rulers, and they had a long history of consorting with foreign elements, a concomitant of their marginal geographical location. And instead of exchanging precious commodities over established trade routes to enrich and display the wealth of traditional Classic rulers, Postclassic trade forged new pathways over territories and treacherous sea lanes, enriching parvenus who dared to assert their marginal authority so that what was central became marginal and what was marginal central. It was a topsy-turvy period. New masters flaunted their newly established power in new centers where new conspicuous public works proclaimed an uneasy dominance over territories and the Maya who inhabited them. If the Books of Chilam Balam are a testament to Postclassic sensibilities, the Maya never really trusted nor did they accept the authority of their new vulgar masters.

However characterized, *when* the change from Classic to Postclassic occurred has been the subject of recent debate. I see no reason to insist that the Postclassic begins at the same time throughout the Maya Lowlands. In fact, I would be surprised if it did. I would expect to see the Classic Period lasting longer at traditional centers of power where the stakes are higher and change less likely to be chanced. And I would see innovation getting its start at the margins of powerful political networks, eventually overwhelming centers where the elite could no longer maintain the *status quo*, as in the Central Peten after 9.19.

Marginal outposts of culture areas are fragile extensions of the societies that produced them. They tend to be extremely conservative, maintaining the traditions, notably material ones, of the center. At the same time, they are susceptible to strong outside influences, being both closer to those external forces and relatively far from the sustaining central ones. For example, the marginal position of traditionally conservative Tancah, on the eastern fringes of the Yucatan Peninsula, makes it ripe for new political orientations introduced from the outside, notably those borne on the commercial sea lanes. Tancah's material record, specifically in the sensitive chronological marker that is mural painting, indicates that change did occur there early, possibly before it occurred in such powerful centers as Coba, the major Puuc sites, and strongholds in Northern Yucatan. A significant reorientation in political alliances, implicit in ethnohistoric data interpreted in the context of architecture and mural painting at Tancah, strongly suggests that rapid and dynamic change occurs there at A.D. 770, and that the change is of such sweeping importance that it not only lasted some four centuries at Tancah-Tulum, but also may have been, at its beginning, a local expression of the dynamic political events associated with Terminal Classic (formerly "Early Postclassic") "Toltec" Chichen Itza. The fundamental nature of the change marked at A.D. 770 at Tancah lies in the new political alliances that are an indirect product of intrusive highland ideas and are manifest in the material culture of the time.

One consensus of the School of American Research seminar on the Postclassic was to include "Toltec" Chichen as a Classic Maya site, placing the onset of the Postclassic Period after the abandonment of Chichen Itza at ca. A.D. 1100–1200, according to the 11.3 correlation. I personally do not favor this realignment of the traditional chronological assignments, although I admit that there are strong arguments for the new chronology in the Northern Plains. However, for Tancah-Tulum on Yucatan's eastern littoral, the Postclassic begins considerably earlier than 1200, and in some classes of material culture, such as mural painting, it may begin as early as A.D. 770, the traditional beginning date for the Terminal Classic at Uxmal.

This paper investigates the nature of the Postclassic change, which is here viewed as a staggered phenomenon (upward change?), occurring first in the margins of the Maya Lowlands and later at the centers. Late eighth-century architecture and murals in coastal Quintana Roo can be seen as testaments of a new Postclassic world view. That Postclassic world view only makes sense within the matrix of archaeological data; for the purposes of this paper those data come primarily from the Tancah-Tulum region.[1]

What is defined as florescence in architecture, murals, and other material expressions does not have to occur in times of peace; it can and does occur in times of political turmoil. In fact, the Postclassic in coastal Quintana Roo was a time of minor warfare, political factionalism, and, in the context of this unrest, florescence in public works. This is not to imply that the creative expressions of the Maya need chaos to stimulate new projects; certainly some sort of order is necessary to coordinate building programs and public works. But it does suggest that creativity can flourish in times of social upheaval and that it is often an expression of new political orientations.

FOREIGN SIGNS ON COASTAL QUINTANA ROO

Until recently, outside influences were thought to have reached coastal Quintana Roo only in the Late Postclassic. Recent archaeological and ethnohistorical data suggest that there were two separate and marked population increases on the littorals of the Yucatan Peninsula: first at ca. A.D. 770 and then at ca. A.D. 1400. Although the presence of foreign elements in material culture on the Yucatan coasts during the beginning and end of the Postclassic implies that the perceived demographic change is a result of foreign groups moving in, the population in both cases was still Maya; they were marginal Maya on the edge of foreign influence from upland territories of Central and South Central Mexico. Architectural evidence for the presence of outsiders is based on a survey of standing architecture on the Quintana Roo Coast and an analysis of its embellishment (Andrews IV and Andrews 1975; Miller 1982; Sanders 1960). And while architecture and its adornment suggest that the source of the new style was upland territories outside the Maya Lowlands, ethnohistoric documents suggest a Gulf Coast origin;[2] because it is not very informative to label this building style as having been the work of the "Putun," the more specific designation "Chontal" is here preferred.

The presence of foreigners on the Yucatan Peninsula's eastern fringe is documented in Scholes and Roys's (1948) study of the Paxbolon Papers, which marshals convincing evidence that the Late Postclassic people who established a long-distance trading network around the

202

Peninsula of Yucatan, including the coastal Quintana Roo region, were the Acalan-Chontal, also known as the Putun. The Chontal are usually described in the literature as traders whose homeland, on its southwestern periphery, borders the Maya area proper (Chapman 1957; Sabloff and Rathje 1975a; Thompson 1970). Anne Chapman's seminal paper on ports of trade established an explanatory model for the trading system that the Chontal controlled during the decades prior to the arrival of European man in the New World (Chapman 1957). Eric Thompson (1970), more than anyone else, has presented the strongest arguments for the Chontal identity of the Late Postclassic occupants of the east coast of the Yucatan Peninsula. Thompson (1970) described these Putun as "foreigners," the "Phoenicians of the New World," tracing them as far back as the eighth century and attributing to them a long line of "Mexicanizing" influence in the Maya area. Evidence from the recent INAH *Atlas* surveys is confirming a marked population increase on the west and north coasts of the peninsula beginning at about A.D. 770 (Andrews and Robles C. n.d.); data collected from the Tancah-Tulum region support the Chontal association for the coastal dwellers of both Early and Late Postclassic Quintana Roo (Miller 1982; Sanders 1960).

Language is a sign of Chontal control of the Yucatan coasts. That both Gonzalo Guererro and Gerónimo de Aguilar learned Chontal from their coastal Quintana Roo captors suggests that the cultural identity of the Contact Period inhabitants of this marine littoral was not the same as that of their Yucatec-speaking inland neighbors.[3] And there are indications that a strange dialect was spoken in the province of Chauaca.[4]

The first east coast entrada is dated at ca. A.D. 770. At this time, several classes of material culture appear that are significantly unlike what came before and can be perceived as the direct or indirect result of cultural stimulus from the outside. Ceramically, the A.D. 770 horizon is indicated by funerary offerings of burials found under the floor of the Tancah Structure 44 Complex. These include examples of Savan Red-on-Cream and Tical-group Thin Slate Ware, both associated with the period between A.D. 750 and 800 (Ball 1982a: 109). A Ticul-group Thin Slate bowl is actually shown in the Tancah Structure 12 mural painting, showing red-painted labial molding. Architectural evidence for the A.D. 770 entrada includes colonnades reminiscent of those from upland South Central Mexico and a distinctive mural style and iconography not unlike "Toltec"-period mural painting known in the highlands of Central Mexico as well as paintings at Chichen Itza and Coba, closer to the East Coast. Construction techniques contemporary with the 770 entrada include pecked masonry and modified boot-shaped vault stones that, while distinct from the boot-shaped vault stones of the Puuc region, employ veneer masonry construction as a basic building technique. Associated with the aforementioned construction technique is the first painting layer on Tancah Structure 12, showing a Ticul-group Thin Slate Ware bowl held by a seated maize god, dating the murals, and the building, to the 770 horizon. The painting style represented by the Tancah Structure 12 mural seems to have had a long duration on the East Coast, lasting beyond and apparently unaffected by the abandonment of Chichen Itza and the possibly coeval Early Postclassic demise of Coba. The latest murals in the 770 horizon style seem to be those painted on Tulum Structure 1-Sub. Sanders (1960) and Barrera Rubio (personal communication 1980) date Structure 1-Sub no earlier than A.D. 1200. If this date is valid, the Structure 1-Sub mural similar to the one associated with Tancah Structure 12 is the latest extant example of the distinctive Early Postclassic painting style on the East Coast.

Significant in the consideration of foreign signs in coastal Quintana Roo associated with the 770 entrada are the Early Postclassic–style murals in an Early Postclassic building at Coba known as Templo de las Pinturas (Miller 1982: 51–53, Fig. 90). These murals are stylistically and iconographically similar to murals in Tancah Structure 12 and a structure at Xelha (Farriss, Miller, and Chase 1975); they are also stylistically and iconographically related to murals painted on Tulum Structure 1-Sub, adding strength to Robles's contention (personal communication 1982) that the East Coast may have served as a port of trade for Coba during the Early Postclassic Period. I conclude that the Acalan-Chontal may have been active on the East Coast as early as A.D. 770, when an intrusive, possibly foreign element appears in the material culture of the Tancah-Tulum zone.

Economy of explanation would argue for a source closer to the East Coast for the "new" mural style associated with the A.D. 770 entrada, and by that logic Coba would be the most likely source. Since the temporal relationship between Tancah and Coba is not yet evident, we cannot be certain of the direction of influence. I suspect that the style appears earlier at Tancah than at Coba, although murals in both places are sufficiently similar to each other in style and iconography to argue for near contemporaneity. They probably both occur somewhere between A.D. 700 and 1100. And because they are both unlike what is generally regarded as Classic Maya mural painting, their appearance cannot now be explained as a product of internal development. Rather, the Early Postclassic mural style and iconography of Tancah, Tulum, and Coba are closest to the "Toltec" mural painting found in the Temple of the Warriors at Chichen Itza and also in the highlands of Central Mexico (Miller 1972).

That there are no data at Tancah, Tulum, Coba, or Chichen to demonstrate that the distinctive Early Postclassic mural style logically develops out of an earlier local style does not mean that internal development is not an explanation for the style. There is no extant Classic Period mural painting from Tancah to prove continuity or its lack in relation to extant Early Postclassic mural art. Understanding of Maya mural painting earlier than A.D. 770 comes from the Southern Maya Lowlands. However, recently discovered murals from Xelha Structure 26 reported by Robles (personal communication 1982) date to the Tzakol ceramic phase and are altogether different from the Early Postclassic murals encountered at Tancah Structure 12, just 10 kilometers to the south. In fact, these Xelha murals, associated with what Robles identifies as "Tzakol" ceramics, are "Teotihuacanoid" in style, suggesting a Middle Classic Period receptivity to visual imagery originating from as far away as the Central Mexican Highlands. Based on the Xelha evidence, I suggest that Classic Period mural painting from both Tancah and Coba would look very different from the Early Postclassic style and that there would be no internal development relationship between the two styles. Because the appearance of new architectural traits, specifically pecked veneer masonry and modified boot-shaped vault stones, is inextricably associated with this new mural style of the Early Postclassic at Tancah, dating as early as A.D. 770 (mural in Tancah Str. 12), the external stimulus for these new forms must be seriously considered, despite the current vogue for seeking internal rather than external explanations of change.

The fact that Coba is a much larger site than Tancah may suggest a Coba origin for the distinctive Early Postclassic mural style, perhaps ultimately from the Puuc. But size does not in itself confirm primacy. And it is difficult to see the beginning of Puuc architecture in the Puuc heartland before A.D. 770. Indeed the coastal location of Tancah may have rendered that site a particularly suitable recipient and local disseminator for new ideas, especially if they were borne over maritime communication networks linking the East Coast with Gulf Coast peoples who transmitted ideas from South Central Mexico and the Mexican Altiplano.

The archaeological evidence that intrusive foreign elements entered the coastal Quintana Roo zone at ca. A.D. 1400 is stronger than that for the A.D. 700 entrada. Tulum Red Ware at Tancah-Tulum has long been associated (Sanders 1956, 1960) with the onset of the Late Postclassic Period; I have argued that at Tancah-Tulum this period began as late as A.D. 1400 (Miller 1982). Recent research at Santa Rita on Belize's northern coast, however, has produced evidence for placing Tulum Red Ware earlier than A.D. 1350 (D. Chase, personal communication 1982), but the ware's occurrence elsewhere on the East Coast, specifically at Tancah, extends well into the Early Colonial Period as well. Chen Mul modeled censers,[5] however, seem to appear on Yucátan's east coast after A.D. 1350, but do not appear after A.D. 1520. Lots from the Tancah Structure 44 Complex's latest excavation level all produced Tulum Red and Chen Mul modeled censer sherds, whereas earlier ones did not.

New architectural forms with no antecedents in earlier periods appear on the east coast after A.D. 1400. These include "three-in-one" buildings, negative battered walls, and miniature shrines. Percussion-cut masonry becomes the exclusive new building material, although available pecked masonry and even modified boot-shaped vault stones find their way into post–A.D. 1400 structures. A distinctive mural style and iconography suddenly appear in the Tancah-Tulum chronological record at this time with no local antecedents, as does the concomitant use of monochrome or dichrome palettes. This new and distinctive mural style was dubbed the "International Style of the Late Postclassic" by Robertson (1970) and the "Mixteca-Puebla" style by Nicholson (1960); while it is found in various media throughout Mesoamerica during the Late Postclassic, the style's most frequent occurrence in the various media of painted ceramics, painted manuscripts, and painted walls is in the South Central Mexican Highlands of Oaxaca.

Certainly the distinctive post-1400 murals and ceramics do not in themselves mean that South Central or Central Mexican highlanders expanded into the Maya Lowlands. The spread of a mural style or a ceramic sphere does not require movements of peoples. However, the fact that there is ethnohistoric evidence pointing to plans of an imminent Aztec takeover of the peninsula at about the time the Spanish arrived in Mesoamerica[6] does give credence to the possibility of incipient Nahua influence on the East Coast during the Late Postclassic Period. Again, as was the pattern during the Early Postclassic Period, the bearers of this upland influence seem to have been the Acalan-Chontal of the gulf coast western periphery.

That the 1400 entrada on the Quintana Roo coast is associated with plundering foreigners is suggested by the superimposed mural paintings and a looted burial from Room 2 of Structure 44 (Fig. 6.1). These superimposed paintings are so radically different from each other that one cannot be seen as developing logically from the earlier (Miller 1982: 73). Partially covering the black-outline painting of the corn god shown in Structure 44's Mural 2 of Room 1 (Fig. 6.2), stylistically identified as belonging to the Middle Postclassic Period (ceramically defined by continuing use of Peto Cream Wares, and the introduction of Matillas Group Orange Paste Ware; architecturally, as employing a combination of pecked and percussion masonry), are small fragments of painting in a style totally different from that in which the corn god is painted.[7] Close examination of this superimposed painting style has shown it to be similar to that of the murals associated with Structures 5 and 16 at Tulum; there are black outlines and blue knot motifs in the surviving fragments, which are leitmotifs of the Tulum mural-painting style. The many small areas filled by lines in these fragments are in marked contrast to the large, flat, simple outlined areas of the Middle Postclassic painting underneath. Apparently the small uppermost fragments are the only surviving evidence of Late Postclassic painting in Structure 44, although more examples may be hidden under the layers of calcium carbonate that encrust the inner wall of Room 1.

The conclusion that these different wall-painting styles are attributable to two different groups with unrelated mural-painting traditions was an important result of excavations below the sealed floor of Room 2 of Structure 44. A trench cut through the center of Room 2 exposed an obviously looted burial located inside the bench centered in Room 2.[8] The area covering the burial had been cut into in ancient times and most of the grave goods removed (Fig. 6.3), although a jadeite tubular bead, three coral beads, two chips of worked greenstone, two human teeth, and several scraps of bone had been left behind. The

Figure 6.1   Mural 2 in Tancah Structure 44. Rendering by F. Dávalos.

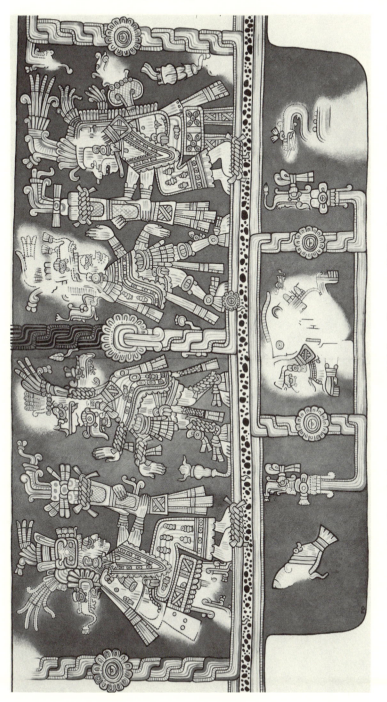

Figure 6.2 Murals from the interior of Tulum Structure 5. Rendering by F. Dávalos.

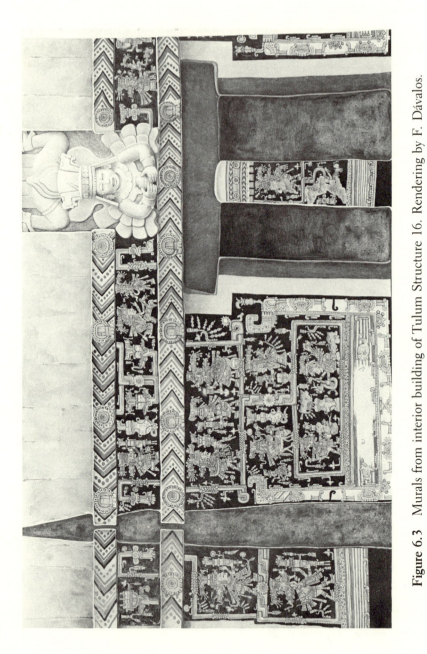

Figure 6.3 Murals from interior building of Tulum Structure 16. Rendering by F. Dávalos.

looted burial area was subsequently filled with small stones and then stuccoed over and painted. This restuccoing was traced to the same layer that bore the Late Postclassic painting superimposed on the Middle Postclassic mural, indicating that the bench repair and possibly the grave looting may have been carried out by the Late Postclassic occupants of Tancah Structure 44.

The restuccoing and repainting of Str. 44 suggests that the people who desecrated the burial inside Room 2 were the Chontal, who may have arrived on the Quintana Roo coast a century prior to the planned Aztec military invasion referred to in ethnohistorical sources, thereby bringing with them the cultural traits that are so clearly intrusive to the region. The Acalan-Chontal of the Late Postclassic, whom I refer to as the Chontal-Nahua, may in fact have been allied with the Aztec *pochteca*, who employed the local marine expertise at Xicalanco to extend their trading networks from the gulf coast around the peninsula to the Quintana Roo coast to gain a foothold there for eventual territorial expansion.

SYMBOLS OF TENSION

Ostentation is usually indicative of insecurity; it is problematic, however, to determine what is considered ostentatious in any given society. In the case of the Postclassic Maya, the Books of Chilam Balam clearly consider foreign "Mexicans" ostentatious. Their over-two-century residence in the peninsula resulted in notable claims to authority. But the peninsular Maya clearly regarded those claims with disdain.

The insecurity that is an inevitable part of any new political system established at the expense of an older one often finds expression in the new order's symbolic forms. In a bid to proclaim legitimacy, great pains are taken to demonstrate the right to rule; the validity of power is most often stressed at times when power is not taken for granted. In such a manner, the modern fascist states, which overthrew traditional governments, often by forceful means, built an architecture invoking the power of ancient Rome and repeated their political logos *ad nauseam* for all to see. More relevant to the Postclassic, the rule of Curl Nose at Tikal, who, Coggins argues (1975), usurped the power of the previous dynasty, is accompanied with lengthy inscriptions establishing legitimacy of rule—so lengthy as to seem to protest too much. And

211

Cauac Sky's rule at Quirigua (Miller 1984; Sharer 1980), festooned with unprecedented enormous monuments celebrating his rule, must have been marked by an anxious arrogance and insecurity.

Ostentatious public monuments erected to celebrate or validate tenuous, unstable political systems are visible expressions of that instability. Evident is a sense of tension that comes from a conflict between the reality of having taken governmental control by means that are often forceful and the wish that all is well with the new political orientation. This tension between reality and wish is evident in murals from Tulum painted after the establishment of Chontal power there ca. A.D. 1400. In fact, the iconological leitmotif of the Tulum murals is the tension between opposing visual characteristics that express, in their unique pictorial language, the conflict between political reality and desire, between what the newly established power unconsciously knows to be the case and what it would like the situation to be. For example, there is a visible mood of anxiety in the confrontation scenes depicted in the Structure 5 and 16 murals at Tulum (Figure 6.3). Although the figures depicted are rigid and their gestures frozen in unnatural positions, a sense of immediacy communicates itself to the viewer: movement is depicted, but it is shown as being immobile. It is remarkable that stereotyped positions and facial expressions encumbered by a plethora of iconographic detail should contain such potential energy. Despite the lack of pictorial realism, the pictures have an aspect of the photographic moment, of frozen movement; yet there is also a very prominent aspect of permanence to these images.

The quality of permanence one senses in viewing the Structure 5 and 16 murals is enhanced by the contrived pictorial sameness in the linear treatment of border motifs, offerings, figures, and costume detailing. One's eye is not attracted to any particular focus in these murals, but rather the viewer's attention is evenly dispersed over the entire surface of the wall; decentralization and the lack of focus contribute to the sense of visual uniformity.

Although it would seem contradictory that something permanent can appear to be momentarily frozen in time and space, such an apparent contradiction is precisely the content of the tension expressed in the murals of coastal Quintana Roo. The clearest expression of this tension, conflict between the reality and the fantasy of the political situation, is evident in Structure 16, where the murals decorate the exterior walls of an inner building encapsulated by an outer gallery The outer shell and the superstructure of this three-in-one building were originally painted in bright pigments of two reds, yellow-ochre, blue, and black. In contrast to this richness of color, the inner building was painted in shades of blue on a black background. The strong visual contrast of these two palettes must have created an overwhelming effect on the observer; the inner room, publicly visible, would have appeared as a dark core surrounded by vibrant color, the inner room all the more dark by being in shadow, and the outer shell all the more bright by being in the direct rays of the sun. The contrasting of monochromatic and polychromatic painting is thus another means of bringing together opposite pictorial characteristics. In the context of archaeology and ethnohistorical sources pertaining to the area, the significance of these visual oppositions is revealed: it is a public symbolic expression of the conflict between the reality of uneasy forceful control over a restless population, who traditionally regard the antiquity of blood lines as the lone real basis for authority, and the fantasy of dominance over submissive subjects, who do not disdain their vulgar masters.

This brief mention of mural imagery suggesting cultural tension is not to say that visual imagery "reflects" society. It does not. The visual imagery evident in a public communicative device such as a mural is a self-referential system that includes information on cultural attitudes of a particular time and place. But it only makes sense in the context of other data sets. In the case of post-1400 Tulum, the pictorial tension to which I refer communicates the kind of unease felt in societies that have experienced fundamental cultural changes such as those that are detectable in the archaeological record at A.D. 1400 in the Tancah-Tulum zone. To illustrate the way public monuments and their particular placement can suggest the kind of cultural tension inherent in the visual language of the post-1400 murals, an analogy from a better known historical situation is presented below.

AN ANALOGY FROM EARLY FEUDAL EUROPE

The homeland of the Chontal is well documented, and their marginal position between Lowland Maya and upland peoples certainly has a lot to do with their long-distance trading activities (Chapman 1956; Sabloff and Rathje 1975a,b; Thompson 1970). It is my intention to comment on their possible political role as well and to characterize the conflicts inherent in Chontal political actions on the Quintana Roo coast, using public art as primary data. Chontal political orientations are as much a function of their marginal location as is their trading vocation. The ethnohistorical record of the Postclassic activities of the Acalan-Chontal Maya shows them to have been entrepreneurs very much on the margins of Classic Maya political power, with an eye to taking political advantage of weaknesses around the edges of the Maya center beginning at 9.17.

In an attempt to understand the sociopolitical process that produced the symbols of tension I have analyzed in Postclassic Quintana Roo, I propose an analogy from European history at the time of the formation of feudal society. In choosing an analogy, one tries to select a situation as comparable as possible to the problem at hand. The past is so varied in time and place that it is impossible to find a perfect fit, but analogies from better known histories can illuminate the process of social interaction in lesser known ones. And there is an advantage in choosing a comparative history that is so removed from that of the Maya and their neighbors that any similarity in cultural process is all the more remarkable. At the same time, obvious differences in cultural history testify to the lack of connection between the two.

From the perspective of cultural process, the conditions in Northern Europe around A.D. 800 parallel those of Postclassic coastal Quintana Roo more closely than do those of modern Europe which have inspired paradigms of economic dependency and its role in state systems. In contrast to the economic and political situation surrounding modern state systems, the early feudal system and the combination of hereditary and elective principles inherent in medieval kingship are closer to the Lowland Maya system where "political power was more fluid, diffused through a hierarchy of lesser lordships, who had some say in the choice of the territorial ruler and on whose support, in the absence of well-developed state bureaucracies and standing armies, his actual power depended" (Farriss n.d.). Transfer of authority was not automatic.

Among the Aztecs the choice was made by senior members of the ruling lineage in consultation with a council made up of the leading nobles. A similar procedure was probably followed by the lowland Maya, with ruling dynasty and the lesser nobility. And we can assume that in all cases more informal political maneuvering accompanied or preceded the final selection. (Farriss n.d.)

214

It was probably such a political system encouraging a degree of fluidity that best describes Postclassic Lowland Maya power on the Quintana Roo coast, a power that was infiltrated by groups of political opportunists who originally hailed from the Gulf Coast. As adventurers and middlemen, these foreigners played political interests of rival political factions to gain their own ends. Opportunities for such machinations were far more frequent during the Postclassic than they had been earlier because the relative stability of rule that was so much a part of Early and Middle Classic life was beginning to disintegrate.

Beginning about A.D. 800 and for a century and a half afterward, the coasts of England and northern Europe were visited by *Nordmän*, "men of the North." These adventurers were neither a collection of tribes nor members of a single state. Included were Danes, Gotar, Swedes, and the various peoples who occupied a disjointed forested coastal land, united by a common sea, that is known today as Norway (Bloch 1974: 15). There was enough likeness among these adventurers that their neighbors gave them a common label: Northmen and, later, Vikings. These labels are as meaningful as is the label *Putun*, also designating foreigners. They were master shipbuilders and mariners for whom the waters were lanes for plunder of the land (Bloch 1974: 16–17). The earliest Viking raids were limited to the coastal shores of northern Europe, but soon, instead of attacking, plundering, and retreating, they established coastal settlements and even bases far inland. They combined piracy with commerce by maintaining a ring of fortified markets around the Baltic which in some cases led eventually to feudal kingdoms. The incorporation of the Viking presence into small competing political entities whose trading and military activities were a means to extend power and prestige is best represented by a descendant of the Vikings who became assimilated into local coastal culture and from there further extended their power:

This same duke of Normandy, the conqueror of England, completely French though he was by speech and manner of life, was also one of the authentic descendants of the Vikings. For, on the continent, as in the island, more than one "sea king" had in the end made himself a territorial lord or prince.

The process there had begun very early. From about 850, the Rhine delta had seen the first attempt to establish a Scandinavian principality within the political edifice of the Frankish state. . . . (Bloch 1974: 26)

The initial influx of Chontal on the Quintana Roo coast may not have been unlike the kind of plunder characteristic of the Vikings in

Northern Europe. Gradually, like the Vikings who had added pagan and Christian elements to their religion, the new Mexicanized Maya Chontal were incorporated into the local cult and political framework, and they subsequently transformed it into a new syncretic religion and political structure. There are indications that these foreigners, who had assimilated and transformed the culture of their hosts (who in turn may have included factions that welcomed the newcomers as means to overthrow the existing rule), introduced new ideas in architecture and mural painting, signs of a new religion carrying with it political control and prestige. These same entrepreneurs established fortified long-distance trading networks, thereby adding vitality to their new-found lordly status. Also like their Viking counterparts, the Mexican-ized Maya may also have established centers of power inland. Perhaps Early Postclassic Coba and Chichen Itza are examples of this process of eventual consolidation of new power within the matrix of old po-litical systems, a process we understand more fully in the better doc-umented Viking parallel.

TWO ENVIRONMENTS

In order to trace the process of establishing a political foothold in new territories, it is revealing to examine the kind of environments chosen for new settlements by the Chontal. Like the Vikings, the Chontal first established networks in coastal areas. In the case of coastal Quintana Roo, the Chontal were fortunate in finding an environ-mental niche which at first set them off and isolated them from the people they sought to control.

As a glance at any map of Mesoamerica quickly reveals, the east coast of the Yucatan Peninsula is a region on the very edge of the Maya world facing onto a cultural void—the sea known today as the Caribbean. This coastal Quintana Roo region consists of two distinct physical environments or microenvironments, only one of which re-sembles the rest of the Yucatan Peninsula. Rocky headlands or sandy beaches face directly onto the sea. Separating this formation of beach rock and sand from *tierra firme* of the mainland are uninhabitable low-lying saline *bajos* or swamps.[9] Most coastal sites of the Yucatan Peninsula's east side, such as Tancah and Xelha, occupy both mi-croenvironments; several of them, such as Tulum, occupy only one. The Tulum locus was first settled during the Early Postclassic Period,

216

and its period of greatest growth corresponds to the Late Postclassic. Our knowledge of Tulum's growth is based on architectural and mural seriations and ceramic evidence excavated by INAH excavations there (Barrera Rubio, personal communication 1978).

The *tierra firme* zones such as inland Tancah are characteristically Maya in material culture: their architecture, ceramics, artifacts, and murals conform to what one would expect to see in a small Maya site throughout the Classic Period. On the other hand, the material remains of architecture, murals, ceramics, and artifacts collected from the rocky headland and sandy beach sites such as Tulum are replete with "non-Maya" features that have been associated with the Acalan Chontal. This pattern suggests that the settlements on the rocky headland/sandy beach result from outside influences whereas the interior ones are the result of indigenous developments. Perhaps the best example of inland indigenous Late Postclassic settlement in the east coast zone is represented by Peter Harrison's Lobil Phase (Harrison 1979).

It is hardly surprising that agriculturalists, which the east-coast Maya certainly were, would prefer to occupy lands favorable to farmers such as the higher, well-watered lands behind the coastal *bajos*. Nor is it surprising that peoples whose major livelihood depended on the maintenance of strong supply networks to the home base around the peninsula should choose to occupy seaside locations, as near as possible to the embarkation and disembarkation points of their goods and reinforcements. The Cozumel Project described a pattern of inland occupation by coastal traders (Sabloff and Rathje 1976b). But I wonder if major inland sites such as the San Gervasio location could have been determined by the availability of fresh water. There are no sources of fresh water on the coasts of Cozumel, whereas seaside freshwater springs are common on the mainland.[10]

Evidence from the Tancah-Tulum zone suggests that there were major population shifts from *tierra firme* to rocky headland/sandy beach zones just when architectural, mural, and ceramic evidence and the ethnohistoric record suggest there were outside intrusions, first during the Early Postclassic Period and then during the Late Postclassic. The relationship between the sites of Tancah and Tulum illustrates this population movement. Prior to the Early Postclassic Period there is no evidence of occupation at the Tulum locus, but Tancah has a long period of continuous occupation beginning at least as early as the Late Postclassic and extending through the Classic Period (Miller 1982: 13–

49, 61–64). Besides the preferability of the land behind the coastal *bajos* for farming peoples, *tierra firme* also offered protection from the hazards of the sea, both natural and human. This is a zone of frequent destructive tropical storms, and coastal exposure would have rendered such settlements vulnerable to attack by marauding vessels looking for easy prey (see discussion in Miller 1982: 3, 46, 76 *n*. 31, 78, 79). When settlement occurs directly on the rocky headland/sandy beach area, it suggests not only an exploitation of marine trading networks but also a political situation that obviates the threat of marine attack. Such a situation implies control of the sea lanes. It is not surprising that after 1521, when the long-distance trading network around the Peninsula of Yucatan is disrupted by the fall of Tenochtitlan, Tulum is abandoned and colonial Tzama is occupied to the west of the Tancah locus (Miller and Farriss 1979). Arguments for the identification of the Tancah locus as the site of the colonial Tzama have appeared elsewhere (Miller 1982: 77–78; Miller and Farriss 1979: 224–27). My purpose in mentioning the perceived occupation shifts in the Tancah-Tulum zone is to correlate the settlement of the rocky headland/sandy beach zone with periods of long-distance marine supply lanes to the Quintana Roo coast. These occupations correspond with the Early Postclassic and the Late Postclassic Period.

Conspicuous coastal sites interspersed with small shrine-like structures, which I interpret as navigation markers, are a practical necessity for the maintenance of long-distance trade along the Quintana Roo coast (Miller 1982: 46, 73); there are no natural features to indicate to mariners where they are situated at any given time. Today, expert mariners from Cozumel depend on man-made markers on the mainland to orient themselves during trips up or down the coast, and it is probable that Postclassic traders did so as well. What strikes me about the rocky headland/sandy beach microenvironment of the Quintana Roo coast is how well such a setting "fits" the needs of coastal traders. Because of the common problems that all long-distance traders face, they tend to live in marginal areas between land and sea, or on the edges of what Polanyi (1971:239) calls "that *alter ego* of the sea"— deserts. [11]

CONCLUSIONS

There are two perceptible periods of outside influence in coastal Quintana Roo corresponding to the Early Postclassic and Late Post-

218

classic periods. Mounting evidence suggests that these periods are represented by a significant change in the material cultural record of the region and that such change occurs in a setting of regional conservatism. The analogy from Northern Europe at the time of Viking expansion may help to explain the process of gradual consolidation of political control on the Quintana Roo coast, first by either force or political opportunism and then by incorporation of existing political systems to establish a new order, the material signs of which are new public works such as architecture and mural painting and a network of trade in luxury goods to enhance tenuous political prestige. Whether or not these entradas, one at A.D. 770 and the other at A.D. 1400, are in fact the result of specific incursions by gulf coast peoples and what kind of military force or power politics were involved cannot be demonstrated given the available evidence. Nevertheless, archaeological data from Tancah-Tulum as well as murals from Chichen Itza (Miller 1977a) and ethnohistoric sources do form a picture of gulf coast–derived foreign-dominated settlements, of which the Quintana Roo coast was an essential part. The choice of a rocky headland/sandy beach environment for such outposts fits in well with what we could expect of such peripheral settlements on the fringes of Mesoamerica.

Peoples of conquered territories, or of lands whose traditional rulership has been usurped by local opportunists, exhibit in their material culture subtle tension between rulers and the ruled. The well-known political and cultural tension between Anglo-Saxons and Normans after 1066 resembles the unease that probably existed between the Chontal and the east coast Maya. Like the defensive towers of the Normans, the walls around Tulum are an architecture of unrest; the murals bespeak an unconscious anxiety (see Miller 1982: 97–98) that betrays the frailty of the cultural fabric. Architecture and murals, signs of foreign dominance, signify the tension inevitable in the newcomers. The Books of Chilam Balam reveal an obsessive concern among the traditional Maya for the antiquity of their blood lines with a concomitant disdain for the new arrivals, who in some cases may have been "residents" for as long as two centuries. The *nouveau riche* Mexicanized Maya of gulf-coast origins flaunted their architecture and commissioned carved and painted imagery on the East Coast as early as 770 in a bid for political legitimacy. In a late manifestation of the same process, gulf-coast peoples made another futile bid for acceptance at ca. 1400. Had the events of 1519 not occurred, they might have succeeded and could have formed the kind of powerful political hegemony that is so obvious in "Toltec" Chichen Itza in northern Yucatan. Yet the fact remains that all the building and its embellishment and the exotic trade goods generation after generation could not disguise the fact that these descendants of the gulf coast Maya were regarded by the peninsular Maya as parvenus who had usurped traditional power whose validity rested on the antiquity of its claims to sovereignty.

NOTES

1. The focus of my argument for Postclassic political upheavals is the coastal zone of eastern Yucatan; the data come primarily from my research there from 1971 through 1976, supported by Dumbarton Oaks, the National Geographic Society, the Brooklyn Academy of Arts and Sciences, and the Mexican-Canadian Foundation. While most of the data have been published in my recent monograph on Tancah-Tulum (1982), the attempt to characterize coastal political organization for the purposes of this seminar is new. Chronological terms used in the following discussion are based on data produced by small-scale stratigraphic excavations conducted in and around Tancah Structure 44 during the 1974 field season at the site. Ten burials containing direct dating evidence in the form of ceramic material (Miller 1982: Table II), which was subsequently evaluated by J. W. Ball (1982a), contributed to establishing the regional chronology for the Tancah-Tulum region. In 1975, excavation of a colonial chapel at Tancah produced 23 burials, all from Early Colonial contexts (Miller 1982: Table III). Combined with data from architecture, murals, and ceramics, a regional chronology of the Tancah-Tulum region was formed (Miller 1982: Table I). Since I use chronological terms from the Tancah-Tulum region to refer to events along the entire Quintana Roo coast, I reproduce the chronological chart below:

Early Colonial	A.D. 1517–1668
Late Postclassic	A.D. 1400–1517
Middle Postclassic	A.D. 1200–1400
Early Postclassic*	A.D. 1000–1200
Terminal Classic*	A.D. 770–1000
Late Classic	A.D. 650–770
Middle Classic	A.D. 550–650
Early Classic	A.D. 250–550
Terminal Preclassic	75 B.C.–A.D. 250
Late Preclassic	300 B.C.–75 B.C.

*The time span A.D. 770–1200 is in this paper combined into one designation: the Early Postclassic Period.

2. See Miller 1982: 64–71 for a discussion of the ethnohistoric evidence for Chontal intrusions in the Tancah-Tulum region during the Early Postclassic Period and 1982: 71–75 for evidence for the Chontal presence on the East Coast during the Late Postclassic.

3. While at Potonchan, Cortés secured the translating services of the Indian woman who later became known as Doña Marina. She knew both Nahuatl and some form of Maya. Cortés was able to talk to her through Gerónimo de Aguilar, who learned his Maya on the east coast of Yucatan while he was captive there. The form of Maya Aguilar learned was most probably the form spoken at Potonchan, i.e., Chontal. See *Cartas de Relación* by Hernán Cortés (1963: 36) for the account that gives the situation from which the above inference is drawn.

4. The *Relaciones Geográficas* report that the form of Maya spoken in Chauaca is distinctly different from Yucatec. See Relaciones de Yucatán, II, Relación de Valladolid, p. 14; Cuidad Real, II, 393.

5. The antecedents for Late Postclassic Chen Mul modeled censers do not seem to be evident in the Maya area, unless one considers Terminal Classic censers from Quirigua as prototypes. Significant is the fact that ceramic forms, functions, and iconography strikingly similar to Chen Mul modeled censers do appear in the Mexican Altiplano at the time they appear in the Maya Lowlands, and the marked similarity has been made more evident by the number of effigy censer wares recently excavated by the Templo Mayor Project in Tenochititlan.

6. In a *Relación de Yucatán* referring to the major conquest-period "port of trade" in southwestern Campeche—Xicalanco, which we know had extensive trade networks around the peninsula—casual mention is made of an imminent military attack on the Maya of Yucatan. A large army of Aztec troops garrisoned at Xicalanco was about to launch an attack on the peninsula under the leadership of a "Captain General" who was Montezuma's brother. The attack never occurred because the Aztec "Captain General" received word in 1521 that Tenochtitlan had fallen to the Spaniards.

7. In a previous publication (Miller 1973b), I did not mention the existence of two painting layers in this mural. During February of 1976, I discussed with Alfredo Barrera Rubio in Mérida the evidence for distinguishing two distinct painting layers; the conclusions are published in Barrera Rubio (1976).

8. Often referred to as "altars," these benches are more likely symbolic and literal seats of authority.

9. The geological characteristics of the coastland on the eastern side of the Yucatan Peninsula have been the object of recent study by several teams of geologists. See Miller (1982: 6–7) for a discussion of this work and Weidie (1974: 102–4) for a technical discussion of geological processes that produced the conditions found along the Quintana Roo littoral.

10. Freshwater springs discharging directly into the sea or into large karst formations directly connected to the sea (such as that at Xelha) are known today as *ojos de agua*. See discussion of their frequency in Miller (1982: 5–6).

11. The changes in coastal Quintana Roo occupation during the Early Postclassic Period and its implications for Postclassic Maya prehistory could be further explored by archaeological research in areas that are particularly attractive to coastal adventurers and at the same time unattractive to mainland

Maya farmers. These areas ideally should be on the sea yet afford protection from storms and, at the same time, be unattractive enough for agricultural settlement. Such an area is the subpeninsula, with its saline *bajos*, extending eastward between Bahía de la Ascensión and Bahía del Espíritu Santo. The sites of Tupak and Chacmool (so named after a chacmool found there by Gann) are particularly intriguing and have never been excavated. The larger Xcalak peninsula between Espíritu Santo and Boca Cacalar Chico is also promising: it features well-watered coastal headlands and small protective inlets, with several sites such as Mahajual and Xcalak among them. Territorial control by maritime adventurers anxious to gain a foothold in new territories seems to be the only explanation for these coastal settlements, since the entire peninsula behind the rocky headlands is composed of saline *bajos* unsuitable for farming. The site of Mahajual is especially attractive because its murals and architecture provide the chance to combine contextual iconographic research with settlement-pattern and trade-network studies—a chance to formulate an interdisciplinary project designed to characterize the poorly known complex dimensions of Maya political interaction with near and distant neighbors of these fringes of Mesoamerica.

7
Stability Through Change: Lamanai, Belize, from the Ninth to the Seventeenth Century

DAVID M. PENDERGAST
Royal Ontario Museum

The conventional wisdom regarding the Postclassic has always been that the six centuries before the arrival of the Spanish were a time of decadence, a sort of descent into the pit from the heights achieved in Classic times. This is, of course, a view rooted in archaeocentrism, which is to say that it rests on the belief that the Classic embodied all that was good and true and noble and beautiful in Maya society, from which it obviously follows that anything in the way of a change must have been a spiral down from the pinnacle. The view is also understandable historically, for among the sites that saw early excavation were several at which decay and collapse had undeniably occurred. Where the cataclysmic events at the end of the Classic were followed by anything at all, it seemed only a feeble glimmer of what had gone before.

Our understanding of the ebb and flow of life at many Maya sites has done much in recent years to dispel the notion of a simple rise-and-fall progression through the Lowlands. For the Central Lowlands, however, one would until recently have been hard-pressed to make a case for the Postclassic as much more than a fast slide down into a very murky sea. The excavations at Lamanai from 1974 through 1982 have provided a body of data that supports a different view of events in the tenth century A.D. and afterward; although the Lamanai data appear unique in many respects, they surely also reflect events that were characteristic of the Postclassic as a whole.

The contrast between Lamanai and Altun Ha, just 40 kilometers to the east (Figure 7.1), in the Terminal Classic and Postclassic is instructive because of its sharpness. Altun Ha saw abandonment of temples at the end of the Classic, and probably of palaces as well. Disappearance of the elite population is strongly indicated not only by the abandonment but also by the desecration of all readily accessible tombs (Pendergast 1979: 183–84, 1982a: 139). Later residential use of at least one temple probably involved nonelite families; ceramic evidence suggests that the temple occupants were the descendants of those who had seen the Classic come to an end not long before. Occupation and some construction continued in outlying areas beyond the final throes in the site center, but the aftershocks of Classic collapse seem to have brought all reconstruction and use of small buildings to an end by or before the early eleventh century.

Following full abandonment of the site center came several burials, and offerings that include a small lot of vessels that are almost certainly of Lamanai origin. Among the vessels are one or more censers and the highly distinctive "chalice" form that marks the twelfth to fourteenth centuries at Lamanai (Pendergast 1982a: 140). Though the vessels' source is clear enough, the identity of their users remains beyond our grasp. Trade between the people of Lamanai and a remnant population at Altun Ha is obviously a possibility, and probably just as likely as pilgrimage by Lamanites to an ancient, totally abandoned city center for the purpose of depositing a single offering atop what must by then have been an almost featureless mound. Whatever the nature of the event, though, it is clear that the offering did not signal any renascence of Altun Ha society; the site core was just as dead a place after the ceremony as it had been before.

When life finally revived at Altun Ha, its pulse was weak and its span was not great. The resuscitation took place primarily in the fifteenth and sixteenth centuries, apparently a time of Postclassic presence at many other sites in northern Belize. At Altun Ha, the occupation was unquestionably a break with the past, and it appears highly likely to have involved people not directly related to those of the Classic and Terminal Classic. Evidence for the presence of the Late Postclassic people consists primarily of Tulum-related ceramics of the Uayeb phase,

Figure 7.1 Location of Lamanai.

a designation that implies the existence of an appreciable body of data. In fact, most of the material is a thin scatter on and in the humus strata atop residential and other small structures in neighborhoods both near and at some remove from the Central Precinct. It is probably true in all cases that Uayeb use of Classic Period structures involved erection of a thatched building atop what was seen by the builders as

225

a mound high enough to be up out of the swamps and mosquitoes, rather than as the remains of an earlier residence.

Late Postclassic use of Altun Ha, and likely of other northern Belize sites, was quite clearly more than a matter of pilgrimage, and may well have been stimulated by the presence of the resources that attracted earlier settlers, perhaps water supply in particular. The data unfortunately do not permit determination of the extent of the occupation, how long it endured, who the people were, or how their activities were related to Postclassic events of quite a different sort near the end of the long occupation span at Lamanai.

At the moment, Lamanai has the seemingly unique distinction in the Central Lowlands of having seen continuous occupation from at least Middle Preclassic times until A.D. 1675 or later, a distinction that is difficult to explain in the face of events in nearby areas during the Postclassic. Lamanai could scarcely have remained a viable community in a vacuum created by collapse of political and social organization at neighboring Lowland centers, with the accompanying dissolution of intersite networks: it is therefore likely that the pattern of events at the site was repeated, at least in its main aspects, elsewhere in the area. Until sites with similar histories are discovered, however, we are forced to take Lamanai as the lone example of a course that may have been followed by a good many Central Lowlands Postclassic communities.

Classic and earlier developments at Lamanai have previously been summarized (Pendergast 1981a: 34–43), and it is only necessary to note here that there are at least as many idiosyncratic features of architecture and ceramics here as at other sites, with the possible exception of Altun Ha and its remarkably catholic taste in buildings and offerings. The earlier centuries at Lamanai were marked by the sort of repetition of architectural and offering components that appears more characteristic of sites in the Peten than of those in northern Belize, and architectural affinities are generally with the Peten. The degree of uniformity present in many facets of the Classic Period archaeological record suggests relatively rigid control over the populace by the ruling class. At the same time, the differences between Lamanai and other Classic centers point up the futility of approaching the period as though all leaders in all communities ruled with similarly heavy hands, or found identical solutions to the myriad problems confronted by their people.

The apparently ordered life at Lamanai seems to have differed from that at Altun Ha, where a more flexible existence appears documented by the great variety in material culture. One might have expected Altun Ha, with its greater potential resilience, to have survived into the Postclassic, but in fact it was Lamanai that bridged the transition with scarcely a ripple. Events at Altun Ha may be partly explainable in terms of the very strongly ceremonial nature of the site, and the characteristics of the ruling group that such a nature produced; one cannot, however, simply view Lamanai as the reverse side of the coin, and use the view as an explanation of what occurred at the site from the late ninth century onward.

At Lamanai, many of the patterns of Classic times continued without change until at least the early tenth century, and some may have persisted with little alteration until nearly the end of the Postclassic. Alongside the retained traditions appeared elements that marked shifts in direction, but were clearly the outgrowths of what had preceded them. The period from about A.D. 850 to 925 was, in fact, a time of continued vibrance, whereas the mood of the times was clearly one of pessimism elsewhere in the Central Lowlands, and with very good reason. The growth at Lamanai in the late ninth and early tenth centuries paved the way for the ongoing vitality of the community in the centuries that followed.

Although a relatively large volume of construction took place in the southern part of the site center in the ninth and early tenth centuries, these years may also have seen the beginnings of withdrawal from the northern and central parts of the zone, from The Harbour southward to the group dominated by Structure N10-43 (Fig. 7.2). It is clear, however, that at the same time small residential groups were being established on the peripheries of the zone, so that it appears that withdrawal was largely or wholly a matter of cessation of major temple renewal, rather than abandonment of the zone in its entirety.

The changes in the site center, and perhaps in portions of the northern residential zone as well, were accompanied by an increased concentration of energy expenditure in the south, the area that was to become the principal focus of the Terminal Classic and Postclassic community. The shift surely had a significant effect on patterns of life at the site, but the inhabitants of Lamanai obviously did not go through the late ninth century staring collapse in the face, nor did they experience any perceptible disruption of their existence as the tenth

227

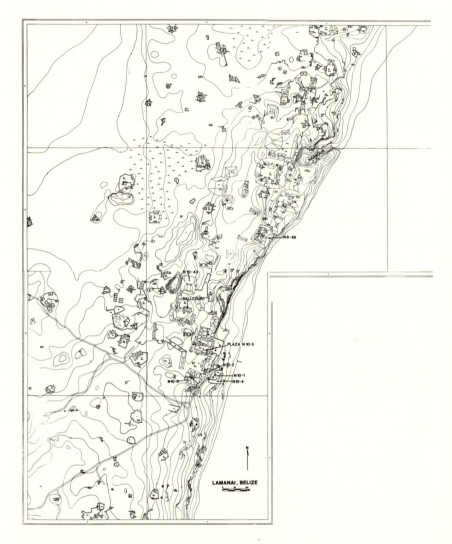

Figure 7.2 Plan of the central portion of Lamanai. Plaza N10/3 ("PA 3") lies immediately north of Structure N10-7.

228

century opened. The impossibility of distinguishing between terminal Late Classic and early Postclassic, in combination with the events of this period in northern Yucatan, argues forcefully for adoption of the term Terminal Classic to refer to events from the late ninth or early tenth century until A.D. 1200. The flow of events past supposed break points was so smooth at Lamanai that the site's occupants were probably no more aware of archaeologically separate stages prior to A.D. 1200 than they were on or after that date.

While the reduction of ceremonial construction in the northern and central portions of the Central Precinct was taking place, and nonelite residences were making their appearance in territory previously too sacrosanct to have served as a dwelling site, the northern residential zone seems to have seen only comparatively minor change. In some groups, evidence suggests continued occupation from the Preclassic through the very late years of the Postclassic, while in others there is no indication of construction, or of use, beyond the Terminal Classic, probably about A.D. 1100 at the latest. One could argue on the basis of evidence now in hand that abandonment of more northerly groups in the Northern Zone occurred by mid–Terminal Classic times as part of a general shrinkage in the physical extent of the community that affected the northern and central parts of the Central Precinct as well. What cannot be determined is the sociopolitical relationship between northern residents and those in the far south from the tenth to the sixteenth century.

It was in the south that Lamanai saw the greatest amount of new development from the late ninth century onward, in which innovation was coupled with a strong sense of continuum. The most striking introduction in architecture at the outset of the Terminal Classic is the lone ball court at the site (Fig. 7.2), from which an offering was recovered that included 9.6 cubic centimeters of mercury (Pendergast 1980: 4). Ceramics from the offering fix the time of court construction in the late ninth or early tenth century, with a date toward the end of that span the more likely. The mercury, the first reported occurrence in the Lowlands, is probably from Honduran sources (Pendergast 1982b: 534), and its presence suggests trade links between Lamanai and Copan or other sites in western Honduras at about A.D. 900–950, a surprisingly late date in view of events at the Honduran centers. The riverine settings of both Lamanai and Copan suggest a water route as the one most likely traveled by the mercury, though of course the metal itself does not constitute evidence in support of such a suggestion. The importance of Lamanai's setting to trade not only in the tenth century but throughout the Terminal Classic and Postclassic is a matter to which we shall return in due course.

Beyond the trade ties, the ball court shows clearly that the inhabitants of Lamanai were intent on, and capable of, undertaking fairly large-scale ceremonial construction at a time when such building had nearly or entirely ceased at many neighboring centers. The court represents less construction than that essayed in the years when its neighbor N10-43, the N9-56 group, and other northern Central Precinct buildings were undergoing periodic face-lifts; from this we can conclude that the labor tax exacted from the populace for ceremonial construction in the tenth century was significantly less than in earlier times. Hence the community's psychological ability to undertake the work emerges as more meaningful than the physical effort expended. This is, as we shall see, true of other Postclassic ceremonial construction; what was vital to the community's continued existence was not simply the presence of a manageable labor force, but rather the spirit required to persist in the face of what must have been appalling news from neighboring sites.

Farther south, Structure N10-9, the only identifiable large Classic temple at the south end of the site, saw continuing use throughout the Terminal Classic and on into the Postclassic. The last major modification of N10-9 in the Classic was probably undertaken not later than the eighth century; from then through the early to mid-eleventh century, maintenance and use of the structure continued with no more than minor changes in the building's form. The continuum of use surely argues for a continuation of at least some of the practices for which N10-9 served as a backdrop during the Classic. From this we can infer that part, if not most, of the structure of Classic religious belief and practice survived into the eleventh century or later with relatively little change.

Maintenance of N10-9, coupled with use of the newly built ball court, seems to have formed the principal element in the ceremonial life of Lamanai during the period in which the larger buildings in the northern and central parts of the Central Precinct were undergoing abandonment. It is of course an inescapable feature of data on structure abandonment that the particulars of the activity and the span of time represented are unlikely to be determinable. For all large central and northern buildings in the heart of Lamanai that we have examined, we know only that there is no evidence of construction following the middle Late Classic, and hence we are free to see abandonment as simultaneous or serial, instantaneous or gradual, as we wish.

It is in the area of residential construction, rather than in the ceremonial face of Lamanai, that evidence on the early portion of the Terminal Classic is most extensive. Work in the large complex immediately north of the N10-9 plaza (Plaza N10/3) has revealed a sequence of construction that spans the period from about the late ninth century to late Postclassic times, with the bulk of the buildings datable to the tenth and eleventh centuries. The structures represent the later stages in the development of an assemblage that had its beginnings in the middle Classic or earlier; while the forms of buildings changed over time, the assemblage enjoyed a continuum of use that bridged the Terminal Classic, and saw the greatest volume of construction during this very period.

By the late ninth century, the group consisted of a series of structures arranged around two contiguous courtyards. While the three eastern structures of this period are typical of the Lamanai Classic in dimensions and other construction characteristics, the masonry is largely or wholly reused material from earlier structures, a reflection of the problem that beset a good many sites in Belize during the Late Classic: lack of stone suitable for facings. The most distinctive feature in the eastern courtyard group is Structure N10-28, the latest of the three structures, which was distinguished by upper-zone stucco decoration that was of complex and highly sophisticated modeling, and painted in a very broad range of colors. This sort of facade treatment has not been encountered in Classic Lamanai, but it resembles an early tenth-century upper zone at Altun Ha, and one of similar date from Seibal (Sabloff, personal communication). The appearance of facades with strong iconographic content in nontemple settings may in all three instances represent a restatement of religious values at a more personalized level, perhaps as part of retrenchment in the face of the upheavals that afflicted many Central and Southern Lowlands sites. The facade at Lamanai may indicate the emergence of semipublic, residence-related religious practice at the outset of the Terminal Classic; at Lamanai, in contrast to the two other sites, such practices may have been an element in the successful staving off of Classic collapse.

The western portion of the residential assemblage resembled its eastern counterpart in that it consisted of three structures, but with the significant difference that the three sat atop a common platform that bordered the court on three sides. While masonry characteristics are essentially those of the Classic, the enclosure of a courtyard with a single multipart platform is a marker of the late Terminal Classic and the Postclassic in parts of the Yucatan. The appearance of the tripartite platform at Lamanai before A.D. 900 might be taken as evidence of the origin of the architectural concept in Belize, but at the moment it is safer to say simply that the occurrence in the architectural form is not peculiar to Yucatan alone.

Whatever the significance of the tripartite platform in Lowland architectural development, its presence at Lamanai bespeaks the existence of innovative approaches to building at the start of the Terminal Classic, blended with techniques that were securely rooted in the Classic. One could argue that use of vertically set facing stones in stair risers of the platform presaged Late Postclassic platform facing construction, but here the relationship is at least as tenuous as that between the joined platform and its northern parallels. A second apparent innovation early in the Terminal Classic was the use of colonnades, although only one structure has yielded reasonably secure evidence of a columned entryway, and we cannot be sure whether the feature was incorporated into the ninth-century assemblage or formed part of the modification that followed.

By the middle or late part of the tenth century, or at the latest by about A.D. 1025, the original Terminal Classic form of the courtyard assemblages was in the process of radical transformation, and it is at this stage that we are best able to assess the construction-labor capabilities of the Lamanai community. As the initial step in the modification, the builders razed the upper portions of all structures but one, and capped the remains with part of the material used to fill both courtyards to a depth of approximately 2.5 meters so as to create a single large platform top. The partly razed rear faces of the northern structures were abutted by a huge platform, with a volume of roughly 3,000 cubic meters, while the west side of the tripartite platform was cased with an extensive new face, and additions were made to platform units peripheral to the principal group. The total volume of construction was approximately 9,860 cubic meters; the weight of core stone in the several units is roughly 21,000 metric tons.

The transformation of the courtyard group was clearly an effort of such magnitude as to have engaged the energies of a very large work force over a very considerable period. Data from a variety of offerings in the core of the courtyard fill indicate that the better part of a century may have been taken up in this effort. During the period, the lone remaining building of the earlier complex, a masonry-walled building probably with wooden roof (Structure N10-15), was also undergoing numerous internal and external modifications, while at the east and west ends of the new large main platform the builders erected residential structures that differed radically from each other and from their predecessors.

The northern extensions of the complex were probably built shortly after the courtyard filling, perhaps in more than one stage, while ceramic evidence from core of the western addition shows that it was almost certainly the last element in the modification, built in the twelfth century or later. The gigantic size of the effort, coupled with the fact that earlier construction must have brought about depletion of core-material sources, means that the rebuilding of the group must reflect the presence of an elite still fully capable of marshaling the populace for a massive undertaking that probably spanned, in all, at least a century and a half. That this was the work of a vigorous, vital community with its goals clearly in view is surely beyond question.

The new architectural endeavors of the early Terminal Classic were accompanied by ceramic developments that followed the same pattern of blending the old with the new. The inventory of vessel forms in the period comprised not only the familiar pedestal-base medial-angle orangeware and redware dishes of San José V (Thompson 1939: fig. 78; Pendergast 1974: fig. 5b, 7a, 10c, d) as well as the distinctive bottles (Thompson 1939: fig. 79a; Pendergast 1970: fig. 11a) and other forms and slips standard for the period, but also tripod bowls of what elsewhere are identifiable as late Terminal Classic or Postclassic shape and foot classes, with paste and slip typical of the Late Classic. Burials accompanied by late ninth- or early tenth-century vessels exhibit the pattern of pre-interment breakage that was to be so omnipresent and headache-producing a characteristic of burials in later centuries. There are, in addition, offerings and burials that mingle early Terminal Classic vessels with pieces that feature shape and surface treatments which appear to be precursors of those of the twelfth century and later at Lamanai.

The first conclusion that can be drawn from examination of the early Terminal Classic ceramics at Lamanai is that previously held

233

concepts regarding the time span represented by San José V–related ceramics are likely to be too short by a considerable factor. Many of the forms introduced in the late ninth or early tenth century persisted in use through much or all of the eleventh century as well, though analysis may reveal subtle changes in shape and slip characteristics that will permit us to refine the use of ceramic time markers in the early Terminal Classic years.

The second conclusion based on ceramics is evident in architecture as well; these two classes of material culture, and others to a lesser extent, show that life at Lamanai did not conform to archaeological pigeonholes in the ninth to eleventh centuries any more than did life at any site at any time. Ceramic, architectural, and other traits refused to come to neat ends to be supplanted by another set; instead, there was a flow of interrelated techniques and ideas, some coming to the end of their time while others showed more staying power.

Both architecture and ceramics demonstrate that passage across the Terminal Classic bar was followed by vigorous development throughout the period and on into the Postclassic, with changes in some areas of life that seem of considerable magnitude but were probably of no greater impact than many that occurred during and before the Classic. One of the changes occurred in the use of N10-9, a structure that was an important part of the traditional aspect of early Terminal Classic life. At some point before the middle of the twelfth century, a part of the tradition was abandoned, as upkeep of the main platform terraces ceased while the building front clearly continued in use. At first glance, abandonment of the temple's body to the forces of decay seems to indicate that the rulers of late Terminal Classic Lamanai were no longer able to bring together a labor force sufficient to keep the now-antiquated building in usable condition. In fact, however, the neglect may reflect an even greater focus on the primary axis than had existed in the Classic, accompanied by the beginnings of a new center of attention and effort on ceremonial construction in the area just east of N10-9.

That N10-9 continued to be an important element in the ceremonial life of the community is demonstrated by the final major modification to the structure, new stair-side outsets sharply different from their Classic predecessors (Pendergast 1981: fig. 14), built sometime between the mid-twelfth century and the mid- to latter part of the thirteenth century near the close of the Terminal Classic. The modification altered no other parts of the structure's front, and this suggests that at the end of the Terminal Classic there was still at Lamanai a strong link with the past, both in building form and in ritual practice.

By the time of the last major addition to N10-9, work was under way in the area immediately east of the plaza, on Structures N10-1 and N10-2 (Fig. 7.2). The area appears to have seen use as early as the Early Classic, but may have lain partly abandoned until work was recommenced on what became a focal point for the Terminal Classic and Postclassic community. In N10-2, the late Terminal Classic saw construction of the first in a series of four structures, all a sharp departure from the architectural traditions of early ceremonial construction, but with one feature that suggests a link with one of the Plaza N10/3 buildings. The first of the N10-2 structures (Fig. 7.3), the only one on which we have something that approximates full evidence, was colonnaded, and therefore seems to resemble the Plaza 3 structure, as well as contemporary and later buildings in the Northern Lowlands. The resemblances cease at this point, however, for the Lamanai structure was a single-room building with wattle-and-daub walls and a floor that amounted to little more than a thick coat of whitewash over the ballast.

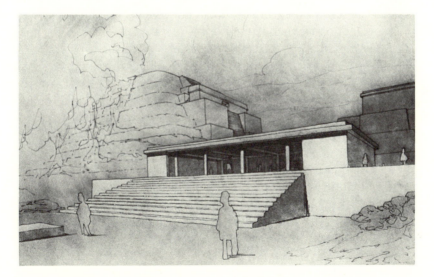

Figure 7.3 Structure N10-2 in the late Terminal Classic.

Identification of the N10-2 series of structures as ceremonial rests on the presence of a small altar at the rear of the room, the only masonry unit in each of the buildings. The placement of N10-2 almost side by side with N10-9 (Fig. 7.3) must have enhanced the visual and psychological effects of continuity accompanied by change, and may suggest related religious practices in the two structures. The juxtaposition of old and new, probably intentional, seems a concrete expression of Lamanai's vitality during a period when a good many neighboring centers were very far along their path to disappearance beneath the forest.

The architectural innovations of the twelfth century were paralleled by the introduction of new forms and surface treatments in ceramics, which, like the buildings, were almost certainly drawn out of earlier traditions. A cluster of radiocarbon dates from N10-2 shows that by about A.D. 1140 there was at Lamanai a fully developed range of distinctive forms, some precursors of which can be seen in burial ceramics from the initial construction in N10-1, a small platform east of N10-2. While a burial in the primary N10-1 structure yielded a combination of locally manufactured and imported vessels not in the full late Terminal Classic tradition, the interment from an addition to the platform was accompanied by vessels closely related to datable N10-2 ceramics (Figs. 7.4 and 7.5), and a single specimen of Silho (Chichen) Fine Orange (Fig. 7.5a). The presence of the Fine Orange vessel demonstrates that by the twelfth century Lamanai was part of a trade network that included many sites in the Northern Lowlands. It is, however, abundantly clear that Lamanai was not part of the Chichen-dominated Northern Lowlands sphere, whereas El Pozito, just 30 kilometers north of Lamanai, shows unmistakable Chichen-sphere ceramic relationships (Ball, personal communication, 1982).

The characteristic vessel forms of the mid-twelfth century and later include large pedestal-based censers with segmented flange, tripod bowls with a broad range of highly inventive foot treatments, and the apparently unique "chalice," a shallow dish set atop a very high pedestal base (Fig. 7.4, and Pendergast 1981a: figs. 15, 20, 26). All of these, as well as a very wide variety of jar, drum, and other forms, are red to orange monochrome, frequently with incised decoration, much of which was originally filled with black pigment. The very small amount of absolute duplication among the more than 600 whole and reconstructable vessels from the twelfth to the early fifteenth cen-

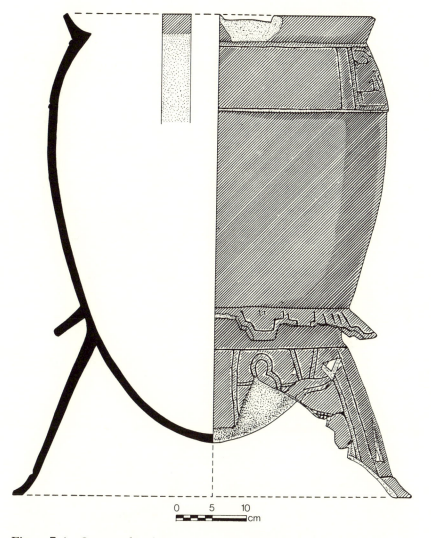

Figure 7.4 Giant pedestal-base censer that contained Burial N10-1/1, and sat atop the vessels shown in Fig. 7.5 Height 66.2 cm.

Figure 7.5 Silho Fine Orange (*a*) and other vessels from Burial N10-1/1. Scale 1:4.

tury conveys the strong impression that individual freedom in manipulation of form and decoration was greater in the Postclassic than it had been at any time in the past.

While construction, together with interment of large numbers of individuals accompanied by vessels broken and strewn atop the graves, was continuing in N10-2 and N10-1, the neighboring Early Classic Structure N10-4 was seeing use as a gravyeard, a use that continued until very near the end of the Postclassic. To the north, Structures N10-17 and N10-18, at the east and west ends of Plaza N10/3, remained in use, perhaps as the principal elite residences of the period. Scattered around their perimeters is midden that contains ceramics and other objects similar to those from burials in N10-1, N10-2, and N10-4. The amount of refuse is considerable, but scarcely enough to represent the full span of use of the buildings. It therefore appears quite likely that the structures were among the sources of a gigantic midden that was deposited as early as the fourteenth century.

The relationship between the midden and Structure N10-2, which it came to abut after filling the east side of the N10-9 plaza, indicates that a fair period of accumulation is represented, and that much of the amassing of the heap took place after the later stages of N10-2 had been built. The huge quantity of ceramics, likely in excess of 300,000 sherds, closely resembles material from N10-2 and N10-4 burials, as well as that associated with N10-18; this suggests that the sources of the refuse were at no greater remove from the deposition site.

The midden bespeaks an attitude toward ceremonial structures that seems rather unusual, as it is apparent that the refuse dump engulfed portions of N10-9 and N10-2 while a bit of the former building and all of the latter were still in use. Its volume also indicates the presence of a considerble population at the south end of the site center, and the nature of the ceramics is a strong argument for ceramic conservatism in the early Postclassic, with retention of form and surface treatment modes that emerged in the final century of the Terminal Classic. As with early Terminal Classic ceramics, it may eventually prove possible to recognize gradations in the sequence, but we are in fact probably seeing long-term persistence of a specific set of attitudes toward what constitute appropriate pottery forms and surface treatments. This is a kind of conservatism also detectable in the N10-2 architectural sequence, but in ceramics the conservative streak ran only as deep as the broad shape and decoration modes, while within those boundaries the potter's imagination continued to be allowed to run riot.

In addition to the chalice and censer recovered at Altun Ha, fragments of a Lamanai-related censer and chalice come from postabandonment strata atop the principal structure at Mayflower, in the Stann Creek District (Graham 1983: 569–70, fig. 169a, b). The Stann Creek occurrence is part of the meager evidence for early Postclassic presence in the area, but in this instance, in contrast with the Altun Ha material, paste characteristics indicate that the vessels were locally made. The significance of the ceramic relationship between Lamanai and Mayflower clearly cannot be assessed on the basis of such limited evidence, but the Stann Creek data suggest that we may eventually be able to identify Lamanai-related ceramics in other parts of the Central Lowlands at some distance from the place of their heaviest occurrence.

While some of the vessel forms of Early Postclassic Lamanai are not known to be duplicated elsewhere, much of the pottery of these times has clear affinities with that of Mayapan. The early radiocarbon-based date for the Lamanai assemblage, coupled with the fact that the beginnings of the distinctive concatenation of traits obviously precede A.D. 1140, appears to document the primacy of Mayapan-style ceramic characteristics at Lamanai. The idea of passage of ceramic innovations from Belize to northern Yucatan is supported by strong indications that the twelfth-century and later Lamanai pottery tradition was a local development, in which earlier techniques overlapped with new concepts. This surely shows that Lamanai was not simply an island in a have-not area, dependent on outside sources for all of its new ideas, but rather was a developing-ground for new ideas as well. The flow of concepts, as of materials, is likely to have been two-way, or in fact multichanneled, as is true of almost all intergroup contacts.

The flow of materials into Lamanai is demonstrated most clearly by the presence of metal artifacts in burials of twelfth-century and later date. Apart from some sheet-gold artifacts, the objects are all of copper, and typological data indicate that most are likely to be from the Oaxaca area. Other sources for metals in the Lamanai area may be identifiable as well, since the presence of a Veraguas-style gold bell in a context of unknown date at El Pozito indicates trade in metals from the south as well as from the north.

While many trade contacts obviously continued to enrich life at Lamanai during the early Postclassic, there is evidence that the importation of obsidian had greatly diminished in volume by or before the end of the twelfth century, if it had not ceased altogether. Obsidian provided everything from a few flake blades to as much as 15 kilograms of cores for Middle and Late Classic offerings, whereas Postclassic offerings and burials are almost entirely devoid of the material. The contrast between Classic and later domestic utilization of obsidian is much harder to determine, but it appears likely that here, too, change took place. Classic and earlier middens generally yield larger pieces of obsidian than those of the Postclassic; much of the obsidian from late Terminal Classic and Postclassic contexts, especially from very late Postclassic middens, consists of small pieces that may represent reuse of material imported to the site in earlier centuries. The breakdown of the obsidian trade is a phenomenon that has received considerable attention as an aspect of Classic collapse; the evidence from Lamanai suggests that if such breakdown occurred, it was probably not earlier than the fifteenth century, though it was preceded by a long period of declining commerce in the highly important material.

In the later part of the Postclassic, some facets of life at Lamanai unquestionably underwent change, although it appears highly likely that both N10-9 and N10-2 continued in use until the fifteenth or early sixteenth century. While use of N10-9 involved only the construction of two tiny units at the structure's base, each faced with typical vertically set facing stones, the relationship of the units to antecedent construction shows that at least the lower portions of the central stair and its flanking outsets had not been allowed to fall into ruin in the preceding centuries. Maintenance of part of the vital primary axis area seems to have been continued despite the fact that much of the stair was strewn with chalices and other pottery deposited during or soon after the final ceremonial use of the upper parts of the temple.

Meanwhile, N10-2 saw a succession of modifications that repeated all the essentials, and perhaps almost the identical form, of the late Terminal Classic structure; rebuilding probably extended through at least the early fifteenth century. Elsewhere in the southern part of the site, new ceremonial construction was essayed in the form of an extensive, low platform in the plaza in front of N10-9 and a pair of small platforms that supported uncarved stelae, west of Plaza N10/3. Construction features indicate that all three platforms are of fifteenth-century date, and artifact matches suggest that all were built simultaneously as part of an extensive ceremonial renewal of the area.

Late ceremonial activity was obviously focused in the southern part of the site center, but was not limited to that area alone. An offering at the base of N10-43 points to at least minimal Late Postclassic religious activity in the central portion of the Central Precinct, while at N9-56 evidence indicates continuing importance for a building that was unquestionably in ruins. Several small platforms that resemble those farther south were built at the base of N9-56; the central one supported a resited Late Classic stela. Atop N9-56 lay a mass of Mayapan-style figurine censer fragments, the products of ritual smashing of between 50 and 100 censers probably at the time of construction of the small platforms. Late Postclassic ceramics elsewhere in the northern and central parts of the Central Precinct suggest that other major temples may have seen ceremonies as impressive as that carried out on the decayed mass of N9-56, but there is no other large body of data on ceremonial activity in this period.

The censers blend the general Mayapan form with a range of specific features of costume, posture, and facial characteristics that are not those of Northern Yucatan. The mixture points to local manufacture, with alteration of a northern pattern to conform to local tastes. One cannot argue from this, any more than one can from the ceramic evidence of preceding centuries, on either side of the question of whether Lamanai was politically bound to any center in the Yucatan, and it is impossible to determine whether the network boundary between El Pozito and Lamanai in earlier times persisted into the Late Postclassic. Indeed, it is impossible to extricate specific evidence on Postclassic political structure at Lamanai from the architecture and other artifacts, and hence to attempt to extend the data northward would be highly dangerous, though it would have the ideal archaeological quality of erecting a hypothesis incapable of proof. What can be shown is that the Mayapan style is reflected strongly in the censers, as it is in some other vessel forms, which demonstrates that Lamanai was linked with Northern Yucatan through ideas in the Late Postclassic, if in no other way.

What are assumed to be links with the north persisted to the end of the Postclassic, in the form of Tulum-related ceramics. The significance of Tulum-style pottery, especially in the Central Lowlands, is impossible to assess at present; at Lamanai, combination of importation with local manufacture seems highly probable. Tulum ceramics appear to have predominated over, but not replaced, locally developed wares in burial accompaniments; the principal interment in N10-4, probably of late fifteenth- or early sixteenth-century date, exemplifies such a combination (Pendergast 1981a: 47, figs. 21, 22). At the domestic level, Tulum-related ceramics initially formed a smaller part of the inventory than in burials, but near the end of the Postclassic Lamanai potters were producing a wide range of Tulum imitations, and also utilizing the Tulum style of incised decoration on wares sharply different from those with which the motifs are usually associated.

Much of the latest Postclassic life at Lamanai continued to be centered on the area that had served as the heart of the community in immediately preceding centuries, but the fifteenth and sixteenth centuries also saw what appears to have been expansion into the far southern part of the site, at least one kilometer south of N10-9. Evidence for such an expansion includes a pure Tulum platform (Structure N12-11) which is the earliest construction at its locus. Though the building was extensively damaged in the early Historic Period, its architectural affinities are clear, and they constitute evidence at least as strong as the ceramics regarding relationships between the Tulum sphere and Lamanai during the Late and Terminal Postclassic.

Finally, there is the Early Historic Period occupation, for which some parallel data are emerging from Tipu in the Cayo District, but are otherwise not identifiable elsewhere in Belize at the moment. At least the southern portion of the Postclassic settlement was still a functioning community in the second half of the sixteenth century, and it is possible that the Spanish arrived about 1570 to find the entire Lamanai community little changed from that of several centuries earlier. Yet placement of the Spanish church about three-quarters of a kilometer south of N10-9 may indicate that the southward extension of the community in immediately preceding centuries had led by or before 1550 to a real southward shift in focus, which was retained until the settlement's dissolution. It is highly likely that the community which surrounded the church was as altered socially and politically as it was structurally, but to date we have been largely unsuccessful in attempts to recover evidence of that alteration.

The tradition of occupation in the southern part of the site may have been a factor in use of the church as a residence by the Maya following its desecration in 1640. From 1641 or slightly later until

243

near the end of the seventeenth century, one or more families dwelt in the masonry chancel of the church, casting their refuse in and around the buildings and burying their dead and their offerings where the chancel floor had been. The midden includes Spanish ceramics as well as a range of locally made pottery that includes at least one reconstructable vessel (Pendergast 1982c: fig. 3). The ceramics illuminate a facet of Postclassic life that is both instructive and unsettling: the materials appear to be indistinguishable from those of immediately preceding centuries, and are identifiable as Historic only because of their context.

The church material includes no identifiable Tulum-related ceramics, but does comprise a considerable sample of Mayapan-like material, among which are numerous figurine censer fragments. The censer material, together with small Tipu-type shrines built in the ruined nave and the offerings from below the chancel floor level, indicates that those who lived in the remains of the church viewed the building both as a sacred spot and as a conveniently sturdy shelter. The absence of "Lacandon-type" censers in this partly ceremonial context raises some questions about the use of such vessels as markers of the Terminal Postclassic or Early Historic Period, although they seem to replace Mayapan-style censers elsewhere in the Central Lowlands.

The nature of the church ceramics points to conservatism in pottery design and manufacture akin to that of the Postclassic, though the sample does not include some of the forms and surface treatments that appear in the late Postclassic middens at the south end of the site center. The retention of prehistoric pottery shape and surface treatment modes in the Historic Period means that recognition of sites of the period in the Central Lowlands, and perhaps elsewhere, may have to rest on a foundation other than pottery, and may therefore prove impossible in a great many cases.

I would not argue that events at Lamanai from the ninth through the seventeenth century are a microcosm of the Postclassic in the Central Lowlands or even in northern Belize, for it is clear that the course of life at many, or perhaps almost all, sites in neighboring areas did not parallel that we have just examined. The Lamanai data do, however, unquestionably give the lie to the view that the Postclassic in the eastern part of the Central Lowlands was entirely a time of stagnation. They also make it clear that the region was not one in which everything of consequence in Postclassic development stemmed from outside sources. It seems to me that the evidence from Lamanai also goes a long way toward dispelling the myth of the Postclassic as decadence writ large; the vitality of the community through much or all of the period, both internally and in its contacts with the outside world, was that of people who were not on a steep descent, but rather on a course different from that of earlier times. Lamanai was, in fact, exactly what one would expect of any community that continued to function in the Terminal Classic and Postclassic: an essentially indigenous development out of Classic and earlier roots, into which ideas and materials from outside sources were introduced as necessary, with the degree of alteration required to make them blend into the local pattern.

The external sources that were of principal importance to Lamanai during the Postclassic seem to have been primarily in the north, as one would expect given the course of events elsewhere in the Lowlands during the period. The exclusion of the site from the Chichen ceramic sphere in the Terminal Classic appears to argue for Lamanai's role in an exchange network yet to be defined. It was this network that brought in the Silho Orange, as well as other materials; what it took outward from Lamanai remains to be determined. Near the end of the Terminal Classic, a shift in network seems to have brought Lamanai into closer contact with northern Yucatan; here, as elsewhere, we should surely view the avenues of communication as two-way streets, which is what one should find in interaction between equals or near-equals.

The maintenance of communications between Lamanai and centers in northern Yucatan and beyond is one of the few critical aspects of Postclassic life at the site that admits comparatively simple explanation. Sitting at the head of the Dzuluinicob or New River, Lamanai had open to it a route of travel that is still one of the more attractive in the rather forbidding northern Belize coastal lowlands. The route must have offered to Postclassic merchants, as it did later to the Spanish, an ideal means of quick movement through the area with minimal outlay of energy. Recognition of the importance of marine and riverine travel as one of the keys to Postclassic interchange and survival not only may provide part of the explanation for events at Lamanai, but also suggests that we should look to other Central Lowlands riverine sites for evidence of a similar Postclassic history.

We are still a very long way from being able to identify the range of goods and information that passed along the Yucatan coast and the Dzuluinicob and from being able to assess the economic significance of that passage to Lamanai. Though we have no way of knowing whether the raised-field system at the northern limit of the site continued in use during the Postclassic, archaeobotanical data show that maize agriculture was practiced at the site throughout the Postclassic, and material from various middens indicates that the community probably came as close as any of this or earlier periods to being self-sufficient insofar as most comestibles were concerned. Here, too, the lagoon and river had a role to play, for turtles and fish provided a high percentage of the animal protein consumed by the Postclassic community. The diet was enriched by importation of a small amount of marine foodstuffs, and the people of Lamanai obviously depended on outside sources for salt, as they may have done for other important foods. It is likely, however, that they had no great need to look to exchange systems to supply themselves with agricultural staples and with most of the meat required by a healthy populace.

Beyond the area of foodstuffs, the people of Lamanai were probably neither better nor worse off than their Postclassic counterparts in other functioning Lowland communities. Cotton and other fibers are likely to have been available locally, while some of the chert used for tools could have been obtained within relatively easy walking distance. Stone for metates was surely an import, but some other basics were almost certainly not. Neutron activation analysis of Postclassic Lamanai ceramics shows that the vessels are an essentially homogeneous group, probably distinguishable from pottery made elsewhere; this does not permit identification of the potting clays as local in origin, but it suggests that something approaching self-sufficiency in this area of the economy existed in the Postclassic, as it had done in earlier times.

I have intentionally omitted cacao from the overview of Lamanai's economic condition in the tenth to the seventeenth century, because there exists at present no shred of solid evidence that cacao was grown at or near the site, or that the site served as any sort of way station in the transport of cacao from the Belize Valley to the northern centers made easily accessible by the river. Absence of evidence is often a help rather than a hindrance in attempts at theorizing, but it is not particularly useful when one is trying to characterize the economic base on which Lamanai depended for its obviously rich Postclassic existence.

246

If cacao was a part of that base, it may always remain a piece we cannot fit into the picture with any sense of certainty.

Lamanai's river avenue to the outside world surely served not as the lone lifeline that kept the community's head above the waves of collapse, but rather as a means whereby an internally strong southern community was able to obtain what it required from outside, and to send out in exchange whatever it possessed that could be used at centers elsewhere in the Lowlands. Hence an understanding of communications between Lamanai and other centers takes us only partway along the path to an explanation of the community's survival in the face of the forces that were at work in other parts of the Central Lowlands during the Terminal Classic and the Postclassic.

No simple environmental explanation for social phenomena is any more satisfactory than a monocausal view of the Classic collapse, or the idea of monodirectional flow of ideas and materials from site to site. The difficulty in moving beyond discussion of environmental bases for survival is that we enter an area in which intangible factors, generally impossible to recover through excavation, surely played as large a part as any economic considerations in Lamanai's ability to weather the ninth and tenth centuries and to continue as an active community in the years thereafter. If we see the high degree of uniformity in Classic Lamanai architecture and offerings as an indication of an essentially conservative, supposedly stable community with a social structure and world view that resembled those in the Peten, then we cannot adduce peculiarities of the Lamanai situation as the cause for the community's survival. This might, in fact, be equally true if we could recognize such peculiarities, since we have no means of imputing survival potential to factors of this sort, nor indeed to any aspect of a community's structure.

The most intangible factor of all, obviously not quantifiable from the archaeological record, is the community's psychological ability to survive, and, as I have suggested, it is precisely this ability that was surely the most important in seeing Lamanai through the transition period. The welding together of individual optimism to form a positive collective will is the function of community leaders, but the techniques used in performing that function leave no archaeological traces.

It is the role of governments everywhere to continue to assure the populace that all is well when a quick glance around shows that disaster is nigh; it is, however, extremely difficult to see how even the most optimistic pronouncements from the Lamanai leaders could have made the difference between success and failure when other Central Lowlands centers were toppling left and right as the Classic drew to a close. That toppling must have resulted in breakdown of intersite relationships enjoyed by Lamanai during the Classic, and this cannot have failed to alter many aspects of life at the site. Yet somehow the community withstood the effects of it all, and kept on forging ahead. The phenomenon can be described, but not explained, as is often true in archaeology, and it is because of this that it would be eminently unwise to see in Lamanai some sort of paradigm of Postclassic life in the eastern Central Lowlands, if one accepts that there were other sites in the area left essentially unscathed by events in the ninth and tenth centuries.

The question remains of whether we can draw from a combination of Lamanai and other site data some sort of model for the Postclassic as a whole. I think that the answer is that we cannot, and indeed should not. It is not simply that we are, especially in the Central Lowlands, a long way from having sufficient data for establishment of a model; it is, rather, that the data from Lamanai combine with those from elsewhere in the Lowlands to suggest that we should see the Postclassic as a time in which various subregions, or in some cases individual communities, pursued various courses, just as they had done in the Classic. There is obviously a level at which unifying features can be recognized among subregions and communities, but it is a level so general, or with concomitants so poorly understood, that it is of little use in explaining events during the last eight centuries of pre-Hispanic Lowland Maya life. It seems to me as true of the Postclassic as it is of the Classic that, especially at our present level of knowledge, we can derive more profit from focusing on the variety in the archaeological record than we can from seeking some means of submerging that variety within a single unifying theory. For the Postclassic in particular, variety may indeed have been the spice of life, a spice that did not just add tang to existence but rather lay at its very core.

I said at the outset, and have repeated several times, that one has to take a very particular view of prehistory in order to see the Postclassic as a time of decadence. No one can deny that many sites in the tenth century and afterward saw not just decay but a decline into oblivion; yet where communities survived, what they experienced was a period of changes in direction, and of life that was in some ways less rich than that of the Classic, but perhaps in other ways was richer. It is only if we persist in seeing the Classic as the embodiment of perfection in all aspects of life that we can view the succeeding centuries as all dross and dreariness.

If one can judge by ceramics alone, as we are often wont to do, there may have been more freedom of individual expression in the Postclassic than ever existed in a Classic community. People may have been no less priest-ridden, but the burdens imposed on them by their rulers in the way of ceremonial construction were, at least at Lamanai, far lighter than they had been in previous centuries. Population in the Central Lowlands was in many instances considerably more dispersed than in earlier times, but where communities hung together, they may have had something of the quality of a solid neighborhood, and for many, or for most, life may in fact have been neither markedly worse nor significantly better than it would have been in Classic times, but simply different. If we reject the idea that the difference is equatable with decadence, we will have come a long way toward a real understanding of what life at Lamanai and elsewhere in the Lowlands from the tenth century onward was all about.

8
The Peten Postclassic: Perspectives from the Central Peten Lakes[1]

PRUDENCE M. RICE

University of Florida

It is ironic and unfortunate, but nonetheless true, that the Postclassic occupation of the Department of Peten, Guatemala, and adjacent western Belize has been largely neglected by archaeologists. This heavily populated "core area" of Classic Lowland Maya civilization has been a focus of intensive archaeological investigation for decades, as the Preclassic and Classic art, architecture, and pottery captured archaeologists' imaginations. But then in the ninth century came the "collapsing": a breakdown of hierarchical social organization, a cessation of construction of architectural centers and erection of stelae, a decline in quantity and quality of craft and trade goods, a major depopulation . . . the litany of disasters is familiar to every Mayanist and bespeaks a general cultural impoverishment.

Paralleling the ninth-century decline of this spectacular civilization, archaeologists' interest in this "post-Classic" period in Peten also faltered. Even ethnohistoric documents, which provided tantalizing glimpses of life in the area during the sixteenth and seventeenth centuries, failed to elicit sustained scholarly attention to the period. By contrast, the mercantile Postclassic societies of Yucatan to the north and the Postclassic "fortress" sites of the Guatemala Highlands to the south enjoyed continuous archaeological research efforts. But the Peten was regarded as essentially uninhabited in the centuries following the Classic "collapse," and the Postclassic cultures of the area represented a demographic as well as an intellectual void in Maya prehistory.

THE PETEN POSTCLASSIC: PREVIOUS RECONSTRUCTIONS

Reconstructions of the Peten Postclassic have generally been formulated on the basis of tacit (usually pejorative) comparison to Classic Period sites and events. Until the mid-1970s comparatively little work was directed specifically toward Postclassic settlement and chronology in Peten. With the exception of the Carnegie Institution of Washington project at Tayasal (Guthe 1921, 1922), Cowgill's (1963) work on Flores Island and the basins of Lakes Peten-Itza and Sacpuy, and Bullard's excavations at Topoxte (1970) and Macanche (1973), the little that was known of the Peten Postclassic had been achieved almost by accident in the course of investigating large Classic Period centers. Resultant syntheses, therefore, not only denigrated the Peten Postclassic as an ignominious successor to a glorious past, but were weighted to the early part of the period and toward site-specific reconstructions. The scenarios were written largely in "catastrophist" terms, critical events being the Classic "collapse" and abandonment of large centers around A.D. 800–900, and later (date or dates uncertain) inmigration and presumed dominance of the area by Itza groups from northern Yucatan. These emphases gave, I think, an erroneous picture of the nature of the Postclassic in Peten.

With respect to the "collapse," it is true that large centers in the interior of central Peten, such Tikal, Uaxactun, and Yaxha (Figure 8.1), seem to have been virtually abandoned by or during the Terminal Classic Period, as is evidenced by the cessation of construction of public and residential buildings and monuments at these sites. Culbert (1973a: 70) has suggested that this abandonment is not hard to explain, because the collapse was primarily an elite-class phenomenon. On the eastern periphery of Peten, however, high population densities continued through the last part of the Late Classic at smaller centers like Barton Ramie and Benque Viejo. Indeed, Barton Ramie appears to have been occupied continuously into the Early Postclassic Period. In the southwest Peten, the Pasión area seems to have experienced a florescence of sorts during the Terminal Classic, with two non-Maya (or "Mexicanized

Figure 8.1 The southern Maya Lowlands and adjacent regions of Mexico, Belize, and Honduras.

Maya") intrusions. The first apparently affected Seibal by A.D. 830 (10.0.0.0.0), while the second overran Altar de Sacrificios by A.D. 909 (10.4.0.0.0). It is uncertain to what extent these groups may have penetrated the interior, disrupting areas perhaps already weakened by other factors. After A.D. 950, most or all sites in the central area of Peten are thought to have been abandoned, and all was quiet on the western front as well.

The most abundant category of data bearing on the Terminal Classic–through–Postclassic transitional period in Peten is, of course, pottery. Three Late-to-Terminal Classic (A.D. 770–930) ceramic spheres have been defined in the areas of interest here, Eznab, Spanish Lookout, and Boca. Each has a unique content, which in most general terms revolves around the presence, absence, or relative proportions of Clas-

253

sic-style polychromes, red monochromes, and fine paste wares. Similarly, each sphere has a particular geographical distribution, being associated with central Peten, western Belize, and the Pasión, respectively. Whatever events were occurring in the Terminal Classic Period in Peten, they had different effects on the ceramic traditions of different areas, and the overall tendencies seem to be conservatism and regionalism in production.

In the Postclassic Period three major ceramic groups—Augustine, Paxcaman, and Topoxte—constitute Bullard's (1973: 222) "Central Peten Postclassic Tradition." These groups are local manufactures, but the inspiration for the corpus of specific decorative and formal (e.g., vessel support) modes (Figure 8.2) cannot be identified in preexisting types either in Peten or in neighboring areas. Initial intuitive impres-

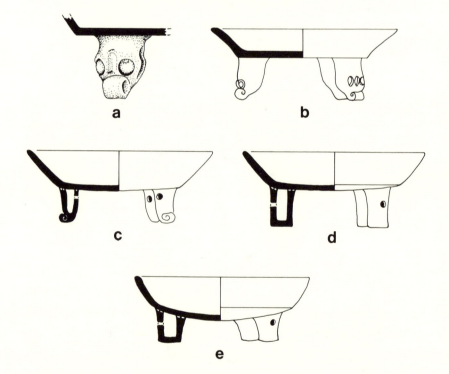

Figure 8.2 Variations on Postclassic tripod dish and support forms. a, b—Augustine Red; c—Paxcaman Red; d—Ixpop and Mul Polychrome (note: examples from Macanche Island lack vent holes in supports); e—Chompoxte Red-on-cream (Redrawn from Bullard 1973: 225, Figure 36).

254

sions of an Augustine-Paxcaman-Topoxte sequencing (Cowgill 1963; Bullard 1970, 1973) appeared to receive confirmation from Bullard's excavations on Macanche Island. This reconstruction also bolstered the general impression that the Yaxha basin experienced a settlement hiatus preceding a late, Mayapan-related occupation of the Topoxte Islands; Topoxte-group pottery, diagnostic of the Isla ceramic sphere (Bullard 1970; P. Rice 1979), was viewed as a late stylistic anomaly in this sequence. Of the relatively well-known Postclassic sites, only Barton Ramie was agreed to have had a probable continuing occupation from the Classic Period into the Postclassic. This was suggested by the presence of Augustine, plus small quantities of Paxcaman, which have been grouped into the New Town ceramic sphere. There has been considerable disagreement, however, as to whether or not Barton Ramie, lacking Topoxte-group pottery and "Mayapan-style" effigy censers, had a Late Postclassic occupation (Sharer and Chase 1976: 289; cf. P. Rice 1979: 77–81).

Since Bullard's original sequencing, new material has been identified, and the ceramic picture has become more complex. The Daylight group was defined as an Early Postclassic entity at Barton Ramie (Sharer and Chase 1976: 300–4), as well as being noted on the Tayasal peninsula (Rivera Dorado 1975). In addition, the Trapeche group was defined for the Early Postclassic on the Tayasal peninsula (A. Chase 1979). At Macanche, new varieties of Trapeche have been extended into the Late Postclassic, and a very late unslipped group, Chilo, has also been identified (P. Rice n.d. a). The Topoxte group has been more explicitly described in type-variety system nomenclature, together with Postclassic unslipped and censer types (P. Rice 1979, n.d. a). Cowgill's (1963: 112–15) tentative Tachis group remains something of an anomaly, although some sherds have been recovered on the Tayasal peninsula (A. Chase 1983).

The available archaeological data tend to confirm the observations of Spanish priests and explorers in the sixteenth and seventeenth centuries, who noted settlements primarily on islands in the central Peten lakes and on the lake shores. The Itza capital of Tayasal or Taiza was situated on what is now Flores Island in the largest of these bodies of water, Lake Peten-Itza (G. Jones, personal communication). Here it functioned at "the heart of a vast concourse of heathendom" (Scholes and Thompson 1977: 48) that resisted Spanish efforts at missionization and conquest. The northwest Peten and adjacent Campeche were largely unoccupied at this time, because Cortés marched five days in this area without seeing anyone. Southeastern Peten also had very few settlements, for Cortés was told it was six days' walk through uninhabited terrain (Pagden 1971: 368). Lake Yaxha and the Topoxte Islands were uninhabited by 1618 when the Franciscan Fathers Fuensalida and Orbita passed through (Lopez de Cogolludo 1867–68: Book 9, pp. 199–200). During these centuries, some former Classic Lowland Maya centers may have been periodically visited—whether by "pilgrims" or by "squatters" is difficult to determine—even in Historic times. Such visits are often indicated, as at Benque Viejo (El Cayo) and Piedras Negras, by the presence of distinctive "Lacandon-type" hourglass censers (Thompson 1977: 15); with their crude appliqued faces, these look like simplifications of Postclassic effigy vessels. Three Lacandon families reportedly lived in Tikal in the nineteenth century (Thompson 1977: 42).

It is frustratingly apparent that archaeologists' attempts to understand events in Peten between A.D. 1000 and 1525 have met with only equivocal success. In part this is so because of the typically poor stratigraphy at Postclassic sites that have been excavated; in part it is also due to a general lack of systematic surveys to determine the broad distribution of Postclassic settlement. Also, the occupational history of Peten has not been clarified at all by legends telling of an Itza migration into Peten from Yucatan in a Katun 8 Ahau, since it is not known if this occurred in A.D. 1201 or 1458. Nor is it clear how to relate these migrations to existing archaeological data on the Postclassic in Peten.

In sum, the general picture that has been painted of the Peten Postclassic is that it is radically distinct not only from the Classic, but from contemporaneous Postclassic traditions in other neighboring areas as well. Recent evidence from surveys and excavations around six of the Peten lake basins, however, suggest that this catastrophist and isolationist view of the Peten Postclassic may be misleading.

THE CENTRAL PETEN
HISTORICAL ECOLOGY PROJECT

The Central Peten Historical Ecology Project (hereafter CPHEP) is a combined archaeological and ecological research program aimed at documenting the impact of Maya populations on the lake basins in Central Peten. Initiated via Expedición Florida-Yaxha in 1973–74 at

Lakes Yaxha and Sacnab (D. Rice 1976; Deevey et al. 1979; D. Rice and P. Rice 1980a, 1984a), the research design was extended westward in 1979–81 by means of Proyecto Lacustre, which focused on the basins of Lakes Macanche, Salpeten, Quexil, and Petenxil (D. Rice and P. Rice 1980b, 1981, 1984b). The project was one of survey, mapping, and test-pitting of settlement remains. Block clearing and excavations were not undertaken, nor were there any excavations into major civic-ceremonial structures.

The lacustrine focus of the overall project conferred several advantages for achieving an understanding of the history of Maya occupation of Peten, especially with respect to the Postclassic. One advantage was that this focus permitted a systematic survey of Late Postclassic/Historic Period settlement, hitherto undocumented, despite being reported to be considerable around the lakes in the sixteenth century. Second, because the work had a regional settlement orientation rather than being a one-site program, the project allowed a wider geographical perspective on Postclassic social/political/economic interactions. Third, this focus allowed the possibility of tracing the developmental history of Postclassic occupation in the centuries during and following the "collapse."

Listed in the chronological order in which they were mapped and/ or test excavated by CPHEP personnel, five Postclassic settlement areas were of interest (Figure 8.3; see also D. Rice, this volume, Figure 9.1):

(1) Cante Island, the westernmost of the Topoxte Islands in Lake Yaxha, was mapped and test excavated in 1974. No Postclassic structural remains were found on the mainland, although occupational debris was noted.

(2) In the Lake Macanche basin, investigations in 1979 and 1980 on Macanche Island, at Muralla de León on the northeast shore, and in three transects in the mainland basin revealed Postclassic construction in all these areas.

(3) The peninsula off the northern shore of Lake Salpeten bore a high density of Postclassic construction, and this site, Zacpeten, was mapped and excavated in 1980. Few Postclassic structures were located on the mainland.

(4) The two islands in Lake Quexil had Postclassic structures, which

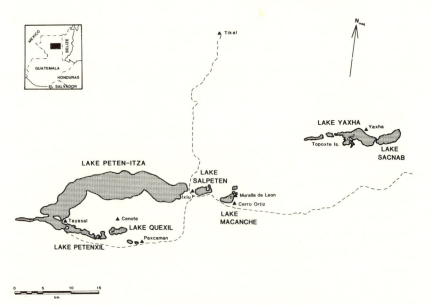

Figure 8.3 The central Peten lakes district.

were test excavated in 1980. Rare Postclassic settlement was noted on the mainland.

(5) The site of Ixlu was mapped in 1981, and although no excavations were undertaken, several Postclassic structures could be identified on the basis of their distinctive form.

In the remainder of this paper I focus on the results of CPHEP investigations in these areas, discussing Postclassic occupation history on a lake-by-lake basis. My emphasis is on the pottery recovered from these excavations and the inferences about culture history and process that can be derived from the ceramic remains. Pottery is not only a ubiquitous artifact category at archaeological sites, it is a very informative one, for the enormous range of variation in shapes, composition, and decorative styles evident in pottery provides a basis for understanding site chronologies, interregional contacts, and changing arrangements of production and distribution of this material. (The settlement and architectural data recovered by CPHEP that pertain to the Postclassic Period are treated elsewhere [D. Rice, this volume].) Following my summary of the ceramic and excavation data, I summarize the implications of these data for revising the chronology of the Peten Postclassic, and offer some tentative scenarios of sociopolitical events from the Terminal Classic through the Historic periods.

Lake Macanche

Lake Macanche is a small lake, roughly triangular in outline, with a large modern community along its southern shore. In the northeast corner of the lake is a small island, site of Bullard's excavations in 1968 and location of Proyecto Lacustre activity in June of 1979. Just off the northeast corner, on a high mesa-like promontory set off by *juleques* (natural small, deep sinkholes) and a dry (in 1979) arroyo, is the site of Muralla de León, consisting of numerous structures enclosed by a defensive wall. On the southeast shore is a small Middle and Late Preclassic center, Cerro Ortiz.

Macanche Island   Macanche Island is approximately triangular in outline, with a low platform mound on its northern apex. This is the highest point of the island, its preconstructional surface estimated at roughly 8 meters above the 1979 lake level. The platform, roughly 35 meters by 55 meters in area, 3 meters in height, and oriented northwest-southeast, apparently had two structures on its summit, to judge from the lines of stone visible on the disturbed surface. Eight test pits were placed on top and at the foot of the mound in order to obtain supplementary data for interpretation of the collection from Bullard's excavations. Five of these pits yielded midden and/or constructional material that served as a basis for preliminary definition of a Terminal Classic component and Early and Late Postclassic phases, as well as faceting within the Early Postclassic (P. Rice 1980, n.d. a).

The early phase of construction of the mound began in the Late Classic Period. Activity included modification of the substrate, and construction of a platform or platforms. Overlying sterile soil in seven of the pits was a disturbed, organically stained or leached, often banded, gray to white marly deposit containing sherds, shell, and frequently charcoal flecks. One area excavated had numbers of semireconstructable vessels, suggesting primary deposition. Two pits excavated into the summit of the platform sampled construction fill, indicating that a platform 1.7 meters high had been built over sterile white subsoil. The lower 70 centimeters of the fill of this platform were devoid of sherds, while the upper meter contained very heavily weathered sherds with little to no slip remaining.

The sherds in both the marl and fill layers are nearly all Late Classic types and/or forms. On the basis of form, the eroded material from the construction fill lots suggests the typical narrow-neck jars and incurved-rim bowls of the red-slipped Tinaja and Subin types and the wide-mouthed unslipped storage jars, often with labial flange, that are common in the Late Classic. Small quantities of dish forms, usually associated with polychrome decoration in better-preserved samples, were also found.

The marl layers included some of the same Late Classic forms found in the fill layers, as well as distinct pastes and shapes. Particularly evident are several new types, varieties, or "wares" not consistently noted in the fill lots. The most distinctive characteristic of many of these is that they are generally thin-walled and hard fired. (They are not, however, particularly *well* fired, as fireclouding is quite evident on many of them.) The materials include the following (see P. Rice n.d. a): (1) a body of cream-slipped sherds that may have some ties to Northern Lowlands pottery (slate wares) as well as to the later indigenous Trapeche group; (2) small quantities of Encanto Striated; (3) a distinctive local Coarse Gray variety of Cambio Unslipped; (4) moderate quantities of Achote Black; and (5) thin-walled, ash-paste jars with indented bases and slip colors ranging from yellow-orange to fireclouded brown and black (Payaso Orange-brown). Together, these distinctive forms, types, and pastes in the marl deposits have been used to define the Terminal Classic Romero complex in the Macanche area.

The problem is that it is not clear what the Romero complex represents in terms of the building/occupational sequence of the island. Because the marl layers contain material distinct from the eroded Late Classic fill sherds, they are presumed to be later, and to represent the debris of the builders of this early platform. Thus Macanche Island may have had some Terminal Classic activity on it, the occupants modifying the surface of the island, then building (by incorporating an earlier construction) a platform ca. 1.7 meters high. This construction may date to the very end of the Terminal Classic Period (ca. A.D. 900–1000), because the builders incorporated into the upper part of the fill Late Classic sherds that had apparently been exposed to weathering for some time.

Early Postclassic activity is evident in another test pit, excavated through mound fill to subsoil, where a black midden deposit overlay the gray mottled marl. This midden may represent later debris of people who lived upon and used the early platform, but this is difficult to determine. The midden contains much of the same ceramic material that was found in the marl layers: Encanto Striated, the Coarse Gray variety of Cambio Unslipped, Payaso Orange-brown, and hard ashy pastes. In addition, three Postclassic groups are represented, the slipped Paxcaman and Trapeche groups, and the unslipped Pozo group. Twelve sherds of Fine Orange were found in the midden. This midden ceramic material has been used to define an early facet of the Early Postclassic Aura complex at Macanche.

Above the early platform, a second platform was built, its surface ca. 80 centimeters above the previous one. The fill between the two platforms is virtually continuous, suggesting that the earlier platform may have been partly torn up in remodeling. The platform was also considerably larger, extending over the earlier dark midden deposit to the southeast of the first platform. Sherds in this later construction include the Paxcaman, Trapeche, and Pozo groups, plus a few sherds of Augustine Red, and comprise the late facet of the Early Postclassic Aura complex. In the late facet, the Terminal Classic types from the preceding early facet no longer consistently appeared in any quantity. In addition, sherds of the Paxcaman and Trapeche groups appeared much better fired in the late facet than in the early facet (P. Rice 1980).

Late Postclassic activity on the island is known from three separate construction or occupational deposits. A structure roughly 9.5 by 6 meters, oriented north-south, was erected over the northwestern end of the Early Postclassic substructure; a single course of double-line foundation bracing was evident for this structure. A second structure, more than 10 meters in length and 4 in width, was erected on the lower southeastern part of the platform. The third category of evidence of Late Postclassic activity is the rich black midden, 20 to 50 centimeters thick, that covers the entire mound area. This midden contains quantities of shell, animal bone, and pottery, much of it indicating primary breakage, and was the occupational episode primarily sampled by Bullard's earlier excavations.

The Dos Lagos Late Postclassic complex has been described on the basis of pottery recovered from these depositional contexts. Pottery types represented include Paxcaman, Trapeche, and Topoxte slipped groups, Pozo unslipped group, and a variety of filleted vase and effigy censers. Topoxte-group sherds were found in the fill of the Late Postclassic platform construction as well as in the overlying collapse and midden. The types that occur at Macanche are principally Topoxte Red monochrome and both varieties of Chompoxte Red-on-cream; few of the sherds could be classed as Pastel Polychrome or Cante Polychrome.

The censers are similar to materials occurring very widely through the Maya Lowlands during the Late Postclassic, and form part of the ceremonial subcomplex that has been linked to the legends of in-migration of Itza peoples from Yucatan. The effigy censers were made of at least three pastes, including the white Clemencia Cream paste characteristic of the red-slipped Topoxte ceramic group and Idolos-group censers of the Isla Postclassic complex at Topoxte (P. Rice 1979), as well as the gray snail-inclusion paste used in manufacture of slipped Paxcaman-group pottery. The finding of two fragments of molds used to form the human faces on these effigy censers suggests that at least some of the censers were made in the Macanche area.

Chilo Unslipped type occurred only in the upper 20–30 centimeters of the midden, and not in construction fill. Chilo is rather crudely made and poorly finished, with a dull orange-brown color, and vessel forms are similar to pottery made in recent times in Peten up to the mid-twentieth century (Reina and Hill 1978: Figure 41).

Macanche Mainland   Proyecto Lacustre investigations in the Lake Macanche basin were spread over the 1979, 1980, and 1981 field seasons, and included mapping and test excavations in three survey transects on the mainland. In addition, two sites were mapped and tested on the east side of the lake, Muralla de León and Cerro Ortiz. One of the surprises of this work was that Postclassic construction was evident on the shores of Lake Macanche (see D. Rice, this volume; P. Rice and D. Rice 1985).

Terminal Classic Romero-complex material was relatively sparse around the lake mainland. Sherds representing the characteristic materials on the island—cream slips, Payaso Orange-brown, and so forth—were not evident either in distinctive locations or in the quantitites in which they were found on the island. Instead, the Terminal Classic material was more like that in other lake basins: Tinaja Red, Subin

Red (including a distinctive hard, bright, pink-orange paste variant named Canjil paste, which usually occurred in incurved-rim bowls), and small amounts of Jato Black-on-gray. A Terminal Classic burial on the north side of the lake was intrusive into a Classic Period mound; an incised Black-on-gray cylinder vessel was the only burial furniture with the extended skeleton (Fig. 8.4).

The Postclassic occupation in the Macanche basin includes an

Figure 8.4 Cylindrical vase of Jato Black-on-gray type from a Terminal Classic burial at Lake Macanche. Vessel is 14.5 cm. in height.

interment of 12 crania, arranged in two rows, uncovered in excavation of the fill of a rather nondescript Postclassic mound in the area near Cerro Ortiz (D. Rice and P. Rice 1984b: 51). Cranial burials seem to have been a rather common Peten Postclassic practice, having been found also at Flores (Cowgill 1963: 20–22), at Lake Salpeten, and at Topoxte (see below). This ceremonial activity calls to mind the seventeenth-century Itza trait of displaying enemy skulls on stakes (Thompson 1951: 394, 1977: 28; López de Cogolludo 1867–68: Book 10, Ch. 2), as well as a recent custom in the modern community of San Jose, on the northern shore of Lake Peten-Itza (Reina 1962).

Lake Salpeten

The Lake Salpeten basin is topographically much like that of Lake Macanche, with a steeply rising northern shore and more gentle slopes on the south. Unlike Macanche, the area has very little modern settlement; this may be in part a consequence of the salinity of the lake's waters, which are high in $CaSO_4$ (the lake is underlain by gypsum). Proyecto Lacustre mapping and excavation activities in 1980 in the basin of Lake Salpeten provided additional evidence of Classic-to-Postclassic continuities in the Central Peten, as well as suggesting Late Postclassic through Protohistoric settlement in this area.

Zacpeten   Zacpeten is the name given to the densely occupied Postclassic site on the peninsula that juts out into Lake Salpeten from its northern shore. The peninsula has a small *juleque* on its western side, opening into the lake, as well as a Maya-made *aguada* (a small natural or artificial rainwater pond, usually shallow and often seasonal) near its center. In the course of mapping the transects in the lake basin, it was found that the area of Operation 1 (see Figure 9.3 in D. Rice, this volume) overlapped this peninsula, and a quick walkover suggested heavy settlement. Mapped in a separate operation, the peninsula had 190 structures arranged on several hills, natural terraces, and bedrock outcrops. The nature of the structures, plus the peninsular setting, immediately suggested a Postclassic settlement even prior to excavation, and the site was given the name Zacpeten. As at Macanche Island, there is evidence from Zacpeten of Late Classic to Postclassic continuity of occupation. Postclassic settlement on the mainland of Lake Salpeten was minor, with only three loci identified in the survey transects. It appears to be primarily a peninsular phenomenon, and began in the

Terminal Classic Period (D. Rice and P. Rice 1984b; D. Rice, this volume).

On the north end of the peninsula, near its join with the mainland, is a small plaza formed by two mounds of distinctly Classic rather than Postclassic form. Near these mounds were found two stelae, one plain and one carved. The carved stela, located between the two mounds, was broken into two pieces and badly eroded, having fallen face up. Nevertheless, it was possible to get an idea of the subject of the carving. A central figure standing in profile faces the viewer's left, holding a ceremonial bar; his feathered headdress flows behind him. No glyphic material or dates are evident on the severely weathered faces of the stela. In shape (being wider at the top) and style, however, it is very similar to 10th cycle Stelae 1 and 2 from Ixlu, a small center at the western edge of Lake Salpeten (see below). Because the Zacpeten stela was not found in a location typical of those in which stelae were commonly erected by the Classic Maya, it is possible that it was moved from its original placement. Similar abnormal stela placements are known from Tikal (Satterthwaite 1958) and Tayasal (A. Chase 1979), as well as Topoxte (Bullard 1970: 271).

Despite the proximity of the two lakes, Macanche and Salpeten, the Terminal Classic and Postclassic pottery from Lake Salpeten is rather different from that of Lake Macanche. One distinguishing marker of the Terminal Classic at Zacpeten was Jato Black-on-gray, found in somewhat greater quantities than at Macanche, but also associated with burials. In one pit on the peninsula a Terminal Classic burial on bedrock consisted of a Black-on-gray tripod dish and jade and shell beads, placed over an inverted skull. As at Macanche, distinctive ceramic pastes seemed to be the most significant characteristics of the Terminal Classic. One was a coarse, red-brown, crudely finished unslipped paste, probably a local variety of Cambio Unslipped. Another is the hard, pink-orange ash-tempered Canjil paste, most typically associated with incurving-rim bowls. Both these materials had been found at Macanche, though they were more common on the mainland than on the island, and seem to be rather widespread Terminal Classic products. Fine Orange sherds were noted on the surface in walking the transect on the south shore of Lake Salpeten, but relatively few sherds were recovered from excavations. In the Salpeten area, there was little or none of the distinctive Macanche Island material, such as Payaso, Coarse Gray, or cream slips.

The excavations at Zacpeten were into structure fill, rather than into middens, and thus did not yield the same quantities of Postclassic materials as were recovered from Macanche Island, particularly from the Late Postclassic midden that covered the platform on the island. In the Postclassic Period at Zacpeten, Trapeche-group sherds were present in extremely small quantities, though at Macanche this group constituted nearly half the slipped Postclassic material. Most of the Postclassic slipped sherds from Zacpeten were of Paxcaman and Topoxte groups. As at Macanche Island, the sherds of the Topoxte group were principally Chompoxte Red-on-cream type, both varieties, or Topoxte Red monochrome; Pastel and Cante polychromes were virtually unrepresented. Chilo Unslipped was also present at Zacpeten, and sherds of this group included a number of vessels with a dull, unpolished, almost fugitive red paint. Pozo Unslipped was common; under one late structure a Pozo jar with a broken rim rested on bedrock, and contained a cache of small seeds (subsequently identified as *Celtis*, related to hackberry; W. Crowe, personal communication) and broken turtle bone.

Censers are also known from Zacpeten, including one complete vessel found on the back "bench" or low wall of an open hall structure. The vessel (Figure 8.5) is a small globular bowl, roughly 15 centimeters in diameter, made of a paste very similar to that of Chilo Unslipped. Five appliqué strips form the limbs and tail of an indeterminate animal; the head is a human face, with a headdress and earplugs. The limbs, head, and lid of the vessel were stuccoed and painted. Inside the vessel were two beads, a tubular bead of jade and a flat disc bead of *Spondylus*. Nothing similar to this vessel has been found at any of the other Postclassic sites excavated by CPHEP.

Ixlu   Ixlu is a small center located on relatively high terrain between Lake Salpeten and the main arm of Lake Peten-Itza. The site was mapped in 1924 by Blom (Morley 1937–38: Plate 210), who showed some twenty structures and two stelae. At the time of Morley's visit, the two stelae were on the front (west) terrace of the large, pyramidal structure on the site. They are Tenth Cycle in date with Stela 1 dated at 10.1.1.0.0.0 (A.D. 859) and Stela 2 at 10.2.1.0.0.0 (A.D. 879).

Ixlu was visited by Bullard in 1968, at the time of his work on Macanche Island, and he excavated two test pits into the principal mound. One of the pits was at the base of the structure, while the

Figure 8.5 A small effigy censer from atop a Late Postclassic "bench" structure on Zacpeten peninsula, Lake Salpeten. Vessel is 14 cm. in diameter.

other was on the low terrace that had held the stelae (Bullard noted only one stela at the time of his visit). The pit at the base of the mound had Postclassic Paxcaman and Pozo types only in the upper 35 centimeters of the excavation, together with a few probable censer fragments. Below a floor (40 centimeters b.s.) the remainder of the material appeared to be mixed Late Classic and Terminal Classic types (P. Rice n.d. a).

In the CPHEP investigations of the Lake Salpeten basin, the site of Ixlu was of interest because Blom's early map had shown some structures that looked as if they could be Postclassic in date. In light of

267

this, plus the known Tenth Cycle dating of the Ixlu stelae, the site was remapped by CPHEP personnel in 1981 in order to assess the possibility of Postclassic construction there. In this remapping effort, numerous structures of typical Postclassic form were noted (see D. Rice, this volume). Although no excavations were undertaken by CPHEP at Ixlu to confirm this inference, material exposed in construction fill in a looter's trench in one of the structures included fragments of a large jar of the Paxcaman Group.

Lakes Quexil and Petenxil

Lakes Quexil and Petenxil lie south of the main arm of Lake Peten-Itza and east of the smaller eastern arm of that lake, on the southern boundary of the Tayasal peninsula. Lake Quexil is dumbbell shaped, with two islands in its western segment; Lake Petenxil, lying to the west, is considerably smaller. Although these two lakes have some similarities in terrain to the other lakes in the chain—the steep northern shore and gentler slopes to the south—in other respects they are quite different. The area around these lakes is very karsted, with numerous small *juleques* and *aguadas* in the surrounding environs. In addition, the south shore of Lake Quexil is distinctive because of its low-fertility soil with oak-savanna vegetation. The basins of the lakes are not heavily occupied at present, despite their proximity to Flores and ease of access by road. Human activity is largely confined to cattle ranching and some milpa farming, especially on the high northern shore.

The area around these two lakes was part of the overall survey region of the University of Pennsylvania's 1971 Tayasal Project, as well as the 1977 extension of that project by Arlen and Diane Chase in the Tayasal-Paxcaman zone (A. Chase 1979, 1983). Sites within the basins mapped by these previous investigations include Cenote (Morley 1937–38) on the north shore, and Finca Michoacan on the southeast, east of CPHEP transect 2 (see D. Rice, this volume).

The two islands on Lake Quexil were likely locations for Postclassic settlement, given the general proclivity for island occupation during this period. Although the Chases mapped the two islands in 1977 and concluded that the structures were Terminal Classic with no evidence for Postclassic occupation (A. Chase 1979: 91), remapping by CPHEP revealed three characteristic Postclassic constructional forms. Also, ethnohistoric accounts suggested a Historic settlement: Spanish documents mention a Lake Eckixil (another name by which Lake Quexil is known), which was said to have two islands supporting Itza houses of idolatry (Villagutierre 1933: 519).

In the four transects surveyed, mapped, and test-excavated by CPHEP personnel in 1980 around these basins (three at Quexil and one at Petenxil; see D. Rice, this volume: Figure 9.1), Terminal Classic and Postclassic settlement was noted on the mainland, but in relatively small amounts. Both Terminal Classic and Postclassic materials were more common on the two north-side transects—one north of Quexil and the one north of Petenxil—than on the south side of Quexil.

It was in the seven test pits on the islands in Lake Quexil that the greatest evidence for Terminal Classic and Postclassic occupation and construction was encountered in the basin. The smaller, western island appeared, from the two test pits excavated there, to have primarily Terminal Classic and very Early Postclassic settlement. The larger, eastern island appeared to have greater continuity into the Late Post-classic.

Terminal Classic pottery at Quexil shows ties to that previously described for Lake Macanche and Salpeten. Among the types and modes shared are: Jato Black-on-gray, Fine Orange, Pantano Impressed jars, Subin Red incurved-rim bowls, jars with indented bases, Canjil paste, and coarse red-brown unslipped paste. Both islands (and the few mainland Postclassic locations as well) showed a much greater quantity of Augustine pottery than was found at any of the outer lake basins. Trapeche-group sherds were relatively rare, as were sherds of the To-poxte group (as in the other sites, the only polychromes were the two varieties of Chompoxte Red-on-cream). Censers—both impressed-fil-let type and effigy figure type—were found in relatively small quantities. Only a few sherds of Chilo Unslipped were identified.

Lake Yaxha

Lake Yaxha and its twin, Sacnab, are the easternmost of the series of lakes in the Central Peten "chain." These lakes were the focus of Expedición Florida-Yaxha in 1973–74, the first program of combined archaeological and ecological investigations of CPHEP (Deevey et al. 1979; D. Rice 1976; D. Rice and P. Rice 1980a, 1984a). On the north shore of Lake Yaxha is the large Classic civic-ceremonial center named Yaxha, which was the location of mapping and test-pitting efforts by the Foundation for Latin American Anthropological Research (FLAAR) in 1969 through 1972 (Hellmuth 1972). In the southwestern portion of Lake Yaxha lie the Topoxte Islands, focus of Postclassic settlement in the basin and the site of Bullard's testing in 1958–60. In the early 1900s, at the time of Maler's visit, a small settlement existed on the isthmus between the two lakes, but it was abandoned by 1945.

Yaxha Center and Mainland

A number of lines of evidence suggest that the civic-ceremonial center of Yaxha had important ties to Tikal in the Late Classic. Yaxha is the only other site besides Tikal to have a twin pyramid complex (C. Jones 1969); Yaxha may have been a second-level center in the geopolitical hierarchy of which Tikal was the head (Marcus 1983: 465); and Yaxha's Terminal Classic Tolobojo Complex indicates full participation in the Terminal Classic Eznab sphere.

The Late Classic demise of the center of Yaxha cannot be traced with any more precision than can that of any other site in Peten. The twin pyramid complex at the site offers some clues, however, in that its construction seems never to have been completed. The "range" structure on the south side of the complex has two levels, as though the construction was abandoned before the building was finished, and no stelae were found in the customary locations, either in the stela enclosure or in front of the eastern pyramid. Stela 13 was found in an abnormal position in the complex, in front of the western pyramid, and its date of 9.18.3.0.0 (A.D. 793; I. Graham, personal communication), makes it the latest dated stela at the site. The relationship of the possibly unfinished construction of this complex to similar complexes at Tikal, where the latest are dated between A.D. 771 and 790 (C. Jones 1969), can only be conjectured.

In the Yaxha center, Terminal Classic Tolobojo material comes from scattered plaza and acropolis locations, but occurs in most significant quantities in the heavy midden in the elite residence compound known as the West Group. The West Group is a small plaza formed by twelve structures. Most of these are Ixbach (Tepeu 2) constructions, to judge from limited excavations and material from the backdirt piles of numerous looters' trenches. Heavy midden material, with quantities of Terminal Classic pottery, bone, and miscellaneous artifacts in a very ashy matrix, surrounds at least some of these buildings, suggesting that the Terminal Classic occupants may have lived on top of these structures. This pattern of reuse is common for the Terminal Classic throughout the basin.

Terminal Classic Tolobojo pottery shares several typological and formal similarities with the Eznab complex at Tikal. The Tinaja group is the most common monochrome ceramic occurring with generally well-preserved red slips on cream-to-tan ash-tempered pastes. Forms include jars (often with recurved neck); flat tripod plates, often with incising and a notched basal flange; and a variety of small and large hemispherical and incurving-rim bowls. Zacatel Cream Polychrome, frequently with a "dress shirt" or "feather" motif, and a variety of "composite" incised, fluted, and/or polychrome painted ceramics also are present. Unslipped vessels include a large jar with an outcurved neck and distinctive "piecrust" lip. These jars occur in such quantities in the Late and Terminal Classic periods in the Yaxha basin (and sparsely in other Peten areas) that they must have been locally manufactured.

Most interesting in the Tolobojo assemblage at Yaxha are the modeled-carved vessel fragments, which are found in at least five pastes (Figure 8.6). These pastes include: (1) a very fine-textured, soft, thin-walled orange paste, probably imported Pabellon Modeled-carved type; and a variety of coarser pastes that appear to be local imitations of Pabellon, including (2) a thick, hard, dense ash-tempered orange paste; (3) a relatively thin-walled somewhat coarser orange paste with mica; (4) a tan ash-tempered paste similar to that used for many vessels in the Tinaja group; and (5) a thick, soft cream-colored, ash-tempered paste, often with eroded slips, that was also used in manufacture of Late Classic polychromes. The occurrence of this variety of pastes at Yaxha suggests not only that the distinctive Pabellon Modeled-carved pottery was being imitated for local consumption, but that it was being imitated by a number of separate producers. Imitation Pabellon Modeled-carved is also known from Tikal and Uaxactun, where it is called Sahcaba Modeled-carved. Culbert's (1973: 81) description of his "Taman" paste, the paste variant used in manufacture of Sahcaba and also in some Tinaja-group vessels, may be equivalent to my variant (4) above.

The distribution of Terminal Classic remains in the Yaxha basin suggests reoccupation of vaulted Late Classic structures in widely scattered areas. Tolobojo material has been found principally on the two transects on the north side of the lake that flank the Yaxha center, as well as in small quantitites in two minor centers on the south side of

271

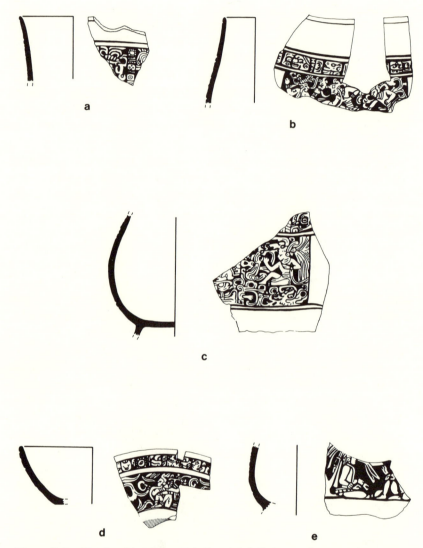

Figure 8.6 Sherds of imitation Pabellon Modelled-carved pottery from yaxha. a—thick ash-tempered paste; b, c—thin, coarse orange paste with mica; d— paste similar to slipped Tinaja group vessels; e—soft, cream-colored paste.

the lake. No Terminal Classic constructions were sampled on the one island of the Topoxte islands group that was the scene of CPHEP activities (although Tolobojo pottery was found in middens), and no Tolobojo pottery was recovered from the Lake Sacnab basin.

The duration of Terminal Classic settlement in the Yaxha basin is not known. The general lack of associated construction and relatively light midden deposition indicated that it was probably relatively brief and "weak," except in the West Group. The existence of well-made imitations of a widespread trade ware, Fine Orange, however, suggests a certain vigor in ceramic manufacture that belies a cultural or de-mographic decline.

Whatever the situation for the Terminal Classic, an occupational "hiatus" has generally been postulated for the early part of the Post-classic Period in the Yaxha basin. This break is of unknown duration, but was followed by the relatively heavy settlement in the Topoxte Islands, which has always been viewed as a Late Postclassic phenom-enon (ca. A.D. 1200–1400; Bullard 1970: 301). Although sparse Post-classic occupational debris was recovered from the Yaxha shores, no Postclassic architectural forms are known from the mainland of either the Yaxha or Sacnab basins (Bullard 1970: 252; D. Rice and P. Rice 1980a: 447).

Topoxte

The "site" of Topoxte consists of three densely occupied islands in the southwestern portion of Lake Yaxha. Actually, each island has been given a separate name (Hellmuth 1974): Topoxte proper is the largest island on the east, Cante Island (Bullard's "Third Island") lies to the west, and Paxte is the small island between them. Each island appears to have varying amounts of ceremonial architecture, indicated by arrangements of large pyramidal mounds, open halls or colonnaded halls with benches, and stelae and altars (see Johnson 1985). Four stelae were sculptured; although very badly weathered, they appear to be of Classic style, and because of their atypical locations probably represent secondary placement (Bullard 1970: 271). Unsculptured—probably stuccoed—monuments associated with small altars were found in the main plaza on Topoxte Island, and may be genuine Postclassic stelae (Bullard 1970: 276).

The islands have been explored, mapped, and photographed by occasional visitors—including Maler, Morley, and Lundell—since the

273

early 1900s (Bullard 1970: 250), but it was not until Bullard's work in 1960 that actual excavations were carried out. The ceremonial complex on Topoxte Island was the site of Bullard's excavations in 1958–60 (Bullard 1961, 1970), one of the first direct investigations into the Postclassic in Peten, and provided the data base for many of the later reconstructions. Bullard's work resulted in the first formal recognition of Postclassic Peten's ties to Yucatan, which existed specifically in the similarities of the colonnaded halls to structures at Mayapan, and in the presence of effigy censers. His work also provided descriptions of the late "Isla sphere" (see also P. Rice 1979), with its "Topoxte Cream Polychrome" pottery, which showed little resemblance to known Peten Postclassic ceramics. The three Topoxte Islands were later completely mapped in 1973 and 1974 by the Foundation for Latin Americna Anthropological Research (Hellmuth 1974; Johnson 1985). These maps revealed ceremonial architecture on all three of the islands, in addition to dense residential architecture.

Cante Island was the location of CPHEP mapping and test-pitting operations in early 1974. Of a total of 112 structures (142 were later mapped by Johnson) on the island, 19 were sampled by test pits, 13 into structural fill, and 6 into midden material adjacent to structures. Three of the pits were in the area of the island's ceremonial assemblage. The pottery recovered from these excavations on Cante Island was significantly different from that recovered by Bullard on Topoxte Island, although the sherds clearly were part of what he had called "Topoxte Cream Polychrome." The Cante Island material was more closely comparable in terms of decorative style to indigenous Peten Postclassic ceramic traditions exemplified in the Paxcaman group than was apparent in Bullard's earlier collection.

Analysis of the Cante Island pottery, and a look at Bullard's collection now in the Peabody Museum, resulted in his Topoxte Cream Polychrome being renamed the Topoxte ceramic group, within which three principal painted types were named (P. Rice 1979). These are Chompoxte Red-on-cream (with two varieties, Chompoxte and Akalche), Pastel Polychrome (decoration in black paint), and Cante Polychrome (red and black paint); very small amounts of incising (Dulces Incised) were also noted. All these types in the Topoxte group have known parallels in the decorated types of the Paxcaman group save Chompoxte variety of Chompoxte Red-on-cream. Whereas the banded, spare designs on dishes of Akalche variety look very much like Ixpop Polychrome vessels, except for being executed in dark red rather than black paint, Chompoxte variety has very complex and intricate decoration on the walls and sides of dishes, featuring loops, dots, combs, and the like (Figure 8.7). The bulk of the material from Bullard's excavations was classifiable as Chompoxte variety. It should be noted that it was not until the CPHEP excavations in the other lake basins that a decorative parallel to Chompoxte Red-on-cream: Chompoxte variety was identified in both the Paxcaman and Trapeche ceramic groups, both types occurring in small quantities and having red painted decoration on unslipped paste (P. Rice n.d. a).

Figure 8.7 A tripod dish of Chompoxte Red-on-cream: Chompoxte Variety; vessel supports are bulbous in shape. Now on display in the Museo de Antropología in Guatemala City, this dish was found in an antiquities shop in Antigua, and was said to have been damaged in the 1976 Guatemala earthquake.

275

The question that then arose concerned the significance of the apparent differences in ceramic content between the two islands, Cante and Topoxte. Were they temporal? Functional? Were they due to differences in status? Evaluation of the possibility of temporal differences was hampered by the general lack of clear stratigraphy, which plagued interpretation of the Topoxte excavation data as it did at many other Postclassic sites in Peten. Nevertheless, some preliminary, largely intuitive, ideas as to temporal differences were suggested in the ceramic report (P. Rice 1979: 11–12). Functional or status differences were perhaps more likely, however, considering the differences in locations of the two excavations. Bullard's material had been recovered from excavations into ceremonial contexts on the largest island; Expedición Florida-Yaxha excavations were primarily into residential architecture and middens on a smaller island. These differences in excavation contexts may have been sufficient to account for differences in ceramic content.

In 1981–82, I was able to spend a few weeks reviewing the Topoxte pottery from Cante Island. With the classification having been accomplished already, I was able this time to concentrate on the excavation context of these materials, and I believe I may now have a more reliable basis for interpreting differences in the ceramic assemblages.

The Postclassic slipped, decorated, and censer materials from 17 of the 19 excavations on Cante Island occurred in three separate "patterns" or clusters.

(1) What I call Group B consisted principally of Pastel and Cante Polychrome decorated types; censer fragments were relatively rare in all but one of the mounds yielding this cluster of materials. Paxcaman sherds, though rare in general on the Topoxte Islands, were usually found in the Group B pattern. This "pattern" occurred in construction fill lots of eight mounds.

(2) The Group A material consisted of principally Akalche and Chompoxte varieties of Chompoxte Red-on-cream, but with Pastel and Cante Polychrome also present. There were greater relative quantities of monochrome slipped and/or eroded (but presumably decorated) dishes in Group A than in Group B. Paxcaman was seldom present. Censers were not abundant, but of the three ceramic "patterns," Group A has the greatest variety of different censer types. Group A was found in only four mound excavations: two (possibly three) are construction

fill, the other is midden material adjacent to a structure. Bullard's original collection would have been classed as Group A.

(3) Group C is late "surface" debris, collapse, and/or midden, occurring in the upper 40–50 centimeters of the excavations. Overall sherd yields were smaller than in Groups A and B, and decorated types formed a much smaller proportion of the total. This is probably not due to erosion, however, because Groups A and B also had "surface" (upper 40 cm.) contexts with preserved polychrome decoration (although it is recognized that circumstances of weathering may be highly localized and variable). Group C overlies Group A in two mounds (one fill, one questionable) and overlies Group B in four mounds. The Postclassic material excavated from three test pits in nonconstructional contexts in the ceremonial center on Cante Island is all Group C.

Group C is clearly later than both A and B, being found stratigraphically above these groups in six excavations. The problem is that A and B were not found in stratigraphic relation to each other. The relationship of these "groups" or "patterns" to the spatial distribution of structures, or structural characteristics, on Cante Island does not resolve questions of functional versus temporal differences. Nor is the search for significance clarified by the fact that Group A was found in only four pits. These locations are all in or around small structures built on the lowest natural terrace near the lake edge on the south side of the island. Only one other structure on this "tier" was excavated; it may or may not be significant that it had evidence of stone structural foundations on top of the platform, and the material recovered from excavations was Group B.

On the basis of circumstantial evidence, I have been inclined to think that Group B was earlier than Group A. Group B was found primarily in construction fill, and in three pits it occurred directly over a construction dating to the Classic Period. Together with the Postclassic types in Group B, there were also some distinctive Terminal Classic materials—e.g., Canjil paste known from Macanche and Zacpeten, and Fine Orange—which were not found in Group A. (Sherds of the Tinaja group occurred regularly in all three "patterns," however.) And Group B contains the ceramic material with the closest typological or decorative ties to other indigenous Postclassic ceramic groups known to occur in the Early Postclassic in Peten. In the absence of stratigraphic associations between the two ceramic "patterns," the argument for the temporal priority of B is not strong, and other explanations may better account for their relationship.

Group A has a mixture of the indigenous-style ceramic decoration, plus the unusual decoration of Chompoxte variety of Chompoxte Red-on-cream. It was found in a rather restricted part of Cante Island, and Chompoxte variety had constituted the bulk of the ceramics from Bullard's earlier excavations into ceremonial contexts on the main island. It was not associated with platforms bearing surface evidence of structures, as was Group B. It may also be worthy of note that it was the polychrome types distinctive of Group A—i.e., the two varieties of Chompoxte Red-on-cream—that were the major representative of the Topoxte ceramic group outside the Topoxte Islands. Pastel and Cante polychromes, more closely identified with Group B, were rarely found at Macanche, Zacpeten, or Quexil. The possibility that Groups A and B are contemporaneous, and differentiated by function or status, is thus quite likely, given the restricted locations of A and the fact that A was found in nonfill contexts and B was not.

The pottery from Cante Island is ambiguous in other respects as well. Despite the presence of some 30 sherds of the Paxcaman group, primarily associated with the Group B "pattern,' and the decorative resemblances of some types to indigenous Peten types of the Paxcaman group, the Topoxte Islands do not share in the other Peten Postclassic ceramic traditions. No Trapeche-group sherds, for example, were found at Topoxte, and no Chilo Unslipped; only one sherd was tentatively classified as Augustine, and only three sherds were identified as being of probably Yucatecan manufacture. The inhabitants of the Topoxte Islands, in short, seem to have sent some of their pottery throughout a relatively broad territory in Peten, but to have brought in very little in return.

Topoxte may have been a bit of an iconoclast in its ceramic traditions, but the islands share several other characteristics of the greater Peten Postclassic tradition. Architecture has already been mentioned (see also P. Rice and D. Rice 1985). Another shared trait is skull burials: three interments of inverted skulls were found on Cante Island. In no case, however, were these associated with whole vessels, as was the one at Zacpeten, so they are relatively difficult to date. One was found on bedrock below a floor, with a metate in place on the floor directly above the burial. All three of the skull burials were found in "Group B" construction fill deposits.

THE PETEN POSTCLASSIC: REVISIONIST SCENARIOS

Central Peten Historical Ecology Project investigations in the basins of six lakes in the Central Peten yielded a substantial body of data bearing on the nature of Postclassic societies in the area. These data have, in some cases, confirmed some longstanding notions, such as the observation that Postclassic peoples tended to settle on islands in the lakes. In other cases, CPHEP investigations have modified, amplified, or disconfirmed earlier reconstructions of the Postclassic. Most significant among the results of these studies, I think, has been the increase in awareness of continuity between Terminal Classic and Postclassic occupations of the basins, and of ties between Peten Postclassic populations and those of neighboring regions. While the main objective of this paper has been simply to present an overview of the Postclassic Period in the Peten lake basins, and the ceramic data from which that overview has been constructed, it is also appropriate here to suggest an outline of broader processes and events occurring during this period.

Terminal Classic Period: "Collapse" vs. Continuity

One of the common tendencies in early reconstructions of the Peten Postclassic has been to see it as a dramatic break with earlier Classic traditions, a view that has been logically and substantively upheld in Mayanists' traditional catastrophist "collapse paradigm" of Peten history (cf. Edmonson 1979). A closer look at settlement and ceramic data from CPHEP investigations and from the broader context of Peten, however, forces some reconsideration of this interpretation. The continuities between the Classic and Postclassic may be stronger than previously allowed.

One perspective on the "collapse" and events in Central Peten during the Terminal Classic Period comes from consideration of the location and content of late (i.e., Tenth Cycle, or post-A.D. 830) stelae. Some of the latest dated stelae in Peten are from riverine or lacustrine locations, such as Seibal and Ixlu. The existence of stelae in these locations argues the presence of new or continuing elites to commission the monuments and craftsmen to carve them. The Pasión area, for example, enjoyed a Terminal Classic florescence associated with "Mexican" intrusions that seemed to be related to the emergence of Seibal as a late "capital" in the shrinking Maya hierarchy (Marcus 1976). Late stelae are also found at large interior sites such as Tikal (dated A.D. 869) and Uaxactun (dated A.D. 889), which suggests that elites continued to exercise the perquisites of status at these centers as well. The appearance of the Tikal emblem glyph on both of the Ixlu stelae and on a Tenth Cycle stela at Jimbal dated 10.3.0.0.0, or A.D. 889 (Marcus 1976), indicates that Tikal continued to be regarded as an important political center in the Terminal Classic (see Culbert 1973a: 89).

Evidence from the lakes area surveyed by CPHEP indicated changes in participation in the Terminal Classic traditions and spheres previously identified at larger Classic centers. Terminal Classic Tolobojo pottery at Yaxha falls into the Eznab with its quantities of Tinaja, cream polychromes, and modeled-carved pottery. At Macanche Island, the Terminal Classic Romero ceramic complex is different, having Tinaja Red and Jato Black-on-gray types as well as a distinct collection of other types, forms, and pastes. These components, plus the relative absence of Fine Orange, tend to support a "peripheral Eznab" rather than Boca sphere affiliation for Romero (P. Rice n.d. a). At Salpeten, Quexil, and Petenxil, the Terminal Classic is different still, characterized by Jato Black-on-gray, Tinaja, and slightly greater quantities of Fine Orange as the principal "fine wares," plus other materials that may or may not be shared with Macanche. None of the lakes demonstrates the same ceramic continuities from Late–to–Terminal Classic that were evident at Barton Ramie, where a single complex, Spanish Lookout, encompasses both periods. Similarly, none of the lakes (except Yaxha) has the distinctive cream polychromes and "dress shirt" motif characteristic of Eznab at Tikal. Probably the materials from all the lakes save Yaxha investigated by CPHEP are part of the Romero complex, and belong in a "peripheral Eznab" Terminal Classic sphere.

The picture is one of very regionalized ceramic content, with variability in both *degree* of change and *kind* of change within the Peten subareas during the Terminal Classic. The regionalization of Late Classic polychrome styles is an acknowledged phenomenon in the Maya Lowlands, but in the Terminal Classic this process seems to be occurring on a more intense or accelerated scale, and not only in decorated wares. Indeed, the overall picture for the Terminal Classic in Peten is one of very localized ceramic styles, in which many of the distinctive horizon markers (e.g., Fine Orange) are present in highly variable quantities. Ceramic changes seem to be most apparent in the variety of new, often localized, pastes more than any other characteristic. This feature accompanies broader changes reflecting an economic reorganization that begins in the Late Classic Period, and that registers a strengthening of heretofore "rural" areas correlated with the decline of elite economic power at the large centers (P. Rice n.d. b).

A broader context for understanding the Terminal Classic in Peten may be developed by looking at events to the north, in Yucatan. A decline in Peten influence is evident on the East Coast by about A.D. 750 (Robles C. and Andrews, this volume), suggesting that the "Peten corridor" had shut down as a central artery of direct transmission of Peten ideas to Yucatan. The Terminal Classic in Peten corresponds to the period of the florescence of the Puuc cities in northwest Yucatan, of "Toltec" Chichen Itza in north-central Yucatan, and of Coba in the east. Becan seems to have enjoyed a brief tenure as an important trading port in the late ninth and early tenth centuries, as the main transpeninsular trading route from the gulf to the Caribbean traversed the region (Ball, this volume). Three coeval ceramic assemblages in these areas, with apparent ethnic, status, and/or functional associations, have been identified: Sotuta, Cehpech, and Xcocom. The constituent types and geographical distributions of these complexes reveal both their mode of spread within Yucatan and their external contacts. Regionalization is evident within the complexes, for example, with differences in composition and slip characteristics of slate wares between eastern and western Yucatan.

What is surprising, however, given the spread and interfingering of Puuc-related Cehpech-sphere characteristics and Itza-related Sotuta sphere materials through Yucatan, is that few or none of these northern ceramics reached Peten. Ball (1974a, 1976) and Adams (1973) have attributed the Terminal Classic florescence of Pasión sites in Peten to incursions of Cehpech-bearing warrior elite groups from Yucatan, and the decline of Altar de Sacrificios to a gulf coast military group (R. E. W. Adams 1973: 155–56). To judge from ceramics alone, however, their impact on Peten was not considerable (but see below).

Taken together, all these data undermine the traditional model of the Lowland "collapse," which emphasized material impoverishment and depopulation. What seems to be occurring in the Terminal Classic is a broad challenge to the Lowland Maya authority structure, manifest in the erosion or decentralization of power, settlement, and production arrangements in the central Peten. The sociopolitical and socioeconomic changes of this period seem to have had variable impact, and the effects were felt differentially in the peripheral regions of Peten, as compared to the large centers.

Early Postclassic Period: Regionalization

There seems to be a good deal of continuity between Terminal Classic and Early Postclassic periods in the central Peten, in terms of settlement location and the still highly regionalized ceramic production. This is evident in the existence of very different pastes, which form the basis for definition of a large number of ceramic groups. Within all these ceramic groups, however, the *structures* of decorative products are virtually identical, as is evident in the parallel ceramic types that have been named in the groups (see P. Rice and D. Rice 1985).

Augustine and Paxcaman are the two major ceramic groups of Peten— "major" in terms of both their geographical distributions and their temporal spans. Although Augustine seems to occur in greatest abundance on the east end of the region, at Barton Ramie, and Paxcaman is more common to the west in central Peten, they have almost fully overlapping distributions. Both, I believe, are Early Postclassic products, and I suspect their overlap may be a phenomenon primarily of the late facet of the Early Postclassic (at least such is true of Macanche). The identity of paste between the Paxcaman and Trapeche ceramic groups, and the great abundance of these two groups in the Peten-Itza/Macanche region (as well as the presence of Paxcaman to the west at Sacpuy; Cowgill 1963), argues for manufacture somewhere in this part of central Peten.

At the same time, there appear to be other Early Postclassic ceramic products with almost entirely local distributions. In Belize, one of these is the Daylight group (see Rivera Dorado 1975), while in central Peten it is the Trapeche group. Impressed-fillet censers are another diagnostic of the Postclassic, and their occurrence may date into the Early Postclassic. These vessels have been found at most Postclassic sites, as well as with the intrusive Caban-phase burial at Tikal (Adams and Trik 1961: Figure 42), but are not reported at Barton Ramie. The

New Town sphere at Barton Ramie is, I feel, entirely an Early Post-classic phenomenon, probably ending ca. A.D. 1200.

A final note to the issue of regionalization in Early Postclassic ceramic production concerns Topoxte. I have concluded that an Early Postclassic occupation of the Topoxte Islands is represented by the decorated pottery contained in "Group B," and probably also by a (status?) subset, "Group A." Group B Topoxte polychromes (Pastel and Cante types) share close similarities of design motifs and arrangement with other indigenous Postclassic polychromes in other ceramic groups. Also, constructional deposits containing Group B have a greater mix of Classic and Terminal Classic types, forms, and pastes than do those of Group A (a phenomenon similar to early-facet Aura material at Macanche). Finally, all types within the Topoxte ceramic group (including both "patterns" B and A) occur in the cream-colored, marly, Clemencia Cream paste ware, which shows very close ties to pastes (especially of Tinaja Red) of the Late and Terminal Classic in the Yaxha basin. It is my feeling that an argument can be made for Terminal Classic through Postclassic continuity of occupation of the basin, and rejection of the traditional model of a major "hiatus" preceding an exclusively late occupation of the Topoxte Islands. Continuity of settlement and land use in the basin area or its peripheries has also been given some support by continuity in the rain of pollen from disturbance species into the lake sediments (Vaughan 1979).

In sum, I think the Paxcaman, Augustine, Trapeche, and Topoxte ceramic groups are all regional Postclassic ceramic products that manifest a shared traditional repertoire of forms and decorative motifs but are manufactured with local resources. Archaeologists recognize these products as different types and "groups," and have tried to place them in some sort of developmental order, but I suspect that they are in large part contemporaneous *regional* rather than sequential *temporal* variants. I believe all the groups identified above coexisted in the Early Postclassic Period. Paxcaman and Augustine were relatively widely traded within the Central Lowlands, and although they are not known from the north in Yucatan, they were apparently traded to the south and west. An Ixpop Polychrome vessel on display at the Museo de Antropología in Guatemala City is reported as being recovered from Salcaja, Quetzaltenango, and one is reported from Tonina, in Chiapas. The other two major ceramic groups, Trapeche and Topoxte, plus

Daylight from Belize, seem to have been more restricted in their distribution. The Topoxte Islands are in some senses anomalous in this reconstruction because they have very little Paxcaman pottery and none of the Trapeche, Augustine, or Daylight groups.

Identification of ceramic spheres for the Early Postclassic is very difficult because of this differential occurrence of ceramic types. The New Town sphere has been identified for the Early Postclassic at Barton Ramie on the basis of a predominance of the Augustine group, but Paxcaman and Daylight groups were also present. The New Town complex also has unslipped jar forms very similar to those of the Pozo group of unslipped jars occurring throughout central Peten (P. Rice 1979). At Macanche, I have named the Aura complex for the Early Postclassic on the basis of large quantities of Paxcaman, Trapeche, and Pozo groups, and extremely small amounts of Augustine (P. Rice n.d. a). The Early Postclassic at Macanche also has Terminal Classic types in its early facet, but only rare sherds of Topoxte in the late facet. I would place the Early Postclassic materials at Zacpeten and Quexil in the Aura complex as well, on the basis of a predominance of Paxcaman and Pozo groups, and variable quantities of Augustine and Trapeche.

As mentioned above, the Topoxte Islands are in some senses (and rather superficially) an anomaly. If Topoxte-group pottery of the Early Postclassic (i.e., Group B, and perhaps Group A) is considered simply a local product of a broader regional ceramic horizon—sharing form and decorative modes with Paxcaman and Trapeche, but differentiated on the basis of paste—then the Early Postclassic at Topoxte is a part of the same sphere that includes the Aura complex. By the same reasoning, the Augustine group is similarly another regional (paste) product sharing the same horizon style. Thus the New Town complex at Barton Ramie, Chilcob at Tayasal, Aura in the central Peten lakes, and an early facet of the Isla complex at Topoxte all would belong in the New Town ceramic sphere. By the succeeding Late Postclassic, however, certain aspects of the ceramics suggest that Topoxte's position vis-à-vis the other Peten lakes is distinctly different, and participation in the same ceramic sphere is doubtful.

The early facet of the Early Postclassic was defined at Macanche Island on the basis of continuation of some Terminal Classic traits and initiation of others characteristic of the Postclassic, most notably the Paxcaman and Trapeche groups. The Trapeche group is interesting, because its paste and fire-clouded pink-to-cream slips resemble the earlier cream-slipped Terminal Classic Harina group (P. Rice n.d. a). Trapeche slips also may be imitations of the widespread slate wares characteristic of Yucatan, an observation made earlier by Bullard (1973: 233). If Trapeche were a slateware imitation, it might suggest some parallels between the Early Postclassic ceramic assemblages of central Peten and those of Yucatan, such as Cehpech or Sotuta. It is interesting to note the virtual absence of Sotuta diagnostics, such as Plumbate, Silho Fine Orange, and "Mixtec" incensarios, in all the lake basins save at Tayasal (A. Chase 1979, this volume). The existence of these materials at Tayasal calls to mind the legends of Itza groups fleeing southward from Chichen Itza to settle on a large lake; however, their absence elsewhere in Peten argues against any widespread penetration of the area by Chichen-related peoples.

Late Postclassic Period: External Relationships

Late Postclassic occupation has been identified at Topoxte, Macanche, Zacpeten, and Quexil. The principal defining criteria for Late Postclassic settlement in these areas are the presence of "Mayapan-style" effigy censers and Topoxte group pottery, which occurs outside the Topoxte Islands almost exclusively in the two varieties of Chompoxte Red-on-cream type.

Mayapan-style effigy censers in Peten are manufactured of at least three pastes, two of which are used for local slipped wares, and all three seem to be widely distributed. One paste is associated with the same cream-colored, marly Clemencia Cream Paste ware used in manufacture of Topoxte-group slipped pottery. Censers of this paste, the Idolos group, have been found at Topoxte and Macanche. Another common paste is the gray snail-inclusion paste associated with Paxcaman and Trapeche slipped ceramic groups. These censers have been found at Macanche and Zacpeten, but not at Topoxte. A third paste is a coarse, heavy tan-to-orange brown paste, and has been found at Macanche and Topoxte. The existence of these several pastes in one characteristic and distinctive censer form suggests a continuity of the regionalization of production and trade networks noted for the Early Postclassic, crosscutting a wide geographic spread of the pan-Maya belief system represented by the censers.

The Peten Postclassic slipped pottery groups show some interesting developments that I believe are peculiar to the Late Postclassic Period.

In the case of Postclassic polychromes, the innovations occur in the style and motifs of decoration, and, like the censers, they show a certain amount of regionalization that seems to be a carryover from the preceding Early Postclassic Period.

In the Topoxte ceramic group, if my sequencing of Groups B and A followed by Group C is correct, a major Late Postclassic change is the increased emphasis on the distinctive dark red-on-paste curvilinear decoration of Chompoxte variety of Chompoxte Red-on-cream, characteristic of Group A pottery. Chompoxte variety, which constituted the bulk of the pottery recovered by Bullard, was not initially thought to have any direct precedents or parallels in Peten or in neighboring areas (P. Rice 1979: 40–42).

Several recent developments, including my brief restudy of the Cante Island materials, suggest that the significance of Chompoxte Red-on-cream and its exterior ties needs to be rethought. One point is that this unusual decoration was imitated in the snail-inclusion paste ceramic groups of central Peten, i.e., in the Paxcaman and Trapeche groups, although these are very minor components. A second point concerns the exterior ties of the style. Bullard (1970: 300) noted vague similarities to San Joaquín Buff Ware at Mayapan, and to late wares from Naco, Honduras. At Mayapan, Tecoh Red-on-buff pottery features red paint on (usually) cream-to-tan backgrounds and "buff" rather than red slips. Some of the designs are rather simple and restrained, occurring in a band on dishes and jars (as in Akalche variety of Chompoxte Red-on-cream), while others include dots and swirls and appear on the entire interior of dishes, including the floors (as in Chompoxte variety of Chompoxte Red-on-cream). A few of the sherds had traces of Maya Blue paint over the decoration, a trait occasionally noted on Topoxte sherds as well (P. Rice (1979: 29).

In Highland areas to the south, the relationships are less specific, in some respects, but broader. The material from the western Highlands, with its red-on-white and white-on-red decoration, shows somewhat greater general similarities to the Chompoxte variety than do the motifs of the central Highlands polychromes, which are executed in red- and black-on-white (Wauchope 1970). Specifically, resemblances are noted in the prevalence of dots, ticks, spirals, and curvilinear and nested motifs. The same can be said for the polychrome and red-on-cream bichrome pottery from Naco, Honduras. Chompoxte variety of Chompoxte Red-on-cream is similar in style and motif to Nolasco

Figure 8.8 The "crested dragon" motif of Sitio Conte, Panama (redrawn from Helms 1979: 100, Figure 16).

Bichrome, which has a relatively long history in Naco going back to the early facet (A.D. 1200–1250) of the Late Postclassic (Wonderley 1981: 306, Figs. 30–35). The closest similarity I have been able to find, however, comes from an area much farther south: the unusual decoration in a nearly complete Chompoxte-variety dish is strikingly similar to the "crested dragon" motif of Cocle cultures in Panama (Figure 8.8).

These comparisons of Peten Late Postclassic pottery with that of neighboring Highland and Lowland Maya areas has prompted me to reconsider some of these relationships. Yucatan ceramics have traditionally been viewed as the general progenitors of Peten ceramic styles. I think it can be argued, however, that the situation is the reverse: Peten polychromes may be earlier, with both Ixpop and Chompoxte Red-on-cream being Early Postclassic styles. The small quantities of Yucatan polychromes, such as Pele and Tecoh, were probably *inspired by* Ixpop and Chompoxte (cf. R. E. Smith 1971: 231–32). A similar view has been expressed by Pendergast (1981a: 49) with respect to incised monochrome redware pottery in Late Postclassic Yucatan.

A second observation concerns the appearance of "reptile," crocodilian, or "earth monster" motifs on Postclassic pottery (P. Rice 1983). Reptilian motifs occur in distinctive patterns that may be significant in illuminating the relationships between the regions of Peten Postclassic settlement. At Macanche and Zacpeten, composite serpent/

287

crocodilian creatures appear on pottery of both the Paxcaman and Trapeche groups, primarily in the incised types Picu and Xuluc, but also in Ixpop Polychrome. The creature is depicted in a consistent manner, occupying one or more panels within an encircling band (Figure 8.9). At Topoxte, the decorative conventions are distinctly different from those of the other lake basins. A reptilian ("dragon") creature is depicted by painting rather than by incising, the painting is in an unusual red-on-cream style, and the creatures appear over the entire vessel interior rather than in a band (Figure 8.7). Many of the curvilinear motifs, J-shaped plumes, and circles that appear in Chompoxte variety, sometimes in positive and sometimes in negative, are abstract or stylized "feathered serpent" elements—eyes, feathers, and jaws—used in much the same way as at Naco (Wonderley 1981), and in the red-on-white and white-on-red vessels of the western Highlands of Guatemala (Wauchope 1970).

These factors, together with the many other anomalies of the Post-classic data from the Topoxte Islands (at least as far as ceramic evidence can be interpreted), suggest that Topoxte was participating in a very different network of relationships, one more closely tied to the High-lands than to the Northern Lowlands, during the Postclassic. The specific nature of these relationships is difficult to identify from available evidence, but "trade" may be a starting point for unraveling them (see below; also Freidel, this volume).

Protohistoric and Historic Periods: Trade and Conquest

The difficulties that beset any archaeological study of the Protohistoric and Colonial periods in the Central Maya Lowlands highlight what is really a much more pervasive problem in the study of the Maya Postclassic in general in this area. The problem is that ceramic change in the indigenous Postclassic types is deceptively slow, and intrusive ceramic evidence for any kind of external contacts, *especially* with the Spaniards, is almost nil.

In the central Peten, as well as in Belize (which G. Jones [1982] terms the "Belize Missions Subregion"), Spanish visitors—from the time of Cortés's first march through Peten in 1525 until the area was brought under Spanish control by Ursua in 1697—mention numerous communities of native Maya populations in the sixteenth and seventeenth centuries. Some of these communities have been identified

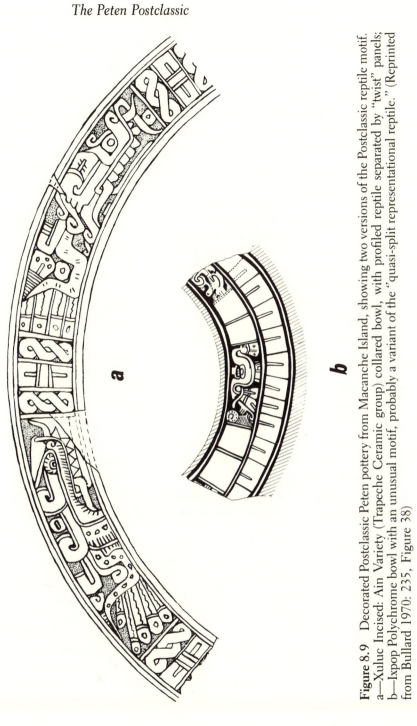

Figure 8.9 Decorated Postclassic Peten pottery from Macanche Island, showing two versions of the Postclassic reptile motif. a—Xuluc Incised: Ain Variety (Trapeche Ceramic group) collared bowl, with profiled reptile separated by "twist" panels; b—Ixpop Polychrome bowl with an unusual motif, probably a variant of the "quasi-split representational reptile." (Reprinted from Bullard 1970: 235, Figure 38)

archaeologically by recent work. For example, both Lamanai in northern Belize on the New River Lagoon (Pendergast 1981a) and Negroman/Tipu (G. Jones and Kautz 1981; E. Graham, Jones, and Kautz 1985) in western Belize on the Macal branch of the Belize River, were locations of Spanish missions in native Maya settlements. At Negroman/Tipu, only a few sherds of European pottery mark this Spanish activity; most pottery on the site consists of the traditional Postclassic Paxcaman, Topoxte, Augustine, and censers, together with heavy quantities of Classic types mixed in (P. Rice 1984a).

In the central Peten, besides the Itza capital of Tayasal, many other contemporary Maya towns have been mentioned in ethnohistoric reports. Among these are Maconche, Zacpeten, and Eckixil, which have been identified with specific areas investigated by the Central Peten Historical Ecology Project. "Maconche" is felt to be equivalent to the archaeologically identified Postclassic settlement around Lake Macanche (D. Rice and P. Rice 1981) and "Zacpeten" is the settlement on the peninsula in Lake Salpeten (D. Rice and P. Rice 1984b). "Eckixil" is believed to be the community on the two islands in Lake Quexil. Another community is "Cazpui," which may be equivalent to a settlement at Lake Sacpuy. Cowgill (1963) did some work around that lake and found quantities of Postclassic pottery, but CPHEP did not undertake any investigations in the area. Interestingly, no populations were ever reported by the Spaniards in the Lake Yaxha basin.

The pottery from the CPHEP excavations at these ethnohistorically reported locations consists of the traditional Paxcaman, Augustine, Trapeche, Topoxte, and censer types, which were in use for as much as 400 to 500 years in the area. No European sherds, such as those from olive jars or majolicas, have been identified at all in CPHEP excavations in central Peten as they have at Negroman/Tipu. To be sure, the nature of European interaction with the central Peten—brief visits by priests or military groups—is not of the sort that would be expected either to introduce a large amount of foreign pottery or have a profound impact on the local manufacture of pots and pans. But there is virtually nothing in the Peten ceramic record that testifies to the cultural upheavals of the Spanish conquest. This lack, combined with the regionalized production and exchange of Postclassic pottery discussed above, makes the ceramic record distressingly ambiguous. I can only echo the opinions of many previous researchers of contact or conquest period sites (Tschopik 1950; Charlton 1968; W. Y. Adams

1979; Pendergast 1981a: 52; see also Thompson 1977: 39; P. Rice 1982), as well as reiterate my own observations above concerning the Classic "collapse," in noting that pottery is in many ways conservative or only indirectly responsive to external change.

The only innovation or addition to the Late Postclassic ceramic inventory that I have been able to identify in materials from CPHEP excavations is Chilo Unslipped. Chilo appears at Macanche and Zacpeten (with red paint in the latter area), and at first I was inclined to use it as a marker of a late facet of the Late Postclassic. In light of the ethnohistoric data, however, ceramic conservatism, and further considerations of the role of the Topoxte Islands (where Chilo was not noted), I am now inclined to identify Chilo as a marker of a Protohistoric-Historic Period Ayer ceramic complex in the central Peten lakes region. Further support for this interpretation is provided by the similarities of Chilo pottery to modern pottery in the area, suggesting extremely long continuity. The extent to which Paxcaman and Trapeche pottery may or may not have continued to be made and used in the Historic Period in Peten is entirely a matter of conjecture at this point.

In the Historic Period, as earlier, the role of the Topoxte Island populations continues to be somewhat anomalous. Although numerous Spanish visitors, from the time of Cortés's first entrada into Peten in 1525, mention specific Itza communities around the lake basins, nowhere has anything been mentioned that could be identified as a settlement on Topoxte. By 1618, when the Franciscan Fathers Fuensalida and Orbita passed in the vicinity of Lakes Yaxha and Sacnab on their way to Tayasal from Tipu, the area was said to be uninhabited. Thus, sometime before 1618—and perhaps before 1525—the thriving and apparently influential settlement on the Topoxte Islands was abandoned. Why?

SUMMARY SPECULATIONS

The following scenario has, as scenarios based on scanty and mostly negative evidence usually do, a distinctly "just-so" quality about it. Nonetheless, it represents a best effort to account for available archaeological and ethnohistoric data in explaining a heretofore perplexing situation in Protohistoric and Historic Peten. In large part, this scenario focuses on the role of Topoxte vis-à-vis the other Terminal Classic and Postclassic settlements in Peten.

As described above, the occupation of the Topoxte Islands in Lake Yaxha is somewhat enigmatic in the Peten Postclassic setting. Identified for a long time with only a very late, Mayapan elite–affiliated settlement, the Topoxte Islands, I suggest, begin their Postclassic florescence as a local variant of a much broader Peten Postclassic tradition of island settlement and polychrome ceramic production. As such, the islands had an Early Postclassic occupation *in addition* to the Late Postclassic settlement emphasized in traditional reconstructions. Throughout their Postclassic histories, the islands are felt to have had more (or at least equally) significant contacts with the Highlands to the south than with the Northern Lowlands.

Lake Yaxha is situated near the bend in the Mopan River, where its direction changes from a northward flow out of southern Peten to an eastward flow to the Caribbean coast. Thus the lake's inhabitants could have played a vital part in trade connections with the Highlands in the Classic as well as the Postclassic periods. Trade items coming into Peten from the eastern Highlands and the Motagua (perhaps through Quirigua in the Early Postclassic; see Ashmore 1980: 27), Naco/Copan, and/or Verapaz areas, would have moved either along the coast, through Belize and into Peten, or overland down the Mopan River and into Peten (R. E. W. Adams 1978; Hammond 1978). These Highland goods would have included basalt manos and metates (which, at sites investigated by CPHEP, occur almost exclusively in Postclassic rather than Classic contexts), obsidian, and greenstone for celts, as well as quantities of perishables. Similarly, Lake Yaxha may have served as a node in the "Peten corridor" channeling movements of people and ideas from central Peten to the east coast of Yucatan in the Classic Period. It is tempting to suggest that the Yaxha settlements served a role similar to that of "gateway communities" (Hirth 1978) in facilitating communication and trade across cultural and/or ecological transition areas.

In the middle of the eighth century, Peten's influence on the eastern part of Yucatan declined. Soon after that, Becan, in the interior part of the peninsula, appears to have taken over important functions of overland trade activities between the Caribbean and eastern Highland areas to northern Yucatan. Contrary to Ball's (1977b: 173–74) interpretation of an "invasion" of Becan by northern groups, I would see greater southern influences on Becan as indicated by Xcocom ceramic complex members Tinaja and Fine Orange, Belizean cherts, Ixtepeque obsidians, and the presence of distinctive "C-shaped" structures characteristic of the Postclassic in Peten. These two shifts—the demise of the "Peten corridor," and the movement of the overland trade route—probably reflect internal dynamics within Yucatan, as well as stresses at the upper echelons of Peten society at this time, including the consequent economic retrenchment known as the "collapse." Concurrent difficulties for Peten polities were presented by intrusions on the western peripheries, plus internal population movements toward the central Peten lakes, which had previously been sociopolitically marginal.

In Lake Yaxha, populations regrouped on the Topoxte Islands following the Terminal Classic Period, and may have continued to benefit from this advantageous location for Highland-Lowland trade. In the case of coastal routes, known to have been important in the Postclassic Period, the position of the Topoxte Islands was such as to facilitate control of movement of these goods, as well as its own ceramic manufactures, into the interior lakes region, thus continuing a "gateway" role. Topoxte also may have continued to enjoy the fruits of contact with northern Belize and the east coast of Yucatan. Contrary to traditional interpretations of the Topoxte Islands, which postulate strong relationships to Mayapan in architecture, it now appears that some of Topoxte's structures are more closely related to those of the east coast of the peninsula (F. Robles C., personal communication).

Participation in the pan-Lowlands Late Postclassic censer cult plus architectural ties to eastern Yucatan indicate that Topoxte was successfully playing those northern connections, too, along with its ties to the Highlands. The success of Topoxte was apparently rather short-lived, however. Events of the fifteenth and sixteenth centuries probably did not work to Topoxte's advantage, and the causes of Topoxte's decline are probably more deeply rooted in long-standing processes of Postclassic history.

Within the central Peten, the early part of the Postclassic witnessed the emergence of competitive ranked societies in the basins of Lakes Yaxha, Macanche, Salpeten, and Peten-Itza. Warfare was said to be endemic in Peten in the sixteenth century; the polity of Yalain, for example, located to the east of Lake Peten-Itza, was said to be hostile to the Itza around Lake Peten-Itza. The evolution of this atmosphere of conflict may be illuminated by means of Helms's (1979) observations concerning chiefdoms in Panama, where warfare was also said to be chronic in the sixteenth century. Given an environmental situation of "resource redundancy" in Panama, Helms doubts (1979: 33–34) that warfare would have been waged for control of subsistence resources or land alone. Instead, she feels that the best means for chiefs and high-status individuals to acquire and reinforce their position was through maintaining access to scarce and exotic resources via long distance exchange:

One likely method of gaining access to exchange benefits was by military competition, and . . . it is noteworthy that warfare is frequently [in ethno-historic reports] indicated between chiefs located at major junctions on long distance exchange routes and groups on their immediate borders. . . . Alliance marriage between chiefs well located in terms of exchange contacts and chiefs most distantly situated could have facilitated access to scarce items from the latter and expanded the political base of supporters for the former. (Helms 1979: 34)

Similar trade-based competition may have existed in Peten throughout the Postclassic Period. It is difficult, however, to suggest archaeological criteria for determining relative power or standing among the various communities around the lakes. In any situation of chronic conflict between chiefly villages the geopolitical relationships are likely to have been somewhat fluid and unstable. Population size, favorable geographical location, and wider extraregional ties (including those to Yucatan, in the case of Peten societies) would have played significant roles. While Topoxte may have had greater ties to the Highlands and to the East Coast, the central Peten lakes area seems—if anything at all about relative sociopolitical ties can be reliably gleaned from decorative styles and motifs on Postclassic pottery—to have had stronger relations to northern and central Yucatan, and to the political center of Mayapan. Indeed, the decorative motifs on the pottery seem to suggest a recalling of traditional symbols of authority and a strengthening of local elites (P. Rice 1983).

In the middle of the fifteenth century, Mayapan fell. This resulted in a stream of refugees moving southward into Peten, a pattern that continued for centuries (Thompson 1977; Farriss 1978; G. Jones 1983). The fleeing Itza may have perceived closer ties to the central Peten lakes area than to Topoxte and settled in this area. This relative demographic strengthening of the Lake Peten-Itza region could have threatened Topoxte politically and economically in a competitive situation, and thereby bolstered Lake Peten-Itza's trading position. The role of Maya calendrical cycles and prophecies would also have given the edge to Tayasal, if, as suggested by Edmonson (1982: 225, 227), the fall of Mayapan as a "holy city" was accompanied by a shift, or "seating of the cycle," to Tayasal in that role.

In the central Highlands, the middle and late fifteenth century seems to have been a time of upheaval as well, with Quiche and Cakchiquel expansion (Guillemin 1977: 229; Fox 1981). To the east, at Naco around A.D. 1450, Nolasco Bichrome decreased in frequency, and a new black-on-white polychrome style appeared in the archaeological record, without a clear history of development (Wonderley 1981: 322–23). This style may be a local version of the Ixpop-like painted decoration common in central Peten, and together these ceramic changes may reflect a shift in trade emphasis from Topoxte to the Peten-Itza communities.

In the early sixteenth century, the Spaniards came into contact with the societies on the borders of Peten, and the effects reverberated even into this remote interior area of the Lowlands. One of the most significant events for Peten geopolitics would have been the Spanish conquest of the Highlands in 1524, together with their disruptions at the trading centers of Nito and Naco, in Honduras, and their later efforts in the Verapaz area. These incursions would have seriously disrupted trade routes and weakened alliances. Closer to home, if Topoxte had survived the earlier challenges, and I doubt that it did, it is likely that the events of the next century would have provided the final blows. The prolonged period of Spanish conquest of Chetumal Province to the northeast between 1531 and 1545 would have severely disrupted any political or economic alliances with that region. Population declines, plus the enforced abandonment of the Tzama (Tulum) port in 1579 owing to harassment by pirates (Miller 1982: 79) further strained the trade relationships to the east. At the same time, in the region to the northwest of Peten, the Spaniards gained control of the Chontal area of Acalan, Tabasco, which dominated overland trade into Peten from the west. After the Spaniards moved the people of Itzamkanac to Tixchel in 1571, the control of overland trade from the west passed into the hands of the Itza in the central Peten (G. Jones 1982: 279). Doubtless these Spanish actions prompted some of the populace to flee, and it is probably significant that the northwest area of Peten, uninhabited in 1525, had settlements in 1580 along the Río San Pedro Martir (Cowgill 1963: 390).

I suggest that during a period of slightly over 100 years, from the time of the fall of Mayapan (taking the 1458 date), through the years of Spanish contact in virtually all portions of the Maya area, to the move of the Acalan Putun in 1571, this series of calamities so severely eroded the political and economic base of Topoxte and its ruling elites that these islands were abandoned. In fact, I would imagine that its role was seriously diminished at about the time of the fall of Mayapan. Control of the southern Peten overland trade, through Manche Chol and Mopan territory, passed firmly to the west into the hands of the Itza of the Lake Peten-Itza region. (But see Thompson [1970: 132–33], who uses Cortés's encounters with natives on his journey through Peten to argue that an overland trade route from Acalan to Nito through Itza territory probably did not exist, and water transport was the preferred commercial mode.) Where the people of Topoxte went is impossible to determine: they may have simply moved out into the forest; they may have moved to the settlements in central Peten (Topoxte's former rivals?); or they might have thrown their lot in with Tipu, located to the east on the Macal branch of the Mopan River. The presence of considerable quantities of Topoxte pottery at Tipu suggests that there were some significant contacts with this area.

Beginning in 1582, ethnohistoric information (the following is summarized from G. Jones 1982, 1983; Scholes and Thompson 1977) suggests that the Tipu area of western Belize was an important political and economic entity in the Maya Lowlands. Tipu was a community that was receiving scores of refugees from the north, fleeing harsh Spanish treatment during the 1531–45 campaign of conquest, and the subsequent Maya uprising of 1546. The economic strength of Tipu appears to have rested in its cacao orchards, together with control of trade by virtue of its favorable location as a "gateway" at the junction of river routes from the coast and interior routes to the Itza of central Peten. At some point in the late sixteenth century, the Spaniards built a church at Tipu and from there attempted to missionize the Itza. These efforts were not only not successful, they were disastrous.

In 1618, Fathers Fuensalida and Orbita went to Tayasal, accompanied by Tipu guides, to begin their conversion attempts. In his zeal, however, Orbita destroyed an Itza idol, Tzimin-Chac, and so angered the Itza that the Spanish fathers were chased out of the area in short order. This incident must have continued to fester in the memories of the Itza, for when in 1623 Father Diego Delgado entered Tayasal with eighty men from Tipu, all were killed as retribution for Orbita's misdeed. Still later, in 1636 a major uprising against the Spaniards broke out in Belize and southern Yucatan (Bacalar), thus freeing Tipu and the general Belize Missions area from Spanish control. In 1641, when some Franciscans bravely pushed once again into the area to try to reconvert the Indians, they were repulsed at Hubelna, east of Tipu, and it is said that Itza warriors, still angry over Orbita's destruction of their idol some twenty years earlier, were among the attackers.

The relative strength and standing of the Itza of Tayasal vis-à-vis Tipu during the nearly two centuries between the first Spanish contact and final conquest of the Itza is difficult to assess. In 1695, Itza nobility and Tipu elite families were regularly intermarrying (Can Ek's sister was married to a man from Tipu, for example). But I suspect that there was a good deal of rivalry between Tipu and Tayasal, on the basis of the trade competition hypothesized above. While Tipu had control of important coastal/river routes and cacao, Tayasal may have been stronger initially. One advantage Tayasal must have had is demographic and military strength, which the Tipuans called upon occasionally for their own protection (G. Jones 1982: 284; 1983). Too, the Itza certainly shared in the phenomenon of continually increasing population resulting from inmigration from the north; Avendano y Loyola estimated the Itza area population at 22,000 souls (Thompson 1951: 390). G. Jones suggests, in fact, that the Itza may have played a central role in the 1636 uprising, as well as in the later stand in 1641 at Hubelna. Second, Tayasal must have served as a center of native religious tradition for the Lowland Maya. Even though they were being aggressively missionized by the Spaniards, the Itza continued to worship their "idols," and it is possible that Tayasal, as a core of resistance to the Spaniards, served as a focal point for native Maya solidarity during these conversion efforts. In 1619 some of the idols at Tipu were said to be from the Itza area (G. Jones 1983). Third, the Itza area was flourishing in its own trade relationships, with cotton cloth its major export, although it apparently did not have the extensive cacao production that is credited for Tipu.

But by the late seventeenth century, on the eve of final conquest of the Itza by the Spaniards, Peten had long since lost the upper hand in political and economic relationships, and dominance had passed on to Tipu. Tipu's economic position relative to that of the Peten Itza had been strengthened by their control of distribution of European steel tools into the interior areas (G. Jones, personal communication). In addition, since 1525 the southern extent of Itza territory had been shrinking, with the loss of the cacao-producing area of southeast Peten (Cowgill 1963: 496). The Mopanes in the southeast, who had funneled trade overland between the Highlands and central Peten (trading with Topoxte before 1450?), were becoming increasingly independent, and this would have undermined the Itza control of this trade. Then too, Can Ek had been having problems with his advisors in dealing with the Spaniards. Cowgill (1963: 414–16) has theorized that Can Ek may have wanted to submit to the Spaniards early in the sixteenth century, in order to consolidate his leadership locally, but was prevented from doing so by various factions, perhaps led by recent immigrants into the area who had fled Spanish control in Yucatan.

In any case, on the morning of March 13, 1697, the forces of Martín de Ursua attacked the Itza of Tayasal from a ship. The Itza fled, abandoning Tayasal, and the Spaniards took over, destroying the idols and founding a church on the island. Much has been made of the fact that this event occurred only 136 days short of a Katun 8 Ahau, the historically and cosmologically mandated period of change and upheaval for the Maya (Puleston 1979: 66).

I will conclude this speculative scenario here. Quite obviously the fabric has been woven out of very fragile threads. But it is clear that the time has come to rethink the entire nature of the Peten Postclassic. Up to the finish, from the Classic "collapse" in the ninth century to the conquest at the end of the seventeenth century, the Postclassic in Peten has always been seen as an adjunct to something else, a shadow, a poor relation, a cultural backwater. And it is true that by the yardstick of Classic civilization—applied to architecture, iconography, ceramics, social organizations—the magnitude and splendor of Postclassic achievements lag behind those of the Classic Period. But viewed in the context of other Postclassic societies of the Maya Highlands and Lowlands, the Peten Postclassic cultures can be seen as participating in broader region-wide traditions, and their role in these interactions is deserving of greater attention.

NOTE

1. The investigations of the Central Peten Historical Ecology Project reported here were carried out under funding of the National Science Foundation: grant CB-32150 to E. S. Deevey supported the work at Lake Yaxha and Topoxte in 1973–74; grant BNS-7813736 to D. S. Rice and P. M. Rice supported Proyecto Lacustre, focused on Lakes Macanche, Salpeten, Quexil, and Petenxil in 1979 and 1980; and grant BSN-8105379 to D. S. Rice allowed completion of the objectives of Proyecto Lacustre in 1981. The courteous assistance of the Instituto de Antropología e Historia in Guatemala and its then director, Lic. Francis Polo Sifontes, as well as the Parque Nacional Tikal, in carrying out these projects, is gratefully acknowledged. Analysis of the Macanche pottery collection, which is curated in the Florida State Museum, was advanced by a University of Florida Faculty Research Award to P. M. Rice in fall of 1981.

Many individuals aided directly or indirectly in contributing data for this study. Among them I offer sincere appreciation to: G. R. Willey and Mary Bullard, for access to the Macanche ceramic collection; G. Jones and R. Kautz, for access to the pottery from Tipu; and N. Hellmuth, for opportunities to study pottery from Yaxha between 1971 and 1974. In Guatemala, CPHEP is forever indebted to Robert Dorion, Rafael Sagastume and the staff of the Hotel Maya Internacional, Antonio Ortiz, Patricia Solis, Meridian Engineering, and scores of dependable and tolerant friends. In Merida, Lic. Fernando Robles C. kindly permitted me to study the Mayapan ceramic collection. And to the many students and workers who helped in the field and lab, my heartfelt thanks.

9

The Peten Postclassic: A Settlement Perspective[1]

DON S. RICE

University of Chicago

This paper represents an inquiry into the internal development of Peten Postclassic society, and to some degree its external connections. I do not undertake this re-examination from the strength of research focused by design on these issues, but rather from the perspective of a recent historical ecology project carried out in the Central Peten's lake region. Nonetheless, the data generated by our program are relevant to an assessment of things Postclassic, and in their presentation I hope to explicate Postclassic events in Peten and perhaps expand the contexts within which they should be evaluated.

THE CENTRAL PETEN
HISTORICAL ECOLOGY PROJECT

The Central Peten Historical Ecology Project was initiated in 1973 with the expressed goal of correlating the environmental and cultural histories of selected lacustrine basins for the purpose of measuring long-term human impact on tropical environments (Deevey et al. 1979). From 1973 to 1981 we carried out ecological studies at Lakes Yaxha, Sacnab, Macanche, Salpeten, Quexil, and Petenxil (Deevey 1978, 1984; Deevey and D. Rice 1980; Deevey, Brenner and Binford

301

1983). The archaeological research program was effected at Yaxha-Sacnab in 1973–74 (D. Rice 1976, 1978; P. Rice 1979; D. Rice and P. Rice 1980a, 1984b) and extended to the other basins in 1979–81 (D. Rice and P. Rice 1980b, 1981).

The archaeological aspect of the project attempted to reconstruct the settlement histories of the lacustrine environs by way of procedures which documented spatial, temporal, and cultural parameters. Approximately 25 percent of the basin areas were surveyed employing transects as the survey units; the transects were randomly located within basins in a manner that would provide for coverage of measured physiographic variability. Conspicuous cultural and natural features therein were located by a pace-and-map technique using brunton compasses and meter tapes (Fry 1969: 44), with the mapping of recovered features accomplished using transits and stadia rods. A total of 20 survey transects and their immediate vicinities were mapped within the six lake basins (Fig. 9.1): 10 at Yaxha-Sacnab; 3 each at Macanche and Salpeten; and 4 at Quexil-Petenxil.

In preparing for the archaeological investigations we were also aware of the potential for recovering Postclassic materials in the areas to be sampled, given the geographical references to Central Peten Postclassic settlements in available ethnohistoric documents and the results of previous archaeological investigations by William Bullard (1970, 1973) and George Cowgill (1963). Our research design allowed for purposive exploration and sampling of loci apparently preferred by Postclassic populations—peninsulas and islands—because these loci were not included in the statistically based program of mainland basin survey. Seven nontransect locales were investigated because it was felt that knowledge of their special characteristics would enhance our understanding of settlement history in the region. These sites were Cante Island at the site of Topoxte in Lake Yaxha (P. Rice 1979); the island in Lake Macanche (P. Rice 1980, n.d. b); the largely Middle Preclassic center of Cerro Ortiz on the Macanche mainland; the fortified site of Muralla de León on a Macanche isthmus (D. Rice and P. Rice 1981); the peninsular site of Zacpeten at Lake Salpeten (D. Rice 1981; D. Rice and P. Rice 1984a); the site of Ixlu on the isthmus between Lakes Salpeten and Peten-Itza; and the two small islands in Lake Quexil.

A total of 1,879 individual structures was mapped by our project within the six basins. Of these, 1,208 loci fell within the 20 formally placed mainland survey transects, and 235 loci were recorded in the

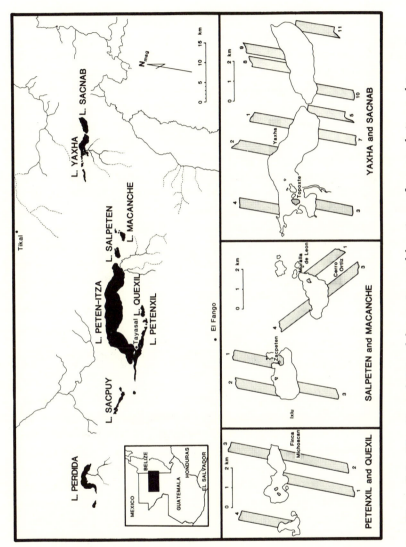

Figure 9.1 The Central Peten lakes region and locations of surveyed sites and transects.

immediate vicinities of those transect boundaries. An additional 436 structures were mapped at the seven nontransect sites. Once all surface manifestations of settlement were known, a stratified random sample of approximately 25 percent of the structure loci was chosen for test excavation, with individual mounds as the sampling units. Sampling was achieved by means of test-pit excavation, in order to maximize sample coverage within the area of the surveys, and test-pit placement at a selected mound depended on structure preservation, location of trees, and the like, and the prospects for sampling relatively undisturbed stratified construction sequences. Our research design demanded that priority be assigned to the testing of transect loci, and mounds located on transect borders or at specific sites were excavated as time and infrastructure permitted. A total of 385 mound loci were sampled, or 20.5 percent of all loci mapped, including 288 structures within survey transects, 41 structures lying on transect peripheries, and 56 construction loci at the seven nontransect sites.

Settlement complexes, structures, and artifacts dating to all periods of Maya prehistory were recovered in all the lake basins investigated. In this presentation, however, I shall pay primary attention to the characteristics of Postclassic architecture and the Classic and Postclassic settlement contexts for these structures.

POSTCLASSIC ARCHITECTURE IN THE CENTRAL PETEN LAKES REGION

Structure Architecture

The form and pattern of Postclassic structures in Peten are very distinctive when compared to those of earlier times. Almost all Post-classic constructions have as their principal component a square-to-rectangular single-level platform that is one-to-several wall courses in height. Two-level and multilevel platforms, which are more characteristic of Classic Period structures in this area, are not common. Postclassic platforms are made up of vertical facing walls that serve to retain a loose rubble fill. While the integrity of exterior platform form is generally excellent, apparently minimal attention was paid to creating even or uniform wall courses and/or smooth facades. The use of cut and shaped blocks is rarer than in the Classic Period, encountered most often in the construction of monumental architecture. In the

304

majority of Postclassic platform wall constructions there is little uniformity in block-to-block relationships or masonry dimensions between courses, and the blocks appear to have been dry-laid with considerable small stone spall chinking. Because rubble fill differs from facing wall stone primarily by position, exterior wall constituents and dimensions and the presence of interior retaining walls are often difficult to determine.

In our test-excavations, the upper surfaces of Postclassic platforms often gave the appearance of having been paved with cobbles or small stone chips. In some instances this paving was sufficiently dense to suggest that it represented a ballast layer for some type of flooring. In other cases, however, the stones were incorporated into a clay matrix and may have constituted the floor itself. We are faced with the problem that lime-base mortar, so common to Classic flooring, was rare on surface remains and in test-excavations at Postclassic loci. It is distinctly possible that these surfaces have eroded away. Given the high degree of general preservation in Postclassic constructions as a whole, however, and the presence of mortar at structure loci dating to all other periods, we would expect at least some mortar surfaces to survive. Instead we may be dealing with a silt-clay flooring for many of the Postclassic platforms, remains of which have long since disintegrated. This might explain the relative absence of evidence for multiple floorings in the excavation units, as well as our relatively greater difficulty in identifying stratified construction phases at Postclassic loci. The latter problem contributes to a concomitant difficulty in categorizing Postclassic building forms chronologically with any assurance, despite a successful preliminary phasing of Postclassic ceramics (see P. Rice, this volume).

Like Classic Period platforms, Postclassic platforms may or may not have supported superstructures. A number of featureless Postclassic platforms were mapped in our surveys, and excavations into this class of building revealed single episodes of undifferentiated fill construction. We found no post molds or other indications of superstructure footings, but, given the nature of the fill, these may have disappeared rather quickly. As a result, we have no idea whether perishable superstructures stood at these locations or, if they did, their possible form, size, and construction.

Where masonry features or superstructural foundations did exist on substructure platforms, their characteristics were quite distinct and, unlike Classic period structures, there appear to have been a limited number of basic plans (Fig. 9.2). The least common of these is a square-to-rectangular quadrilateral wall consisting of one course of shaped and fitted blocks (Fig. 9.2a). This might best be described as a foundation brace, because the single stone width of the wall did not provide a footing into which a perishable superstructure could be secured. The wall did not serve to retain soil or masonry fill, as might be expected with a building platform for a superstructure or a bench feature. Rather, it appears to have functioned as a sill and brace to the interior or exterior of a perishable superstructure.

Considerably more prevalent than the open single-line quadrilateral wall as a Postclassic superstructural form were masonry foundation walls and/or benches made up of interior and exterior facings that hold a rubble core. Most of these were low, usually only a few courses high, with facing walls made of cut or shaped block, unmodified stone, or both. As with substructure platform retaining walls, these appear to

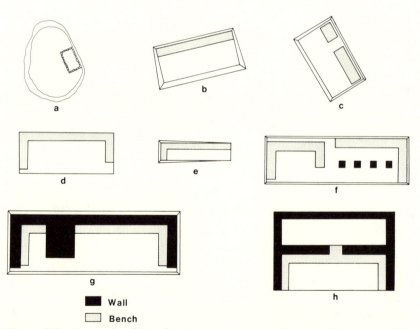

Figure 9.2 A sample of Postclassic superstructure plans (not drawn to scale) found in the Central Peten lakes region (lettered variants are referred to in the text).

have been dry-laid and heavily chinked, although we acknowledge that evidence of silt-clay binding, facing, or surface washes would be long since gone. Occasionally the interior facing of a long-axis wall was the best constructed and the best preserved, giving the impression of a surface feature consisting solely of a single line of stone. It was apparent, however, from the observation of many cases and test-excavation of a number, that the majority were originally "double-line" constructions—two facings that retained a core. The core consisted of a fill of smaller undifferentiated stone which, like platform fill, contained cultural debris. The width of the wall varied from less than half a meter to more than one meter, and several of the better preserved examples exhibited a paved or ballast-layered upper surface.

In our samples, double-line architectural features are generally found in one of three basic configurations. These include a single straight wall aligned with the long axis of the substructure and situated on or near the rear edge of the platform surface (Fig. 9.2b), L-shaped foundations with the long arm aligned on the platform end (Fig. 9.2c), and C-shaped walls that sit atop and border three edges of the substructure surface (Fig. 9.2d). In some instances several of these forms may be combined on the same substructure (Fig. 9.2e). The most common of these is the combination of straight line and/or L-shaped walls of equal or different lengths, where a space or portal separates the two segments (Fig. 9.2c).

Perishable structures are assumed to have sat on or surrounded these foundation structures. Given that the number of "sides" of structural support provided by these constructions is variable, however, and never includes four facades of a presumed quadrilateral superstructure, a nonfoundation function for many of the walls is suggested. It is apparent that these double-line wall forms were not intended solely as a footing for superstructure walls, and that they may have functioned more as benches than as foundations—with foundation support perhaps provided only in that the bench served as an interior brace to a perishable superstructure. This interpretation is supported by evidence from some of the larger masonry superstructures, where higher foundation walls of similar construction definitely back such bench features. There are also many low platforms supporting small interior masonry bench features which appear ill-suited in size or position to function as foundations of any kind. Where masonry walls are indicated in addition to benches, the quantity of collapse suggests that the wall

307

itself probably fell short of a roof zone, requiring that a perishable upper wall and roof structure be set onto the foundation wall surface.

With respect to superstructure plan, it is important to recognize that regardless of the presence or absence of superstructural walls, or the extent of the bench work, there is no instance in which either a wall or bench extends across the front of the building platform. Where there are distal and side structure walls in addition to a bench or benches, proximal corner jambs may be present, but there are no interjambs and no imperishable indications of restricted entryways.

The absence of masonry walls or interjambs on the building fronts, the low height of foundation walls, the general lack of evidence for masonry roof collapse, and our assumption that all interior space was roofed combine to suggest that the roof was not vaulted, but rather consisted of perishable beams and stringers with interior roof supports. The possibility of two types of interior supports, masonry and perishable, is indicated by surface remains. The exact form and size of masonry pillars or columns is difficult to determine because none have been discovered intact by us. The presence of limestone "drums" at several structure locations in our survey area may suggest that some supports were limestone columns, or masonry pillars with limestone cores (Bullard 1970: 261).

The use of perishable pillars is suggested by the limited number of drums recovered and the limited amount of masonry collapse encountered in superstructure interiors. In several instances the presence of solitary drums and/or minimal masonry debris aligned at regular intervals hints that these features may have served as pillar bases or pedestals for wooden supports. Possible column positions have been suggested on either the medial or proximal long axes of superstructures, the latter between the jambs or proximal ends of the lateral exterior walls, but in no case thus far have we recognized the two alignments within the same building. Proximal axis supports suggest a roof structure consisting of a lintel and stringers, while the medial axis columns may indicate the presence of both a lintel and ridgepole.

Most of the Postclassic superstructures we mapped appear to have consisted of a single room; internal partitions in these rooms are rare. We have recognized two exceptions, both of which occur within C-shaped plans where both benches and foundation walls are present. The first exception (one case recognized in a total of 56 mapped C-shaped units) finds a short and wide partition sitting several meters from, and parallel to, an end (side) wall of the building (Fig. 9.2g). The length of this partition is only slightly less than that of the lateral facade wall and it sits at the same height, but it appears to be double the exterior wall width, or more. We did not excavate this feature and cannot say with any assurance whether it served as a structural partition, or as a specialized addition such as an altar or table hearth. The effect of the feature, however, is to create an off-axis compartment of interior space which, like the main room, has an open front.

The second elaboration of the C-shaped architectural form is the addition (in 10 cases) of a rear room, creating a single-zone, double-range floor plan that might be called a tandem-room or "tandem-plan" structure (Freidel 1976: Fig. 15, 1981a: Fig. 12.1; Smith 1962: Fig. 8). Here the second room sits directly behind the first and was apparently entered from the front room through one or more doorways, as suggested by slumps in the collapse of a medial spine wall (Fig. 9.2h). The rear room is most often defined by rear and lateral walls, together with the shared spine wall, although there are instances (4 of the 10 cases) where the rear wall, or the rear and a side wall, was not detectable. While all the mapped walls appear to be of the same double-line and rubble-core construction, comparison of relative amounts of collapse suggested that the end and back walls of the second room were in some instances lower in height than the spine wall or its adjoining front range end walls. In several cases the entire rear room appeared to sit at a lower elevation than its foyer. There is no visible evidence of any doorways in the exterior facades of the rear rooms, nor is there evidence to date of any bench structures in these ranges.

Structure Arrangements and Functions

Unlike Late Classic settlement, Postclassic architecture is not broadly distributed across the landscape of the Central Peten lakes region. While there are platforms and structures at mainland loci within specific basins, the majority of Postclassic occupation is situated in densely settled nucleated communities or "centers" located on naturally defensible landforms that are physiographically circumscribed. These include the islands in Lakes Yaxha and Quexil, the Zacpeten peninsula, and the Isthmuses of Muralla de León and Ixlu, all of which are largely surrounded not only by water but also by broken terrain. The island in Lake Macanche was also occupied during the Postclassic, but less densely so (P. Rice n.d. a, this volume).

The Postclassic constructions that have been mapped in mainland transects tend to stand alone rather than being arranged in groups. Hence there is no good evidence for the regular alignment of buildings or focus on central patios or plazas that is common in Classic Period architectural groups. Not only do mainland Postclassic structures tend not to cluster in groups, but occupation loci fail to cluster on the mainland landscape. High, well-drained terrain appears to have been preferred for structure location, but settlement does not dominate any particular topographic feature. Rather, construction loci are spaced across a range of the higher physiographic features, eschewing possible nucleation in the vicinity of any one attractive locale.

A preference for high terrain was not unique to Postclassic populations, and more suitable sites in the lake basins had been occupied and modified previously. It is not uncommon to find Postclassic platforms situated among earlier architectural remains. Postclassic architecture that does occupy a portion of an earlier, formally arranged mainland group is most likely to be located in the formerly open patio or plaza. There is little evidence that these buildings were positioned in any significant alignments with earlier structures. We also test-excavated several mounds bordering such re-used spaces and found no evidence that the spatially associated earlier constructions were re-modeled during the Postclassic Period.

The spatial arrangement of Postclassic architecture in the densely settled "island" centers of Peten is quite different from that described for the mainland transects. The limited area and very uneven terrain of the island centers were partly overcome by effective use of architectural terracing and the packing of structures on the artificial surfaces and available level ground. The density and configuration of building construction depended, therefore, on the underlying topography and the elevation of the landform.

Structures situated in these Postclassic settlements are clustered in groups largely because they share terraces. It is difficult, however, to identify discrete units, even though buildings are situated side by side. Courtyard arrangements, where they are deemed to exist, are nowhere near as compact or as restricted in access as are Classic Period complexes. One reason for this difference in organization of Classic and

Postclassic sites in the Peten is an apparent disregard for the orientation of adjacent structures in the latter (Johnson 1985). Generally, the direction of topographic slope is more critical than the alignment of nearby architecture in determining the position of any individual platform. As a result, structurally defined formal patio or plaza space is rare, or at least hard to isolate conceptually.

The alignment of adjacent Postclassic buildings increases and becomes more normal, or perpendicular, as slope increases and as the crest of plateau of the site terrain is approached (Johnson 1985). The distribution of architectural types also tends to change along the same gradient. On the lower, peripheral terraces of the center, for the most part, a greater percentage of platforms lack visible evidence of surface features or support modest bench arrangements. With an increase in elevation the incidence of superstructural components—benches, foundations, walls, stairways, and columns—increases, as does the formality of architectural arrangements. The largest structures and the highest quality masonry are usually recovered at the highest elevations of the site. Here there is also a greater emphasis on interstructure alignments, which, together with a relatively larger extent of level terrain, contributes to the presence of structurally delimited plazas.

If we assume a positive correlation between the quantity and quality of architecture and the relative sociopolitical and/or economic status of the occupants, the settlement pattern of these island centers suggests a concentric model for Postclassic Maya nucleated communities. This model finds elite residences and civic-ceremonial precincts located at the center of the site; status and specialized functions decline as the distance from the central zones increases. A similar pattern is implied for the arrangement of administrative and residential structures in the Postclassic towns of Yucatan:

In the middle of the town were their temples with beautiful plazas, and then the most important people. Then came the houses of the richest and of those who were held in the highest estimation nearest to these, and at the outskirts of the town were the houses of the lower class. (Bishop Diego de Landa, quoted in Tozzer 1941: 62–64)

In the Peten proper, the Spaniards characterized the Itza island capital of Noh Peten in similar terms, indicating that the high center of the island was dominated by temples for the worship of idols and that private dwellings were interspersed among the temples, surrounding them on the slopes and shoreline below (Thompson 1951).

The Itza houses of Noh Peten were described by the Spaniards (Thompson 1951) as having stone walls more than one "vara" (yard) high, above which was a wall of wood, or exterior walls that were entirely of wood, and in both cases the roofs were thatched. In his discussion of architecture on the main island of the site of Topoxte, Bullard observed that house ruins most likely included those loci of limited substructure preparation and/or low, stone-filled platforms, with or without bench features (1973: 269). Jay Johnson concurs with Bullard's assessment, arguing on the basis of his cluster analysis of site structure at Topoxte that the buildings' relatively small size and large number, and the presence of interior benches suggest that these constructions may have been house platforms (1985). Johnson also hypothesizes that these forms, with the addition of architectural features such as walls and stairways, may represent elite residential architecture. Postclassic elite residences in Yucatan, as described in Landa's *Relaciones de las Cosas de Yucatán*, offer some insights into the construction of structural equivalents in the Peten:

> . . . they build a wall in the middle, dividing the house lengthwise leaving several doors in the wall into the half which they call the back of the house, where they have their beds; and the other half they whitened very nicely with lime. And the lords have their walls painted with great elegance; and this half is for the reception and lodging of their guests. And this room has no doors, but is open the whole length of the house; and the shape of the roof comes down very low in front as a protection against sun and rain. (Tozzer 1941: 85–86)

The construction of these Yucatecan residences appears to resemble the tandem-plan structures of the Central Peten Postclassic. At the site of Mayapan, where this floor plan is quite common, benches are normally found in the front room on either side of the doorway leading into the back room (Smith 1962: 217). Given the ethnohistoric descriptions of domestic architecture, and the prevalence of the double-range plan at Mayapan, A. L. Smith interprets most single-room plans there as also representing double rooms, proposing that "it seems to have been a fairly common procedure to have the exterior walls of the back room made out of wood" (1962: Fig. 8). While this may have been the case at some C-shaped bench/wall loci in Peten, a great many of the substructures supporting these buildings are too narrow to have accommodated rear rooms. Likewise, the structures are often positioned vis-à-vis topographic features, or other buildings, in such a way as to preclude a second range. These single-room C-shaped plans with their putatively open front sides give no privacy, suggesting that perhaps they were used only as reception halls. Nonetheless, Landa states that guests were lodged in the front rooms of the tandem-room structures, and a domestic function for many of the single-room structures is possible.

With the addition of architectural embellishments such as columns, stairways, and benches, and incorporation of structures into more formal arrangements, it becomes increasingly difficult to attribute solely domestic functions to the single- and tandem-room buildings. Bullard calls the most formal of these masonry structures at Topoxte "open halls"; he classifies them as "ceremonial" architecture (1970: Fig. 11). Fray Andrés de Avendano y Loyola may well have been describing this class of construction in his eyewitness account of the palace of the chief of the Itza at Noh Peten:

> Of this same workmanship is the hall which the king or Ah Canek has as a vestibule to his house, in which he received his guests as he did us . . . [and] we understood that here was the room of welcome for all. At the entrance of said hall stands a large stone table more than two 'varas' long and proportionally broad, placed on stone columns, with twelve seats of the same number around it for the priests . . . [and] the number of people who ran together at the novelty of seeing us was so great, that besides filling all the hall inside, those who could not find a place there, obstructed on the outside all the light which the hall had, and which came in all around it. . . . (Means 1917: 19)

Although the hall is described as a vestibule to an elite residence, it is apparent that the structure sat sufficiently apart from other architecture to allow people to crowd around its sides. The fact that light was admitted from those sides confirms that the masonry walls were of limited height. Avendano also gives the impression that this was a structure for public audiences or public forums, located in a public place. It is also interesting to note that the table in Ah Canek's hall was placed on stone columns, which may indicate that the few stone drums recovered in Postclassic structures may have less to do with roof supports than with furnishings of some kind.

Avendano's description suggests a functional similarity with the "big houses" that were an integral element of sociopolitical architecture at the Highland Guatemalan site of Utatlan (also known as Gumarcaj) at the time of the Conquest (Carmack 1981: 159–60). Within this Quiche Maya capital, the principal lineages were closely identified with the buildings in which they carried out their affairs. These big houses, long colonnaded structures with benches against their back walls, were expressly used for ceremonial lecturing, bride-price giving, eating and drinking at celebrations, audiences, and councils for setting of policy.

Also found in the nucleated Peten Postclassic settlements are temples, not unlike their Classic Period counterparts. The Postclassic temple substructures encountered in our surveys do not appear to have functioned primarily as funerary mounds, however, as did a number of the monumental Classic Period pyramids (Coe 1956). We did not test-excavate any of these platforms, nor did Bullard, but a majority of those recorded in our survey areas had been excavated and exposed during looting activities, in such a manner as to make it possible to verify the absence of a formal crypt or tomb in the base. We cannot speak with any certainty on the possibility of burials elsewhere in the structures. Regardless, it would seem that these multitiered substructure platforms were intended largely to elevate temple superstructures above other public buildings.

The most conspicuous feature of these buildings is the presence of a temple standing on the terraced substructure. The Spaniards indicate that such temples at the Itza center of Noh Peten had:

. . . a wall about a yard and a half high and of the thickness of six quarters; the bench or seat all around, which stands out from the middle inwards, is three quarters thick and the rest, which stands out above, is three quarters thick; so that both together form two rows of seats around the said churches, and all repainted and polished. (Means 1917: 18)

Open halls and temples are found together in the central zones of Postclassic sites, and these precincts of relatively monumental architecture exhibit formal plaza arrangements like those of Classic centers. They are, however, limited in both number and complexity. Several Postclassic plaza plans of civic and religious structures were defined at the Yucatecan site of Mayapan in the 1950s (Proskouriakoff 1962), prior to any organized investigation of Postclassic society in Peten, and variants of these plans have subsequently been identified at a number of Postclassic centers in the latter region (D. Rice and P. Rice 1981, 1984b; Johnson 1985; P. Rice and D. Rice 1985).

At Mayapan, a "basic ceremonial group" includes a colonnaded hall, a raised shrine, and an oratory (Fig. 9.3a). The colonnaded hall is the Mayapan architectural equivalent of the Peten open hall, a large, long room with benches and colonnaded open facade, usually lacking rear compartments. The raised shrine stands as a low block-like sub-structure, occasionally supporting masonry foundation walls and bench altars, which is centered in front of the colonnaded hall. Beyond the shrine and facing the hall is the oratory, a low substructure supporting a C-shaped bench structure which resembles in plan those buildings identified as temples. Its relatively low height and its subordinate po-sition with respect to temples in plaza plans prompted the separate oratory category (Proskouriakoff 1962: 90–91, Fig. 2a).

A second plaza plan, the "typical temple assemblage," combines the basic ceremonial group with larger pyramidal temples (Fig. 9.3b). These stand at right angles to the hall, facing the shrine, with the oratory remaining opposite the hall, facing the shrine, also more or

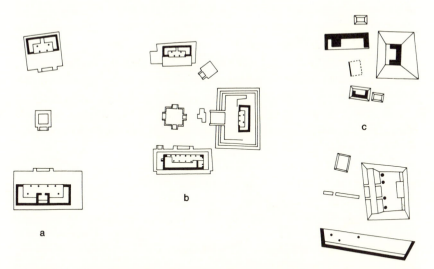

Figure 9.3 Postclassic plaza plans (not drawn to scale): a. basic ceremonial group (after Proskouriakoff 1962: fig. 2a); b. typical temple assemblage (after Proskouriakoff 1962: 91, fig. 1); c. Peten variants of the typical temple as-semblage (upper—Muralla de Leon, lower—Zacpeten).

315

less at right angles to the temple. Between the temple and the shrine is often a low, irregular platform that supported statuary (Proskouriakoff 1962: 91).

Variants of the typical temple assemblage plan are more readily identifiable at Peten Postclassic sites (Fig. 9.3c) than is its basic ceremonial group component (D. Rice and P. Rice 1981: fig. 8; Johnson 1985). Peten examples are not completely isomorphic with those from Mayapan, however, largely as a result of the difficulty in identifying oratories and shrines in the former. In the case of the oratory, the Peten equivalent in the temple assemblage is often less formal than that recorded at Mayapan assemblages (Johnson 1985). Peten shrines are rare, or at least are difficult to detect on the surface, and where identified they consist of small quadrilateral foundation braces or featureless masonry platforms. Long, low bench-like structures have been found to bisect the plazas of temple assemblages on the central axis of the temple, much as did the statuary bench in Mayapan groups, but where these occur, shrine structures are absent. A final Peten deviation from the Mayapan type is the occasional addition of unidentified, generally featureless structures in association with the assemblage. These may be peripheral, or situated in the plaza area, and we have no excavation data or spatial equivalents from other sites by which to determine their ancillary functions.

It would appear that Postclassic communities, with their monumental and residential architecture, were founded on landforms relatively devoid of earlier occupation, or where earlier construction was removed or greatly modified. This tendency, and the apparent absence of more than minor structural alteration to buildings during the Postclassic Period, minimized the mass and complexity of Postclassic sites and to some extent contributed to their distinctive style. The form and location of these settlements are the product of an interplay of previous history and pan-Maya Postclassic events, however, and I would like to review the spatial and temporal distribution of Postclassic architectural forms as a basis for speculation on the possible processes involved.

THE SPATIAL AND TEMPORAL DISTRIBUTION OF POSTCLASSIC ARCHITECTURE

Table 9.1 presents the Early Classic, Late Classic, and Postclassic occupation distributions for settlement mapped in our surveys, as determined from the datable structures sampled within transects (the table does not include 41 mainland structures tested on the peripheries of transects, nor 4 undatable mainland tests) and at the seven special nontransect sites. The latter are utilized here to demonstrate construction characteristics and change at those specific loci only; they are not considered in the derivation of any overall settlement percentages for mainland occupation. Table 9.2 indicates the overall magnitudes of change in settlement numbers from one time period to the next, within the various survey units. While there is a continuum of occupation and culture change during the temporal span under consideration, discussion of the distributions will follow the traditional Peten periodization, defined by significant disjunctions in the artifact inventories from our test-excavations (see P. Rice, this volume).

Late and Terminal Classic Settlement: A.D. 550–950

Classic Period occupation was identified in all transects that we surveyed. More than 83 percent of all mainland structure loci tested were occupied during the Late Classic, an increase of 280.6 percent in loci of construction over the preceding Early Classic Period. This increase is highly variable from basin to basin, however. In the Yaxha-Sacnab area, where earlier settlement was substantial, there was a 118.5 percent increase in Late Classic mainland structure loci in the combined basins. In the Macanche-Salpeten and Quexil-Petenxil basin pairs, which were almost devoid of Early Classic construction, the growth of Late Classic settlement was more dramatic still, with increases of 1,183.3 percent and 1,950.0 percent respectively. The highest individual increase occurred in the Quexil basin, where there was a 3,100.0 percent increment in the number of occupation loci over the Early Classic level. Late Classic structure densities in the individual basins ranged from a high of 66.6 structures per square kilometer at Macanche to a low of 27.2 structures per square kilometer at Lake Sacnab.

The Terminal Classic Period is generally thought to follow whatever event or events contributed to the Maya "collapse," roughly beginning with the start of the 10th cycle, ca. A.D. 830 (Rands 1973a). Only 15.1 percent of all mainland structure loci tested produced artifact evidence of Terminal Classic occupation, which represents a decline of more than 81 percent in the total number of structures occupied

Table 9.1: Central Peten Lakes Survey Occupation Distribution

Lake/Site Operation	Total Strs. Excavated #	Early Classic #/%	Late Classic #/%	Terminal Classic #/%	Early Postclassic #/%	Late Postclassic #/%
YAXHA						
Op. 1	14	3/21.4	9/64.3	5/35.7	0/0	0/0
Op. 2	28	11/39.3	24/85.7	6/21.4	9/32.1	0/0
Op. 3	22	6/27.3	19/86.4	1/4.5	0/0	0/0
Op. 4	28	9/28.6	26/92.9	0/0	1/3.6	0/0
Op. 5	16	8/50.0	13/81.3	0/0	0/0	0/0
Total	108	36/33.3	91/84.3	12/11.1	10/9.3	0/0
Cante Island	19	2/10.5	3/15.8	0/0 (?)	9/47.4	14/73.7
SACNAB						
Op. 8	1	0/0	1/100	0/0	0/0	0/0
Op. 9	17	4/23.5	15/88.2	0/0	0/0	0/0
Op. 10	16	8/50.0	10/62.5	1/6.2	0/0	0/0
Op. 11	6	6/100	1/16.6	0/0	0/0	0/0
Total	40	18/45.0	27/67.5	1/2.5	0/0	0/0

MACANCHE

Op. 1	14	0/0	10/71.4	3/21.4	4/28.6	2/14.3
Op. 3	17	0/0	14/82.4	1/5.9	1/5.9	1.5.9
Op. 4	22	3/13.6	17/77.3	3/13.6	6/27.3	4.18.2
Total	53	3/5.7	41/77.4	7/13.2	11/20.8	7/13.2
Cerro Ortiz	3	0/0	2/66.7	0/0	0/0	0/0
Muralla de Leon	8	0/0	2/25.0	0/0	2/25.0	2/25.0
Macanche Island	1	0/0	1/100	1/100	1/100	1/100
SALPETEN						
Op. 1	19	0/0	18/94.7	8/42.1	1/5.3	0/0
Op. 2	6	1/16.7	5/83.3	1/16.7	1/16.7	1/16.7
Op. 3	14	2/14.3	13/92.9	6/42.9	2/14.3	0/0
Total	39	3/7.7	36/92.3	15/38.5	4/10.3	1/2.6
Zacpeten Peninsula	18	1/5.6	4/22.2	7/38.9	8/44.4	13/72.2
QUEXIL and PETENXIL						
Op. 1	7	1/14.3	6/85.7	2/28.6	0/0	0/0
Op. 2	14	0/0	12/85.7	1/7.1	0/0	0/0
Op. 3	14	0/0	14/100	2/14.3	1/7.1	0/0
Op. 4 (Petenxil)	9	1/11.1	9/100	3/33.3	0/0	0/0
Total	44	2/4.5	41/93.2	8/18.2	1/2.3	0/0
Quexil Islands	7	2/28.6	3/42.9	5/71.4	6/85.7	4/57.1

319

Table 9.2: Magnitude of Change in Settlement Distribution
(the # of occupied structures, and the % of change from the preceding period)

Lakes/Site	Total Strs. Excavated #	Late Classic #/%	Terminal Classic #/%	Early Postclassic #/%	Late Postclassic #/%
YAXHA-SACNAB					
Yaxha	108	91/+152.8%	12/-86.8%	10/-16.7%	0/-100%
Sacnab	40	27/+50.0%	1/-96.3%	0/-100%	0/0
Combined basins	148	118/+118.5%	13/-88.9%	10/-23.1%	0/-100%
MACANCHE-SALPETEN					
Macanche	53	41/+1266.7%	7/-82.9%	11/+57.1%	7/-36.4%
Salpeten	39	36/+1100%	15/-58.3%	4/-73.3%	1/-75.0%
Combined basins	92	77/+1183.3%	22/-71.4%	15/-31.8%	8/-46.7%
QUEXIL-PETENXIL					
Quexil	35	32/+3100%	5/-84.4%	1/-80%	1/-100%
Petenxil	9	9/+900%	3/-66.7%	0/-100%	0/0
Combined basins	44	41/+1950%	8/-80.5%	1/-87.5%	0/-100%
All Mainland Transects	284	236/+280.6%	43/-81.8%	26/-39.5%	8/-69.2%
Cante Island	19	3/+50%	0/-100%	9/+900%	14/+55.6%
Muralla de Leon	8	2/+200%	0/-100%	2/+200%	2/0
Cerro Ortiz	3	2/+200%	2/0	0/-100%	0/0
Zacpeten	18	4/+300%	7/+75.0%	8/+14.3%	13/+62.5%
Quexil Islands	7	3/+50.0%	5/+66.7%	6/+20.0%	4/-33.3%
Macanche Island	1	1/+100%	1/0	1/0	1/0

within the basin transects. Whereas the levels and rates of growth were highly variable from basin to basin in the Late Classic Period, the decline in mainland construction was somewhat more uniform in the Terminal Classic: at Yaxha-Sacnab, 89 percent; at Macanche-Salpeten, 71.4 percent; at Quexil-Petenxil, 80.5 percent.

Terminal Classic ceramics have commonly been found in a context of postcollapse reuse of structures fabricated in the Late Classic or an earlier period, particularly Late Classic vaulted structures in or near centers (Fry 1969: 166; Culbert 1973b: 67–69). Such occupation has been considered the ephemeral remains of "hangers-on" at the centers, and there has been little evidence recovered in Peten of Terminal Classic architectural endeavors. Our test-excavation in several basin pairs produced data that generally support this view. In the basins of Yaxha, Sacnab, Quexil, and Petenxil, all mainland Terminal Classic deposits were found at loci of previous construction and in humus and collapse contexts, which suggests minimal Terminal Classic investment in the occupation sites. The low incidence of Terminal Classic material recovered in our survey may be due in part to our focus on recovering construction sequences, which dictated the placement of our test-excavations. Because there appears to have been little Terminal Classic construction, and most Terminal Classic debris is likely to have been discarded away from the immediate living floor or structure area, it is possible that our excavation data do not reflect accurately the quantity and character of Terminal Classic occupation (cf. Ford 1981: 115–17).

In the Macanche basin, several of the Terminal Classic deposits are from well-defined contexts of architectural remodeling of earlier settlement loci, but no new loci were occupied. Only on the Salpeten mainland do we find both Terminal Classic reconstruction of buildings and initiation of construction at previously unoccupied locations. In addition, the Salpeten transects yielded the highest percentage of Terminal Classic occupation, 38.5 percent, and the lowest rate of decline from the Late Classic to Terminal Classic, a loss of 58.3 percent.

While the mainland transects suffer a decline in the Terminal Classic, this is not necessarily the case with most of the island and special locales that we investigated. The nontransect sites tested in our survey, all but one of which were locations of significant Postclassic settlement, were all occupied in the Late Classic Period. In contrast to the transects, however, that occupation appears to have been relatively light. Only

24.4 percent of the island/peninsular loci sampled, for example, revealed Late Classic construction, none of it substantial. On the basis of the excavation samples, it would seem that none of these sites functioned as centers of dense settlement in the Late Classic, and certainly none of the tested loci revealed Late Classic monumental construction. Several of the sites, however, exhibit characteristics that suggest a Classic Period base for Postclassic settlement and polity.

On the main island of the site of Topoxte, Bullard observed Late Classic veneer masonry that belonged to a platform retaining wall that had been buried beneath a later terrace near the large but heavily collapsed temple Structure A (1970: 255, Fig. 3). Two sculptured stelae were also located in the central group of this main island, lying on the steep slope of the terrace edge on the west side of that plaza. A second pair of carved stelae was erected in the central ceremonial group of Cante Island (Bullard 1970: Fig. 12; Johnson 1979: Fig. 1; Hammond 1982: Fig. 4.20). All four stelae are heavily eroded, their artistic details difficult to discern. Each carries the image of an elaborately dressed human figure in either a seated or standing position, and they are all assessed as having been carved in the Late Classic style, dating to the "Late Classic Tradition," or A.D. 652–869 (Proskouriakoff 1950: 149–50). Given the location of these monuments in Postclassic architectural groups, Bullard suggested that they were obtained from elsewhere, or from an earlier construction period at Topoxte, and reused during the Postclassic period (1970: 271). While evidence for major Late Classic construction in the islands is slight, Bullard assumed that the islands were occupied during the period and were subordinate to the nearby mainland civic-ceremonial center of Yaxha (1970: 255).

At Topoxte the Terminal Classic situation is likewise a bit confused. Terminal Classic materials were recovered in both Bullard's work on the main island and our test-excavations on Cante Island, but in both cases these are mixed with later materials and there are no confirmed Terminal Classic occupation loci or constructions. At the island in Lake Macanche, on the other hand, a Late Classic platform was rebuilt during the Terminal Classic period, incorporating weathered Late Classic sherds into the Terminal Classic fill (P. Rice n.d.a).

It is on the Quexil Islands and the peninsular site of Zacpeten at Lake Salpeten that the trajectories of occupation from Late Classic to Terminal Classic deviate most widely from the aforementioned basin transitions. On the Quexil Islands there was a 66.7 percent increase in structure loci occupied in the Terminal Classic, 50 percent of which were new constructions not overlying or incorporating previous architecture. While the Quexil Islands are small, with only 26 total structures between them, it is significant that the islands experienced an increase in occupation, while the Quexil-Petenxil mainland transects underwent an 80.5 percent decline.

At Zacpeten 38.9 percent of the tested loci were occupied in the Terminal Classic. All of these occupations involved architectural construction, and 71.4 percent of those constructions were initiated at previously unoccupied/unmodified loci. The peninsula of Zacpeten was ultimately a densely settled land form (Fig. 9.4), with 190 structures mapped, and a Terminal Classic occupation percentage of 38.9 percent translates into a Terminal Classic population of 73.9 occupied structures and an occupation density of 318 structures per square kilometer.

A carved stela of Late Classic style was also recovered at Zacpeten in association with two small, heavily collapsed temple structures and a second, plain stela at the northern end of the peninsula (see P. Rice, this volume). The nearby temple structures were not test-excavated by our project, but they are the only architectural forms on the island that do not exhibit obvious Postclassic attributes of construction or plan. Tentative confirmation of a possible Classic date for their manufacture comes from ceramic materials recovered from the spoil of looter's trenches into both of the substructures, sherds considered to be Late Classic in date. This recovery must be tempered, however, by a lack of context and by the knowledge that it is not uncommon to find Classic Period ceramics in Postclassic construction.

While the presence of Late Classic artifacts and Classic Period stelae at these Postclassic sites is only suggestive of potential Classic-to-Postclassic continuity, it is in association with apparent Late Classic architectural complexes elsewhere that we may have found our earliest examples of Postclassic structure forms. These examples come from the south shore of Lake Quexil at the site of Ixlu.

In the Lake Quexil basin, 76 structure loci were mapped within survey Operation 2, and an additional 59 mounds were mapped immediately to the east of that transect in a pasture area that is part of the modern Finca Michoacan. Better than 85 percent of all structures sampled within the transect were occupied in the Late Classic Period.

323

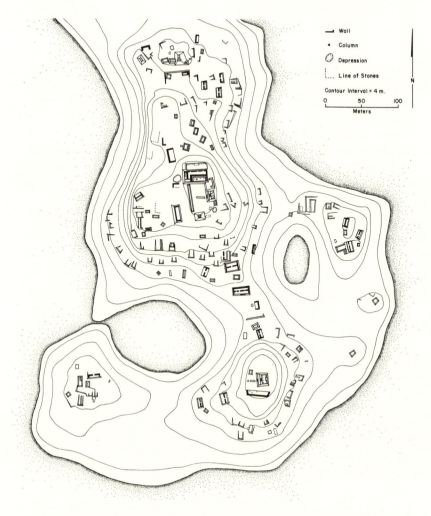

Figure 9.4 The peninsular site of Zacpeten, Lake Salpeten.

Many of the Michoacan structures had been mapped previously by Arlen and Diane Chase in 1977, during their surveys to supplement the Tayasal peninsula data of the University Museum's 1971 Tayasal Project (A. Chase 1979, 1983). The structures within Operation 2 and Michoacan are largely arranged in plazuelas, although there are several large and less formal complexes, particularly east of the operation, which A. Chase considered "an anomaly in the region . . . [because]

324

it had a different settlement pattern from other sites in the zone" (1979: 91).

While most of the Quexil basin structures manifest form and collapse characteristics normally indicative of Late Classic architecture, double-line bench structures have been identified by our project in four complexes in the Michoacan area, one within the survey transect. Seven structures in all are confirmed bench constructions. Three of these are C-shaped benches, while the others appear to be single-line forms. Two of the bench structures sit on cardinal points within plaza groups, while the others are constituents of larger groups (Fig. 9.5). None of the identified structures was selected for test-excavation, but surface materials and sherds from looting activities at the complexes of interest were determined to be Late Classic in date. I would tentatively attribute a Late/Terminal Classic date to these architectural forms because of the presence of these ceramics, the total absence of Postclassic materials in the vicinity, the apparent planned integration of the bench structures

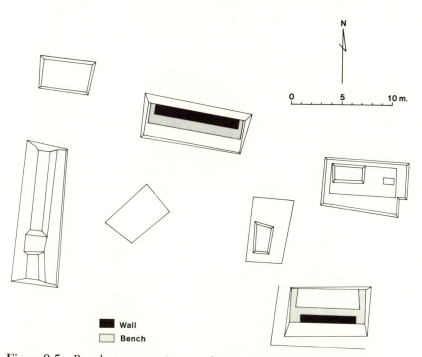

Figure 9.5   Bench structures in an architectural group at Finca Michoacan, east of Operation 2, Lake Quexil.

into several groups of seemingly Late Classic design, and the occupation distribution for the immediate area, as reconstructed from the excavated loci in Quexil's Operation 2 and the basin as a whole.

Ixlu, which sits on the elevated spine of an isthmus between Lakes Salpeten and Peten-Itza, is a small site that was mapped by Franz Blom in 1924 (Morley 1937–38: Plate 210a) and by Eric von Euw in 1975. Our permit did not allow us to pursue test-excavations at Ixlu, but in 1968 Bullard did excavate two test pits at the site (see P. Rice, this volume) and he recovered Late Classic, Terminal Classic, and Postclassic ceramics (1973: 237). Two carved stelae from Ixlu date to A.D. 859 and A.D. 879, making them two of the latest monuments in the Peten. Solely on the basis of these stelae, Ixlu has been considered a Late and Terminal Classic center with relatively brief occupation and limited construction.

We turned our attention to the site of Ixlu in 1981 after the discovery of an Ixlu-style stela at Zacpeten. Our intention was to search for architectural parallels between Zacpeten and Ixlu, even though we would not be able to sample the latter site in order to document its construction history. A total of 50 structures was mapped by us at Ixlu, and 11 of these have surface remains comparable to those forms of confirmed Postclassic architecture already described herein (Fig. 9.6). Two of the 11 structures are L-shaped bench superstructures, while the remainder are C-shape in plan. All these structures appear to be composed of both exterior foundation walls and interior benches.

Several of the Postclassic forms at Ixlu are situated without significant structural associations, while others are located on plaza peripheries or in plaza positions in front of other buildings that do not appear to be Postclassic in form. At least two other of the Postclassic structures at Ixlu, one possibly a tandem-room plan and the other an open hall, have been integrated into a plaza made up of large buildings which exhibit collapse characteristics that are in keeping with Classic Period architecture and plaza arrangements elsewhere. As with the Michoacan case at Quexil, I believe it possible that at least some of the bench structures may be Late/Terminal Classic in date because of the presence of Classic stelae, ceramics, and architecture at the site, and because of the apparent incorporation of the Postclassic forms into a plaza that includes both substructure and superstructure architecture that looks to be Classic in date.

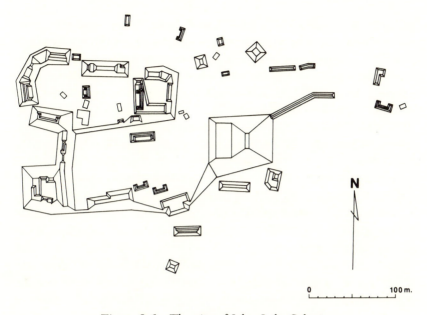

N

0   100 m.

Figure 9.6   The site of Ixlu, Lake Salpeten.

Early Postclassic Settlement: A.D. *950–1200*

The reorganization in Central Peten lakes settlement that began in the Terminal Classic Period, and that is manifest in a decline in mainland occupation and an increase in the numbers of island and peninsular structures, continued in the Early Postclassic Period. There was a 39.5 percent decrease in the occupation of sampled mainland transect loci from the Terminal Classic to Early Postclassic, while our limited testing suggests that island/peninsular sites experienced a 84.6 percent growth. The pattern of transition is variable from basin to basin, however.

In the Yaxha-Sacnab samples, the Lake Sacnab basin yielded no architecture or artifacts attributable to the Postclassic, and the Lake Yaxha transects witnessed a 16.7 percent decline in occupied loci from the Terminal Classic to Early Postclassic Period. Ninety percent of those identified Postclassic loci were found on Operation 2 in the immediate vicinity of the Classic center of Yaxha (D. Rice and P. Rice 1980a: Fig. 11), even though there has been no Postclassic activity

327

recognized thus far in the center itself. In fact, there have been no Postclassic architectural forms noted anywhere on the Yaxha mainland within the basins. The identified habitation loci consist of quantities of artifact material recovered in humus and collapse contexts at previously constructed sites. On an intersite transect between the centers of Yaxha and Tikal, Anabel Ford tentatively identified two Postclassic structures consisting of quadrilateral dressed-stone foundation braces, lying approximately seven kilometers north of Lake Yaxha, but no Postclassic artifact material was found in her survey, and abandonment of Late and Terminal Classic occupation areas appears extensive (1981: 105).

While there was mainland decline in the Yaxha-Sacnab basins, there is evidence for major Postclassic occupation on the Topoxte Islands, at least on the island of Cante. Here 47.4 percent of the sampled structures were constructed in the Early Postclassic Period. We have no similar occupation figures for the main island of Topoxte because Bullard focused on clearing and recording architecture rather than sampling construction episodes at the various structure loci (1973).

The Early Postclassic pattern in the Quexil-Petenxil basins is very similar to that from Yaxha-Sacnab. Postclassic material was not recovered from the Lake Petenxil survey transect, and the Quexil mainland occupation level was only 2.9 percent in the Early Postclassic, an 80 percent decrease from the preceding period. These few occupations are evenly distributed around the lake, and all are in humus and collapse contexts overlying earlier construction. While there is a decline in mainland occupation during the period, 85.7 percent of the Quexil Island structures were occupied, a 20 percent increase from the Terminal Classic Period.

As in the Terminal Classic, the Early Postclassic settlement figures for the Macanche-Salpeten basins deviate somewhat from those of the other two pairs. The platform on the island in Lake Macanche was further remodeled and occupied in the Early Postclassic (P. Rice n.d.a), but, more important, Macanche was the only sampled basin to experience a mainland settlement increase during the period. There was a 57.1 percent increment in mound construction from the Terminal Classic, with 20.8 percent of the sampled transect loci occupied. The Early Postclassic constructions included large featureless platforms, quadrilateral foundation braces, and variants of the double-line bench structures. The largest number of Postclassic buildings in the Macanche mainland samples were C-shaped structures, most with exterior foundation walls and internal bench arrangements, but generally lacking the overall size of open halls found at nucleated island or peninsular sites elsewhere. Most of these Early Postclassic structures stood alone, spaced some distance from one another across the sampled landscape. There were, however, several sizable groups of Postclassic architecture in and around Operation 4, the transect nearest Lake Salpeten and the site of Zacpeten.

While none of the Postclassic groups mapped in the Macanche mainland transects appear to constitute a civic-ceremonial complex, a temple assemblage was constructed during the Early Postclassic Period at the fortified site of Muralla de León, situated on a very high isthmus of land defined by Lake Macanche and two large cenotes on the northeast corner of the lake (D. Rice and P. Rice 1981: fig. 2). We believe that the walled perimeter of the site was constructed during the Protoclassic Period, the period of peak settlement on that mesa, but apparently in the Early Postclassic a small temple assemblage was begun on the highest terrain of the site. There is minimal Postclassic residential architecture associated with the assemblage within the confines of the wall, however.

While the Macanche mainland transects exhibited structure growth during the Early Postclassic, mainland occupation at Salpeten continued to decline. Only 10.3 percent of the sampled transect loci were occupied, down 73.3 percent from the preceding period. At Ixlu, where some of the mapped Postclassic structures may well be attributable to the Early Postclassic Period, Bullard's test-pit material at least confirms a Postclassic presence at the site. There are not enough data from enough locations, however, to enable us to tell if that presence is early, late, or both.

As with the island sites of Topoxte and Quexil, the site of Zacpeten continued to experience construction. Over 44 percent of the sampled structure loci were occupied in the Early Postclassic, 28.4 percent of these being new building starts, for an overall increase of 14.3 percent over the Terminal Classic Period. It is interesting to note that this occupation percentage is very similar to that at Topoxte.

Late Postclassic Settlement: A.D. 1200–1524

In our surveyed basins the Late Postclassic Period appears to have been one of settlement nucleation, centered on the sites of Topoxte and Zacpeten. The mainland transects at Quexil and Petenxil were devoid of evidence for construction during this period, and only 57.1 percent of the sampled Quexil Island loci were occupied, a 33.3 percent decline. While the island platform in Lake Macanche continued to be utilized (a basal platform with a superstructure on it was a Late Postclassic construction), mainland settlement was reduced by 36.4 percent and there was no elaboration of the monumental architecture at Muralla de León or increase in settlement there.

At Yaxha-Sacnab, transects in both basins are empty of recognizable Late Postclassic settlement, but there was a 55.6 percent increase in occupation loci on Cante Island of Topoxte, where 73.7 percent of the test excavations yielded Late Postclassic materials. On the basis of architectural similarities between the buildings on the main island of Topoxte and those from Mayapan, and his assumption of a late date for the latter site, Bullard felt that these Peten constructions dated to the Late Postclassic (1973: 232). The ceramics recovered by Bullard include types that are late, and the main island was certainly occupied in the Late Postclassic, if not earlier.

There is a 75 percent decrease in the Late Postclassic settlement of mainland transects at Lake Salpeten, with only 2.6 percent of the occupation loci tested being occupied. We have no data on the state of activity at Ixlu during the period. Zacpeten, however, definitely continued to grow, with a 62.5 percent increase from the Early Postclassic, and it is ironic that again the 72.2 percent occupation percentage for the Zacpeten excavation samples is approximately equal to that of Topoxte's Cante Island for the same period.

The Zacpeten peninsula is the only sampled location in all of our surveys, whether transect or site, for which we can demonstrate continued increase in settlement size and density from the Late Classic through the Late Postclassic. The evidence for long-term "growth" at Zacpeten, together with stratigraphic superposition of Late Classic, Terminal Classic, and Postclassic materials in test excavations at the site, is suggestive of population continuity in the immediate area through the Maya Collapse and up to the Historic Period.

DISCUSSION

It is apparent from our survey data that a remarkable settlement transition followed the Early Classic Period in many of the lake basins investigated. The Late Classic witnessed a great increase in construction, which I believe represents an increased investment in domestic architecture and which I would interpret as indicative of an overall population increase in the region. Given that such an investment in construction is contingent on the social and economic interests of the individual household members, including their wealth, status, access to property, and generational continuity of occupation (Netting 1982; Wilk and Rathje 1982), it must be acknowledged that differences between the Early Classic and Late Classic patterns may also have resulted from a major shift in household organization, and the diversification and scheduling of labor on a large scale. There is some paleolimnological evidence for a relaxation of human impact in the basins of Macanche and Quexil during a timespan equivalent to the Early Classic (M. Binford 1983), however, suggesting that the relative paucity of archaeologically measured settlement in those basins during that period is a real demographic phenomenon. It is likely, then, that there was a sharp increase in the numbers of basin occupants during the Late Classic, and perhaps a change in their socioeconomic organization as well.

In the Central Peten lakes survey region, the highest Late Classic settlement densities and most dramatic structural increases were recorded in those basins which lacked established communities of any duration or consequence. For these basins exhibiting minimal Early Classic seed population, such increases may initially have involved inmigration, although it is at present difficult to pinpoint potential sources for the migrants. This increase in settlement density in the region may well reflect a general Late Classic trend of population growth and radiation out from Early Classic centers of settlement. It is not possible to discern, however, if that movement was the result of established elites attempting to settle and extend control over surrounding unoccupied areas (Cowgill 1979), or if it was linked to the kinds of shifts in political fortunes and declines and abandonments that have been proposed for civic-ceremonial centers in the Late and Terminal Classic periods (Marcus 1976), or perhaps both in some sequence of events. Whatever the motivation or process, and on whatever scale, such transition is one of major alteration in the demographic bases of site regions, and would have repercussions for systems of social control, craft production, trade, and food provision throughout the Peten.

The economic and sociopolitical reorganization which must have accompanied such changes constitutes the context from which subsequent events of the Maya collapse should be evaluated. While it cannot be denied that some dramatic episode(s) may have been responsible for such a phenomenon, the proposed 120-year duration of the Terminal Classic Period itself argues against such catastrophism. Societal configurations and manifestations were markedly transformed, but those changes are the culmination of almost four centuries of cultural dynamics that we are only now beginning to document. One characteristic that can be attributed to the period of the collapse, however, regardless of how it is defined, is the introduction of foreign elements into the Central Peten by the close of the Classic.

At some point during Late Classic and/or Terminal Classic times, I believe, there was an intrusion of non–Peten Maya influence into the lakes region. This view is based on three considerations: (1) the foreign flavor and projected sources of the Terminal Classic ceramics (Adams 1973; Sabloff 1970; Rands, Bishop, and Sabloff 1982) and their presence in the basins (P. Rice, this volume); (2) the foreign elements or styles detected on stelae at the sites of Flores and Ixlu (Graham 1973); and (3) the presence of double-line bench structures in the Quexil basin and at the site of Ixlu. While the latter structures were not test-excavated, and associated artifact material is circumstantial, they appear to have been purposefully integrated into functioning Classic Period architectural groups and settlement. This is very unlike the later Postclassic pattern. The presence of all three non–Peten Maya attributes at Ixlu, a site which lacks the density characteristics and distinct plaza plans of confirmed Postclassic centers, further suggests a possible early date. Whether the presence of these structural forms represents the incorporation of some new functional unit, the diffusion of a non–Peten Maya style, or the actual presence of foreigners at these locations is another question, however.

Architecture represents a considerable labor investment; it is both nonportable and relatively rarely replaced, which contributes to a general conservatism of architectural styles. Both domestic and civic-ceremonial architecture are also conservative because the social units and institutions which are housed tend to be conservative. Architectural style can be a major symbol of personal identity, and choice of residential form can be "construed as a sign of one's personal values, self-perceptions, and socioeconomic position" (Sircar 1982). Where distinct civic-ceremonial structures accommodate social and domestic functions for elite groups, for example, it is understandable that other contemporary domestic buildings would to some degree emulate the style and forms associated with status and authority.

Style, together with construction techniques and architectural concepts, is likewise embedded in the repertoire of architects and builders and is diffused throughout society as training and cultural transmission occur. Therefore, architectural styles often serve as ethnic identifiers and symbols of corporate identity. The tenacity of that identity, and of architectural concepts and techniques, can be seen among modern Peten migrants, whose house styles betray their regions and communities of origin in the Guatemalan Highlands.

For these reasons I believe that we have foreign influence, or perhaps even small non–Peten Maya populations, in the lakes region by the close of the Classic Period. Indigenous sources or processes of architectural innovation are certainly possible, but the contexts and timing of the additions in this instance suggest otherwise. The presence of putative foreign influence raises questions about the origin of that influence or population and its mode or motivation for entry into the Central Peten.

In his evaluation of structure forms on the main island of Topoxte, Bullard looked primarily to late Yucatecan sites for parallels, including Chichen Itza, Mayapan, and Tulum (1970: 302, 1973: 232–33). While Late Postclassic similarities between Yucatecan and Peten architecture have been acknowledged in this review, it would appear from our Quexil and Ixlu mapping that we have Postclassic structure variants in Peten which predate those confirmed thus far at Topoxte. Furthermore, the dating of these Yucatecan sites is still a matter of considerable debate (see Ball; A. Chase; and Lincoln, all this volume). These facts, together with the general paucity of information on the architectural forms themselves, make it difficult to trace potential precursors for the Peten units or to define vicinities of origin for the styles.

There are reports of early structures from Yucatan and adjacent regions which bear resemblances to the Peten examples, but often their dating is not exact or their contexts are nebulous. At the site of Becan, for example, Structure 6F-1 consisted of a single long room and transversely parallel "porch," the latter left open along its front side. Despite its dearth of artifacts, not uncommon in Peten Postclassic structures, Ball has suggested on the basis of location and reuse of Classic building

stone that the structure dates to the Xcocom ceramic phase (1979a),
A.D. 800–1100 (Hammond and Ashmore 1981: Fig. 2.2). Other units
of dry-laid rubble foundation walls and similar morphology have been
noted in the area of Becan, however, and the only other tested structure
of this type yielded a small collection of Late Classic sherds from a
subfloor trenching (Eaton 1975, cited in Ball 1979a).

A single Terminal Classic colonnaded structure was recovered at
Altun Ha (Pendergast 1982a: 248, 251, Fig. 118), and one is also
reported from Lamanai (Pendergast 1981a: 44, Fig. 17) with a radio-
carbon-indicated date of ca. A.D. 1140. The latter date also appears
appropriate for similar architectural units at the Belizean sites of Santa
Rita (D. Chase 1981, this volume) and Negroman/Tipu (P. Rice personal communication). At Barton Ramie, Belize, structures BR-19
and BR-145 are both "plazuela" type mounds which might qualify as
C-shaped structures, although the construction materials and techniques are considerably different from those found in Peten. The BR-
19 locus contained refuse from the Late Classic and Early Postclassic
Spanish Lookout and New Town ceramic phases, with principal construction of the mound attributed to the former (Willey et al. 1965:
164–65).

These isolated instances of architectural similarity are intriguing,
but they lack for me the force of numbers in identifying potential
routes for foreign influence in Late Classic Peten. A more promising
immediate source may be the Rio Pasión site of Seibal, where more
than 70 percent of the domestic structures had C-shaped benches or
upper levels (Tourtellot personal communication). In the Late Classic
at Seibel these coexist with simple multilevel structures like those found
in the Central Peten during the same period, and they may be the
primary form constructed there during the Terminal Classic Period,
when the non–Classic Maya attributes of Seibal became prominent
(Tourtellot 1983). Gair Tourtellot has suggested that structures with
these bench forms "may eventually fit into a larger reconstruction of
ethnic or cultural ties between the Usumacinta-Pasión Valley and the
Yucatan" (1982: 623).

While the relationships between these two areas over time appear
to have been quite complex (Ball 1974a, 1977b, this volume; Miller
1977a), one possibility is that ties may have been initially forged by
Chontal-Putun Maya groups migrating both north into the Yucatan
and south up the Usumacinta River, during the Late Classic Period,

from their homeland in the Chontalpa of Campeche and Tabasco (Thompson 1970). This hypothesized migration coincides in area with the early distribution of "Mexicanized" architectural features in the Puuc and Pasión, although the ultimate inspiration for these Mexicanized forms is still a matter of speculation.

The southern Chontal migration, which would have brought the initial C-shaped benches and other non-Maya attributes to the Rio Pasión sites, may also have been responsible for the introduction of similar forms into the Guatemalan Highlands. John Fox believes that after political interaction at Seibal and Altar de Sacrificios, Chontal lineages followed the river to the Negro and Motagua river valleys (personal communication). Here are found intrusive Puuc/Chontal–like sites dating to the Epiclassic Period, or A.D. 800–1100 (Fox 1980). Among the foreign architectural features exhibited by these sites are colonnaded long buildings and C-shaped bench structures, the latter becoming the dominant house type through the Postclassic (Fox personal communication; Ichon et al. 1980; Ichon and Grignon 1981). During the Early Postclassic Period additional Mexicanized influence becomes crystallized in the form of the "Chichen Itza acropolis pattern," which includes both colonnaded structures and four-stairwayed pyramids (Fox 1980). Fox suggests that these migrations, and those of the Epiclassic Period, were demographic thrusts following established trade routes and represent attempts to control high-yielding agricultural lands and, secondarily, deposits of notable trade materials.

It is projected from our survey data that foreign influence in the Peten at the close of the Classic is not confined to the Río Pasión area. As in the Highland Negro and Motagua river valleys, Chontal-Putun influence, or people, may have moved into the Peten interior from the Pasión region. If this was the case, then the early non–Peten Maya architecture in several of our sampled lake basins may represent implicit ethnic and political reflections of that influence or intrusion from the outside. That the foreign structures are few may reflect a specialized function, or preferential association with more prestigious individuals or households.

If the possibility of an actual population intrusion is considered, then the limited number of such structures suggests that it was without great demographic base. By extension, the degree to which such a foreign presence, in and of itself, would have been a precipitating factor in the Maya collapse is questionable. Instead, that presence might be symptomatic of broader internal transitions. Additionally, it is apparent that in our survey samples the proposed foreign influence, or intrusion, was centered on areas where the demographic impact of the collapse is least apparent. Given the later ubiquity of the non–Peten Maya architectural forms in these same areas, I would suggest that the foreign presence, whatever its embodiment, formed the core around which Peten society re-established itself sociopolitically in the Postclassic Period.

Why there should be a foreign presence in the lakes region is as difficult to explain as Seibal's resurgence under non-Maya influence at the close of the Classic Period. Given our survey results, I would expect that in many areas of the Central Peten there was considerable Late Classic change in demographic structure, that political and economic relationships may have been in a constant state of flux, and that there may have been periods or areas of minimal resistance to intrusion. Perhaps, as Fox suggests for the Epiclassic intrusions in Highland Guatemala (1980), foreign activity in the Peten might then have resulted from attempts to extend control over lucrative markets, populations, or landscapes which were vulnerable in the Late Classic Period.

The continued presence of exotic goods such as jade, obsidian, and volcanic metates in our survey area through the Terminal Classic and Postclassic periods, and the recovery of these and Terminal Classic and Early Postclassic foreign ceramic pieces at Flores (A. Chase 1979: 102), attests that the Central Peten maintained active participation in interregional trade. The structure of that trade may well have changed at the close of the Classic, however. A dramatic shift in the dominant source of one commodity, obsidian, from primarily Chayal in the Classic to Ixtepeque in the Postclassic (P. Rice 1984b, n.d.b), may in part be the result of a realignment of mercantile activities and motivations, born of Terminal Classic foreign presence in the Peten and/ or the political machinations of 10th cycle centers like Ixlu and Seibal.

It is possible that the non–Peten Maya architecture at the site of Ixlu in fact reflects administrative ties with Seibal. The Central Peten and Río Pasión were apparently two of five regional zones in the Maya Lowlands in the Terminal Classic Period (Bove 1981: 109; Marcus 1976: 193), and they are to date the only two which have yielded early examples of the architectural forms discussed. Joyce Marcus has interpreted the available hieroglyphic information from these zones to suggest considerable Terminal Classic interaction between the two (1976) and a Central Peten–Río Pasión connection is perhaps reflected in apparent similarities between the stelae of Seibal and those of Ixlu (Graham 1973: 213). The ceramics recovered in Terminal Classic contexts on the Macanche island also share a number of types and modes with Seibal's Terminal Classic Bayal complex (Bullard 1973; P. Rice n.d.a) that are not evident in contemporary deposits recoverd at Uaxactun, Tikal, or other interior Peten sites.

Any relationship which may have existed between Seibal and Ixlu perhaps also incorporated intervening terrain. Late Classic bench structures have been identified in the Peten approximately midway between the Rio Pasión and the Central Peten lakes at a savanna site called El Fango. El Fango, which sits in a finger of grassland near the modern town of San Francisco, was found to be a dense community of Late Classic residential architecture (D. Rice and P. Rice 1979; P. Rice and D. Rice 1979). It was a settlement of short duration and may represent another example of Late Classic populations seeking and occupying previously unoccupied and unmodified terrain. Most structures at El Fango are arranged in plazuela groups in the grassland flats and the lack of high forest or heavy overburden makes their Late Classic construction readily distinguishable. Situated among the Late Classic groups, however, are four structures with C-shaped bench or foundation features (D. Rice and P. Rice 1979: Fig. 13; P. Rice and D. Rice 1979: 24). A fifth building of similar plan, a large open hall with C-shaped exterior foundation walls and interior bench arrangements, is the only monumental architecture recovered at the site; it sits on a hill overlooking all other structures in the settlement (Fig. 9.7). Located as it is between the Rio Pasión and the lakes region of Central Peten, El Fango may have been situated within the territory of a sociopolitical alliance.

Judged in the context of other data available from the Peten interior, our surveys suggest that the demographic and sociopolitical changes previously attributed to the Terminal Classic and Postclassic periods actually began in the Late Classic, and that the transition was at least in part focused on the Central Peten lakes. A salient feature of that transition within the basins is settlement continuity, a continuity that is apparent from both our architectural information and the ceramic data (P. Rice 1979b, 1980, this volume; cf. Bullard 1973). Population continuity from the Classic through Postclassic periods is also suggested

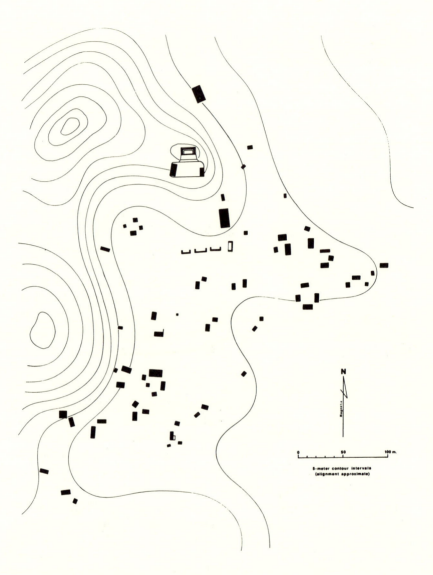

Figure 9.7 The western sector of the savanna site of El Fango.

for the Tayasal peninsula, immediately west of our survey region (A. Chase 1979: 96–97).

By the end of the Terminal Classic Period we do have undeniable evidence for a decline in architectural loci in the lakes area from projected Late Classic levels, but in several basins this was not the traumatic Classic-to-Postclassic loss which has generally characterized the Peten Maya collapse. When taken only as change, divorced from the connotations of rise or fall, the transition of the collapse, integrated over time, is no more dramatic than the similarly integrated magnitude of Early Classic–to–Late Classic settlement changes in the lakes region. Our chronological control is so tenuous at present that we should acknowledge that these may have been gradual changes which began in the Late/Terminal Classic Period and continued into the Postclassic. Also, if Postclassic structures accommodated both multiple functions and multiple domestic units, which in the Late Classic may have been housed individually, then larger numbers of residents might be attributed to each (Haviland 1972a; Thompson 1971), and the demographic decline may have been even less than the construction percentages would imply. A population of disenfranchised farmers, or the failure of households to invest in domiciles for reasons of sociopolitical and economic instability (Netting 1982; Wilk and Rathje 1982), would have a similar impact on our perception of the collapse transition. That is, it should be kept in mind that survey focused on visible remains, and our test-excavation program was designed to sample construction fill, which may have biased our ability to detect more ephemeral, nonstructure midden or occupation loci.

During the course of the subsequent Postclassic periods, a decided interest was maintained in settlement of islands, peninsulas, and isthmuses within the lakes. It is difficult to ascertain why these locations would be selected in addition to, or in lieu of, mainland ones. Occupation in the vicinity of lakes ensures the availability of lacustrine protein and potable water, although Salpeten's waters are too saline for human consumption. However, this does not really explain island residence when riparian choices were available. Movement to these confined loci would make terrain available for economic pursuits on the mainland, but this advantage may have been secondary to more critical considerations. I would suggest that the focus on islands results from a concern for protection. The events of the Late and Terminal Classic undoubtedly produced an insecure social environment and, if this was a period of economic and political reorientation, there may have been substantial local movement and raiding as short-term adaptations to an unstable situation.

In addition, the presence of small, side-notched, chipped obsidian projectile points in Terminal Classic contexts at Macanche Island (P. Rice n.d.a) and Seibal (Willey 1982: 127), and at other sites in the Peten and Belize (Willey et al. 1965: 411, 423, Fig. 268), may well indicate the presence of the bow and arrow in the Maya Lowlands by this time. It has been suggested that Mexican mercenaries from Tabasco introduced the bow and arrow into Yucatan in the later Postclassic Period, under the patronage of an Itza lineage that enlisted their aid in seizing control of government at Mayapan (Porter Weaver 1972: 229). If on the basis of the Terminal Classic small projectile points we entertain the possibility that the late date of introduction might be incorrect, the Terminal Classic and Postclassic populations may have found themselves seriously vulnerable to attack over greater distances, and by smaller groups, than would have been possible with spears, atlatls, or hand weapons. A natural response would have been to nucleate residences in those locations which physiographically impede easy or unnoticed access to within a bow shot. Islands, peninsulas, and isthmuses offer such a degree of natural defense to those settlements and centers of authority situated thereon, which may explain why we have recovered no Postclassic civic-ceremonial groups on open mainland terrain.

If the late date for the introduction of the bow and arrow is in error, we must question the mode of introduction. Fox indicates that, like the Quiche, the Chontal (and Xiu, Yucatecan Itza) were organized into a complex hierarchy of lineages with the less highly ranked warrior lineages being the first to migrate into less densely settled new territories, a process which can be demonstrated clearly and frequently in the Guatemalan highlands. In the Quiche area, these military lineages established plazas with "a single temple on the plaza grate, and with several colonnaded rectangular structures" (personal communication). Given the simultaneous Terminal Classic appearance in Peten of small projectile points and non–Peten Maya architectural elements, each of which is characteristic of the later Postclassic, we might consider the possibility that both were introduced by a Chontal-Putun–like group. It is intriguing to speculate that this introduction could have resulted from Chontal mercenaries serving the Classic Maya with greatest access to them, such as "buffer zone" Seibal and its allies, or that the Chontal-Putun were expanding into an already politically and demographically troubled area. In either case they would have exacerbated existing hostilities and the propensity to shift settlement to protected locations. At the moment, however, the best we can say is that the latter occurred.

Not only was there a preference for lacustrine settlement areas, but a number of basins appear to have been preferred over others. Within our survey region, the Macanche and Salpeten basins were apparently more heavily settled in the Late/Terminal Classic period than the rest. Here we also found the greatest percentage of Postclassic occupation and both significant mainland settlement and island nucleation. I would suggest that this focus was initially due to the Terminal Classic authority of the site of Ixlu, a center whose stelae acknowledge Tikal (Marcus 1976) and demonstrate affinities with Seibal, and a center which by virtue of its small size (and concomitant scale of infrastructure, demands, and support) may have been more capable of surviving demographic change and/or sociopolitical and economic reorganization.

Ixlu is the only Classic Period mainland center at which we have tentatively identified a continuity of settlement and the possibility of Postclassic residence and use on a large scale. I attribute an important Late Classic, Terminal Classic, and Early Postclassic status to Ixlu because of the results of Bullard's test-excavations, the presence of 10th cycle stelae, and the presence of foreign structures in a plaza of Classic Period style. I doubt, however, that the center functioned as a seat of central authority into the Late Postclassic Period. I say this because the isthmus never became a location of dense and varied Postclassic architecture, and because currently recognizable Postclassic civic-ceremonial plans were not constructed there.

At this stage in our research I cannot indicate the longevity of the site in actual years, or even periods, nor can I define its relationship to the peninsular site of Zacpeten in the same basin. My inclination is to suggest that the latter replaced the former in administrative importance at some point in the Postclassic. In light of apparent settlement continuity in the area, I would opt for considerations of defense as the reason, but there remain the possible effects of events or functional relationships which cannot be anticipated until both sites are investigated further. A bond between the two centers is suggested by the presence of an Ixlu-style stela at Zacpeten. The erection of stelae at

Postclassic sites, particularly stelae carved during the Classic Period, or in the Classic Maya style, may reflect a continuity with the political history of the Peten. Their use or reuse is a statement about heritage, rulership, and domain that the resident population understood.

While the Terminal Classic occupation of the site of Ixlu and its environs, and its 10th cycle stelae, suggest demographic and political continuity from a Classic base, the non–Peten Maya architectural forms in these locations may be indicative of changes in civic-ceremonial behavior, changes which we see elaborated and carried through to the Historic Period in the Central Peten. The most dramatic change in the organization of space is the openness of the temple and colonnaded hall superstructures, a change which I believe may reflect a different social fabric and administrative type. The activities performed therein involved a number of participants and were open to a large audience. Gone is the restricted access and privacy of the Classic Period elite palace and acropolis, and in their place are "flexible multi-functional public buildings" and "public administrative centers" (Freidel 1976: 240). Gone also are the large funerary monuments with their closed temple superstructures. Perhaps gone is government embodied in a closed elite class and a divine king. The presence of several separate, but equivalent, formal plaza plans at a site like Zacpeten suggests decentralized civic-ceremonial functions, perhaps a pattern of multiple and separate kin-group loci of administration and ritual like that documented for the segmentary lineages of the Quiche Maya at Utatlan (Carmack 1981: 156–63).

The fact that Peten Postclassic plaza plans and architectural forms were shared with non–Peten sites, particularly those of Postclassic Yucatan, calls into question the degree to which external influences continued to affect Peten Postclassic populations and politics. The presence of quantities of trade goods suggests that pan-Maya contacts were maintained throughout the Postclassic Period, but evidence of major outside impact on Peten is at present difficult to isolate (see P. Rice, this volume, for a broader discussion of this issue). At the time of Puuc development in the Yucatan, the associated Cehpech ceramic assemblage is absent in the Central Peten. Bench structures do occur at Uxmal (Ruppert and Smith 1957: 581–82, Fig. 3), but the two zones apparently shared little else in architectural style. While there are structure forms common to Chichen Itza and Peten Postclassic sites, no known Chichen Itza acropolis pattern has been identified at the latter during the period of Chichen Itza hegemony in the north, nor have the diagnostics of the Chichen Itza–related Sotuta ceramic complex been found in Peten.

In the Late Postclassic Period, architectural similarities obtained between Peten communities and a number of Yucatecan sites, including Cozumel (Freidel 1976; Sabloff and Freidel 1975), Tulum and El Meco (see Andrews and Robles C., this volume), and the center of Mayapan. Of all known Yucatecan contemporaries, however, only Mayapan appears to manifest the formal plaza plans that are found in Peten Postclassic settlements. The sharing of these plans tends to reinforce traditional reconstructions of Mayapan as a source of inspiration and population for the Peten Postclassic, a population which has been identified ethnically as the Itza Maya.

From the perspective of his work at Topoxte in the 1960s, Bullard suggested that expansionist elite groups from the north brought political and religious control to the Central Peten (1973: 241). They were able to do this because Peten settlement was assumed to have been sparse and unorganized, and "left to their own devices, the native population of the Peten Postclassic Tradition did not construct specialized ceremonial buildings of a monumental nature" (1973: 238). Bullard fell short of saying, however, that the missionary group from the Northern Yucatan was the Itza of the migration myths.

I have attempted to make a case for a non–Classic Maya presence at the center of early Peten Postclassic developments, but I believe that our current data do suggest the existence of a native population and political infrastructure at the close of the Classic. While the details of the subsequent record of development are still vague, I do not feel that the Late Postclassic sites in Yucatan can be seriously considered as primary sources of organization for the Postclassic Peten.

Certainly by the Late Postclassic Period we cannot deny Itza presence or influence: ethnohistory, linguistics, and myth all reflect an Itza affiliation. We should seriously question, however, the direction of the influence and its mode, timing, and scope. Given the long and varied history of the Itza in Yucatan, and our settlement data from the Central Peten lakes area, interactions and movements may just as easily have been long-term and reciprocal as late and one-sided.

At the time of Spanish contact we know that an Itza polity, centered on the capital of Taiza and its main island of Noh Peten, controlled the region of Peten. There were a number of provinces within that

343

polity, one of which was Yalain or Alain, with its town of Zacpeten, and another was Maconche. I believe that these provinces were centered on the Macanche and Salpeten basins of our survey and that we have demonstrated that a considerable Postclassic history exists for those zones. Based on that longevity, I am inclined to see the Itza ethnicity attributed to Historic Period Peten as having deep internal roots, the result of complex interactions going back to the Classic Period. It remains to isolate the archaeological correlates of that ethnicity and to recover the substance and structure of that history.

NOTE

1. The author would like to acknowledge the support of National Science Foundation funding for various aspects of the research in the Central Peten lakes region reported herein: grant GB-32150 to E. S. Deevey for work at Lakes Yaxha and Sacnab; and grant BNS-7813736 to D. S. Rice and P. M. Rice, and grant BNS-8105379 to D. S. Rice, for work at lakes Macanche, Salpeten, Quexil, and Petenxil. The research reported from the Central Peten savannas was funded by a National Geographic Society grant to D. S. and P. M. Rice. I would also like to acknowledge the Florida State Museum and the University of Chicago for assistance and support during the various phases of fieldwork and analysis. In Guatemala, the research projects were made possible by the Instituto de Antropología e Historia de Guatemala, its former director Lic. Francis Polo Sifontes, the personnel of the Parque Nacional Tikal, and our many friends in Guatemala City, Flores, Macanche, and Tikal. This manuscript has benefited greatly from the comments and constructive criticism of Wendy Ashmore, John Fox, Jane Kepp, Joyce Marcus, Gair Tourtellot, and the editors of this volume. A special debt of gratitude is owed to Pru Rice, who has shared the direction of the Central Peten research and analyses of the results, and who provided advice and data during the writing of this paper.

PART FOUR

Interpretations

10

Social and Political Organization in the Land of Cacao and Honey: Correlating the Archaeology and Ethnohistory of the Postclassic Lowland Maya

DIANE Z. CHASE

University of Central Florida

Present knowledge of Lowland Maya social organization prior to the Historic Period is derived primarily from syntheses of ethnohistoric descriptions of the Maya by Spaniards during and following their conquest of Middle America. Analysis of these documents reveals substantial information concerning Lowland Maya cultural practices. However, the descriptions are clearly not all-embracing, particularly when they concern material culture. The accounts are also known to vary in their reliability. Given the continued use of ethnohistory for interpreting the Classic Maya (M. Coe 1965; Haviland 1968; Kurjack 1974; Thompson 1970) as well as Postclassic Maya archaeological remains, it seems appropriate to assess the ethnohistoric descriptions through archaeological information from sites occupied immediately prior to the Conquest. While such an assessment was undertaken on a limited scale for Mayapan (Pollock et al. 1962), recent archaeological work on the Lowland Maya Postclassic Period (see other papers this volume and A. Chase and P. Rice 1985) has added significantly to the available data. Archaeological data may often be used to clarify ethnohistory and may occasionally serve to correct garbled accounts. This paper, therefore, seeks to combine and contrast what is now known from both archaeological and ethnohistorical studies concerning the

347

Protohistoric social and political organization of the Lowland Maya.

It is astonishing that after a century of study Mayanists can still not archaeologically define what is "Maya" at the point of the Spanish conquest as opposed to what is "Mexican" or "Putun," particularly given the ethnohistoric data that are available concerning the location of various ethnic groups at the time of the Conquest. In order to discuss interactions between various groups and regions, it is necessary first to define the realities of the situation at contact. Without such a definition, researchers can find themselves speculating unnecessarily about matters that can actually be resolved by reference to hard data.

The ethnohistoric information used in this paper will be drawn primarily from the most accessible works, such as the numerous synthetic writings of Roys (1933, 1943, 1957; Scholes and Roys 1948) and the descriptions of Diego de Landa as translated by Tozzer (1941). Archaeological discussion will be limited to the Late Postclassic Period (ca. A.D. 1300–1520) and will be presented predominantly from the site of Santa Rita Corozal, with additional information being added from the site of Mayapan.

Although Mayapan was largely unoccupied after A.D. 1450, this site was probably the most important administrative center in the Northern Lowlands for much of the Late Postclassic Period. Excavations there by the Carnegie Institution have provided an extensive body of archaeological data on the Postclassic Maya (Pollock et al. 1962). Mayapan also lies squarely within the Yucatec area best described in the ethnohistoric documents (Relaciones de Yucatan 1898–1900; Tozzer 1941), and tentative correlations between the archaeology and ethnohistory have been made (Roys 1962).

The site of Santa Rita Corozal, located on the extreme southeastern part of the Northern Lowlands, was first investigated by Thomas Gann (1900, 1911, 1914–16, 1918) and more recently by the Corozal Postclassic Project (A. Chase 1980; A. Chase and D. Chase 1981; D. Chase 1981, 1982a, 1985; D. Chase and A. Chase 1980). Both sets of investigations serve to underscore not only the Late Postclassic Period remains, but also the long history of occupation at the site. While continued investigation at Santa Rita Corozal is planned, the 1979 and 1980 seasons unearthed substantial information relevant to Protohistoric Lowland Maya cultural practices.

Santa Rita Corozal is located within the southern province of Chetumal, noted for being rich in cacao and honey at the time of contact

(Oviedo y Valdez 1851–55, book 32, chapter 6). The site has been tentatively identified as the capital of the province of Chetumal during the early sixteenth century based both on its location and on its archaeological remains (for discussion see D. Chase 1981, 1982a: 571–73; Sidrys 1976: 325–31; Thompson 1972: 6). It has been further argued (D. Chase 1982a) that the archaeological links between Mayapan and Santa Rita Corozal are such that the Yucatec documentary references probably apply to the latter site as well as the former. While archaeological remains from Santa Rita Corozal are not identical to those from Mayapan, they clearly derive from the same tradition. Recovered archaeological patterns at Santa Rita Corozal also fit ethnohistoric descriptions for central Yucatan (D. Chase 1982a, 1985). The archaeological work at Santa Rita Corozal may therefore be viewed as providing insights into the organization of Protohistoric Yucatec Maya society from a point in time following Mayapan.

ETHNOHISTORIC DESCRIPTIONS OF LOWLAND MAYA SOCIAL ORGANIZATION

According to Roys (1943: 33), Postclassic "Yucatecan Maya society was definitely divided into three classes: nobles, commoners, and slaves." The nobles were not only the ruling class, but were also the most important and/or wealthiest warriors, priests, farmers, and merchants. While commoners could be wealthy, too, they were reportedly separated from the true nobility by their lack of knowledge concerning ritual. Commoners were "artisans, fishermen, and small farmers and merchants generally" (Roys 1943: 34). More recent archaeological work (Adams 1970; Becker 1973) would indicate that artisans during the Classic Period may have been considered nobles. Slaves were generally commoners captured during war and were evidently used as laborers for various kinds of activities, including farming, fishing, trading, and domestic chores. There may have also been a class of individuals whose position was below that of commoners but above that of slaves, "the members of which might be considered serfs" (Roys 1943: 34).

Roys further describes (1943: 35) Yucatec society as having been divided into patrilineal groups (*ch'ibal*) that, at least in some instances, included both nobles and commoners and, as Roys suggested, undoubtedly aided in maintaining the solidarity of the group. These lineage groups were exogamous and each had a patron deity—in some

349

cases a deified ancestor. While patrilineal descent was clearly important, matrilineal descent was also evidently recorded, as the mother's first name was transferred to her children as a first name (*naal*) following marriage, at which point the person's childhood first name was technically dropped (Roys 1943: 36). Roys (1943: 33) suggests that descent in both the male and female line was acknowledged in the meaning of the Maya word for noble, *almehen*—"*al*, a woman's off-spring, and *mehen*, a man's progeny."

Marriage between bearers of the same patronymic was generally prohibited, as were marriages between close relatives on either side. After marriage the couple lived for at least five years with the bride's parents and then generally moved to the husband's father's home for permanent residence; this was apparently in direct contrast with Chontal practice, where matrilocal residence has been described as being common (Roys 1965: 663). While monogamy was the general custom, polygyny was evidently practiced among the upper class. The principal wife would have been of the noble class, while subsequent wives could be "slave concubines." While children of the principal wife retained the status of their father, children of slaves most likely did not and were apparently sometimes sold (Roys 1943: 26–27).

Property and major offices/titles were held primarily by men. Titles were handed down from father to eldest son (where possible) and property was generally divided among the sons (Roys 1943: 28, 164). While women could inherit chieftainships in certain parts of Mexico, this pattern is not described for the Yucatec Maya (Roys 1962: 63).

According to Landa, each town had four ceremonial entrances, which were associated with the cardinal points. At each of these entrances were two opposing mounds of stone. The town itself was oriented around a central area containing plazas and ceremonial structures. Houses nearest the center were those of the nobles and priests; the lowest class had their residences at the very outskirts of town (Landa in Tozzer 1941: 62–64). Roys (1943: 20) points out that the larger towns were composed of a series of subdivisions or barrios (1965: 662–64) and that members of the same name group, while distributed throughout the town, might be concentrated in specific barrios. This barrio model may either be viewed as directly opposing the concentric ring model provided by Landa or it may be viewed as complementing it.

At the time of the Spanish entrance into Yucatan in the early sixteenth century and following the fall of Mayapan (mid-fifteenth century), there were at least 18 independent Maya territories (see Figure 10.1), each called a *cuchcabal* (Roys 1943: 1; 1957). These had at least three types of government (Roys 1965: 669; 1957). In the first type of territory or state, a *halach uinic* governed the entire province (examples included Cehpech, Mani, Sotuta, Hocaba, Cochuah, Ah Kin Chel, and probably Chetumal, Chanpoton, and Tah Itza); below him were the *batab*s of the various towns. In the second type of territorial organization, the province did not have a *halach uinic*, but was ruled primarily by members of the same name group (examples included Ah Canul and Cupul). A third type of organization was characterized by only a loose alliance of independent towns (examples included Chakan and Chikin Chel and possibly Tases).

In the territories where a *halach uinic* was present, he was the military and judicial administrative head or *batab* of his own town and was also superior to the *batab*s of other towns in the province. Below each *batab* were a series of individuals with duties toward a specific portion or division of the town—each called an *ah cuch cab* or, in Spanish, a *principal*. In the hierarchy below the *ah cuch cab* were a number of individuals with the title *ah kulel*, and below this the *tupil*. Two other individuals, the *holpop*, possibly the local head of the most important name group (Roys: 1965: 669), and the *nacom*, or war chief, were sometimes present within a town hierarchy. While not suggested by Roys, it seems likely that the *holpop* was present primarily in those instances where the ruling lineage was not either the most populous or most prestigious one in a territory.

Towns within a territory might have joined together formally under a *halach uinic*, because of name groups, or due to ceremonial activity (Landa in Tozzer 1941: 164–66), and other less formal affiliations undoubtedly existed. Lands may have been held in common within the province; it is unclear whether lands and salt beds were sometimes held in common by several towns (Roys 1943: 37). Territories appear to have been only loosely allied at the time of the Spanish Conquest and often at war with each other.

The organization of Maya society at the time of the Spanish Conquest appears, in sum, to have been based upon a number of interwoven systems. Individuals of the same patronym were linked together by their lineage regardless of social status. Lineage heads and ancestral deities may have been important in effecting this union. At the same

351

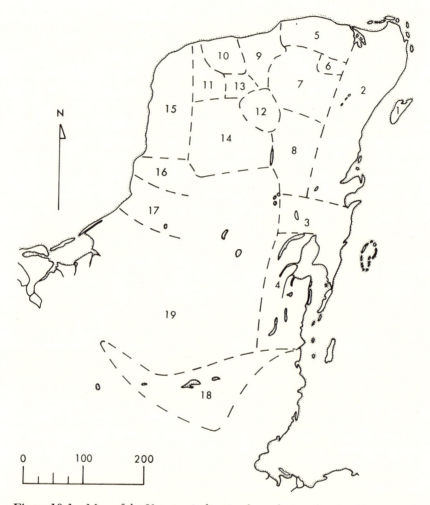

Figure 10.1 Map of the Yucatan indicating boundaries of native Maya provinces in existence at the time of Conquest (after Roys 1957: Map 1). 1. Cozumel or Cuzamil; 2. Ecab or Ekab; 3. Uaymil; 4. Chetumal or Chactemal; 5. Chikincheel or Chauaca; 6. Tazes; 7. Cupul; 8. Cochuah; 9. Ah Kin Chel; 10. Ceh Pech; 11. Chakan; 12. Sotuta; 13. Hocaba or Homun; 14. Tutul Xiu or Mani; 15. Ah Canul; 16. Canpech; 17. Champoton; 18. Tayasal or Tan Itza; 19. Cehaches (?).

time, however, towns were most likely organized spatially into a series of barrios, which formed administratively distinct units. Whether these correlated with lineage groups is unclear; apparently in certain cases this was true. Members of the various social classes appear to have resided in each barrio. The barrios themselves were tied together not only by a larger administrative system, but also by a system of ritual. This system, maintained by the noble class (and, of course, specifically by "priests"), integrated the various subdivisions of a town through rituals that were concerned with the Maya calendar and the cardinal directions. These towns were further organized along similar lines into territories or provinces, each with a regional capital and many with a regional ruler, or *halach uinic*.

THE ARCHAEOLOGICAL DATA BASE

The reconstruction of the social organization of a group of people from material remains is a problematic task (Allen and Richardson 1971), but one that is continually attempted by archaeologists. While it is unlikely that archaeological evidence will be found incontrovertibly to confirm or refute all ethnohistorically derived interpretations of Protohistoric Lowland Maya social organization, certain aspects of social organization can be viewed relatively usefully from an archaeological perspective. This essay will differ somewhat from previous correlations of ethnohistoric and archaeological data concerning the Late Postclassic Lowland Maya (such as Haviland 1968) in focusing on only three topics for which there is pertinent evidence: status, site organization, and regional organization.

Archaeologial Evidence for Differential Status

There is little direct archaeological evidence for the presence of classes in Postclassic Maya society, but there are indirect indications that such may well have existed. Two sets of data that can be analyzed with regard to determining status differentiation are architectural constructions and burials (cf. Haviland 1968; Kurjack 1974). The juxtaposition of these two sets of data produces additional information.

If one examines constructions that have been identified as dwellings at the sites of Santa Rita Corozal and Mayapan, it soon becomes apparent that these buildings are not all equal in size, plan, or technique of construction. Residences vary in sheer mass and in number of rooms. The quality of construction and the amount of imperishable building material utilized likewise vary; excavated Postclassic building remains range from simple lines of stones to multiple-course base walls and, occasionally, to completely stone-walled buildings.

Thomas Gann excavated approximately 47 structures at Santa Rita Corozal; of these, at least 13 yielded evidence for Late Postclassic use. Unfortunately, little extant information from these early investigations can be used to determine architectural or residential types. Recent work at the site has led to investigation of 20 structures of which at least 17 evinced Late Postclassic use. Six basic structure types have been identified from the site of Santa Rita Corozal; examples of each of these six types, used during the Late Postclassic Period, are illustrated in Figure 10.2. While an absolute assessment of structure function based on form may be impossible, investigations have suggested probable correlations between building form and archaeological materials that may be indicative of the functions for the various structure types excavated to date (D. Chase 1982a).

The simple structure (Figure 10.2: Type 1) is frequently visible on the surface only as lines of stone. Like most Postclassic constructions at the site, these were once surmounted by perishable superstructures. The occupational refuse associated with Type 1 buildings suggests that these constructions served as residences or possibly for other domestic-related activities. Simple structures with frontal platforms (Figure 10.2: Type 2) frequently have higher substructures than Type 1 and are sometimes associated with more finely dressed masonry. While these may also have served a multitude of possible functions, the lack of domestic and ritual objects, in combination with the occurrence of a core cache in one of the excavated examples, could indicate that such structures were employed in administrative-related activities. Single structures on larger platforms (Figure 10.2: Type 3) sometimes have partially standing walls. Their form is suggestive of shrines found in the Northern Lowlands. The single investigated example had no associated refuse to indicate either residential or purely ritual function, but did have a cache and numerous burials placed within it. Based upon this example (Str. 58), Type 3 buildings are thought to have served civic-ceremonial functions. Large platforms with multiple structures resting on them (Figure 10.2: Type 4) are believed to have served a variety of functions based on the variety of associated buildings. Most

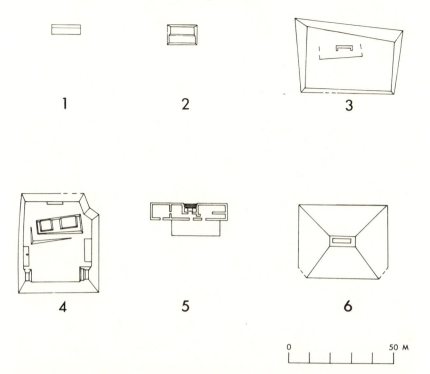

Figure 10.2 Santa Rita construction types in use during the Late Postclassic. Type 1: Simple structure (Ex. Str. 74). Type 2: Simple structure with frontal platform (Ex. Str. 36). Type 3 Single structure on a larger platform (Ex. Plat. 1—Str. 58). Type 4: Multiple structures on a platform (Ex. Plat. 2—Strs. 73, & 76–80). Type 5—Multiple room construction (Ex. Str. 81). Type 6: High elevated construction with or without multiple rooms (Ex. Classic Period Str. 7 which was re-used during the Postclassic).

of the constructions atop large platforms are variations of Type 1 simple buildings, but others represent Type 2 or Type 3 constructions. Based upon associated debris, the platform as a whole has been suggested as the locus of both residential and ritual activity (D. Chase 1982a: Table 20). Multiroom constructions (Figure 10.2: Type 5) may have basal wall stubs and an enclosed shrine with altar. The remains associated with the excavated Str. 81 have been interpreted as indicating that the building was most likely the residence of a *principal* (D. Chase 1982a: 301–2), thus serving combined residential, ritual, and administrative functions. Raised temple constructions (Figure 10.2: Type 6) are thought

355

to be primarily ritual in use and are frequently associated with censer deposition. These may be either reused Classic Period constructions or entirely Postclassic Period buildings.

While it would be difficult, if not impossible, to define three formally distinct types of house each of which could be associated with one social class (nobles, commoners, slaves), the two polar extremes recovered to date in investigations at Santa Rita Corozal are easy to identify (Type 1 and Type 5). These extremes do not necessarily represent class differences; certain simple structures are located in close proximity to multiple-roomed buildings, allowing the possibility that the former were either specialized activity areas or housing for newly married individuals (see Landa in Tozzer 1941: 41, 101). Alternatively, the Type 1 constructions within a grouping including Type 5 buildings may have been the houses of servants while Type 1 buildings elsewhere may represent residences of commoners, loci for food preparation or storage, or some combination thereof. Further investigation of domestic residences is necessary in order to define these relationships more accurately.

The distinction between elaborate and simple dwellings at Santa Rita Corozal and at Mayapan (A. L. Smith 1962; R. E. Smith 1971: 106–7) may not be as clear cut as is indicated by delineation of structure types. Material remains associated with Type 1 and Type 5 constructions, with the exception of ritual items (see below), do not necessarily suggest differing wealth in material goods. The archaeological situation may in fact be taken to indicate the existence of a continuum in classes below the elite. Such a continuum might indicate that commoners could accumulate wealth to the point that they were difficult to distinguish materially from the elite. This much has been suggested from a study of early documents by Roys (1943: 33). Interestingly, only the more elaborate of the dwellings and platforms (Types 4 and 5)—those presumably utilized by the nobles—are predominantly associated with ritual activity in the form of caching and censer deposition. This association agrees with statements by Roys (1943: 33) that the elite differed from the common people not solely by virtue of wealth, but, more importantly, in their knowledge of ritual.

There is no direct archaeological evidence for occupational differences between classes at Santa Rita Corozal with the exception of ritual activity (as determined by censer or other modeled pottery deposition and caching). Lithics and objects usually assumed to be net weights

356

appear to be distributed nearly universally at the site, although their frequencies may possibly vary. It may, however, be significant that small notched points are more common in what are interpreted to be elite areas of the site.

Ideally, in order to archaeologically identify the several ethnohistorically defined classes, burial data should correspond with dwelling type to indicate at least three mutually exclusive groups, each including members of both sexes and individuals of all age groups. Instead, excavation thus far has revealed a variety of burial patterns; most of their cultural associations are unknown.

Excavations in the vicinity of Santa Rita Corozal by Thomas Gann (1900, 1911, 1914–16, 1918) yielded at least 92 burials containing 95 individuals. Of these burials, seven are clearly Postclassic in date. The 1979 and 1980 Corozal Postclassic Project investigations at the site encountered 62 burials containing 78 individuals. Twenty burials with 32 individuals were deposited during the Postclassic Period.

The Gann and Corozal Postclassic Project burial patterns are consistent. Unlike Mayapan, the site has not been reported to contain any crypt burials for the Postclassic Period. Deposition was either in a simple burial with no clear outline or in a cist (i.e., with clear outline), sometimes lined or covered with stones, but always filled with earth. However, certain of the cist burials, specifically those cut into bedrock, may actually have required effort nearly equivalent to that involved in creating a crypt. Burials at Santa Rita Corozal range from single, articulated primary interments to multiple secondary ones. Bodies are sometimes placed with no artifacts but are sometimes associated with one or more objects. Accompanying grave goods include pottery, flint tools, copper artifacts, and jade, shell, or ceramic beads. Articulated individuals are generally found flexed with skull toward the north of the pit; however, extended burials are also present as are interments in which the skull is located toward the east or south. The present sample includes male, female, and subadult human remains; there appear to be more females and children than adult males.

While burials at Santa Rita Corozal range from individuals with no associated items to individuals accompanied by a wealth of material goods, this range may not be indicative of class distinctions. Apart from the archaeological evidence reviewed below, ethnohistoric data may also illuminate the problems involved in archaeological determinations of status and wealth. Specifically, Landa (Tozzer 1941: 130–

357

31) relates that Maya nobles were cremated in northern Yucatan; obviously this practice could obscure archaeological evidence of a continuum of status distinctions in burial "wealth."

The locations of burials relative to recognizable structure types, however, may prove instructive. Investigations at the site have thus far (with one possible exception) encountered no simple residences associated with burials, and this may indicate that the excavated sample is only indicative of the range in status and/or wealth of individuals within a single class. However, based on investigations to date at Santa Rita Corozal, burials appear to be associated primarily with non-domestic constructions (Platform 1, a Type 3 construction), platforms with multiple constructions (Platform 2, a Type 4 construction), or with an altar within a presumed elite residence (Structure 81, a Type 5 construction). Platforms 1 and 2 at Santa Rita Corozal contain a number of burials and thus resemble Western graveyards.

Santa Rita Corozal Structure 58 in its latest phase was a small structure, measuring 3 by 8 meters, situated atop a larger platform, measuring 34 by 37 meters (see Figure 10.2: Type 3). The form of this latest construction is suggestive of a shrine; although there is not enough significant associated refuse to confirm this, a cache was located on axis with the structure. The earlier Late Postclassic structures, which were buried within Platform 1, may have functioned as either shrines or residences. Burials were found throughout the trench dug into Platform 1; these were associated with either the latest or the penultimate construction of the structure and platform, but were cut through an earlier, probably Early Classic, plaster floor. The interred individuals included adults of both sexes as well as subadults; they were found in both the flexed and the extended position, generally with their heads to the north. While most interments were of only a single individual, there were occasionally two individuals (or parts of two individuals) within one grave. Of all the burials in the vicinity of Structure 58, the most elaborate one belonged to a woman. She had been placed in a flexed (fetal), upright position and had been buried with a jadeite and spondylus necklace as well as two copper rings.

Platform 2 is a large platform measuring 44 by 36.5 meters (see Figure 10.2: Type 4). There are a number of structures located on its summit, specifically Structures 73, 76, 77, 78, 79, and 80. These were apparently residential and/or administrative buildings as well as ritual constructions. While burials were encountered throughout the platform, they were most abundant adjacent to it. An excavation along the eastern portion of the southern platform face encountered seven interments (see Figure 10.3). Like those in association with Platform 1, these were placed in cists cut through a floor and then filled with earth; a few were cut into bedrock. Objects recovered with these interments ranged from nothing to one or more beads to beads and copper rings to multiple smashed vessels. The individuals placed in graves in this area appear to have been only children and women. While men may have been interred elsewhere in Platform 2, none were encountered in this southern burial area. An extensive refuse deposit was located above the majority of these graves. Pottery in this deposit included redwares (Figure 10.4a & b), unslipped ollas (Figure 10.4d & e), modeled vessels, modeled cups (Figure 10.4c), effigy censers, and ring-based censers.

The two graveyard-like areas from Platforms 1 and 2 at Santa Rita Corozal include interments that vary both in the amount of preparation necessary to create the grave and in the kinds and numbers of items included with the burials. Not everyone who died at Santa Rita Corozal was buried in these two areas. At most, this sample is indicative of the range in status of a limited group of individuals, most likely those from a single family or lineage; alternatively, it may possibly be representative of everyone living within a particular area, regardless of their family ties. The significance of age and sex in the placement of individuals in parts of northeastern Santa Rita Corozal suggests that the location of the burial itself is an important variable.

While Roys (1943: 28, 164, 1962: 63) and Landa (in Tozzer 1941: 99) indicate that women did not generally hold important positions or inherit wealth, the burials of women at Santa Rita Corozal suggest that their worldly existence was not always devoid of material pleasures. While there are differences in the burial patterns among men and women at Santa Rita Corozal during the Late Postclassic Period (no men were interred with copper rings; men and subadults seem more likely to be found in secondary burials), several female interments are "rich" in terms of number and kinds of objects, and at least one was located in a place of presumed importance (S.D. P3B-3, located in a Type 3 construction). While prominent status has been inferred for certain Classic Period Maya female interments (Adams 1963; A. Chase n.d.; Pohl & Feldman 1982), the Santa Rita Corozal data may indicate that women were much more important in Protohistoric Maya society

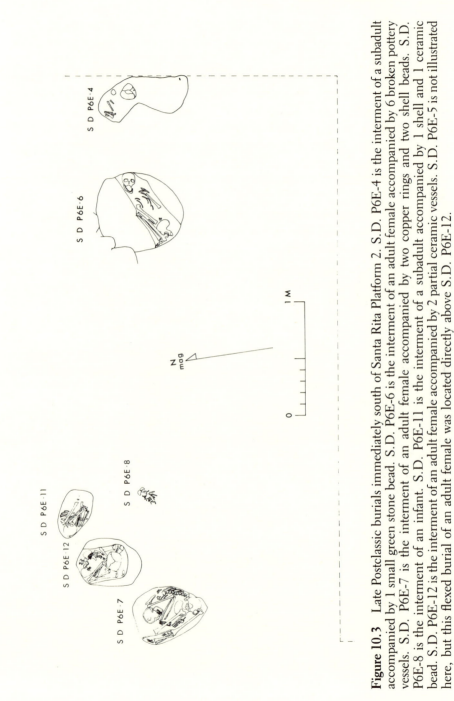

Figure 10.3 Late Postclassic burials immediately south of Santa Rita Platform 2. S.D. P6E-4 is the interment of a subadult accompanied by 1 small green stone bead. S.D. P6E-6 is the interment of an adult female accompanied by 6 broken pottery vessels. S.D. P6E-7 is the interment of an adult female accompanied by two copper rings and two shell beads. S.D. P6E-8 is the interment of an infant. S.D. P6E-11 is the interment of a subadult accompanied by 1 shell and 1 ceramic bead. S.D. P6E-12 is the interment of an adult female accompanied by 2 partial ceramic vessels. S.D. P6E-5 is not illustrated here, but this flexed burial of an adult female was located directly above S.D. P6E-12.

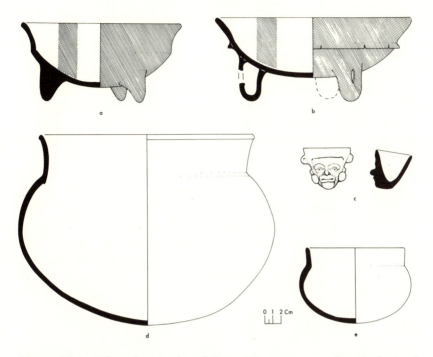

Figure 10.4 Selected examples of Santa Rita pottery. a. Rita Red tripod bowl. b: Rita Red tripod bowl. c: Kol Modeled cup. d: Santa Unslipped olla. e: Santa Unslipped olla.

than has been suggested so far in ethnohistoric work. Alternatively, this apparent significance may be an indirect result of the recorded practice of cremating noble men and rulers and placing them in urns (Landa in Tozzer 1941: 130–31), although there is no evidence for this at Santa Rita Corozal.

Burials at Mayapan (A. L. Smith 1962: 232–55; R. E. Smith 1971: 114–19) were of several different types: simple burials with no definite outlines, cists, and more elaborate stone-lined and vaulted crypts. Each of these burial types involved different amounts of labor. It is tempting to suggest that the elaborate Mayapan crypts were the final resting places for important nobles, yet many of these yielded no evidence of ever having contained a body. However, several crypts in places of presumed importance did contain one or more individuals and perhaps represented family tombs; only one elaborate crypt contained a single

361

interment. It would further seem that the care taken in the preparation of a grave was not always proportional to the quantity or quality of accompanying objects, for simple burials at Mayapan are not all devoid of goods (see, for example, Mayapan Str. K52a).

Work at both Santa Rita Corozal and Mayapan supports the notion that type of burial, burial objects, and location all have implications for the status of the deceased individual. However, it is difficult, based upon the present archaeological sample alone, to state with confidence precisely what these status differentials might be. It is evident, however, that the burial types are dispersed throughout both sites and that interments in any one area or structure vary as to type of grave and contents. This suggests either nonstandardized burial practices or much variation in the status and wealth of individuals living within any locale. While age and sex do apparently affect the grave type, burial objects, and location of burial, there is enough variation within burials of adults of the same sex to suggest the presence of wealth and/or status differences.

In summary, investigations to date indicate that there are neither three distinct burial patterns nor three distinct residence plans that can be related to class differences; this in turn suggests a status gradation that blurs these categories. Maya social organization during the Late Postclassic was clearly more complicated and less rigid than the terms *noble, commoner,* and *slave,* found in the ethnohistory, imply.

Site Organization

The spatial organization of towns described ethnohistorically is less difficult to compare with the archaeological data than is the social organization. The "concentric ring" model (see Figure 10.5a) for Postclassic or early Historic Maya towns, first described by Landa (Tozzer 1941: 62–64), holds that the most important temples and plazas were located in the center of a Maya town, with the houses of the nobles located directly outside this area and the houses of those of lesser status still farther from the center. It must be noted here that this model not only bears a strong resemblance to colonial Spanish villages but also was generally held by the majority of the early ethnohistorians for much of Latin America. These facts are important when one realizes that Landa, who defined the pattern for the Yucatec Maya, was described by Genet (1934) as "one of the greatest plagiarists of his period."

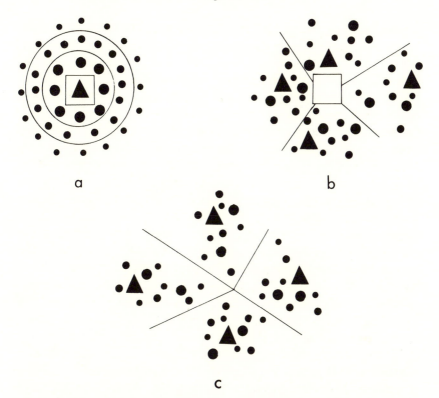

Figure 10.5 Schematic drawings of possible Postclassic site organization. a: Concentric organization. b: Barrio organization with defined site center. c: Barrio organization with no defined site center.

Landa's description of the organization of a typical Maya town reads uncannily like earlier descriptions of Central American towns (see Anghiera 1516: VI, V, 4; López de Gómara 1552, *Serie de Cronistas* 1: 120; and Oviedo y Valdés 1851–55). Landa probably had access to the works of Gómara and Oviedo when he was composing his *Relación* (Tozzer 1941: vii). In short, Landa's account of the organization of a Maya town may be neither original nor descriptive of the Maya. In any case, if the model is applicable to the Maya, we can expect to find distinct archaeological traces of a compact center with complex architecture and to find buildings of decreasing size and complexity radiating from it.

An alternative model for the organization of a Maya town may be postulated both on the ethnohistory (Roys 1943: 62–63; 1957: 7–8) and the archaeology (D. Chase 1982a: 578–83). Two alternate versions of this sector or barrio model may be postulated (see Figures 10.5b and c); in the first there is a single central civic and ceremonial area per site while in the second the important civic and ceremonial constructions are found in each barrio. In either form of this barrio model, there were different subdivisions (barrios) within a town, each governed by an *ah cuch cab*. If each barrio included members of the three Maya social classes noted in the ethnohistory, they should be expressed archaeologically in what might appear to be a random distribution of residential architecture and burial types. The various activities and constructions (certain structures, burials, and caches) that are generally considered elite would therefore not be concentrated solely in the center of the site. In order to delineate a barrio, however, it is necessary both to define the minimum number of constructions and/or traces of activities expected to be found within a barrio and to note the patterned replication of these remains at a site or to find actual walled subdivisions within the town.

Whether or not the Late Postclassic site of Santa Rita Corozal ever had a core area that was the primary locus for ritual and administrative buildings is difficult to ascertain because of the destruction of the site in the course of modernization. Gann's (1900, 1918) work, however, suggests that although there may have been a slightly greater concentration of higher Classic Period mounds in a core area, there was no specialized Postclassic Period site core like the one at Mayapan. Thus, both postulated barrio models (Figures 10.5b and c) may have been extant during the Postclassic Period. Construction types at Santa Rita Corozal appear to be distributed more or less equally throughout the site; the most complex constructions are not restricted solely to the core area. The same is true for caches and burials. This distribution indicates that a strict interpretation of the concentric ring model does not apply to Santa Rita Corozal. This site, in fact, appears to be organized into what may be interpreted as a noncentralized barrio or sector pattern (Figure 10.5c).

At Santa Rita Corozal, the recovered caches clearly do not correlate with any "central" area as they should according to Landa's model. Differences in coeval caching patterns may in fact be correlated with different parts of the site and are believed to be representative of some combination of barrios and the various Uayeb or New Year's rites (D. Chase 1985).

Work at Santa Rita Corozal also suggests that at least one of each of the six structure types defined above (see Figure 10.2) is likely to be present in any barrio (D. Chase 1982a: 580–83). The distribution of the six structure types should allow definition of site sectors and, thus, understanding of overall site organization.

A single elaborate multiroomed residence (Structure Type 5)—presumably the home of the *ah cuch cab* (or *principal*), the head of a barrio—should be in use at any one time in a barrio according to the model. The archaeological identification and dating of Structure Type 5 buildings should, therefore, aid significantly in defining site organization. While smaller house constructions (Structure Type 1) should be abundant throughout the site, elevated platforms supporting several buildings (Structure Type 4) and isolated constructions on large platforms (Structure Type 3) may be barrio-specific and possibly useful indicators for determining site sectors. Structures with frontal platforms (Structure Type 2), believed to have served an administrative function, may also be barrio-specific. If there was any one unifying characteristic of a Late Postclassic town, however, it may have been a centrally placed large temple; this temple may, however, have been replaced to a certain extent in Protohistoric times by smaller temples in each ward (Structure Type 6).

While M. Coe (1965: 107) interpreted Landa's descriptions of the Uayeb rites and the four entrances to the town as indicating the existence of four barrios in every town, such was apparently not the case at Santa Rita Corozal. The replication of the above-defined construction suggests that there were minimally five barrios at the site during Late Postclassic times (D. Chase 1982a).

The identified barrios at Late Postclassic Santa Rita Corozal do not seem to have been organized in a rigid fashion. They tend to be composed of clusters of structure groups with less formalized constructions scattered about them. This is a pattern which has been indirectly defined for earlier Classic Maya sites (Kurjack 1974; Willey 1956; see also Haviland 1968). Neither Mayapan nor Santa Rita Corozal evince the gridded layout evident at certain Mexican sites (Haviland 1968: 97); if any sites may be considered to be organized in such a fashion it would be some of those along the Quintana Roo coast such as Tulum (Lothrop 1924) or Cancun (Vargas Pacheco 1978).

Although Mayapan does have a core area composed of what are presumably administrative and religious constructions (see Figure 10.5b), the rest of the site was apparently organized in a fashion similar to that found at Santa Rita Corozal. Certain dwellings and elaborate burials or caches were near the site center (which was also the focus for archaeological work); however, equivalent ones were also dispersed throughout the site. Residences do not seem to diminish in size away from Mayapan's center in a radiating fashion; likewise, elaborate caches were found outside the site center, and crypt burials were found to the limits of the town wall. The structure types at Mayapan also appear to be similar to those noted for Santa Rita Corozal, but both platforms supporting multiple structures and multiroomed constructions appear to be more common, while isolated (nongroup) shrines and temples may not be as prevalent. Formal, clustered groups of structures are also found outside the site center.

Investigations at Santa Rita Corozal and Mayapan may be interpreted as verifying a barrio-type occupation model in the Late Postclassic. The concentric-ring class-linked residence pattern described by Landa does not appear to have existed. Many Late Postclassic sites, however, probably had a distinct central area, which may have been largely nonresidential; this is particularly visible at Mayapan. The barrio site organization, with its dispersion of individuals belonging to the noble class throughout the site, might actually have served as a more effective mechanism for integration within a town.

The differences between Santa Rita Corozal and Mayapan, specifically the greater decentralization evident at Santa Rita Corozal, may be due to regional or political factors or to the slightly later Protohistoric Period occupation at Santa Rita Corozal. I would suggest that regional capitals and perhaps major and populous Late Postclassic towns all had a site organization organized along one of the two barrio models. Those in the northern part of the Yucatan Peninsula may have comprised a center surrounded by barrios with clusters of constructions, while those to the south may have been more decentralized.

Alternatively, it is possible that Mayapan symbolically represented the heart of the Maya Late Postclassic world, emulating in its plan the allegorical world tree and fifth world dimension of the Maya (cf. M. Coe 1981: 161–62). Thus, Mayapan's ethnohistorically noted role as the preeminent center of the Late Postclassic Northern Lowlands may have been replicated symbolically in its physical layout; this focal plan may not be present at any other Late Postclassic site. This symbolism would be in keeping with a wider Mesoamerican world view, for the Aztec capital Tenochtitlan was also considered to be the center of the world and its nulceus symbolically portrayed this concept.

Other material evidence of specialized activities may also be expected to be present in important Postclassic Maya sites. In addition to trade items, greater indications of ritual activity, specifically caching and censer deposition, should appear in leading towns. Landa noted at least one occasion when people from smaller villages gathered at a larger one for ceremonies (Tozzer 1941: 164–66). The abundance of caches at Santa Rita Corozal and Mayapan in the Late Postclassic Period versus their relative absence elsewhere suggests that people may have gotten together more frequently than was suggested by Landa— perhaps along the lines of the pilgrimage fair pattern proposed by Freidel (1981b). The ritual knowledge of the elite, who were more likely to live in these larger centers, may well have encouraged such activity.

Structure 81 at Santa Rita Corozal includes a component that may be a useful indicator of religious organization and interactions during Protohistoric times: an enclosed shrine room with a false back wall. The plan of this shrine room and false wall is very similar to that projected for the shrine of the talking idol at Cozumel (Freidel 1975), and it has been suggested (D. Chase 1982a, 1985) that Structure 81 was the home of such an oracle. The location of similar shrines elsewhere should lead to a more comprehensive understanding of Maya belief and interaction systems. Given the existence of similar phenomena at both Cozumel and Santa Rita Corozal, it would not be surprising if oracles proved to be important components of most major Late Postclassic towns.

Provincial Politics

The differences in political organization among the territories of the time of the Conquest—specifically, the presence of a territorial capital with a *halach uinic* versus the existence of loosely allied towns without a dominant leader—do not appear to correlate with larger alliances as indicated by the various documents. The provinces known to have *halach uinics* (Sotuta, Cehpech, Hocaba, Mani, Ah Kin Chel) included ones that were constantly warring with each other, such as

Sotuta and Mani. Most of those provinces noted as having *halach uinicob* were reportedly established by lineages from Mayapan (Sotuta, Mani, Ah Kin Chel, Cochuah). There were, however, people from at least one former Mayapan lineage who became rulers of a province without holding the title of *halach uinic*. The Canul, who have been referred to as the guardians of Mayapan (Roys 1957: 11), left the city following its "destruction" to become the ruling lineage in the province of Ah Canul; they did not, however, establish themselves as *halach uinicob*. That the Canul were purported to be of Mexican origin should not have prohibited them from assuming this role, as the province of Hocaba was known to have a *halach uinic* of the Iuit lineage. *Iuit* is Nahuatl for "feather" (Roys 1957: 55) and presumably indicates a Mexican origin for this lineage.

Not all provinces were controlled by former ruling lineages at Mayapan. Ah Kin Chel, for example, was named for the leader of a military group at Mayapan. It has also been argued (Roys 1957: 110) that Tases, which had no *halach uinic*, was formerly part of the confederation of Mayapan. As most of the territories with *halach uinicob* were ruled by members of what are believed to have been important lineages from Mayapan, the ability to set up a territory with a *halach uinic* may have depended on the status and/or size of a particular lineage in the League of Mayapan prior to the league's disruption.

Whether the differences in internal organization within the territories, as outlined by Roys (1957), can be identified archaeologically is as yet unclear. It is possible that those territories with *halach uinicob* residing in a capital town will be found to have more easily identifiable capital sites. Work at the site of Mayapan (Pollock et al. 1962) and Santa Rita Corozal suggests that these sites would also have greater numbers of certain other features, such as modeled-figure cache vessels, than would contemporary neighboring sites.

It has been suggested that the territory of Chetumal had a *halach uinic* (Roys 1965). There is no evidence for the presence of one in Ecab (Roys 1957: 143) in northeast Yucatan, and it is unlikely that such a ruler was present in Uaymil to Ecab's south at the time of the Conquest, since Uaymil was organizationally combined with Chetumal by the Spanish. If the site organization and caching patterns identified at Santa Rita Corozal correlate with more than just its role as a regional capital, these patterns may also be indicative of the type of organization we can expect from towns with presiding *halach uin-*

icob. The lack of other such sites in southern Quintana Roo, where the lower part of Ecab and all of Uaymil were located, may reflect differences in political organization.

Some Late Postclassic sites, such as Mayapan (Pollock et al. 1962), Tulum (Lothrop 1924), and possibly Muralla de León, far to the south (D. Rice and P. Rice 1981), were fortified (see also Webster 1979). Other sites may have been fortified with perishable materials (Landa in Tozzer 1941: 123). In any case, the presence of defensive features must be regarded as a significant indicator of political insecurity. There are also sites, such as Cozumel (Sabloff and Rathje 1975a, 1975b), Tancah (Miller 1982), and Mayapan (Bullard 1952, 1954) with internal boundary walls. These latter features, while primarily delineating house or garden areas, may also reflect barrio relations within the site.

The presence of three different kinds of political organization during the Protohistoric Period may be connected with geographical location and may be interpreted as correlating with the archaeological differences noted between the east and west coasts of Yucatan (see Andrews and Robles C. this volume). The *halach uinic* provincial organization has been found primarily in territories located in the middle of the Yucatan Peninsula rather than on the east or west coast. This form of Postclassic Maya government is also the most politically centralized. The geographical distribution of *halach uinic* government may indicate that the inland territories required a strong central government to maintain their political and economic status in the midst of east-west stresses and competition. The decentralized organization and possibly fluid alliance patterns of the coastal provinces may have been a direct result of increased exposure to outside stimuli (see Miller, this volume). If this is the case, the *halach uinic* form of provincial organization can perhaps be interpreted not only as the strong governing force needed in a tenuous political situation, but also as a vestige of the indigenous Maya political organization.

The Land of Cacao and Honey: Time and Space

Unlike political organization within provinces, the territories and larger alliances of the Maya should be relatively easy to define through archaeology. On the basis of the known excavated sample, architecture and ceramics appear to be prime indicators of regional variation. Regionalization was apparently present prior to the Late Postclassic in

Yucatan and can be seen in Early Postclassic Cehpech, Hocaba, and Sotuta ceramics (Ball 1979a) as well as in what is called Puuc as opposed to "Toltec" architecture. The obvious differences in the spatial distribution of these archaeological remains have led to major disagreements concerning the temporal placement and meanings of these archaeological traditions (Smith 1971; Ball 1979a, 1979b; D. Chase and A. Chase 1982; A. Chase this volume).

While there are overall similarities in Late Postclassic Lowland Maya architecture, specifically in the use of relatively crude masonry constructions (at least by Classic Period standards) and the increased importance of stucco in surface finishing and decorating, several differences in building components are also identifiable (see Figure 10.6). These

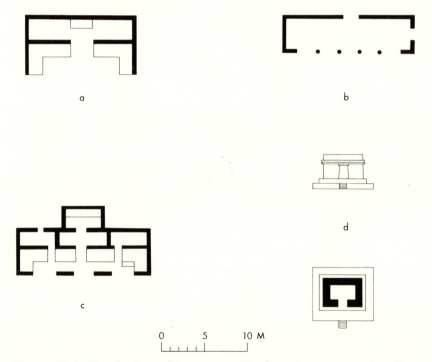

Figure 10.6 Postclassic architecture. a: Tandem-plan construction (Ex: Mayapan Str. S-30c after A. L. Smith 1962 Figure 5c). b: Columned construction (Ex. Mayapan Str. K-79a after A. L. Smith 1962 Figure 7b). c: Multiple roomed construction (Ex: Mayapan Str. K-52a after A. L. Smith 1962 Figure 5b). d: Flat masonry roofed construction (Ex: Tulum Str. 54 after Lothrop 1924 Figure 106).

variations include the use of tandem plans (Freidel 1981; Figure 10.6a), multiroom (Figure 10.6c) and "dwarf" constructions (called shrines by Lothrop 1924), stone columns (Lothrop 1924; Figure 10.6b), and flat masonry roofs (Andrews IV 1943; Sanders 1960; Figure 10.6d). Sites along the Quintana Roo coast (Andrews and Andrews 1975) best exemplify a combination of these assorted architectural traits; Proskouriakoff (1962: 137), in fact, noted that the East Coast building plans were far more variable than those at Mayapan. Interestingly, this synthetic East Coast architectural tradition appears to have emanated primarily from the province of Ecab (El Meco to Chacmool?) and also occurred in northern Chetumal (Ichpaatun); it is not known to occur in what may be interpreted as the intervening province of Uaymil south of Espiritu Santo Bay (Harrison 1979; Lothrop 1924). While its absence may be due to a lack of archaeological work in this vicinity, it is also possible that the void noted here is due to the existence of a different Postclassic architectural tradition in this area, possibly that of a different, diminished population (Harrison 1979: 206).

Certain Postclassic building plans have been cited as useful in determining relationships between sites, including those located at some distance from each other. Freidel (1981a) proposed that the presence or absence of the tandem-plan constructions might be indicative of regional housing preferences and that their distribution within sites (Mayapan, Quintana Roo, Cozumel, and Cilvituk) might reflect the use of tandem-plan buildings as elite residences. He saw their presence at Cozumel as indicative of close ties between Cozumel and Mayapan. Freidel did note, however, that tandem-plan constructions (Figure 10.6a), which are abundant at Mayapan, are not as common at Cozumel. This is surprising because, according to the Books of Chilam Balam (Roys 1933: 168), Cozumel was the origin point for the population of Mayapan (via the Little Descent). It may thus be possible that tandem-plan constructions were largely a Mayapan innovation and that their presence at other sites followed contact with Mayapan.

At Santa Rita Corozal, as at Cozumel, the predominant construction type appears to have been the single-room building (see Figure 10.2: Type 1). As at Cozumel and Mayapan, multiroom constructions (Figure 10.2: Type 5; Figure 10.6c) appear to be indicative of elite occupation. Columns (see Figure 10.6b), although present to the north at Ichpaatun and apparently in Structure 2 at Santa Rita Corozal (Gann 1900: 678–82), are not characteristic of Santa Rita. Likewise masonry roofed constructions (see Figure 10.6d) are not known from the site, although Structure 1 may have been an exception (Gann 1900: 662–77). That there were few masonry tandem-plan rooms at Santa Rita Corozal does not, however, exclude the possibility that they were made of perishable materials. Assuming that there was a front room constructed solely of perishable materials, some of the line-of-stone constructions at Santa Rita Corozal may correlate with the open halls noted by Bullard (1970) for Topoxte.

Recent work in the Peten indicates that both Topoxte (Bullard 1970; A. Chase 1976, 1982; Johnson 1985; P. Rice and D. Rice 1985) and Macanche (D. Rice and P. Rice 1981) have constructions in the Yucatec tradition. In contrast, work in the vicinity of Lake Peten indicates the existence of simple line-of-stone Postclassic constructions, but with an apparent lack of the formalized Yucatec architectural tradition (A. Chase 1979, 1982, 1985). Investigations at Barton Ramie, Belize (Gifford 1976; Willey et al. 1965), also revealed Postclassic occupation, but without any identifiable Yucatec component; this material probably predates that found to its west in Lake Yaxha (A. Chase 1982; Sharer and Chase 1976).

Late Postclassic redware ceramics and censerware vary considerably in vessel forms and types. These ceramic differences, in combination with architecture, may be suggestive of the kinds of material-culture distinctions to be expected between territories or allied groups of territories. At the site of Tulum, for example, generally believed to be at least partially coeval with the site of Mayapan, distinctive ceramic forms within the general redware tradition (Sanders 1960; see also Figure 10.7a & c) include sag-bottom bowls, double-vented feet, and banded curvilinear incised designs. There is, however, a problem in the absolute definition of the Late Postclassic red slipped groups. Tulum-related ceramics evidently occur outside Tulum both at nearby sites such as Cozumel (Connor 1975; Escalona Ramos 1946) and at more distant ones such as Ichpaatun in southernmost Quintana Roo (Sanders 1960) and Colha in northern Belize (Adams and Valdez 1980).

While Tulum (Paybono) red pottery has generally been seen as an indicator of the Late Postclassic Period, these ceramics at Colha are dated to the Early and Middle Postclassic periods (Adams and Valdez 1980). This dating is evidently confirmed by other associated artifactual classes (Hester 1980: 12; Hester, personal communication; Shafer, personal communication). The similarity in ceramics may well indi-

372

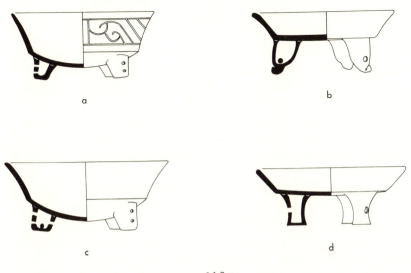

0 1 2 cm

Figure 10.7 Selected Postclassic red slipped tripod bowls. a: Tulum Red bowl with incision (Ex. from Tulum, after Sanders 1960: Figure 4a-3; incision such as that present on this bowl occurs in the early facet of the Late Postclassic at Santa Rita). b: Augustine Red bowl (Ex. from Tayasal, after A. Chase 1983: Figure 3-94). c: Tulum Red bowl (Ex. from Ichpaatun, after Sanders 1960: Figure 4 b-10). d: Paxcaman Red bowl (Ex. from Punta Nima, after A. Chase 1983: Figure 5-2, this vessel is actually an Ixpop Polychrome).

cate interaction between peoples. The violent nature of the end of the Late Classic Period at Colha (Hester 1980) suggests a warlike interaction.

The possibility that at least certain forms of Tulum Red are Middle Postclassic or earlier cannot be overlooked given the occurrence of Tulum Red forms only in fill for Late Postclassic constructions and of related modes in early-facet Late Postclassic lots at Santa Rita Corozal; it is possible that the slight variations within the type between Tulum and Ichpaatun also indicate temporal variations (Figure 10.7a & c; Sanders 1960). Pendergast (1981a, 1981b, 1981c) has suggested that there may be a Belizean origin for certain Late Postclassic red wares, specifically Mayapan Red. The coexistence but mutually exclusive distribution of northern Belize Mayapan or Tulum-like red wares with the Terminal Classic–Early Postclassic complexes consisting of San

Jose V red wares, double-mouthed jars (Sidrys 1976), trickle and slate wares (such as in the Ikilik Ceramic Complex at Nohmul [D. Chase 1982b]) indicates the presence of at least two and probably three interaction spheres during this era (see A. Chase, this volume).

During the late facet of the Late Postclassic, ceramics at Santa Rita Corozal appear to be both coeval with and later than, as well as derivative from, the Mayapan tradition (see Figure 10.4). Thus far, the Santa Rita Corozal red slipped type known as Rita Red (Figure 10.4a & b) has been found only in limited distribution outside northern Belize. (It has also been found at Yakalche in northern Belize [Pendergast, personal communication] and at Aventura [Ball, personal communication].) What appear also to be Rita Red vessels, however, are evidently among the latest pottery noted by Brainerd for Yucatan (1958: Figure 95c). There is little overlap between vessel forms and types at Santa Rita Corozal and Ichpaatun. Santa Rita Corozal is closer in support and vessel forms to some of those pieces illustrated from Tulum (see Sanders 1960) than to Ichpaatun ceramics.

Farther south in Belize, the pottery traditions appear to be less closely related to the Yucatec tradition. The Augustine Red (Figure 10.7b) and Paxcaman Red (Figure 10.7d) ceramic groups appear to be distributed in a belt extending from Lake Salpeten, in the Peten of Guatemala, to Tayasal, on Lake Peten, to Barton Ramie, in Belize (A. Chase 1982, 1985; Sharer and Chase 1976). Pottery found in the vicinity of Topoxte and Macanche in the Peten (specifically the Topoxte Red ceramic group; Rice 1979) appears to be modally related, albeit distantly, to that from the Northern Lowlands or from Santa Rita Corozal. The historic site of Tipu (Jones 1982) appears to continue the usage of the traditional New Town sphere Postclassic ceramics with the introduction of some Spanish wares.

The above-mentioned archaeological data may be interpreted in a number of ways and may in fact enable us to delineate more precisely the boundaries of Protohistoric provinces, specifically those of Chetumal. The site of Santa Rita Corozal (the capital of Chetumal) is distinct architecturally and artifactually from Ichpaatun, the only other relatively well-known Postclassic site in northern Chetumal. This may be due to the imposition of a new ruling group at Santa Rita Corozal following the demise of Mayapan or to an incorrect accounting of the boundary of the province of Chetumal. It seems more likely, however, given the proximity of the sites and the descriptions of the province, that the archaeologically known aspects of Ichpaatun predate those of Santa Rita Corozal and that further work in the northern portion of the province of Chetumal will reveal evidence of occupation like that known from Santa Rita Corozal.

The site of Lamanai, near the limits of the New River, represents either the southern boundary of the province of Chetumal during the Late Postclassic or possibly the leading town within a completely different (and unknown) province; it was probably a regional capital in its own right on an earlier temporal horizon and, in fact, may have continued in this role and been a contemporary of Late Postclassic Santa Rita Corozal. The province of Tayasal as defined archaeologically by the sites of Tayasal and Barton Ramie (and the Central Peten Postclassic tradition [Bullard 1973]) extended in a wide band from the central Peten of Guatemala east to include the Belize River drainage, but apparently included a distinct, probably Yucatec-inspired (A. Chase 1976, 1982) enclave, minimally comprising Topoxte and Macanche.

The similarity in archaeological remains between sites in the provinces of Ecab and what may be called northern Chetumal is also suggestive of a number of prehistoric possibilities, among them the inclusion of Ichpaatun in the poorly defined province of Uaymil and, if this situation can be confirmed, perhaps an alliance between Ecab and Uaymil. This reconstruction would fit the known archaeological distinction between the material remains from Santa Rita Corozal and those from Ichpaatun and Chacmool (to its north) and Chamberlain's (1948: 101–2) assertion that "the lords of Uaymil . . . accepted the overlordship of the cacique of Chetumal only with reluctance." Alternatively, Ichpaatun and/or Tulum may have been abandoned prior to the Conquest, and the apparent similarity in both ceramics and architecture could mirror political unity prior to the establishment of the Protohistoric provinces of Chetumal, Uaymil, and Ecab. Two additional points may support the latter interpretation. The first consists of ethnohistoric references to Tulum which describe a situation in 1579 where none of the residents in the area could remember who had constructed the site (Scholes and Roys 1948: 75), implying that the major occupation at Tulum may have ended prior to 1520. The native documents also describe a series of events, which may have a bearing on Ichpaatun, Tulum, or another site along the coast, culminating in the overthrow of Ah Ulmil Ahau in Katun 8 Ahau (A.D. 1441–61) (Roys 1962: 74; A. Chase, this volume). The similarity between Ulmil and Uaymil is apparent; this event takes place during the same katun as the depopulation of Mayapan. Yet a third possibility might be that the archaeologically recognized discontinuities between Santa Rita Corozal and Ichpaatun are an expression of the internal organization of the provinces themselves.

CONCLUSIONS

A number of topics relating to Late Postclassic or Protohistoric Maya social and political organization can be cross-checked through both ethnohistoric and archaeological investigation. Excavations at the site of Santa Rita Corozal, in combination with those from the site of Mayapan, in fact offer a few new twists to traditional ethnohistoric perspectives.

Archaeological work indicates that if status distinctions are present during the Late Postclassic Period, they are not clear-cut along three class lines. While elite residences and burials may be relatively elaborate and commoners' residences and burials less distinguished, the situation is one of obvious overlaps and gradations. It is uncertain what, if any, archaeological data can be associated with slaves. The association of elites with ritual that is indicated in the ethnohistory can be documented archaeologically. Ritual activity at Santa Rita Corozal appears to have occurred principally around the more elaborate constructions, many of which presumably represent elite residences, and does not appear to have been associated with all family groups. As has been pointed out elsewhere (D. Chase 1982a, 1985), the archaeological investigations at Santa Rita Corozal have provided data that contradict earlier interpretations of Postclassic ritual (Proskouriakoff 1955; Thompson 1970).

While grave type and associated objects are significant, one of the other important factors in suggesting status in Postclassic burials appears to be location. Differences between male and female interments and adult and child burial patterns exist. Female burials at Santa Rita Corozal appear to be in favored locations, in graves requiring much effort, and often accompanied by elaborate objects. This evidence suggests that women in the Late Postclassic were more prominent than is indicated by the ethnohistory.

Important Late Postclassic sites appear to be organized in a sector or barrio arrangement rather than in the concentric configuration described by Landa (in Tozzer 1941). Two basic types of barrio settlement pattern are archaeologically evinced in Late Postclassic site organization. In the first, exemplified by Mayapan, a site center was surrounded by barrios. The second, exemplified by Santa Rita Corozal, had no obvious center. In both cases, the barrios were composed of clusters of smaller constructions organized about more formal groups in a manner similar to that found at Classic Maya sites. In combination with the continuities in caching patterns, burial practices, and certain construction techniques from the Classic to the Postclassic Period, this pattern may be interpreted as an indication of the predominantly "Maya" nature of these sites.

While more work must be carried out, the regional nature of the archaeological remains of the Late Postclassic is apparent. The architecture and pottery found at sites in the presumed Protohistoric provinces of Ecab, Uaymil, Chetumal, and Tah Itza indicates that the boundaries of the provinces or allied areas, which were initially defined from documentary evidence, can be assessed and partially confirmed archaeologically.

I suggest that the organization of the site of Santa Rita Corozal is representative of the organization of Lowland Maya regional capitals at the time of the Conquest. This organization can be seen both as derivative of that known archaeologically for the Classic Period and as homologous to that which can be reconstructed from documents for the early Historic Maya. The archaeological patterns I have defined can also be utilized to attempt a discussion of larger Protohistoric interactions. The archaeological differences between Santa Rita Corozal and sites along the east coast of Yucatan reflect temporal, regional, and organizational distinctions between Quintana Roo and contact-period northern Belize. It is doubtful that enclaves of purely non-Maya peoples will be securely defined archaeologically anywhere in the Maya Lowlands for the Late Postclassic Period; if any site organization within this area hints at Mexican influence, however, it is that seen in coastal Quintana Roo.

In conclusion, ethnohistory and archaeology in the Maya area may be more complementary than has been previously proposed. Their relationship, however, is neither static nor unidirectional. Late Postclassic archaeological data and their interpretations can clearly be utilized to identify, elucidate, and correct problems in the sometimes nebulous documentary accounts.

377

11

Campeche, the Itza, and the Postclassic: A Study in Ethnohistorical Archaeology[1]

JOSEPH W. BALL

San Diego State University

Realizing that the plans for the ceiling are not what they should be, a discouraged Michelangelo stops in a nearby tavern for a glass of wine. The wine turns out to be sour, and the innkeeper smashes the cask shouting at the artist, "If the wine is sour, throw it out!" Those words send Michelangelo running back to the chapel. Taking a stone hammer, he slashes his frescoes beyond repair . . .

> P. Dunne, screenplay
> synopsis for *The Agony*
> *and the Ecstasy*

KATUN 1 AHAU: *uac kal haab, cu tepalob chichen itzaa ca paxi chichen itza, ca binob cahtal Chan putun ti yanhi u yotochob ah itzaob kuyan uincob lae: lai u habil lae.* "one hundred twenty years they governed in Chichen Itza when it was destroyed causing them to establish themselves in Champoton where the Itzas, a believing people, lived." (Craine and Reindorf 1979: 135, 138)

So began the Postclassic era in central Campeche, a fact not generally appreciated by either archaeologists or ethnohistorians. Neither the known archaeological record of the site today called Chichen Itza nor the most widely accepted correlation of the Maya Initial Series and Christian calendars at 11.16.0.0.0 in the former seems to provide more than the most tenuous support for such a scenario (see Ball 1974a for a somewhat procrustean approach to the matter). Nonetheless, closely critical study of the Yucatec Books of Chilam Balam and early Colonial Period Spanish documentary sources in conjunction with a careful consideration of the overall known Lowland Maya archaeological record does indeed suggest such to be the case. Acceptance of this scenario does require the utilization of one or more interpretive paradigms at odds with some of those most cherished by Maya scholars today, however, and it is the intent of this paper to examine the historical-behavioral ramifications of these paradigms for the northern Maya Postclassic archaeological record.

Two of the alternatives are discussed at length in other seminar papers. One is the so-called total overlap model, which places Toltec Chichen Itza in the Terminal Classic Period, overlapping completely in time with the Puuc architectural style (Lincoln 1982, this volume; see also Ball 1979a). One is correlation of the Christian and Maya calendars at 11.3.0.0.0 in the latter (A. Chase 1978, this volume). The third, which might be called the mistaken identity model, is outlined below.

As its title indicates, the primary orientation of this essay is "historical" rather than "processual," although I perceive these approaches as aspects of the same endeavor: valid elucidation of the archaeological record. The archaeological record of any region can be interpreted ("explained," if one prefers) in terms of historical events or cultural processes or both. Such records are products not of cultural processes but of human behavior. Processes manifest themselves in patternings of human social behavior and temporal sequences of these patterns (i.e., histories). These recurrent behavioral events and sequences in turn produce the tangible archaeological record.

If we hope to explain a given regional archaeological record in terms of underlying cultural processes, we must first seek to ascertain the behavioral events and sequences of events responsible for that record. This paper consequently is concerned with establishing what happened in Campeche and other parts of the Northern Lowlands during the Postclassic era as a necessary step in understanding why whatever happened did so.

To comprehend the history and anthropology of Postclassic Campeche requires knowledge of several distinct bodies of data. First, there

380

is the archaeological record, as yet but partially and imperfectly known. Especially problematic are some quite crucial zones including the Cilvituk lakes region (see Andrews IV 1943); the Río Champoton drainage; the circum–Laguna de Términos floodplain (see Ruz Lhuillier 1969; Matheny 1970; Eaton 1978; Ball 1978); and the overall gulf coastal lowlands of southwestern Campeche–northeastern Tabasco (see Berlin 1956; Ochoa and Casasola 1978; Ball 1985a). Even in such well-investigated zones as the central eastern Campeche Río Bec region scant attention has been paid to Postclassic remains.[2]

Next, there are the early Colonial Period Spanish documentary sources dealing specifically with the Campeche area. As these and their import to late preconquest Maya culture history have been treated at length on several previous occasions, they will not be reconsidered again here (Tozzer 1941; see Scholes and Roys 1948; Thompson 1970; Ball 1978).

Finally, there are the much maligned Books of Chilam Balam, native Maya compositions purporting to forecast future events on the basis of those of the past in conjunction with a cyclical conception of time and history, and in fact containing modest amounts of actual preconquest history (see Morley 1911; Thompson 1970; Edmonson 1982). These works have been attacked for their garbling of dates, persons, myths, and real events, and it is certainly true that anyone reading them cannot but be impressed by the apparent utter confusion of their compilers. A groping for prophetically reliable historiography is clearly evident, but it is confounded and confused by a conception of time and history that is alien to our own; one that melds past, future, and present into a single indistinguishable round in which what was will be and what is must have been and so will be and so must have been.

By the late eighteenth to early nineteenth centuries, to which the surviving copies of the Chilam Balam books date (Roys 1967: 6; Edmonson 1982: xi–xii), it is doubtful that their compilers had any real grasp of the correct temporal relationship of the preconquest events they were relating or of the precise personages and places involved in those events. Given their purpose and cosmological stance, I doubt very much that these incidentals were even of any great concern to them. Still, the requirements of dependable prophecy should have ensured that dramatic events were at least placed within the proper predictive interval (katun) of their actual original occurrence even if some leeway was acceptable with respect to the precise persons, groups, or locales concerned.

Moving from the realm of prophetic historiography to that of archaeological history, I would emphasize that the major events and event sequences recorded in the Books of Chilam Balam represent more than mere idiosyncratic occurrences. They are, rather, the historical-behavioral correlates, the perceived or apparent manifestations, of sociocultural processes. To reconstruct them correctly, therefore, contributes directly to understanding the archaeological record of the Postclassic Maya Lowlands in terms of such processes.

As on previous occasions (Ball 1974a, 1974b, 1979a), I offer the following thoughts primarily as models for future testing along with other alternatives rather than as formalized historiographies. Far too much needs to be learned of not only Campeche but also Yucatan and Quintana Roo archaeology before we are in any position to produce the latter.

THE CAMPECHE "POSTCLASSIC": A WORKING DEFINITION

Over the past decade, I have experimented with several different formulae for defining the Postclassic era in Campeche but have not yet received any genuinely satisfactory results (see Ball 1977a, 1978, 1985a). The reasons for these failures have varied and are not really relevant to the present discussion. Suffice it to say that I believe all my definitions suffered from geographic overextension; I now consider it necessary as well as most useful to define the era individually and specifically on a subregion-by-subregion basis. In this essay I will attempt to deal seriously with only one region, the central or central eastern Campeche Río Bec zone. To its west, the known existence of several "non-Classic" Maya culture traditions and their vigorous survival of the Classic Maya collapse make defining a Postclassic stage or period both meaningless and difficult—if not impossible—at this time. Their very existence is, of course, significant, but present data really do not permit more than the recognition of this fact.

Review of the central eastern Campeche archaeological sequence suggests it is most reasonable to define a local Postclassic era as beginning with the appearance of the Xcocom ceramic phase and its correlates in that zone. It should be noted clearly that this involves a sequence of events that cannot currently be dated by purely archaeological means. On ethnohistoric grounds (see below), however, I will suggest a probable dating of ca. 10.2.0.0.0 to 10.3.0.0.0 (A.D. 869–889 or 1125–1145).[3]

Fixing the termination of the Campeche Early Postclassic has proved no less problematic. It is most useful archaeologically to place it at the end of the Xcocom occupation. This is more than a mere solution of convenience, for once again, while archaeologically rooted absolute dates for the phase are not available, the Books of Chilam Balam provide reasonable grounds for assigning the historical event represented by its end a date of about 10.5.0.0.0 to 10.6.0.0.0 (A.D. 928–948 or 1184–1204).

The rather short duration of the central eastern Campeche Early Postclassic Period thus suggested is in accord with the character of Xcocom occupational deposits at the two intensively investigated Río Bec Zone sites of Becan and Chicanna, although none of the numerous associated hearths located there during the 1969–70 excavations was sampled for radiocarbon dating. As things stand, I propose that the central eastern Campeche Early Postclassic can be validly terminated with the withdrawal from the region of the *yala Itza* ("other" Itza; see below) sometime following Tun 7 or Katun 8 Ahau (A.D. 935 or 1191). I eagerly await the substantive testing of this proposition.

A genuine void lasting well into the sixteenth century follows this date and so removes it from our present concern (Ball 1985b). To the far west, the archaeological record as known does not suggest any valid division of gulf coastal prehistory into Classic and Postclassic periods. It is, however, possible to discuss this record in terms of pre– and post–Classic Maya collapse times, and I have attempted to do so in the concluding section of this paper.

THE CAMPECHE POSTCLASSIC:
WHAT HAPPENED?

To answer this question, it unfortunately is necessary at present to rely heavily on the postconquest literary materials of northern Yucatan. On initial examination, as already noted, these present a formidable morass of chronological, nominal, and locational hearsay, but they probably do contain a modicum of historical—and therefore processual—truth. Abstracting this truth is not easy, however, and requires employment of one or more interpretive paradigms likely to prove unpalatable to many Mayanists. In the following sections, I present these paradigms and discuss their interpretive significance for Postclassic Campeche. I am in no way wedded to any of the historical scenarios, and I offer them purely as illustrations of what might be accomplished through the serious but critical conjunctive examination of extant literary materials and archaeological data pertaining to the late preconquest history of the Yucatan Peninsula.

Paradigm 1

The underlying assumptions of this paradigm include (a) the validity of the total overlap model (Ball 1979a; Lincoln 1982, this volume); (b) the validity of an 11.16.0.0.0 correlation of the Maya and Christian calendars; (c) the probability of some historically significant locative confusions in both the early Colonial Spanish sources and the Books of Chilam Balam.[4] Several quite complex factors are concerned in the last instance, and I will attempt to do no more here than indicate their general character. A planned future study will examine them in depth.

One factor of considerable importance was the traditional association of particular place names with specific ethnic groups or lineages. Examples include "Uxmal" and the Xiu, "Mayapan" and the Cocom (Itza), and "Chichen Itza" and the Itza (in general).[5] To Maya chronicler and bard, the traditional seat or primate center of the Itza was "Chichen Itza," but I submit that to both chronicler and bard it was far more important to pair the canonically right center with the traditionally right group than to make any accurate locational identifications. Similarly, placing the historically right event-type in the traditionally right prophetic interval was more important than achieving any real historical accuracy.

"Mayapan," or the "water-place cycle" seat, was the traditional center of Cocom Itza socioceremonial and political power before their destruction by the Xiu and yala Itza in Katun 8 Ahau. Open-minded comparative readings quickly show, however, that this appellative was applied rather freely to various premier centers or cycle (*may*) seats by both the early Spanish authors' Maya informants and the Maya chroniclers themselves. On some occasions adjectival identifiers were added (e.g.; *ychpaa, tancah, zaclactun*), on others not. Again, it seems clear that associating the right locational appellative with the right group or person was what mattered rather than actual geographic accuracy. One somewhat less ambiguous instance of such geographically indifferent usage involves the cycle-seat appellative "Siyan Can" or "Ziyancaan" ("Born of Heaven"). Edmonson (1982: 5n.26) points out that this was applied, as appropriate, variously to Chichen Itza, Mayapan, Merida, Valladolid, Bacalar, and other places.

Archaeological data provide one standard by which documentary histories may and should be evaluated. In the present case, their weight is to associate the Cocom Itza of "Mayapan"; their "valiant captain," Kakupacal; and their legendary ancestor-founder, Kukulcan-Quetzalcoatl, with the place known to us as Chichen Itza rather than any other (Kelley 1968, 1982; Ball 1979a; Davoust 1980; Lincoln 1982). Recognizing the foregoing, we may more easily appreciate the probability of significant locative mix-ups in the Colonial writings.[6]

Also complicating matters was the natural tendency of Colonial Period Maya informants and chroniclers to identify the major traditional centers with the more imposing ruins known to them or located within their own provinces. Special interests as well might have contributed to identifying one's own group with traditionally important place names or territorially advantageous locations, particularly when boundary questions were involved.

Beyond all the foregoing lies a still more serious problem: locative misassignments were not consistent or inevitable. "Chichen Itza" sometimes is Chichen Itza; Coba sometimes is "Coba." Identifying the occurrence and significance of misapplied locatives is where the rub really lies.

On the foregoing premises, I have developed a new "historical" scenario for the overall Northern Lowlands using a combination of selected prophetic (Maya) and documentary (Spanish) texts.[7] Originally intended to cover only the traditional Postclassic Period, this scenario unexpectedly extended backward well into the Late Classic. A few major events remain frustratingly elusive as to both placement and significance and will require further analysis if they are to be resolved.[8] On the whole, however, I believe a coherent, internally and archaeologically consistent ethnohistoric picture of Itza ("Postclassic") Yucatan is beginning to emerge. This picture, as I interpret the relevant literary materials, is as follows:

(ca. A.D.)

672–692   "Chichen Itza" (*Coba archaeological locality*) occupied, formally established, or recognized as a center of major socioceremonial and political import by a group (of Itza Maya) from the eastern lowlands.
Suggested source references: CBT—"8 Ahau had been revealed; Chichen Itza had been manifested: the grove, Born of Heaven, there."

770   The Tutul Xiu arrive in Yucatan.
Suggested source references: CBT—"It was 13 Ahau. 8 Ahau. . . . 2 Ahau. Then arrived the East priest Bi Ton, the chief of the Tutul Xiu, one year before it was one hundred years." CBM—"Katun 8 Ahau . . . Ah Mekat Tutul Xiu came . . . One year was lacking to complete 100 when he arrived . . ." (See also Tozzer 1941: 29–31).

751–771   "Mayapan" (*Chichen Itza*) established as the primate socioceremonial and political center of the Cocom Itza Maya.
Suggested source references: CBC_2—"13 Ahau was the katun when they founded the Mayapan, the Maya men, as they were called."

870–889   "Chichen Itza" (*Coba*) "lost" as a major socioceremonial and political center. Its onetime lords emigrate southward.
Suggested source references: CBT—"1 Ahau: two hundred years Chichen Itza ruled. Then it was destroyed. Then they went to the settlement of Champoton [Chakanputun] where there were then the homes of the Itza . . ." CBM—"Katun 1 Ahau: 120 years they governed in Chichen Itza when it was destroyed causing them to establish themselves in Champoton [Chan putun] where the Itzas, a believing people, lived." CBC_3—"1 Ahau was when the remainder of the Itza [yala Ah Itza] were driven out of Chichen. It was the third tun of 1 Ahau (A.D. 872) when Chichen was depopulated."

872+   "Chakanputun/Champoton (*Champoton, the prov-*

ince or region) occupied by southward-moving individuals from the formerly ascendant center "Chichen Itza." Here they joined an already resident local group of Itza Maya.

Suggested source references: CBT—see above. CBM—see above. CBC₁—"4 Ahau [?] was when the land was seized by them at Chakanputun. [reprise] There were thirteen folds of katuns when they established their houses at Chakaputun."

928–948   "Chakanputun/Champoton" lost to the Itza and their immigrant (Itza?) guests from "Chichen Itza" through their conquest by Kakupacal and Tec Uilu of the Cocom Itza, ca. A.D. 935.

Suggested source references: CBT—"8 Ahau. Destroyed was Champoton." CBM—"Katun 8 Ahau: Champoton was destroyed. . . . they lost Champoton." CBC₁—"8 Ahau was when Chakanputun was abandoned by the Itza men." CBC₃—"In the seventh tun of Katun 8 Ahau [A.D. 935], this was the katun when Chakanputun perished at the hands of Kakupacal and Tec Uilu."

968–987   "Ichpaa Mayapan" (*Mayapan, the site and region*) occupied and established as a political and socioceremonial center by those who "lost" Champoton.

Suggested source references: CBT—"Destroyed was Champoton. . . . Then they came on and returned to their homes for the second time. They destroyed [or "lost," cf. Brinton 1882: 145; Barrera V. 1948: 61] the road of Champoton. . . . Then they destroyed [or "lost," as above] the road of Champoton" [note the reiterated emphasis on this fact]. CBC prophecies—"Katun 4 Ahau. . . . The katun is established at Chichen Itza. . . . Kukulcan shall come with them for the second time. . . . The Itza shall come."

987–1007   Uxmal established as the paramount socioceremonial and political center of the Xiu by Ah Zuytok Tutul Xiu. "League of Mayapan" formed by Cocom Itza of Chichen Itza ("Mayapan"), the Xiu of Uxmal, and

the yala ("other") Ytza of Mayapan ("Ichpaa Mayapan").

Suggested source references: CBT—"Second Ahau
. . . They established the land of Zuy Tok, a Tutul
Xiu of Uxmal. Two hundred years had passed since
they established the land of Uxmal." CBM—"In Katun 2 Ahau, Ah Cuytok Tutul Xiu established himself
in Uxmal. Katun 2 Ahau . . . Katun 10 Ahau: 200
years they governed along with the governors of
Chichen Itza and Mayapan."

1194   Chichen Itza ("Mayapan"/"Chichen Itza") destroyed
as a major political power; Cocom Itza massacred by
Uxmal Xiu and Mayapan ("Ichpaa Mayapan") or yala
("other") Ytza. Cocom survivors resettled at Sotuta.
Uxmal possibly abandoned for Mani (the province)
at this time.

Suggested source references: CBT—"8 Ahau, they
destroyed the governors of Chichen Itza by the sinful
words of Hunac Ceel." CBM—"Katun 8 Ahau, the
halach uinic of Chichen Itza and the Itza men abandoned their homes . . . in the tenth year [tun] of
Katun 8 Ahau they were dispersed. . . ." CBC$_1$—"8
Ahau was when Chichen Itza was abandoned . . . 8
Ahau was when the Itza men again abandoned their
homes because of the treachery of Hunac Ceel. . . ."
CBC$_2$—"8 Ahau was when their town was abandoned
and they were scattered throughout the entire district
. . . then they ceased to be called Maya."

1224–1244   Emergence or formal recognition of *Mayapan* ("Ichpaa Mayapan") as the paramount northern political
and socioceremonial center.

Suggested source references: CBT—"6 Ahau, 4 Ahau:
forty years. Then it was completed, the land within
the walls of Mayapan . . ." CBC$_1$—"4 Ahau was when
the land of Ichpaa Mayapan was seized by the Itza
men (who had been separated from their homes because of the people of Izamal and because of the
treachery of Hunac Ceel)."

1441–1461   *Mayapan* ("Ichpaa Mayapan") destroyed; *Mayapan* or yala Ytza emigrate southward into the Peten lakes region.

Suggested source references: CBT—"8 Ahau, fighting took place in *ichpaa Mayapan* . . ." (after Brinton 1882: 147; cf. Barrera V. 1948: 63; Edmonson 1982: 10). CBM—"In the Katun 8 Ahau, Mayapan was destroyed . . . Katun 2 Ahau was in progress when the Spaniards came the first time, when they were seen for the first time in the province of Yucatan, sixty years after the destruction of *ichpa* Mayapan." CBC₁—"8 Ahau was when there was fighting with stones at ichpaa Mayapan . . ." CBC₃—"8 Ahau was the katun when the *yala* Itza founded their town, coming forth from beneath the trees and bushes at Tan-Xuluc-Mul. . . . They came out and established the land of *zaclactun* Mayapan. . . ."

The following discussion is not intended to be a detailed commentary on the foregoing scenario, but rather to point out some of its decidedly attractive consistencies with the known archaeological record.

Munro Edmonson (1982) has elegantly discussed the structural and stylistic complexities of the Books of Chilam Balam in the context of his own masterful translation of the *Tizimin*. As has Arlen Chase (1978, this volume), he has pointed out that the chronicles are not, as generally assumed, entirely sequential in their organization. After considerable study, however, I have become convinced that much greater use was made of such standard epic literary devices as the reprise and flashback than even Edmonson and Chase have suggested, and also have identified several probable instances of anachronistic temporal juxtaposition, temporal glissading, and time-interval jumping.[9] The foregoing scenario takes all of these into consideration, and the reader should be aware of their incorporation in evaluating it against the source references suggested.

The seating of the earliest Itza *may* or cycle recorded in the Books of Chilam Balam at "Chichen Itza" (*Coba*) in Katun 8 Ahau (A.D. 672–692) is consistent with several lines of data and contradicted by none. The center already was politically and economically important, as befits a place chosen to be the socioceremonial heart of a people.

A seemingly obvious fact which nonetheless has been persistently overlooked or ignored by most Mayanists is that the time of a center's rise to preeminence in most cases probably did not correlate with its initial establishment. This fact is especially evident in the cases of Mayapan and Uxmal, and I suggest its application to that of "Chichen Itza" (Coba) as well.

The existence of well-established lines of interaction between the greater Coba region and that of northeastern Peten–northern Belize has been documented in ceramics, architecture, and epigraphy (Thompson, Pollock, and Charlot 1932; Ball 1978, 1982a; Robles C. 1980). Peter D. Harrison (1974) has established the existence of a "Peten corridor" linking these zones through southern Quintana Roo.

The way thus lay open for the "discovery" of "Chichen Itza" (Coba) by the Itza of the Peten, and interestingly enough, it lay through Bacalar, just as the Mani Chilam Balam indicates (Craine and Reindorf 1979: 134, 138). In this light, it is significant rather than coincidental that in Tun 7 of Katun 8 Ahau, Coba commemorated an event of dynastic import involving the southern Peten center of Naranjo (Stela 1, Coba: 9.12.10.5.12 4 Eb 10 Yax; see Marcus 1976: 164–69).

The Itza had established their order at Coba, and there they would reign until the fateful Katun 1 Ahau.

. . . in the olden times they called the east *cenial* [dze-emal], "the little descent" and the west *nohenial* [noh-emal], "the great descent." And it is a fact that they say that from the east there came to this land but few people and from the west a good many. . . . (Lizana 1633)

Whether considered independently or together, both the archaeological and literary data bearing on Uxmal and the Tutul Xiu seem all but incapable of satisfactory interpretation. Underlying this apparent problem, I suggest, has been the assumption that only one or two chronologically distinct events are concerned whereas actually there are four: (a) the arrival of the Tutul Xiu in Yucatan, (b) the "foundation" of Uxmal, (c) the recognition of Uxmal as the premiere Xiu socioceremonial center, and (d) the formal establishment of the Yucatan Xiu dynasty.

Edmonson (1982: 3–5) has provided a convincing assessment of the Tutul Xiu arrival in Yucatan in A.D. 770. A closely comparable dating for the establishment of Puuc-style Uxmal and the emergence of the Puuc architectural tradition has been documented extensively over the last decade (Ball 1974a, 1979a, 1979b; Ball and Andrews V 1975; Andrews V 1979; Andrews IV and Andrews V 1980).

Turning to the emplacement of Xiu regency at Uxmal, I am impressed by the consistent traditional insistence on this for Katun 2 Ahau and am most inclined on archaeological grounds to place it in 10.9.0.0.0 (A.D. 987–1007). On the issue of Xiu dynastic establishment, I have no comment.

The dating here suggested for the establishment of Chichen Itza as the premier Cocom Itza center is predicated upon the assumed original correct association of the Cocom with this site rather than with that today known to us as Mayapan. In this light, it is worth taking a fresh look at the relevant radiocarbon data from the Northern Maya Lowlands as recently summarized by Andrews IV and Andrews V (1980: 281–85).[10] As presented here, all determinations have been corrected and, when appropriate, averaged using the Damon et al. (1974) and Long-Rippeteau (1974) formulae.

From Chichen Itza, an averaged and corrected date based on two separate runs of an El Castillo lintel is A.D. 830 ± 75. A Las Monjas lintel yielded a comparable determination of A.D. 830 ± 110, while two beams from La Iglesia and one from the Casa Colorado were dated respectively to A.D. 805 ± 85, A.D. 610 ± 75, and A.D. 640 ± 65. While the last two seem early from any reasonable perspective, the others all conform nicely with the suggested scenario.

From the Puuc Hills, we have three corrected Uxmal dates of A.D. 900 ± 130, 755 ± 80, and 590 ± 55, as well as one Sayil determination of A.D. 735 ± 80. Again, excepting one unacceptably early date, all are compatible with the proposed scenario.

It should be kept in mind that the foregoing determinations all derive from structural beams, and that past sampling naiveté very probably has been sufficient to throw the real significance of such samples into question. In this light, undoubtedly the most reliable and crucial dates currently available from the Northern Zone are the four from Balankanche Cave. Averaged and corrected, the *incensario*-associated twig charcoal samples yield ages of A.D. 900 ± 70 and 920 ± 50. Assuming the shrine's establishment and utilization were associated with the introduction from the Tabasco-Campeche coastal plain of "Mexican" forces by the Cocom Itza (Tozzer 1941: 32–35, 216), these results are in excellent accord with the scenario presented.

A second major body of Northern Maya Postclassic chronological data is epigraphic in nature. The inscriptions of Chichen Itza and the Puuc Hills sites only recently have begun to receive the attention they deserve. It is already evident, nonetheless, that they contain much of significance concerning politico-dynastic affairs during the general Florescent Period (i.e., the Terminal Classic–Early Postclassic) as defined by Andrews IV (1965a).

With reference to chronology, Kelley's (1983) new analysis of the known Chichen Itza inscriptions places all but one between A.D. 866 (10.1.17.0.0) and 906 (10.3.17.0.0). A somewhat later reading of A.D. 997 (10.8.10.0.0) is associated with the Tomb of the High Priest.

Thompson (1937, 1973) has provided a small set of epigraphic readings from Uxmal spanning an interval of A.D. 897 to 907 and one from Labna of 862. Kelley (1983) does not entirely agree with these and would place one as late as 11.12.17.11.1 (A.D. 1477 or, using Kelley's own 11.5 correlation, A.D. 1693). Kowalski (1981), however, finds Thompson's readings acceptable, and on grounds of reasonable intrasite and regional consistencies, I, too, favor them.

Both Davoust (1980) and Kelley (1983) argue that most of the monumental architecture and all of the hieroglyphic inscriptions from "Old" or "Maya" Chichen Itza pertain to the reign of the ruler Kakupacal and one of his successors. Those specifically mentioning Kakupacal, however, all fall between A.D. 869 and 881 (10.2.—; 10.2.12); that is, within Katun 1 Ahau.

The martial character of most public sculptural and mural art at Chichen Itza is well known, and my intent here is to propose as its probable impetus the triumphal celebration of historical fact rather than some attempt at dynastic glorification. More specifically, I suggest that the destruction of "Chichen Itza" (Coba) by the Cocom of "Mayapan" (Chichen Itza) and their Mexicanized Xiu allies underlies the Katun 1 Ahau programs of architectural activity at both Chichen Itza and Uxmal.

The latest known inscription from Coba, in contrast, dates to A.D. 780 (9.17.10.0.0), and while Robles (1980) has presented strong evidence supporting the chronological overlap of the Copo-Cehpech and Sotuta ceramic complexes, he provides *none* for the uninterrupted continuity of the local (Coba) Oro Copo-Cehpech into the local Seco Hocaba-Tases. I suggest that no such continuity did occur, and that as a center of socioceremonial as well as political and economic prominence, "Chichen Itza" (*Coba*) ceased to exist in the late ninth century A.D.

Some years ago (Ball 1974a), I suggested the possible identification of "Chakanputun" with the archaeological site of Seibal. I here disavow that in favor of the more generally accepted correlation of "Chakanputun" with Champoton. At the same time, however, I propose that while most scholars have identified such locatives as "Chakanputun/ Champoton" or "Mani" with individual sites, it is far more probable in many cases that they refer to entire provinces or regions. The "Chakanputun/Champoton" of the chronicles, thus, I would equate with Champoton, the region, rather than with Champoton, the town. Ninth-century provincial boundaries remain conjectural, of course, but what is known of later sixteenth-century ones suggests inclusion of central to central eastern Campeche within the Chakanputun/ Champoton province of that time.

It was into this general Chakanputun/Champoton region, then, that those driven from "Chichen Itza" moved in the late ninth century. The chronology of their flight and reestablishment is understandably muddled and seems to have become interwoven with a reprise of the original regional occupation by yet another "Itza" in each of the known Chilam Balam accounts. Their material culture was that which comprises the Xcocom archaeological complex in central eastern Campeche. This complex possesses two quite distinct manifestations as currently known. One involves an unbroken although somewhat impoverished continuity of the local Late Classic material cultural tradition and appears to be restricted in distribution to the dispersed rural rancherias of the zone (Ball n.d.). Locally produced finewares or exotic goods of any kind are rare or absent among these households as are apparent weapons. In contrast, standing masonry buildings throughout the zone frequently are associated with primary refuse deposits rich in ceramic, lithic, and molluscan exotica as well as finely made articles of probable local manufacture (Rovner 1975b; Ball 1977a; Taschek n.d.). Weapons are heavily represented among the chipped-stone artifacts. While most directly and tightly tying Xcocom into an east-west interaction network linking the Laguna de Términos and Bahía de Chetumal, these materials also show a general "Northern" affinity strong enough to suggest derivation from that direction (Ball 1974b, 1977a; Rovner 1974, 1975b).

Large-scale architectural undertakings currently seem to have been rare or nonexistent during Xcocom. On the other hand, the practice of erecting sculpted stelae was maintained or possibly even introduced during this phase. Of the datable monuments known from central eastern Campeche, one (Stela 1, San Lorenzo) can be read as 10.5.0.0.0 (A.D. 928; Thompson 1953); two others (Stelae 1 and 2, Pasión del Cristo) respectively as 10.3.0.0.0 and 10.3.10.0.0 (A.D. 889 and 899; J. Andrews 1976). Stelae 3, 7, and 8 at Becan can be assigned to Xcocom by ceramic associations. Those remaining (Stelae 1 and 2, Becan) are uncarved shafts contextually assignable to the fifth century. No stylistic assessments of these monuments have been attempted.

Overall, the Xcocom archaeological complex appears to reflect a vaguely northern intrusion into and short-term control over the central eastern Campeche inland entrepôt on the transpeninsular passage between the Bahía de Chetumal and Laguna de Términos. Neither the Xcocom archaeological record nor the prophetic accounts I would associate with it bespeaks any great duration: "In the seventh tun of Katun 8 Ahau, . . . Chakanputun perished at the hands of Kak-u-pacal and Tec Uilu" (Roys 1967: 141). As I have elected to read it, this date would have fallen in A.D. 935. That the "Great Man" (Kak-upacal) was himself physically involved is unlikely, but a prominent lieutenant or immediate successor of his probably is referred to in Tec Uilu. Read this way, the account describes the logical continuation of active hostilities between two historically competitive groups.

I would call attention at this point to the somewhat unusual manner in which the conquest of "Chakanputun/Champoton" is described: the yala Itza are said to have "lost" not Champoton but its "road" or "way." This is an extremely significant point to which I will return in the next section.

There is sufficient recurrent insistence among all the literary sources on a Katun 4 Ahau (A.D. 968–87) resurgence of the yala Itza on the Yucatan plains to make it difficult to believe that some such event did not take place. On archaeological grounds, it is not unlikely that this in fact involved establishment of the fortified settlement "Ichpaa May-apan," known today simply as Mayapan.

The following Katun 2 Ahau (A.D. 987–1007) was a politically eventful period, particularly from the Xiu perspective. It saw both the formal establishment of Xiu hegemony at Uxmal and the formation of a triple entente involving the Xiu, the Cocom Itza, and the yala Itza. Whatever its perceived intent,[11] this league was to survive for some 200 years.

In A.D. 1194, the Xiu and yala Itza joined together to destroy the Cocom. Their success in this venture corresponds archaeologically to the collapse of Chichen Itza as a major political and economic power, but not as a center of considerable ceremonial import (Ball 1982b). Following it, the Cocom were resettled in Sotuta where their western conquerors might better monitor their activities. At the same time, the Xiu appear to have adopted a less obviously defense-oriented pattern of settlement on the rich, open plains of Mani to the north of the Puuc Hills.

The yala Itza now assumed politico-economic dominance on the peninsula, a fact reflected archaeologically in the horizon-like spread of Mayapan-style material culture and the florescence of Mayapan itself. The mercantile, maritime orientation of their culture has been documented exhaustively over the last decade, as has its integration into the larger Mesoamerican–Central American interaction networks of the time (e.g., Scholes and Roys 1948; Thompson 1970; Ball and Rovner 1972; Sabloff and Rathje 1975a; Freidel, this volume). Generally overlooked, however, has been the probable historiographic impact of "Ichpaa Mayapan" yala Itza cum Xiu success on subsequent traditional history.

In A.D. 1451 or thereabouts, "Ichpaa Mayapan" was destroyed. With the loss of their principal northern powerbase, the yala Itza withdrew southward along traditional routes of passage to the northeastern Peten lakes region whence had come their ancestors some eight centuries before.

Paradigm 2

Like the first paradigm, this one is predicated on a total overlap model and Maya-Christian calendrical correlation at 11.16.0.0.0. For those unwilling to accept the equation of "Chichen Itza" with Coba, it offers as an alternative possibility the establishment of formal recognition of Chichen Itza as a premier center sometime between A.D. 672 and 731—most probably 711—and its "loss" in 889.[12] The southward emigration of Chichen's former lords and their reestablishment in the Champoton area would follow this.

The Champoton episode would date as above, and as above would be followed by an Itza resurgence on the Yucatan coastal plain in

Katun 4 Ahau (A.D. 968–87). Again I would argue that Mayapan rather than Chichen Itza was the likely site of this comeback, although I will admit the existence of the latter possibility. In either event, Chichen Itza itself probably did regain substantial ceremonial importance at this time.

While the available radiocarbon dates from Chichen Itza and the Puuc sites are in harmony with such a reconstruction, two important assumptions must be made if the reconstruction is also to agree with the crucial Balankanche and epigraphic data. First, the known Chichen inscriptions that postdate and do not mention Kakupacal also must postdate the Itza exodus. Second, some alternative, non-Itza Mexican Maya hybrid group must be identified and assigned responsibility for the Katun 1 Ahau "loss" of Chichen to the Itza, the post-loss hieroglyphic inscriptions, and the Balankanche Cave ceremonies.

Obvious candidates for the foregoing role are the Tutul (Toltec) Xiu, proclaimed by both themselves and others to be foreigners with close ties to Nonohualco, Zuyua, Chiconauhtla, and, possibly, Tollan (Tozzer 1941: 30,40,45,54,56; Barrera V. 1948: 57–58; Edmonson 1982: 5). The A.D. 889 and later Xiu presence at and around Chichen Itza would be reflected in the Caracol inscriptions of 10.3.0.15.1 and 10.3.17 (A.D. 889; 906), the Balankanche ceremonies (ca. A.D. 915 ± 40), and the Puuc-style architectural complex at Culuba (Andrews V 1979).[13]

The High Priest's Grave, with its 10.8.10.11.0 (A.D. 997) inscription, on the other hand, probably should be assigned to the period following the "return of the Itza." Its existence does not necessarily indicate Chichen's politico-economic revival at that time, merely its restored socioceremonial import.

The Paradigm 2 scenario possesses a number of attractive features from both the literary and archaeological perspectives. In the first place, it allows for association of Itza groups with both Chichen Itza and Mayapan. This accords well with traditional history, and also with the occupational sequencing recorded by Landa and Herrera (Tozzer 1941: 20–26, 215). Whether the Cocom Itza should be identified with Chichen, Mayapan, or both, however, is somewhat unclear in this instance (compare, for example, Tozzer 1941: 23–37 and Roys 1962: 66; also see Kelley 1968). Equally appealing is the logical appellative progression of this scenario in which the first major northern Itza center,

"Mayapan"–*Chichen Itza* would be replaced by "Ichpaa (Fortress) Mayapan." This also accords well with the testimonies of Landa and Herrera as to persons, places, events, and sequencing (Tozzer 1941).

The architectural continuities betwen Chichen Itza and Mayapan are manifest (Tozzer 1957: 68; Proskouriakoff 1962: 132–39). Important differences exist, however, and Mayapan shows at least as many similarities to the east coast architectural tradition as to that of Chichen. Nonetheless, a derivative relationship between the two centers is certain.

Ceramics suggest a similar situation; the combined Hocaba-Tases assemblage of Mayapan shows strong modal and typological linkages to the Chichen Itza Sotuta complex despite the surprisingly limited recognition of this fact over the years (see, however, Smith 1971: 253–56). In addition to many general formal and stylistic ties, close affinities exist between the cream Kukula and slate Dzitas, red Mama-Panabchen and red Dzibiac, and the Fine Orange Matillas and Fine Orange Silho groups (Smith 1971: 15–100; figs. 11–56). The Mayapan assemblage can be linked as well to ceramic traditions of the Puuc Hills and the East Coast, but the possibility of a Sotuta connection is strong.

The apparent attractiveness of the Paradigm 2 scenario is diminished somewhat by the serious inconsistencies involving both the postconquest literary accounts and the preconquest epigraphic data that its acceptance assumes. These are particularly obtrusive with respect to the interrelationships of Kakupacal, the Itza in general, the Cocom, "Mayapan," "Chichen Itza," and "Chakanputun/Champoton." Either the self-contradictory prognostic recountings of the Chilam Balam chronicles and the self-serving accounts of the early Spanish *relaciones* must be resolved or they must be adjudged worthless. One cannot excoriate such sources as quasi-historical and simplistic on one page of a paper and then employ them in any explanatory manner several pages later.

The Paradigm 2 scenario would also place the principal Itza occupation at Chichen during preplumbate (i.e., pre-10.4.0.0.0) times. Were the Tutul Xiu the Katun 1 Ahau conquerors of Chichen Itza, as suggested, they could easily have been responsible for the introduction of this tradeware. As Lincoln (1982, present volume) has documented, plumbate was not unknown at the Xiu center, Uxmal.

Paradigm 3

This total-overlap paradigm assumes a Maya-Christian calendrical correlation at 11.3.0.0.0. My reassessment of the conjunctive archaeological and literary data pertaining to the late preconquest cultural history of Campeche, Yucatan, and northern Quintana Roo was inspired largely by the suggestions of Arlen F. Chase concerning an 11.3.0.0.0 correlation of the Maya and Christian calendars. The principal attraction of this correlation from my perspective is its resolution of the "overlap question" (Ball 1979a). By shifting the Gregorian equivalent of any Initial Series date 256 years forward in time, it neatly eliminates the gap between about A.D. 950/1000 and 1200 and makes contemporary the traditionally distinguished Terminal Classic and Early Postclassic periods.

Some, but not all, of the locative quandaries discussed above are resolved by use of an 11.3.0.0.0 correlation. Those remaining can be dealt with as already described. Probably the most serious obstacle to this alternative's ready acceptance is its incompatibility with the extant Classic and Postclassic radiocarbon determinations. From the Northern Zone, the Balankanche dates can be interpreted as fitting (and verifying) the Paradigm 3 scenario, but few others complement them, and I remain uncertain about its validity.[14]

In his own contibution to this book, Chase details the arguments supporting a correlation at 11.3.0.0.0 and offers a revised reconstruction of Terminal Classic–Postclassic cultural history. I believe this reconstruction is flawed by a number of serious inconsistencies with respect to both the limited relevant stratigraphic and epigraphic data from the North and the comfortable meshing of these with the pertinent literary data. In its place I offer what I believe to be a considerably more acceptable alternative. The following presentation returns to the format used in outlining the Paradigm 1 scenario.

(ca. A.D.)

918	Itza arrive in Yucatan and establish a center of major socioceremonial and political importance at Chichen Itza.
935	Mayapan established as a settlement center of minor importance (by the Cocom?).
948	New cycle (*may*) "seated" at Chichen Itza, which is

	thus recognized as the premier (Itza?) socioceremonial (and political?) center on the northern plains.
986–1006	The Tutul Xiu arrive in Yucatan. Uxmal established as their paramount socioceremonial and political center. "League of Mayapan" formed by the Uxmal Xiu, Chichen Itza Itza, and Mayapan Cocom(?) (but cf. Chase, this volume).
1145	Chichen Itza destroyed as a major political power and socioceremonial center. Its Itza(?) lords emigrate southward.
1128 +	"Chakanputun/Champoton," the town or the region, occupied by southward-moving individuals from Chichen Itza.
1184–1204	"Chakanputun/Champoton" lost to the Itza.
1243	"Chichen Itza" reoccupied by Itza from "Chakanputun/Champoton."
1263	Rise of Mayapan and the Cocom to political ascendancy on the northern plains.
1450	Chichen Itza again assaulted (by the Mayapan Cocom) and abandoned by the Itza.
1451	Mayapan destroyed as a political power and abandoned by its ruling families.
(1451)	(Uxmal possibly abandoned by the Xiu for "Mani": see A. Chase, this volume.)

In evaluating the foregoing scenario, the reader should keep in mind several archaeological-epigraphic data correlates. First, the Balankanche Cave shrine and its radiocarbon-dated ceremonial utilization equate precisely with the inferred time of Chichen Itza's recognition as the principal center of Itza ceremonial activities. Next, the Kakupacal-associated inscriptions known from Chichen terminate in the A.D. 1145–equivalent 1 Ahau. Both Davoust (1980) and Kelley (1983) see these inscriptions as having been executed very near the end of Itza dynastic hegemony at the center. Finally, the archaeological sequence at the Cuidad Champoton site on the central-western Campeche coast fits the expectations of the scenario with reference to the "Chakanputun exile" episode (see Ruz L. 1969; Ball 1978, 1985a). In sum, Paradigm 3 ought not be too quickly dismissed.[15]

THE CAMPECHE POSTCLASSIC:
AN EXPLANATORY INTERPRETATION

It has been argued above and elsewhere (Ball 1974a, 1974b, 1977a; Rovner 1974, 1975b) that the central-eastern Campeche Xcocom archaeological assemblage is the product of that region's late-ninth–early-tenth-century occupation by displaced Itza Maya from the Northern Lowlands. This now seems reasonably certain. What the Itza Maya were doing there and why is not known.

Roughly 1,150 maritime kilometers separate the mouth of the Río Nuevo and Guarixes, Isla Carmen, by the shortest circumpeninsular route. Only 340 overland kilometers separate these same points by an easily negotiable transpeninsular route passing near Becan. Using available "best possible" estimates (see Adams 1978), I would set the round-trip averages for these alternatives at 32–34 days (circumpeninsular) and 20–28 days (transpeninsular), discounting seasonal weather factors. Adams (1978) also has considered the trade-offs involved in overland vs. maritime haulage, and his findings suggest that the overland Bahía de Chetumal–Laguna de Términos route would have been a viable alternative to the circumpeninsular one. This possibility has not been systematically investigated, but has been suggested by several authors (e.g., Rovner 1975a; Ball 1977a). In its light, let us again review the material record left by the Xcocom occupation.

What might be designated the "urban component" of the Xcocom archaeological complex has been asserted to consist of two successive facets (Ball 1974b, 1977a; Rovner 1974, 1975b). Recently, however, Charles E. Lincoln (1982, this volume) has argued very convincingly that early and late Xcocom actually represent two somehow otherwise differentiated but entirely synchronous subcomplexes.[16]

As indicated above, the clearest and most precise ceramic ties of Xcocom are with assemblages found to the west and east of central-eastern Campeche. This is true whether qualitative or quantitative measures of nearness are employed, the most numerous and closest correspondences linking the Becan-Chicanna complex to those of Guarixes (Isla Carmen) and Aventura (Bahía de Chetumal). These correspondences are limited, however, to ceramic units best characterized as tradewares, finewares, or other exotica. Ties do not seem to exist among the domestic and utility plainware assemblages of the three locales. Unusually high percentages of the more exotic materials do serve to link them, however.

Somewhat looser, more generalized ties link the Xcocom domestic ceramic and lithic assemblages to the Northern Lowlands, but since these ties cannot yet be precisely defined, the question of Xcocom–Northern Zone affiliations is still open.

How do the urban Xcocom subcomplexes differ in composition? Are these differences significant? Urban Xcocom subcomplex a (formerly "early facet" Xcocom) is defined by the occurrence of Balancan-Altar (Z-Y) group Fine Orange pottery; elaborate gouged-incised, molded-carved, and modeled decoration; and the absence of Tohil-group Plumbate pottery. Urban Xcocom subcomplex-b ("late facet" Xcocom) collections are distinguished by the presence of Tohil-group Plumbate and the absence of all subcomplex-a diagnostics.

Rovner (1974, 1975b) has described comparable distinctions between the lithic assemblages of the two subcomplexes. A predominance of Campeche coarse-grained cherts worked into implements and points typical of the pre-Toltec Maya lowlands and the southern Mexican plateau (Oaxaca and Puebla) characterizes subcomplex a. A larger and more diverse inventory of points and implements worked from fine-grained dark brown chert of probable Belizean origin is associated with subcomplex b. Other subcomplex-b stone items included basalt manos and bark beaters as well as several celts and palette fragments of polished serpentine (Rovner 1975b; Taschek n.d.).

Obsidian blade fragments and debitage occur in both subcomplex a and subcomplex b deposits, but recent characterization studies suggest a strong positive correlation between subcomplex-a deposits and obsidian originating in Central Mexico and at the Highland Guatemala "western route" source, El Chayal (Rovner 1981). Subcomplex-b deposits appear to lack obsidian from these sources, containing instead obsidian from the "eastern route" quarries at Ixtepeque, Guatemala (Rovner 1981).

To summarize, urban Xcocom subcomplex a is distinguished by the presence of gulf coastal–Mexican and "western obsidian route" exotica in association with Xcocom general pottery. Subcomplex b, in contrast, comprises a mixture of Xcocom general wares and items primarily of Caribbean–Central American or "eastern route" origin. The overall ceramic and lithic compositions of the two subcomplexes as well as their recorded depositional contexts strongly imply their coexistence at Becan and Chicanna (see Rovner 1975b; Lincoln 1982, this volume). Individual subcomplex and combined assemblage features indicate considerable interaction between Xcocom-phase Becan, Guarixes to its west, and Aventura to its east, but they also show clear differences in the domestic utility wares at these three sites.

I suggest that the Becan locality functioned as an inland entrepôt during the Early Postclassic Period, and that urban Xcocom subcomplexes a and b are the archaeological reflections of this role and of the correlative arrival and interchange at Becan of goods moving eastward and westward across the narrow base of the peninsula. The zone possesses the two locational criteria suggested by Rathje and Sabloff (1975: 7) to be typical of most trading centers and also reveals the severely restricted local retail distribution pattern that generally characterizes them. What leakage of freight did occur was in the form of damaged goods or fragments thereof and was concentrated in the refuse of reoccupied architectural complexes. On-floor *de facto* (Schiffer 1976: 33–34) and use-related (Sharer and Ashmore 1979: 87) primary-context deposits typically contain materials characterizing them as pertaining to urban Xcocom subcomplex a or b. Off-terrace, transposed (Sharer and Ashmore 1979: 87) primary deposits inevitably include both Caribbean and Gulf Coast articles.

Several quite different movement-interaction patterns might be inferred from the data, but I personally favor a schema in which Becan was a stationary facilitator for trade between southern Gulf Coast and Caribbean principals.

The on-floor *de facto* primary context of so many Xcocom deposits suggests an abrupt end to that phase together with rapid abandonment of the locality and no subsequent reoccupation. When settlers did once again enter the region several centuries later, it was as pioneering refugees withdrawing from the demands of invading foreign colonialists (Ball 1985b).

Who controlled the Early Postclassic Becan entrepôt and why, I submit, is documented in the Chilam Balam chronicles. When the lords of "Chichen Itza" emigrated southward following their Katun 1 Ahau loss of power in the north, there was far more purpose and direction to their travel than has generally been assumed. Their aim was "the road of Champoton"—the traditional overland transpeninsular route providing a realistic alternative to the "lost" circumpeninsular one. The commercial viability of this route is documented incontrovertibly by the contents of Xcocom refuse deposits. Its competitive efficacy is equally well documented, I suggest, in the necessity for its destruction perceived by the Itza followers of Kakupacal.

For a short but significant interval during the late ninth and early tenth centuries, the principal commercial route between the southern Gulf Coast and Caribbean Central America lay across the base of the Yucatan Peninsula via Becan. Its eventual failure might have resulted from any of several factors, including in particular (a) deliberate interruption of the route by an economic competitor, (b) strangulation of the route by the success of a circumpeninsular alternative, (c) abandonment of the route upon its becoming strategically unnecessary in political terms, assuming that it in fact was economically less attractive than its maritime alternative.

As I read them, the Books of Chilam Balam appear to support alternative (a) or possibly (b), but (c) should also be kept in mind pending further research.

When the yala Itza "lost the road of Champoton," what they in fact lost was control over the overland route that had made them effective mercantile competitors to Kakupacal's Itza in the lucrative trade between Central Mexico and Central America. The experience was traumatic, and was so recorded in the prophetic traditions. There followed an eventual yala Itza retrenchment in the North; the eventual conclusion of an alliance of convenience involving them, the Chichen Itza, and the Uxmal Xiu, and ultimately, their violent political subversion of the Chichen Itza and recapture of the circumpeninsular maritime route linking Central America and the Mexican Highlands.

The foregoing interpretation would be accommodated most comfortably either by Paradigm 1 as proposed, or by Paradigm 3 in conjunction with some locative adjustments. Paradigm 2 does not really allow for such a reconstruction without considerable distortion of data; in my opinion, it actually produces more complications than anything else.

Acceptance of Paradigm 3 with some locative changes alters the absolute chronology of events but is not otherwise disruptive. Acceptance of this paradigm without any locative adjustments, however, opens up the possibility of an entirely different sequence of events, one directly involving the central-western Campeche coast.

The interpretive effects of a paradigm change on the archaeological record of late preconquest coastal Campeche are easy to specify. Its explanatory consequences remain to be determined, however. I have shown elsewhere (Ball 1985a) that the greatest single problem involving this record of which we are currently aware concerns an apparent gap in the archaeological sequences of the western Campeche–eastern Tabasco coastal plain extending from approximately A.D. 950 or 1000 to approximately A.D. 1200 or 1250. Paradigm 3 would eliminate this gap by shifting the Balancan-Altar Fine Orange–associated Jonuta complex and related assemblages forward in time from their present ca. A.D. 750–1000 slot to ca. A.D. 1000–1250 without displacing those assemblages currently dated to ca. A.D. 1200 and later.

It is interesting that the known archaeological record of Ciudad Champoton fits the Itza peregrination scenario that seems most likely if an 11.3.0.0.0 correlation is correct (see Ruz L. 1969; Ball 1978, 1985a). In this case, the "Chakanputun" referred to in the chronicles would have been Champoton, the town, rather than Champoton, the region, and Itza occupational history would have had to progress as follows: "?"/⟶/Chichen Itza/⟶/Champoton/⟶/Mayapan. Serious inconsistencies involving the persons, places, groups, and event sequences denoted in the postconquest literary and preconquest epigraphic sources would remain, however.

Paradigms 1 and 2 would close the gap by adjusting the traditionally ascribed limits of pre-1000 and post-1200 assemblages upward or downward to overlap. Unfortunately, the nature and extent of adjustments required remain uncertain on the basis of available data.

Any of the three paradigms would link the Balancan–Altar–Silho group–associated assemblages of the Gulf-Coast Jonuta horizon (Berlin 1956; Ball 1985a) and the Matillas-Cunduacan group-associated ones of the Cintla (Ball 1985a). These now are believed to have been separated by about 150 to 250 years, and so to have had little if any meaningful relationshp to each other. This belief is probably wrong, and I urge its critical testing and rejection.

CONCLUSION

The foregoing essay has examined the archaeology and cultural history of Postclassic Period Campeche in terms of several long-unquestioned assumptions that I believe no longer to be tenable and has suggested a number of alternatives to them. Treatment has been selective because of the constraints of the available data and of space. One important issue I have not addressed is the kinds of archaeological data needed to test each of the paradigms.

What I have attempted to do is to regenerate appreciation for the tremendous wealth of historical as well as cultural information concerning the preconquest Maya preserved in the bountiful literature of the Colonial Period. Although it is not to be abstracted easily or used without caution, it is there.

It has also been my intent to demonstrate the importance of accurate historical reconstructions in the study of cultural processes in complex prehistoric societies. For example, when archaeologists state that two typologically dissimilar ceramic spheres equate with and reflect the politico-economic activities of two competing social systems—or, worse, polities—they are making unwarranted assumptions since the correlations between ceramic units, ceramic systems, or other material classes and human sociobehavioral units are neither easily nor reliably defined. I believe that an understanding of *what* happened in the past and *why* what happened did so is to be found through the questioning and discarding of such assumptions and meticulous reconstructive research.

Finally, I hope that my arguments will force some scholars to consider seriously the interpretive constraints of our current operational paradigm, the potentially fruitful effects of a paradigm change, and the possible significance of the recurring major inconsistencies between the growing Terminal Classic/Postclassic Lowland Maya data base and our current interpretative paradigm. "If the wine is sour, throw it out!"

NOTES

1. The rather unparochial thoughts expressed in the foregoing essay owe their genesis to many long hours of talk and argument with a relatively small number of intellectually unfettered colleagues. Chief among these have been my wife, Jennie, and my friend Arlen Chase. Others whose ideas have contributed to or served as constructive irritants in its writing include Charles Lincoln and David H. Kelley. While also holding forth on a variety of other pertinent topics at the family dinner table, Dr. Richard F. Taschek provided some genuinely invaluable insights into the nature and effects of paradigm shifts in the hard sciences which I have incorporated in the final sections of this paper. Finally, Mrs. Barbara Schloss of the SDSU Anthropology Department deciphered and typed the manuscript, for which I am indescribably

appreciative. To all of the foregoing, my thanks. To all of them as well, my apologies for the way in which their thoughts have herein been mangled, reshaped, and expressed. Responsibility for the hybrid end product is, of course, entirely and exclusively mine.

2. The Postclassic Campeche archaeological data have been presented in both synoptic and detailed form on several recent occasions and are not presented here. In addition to those sources already cited, the reader is referred to Adams 1977: 90–91; Ball 1947b, 1977a, 1977b, 1985b; Ball and Rovner 1972; Rovner 1974, 1975b, 1981; Thomas 1981.

3. Throughout this paper Gregorian dates separated by the word "or" represent the alternative 11.16 and 11.3 equivalents of Initial Series positions.

4. A situation quite closely paralleling that discussed here is described by Sanders, Parsons, and Santley (1979: 137–38) with reference to "Tollan," Tula, Teotihuacan, and Cholula in the Mexican Highlands.

5. Throughout this paper, place-names not set off in any manner refer to sites or regions as they currently are known. Those enclosed by quotation marks represent designations as given in the historical or traditional literature. Italicized names stand for the places I believe were actually being referred to by the literary sources when their designations differ from those by which sites or regions are known today.

6. Not all documentary sources controvert a Cocom–Chichen Itza linkage. The decidedly pragmatic Valladolid Lawsuit of 1618 describes the selection of "a certain Cocom to rule in Chichen Itza. . . . and those of the island of Cozumel were subject to him; and from there [Chichen Itza] they passed to the province of Sotuta, where they were when the conquerors came. . . ." Landa further records that when "they conspired to put Cocom to death . . . killing at the same time all his sons, . . . They sacked his house and took away the lands which he had in cacao" (Tozzer 1941: 36–37). The only cacao groves known to us on the sixteenth-century Northern Plains were located in the province of Cupul, within which the ruins of Chichen Itza are situated.

7. The prophetic text editions used were those of Edmonson (1982), Craine and Reindorp (1979), and Roys (1967). These were supplemented as possible by piecemeal literal translations of isolated relevant text portions. In referencing this material, the following abbreviations are used: Chilam Balam of Tizimin: CBT; of Mani: CBM; of Chumayel: $CBC_{1,2,}or_3$.

8. Among the unresolved episodes are the Hunac Ceel adventures, possibly in fact involving two or more chronologically discrete sets of persons and places, and the entire event sequence following the Katun 8 Ahau destruction of "Chichen Itza" as recorded in the CBM and CBT.

9. David P. Henige (1974) has described the distorting effects of comparable processes on the chronohistorical structure of African oral traditions. In fact, they would appear to be anything but uncommon among most bodies of material belonging to this genre.

10. Full referencing and presentation of the radiocarbon record from the

Northern Lowlands is provided in this source, to which the interested reader is referred.

11. As I see it, the league most probably comprised an intersocietal mercantile conglomerate, its primary impetus being economic. Edmonson (1982: xvi) has argued that it represented an Itza-Xiu socioceremonial compact with ritual chronology as its chief concern. The Maya themselves may have perceived it in more pragmatic sociopolitical terms with the termination of endemic intergroup warfare as the immediate goal.

12. Admissible source references to the establishment or formal recognition of Chichen Itza as the premier northern Itza socioceremonial and political center in this case include: CBT: "8 Ahau had been revealed; Chichen Itza had been manifested. . ."; CBC_1: "6 Ahau was when the discovery of Chichen Itza occurred." CBC_2: "4 Ahau was the Katun when they sought and discovered Chichen Itza." CBM: "4 Ahau, 2 Ahau, 13 Ahau: 60 years they governed in Ziyancaan. During these years, Chichen Itza was discovered."

13. In this connection, Kelley (1968: 262) reminds us that the oft referred to linguistic ineptitude of the Itza actually reflects the views of the Mexican-oriented Xiu: "The word which they use to say that the Itza speak badly is . . . a Nahua word. . . . I would suggest . . . that the description of the Itza as 'foreigners' is from the viewpoint of the Mexican intruders, . . . the Xiu. . . . I would also suggest that the original language which the Itza spoke badly was Nahua and that they spoke it badly because their native tongue was some Mayan language. . . ."

14. Three corrected dates from Mayapan (A.D. 1235 ± 120; 1300 ± 70; 1525 ± 135) and one from Tulum (A.D. 1080 ± 70) also support the 11.3 paradigm, but work equally well with Paradigms 1 and 2.

15. In addition to the scenarios discussed, at least one other viable but significantly different reconciliation of the relevant literature and archaeological data is possible. Its elaboration and discussion are sufficiently complex and divergent from the reconstructions suggested, however, as to require a presentation elsewhere. Here I will simply note that it involves acceptance of an 11.16.0.0.0 correlation of the Maya and Christian calendars; establishment or formal recognition of Chichen Itza by Kakupacal and his followers in A.D. 866 (Ball 1979b); a heyday for Chichen Itza from the late ninth through mid-to-late tenth centuries; assignment of the 1 Ahau abandonment of Chichen Itza to the twelfth century (A.D. 1125–1145); effective "Chichen" Itza occupational control of the Champoton region during the late twelfth century; establishment or formal recognition of the Ichpaa-Mayapan center by former occupants of Chichen Itza or Chichen Itza and Champoton in the early thirteenth century; and final destruction of Mayapan in A.D. 1441 (8 Ahau). Substantial overlap of the major occupational episodes at Chichen Itza and the Puuc centers is assumed in this reconstruction.

Both the archaeological and epigraphic data and the pertinent literature support such an event sequence, although as with the suggested Paradigm 2

and 3 scenarios, it entails some seemingly major inconsistencies and contradictions involving these. Further, its acceptance makes the ostensibly straightforward chronological, cultural, and historical position of the central eastern
Campeche Xcocom complex highly ambiguous. I plan to discuss this alternative and its archaeological testing at length in a future paper.

16. Irvin Rovner recognized and suggested the probable contemporaneity
of the two urban Xcocom subcomplexes as early as 1971. He was dissuaded
from pursuing this possibility, however, by my own convictions concerning
the chronological relationships of Balancan-/-Altar (Z/Y) Fine Orange pottery
and other Terminal Classic horizon markers on the one hand and Tohil
Plumbate on the other. In his dissertation, Rovner (1975b: 219) nonetheless
maintained that "the limited distribution of early fact material suggests it is
not a true chronological facet but an intrusive group occupying specific
structures during the course of the Xcocom phase. Late facet Xcocom material
in many respects is derived from Chintok material and at Chicanna is intermingled with Chintok indicating a direct Chintok to late facet Xcocom sequence. In this sense, late facet Xcocom probably wholly overlaps early facet
Xcocom in time. . . ."

12
Terminal Classic Lowland Maya: Successes, Failures, and Aftermaths

DAVID A. FREIDEL

Southern Methodist University

THE MAYA DARK AGE

Was Lowland Maya civilization tragically "flawed"? Subordination of this vast region to the expanding imperium out of highland Mexico at the time of the Spanish conquest is undeniable (Willey, this volume). Despite the impressive florescence of Lowland civilization in the north during and following the great collapse in the south, that regional catastrophe lends a certain inevitability to the clearly lower level of social organization in the Contact Period. Nearly a decade has passed since this perennial issue in Maya studies last underwent programmatic analysis (Culbert 1973b). If the Maya evolutionary trajectory was flawed, new information and research perspectives suggest that it was flawed in ways not considered in the first School of American Research Advanced Seminar on the Maya.

My position in this speculative overview of Late Maya civilization involves three premises that are amenable to field investigation. First, the southeastern tropical lowlands of Mesoamerica, and the Maya Lowlands in particular, were a primary source region for commercial agricultural commodities used in the overall Mesoamerican interaction sphere. Second, prior to the advent of conquest states whose govern-

409

ments relied on the tribute they exacted, the political economies of Mesoamerica were based upon control of redistribution and local exchange through commodities that served as currencies. These goods were either labor intensive or obtained in volume by means of administered trade over long distances, or both (Dalton 1975; Polanyi, Arensberg, and Pearson 1957). In other words, these were administered economies. Third, the shared economic organization of Mesoamerican polities through these currencies encouraged the long-term development of Highland-Lowland symbiosis (Sanders 1956), which maintained the flow of commodities from regions of abundance to regions of scarcity. Viewing the Maya Lowlands as part of the Mesoamerican interaction sphere (MacNeish 1978) can help explain the pronounced fluctuations and final decline of this civilization.

SOME OLD FLAWS

For many years the ancient Maya were thought to be swidden farmers whose agricultural production was aimed primarily at local consumption (cf. Adams 1977 passim). This premise made the possibility of substantial surplus for trade and for large-scale economy seem unlikely (Webb 1973). It also made the vision of a precarious and impractical economy shored up by theological maxims and luxury trade seem a reasonable one (Sanders and Price 1968). Harrison and Turner (1978), Adams, Brown, and Culbert (1981), and others (Freidel and Scarborough 1982; Sabloff and Freidel 1975) are well on the way to rendering this postulated flaw obsolete.

From the Late Preclassic Period (350 B.C.–A.D. 1) onward, there is now clear evidence of intensive agriculture in the Lowlands. Whole vessels dating to the Late Preclassic Period were intentionally placed in a main canal surrounding the site of Cerros in Belize, and there is evidence in the form of pottery deposits, C-14 dates, and overall plan (Scarborough 1980, 1983) to show that the entire waterworks there dates to the Preclassic Period. Moreover, recent palynological analysis (Crane n.d.) has documented the presence of domesticated cotton— a traditional lowland commercial product—in the Cerros deposits.

The research of Adams and his colleagues (1981) and of Turner and Harrison (1981) and others indicates that the Maya were practicing intensive agriculture on a scale rivaling any other region in Mesoamerica (B. L. Turner 1983: 31). Regulation of land tenure and ag-

410

ricultural production is extensively documented in other sectors of the Lowlands where dryland farming is the only practical technique: around Becan (Turner 1974), on the east coast of Quintana Roo (Barrera 1985), on the west coast of Yucatan (Vlcek, Garza T. de González, and Kurjack 1978), on Cozumel Island (Sabloff and Freidel 1975). This last system is definitely a Late Postclassic phenomenon. Agricultural intensification, then, spans Maya civilization and the Lowlands (B. L. Turner 1983).

The discovery of intensification of agriculture combined with data on variable soil regimes (Sanders 1973, 1977) reveals a much more complex and diversified picture of agricultural production than was previously envisioned. No doubt swidden techniques were always employed as a complement to these other means of production, but the various strategies would have had different liabilities and potential in the face of such factors as drought, flood, and parasite load. A complicated food economy based upon redistributive institutions seems likely to have operated throughout Maya prehistory (cf. Culbert in press), not just at the outset of civilization as postulated by Sanders (1977), Webster (1977), and Ball (1977c).

Not only does the existence of intensive agriculture enhance the likelihood of political regulation of subsistence production (Sanders and Price 1968; Adams and Smith 1981), it also suggests the strong potential for surplus production. Commercial agriculture is clearly present in the Late Postclassic Period (Scholes and Roys 1948), and in light of current data there is every reason to believe that it was present earlier. In Tabasco, some Contact Period communities chose to import their food and devote themselves full-time to the production of cacao (Scholes and Roys 1948). Recent research at the extraordinarily dense communities of Komchen (Andrews V 1981) and Chunchicmil (Vlcek, Garza T. de González, and Kurjack 1978), both located on marginal land near coastal salt beds, suggests the possibility of such intercommunity food exchange in earlier periods.

Beyond the prospect of interdependency between Lowland Maya communities, there is the whole question of commercial production for foreign export. The Late Postclassic and Contact Period Maya, despite their "decadence," participated in a thriving trade in salt, cacao, cotton, dyes, feathers, and other products destined for distant markets in Mexico. The Yucatec of this time were famous all over Mesoamerica for their textiles (Roys 1972), and every Classic artistic medium cele-

411

brates the even greater mastery of earlier Maya weavers. The volume of exotics found in Lowland sites attests to sustained trade with Highland societies throughout the development of Maya civilization. On the face of it, there is no reason to suppose that Preclassic commodities differed substantially from those found in the Contact Period.

Related to the question of export trade is the matter of resource redundancy and the absence of a clear impetus for government management of the distribution of goods. Rathje (1971) suggested that salt, among other things, might have been a necessity requiring high-volume redistribution. A. P. Andrews (1983) has presented convincing data to support this notion based upon average requirements, population estimates, and productive potential for the various sources of salt.

Mayanists have at last discovered evidence of industrial stone-working operations in a Lowland context (the Belizean site of Colha [Hester, Eaton, and Shafer 1980]) that are analogous in function, if not in scale, to the justly famous obsidian fields and centers of the Highlands (Charlton 1978). The distribution of Colha chert still needs to be plotted out in the Lowlands and beyond, but it is clear that already in the Preclassic Period and continuing thereafter, this localized resource was of regional importance to the Maya. The size and intensity of the works registers the existence of a complicated and sustained network of distribution and consumption. There is no more reason to suppose that Colha is unique than that the industrial stone-working sites at one Highland source are unique.

A final old flaw is the notion that Lowland Maya economy, as an aspect of the larger economy of civilized Mesoamerica, was from the beginning dominated by the strategies, demands, and destinies of polities in the Highlands of Mexico. This view underlies C. Jones's (1979) postulate that successful Lowland polities, such as Tikal, flourished through the control of trade that crossed the Lowlands on the way to other regions. It is also behind Webb's (1973) suggestions that the Lowlands served as a relatively passive market for Highland imports. Tikal no doubt did control important trade with Highland polities, especially with Highland Guatemala, but not because it lacked local products or because interior trade was more efficient (Freidel 1978). Tikal and other great Peten centers, beginning with El Mirador in the Late Preclassic (Matheny 1980), are surrounded by vast swamps. We

412

know that such swamps were used for intensive agriculture in Belize and Quintana Roo (Harrison 1982). There is every reason to suspect that the florescence of the Peten Maya was due to, rather than in spite of, their swampy environs. If we combine the evidence for surplus production for export from the Contact Period with the manifestly greater political power and hierarchical organization of the Classic society, then it is only realistic to envision trade as controlled and manipulated at both ends. The question is, how and why had such long-distance economic organization developed?

MESOAMERICAN POLITICAL ECONOMY

An explanation for the role of long-distance trade in Mesoamerica requires an overarching model for the relationships between localized economy and extralocal export and import. Several scholars, most recently Adams and Smith (1981), have argued that in the Maya case the relationship between the manipulation of scarce, precious, or labor-intensive goods and the control of the bulk of economic means in agricultural production was a tenuous one at best. The increasing evidence for large-scale definition of land in the Lowlands through terraces, walled plots, and raised fields does indeed enhance the prospects for political manipulation of agricultural production (B. L. Turner 1983: 33). Similar dynamics are evident elsewhere in Mesoamerica. In practical terms, however, ownership of the land must be expressed in control of the products of the land in order to be a political force. One such expression is centralized storage. The evidence for the display of ownership in the form of centralized storage facilities remains problematic in the best of cases, such as Teotihuacan (Millon 1973), and it is certainly not a generally recognized feature of Mesoamerican central places. There are plenty of permanent facilities which might have served such a function, both in the Maya Lowlands and elsewhere. Yet archaeological corroboration for storage function has not been forthcoming.

Redistribution along the lines of the "palace economy" model developed, among other places, in substantive economics (Dalton 1975) does not seem to have been widespread in Mesoamerica before the rise of the conquest state. Dispersed storage of surplus, and indeed generally dispersed production of commodities within households, sug-

413

gests that the elites of Mesoamerica concentrated their efforts on control of the mode of distribution—that is, raw materials and finished products—more than on control of the mode of production.

One form of redistribution, tribute, is certainly a feature of Mesoamerican political economy. In the Maya Lowlands, the residents of Mayapan were maintained in part by such tribute (Roys 1962), and Maya lords were generally sustained by tribute in the forms of such labor services as the cultivation of some fields and the refurbishment of homes. Sustaining tribute of this kind, however, can be given directly by a constituent to a patron and requires no elaborate organization. Moreover, as reported ethnohistorically, the elite demanded relatively small amounts of tribute from the populace. Coerced tribute became an important political force with the rise of the Triple Alliance (Brumfiel n.d.), but with the possible exception of the Chichen Itza state, there is little evidence to support coercion as a major economic force in Maya civilization. How far back in time the conquest state goes in the Mexican Highlands remains unresolved; but we might expect massive tribute, like direct ownership of the means of production, to be evidenced in centralized storage facilities, as it is in Tenochtitlan (Simpson 1966: 155). In the last analysis, tribute is a form of economic exploitation that presupposes the prior existence of other institutions to organize production and distribution (Brumfiel n.d.)—institutions responsible for the surplus that a tribute system preys upon. The question is, What infrastructure does tribute build upon?

The archaeological record in Mesoamerica does not show that scarce, precious, or labor-intensive goods circulated only among the elites. To be sure, these goods are found in rich tombs and offerings in vastly greater quantities than in other contexts. Yet such things pervade the record from the top to the bottom of the social hierarchy. Perishables such as cacao, salt, and cotton are only known historically, but they, too, circulate throughout societies (Blanton and Feinman 1984: 679). We cannot allow ourselves to be impressed by their scarcity (for they were quite intentionally scarce) into thinking that they were ever economically superfluous (see Drennan 1984). These goods provide a material link between the household and the palace, the village and the center. It is only logical to presume that such links were central to Mesoamerican political and social cohesion. If these goods served as currencies in earlier periods, as most of them did at the time of contact (see Millon 1981), they would have provided a practical means of controlling a very much wider range of goods and services connected to them by equivalency. Monopoly over such currencies would provide significant control over the mode of distribution. And if control of the mode of distribution was central to Mesoamerican political economy, then governments would have been as concerned with the places and events as with the means of exchange.

EXCHANGE PLACES AND EVENTS

Where we can clearly and indubitably see Mesoamerican governments controlling economic means is in the massive labor invested in public pyramids and plazas. No doubt these were devout people, but the high concentration and organization of labor expressed in these facilities suggests that they were as important to the economy as to state religion (Rathje 1975). The logical facility for carrying out major exchange events in Mesoamerica is the open plaza space found in every center. Central plazas are inextricably bound to the ritual life in the community, and pyramids display the cosmic underpinning of the political and social orders. There is no reason to think that there was a spatial or conceptual separation of these concerns from economic exchange.

Elsewhere (Freidel 1981b) I have postulated that the primary economic event in Maya civilization was the pilgrimage-fair, a regular and periodic gathering of locals and nonlocals in central places for purposes of religious celebrations and exchange. A similar connection of the religious, economic, and political dimensions of state organization has been postulated by Millon for Teotihuacan (1981). Although purely a theoretical construct, the pilgrimage-fair allows for the political manipulation of surplus when storage is dispersed through the management of commodity collection, scheduling of the exchange events, and direct supervision of the events themselves. The pilgrimage-fair is the kind of institution that necessarily integrates extralocal with local economy and presents what would normally be local redistribution in the guise of an encounter between polities. This brings us back to the issue of exchange equivalencies, or currencies, operating between as well as within polities.

415

EXCHANGE MEDIUMS AND THEIR FUNCTION

The kinds of money or valuables and the kinds of external trade that are employed in any economy are direct and sensitive expressions of the dominant internal mode or modes of transaction in that economy. (Dalton 1975: 92)

Dalton provides a full and stimulating discussion of currencies in nonmarket economies (1975), but both his thinking and that of Polanyi (1975) are predicated on the existence of redistribution by means of centralized storage. As a result, the distinctions and functions they propose do not easily fit the Mesoamerican case:

Primitive money, such as cowrie, twists of wire, iron hoes, and slabs of salt, consisted of divisible and relatively uniform objects used in ordinary commercial purchase and sale in the market sector of aboriginal economies in which variants of reciprocity and redistribution were usually more important modes of transaction. These primitive monies were usually confined to petty, marketplace transactions of foodstuffs and other ordinary consumption goods and small tools, whereas land, labor, and the bulk of livelihood were acquired in ways not requiring the transaction of primitive monies. (Dalton 1975: 97)

Dalton goes on to contrast the roles of primitive monies with those of primitive valuables and "treasure"—goods circulated among elites for purposes of maintaining status boundaries and displaying high-level political relationships. In the first place, it is well established that some currencies, such as cacao beans (Millon 1955), were pan-Mesoamerican in distribution at the time of the Spanish conquest and were exchangeable for a wide range of goods and services. The economic centrality of cacao currency, even to the tribute-based government of the Aztecs, is unequivocal. In the second place, the distinctions drawn by Dalton between monies, valuables, and "treasure" are significantly blurred in Mesoamerica. Imperishable materials used for currency, such as metal, greenstone, and red shell (Tozzer 1941: 80, 89, 90, 117, 231), were the same materials used to fashion valuables and "treasure." The great fungibility of the materials used as currencies in Mesoamerica, and their interconnection with other vital commodities, is well described by Landa:

The occupation to which they had the greatest inclination was trade, carrying salt and cloth and slaves to the lands of Ulua and Tabasco, exchanging all they had for cacao and stone beads which were their money; and with this

416

they were accustomed to buy slaves or other beads, because they were fine and good, which their chiefs wore as jewels in their feasts; and they had others made of certain red shells for money, and as jewels to adorn their persons; and they carried it in purses of net, which they had, and at their markets they traded in everything which there was in that country. . . . And the greatest number were cultivators and men who apply themselves to harvesting the maize and other grains, which they keep in fine underground places and granaries, so as to be able to sell (their crops) at the proper time. (Landa in Tozzer 1941: 94–96)

The gradations in size, quality, and workmanship in objects of greenstone and shell do not show the kinds of sharp breaks in archaeological assemblages that might denote the distinctions made by Dalton. Significantly, widespread circulation of these materials, among others, is well documented from the Preclassic Period onward. Rather than postulate some drastic change in value and function for such materials between the Contact Period and previous eras—a change for which there is no archaeological evidence—it is more reasonable to hypothesize that these imperishables, and perhaps others, functioned as exchange equivalencies in antiquity. Metal, although a late development in Mesoamerica, ranged from standard small axes and bells used for money through the exotic "treasure" of religious artifacts and state gifts (see Pagden 1971: 40–45).

The primary currency at the time of the conquest was a Lowland product, cacao, but it is clear that other Lowland commodities, while not specifically currencies, were highly strategic and fungible. When the Aztecs attempted to economically strangle Tlaxcala, the goods most focused upon were cotton and salt (Pagden 1971; Simpson 1966). Indeed, López de Gómara (Simpson 1966: 161), in describing the marketplace of the Aztecs, stipulates that cotton and salt were the most valuable goods, a curious statement in light of the gold, silver, and featherwork he proceeds to describe. Clearly he is referring to the high demand for, and exchangeability of, these goods. The same qualities would explain why cotton was a major tribute item in the Aztec state, for as Brumfiel (n.d.) notes, it is likely that cotton tribute mantles redistributed by the government were exchanged for other goods and services in the major markets. Cotton, like the imperishable currencies, could vary from plain and standard units to valuable items with woven designs to "treasure," embellished with feathers and furs.

Mesoamerican currencies, then, more closely approximate what

Dalton defines as "generalized money" as found typically in market economies than they do the "special purpose" monies typical of administered economies predicated on centralized storage and redistribution. Rather than acting as a minor component of economic control, Mesoamerican currencies were central because of their manifold functions: regulation of normal transactions through exchange equivalency, regulation of ritually necessary gift exchange and consumption, and regulation of status relationships through access to quality and quantity of commodities in demand throughout society. The main economic rationale for the exchange event, the motivation employed by governments to get people to collect surplus in the center at pilgrimage-fairs, was access to extralocal goods used in these many ways.

HIGHLAND-LOWLAND SYMBIOSIS

The primary currencies of Mesoamerica—cacao, jade, shell—were goods designed to travel over long distances. These substances were used as currencies because goods acquired by long-distance trade are easily monopolized by governments. The Contact Period situation, however, differs from that in earlier periods in two important ways, and hence can be misleading. First, the major currency was a Lowland product, cacao. Second, a major commodity and possible currency of earlier periods, obsidian, was no longer used as an exchange equivalency. These changes appear to coincide with the rise of conquest states in Mexico, but that argument is beside the point here. For the moment, note that major long-distance trade in Mesoamerica links Lowland areas producing primarily agricultural products used for currency with Highland areas producing primarily minerals used as currencies. The values of these items are not determined simply by scarcity, for in the regions of production these commodities were not necessarily scarce. It is a matter of high-volume production in some regions and controllable scarcity in others.

The goods used as currency were those amenable to mutually beneficial monopoly linking Highland and Lowland polities. Symbiosis of this kind characterizes the Mesoamerican interaction sphere throughout prehistory (MacNeish 1978), and no subregional civilization can be understood in economic isolation. The cultural strategies employed to sustain symbiosis over long distances and between societies varying widely in social organization and world view are of major theoretical

418

interest. In this essay I will focus on the development of one particular social means to the objective of symbiosis, a phenomenon I call the *cartel*.

CARTEL: PRELIMINARY DEFINITIONS

Long-distance trade in volume requires at least a mutual tolerance of cultural differences, a certain cosmopolitian sophistication. By Middle Classic times Mesoamerica witnessed the development of much more substantial relationships over distance. In the Maya area, Tikal and Kaminaljuyu have been focal points for examination of this issue. It has been suggested that Tikal constituted a secondary state under the aegis of Teotihuacan (Coggins 1975; Sanders and Price 1968; Webb 1973) by way of Kaminaljuyu. In light of the foregoing discussion, I suggest that the advantages and liabilities of these relationships worked in both directions: Kaminaljuyu and Teotihuacan depended as much on such relationships as did Tikal. What is significant is the nature and scope of cultural syncretism evinced in this network.

The impact of Mexican-style goods and symbols on the Lowland Maya has been much discussed. Actually, in terms of major public symbols such as *talúd-tablero* architecture, the Lowland Maya were the least affected of the civilized societies of Middle Classic Mesoamerica. The concentrated impact is on portable goods of the kind that would figure prominently in economic and ritual activities without suggesting major deviation from the sacred tenets that underwrite political power. The most dramatic affiliation is the marriage of a presumable foreigner, Curl Nose (Coggins 1975), into the royal dynasty of Tikal, a major departure from Lowland Maya sacred tenets. The primary affiliation appears to be between Tikal and Kaminaljuyu, and then through Kaminaljuyu to Teotihuacan (Brown 1977). Economically, this would be a southeastern Mesoamerican symbiosis between Maya Lowlands and Maya Highlands under the general aegis of the larger network dominated by Teotihuacan. Kaminaljuyu shows strong affiliation with the Mexican city and other allies in the gulf region.

This is an instance of a cartel relationship. By *cartel* I mean a symbiotic economic trade relationship in which there is an actual merging of political economies over distance. Merging occurs through the syncretism of the theological charters underwriting political policy, through the merging of the elite through intermarriage, and by means

419

of the creation of an overarching "superculture" binding at least elites and often whole societies into coherent totalities. As a means of insuring access to markets and resources, cartel is surely more effective than mutual tolerance of differences. What I am suggesting is that the well-recognized syncretism of the Middle Classic era is not the result of cultural imposition from any one polity, nor is it the reflection of haphazard adoption of foreign fashion; rather it reflects deliberate and selective merging of powerful icons to underwrite the establishment of political economies linking distant societies.

The advantages of cartels over trade relationships based upon mutual tolerance are stability and more enforceable monopoly. But if cartels are less vulnerable to the capriciousness of trading partners, they are more vulnerable to drastic changes in the polities with which they are allied. Willey (1974) underscored such vulnerability in his suggestion that the Tikal "hiatus" might be attributable to the Metepec-phase collapse at Teotihuacan and its subsequent repercussions at Kaminaljuyu. In my view, it is just as reasonable to propose that disruptions in cartel relationships extending out from Teotihuacan were instrumental in the collapse there.

CARTELS AND COLLAPSE

However the fates of Tikal and Teotihuacan are conjoined, it is clear that the sort of sociocultural symbiosis that might be symptomatic of cartels is well evinced by such Terminal Classic relationships as that between Puuc communities and Oaxaca/Puebla (Sharp 1973) and that between Chichen Itza and Tula (c.f. Andrews V 1979; Kubler 1975; Lincoln, this volume; Tozzer 1957). The precise nature of the sociocultural links between Maya and Mexican polities as such remains controversial. The chronological placement of Chichen Itza relative to the Puuc centers and Coba is not settled and is subject to various "overlap" models (Ball 1979b). In order to highlight the importance of this chronological issue, I will take a side and follow some of the cultural historical and theoretical implications for Terminal Classic Maya Lowlands and the subsequent periods.

Lincoln (this volume) has reviewed the ceramic, architectural, and settlement data germane to the overlap of Sotuta/"Toltec"/Modified Florescent developments with Cehpech/"Maya"/Florescent developments. I find his arguments persuasive to the effect that these generally reflect geographic syndromes rather than chronological phases. Among the data that can complement his argument is the general site plan at Chichen. Like several of the major Puuc communities (excluding, notably, Uxmal) Chichen Itza is laid out on a major north-south axis when the so-called "Toltec" center is included with the "Maya" districts (buildings) to the south. This axis is reified in *sacbeob*, as Lincoln notes. Not only is this site plan documented for such Puuc sites as Sayil and Kabah (Pollock 1980: 561), but it is postulated to occur—lacking *sacbeob*—in Terminal Classic Quirigua and other Southern Lowland sites (Ashmore n.d.).

Chase and Chase (1982) have suggested that Sotuta is contemporary with Terminal Classic materials in Belize; Robles and Andrews (this volume), argue similarly for contemporaneity between Coba and Chichen Itza in Terminal Classic times, or at least between Cehpech and Sotuta ceramics. In brief, there is a trend toward viewing the northern florescence and southern collapse as contemporary episodes. If this is the case, then Terminal Classic times witness a complex splitting of Lowland Maya destiny into success and failure. On the assumption that these events are interrelated, I will examine the northern success story as a possible avenue to better understanding the failure in the Southern Lowlands.

NORTH AND SOUTH: BRIEF BACKGROUND

The most pressing issue in Lowland Maya archaeology is the relationship between the histories and evolutionary developments of the Northern and Southern Lowlands. The apparent divergence in the Terminal Classic seems symptomatic of long-standing differences in culture and social organization in these subregions (Andrews IV 1965a), but these differences occur in a context of sustained and ill-understood affinities. Some contrasts, such as the natural environment of the northern plain versus the southern rain forest, are quite clear, but most of the significant contrasts register not in basic technology, demographics, or settlement patterns so much as in material culture reflecting cultural outlook and ethos, the rationale and expression of power. The differences in approach to public art and architecture, the use or non-use of free-standing stone monuments (Proskouriakoff 1950), the deployment of symbol systems on a variety of subsidiary mediums such as pottery, shell, and exotic stone are already documentable in the record—as are the affinities cross-cutting them. The underlying notion of what it was to be "civilized Maya" in the South has a distinctive, albeit related, expression in the North.

At this point, I will confine myself to some general observations of trends in the South and North that bear on the events of the Terminal Classic Period. First, public material symbols burst onto the Southern Lowland scene in the Late Preclassic Period (100 B.C.–A.D. 1) in the form of decorated pyramids (Freidel 1981b, 1983a). The well-investigated Preclassic community of Komchen lacks this political art (Andrews V 1981) and in fact appears to go into decline during this period. Nevertheless, a monumental stucco mask at Acanceh (Seler 1915) clearly falls into the Late Preclassic style of the South, and I suspect that there were several "salient" polities in the North that participated in the establishment of the basic cosmology underwriting hierarchical authority and royal power found in the South. During the Early Classic Period, the southern polities incorporate stelae and hieroglyphic writing into this political ethos as a complement to sculptured pyramids (Freidel and Schele 1982). The Early Classic is perhaps the least understood period in the North, but again there are indications of affinities with the South, in particular, the monumental "Kinich Ahau" masks at Izamal (Stephens 1843), the scattered occurrence of Early Classic Long Count dates at such sites as Oxkintok (lintel in Structure 3C6; Pollock 1980: 301), and the displaced stela at Tulum (Proskouriakoff 1950). Significantly, these elusive indications of affinity to the South are hardly more apparent than the affinities to Mexico registered in such buildings as the extraordinary one with stucco freize at Acanceh (Andrews IV 1965a) and Structure 612 at Dzibilchaltun with its talúd-tablero (Andrews V 1981: fig. 11.9).

Despite the paucity of data, there are reasons to believe that the Early Classic (Early Period I) witnessed a fundamental divergence between the South and the North in political religion as used to affirm complex social organization. In the South, the stela cult ushers in a direct focus on rulers and royal dynasty as the core of the political order. Religious art is diverted from the subject of "gods" as such to the relationship among sacred bloodlines, rulers, and these supernaturals. On pyramids, images of the "gods" take on human aspect during the Early Classic (beginning in the Protoclassic) and ultimately portray rulers, as on Structure N9-56 at Lamanai (Pendergast 1980 and personal communication). Given the human god-mask at Izamal, it seems likely that some polities in the North followed the trend more clearly documented in the South. In the South, however, decoration on pyramids shows a marked decline, particularly on substructures (W. Coe, personal communication), in the transition between Early and Late Classic times. This trend is accompanied by the general expansion of art in other mediums and the deployment of public symbolic statements on stelae and on less accessible parts of buildings, such as interiors, roof combs, and lintels. Essentially, the building as cosmic sculpture to be viewed from the exterior is gradually phased out in the South. The contrast with the North is here striking (and I use *North* to include the central peninsular region). Rather than being phased out, the sculptured building remains the single most important medium for symbolic statements pertaining to power and authority. Indeed, while individuals who might be discerned as rulers are a component of the symbolism, they are encompassed by a panoply of polymorphic imagery which can be viewed as generally expressing broad cosmic statements (c.f. Pollock 1980; Potter 1977). In brief, the Río Bec, Chenes, and Puuc architectural styles not only retain the original focus on the sculptured building, but persist in emphasizing general cosmology, a feature of the Late Preclassic Southern Lowlands. The Northern Maya do not harness buildings to the cult of the ruler and sacred bloodline in the pronounced fashion found in the South. The cosmology on these northern buildings appears to relate well to that expressed in the South, the same sorts of polymorphic entities are there, but the political implementation of religion is clearly distinctive. The sporadic, peculiar distribution of iconography—particularly on stelae—pertaining specifically to royal dynasty and to rulers in the North (Proskouriakoff 1950) need not reflect simpler political or social organization there. Instead, it may reflect religious schism and the perpetuation of a cosmology and theology in which sacred bloodlines are a relatively minor component rather than the central theme as in the Southern Lowlands.

There are some indications in site planning and architecture that Northern Lowlanders were more concerned with the religious affirmation of political entities than other ruling lines. No doubt the Southerners did not live by rulers alone; there must have been councils, officers, and ritual means of distributing authority (Freidel 1983b). Beyond such indirect expressions as the fourteen lords on the Bonampak murals (Miller 1980), the many visiting dignitarites found on

Classic painted pots, and the ritual advisers accompanying rulers on stelae and other monuments, it is difficult to find the rest of the Southern political structure in the art. Architecturally, the spatial separation usually seen in Southern sites of temples and pyramids, public buildings devoted to the cult of the ruler, from other buildings with interior space appropriate to the congregation of councils and courts (palaces or "range structures") (see Ashmore n.d.) suggests a balance between the political authority of ruling lineages and that of their councils.

In contrast, the Northern public places show a routine conflation of "temple" and "palace" architecture (Potter 1977: 88 for Rio Bec–Chenes) or a strong orientation to decorated superstructures over pyramidal "temples" (Pollock 1980: 565–70). Andrews V (1982) suggests that rotation of office among elite kin groups might well account for the site plan at Dzibilchaltun, and C. C. Coggins (1983: Chapter 3) believes that the quadripartite arrangement of the center of that site (Andrews IV and Andrews V 1980) is related to circulation of council office in the Contact Period. In other words, the architectural expression of dynastic power in the North is clearly overshadowed by the architectural accoutrements of the power of council or court. Coba is, of course, a notable exception to this general rule but also shows many affinities to the South.

To summarize, Southern Lowland political religion by the Early Classic Period focused on the notion of royal bloodlines, all of which probably traced their descent from the hero-twin founders of the Maya (Freidel and Schele 1982; Schele 1976). It is reasonable to suppose that concomitant political organizations, such as councils, were composed of related lineages and that they circulated offices by means of ritual cycles other than the royal Long Count. Obsession with the transfer of political power through "pure" descent lines no doubt reinforced a notion of ethnic purity among all participating nobility. While this concept no doubt accounts in part for the great stability and internal integration of Southern Lowland civilization, it may also account for this system's vulnerability in the face of changing political and economic circumstances in Mesoamerica generally during Epi-Classic and Terminal Classic times.

In the North, the basic cosmology is shared—presumably including the notion of hero-twin founding ancestors, who are depicted in their grotesque forms on buildings. The sacred royal bloodlines as the living incarnation of the Maya supernaturals are not a major feature of political religion here as they are in the South, however, or at least are not the overriding feature. Religion affirms the general political order, including the council officers, and celebrates individual rulers rather than whole dynasties. On the one hand, the Northern polities lacked the overall integration characteristic of the South; on the other, they eschewed the obsession with "pure" bloodlines and more generally, the notion of ethnic and cultural purity this central focus entailed. I suspect that this attitude constituted an important adaptive advantage as the Classic epoch drew to a close.

THE MAYA-MEXICAN CARTELS

The syncretistic "Mexican" flavor of Northern Lowland material symbolism of the Epi-Classic and Terminal Classic (Florescent–Modified Florescent) is currently attributed to a complex panoply of hostile and beneficent relationships between Lowland Maya and foreigners of the Gulf Coast and Highland Mexico (Kubler 1975; Thompson 1970; Webb 1973). Webb (1973) specifically suggests that such cultural cross-fertilization went hand in hand with the development of economic trade networks that ultimately outcompeted the Southern Lowland polities (or filled the vacuum left by collapse, depending on the timing). In essence, Webb is proposing the existence of cartels, but whereas he suggests fundamental changes in trade from limited luxury trade to more broadly based trade in a range of commodities (mostly the monies of the Contact Period), I believe that Classic trade was essentially of the same nature as that found by the Spanish. If there is not a major shift in the nature of long-distance trade, then there must be other reasons why the Northern Lowlanders succeeded in linking up with the major centers of Highland and Gulf power while the Southern Lowlanders failed.

I suggest that the Northerners were able to cope culturally and politically with the major innovation of the time: international "super cultures" welding political economies over distance into something more stable and substantial than trade networks. The consolidation of such "supercultures" would entail noble intermarriage and innovative theological solutions relating the religious underpinnings to political power, in short, mutual acculturation far beyond mere tolerance of differences.

425

The precise nature of these Northern cartels is beyond the scope of this essay, but there are clearly iconographic materials, such as the "sun captain" and "serpent captain" murals at Chichen Itza (Miller 1977a) and the Cacaxtla murals depicting "jaguar" and "bird" captains (Abascal et al. 1976) which deal with initial conflict and subsequent reconciliation of what appear to be Maya and Mexican contingents. It is too early to say how these solutions to multiethnic power bases work. My hunch is that the Chichen Itza example will be shown to deal with the conflation of Lowland Maya ideas of the hero-twin ancestors, the Sun and Venus, with highland Mexican ideas of analogous dyads, including the famous Kukulcan/Venus—Tezcatlipoca. Whatever the solutions, the result is a nobility in the North which, even at the time of the Spanish Conquest, claimed descent not from the ancestral twins but from foreign heroes (Roys 1962).

THE SOUTHERN FAILURE

With the notable exception of Early Classic Tikal, none of the Lowland Maya polities in the South shows evidence of having established enduring cartel relationships with Highland Mexican or Gulf Coast polities. It is equally clear that the many Southerners were well aware of their predicament and were attempting to solve the ideological impasse of "pure" sacred bloodlines. The result was not the florescence of a new political order but a brief and iconographically (presumably theologically) bizarre grafting of foreign ties onto the traditional order. Some such experiments, as at Seibal (Graham 1973), were indeed successful for a time; but they proved the exceptions to the rule. Some very successful Classic frontier polities, such as Palenque (Rands 1973b) and Copan (Willey, Leventhal, and Fash 1978; R. M. Leventhal, personal communication) show foreign ties in ceramics yet held staunchly to the traditional ethos in their monumental art up to the end. Perhaps such communities, in constant contact with foreigners, were especially adamant about the purity of their nobility.

It is unreasonable to suppose that the Southern Lowland polities lacked effective trade relationships with Highland communities in Guatemala and Mexico. I suggest, however, that these relationships were maintained primarily on a commercial basis; a relatively secular trade involving professionals (*ppolom* sodalities of the Contact Period). With the innovation of cartels linking Northern Maya (and perhaps Highland

Maya) to polities controlling the major markets and resource areas of Highland Mexico, the Southern Maya would have been hard pressed to compete effectively for the trade, even if their productive systems were on a par with or exceeded those of the North. Locked into traditional trading relationships, the Southern polities would have found themselves straining after shrinking markets. This situation may well have upgraded Southern Lowland warfare from a traditional sacred competition between bloodlines (Freidel n.d.) into strategic attempts to divest rivals of their trade routes and partners—a pattern attested in the Contact Period (Scholes and Roys 1968). Disruption in the flow of currencies would have had serious repercussions in the control of goods and services by Southern Lowland governments. The various sociopolitical conditions for collapse can be partly accounted for by a failure to adapt to a new kind of society cross-cutting traditional boundaries.

COLLAPSE OF THE CARTELS

If the foregoing scenario is on the right track, then the collapse experienced by the North was a phenomenon distinct from that suffered earlier in the South. One might imagine that "supercultures" sustained over long distances were vulnerable to disruption by intervening peoples and rivals, but if the odds were against them, they evidently overcame adversity for a considerable period of time. Militarism no doubt played a significant role both in the initial consolidation of the cartels and in their downfall, but the essential role of military effort appears to have undergone important changes subsequent to the collapse of the Terminal Classic cartels, and these changes may also have contributed to the premature demise of this innovative cultural form: a shift from wars over trade routes and markets to wars of conquest for purposes of tribute extraction.

The impact of the conquest state on Mesoamerican political economy cannot be overestimated. There are good reasons to believe that earlier state economies were administered through the control of exchange events, such as fairs in the context of pilgrimage convocation (Freidel 1981b), and by control of exchange equivalencies through monopolized currencies. Direct manipulation of productive surplus through collection and disbursement prior to the Contact Period has left no clear archaeological record in the form of centralized storage anywhere in Mesoamerica. No doubt storage facilities existed, but they were not focused upon by government. The various facilities thought to be marketplaces in Mesoamerica are just the same places that could well serve a variety of other functions for congregation, most notably religious festivals. On the other hand, there is clear evidence at such centers as Teotihuacan, Tula, and Kaminaljuyu for centralized control of the production in residences of obsidian, a commodity broadly exchanged from the outset of civilization in Mesoamerica. In the Lowlands, such huge communities as Dzibilchaltun and Chunchuc-mil (Andrews V 1981; Vlcek, Garza T. de González, and Kurjack 1978) no doubt owed their prosperity to the commercial exploitation of salt. In the case of obsidian, there is a dramatic shift in production control between the era of cartels and that of the conquest state: obsidian is no longer under the direct aegis of political capitals but rather is the product of minor settlements. Obsidian remains a major trade item through the Contact Period, but it is no longer a currency anywhere in Mesoamerica. With the exception of jade and metals, all of the major currencies of the Contact Period are Lowland products: cacao, cotton cloth, feathers, shell, and salt.

On the face of it, this distribution would appear to make the major Highland polities very vulnerable economically. Indeed, had the dominant Highland polities not shifted their bases of economic support from exchange administration to tribute exaction they would have been in dire straits. Tribute, combined with direct control of strategic Lowland regions producing currencies, freed the Triple Alliance from the necessity of promoting the maintenance, through alliance or cartel, of large-scale polities in Lowland areas. At the same time, this changed political atmosphere must have limited the potential of Lowland polities.

AFTERMATH OF THE SECOND COLLAPSE

Despite a superficial resemblance to the cartels that preceded it, the final episode of state formation in the Maya Lowlands, the Mayapan Confederacy, is clearly a distinct phenomenon. Lowland groups previously affiliated with Mexican polities seem to have consolidated for mutual benefit in the absence of any prospect of re-establishing cartels. Many of the institutional means hypothesized to exist in the cartels are retained: royal intermarriage over long distance, exchange tied to pilgrimage-fairs, shared or analogous deities, and an ethos emphasizing the foreign blood of the ruling houses. At the same time, ties beyond the peninsula are tenuous and vague; and there is an evident resurgence of Maya symbology, albeit in syncretized form. It seems likely that polities which managed to survive the first collapse and the cartel era through assiduous diplomacy and economic accommodation, perhaps Coba (Robles C. and Andrews, this volume) and Lamanai (Pendergast, this volume), are the sources of this resurgence. In brief, there is something of a reintegration of the peninsula as a political entity following a period of ethnic and political factionalism. No doubt the economies of the confederacy still involved symbiosis with Highland regions, but this trade, whatever its volume, was carried out in terms set by the Triple Alliance and its subordinate polities by means of peripheral intermediaries in the Gulf region and the Bay of Honduras. An Aztec-related equivalent of Chichen Itza or the Puuc communities did not emerge, not because the Aztecs were incapable of such action at a distance (surely they were more powerful than previous Highland states), but rather because they did not need such alliances. Despite the maintenance of trade in volume during this Late Postclassic era, the economic basis of the confederacy and the petty states that followed was surely more precarious than that of the earlier Lowland states. I would attribute the "decadent" quality of architecture and the arts and crafts of this time to a reluctance on the part of governments and elites to invest heavily in material mediums lacking easy "liquidation" in the face of economic uncertainty (cf. Sabloff and Rathje 1975a, 1975b). Whatever problems the Lowland Maya may have had in reformulating their culture after centuries of cartel experimentation, conservative "hold-outs," and general chaos in the South, the Late Postclassic is less a decadent than a stymied socioeconomic development.

CONCLUSIONS

The general position taken in this essay is that the Lowland Maya developments of the Terminal Classic and its aftermath can only be understood as an aspect of larger developments encompassing Mesoamerica in its entirety. The central hypothesis is the importance of Highland-Lowland symbiosis in the development of complex societies in the region, more specifically stated here as mutually beneficial interregional monopolies over commodities used as currencies in local, administered economies. The cultural means of establishing and maintaining such monopolies varied significantly in time and space, but the general impetus was toward the cartel phenomenon: the creation of "supercultures" cross-cutting ethnic and language boundaries. This phenomenon is presaged already in the Middle Preclassic Olmec interaction sphere (Early Horizon), is clearly expressed in the Middle Classic, and reaches its apogee in the Epi-Classic. It is superseded by the development of a new economic order in the conquest states. The Southern Lowland Maya civilization was the major exception to this trend. Having established an ethos of ethnic purity based upon the central axiom of sacred bloodlines, the Maya were capable of an internal coherence and cohesiveness never rivaled elsewhere in Mesoamerica. As a rule, their external economic relationships were successfully based upon mutual tolerance of differences and ingenious innovations of syncretic trade goods, such as Copador Ware (R. M. Leventhal, personal communication). The internal productive strength and reliability of the Southern Lowlands made these polities a force to be dealt with on their own terms. In the face of pervasive cartels surrounding them and monopolizing their markets, however, the Southern polities entered a crisis from which they could not emerge; out of step with the general evolutionary trends in the region, they became extinct. The Northerners succeeded in establishing visible cartels, but when these were superseded by tribute-based Highland states, the Lowland Maya truly lost status.

The power vacuum in the Lowlands, maintained as a matter of economic opportunity and political exigency by Highland polities, is a decline only from the Lowland point of view. From the perspective of Mesoamerica, the Maya decline is a symptom of evolutionary advancement through the innovation of the tribute-based government and the development of market economy. The imperative was the establishment of one government over one world, an imperative not to be denied by any one culture, no matter now transcendent or entrancing.

430

PART FIVE

Summary

13
Classic to Postclassic: A Summary Discussion

E. WYLLYS ANDREWS V
Middle American Research Institute, Tulane University

JEREMY A. SABLOFF
University of New Mexico

This summary differs from the ones which Gordon Willey has prepared for the three previous Maya volumes in the School of American Research Advanced Seminar series (Maya collapse [with Demitri Shimkin] in 1973; Maya rise in 1977; and Maya settlement in 1981). We do not offer a consensus statement that tries to summarize the views of the seminar participants, since we feel that any such attempt would fail to do justice to the diversity of opinions expressed in the chapters above and in the seminar discussions. Moreover, much of the discussion was concerned with restructuring our thinking on the Postclassic and looking at future research directions, not with synthesizing the state of the art.

We believe that the principal thrust of the papers in this volume and the seminar discussions is a reorientation of our view of ancient Maya civilization away from the traditional perception of the time from the Late Classic until the Spanish conquest (see Gordon Willey's introductory chapter for a clear presentation of this traditional viewpoint). So the challenge that faces us in this final chapter is how best to communicate the nature of the ideas presented during the seminar and in the papers of this volume. In effect, how can we communicate the content of our own reeducation to other scholars? Many important and fascinating ideas were presented at the seminar, but we believe two major themes dominated the conversations and papers. These have been around for a long time and have been expressed by seminar participants in earlier papers, but we think that their time has come and that their utility should now be confirmed.

The first theme we will examine is the extent of the overlap among the Terminal Classic occupations in the Southern Lowlands, the Puuc region sites, and Toltec Chichen Itza. The second concerns the time of the Classic-Postclassic transition in the Maya Lowlands.

THE RELATIONSHIP OF CHICHEN ITZA TO THE PUUC CITIES

It was clear to us when the conference was organized that one of the most significant problems we would be discussing was the relationship of Chichen Itza to other Terminal Classic and Early Postclassic sites in Yucatan and in the Central and Southern Maya Lowlands. A number of archaeologists working in northern Yucatan and elsewhere in the early and mid-1970s had become increasingly uneasy with the traditional and prevalent interpretation of this segment of the northern Maya culture-historical record. The most widely accepted reconstruction of events, one that is at least implicitly followed in the vast majority of the archaeological literature, is that sites with Puuc architecture, both in the Puuc Hills and on the Northern Plains, date to the Late and Terminal Classic periods and that Toltec-influenced architecture at Chichen Itza dates to the Early Postclassic, with little or no overlap in time between the two. A correlate of this, of course, is that Toltec Chichen Itza postdates the last manifestation of the Terminal Classic in the Southern Lowlands between about 10.3.0.0.0 and 10.5.0.0.0 or 10.6.0.0.0 in the Maya calendar (ca. A.D. 890 to 930 or 950).

We believe that this interpretation of the archaeological data is partly in error and that in fact the Puuc and Toltec architectural and ceramic traditions of northern Yucatan overlapped in time. We think sites with fully developed Puuc concrete-and-veneer masonry coexisted with Toltec Chichen Itza for an as-yet-undetermined number of years, and that the overlap of Puuc and Toltec ceramic complexes was very substantial. In this view we are joined by most, if not all, the participants in the School of American Research Advanced Seminar and by a number of other archaeologists who were not with us in Santa Fe.

434

The extent and nature of these overlaps, however, find less of a consensus. In the months before the seminar we learned that Charles Lincoln, a graduate student at Harvard, was writing a paper on the subject of this possible overlap, and we asked him to submit a shortened version of his work for this volume, although at that point we could not include him in the seminar itself. Lincoln's work, the most careful and detailed consideration of this problem to date, vigorously supports a revision in this portion of the archaeological record and indeed goes beyond the position we favor, suggesting a more complete overlap of the architectural styles than we believe likely. Lincoln also favors a shortened chronology that would force archaeologists to consider a correlation of the Maya and Christian calendars at 11.3.0.0.0 instead of the widely accepted 11.16.0.0.0 solution, a position that finds congenial company in Arlen Chase's chapter in this volume but is not generally adhered to by most seminar participants.

The genesis of these ideas is far earlier than the 1970s. Seeds of doubt were cast by the works of several scholars as far back as the late 1940s and early 1950s. Tatiana Proskouriakoff's study of Classic Maya sculpture (1950) and her paper on nonclassic sculptural traits in Yucatan (1951) showed that Toltec and Toltec-related themes and motifs could be found in the sculpture of a variety of sites with Puuc architecture, including Edzna, Oxkintok, Kabah, Uxmal, and Halakal. This suggested to her that Toltecs were present in Yucatan for some time before they dominated Chichen Itza. She also noted that the carvings in the Lower Temple of the Jaguars at Chichen Itza, a Toltec building, more closely resembled Classic sculpture than they did any Toltec sculpture at that site. Robert Rands (1954) also suggested close ties between Classic Maya art and the art of Chichen Itza.

Harry Pollock in 1952 included a long and thoughtful comment on the relationship between the Puuc sites and Chichen Itza in the annual report of the Carnegie Institution of Washington Department of Archaeology, and a decade later (1962: 5) he reiterated his caveat. He considered the chronological placement and external relationships of Toltec Chichen Itza to be far from settled, and his own interpretation of the data clearly presaged those that developed a quarter of a century later. Near the end of his discussion he stated:

A position that seems more tenable is to assume that the invader and his culture were confined to the Chichen Itza area or possibly the eastern part

435

of the peninsula. This would not be unlikely if the foreign elements entered Yucatan when the Puuc culture was still vital. In any event, the older forms of art and architecture might have continued in use in the west. (1952: 239)

Lee A. Parsons's report on Bilbao, Guatemala, argued for a Middle Classic Period in Mesoamerican history, when he thought Teotihuacan-related architectural and artistic elements spread into several parts of the Maya area. Parsons regarded much of the early Toltec architecture at Chichen Itza as belonging to this Teotihuacanoid horizon (1969a: 172–84, Table 7), which he dated to about A.D. 600 to 700 or 750. His arguments have not received wide support among Maya archaeologists, but his work did point out again that Toltec sculpture bore close resemblances to Late Classic art in other regions of Mesoamerica. Marvin Cohodas (1978) pursued Parsons's views on the Middle Classic in northern Yucatan, arguing that the Chichen Itza ball courts dated to the second half of the seventh century and were contemporary with early Puuc architecture. His dates seem too early to us, although we agree that the northern Maya area contained more than one contemporary regional style, a position echoed by Lincoln's paper in this volume.

The prevailing opinion, nevertheless, remained that Puuc architecture, with its associated Florescent, or Cehpech, ceramic complex, preceded the Toltec period of construction at Chichen Itza and its Early Mexican or Sotuta ceramic complex. George W. Brainerd (1958: 34–45) noted that there was little stratigraphic evidence for this succession of ceramic complexes at Chichen Itza itself, but he continued to support this view, which was based largely on the hypothetical architectural sequence at Chichen Itza developed by Alfred M. Tozzer (1930, 1957). Brainerd (1958: 4) clearly favored the beginning of the Toltec architectural style at about 10.8.0.0.0 (A.D. 987) as had J. Eric S. Thompson (1937: 190), and he did not think the ceramic evidence would allow more than a "minimum" overlap of Puuc and Toltec, if any. Robert E. Smith's study of Mayapan pottery (1971) followed Brainerd's in dating the Puuc Cehpech complex to A.D. 800–1000 and the Toltec Sotuta complex at Chichen Itza to the following 200 years. E. Wyllys Andrews IV regarded architecture at the Puuc sites and Toltec Chichen Itza as very similar, with the latter adding Central Mexican–derived stylistic elements to a basic Maya repertoire of construction techniques, masonry, and architectural styles shared by both. His new terminology reflected this perception. Brainerd's Florescent stage became his Pure Florescent Period, and Brainerd's Early Mexican substage he termed the Modified Florescent. In spite of this revision, Andrews IV did not accept any overlap of the two. In 1965 he stated that Kabah and Uxmal "were abandoned before the start of the Modified Florescent," although he believed that "many of the cities on the flat northern plain . . . remained inhabited [he was thinking here of Dzibilchaltun]" (1965a: 315–16).

Several northern Maya archaeologists, including Joseph W. Ball, Norberto González C. and others at the Southeast Regional Center of INAH in Merida, Edward B. Kurjack, Michael P. Simmons, and Andrews V, began to suspect in the early 1970s that the linear succession model was inadequate and that the Toltec tradition was a regional one. Major themes of a 1977 symposium on Puuc archaeology at central College, in Pella, Iowa (Mills 1979), were the extent to which an overlap did exist and the implications such an overlap would have (Ball 1979a, 1979b; Andrews V 1979). In the years since that conference, reevaluation and speculation have continued, but relatively few data have been added that bear directly on the chronological position of Toltec Chichen Itza. As we write, Charles Lincoln is beginning a program of investigation at Chichen Itza that may help clarify the issue. In the meantime, however, we realize our views are based on limited evidence and no small amount of inference and speculation.

The evidence for an overlap of Puuc and Toltec is of various kinds and varying degrees of signficance and reliability. Most of it has been described or alluded to earlier in this volume, but we will summarize what seem to us the most compelling data.

The finest masonry at Chichen Itza is found in the Toltec structures, not in the buildings that have been ascribed to the pre-Toltec Maya period, some of which bear early Cycle 10 inscriptions. The masonry of the Casa Colorada, for example, although definitely of Puuc concrete and veneer, is cruder than that found in the Temple of the Warriors, the Castillo, and other later buildings. It is to the latest buildings at Uxmal, such as the Palace of the Governor, the Nunnery, and the Ball Court, that the Toltec masonry at Chichen Itza shows the closest resemblances, suggesting that the time separating their construction was not great. J. Eric S. Thompson (1937b: 194) gave possible readings for the Uxmal Ball Court rings at 10.3.16.16.19 and 10.3.16.17.0 (A.D. 906) (1950: 199) and 10.3.8.7.12 (A.D. 897) or 10.3.18.9.12 (A.D. 907) (1973: 61–62). David Kelley (1982: 15) has suggested that the east ring records the date of 10.3.15.16.14 (A.D. 905). These readings correspond well to the radiocarbon date of A.D. 885 ± 120 (GrN-613) from a lintel in the North Building of the Nunnery (Andrews IV and Andrews V 1980: Table 4. Radiocarbon dates in this chapter have not been recalibrated.).

Despite extensive excavations at Chichen Itza, archaeologists of the Carnegie Institution did not encounter pure deposits of the Cehpech (Puuc) ceramic complex underlying levels with Sotuta (Toltec) materials, nor did they find incontrovertible evidence for a sequential relationship of the two architectural styles. As Lincoln argues in this volume, the failure to find this ceramic stratigraphy is one of the strongest reasons we now have for believing that the Toltec intrusion was a regional, rather than a pan–northern Maya phenomenon, and that not all Toltec architecture postdated late Puuc constructions at other sites. H. B. Roberts's trenches near the Temple of the Three Lintels, reported by Brainerd (1958: 38–40), provide hints of a transition from Cehpech to Sotuta ceramics at Chichen Itza, but the evidence is weak and ambiguous. The architectural sequence at Las Monjas likewise gives the overall impression of Toltec additions to a Puuc architectural complex (Bolles 1977), but the ceramic stratigraphy suggests mixing or overlap of Puuc and Toltec pottery.

Tatiana Proskouriakoff's (1950) study of northern Maya sculpture documents the presence of Toltec and other nonclassic styles at several Puuc sites. Certainly a possible inference to be drawn from this situation is that the Toltec style entered early or developed gradually in Yucatan, and that during at least part of this time many Puuc sites were thriving.

Lincoln (this volume) argues that the site of Chichen Itza consists of "an integrated, whole community," rather than two temporally distinct complexes of ruins. He cites as evidence the overall distribution of the ruins (Maya and Toltec buildings interspersed in many areas) and radial causeways linking the Toltec center to groups with predominantly Maya ruins. Lincoln's argument is a strong one, but we believe not entirely conclusive. The bulk of the Toltec architecture is concentrated in one area of the site, and the raised causeways may have been constructed at a relatively late date specifically to link the Toltec center to other groups that were still occupied and in which Toltec structures were being built. The absence of Toltec structures directly overlying Puuc buildings strengthens Lincoln's position, but room is still left for the alternative explanation.

About a dozen inscribed dates at Chichen Itza have been placed in the third katun of Cycle 10 (Thompson 1937: 186, 1950: 199; Kelley 1968: 264). All of these are found in buildings thought to predate the Toltec occupation and fall in a span of twelve years from A.D. 869 to 881 (10.2.0.15.3 to 10.2.12.2.4). David H. Kelley (1968: 264) notes that they all seem to refer to the Itza captain Kakupacal. After this, known Cycle 10 dates cease until 10.8.10.11.0 (A.D. 998), when a date was inscribed on the High Priest's Tomb, a Toltec structure. It is difficult not to suspect that the cessation of inscriptions on Maya-style structures and the subsequent appearance of Toltec-influenced architecture were related. If they were, and in the absence of contradictory evidence we think this the most economical argument, the door is open for a Toltec presence at Chichen Itza by about 10.3.0.0.0, when Uxmal, Kabah, and probably many other Puuc sites were in full flower, although nearing the end of their florescence.

Two radiocarbon dates from twig charcoal in a shrine at Balankanche Cave, a few kilometers from the center of Chichen Itza, suggest a Toltec presence by or before A.D. 900 (Andrews IV 1970). The first determinations were both A.D. 860 ± 200 (LJ-272 and LJ-273); when rerun, the samples yielded dates of A.D. 878 ± 51 (P-1132) and A.D. 922 ± 42 (P-1133) (Andrews IV 1970: 69–70). The shrine, apparently sealed immediately after the offerings were made, contained many painted Toltec Tlaloc censers. Although only two samples were dated, the fact that the dates did not change greatly when the charcoal was retested by a different laboratory adds to their importance.

Five other C^{14} samples from Chichen Itza have been run (Andrews IV and Andrews V 1980: Table 4), from both Pure and Modified Florescent contexts. Most of these seem too early for the likely ages of the structures from which they derive, perhaps, as one of us has suggested (Andrews IV and Andrews V 1980: 285), because they were taken from inner portions of beam and lintels. Most are too early to be acceptable for an 11.16.0.0.0 correlation, and we do not think they bear on the question of overlap.

Recent excavations at Uxmal have documented the presence, in apparently large quantities, of Sotuta complex ceramics. With the exception of a Silho Orange bowl found inside the east range of the Ball Court (Maldonado 1979c), the context of the Sotuta pottery is not entirely clear. César Sáenz's material is primarily from clearing and other superficial contexts (Sáenz 1972, 1975b). The Sotuta ceramics recovered by Barbara Konieczna and Pablo Mayer (1976) derive from a number of late residential rooms built along the north base of the Temple of the Magician and from trenches beside the East and North buildings of the Nunnery, and they are mixed with larger quantities of Cehpech types. Toltec pottery at Uxmal appears to be late. Most of it probably postdates construction of the major buildings, but it seems certain that it was contemporary with Cehpech after A.D. 900.

Anthony P. Andrews (1978b) has argued that Isla Cerritos, just off the coast, north of Chichen Itza, was a port for that site in the Toltec period. A small ceramic sample collected by Jack D. Eaton in 1968 (Eaton 1978: 41–42; Ball 1978: 137–38) contained primarily sherds of the Sotuta complex, without ceramics of the Cehpech complex, except for Chablekal Gray, a diagnostic type of Puuc and pre-Puuc ceramic assemblages elsewhere in northern Yucatan not previously found in direct association with Modified Florescent pottery. Much larger surface samples collected later by A. P. Andrews and Andrews V confirm this association. The appearance of Chablekal Gray with Sotuta Chichen Slate, Silho Orange, Tohil Plumbate, and other late types indicates at least partial overlap of the Cehpech and Sotuta ceramic complexes. Investigations in 1984 and 1985 produced small numbers of Balancan Orange. In 1984, with Fernando Robles C. and Tomás Gallareta, Tony Andrews began what we hope will be a multiseason project of investigation at this island site.

Recent excavations in Quintana Roo by archaeologists of the Southeast Regional Center of INAH have added a new and extremely important perspective to the impact of Toltec Chichen Itza on the northern Maya area. Robles, who has been responsible for the ceramic analyses on these projects, states that at the vast archaeological zone of Coba no Toltec or Modified Florescent Period can be documented (1980: 45–47). Types of the Chichen Slate group appear in limited numbers, but they are always mixed with far greater quantities of sherds of his

Oro Cehpech complex, including Puuc Slate, Ticul Thin Slate, and Puuc Red. The Sotuta types Silho Orange and Tohil Plumbate are absent.

At El Meco, a few kilometers north of Puerto Juárez on the north coast of Quintana Roo, the Sotuta ceramic sphere is well represented (Robles C. 1980: 45–47, Robles's comments to the seminar). Chichen Slate, Silho Orange, and Tohil Plumbate are found in amounts about equal to Cehpech types, but they are always inextricably mixed with them, and also with Peto Cream Ware (Xcanchakan Black-on-cream, called Coarse Slateware by Brainerd), a major group that in northwestern Yucatan follows Terminal Classic Cehpech Puuc Slate and precedes the Late Postclassic Tases complex. At Mayapan (Smith 1971) Peto Cream Ware is diagnostic of the Hocaba complex (suggested to date to A.D. 1200–1300), in which it is associated with Mayapan Red, but it begins at other sites before A.D. 1200.

Robles noted that Sotuta ceramics are very common at north coastal sites in Quintana Roo but that they are invariably associated with Peto Cream and often with Terminal Classic Cehpech materials. The central coast of Quintana Roo, in contrast, has produced very few Sotuta complex ceramics, and at most sites in this zone the ceramic sequence runs directly from Cehpech to levels with Peto Cream and ultimately to Tases levels with Tulum Red ware. At Xelha, however, Robles reports levels including Muna Slate, Chablekal Gray, and Vista Alegre Striated, overlain by deposits containing Muna Slate, Ticul Thin Slate, Vista Alegre Striated, large amounts of Chichen Slate and Peto Cream, and little Silho Orange (personal communication).

San Gervasio, on Cozumel Island, has provided the most useful ceramic sequence, from the point of view of placing Sotuta ceramics relative to other complexes. The stratigraphy here runs from Cehpech to levels with mixed Sotuta and Hocaba (Peto Cream), then to levels with pottery of both Hocaba and Tases complexes, and finally to Tases, with both Mayapan and Tulum Reds, but without Peto Cream. San Gervasio, therefore, provides evidence that the Sotuta ceramic complex postdates, to some extent, the Terminal Classic Cehpech complex (Robles, comments to the seminar and Robles and Andrews, this volume).

Robles concludes in his Coba report that "according to the ceramic evidence presently available, the Cehpech and Sotuta horizons represent essentially a geographic, rather than a temporal difference. At some sites, as at El Meco and to a lesser extent at Coba, they are found together. . . . In our opinion, Sotuta ceramics are a regional or zonal manifestation, limited to the northcentral portion of the Yucatan Peninsula" (1980: 46–47). His view, expressed at the seminar, is that the spread of the Sotuta ceramic sphere represented an expansion of Chichen Itza's political power, that this took place in some areas but not in others, and that the Toltec presence was an intrusion that coexisted with local cultural traditions, rather than a distinct period.

Evidence for the chronological position of Toltec architecture has recently come from as far away as Belize. Diane and Arlen Chase (1982) have reported two structures from Nohmul, both near the center of the site, that are clearly related to Toltec-style structures at Chichen Itza. Structure 20, a "patio-quad," is similar to those Karl Ruppert (1950, 1952) called gallery-patios, and Structure 9 is a small, round building the Chases compare to the Caracol. Associated pottery includes Puuc Slate and Thin Slate, grater bowls, San Jose V types, and Peto Cream Ware (but not Chichen Slate). The Chases argue that at Nohmul, therefore, Toltec structures correspond in time to the Terminal Classic, or Tepeu 3, horizon (see also Hammond 1974, 1985; Chase and Hammond 1982). The occurrence of Peto Cream with slate wares, however, would seem to parallel the situation that Robles reports on the north coast of Quintana Roo and raises the possibility that this ceramic assemblage and the two buildings are as late as or postdate A.D. 1000.

The effect of most of the foregoing bits and pieces of evidence has been to indicate an overlap of Puuc and Toltec ceramics, rather than to clarify the duration of the Toltec style and the Sotuta ceramic complex. From Lamanai, northern Belize, David Pendergast (this volume, and comments to the seminar) notes a series of C-14 dates that cluster around A.D. 1140 and are associated with a vessel of Sotuta complex Silho Orange. Although this is only one vessel from a burial, the find provides one of the very few reasonably firm dates we have for this pottery type.

The ceramic sequence on the east coast of the peninsula (reviewed above), especially at San Gervasio, resembles what we believe the situation to have been at Dzilbilchaltun, 75 miles west of Chichen Itza. At this site there is enough stratigraphic evidence to place types of the Sotuta ceramic complex relative to earlier and later ceramic materials (Andrews V 1978: 378–79; Andrews IV and Andrews V 1980: 274–75, 278–81; Andrews V 1981: 334–37), although the implications of the sequence for the overlap question are not entirely clear. The formulation of the sequence as it now stands is largely the work of Michael P. Simmons. The Copo 2 ceramic complex, associated with Puuc architecture, is equivalent to Smith's Cehpech complex, except that Ticul Thin Slate appeared here relatively late, considerably after the development of the full Puuc architectural style. Puuc Slate at Dzibilchaltun developed in late Copo 2 into a coarse-paste slate type that Simmons has named Hunucma Slate. This type continued well into the following Zipche (Sotuta) phase and was in turn replaced by Peto Cream Ware sometime during Zipche. The final preconquest Chechem complex, equivalent to Smith's Tases complex at Mayapan, was marked by the appearance of Mayapan Red, Chen Mul Modeled, and other late diagnostics.

Simmons stresses that this is a local sequence and that there is considerable overlap among the major sequential wares. Chichen Slate, Silho Orange, Plumbate, and other Sotuta types were present only during the Zipche phase, and they were always greatly outnumbered by what are presumed to be local ceramics. The Sotuta presence, therefore, was intrusive at Dzibilchaltun, as it apparently was on the east coast of the peninsula. Construction during the Zipche phase was minimal, and all indications are that the vast population of the Copo phase was reduced to a small fraction of its former size. It seems highly likely that the intrusion of Toltec pottery was in some way related to the cessation of Puuc-style construction, the rapid demographic changes, and the end of the site's importance.

The intrusion of Sotuta ceramics at Dzibilchaltun only when or after Puuc architecture ceased to be built could be taken to indicate that no overlap existed between Puuc and Toltec in northern Yucatan. We nevertheless think the Dzibilchaltun sequence is compatible with an overlap. To state it simply, Toltec ceramics probably reached Dzibilchaltun some time after they were present at Chichen Itza. There is no compelling reason to deny that Toltec Chichen Itza coexisted with a limited part of Copo 2 (the Pure Florescent) at this northwestern site. Both groups, Toltec and Puuc, were almost certainly exploiting north coast salt and participating in circumpeninsular and internal trade, and they were probably competitors and antagonists. This competition could well have prevented the intrusion of Toltec pottery into northwest Yucatan until Chichen Itza was able to extend its domination over the area, an event that, if we are to judge from the collapse of all known important Terminal Classic sites in this zone, surely happened.

THE EXTENT OF THE OVERLAP

The origins of the Puuc architectural tradition have been discussed at length in recent years (for example, Andrews V 1979, Ball 1979b, Pollock 1980), and we have little to add here. A beginning date for early Puuc architecture somewhere in the second half of the eighth century, perhaps about A.D. 770, would leave few of us uneasy.

The end of the Puuc tradition is far more difficult to place. The latest inscriptions and C-14 dates come from the Nunnery and the Ball Court at Uxmal, as noted above, and they indicate that construction of important public buildings continued until at least A.D. 900, the approximate date Jeff K. Kowalski (1981: 155) suggests for the House of the Governor at that site. Kowalski also believes that no major building was finished after this time, although he thinks some were begun. Possible epigraphic ties at about A.D. 900 with Kabah, as well as the causeway connecting these two sites and Nohpat, halfway between them, make it likely that this entire area remained vigorous until this time. The early Cycle 10 inscriptions at Chichen Itza associated with Puuc architecture are nearly this late.

It is certainly conceivable that at some Puuc sites major building efforts extended into the tenth century, but of this we have no direct evidence. At Dzibilchaltun, for example, the end of the Puuc architectural tradition is signaled by changes in ceramics and is not dated by radiocarbon. Even if the early years of the tenth century saw the decline or cessation of large building projects at most Puuc sites, occupation at most centers undoubtedly would have persisted, perhaps for more than a century. Kowalski (1981: 155) suggests that Uxmal was abandoned by A.D. 925–75. This may be a bit early, if we are to judge from construction of the late rooms north of the Temple of the Magician, but these rooms could have been built, used, and abandoned before A.D. 1000. The apparent absence of Peto Cream in these excavations indicates an abandonment perhaps this early. On much of the east coast of the peninsula, the development of Cehpech directly

444

into Hocaba also leads one to see a long duration of Terminal Classic pottery, if not architecture.

The traditional date for the end of the Puuc tradition is ca. A.D. 1000. Ball (1979a: 48) would not be unhappy with an extension of another 50 or 100 years at the major Puuc sites, but we agree that hard evidence is lacking. One strong possibility is that the Puuc architectural tradition in northern Yucatan met its demise not too many years after A.D. 900, especially if Chichen Itza was directly involved in this collapse, but that in other parts of Yucatan, and perhaps in the north as well, the Puuc ceramic tradition continued with little modification, sometimes mixed with Sotuta types, for years afterward.

The beginning of the Toltec style in architecture, sculpture, and pottery can be traced back to the Terminal Classic at a number of sites and in more than one area. The inception of Toltec architecture at Chichen Itza cannot yet be firmly placed, but we think that it began shortly after the end of the series of early Cycle 10 inscriptions, perhaps by A.D. 890. Ball, in 1979, suggested a date about 100 years later for the inception of the Toltec architectural style at Chichen Itza. Combining Kelley's (1968) arguments concerning the Itza with the traditional beginning date for Toltec architecture (A.D. 987) that Thompson (1937: 190) espoused, Ball argued that the Puuc style of architecture at Chichen Itza began with the arrival of the Itza leader Kakupacal about A.D. 866 and continued until A.D. 987, when it was replaced by the Toltec style. To us the A.D. 987 date seems late, in part because of the relevant radiocarbon dates from Chichen Itza and Balankanche, in addition to external evidence suggesting an earlier Toltec presence in northern Yucatan and elsewhere, and in part because this scheme creates a century at Chichen Itza for the further development of the Puuc style without obvious candidates to fill this architectural gap. We also wonder if A.D. 866 is not too late for the introduction of Puuc architecture at Chichen Itza. This would be possible only if the style was somehow hindered from spreading 60 or 70 miles to the east for almost a century. Ball's reconstruction might be correct, however, if the early Cycle 10 dates at Chichen Itza are not contemporary with the structures on which they were carved, but rather refer back to earlier events. In this case, though, the A.D. 987 date for the introduction of what Ball (1979a: 50) calls "emphatically Toltec traits" would preclude an overlap of Puuc and Toltec architecture.

Determining the end of the Toltec period at Chichen Itza with any

445

precision is not possible using available archaeological data. The traditional view is that Toltec Chichen Itza fell in a Katun 8 Ahau (A.D. 1185–1204). Given its inception about A.D. 900, this would leave almost 300 years for the Toltec-style architecture at the site, a span that is probably unnecessary. The date of 10.8.10.11.0 (A.D. 998) from the High Priest's Tomb is widely accepted, and if this building is relatively late in the Toltec architectural sequence at the site, the probability that Toltec construction stopped long before A.D. 1200 is high.

One implication of the preceding arguments for a closer cultural relationship between and probable chronological overlap of the Puuc sites and Chichen Itza is that the two formed part of one northern cultural climax that was distinct from and mostly later than the Southern Lowland Classic peak. We are reminded of Morley's (1946) Old and New Empires. The Southern collapse began in some areas shortly after A.D. 800, near the beginning of the Puuc Florescence in the North. By A.D. 950 the Southern decline was complete, whereas in the North the modified Classic tradition at Chichen Itza probably continued for another century and perhaps two.

Archaeological and ethnohistoric data place the founding of Mayapan at ca. A.D. 1200–1250. Although this site copied many of the Toltec architectural features at Chichen Itza, a large number of building types and arrangements were new and different, construction techniques degenerated noticeably, and the overall organization of the site is quite different from what went before. The ceramic assemblage also represents a major shift from the Toltec Sotuta complex, which closely resembles that of the Puuc sites (although Ball, in this volume, stresses the similarities between Chichen Itza and Mayapan pottery). Given these marked changes, many of which may derive from areas to the south, from the East Coast of the peninsula, and from Central Mexico, rather than from northwestern Yucatan, we think a considerable time must separate Toltec construction at Chichen Itza and the beginning of Mayapan. This span would have seen the predominance of Peto Cream Ware in most of northern Yucatan, accompanied early by Puuc Slate and its late variants, in some areas by Chichen Slate, and finally by Mayapan and Tulum Red.

In summary, we see varying amounts of overlap among the different components of the Puuc and Toltec traditions. Toltec sculptural traits are found in late contexts at several Puuc sites. They may precede in time the Toltec buildings at Chichen Itza. The limited number of relevant inscribed dates and radiocarbon determinations also indicates an overlap of late Puuc architecture in the Puuc Hills and elsewhere with Toltec construction at Chichen Itza. This overlap may have been relatively brief, even if Toltec buildings are as early as 10.3.0.0.0, because we have so far almost no evidence of major Puuc construction much beyond this time anywhere in the Lowlands. This may mean that the construction of buildings in the Puuc and Toltec styles overlapped less than 50 years.

The situation with regard to ceramics is quite different. The Cehpech ceramic complex continued in most areas long after A.D. 900, sometimes developing gradually into the Hocaba complex and in some cases being mixed with Toltec Sotuta ceramics. At some sites, such as Dzibilchaltun, Chichen Slate and associated Toltec types definitely continued past the end of Cehpech ceramics; at others, especially in the east and possibly at Uxmal, they did not. These data mean that in some zones the overlap of Cehpech and Sotuta was partial and that in others it was total.

THE CORRELATION QUESTION

We believe that the archaeological data fit best a correlation of Maya and Christian calendars at 11.16.0.0.0, rather than at 11.3.0.0.0, a judgment in which the majority of those attending the seminar, although by no means all, would probably concur. An 11.3.0.0.0 correlation would force Maya history after the end of the Initial Series period into a span 256 years shorter than would an 11.16.0.0.0 solution, an interval we think is uncomfortably brief. It would also force us to discard almost all of the radiocarbon chronology for the Maya area. Many C-14 dates from northern Yucatan appear too early for an 11.16.0.0.0 (Andrews IV and Andrews V 1980: Table 4), but none, as far as we know, supports an 11.3.0.0.0 correlation.

An 11.3.0.0.0 solution would place the early Cycle 10 dates from Uxmal and Chichen Itza at ca. A.D. 1125 to 1163. Occupation may have continued at Uxmal for another century, but abandonment of the site preceded the introduction of Peto Cream Ware. The 11.3.0.0.0 correlation, therefore, would place the entire span with Black-on-cream pottery, including the Hocaba phase at Mayapan, after ca. A.D. 1225 or 1250, by which time Mayapan had probably been founded.

The earlier correlation also does violence to the situation at Chichen Itza. It places the 10.8.10.11.0 inscription from the High Priest's Tomb at A.D. 1254. Ralph Roys (1962: 43) put the "founding" of Mayapan by the Itza at Katun 13 Ahau (A.D. 1244–63, also 11.16.0.0.0). (These Christian dates for Mayapan will not change significantly if one uses an 11.3.0.0.0 solution.) We think, as did R. E. Smith (1971), that the Late Postclassic settlement and the Hocaba complex there went back somewhat before this, perhaps to A.D. 1200.

Not only, therefore, does an 11.3.0.0.0 correlation fail to allow for the interval between Toltec Chichen Itza and Mayapan that we think the great changes in material culture indicate (although admittedly this argument is based on an unconfirmed judgment), it in fact has the two very different florescences overlapping by at least 50 years.

Joseph Ball suggests in this volume that the Books of Chilam Balam can be used to create more than one reconstruction of late Northern prehistory, especially if one accepts the possibility that some place names recorded in these books actually refer to sites we know by different names and if an 11.3.0.0.0 correlation is used, rather than an 11.16.0.0.0 one. Arlen Chase also urges us to pay greater attention to native documents as we attempt to reconstruct history. We are somewhat wary of relying too heavily on the dates and events recorded in the Books of Chilam Balam for a reconstruction of late Yucatecan culture history, because it is almost impossible to choose among the various scenarios. It seems to us that, in the end, any chronicle of events created from the ethnohistorical records must depend on archaeological data for its plausibility and eventual verification, and not the opposite. It is in such a context, we believe, that a new emphasis on ethnohistoric studies will have its greatest payoff.

We will not attempt to discuss the ethnohistoric and astronomical evidence in favor of an 11.16.0.0.0 correlation, although we believe it is stronger than that for either an 11.3.0.0.0 or a 12.9.0.0.0 one. Mention should, however, be made of a recently published analysis that further weakens the case for the 11.3.0.0.0 correlation. Harvey M. and Victoria R. Bricker (1983) have presented a convincing model for the use of the eclipse-warning table on pages 51a through 58b of the Dresden Codex (but cf. Kelley 1983). The use of the 11.16.0.0.0 correlation in conjunction with their model allows the table to predict correctly all of the 78 solar eclipses that occurred during the 33-year life of the table, as well as all but one of the 53 lunar eclipses. The

Brickers, in response to our request, calculated the success of the table in predicting eclipses using an 11.3.0.0.0 correlation. They note (personal communication) that this correlation misses 16 of the 78 solar eclipses and 34 of the 52 lunar eclipses.

SOME IMPLICATIONS OF THE OVERLAP

The most obvious implication of the overlap of Puuc and Toltec, or of the Pure and the Modified Florescent Periods, is that Toltec Chichen Itza overlaps in time, to some extent, the Terminal Classic manifestations throughout the Maya area. The overlap was longest in the realm of ceramics and less in architecture and sculpture. The Toltec phenomenon was at least partly contemporaneous, then, with the latest Classic materials at Coba, sites on the east coast of Quintana Roo, Becan, Altar de Sacrificios, Seibal, San José, Nohmul, and many other sites in the Lowlands. Toltec Chichen Itza can no longer be viewed as occurring entirely after these occupations, many of which were extremely vigorous, although it probably continued after the decline of most of them.

As a number of archaeologists have argued, more or less forcefully, over the past years, the Toltec presence was a regional tradition that affected the rest of the Lowlands in varying degrees at different times. It was not a uniform cultural period that inevitably followed the end of the Classic Maya tradition, in the North or in the South. The data presented in the preceding pages give us at least an idea of the varying degrees to which Chichen Itza came in contact with and exercised control over neighboring and distant polities. It follows that we cannot reasonably infer, in advance, what events in any one area characterized this period. David Pendergast's discussion in this volume of what happened in the Postclassic at Lamanai is a good example of what we mean.

Steadily accumulating, though still sadly inadequate, information from excavations throughout the Lowlands has led us to revise, in this case, one portion of the strongly linear sequence of culture periods developed for northern Yucatan. There is a lesson here, and it is that similar situations almost certainly occurred at other times and in other places, from the beginning of the Formative until the Spanish Conquest and afterward. In an effort to make sense of what is always a limited sample, we sometimes tend to project our glimpse of the pattern beyond the small area we see from our window, inferring far greater regularities across the human landscape than may turn out to be warranted. We must be wary of doing so.

It also behooves us to remember that different classes of material culture may not be telling us the same things and that the associations among then cannot be assumed. Archaeologists have been rediscovering this seemingly obvious fact in prehistoric cultures of diverse degrees of complexity around the world for many years, perhaps especially in the past two decades. Yet we tend easily to forget this lesson, and when, in the course of our own work, we again arrive at the realization that the relationships between different subsets of material remains, far from being straightforward, are often bafflingly complex, it comes as a heady surprise. The recognition of these complexities and disjunctions in the archaeological record is apparent to some degree in all the contributions to this volume and constitutes, we think, one of its major strengths.

One forms very different conclusions, for example, about the nature of the Toltec presence in the Maya Lowlands by looking at Toltec and Puuc architecture and art, on the one hand, and at the Sotuta and Cehpech ceramic spheres, on the other. They did not go hand in hand, and what understanding we have of the Toltec phenomenon results in part from tracing their interaction.

The overlap of late Puuc and Toltec centers; the strong possibility that major Puuc construction ceased not long after A.D. 900, after which Chichen Itza continued as a potent force in northern Yucatan; and the spread of the Sotuta ceramic sphere at about this time to many sites, including Uxmal, Dzibilchaltun, and Cozumel Island, again raises questions about the nature of this interaction. Did, in fact, the dominion of Chichen Itza spread over much of northern Yucatan, and was this political force responsible for the decline of the Pure Florescent sites? We think the answer is yes, but the nature and force of the contact must have varied enormously. And if Chichen Itza did emerge, perhaps by A.D. 950, as the primate city in the North, why and how did it do so? A. P. Andrews (1978b) thinks control of the salt trade was the magnet, but other economic and political lures must have been strong, too. Was the Toltec presence, or tradition, more militaristic than that of the societies surrounding it? Warfare among sites was endemic by the Late Postclassic, and it likely was a powerful stimulus in the development of increasingly large and influential political units, as Webster (1976a, 1976b, 1977) has argued, but the sheer effectiveness of Chichen Itza in this form of interaction seems to have surpassed that of any earlier Maya site. David Freidel's contribution to this volume suggests that the formation of Maya-Mexican economic cartels and less emphasis on the maintenance of pure dynastic lines in the North contributed to its economic and political success at a time when the Southern cities were failing. Arthur Miller (1977a) argued that the battle murals painted in the Upper Temple of the Jaguars in the Ball Court Group at Chichen Itza show events in Oaxaca. The red hills in these scenes look to us suspiciously like the kegelkarst haystack-shaped hills of the Bolonchen district of the Puuc (Kurjack, Garza T. de González, and Lucas 1979), where much of the soil is red. A depiction of victorious battles in this area seems more probable than one of conflict in distant Oaxaca, where the ties of Toltec Chichen Itza must have been rather tenuous, a point with which most of the Advanced Seminar participants would agree (see Robles C. and Andrews's paper in this volume).

We discussed the problem of Toltec origins in Yucatan at the seminar but have little to add to what is currently known. It seems unlikely to us that, given the depth of the Toltec tradition in Yucatan, we can trace it simply to Tula, and no one argued for the derivation of Toltec Tula from Chichen Itza. Strong Central Mexican features are present at Chichen Itza, but some, such as the form and decoration of the terraces of the Castillo, are not found at Tula. It seems most probable that groups of nonclassic, Mexicanized Maya, as they have been called at Altar de Sacrificios and Seibal, from unknown areas near the southern Gulf Coast, were in large part responsible for the new cultural configuration that we call Toltec, and that they channeled Mexican influences into northern Yucatan. These groups, perhaps allied with the dominant Mexican political units of the time, may well have been a driving force behind the military, political, and economic success of both Tula and Chichen Itza.

THE BEGINNING OF THE POSTCLASSIC PERIOD

It is the accepted wisdom in the field, as expressed in virtually all the texts on the ancient Maya, that a major change in the development of Maya civilization occurred with the Classic Maya collapse in the ninth century A.D.. However, we would argue that another significant implication of the overlap model is that the major change came with the fall of Chichen Itza in the thirteenth century A.D. and not with the fall of the Classic centers in the South or with the rise of the Puuc sites in the North. In other words, we believe that there is greater continuity from the Late Preclassic phenomena that we now know at Mirador, Cerros, Komchen, and other sites up through the fall of Chichen Itza itself, than there is between the decline of Chichen Itza and the rise of Mayapan.

Like those presented in the first part of this chapter, this interpretation is not without precedent. In his introduction to the final report on Mayapan, Pollock stated:

Another matter worth recording is that our recent work in Yucatan has made it amply clear that a major break in cultural tradition, as witnessed by a sharp degeneration of the quality of the remains, came about at the end of Maya-Toltec times. This event tends to be obscured in being marked only by the passage from one substage to another (Early Mexican–Middle Mexican) in Brainerd's arrangement of cultural stages. It does not affect the sequence of the relative chronology, but it may have implications concerning history. (1962: 5–6)

The same point was made by Andrews IV:

A number of years of intensive excavation since the war have made it even more abundantly clear that what used to be called the "Puuc" or "Florescent" and the "Toltec" periods are manifestations of a single cultural tradition and that each of these components much more closely resembles the other than they do the major periods which preceded and followed. (1965a: 318–19)

We think this argument is compatible with either the 11.16.0.0.0 or the 11.3.0.0.0 correlation, although we strongly favor the former. The correlation question does not seriously weaken the argument that significant change in the developmental trajectory of complex society in the Maya Lowlands accompanied the demise of Chichen Itza.

On the basis of architecture, use of space, ceramics, and other material items, it can be argued that the major elements of classicism persisted in the Puuc region and at Chichen Itza through the Modified Florescent or Early Postclassic Period. Although we admit that our bias is toward lumping rather than splitting, it still seems to us that a dispassionate examination of the sites in the Puuc region, Puuc-

452

influenced sites, and Chichen Itza itself shows that they are much closer in appearance to the earlier Classic sites of both the Southern and Northern Lowlands than they are to Mayapan and other late sites. Thus, we would argue that there is a significant break in site layout and construction and in a variety of material classes, as well as in the sociopolitical and economic inferences we can make from them, between Chichen Itza and Mayapan. We also see a significant change in political organization with the rise of the Mayapan confederacy, the idea of depositing families (held in effect as hostages) at a major center, and political centralization of large areas. Although some of these practices may have had antecedents in earlier periods, we are suggesting that the basic organization of the confederacy of Mayapan was quite different from anything that had been seen before in the Maya Lowland world.

Looking at Mayapan and its contemporaries, one sees a near abandonment of what traditionally has been called Florescent architecture and pottery. For example, in comparing Temple 1 at Tikal, the Temple of the Magician at Uxmal, or the Castillo at Chichen Itza with any of the buildings at Mayapan, Tulum, or other late sites, one sees in the latter group much cruder construction, significantly less decoration, and other indications of less rigorous standards. Willey, in Chapter 2 (this volume), refers to the Late Postclassic "as a reduced, shrunken, impoverished version of its former Classic condition." Although emphasizing the changes that appear with the rise of Mayapan, we would not be inclined to use such strong, value-laden terms. In fact, Sabloff has argued, along with Rathje (see Sabloff and Rathje 1975a, 1975b; Rathje 1975), that from an economic or political point of view, the Late Postclassic was anything but impoverished.

In addition, one can argue that there is more Central Mexican influence in the architecture at Mayapan than there is in the architecture of the Puuc sites or Chichen Itza, especially in the conception of buildings, their proportions and perspectives. We think that a significant change occurred in both public and private construction at Mayapan, although this point could be argued. Moreover, there was a virtual end to what we might call, in the largest sense, Classic carving at Mayapan. In certain places a new emphasis was placed on murals or plaster decoration, but the conception was no longer Classic.

We also conclude that there was significantly less investment in large public architecture after the fall of Chichen Itza (see Rathje 1975). Even though one might argue about the labor involved in stone carving versus working in plaster, it seems clear that public architecture of the type, size, and extent found at Mayapan and other sites on the East Coast could not have required a labor force comparable to that indicated for Chichen Itza, the Puuc region sites, or the Classic centers that preceded them.

It is important to recognize that the acceptance of the overlap model leads one to see that with the demise of the Puuc region sites and Chichen Itza, for the first time there was, with the rise of Mayapan and the Mayapan Confederacy, a virtual absence of large sites anywhere in the Northern Plains, except at Mayapan itself. We must look to the East Coast, northern Belize, or the lake region of the Peten for major sites. Thus, there appears to have been a significant shift in regional settlement patterns in the north with the rise of Mayapan.

Older arguments about growing mercantilism and changes in religious organization with the rise of Mayapan, made by Rathje and Sabloff (Sabloff and Rathje 1975a, 1975b; Rathje 1975) among others, also would be applicable, although such arguments (which would not be accepted by many of the seminar participants) certainly are not crucial to the main point being made here.

The disjunction we posit between the fall of Chichen Itza and the rise of Mayapan, however, was not total. On the basis of new research reported in several of the preceding chapters, it is becoming increasingly clear that the rise of Mayapan and its confederacy probably had some of its roots in the Southern Lowlands, where there seems to have been much more continuity between what traditionally has been called the Early and Late Postclassic, in northern Belize, and on the East Coast. Moreover, we can see the addition of elements from the west, including the Gulf Coast and Central Mexico. Thus, what we are now seeing, we would argue, is a much more complex picture of interchange, competition, and influence than was possible in the older view of a simple linear development through time (and space) in the Maya Lowlands.

It should be clear from this discussion that we are talking about much more than where to draw the line between the Classic and Postclassic. We are striving to understand the nature of the development and changes in complex society in the Maya Lowlands. According to traditional views, the fall of Classic civilization in the Southern Maya Lowlands began a decline that continued until the Spanish Conquest in the sixteenth century. The weight of recent research and analyses, however, indicates that the demise of many major centers in the Southern Lowlands during the late eighth to early ninth centuries A.D. may not have been as radical an event in the trajectory of ancient Maya civilization as was once believed. Although the collapse of most of the southern centers may have ushered in significant demographic shifts in the Maya Lowlands, if one adopts an overall view of the Lowlands, the continuities appear to outweigh the changes heavily. The evidence for strong continuities casts new light on the ability of the Maya to adapt to the changing economic and political realities of the Mesoamerican world and challenges the belief that the so-called Classic collapse had a disastrous impact on the ancient Maya cultural system. It focuses attention on the reasons for the demographic and economic shifts around A.D. 800 and also directs research toward understanding the reasons for the emergence of the Postclassic sociopolitical system at Mayapan and other sites after A.D. 1200. In sum, the overlap model not only necessitates the re-evaluation of the relationships among Terminal Classic sites in the South, the Puuc region sites, and Chichen Itza, but it additionally implies that archaeologists must rethink the whole question of the nature, adaptability, and persistence of the Classic Maya social, political, and economic system.

One of the great problems we face is that our formulation rests on insufficient information, with isolated individual sites dominating our thinking. Almost certainly, years from now we will look back and say that our discussions were naive, because we relied too greatly on too few data both for historical reconstructions and for the foundation of most of our hypotheses. Thus, one of the goals all the seminar participants have tried to reach in this volume, as a means of strengthening our grasp of the post–A.D. 800 era in the Maya Lowlands, has been the offering of preliminary suggestions of very specific sites, regions, periods, and questions which the field could profitably address in coming years.

To conclude, we believe that it is worth emphasizing that one effect of the ideas presented in this book is a long-overdue redress of the domination of Maya studies by a Southern Lowlands, Classic Period point of view. Here, we are attempting to look at the totality of developments in the Maya Lowlands. Whether one is looking at the overlap argument, the disjunction argument, or some other question, an underlying theme in all the discussions is that we have to adopt a much wider perspective in *all* periods in order to do away with the older, restricted viewpoints that have dominated Maya archaeology for so many decades.

References

ABASCAL, R., P. DAVILIA, P. J. SCHMIDT, AND D. Z. DAVILA
1976   "La arqueología del sur-oeste de Tlaxcala (primera parte)," *Communicaciones Proyecto Puebla-Tlaxcala 11.*

ADAMS, RICHARD E. W.
1963   "A Polychrome Vessel from Altar de Sacrificios, Peten, Guatemala," *Archaeology* 16 (2): 90–92.
1969   "Maya Archaeology 1958–1968, A Review," *Latin American Research Review* 4 (2): 3–45.
1970   "Suggested Classic Period Occupational Specialization in the Southern Maya Lowlands," in *Monographs and Papers in Maya Archaeology*, ed. William R. Bullard, pp. 487–98. Papers of the Peabody Museum, vol. 61 (Cambridge, Mass.: Harvard University).
1971   *The Ceramics of Altar de Sacrificios*, Papers of the Peabody Museum, vol. 63, no. 1 (Cambridge, Mass.: Harvard University).
1973   "Maya Collapse: Transformation and Termination in the Ceramic Sequence at Altar de Sacrificios," in *The Classic Maya Collapse*, ed. T. Patrick Culbert, pp. 133–63 (Albuquerque: University of New Mexico Press, School of American Research Advanced Seminar Series).
1977   "Rio Bec Archaeology and the Rise of Maya Civilization," in *The Origins of Maya Civilization*, ed. Richard E. W. Adams, pp. 77–99 (Albuquerque: University of New Mexico Press, School of American Research Advanced Seminar Series).

1978   "Routes of Communication in Mesoamerica: The Northern Guatemalan Highlands and the Peten," in *Mesoamerican Communication Routes and Cultural Contacts*, eds. Thomas A. Lee, Jr., and Carlos Navarrete, pp. 27–35. Papers of the New World Archaeological Foundation, no. 40 (Provo: Brigham Young University).

ADAMS, RICHARD E. W., W. E. BROWN, JR., AND T. PATRICK CULBERT
1981   "Radar Mapping, Archaeology, and Ancient Maya Land Use," *Science* 213: 1457–63.

ADAMS, RICHARD E. W., AND NORMAN HAMMOND
1982   "Maya Archaeology, 1976–1980: A Review of Major Publications," *Journal of Field Archaeology* 9: 487–512.

ADAMS, RICHARD E. W., AND W. D. SMITH
1981   "Feudal Models for Classic Maya Civilization," in *Lowland Maya Settlement Patterns*, ed. Wendy Ashmore, pp. 335–49 (Albuquerque: University of New Mexico Press, School of American Research Advanced Seminar Series).

ADAMS, RICHARD E. W., AND A. TRIK
1961   *Temple I (Str. 5-I): Post Constructional Activities*, University Museum Monographs 7 (Philadelphia).

ADAMS RICHARD E. W., AND FRED VALDEZ, JR.
1980   "The Ceramic Sequence of Colha, Belize: 1979 and 1980 Seasons," in *The Colha Project: Second Season, 1980, Interim Report*, eds. Thomas R. Hester, Jack D. Eaton, and Harry J. Shafer, pp. 15–40 (San Antonio: Center for Archaeological Research, The University of Texas at San Antonio and Centro Studi e Ricerche Ligabue, Venezia).

ALLEN, WILLIAM L., AND JAMES B. RICHARDSON III
1971   "The Reconstruction of Kinship from Archaeological Data: The Concepts, the Methods, and the Feasibility," *American Antiquity* 36: 41–53.

ANDREWS, ANTHONY P.
1973   "A Preliminary Study of the Ruins of Xcaret and a Reconnaissance of Other Archaeological Sites on the Central Coast of Quintana Roo, Mexico," *Atti del XL Congressi Internazionale degli Americanisti* (Rome, 1972), I: 473–77 (Genova: Tilgher).
1976   "El proyecto Xcaret y reconocimiento de la costa central de Quintana Roo," *Boletín de la Escuela de Ciencias Antropológicas de la Universidad de Yucatán* 4 (19): 10–20.
1977   "Reconocimiento arqueológico de la costa norte del Estado de Campeche," *Boletín de la Escuela de Ciencias Antropológicas de la Universidad de Yucatán* 4 (24): 64–77.

References

1978a   "Breve addenda al 'Reconocimiento arqueológico de la costa norte del Estado de Campeche'," *Boletín de la Escuela de Ciencias Antropológicas de la Universidad de Yucatán* 6 (33): 40–43.

1978b   "Puertos costeros del Postclásico Temprano en el norte de Yucatán," *Estudios de Cultura Maya* 11: 75–93.

1980a   "Salt-making, Merchants and Markets: The Role of a Critical Resource in the Development of Maya Civilization," Ph.D. diss., University of Arizona.

1980b   "The Salt Trade of the Ancient Maya," *Archaeology* 33 (4): 24–33.

1982   "Archaeological Mollusca from Tancah, Quintana Roo: A Brief Report," Appendix III in *On the Edge of the Sea: Mural Painting at Tancah-Tulum, Quintana Roo, Mexico*, by Arthur G. Miller, pp. 129–30 (Washington, D.C.: Dumbarton Oaks).

1983   *Maya Salt Production and Trade* (Tucson: University of Arizona Press).

ANDREWS, ANTHONY P., AND FERNANDO ROBLES C.

1985   "Chichen Itza and Coba: An Itza-Maya Standoff in Early Postclassic Yucatan," in *The Lowland Maya Postclassic*, eds. Arlen F. Chase and Prudence M. Rice (Austin: University of Texas Press). In press.

n.d.   *Excavaciones Arqueológicas en El Meco, Quintana Roo*. In preparation.
(eds.)

ANDREWS IV, E. WYLLYS

1940   "Chronology and Astronomy in the Maya Area," *The Maya and Their Neighbors*, eds. Clarence L. Hay et al., pp. 150–61 (New York: Appleton-Century).

1943   *The Archaeology of Southwestern Campeche*, Carnegie Institution of Washington Publication 546, Contribution 40 (Washington, D.C.).

1965a   "Archaeology and Prehistory in the Northern Maya Lowlands: An Introduction," in *Handbook of Middle American Indians*, vol. 2, eds. Robert Wauchope and Gordon R. Willey, pp. 288–330 (Austin: University of Texas Press).

1965b   "Progress Report on the 1960–1964 Field Seasons, National Geographic Society–Tulane University Dzibilchaltun program," in *Archaeological Investigations on the Yucatan Peninsula*, pp. 23–67. Middle American Research Institute Publication 31 (New Orleans: Tulane University).

1969   *The Archaeological Use and Distribution of Mollusca in the Maya Lowlands*, Middle American Research Institute Publication 34 (New Orleans: Tulane University).

1970   *Balankanche, Throne of the Tiger Priest*, Middle American Research Institute Publication 32 (New Orleans: Tulane University).

1973   "The Development of Maya Civilization after Abandonment of the Southern Cities," in *The Classic Maya Collapse*, ed. T. Patrick

Culbert, pp. 243–65 (Albuquerque: University of New Mexico Press, School of American Research Advanced Seminar Series).

ANDREWS IV, E. WYLLYS, AND ANTHONY P. ANDREWS

1975   *A Preliminary Study of the Ruins of Xcaret, Quintana Roo, Mexico, with notes on other archaeological remains on the east coast of the Yucatan Peninsula*, Middle American Research Institute Publication 40 (New Orleans: Tulane University).

ANDREWS IV, E. WYLLYS, AND E. WYLLYS ANDREWS V

1980   *Excavations at Dzibilchaltun, Yucatan, Mexico*, Middle American Research Institute Publication 48 (New Orleans: Tulane University).

ANDREWS IV, E. WYLLYS, AND IRWIN ROVNER

1973   "Archaeological Evidence on Social Stratification and Commerce in the Northern Maya Lowlands: Two Masons' Tool Kits from Muna and Dzibilchaltun, Yucatan," in *Archaeological Investigations on the Yucatan Peninsula*, pp. 81–102. Middle American Research Institute Publication 31 (New Orleans: Tulane University).

ANDREWS V, E. WYLLYS

1972   "Comments on the Archaeological Sequence in the Northern Maya Lowlands," xeroxed manuscript on file at the Middle American Research Institute, Tulane University.

1978   "The Northern Maya Lowlands Sequence," endnote to "Eastern Mesoamerica" (Gareth W. Lowe), in *Chronologies in New World Archaeology*, eds. R. E. Taylor and Clement W. Meighan, pp. 377–81 (New York: Academic Press).

1979   "Some Comments on Puuc Architecture of the Yucatan Peninsula," in *The Puuc: New Perspectives*, ed. Lawrence Mills, pp. 1–17. Scholarly Studies in the Liberal Arts 1 (Pella, Iowa: Central College).

1981   "Dzibilchaltun," in *Supplement to the Handbook of Middle American Indians* 1, eds. Victoria R. Bricker and Jeremy A. Sabloff, pp. 313–44 (Austin: University of Texas Press).

ANDREWS, GEORGE F.

1975   *Maya Cities: Placemaking and Urbanization* (Norman: University of Oklahoma Press).

1982   "Puuc Architectural Styles: A Reassessment," paper presented at the Symposium on The Northern Maya Lowlands: New Data, Syntheses and Problems, Universidad Nacional Autónoma de México, Mexico, D.F., June 1982.

ANDREWS, JOANN M.

1976   "Reconnaissance and Archeological Excavations in the Rio Bec Area of the Maya Lowlands," in *National Geographic Society Research Reports, 1968 Projects*, pp. 19–27 (Washington, D.C.).

ANGHIERA, PEDRO MARTYR DE

1626   (1516) *The historie of the West Indies, containing the acts and adventures of the Spaniards, which have conquered and peopled those countries*, trans. M. Lok, Andrew Webb (London).

ASHMORE, WENDY

1980 "The Classic Maya Settlement at Quirigua," *Expedition* 23: 20–27.

n.d. "Ideological Structure in Ancient Maya Settlement Patterns," paper presented at the Eighty-second Annual Meeting of the American Anthropological Association (1983), Chicago.

AVENI, ANTHONY F.

1975 *Archaeoastronomy in Pre-Columbian America* (Austin: University
(ed.) of Texas Press).

1977 *Native American Astronomy* (Austin: University of Texas Press).
(ed.)

1980 *Skywatchers of Ancient Mexico* (Austin: University of Texas Press).

BAKER, B. LEA

1976 "Maya Inter-Center Spatial Organization," paper presented at the Seventy-fifth Annual Meeting of the American Anthropological Association, Washington, D.C.

BALL, JOSEPH W.

1974a "A Coordinate Approach to Northern Maya Prehistory: A.D. 700–1000," *American Antiquity* 39 (1): 85–93.

1974b "A Regional Ceramic Sequence for the Rio Bec Area," in *Archaeological Investigations on the Yucatan Peninsula*, pp. 113–17. Middle American Research Institute Publication 31 (New Orleans: Tulane University).

1976 "Ceramic Sphere Affiliations of the Barton Ramie Ceramic Complexes," in *Prehistoric Pottery Analysis and the Ceramics of Barton Ramie in the Belize Valley*, by J. C. Gifford, pp. 323–30. Memoirs of the Peabody Museum, vol. 18 (Cambridge, Mass.: Harvard University).

1977a *The Archaeological Ceramics of Becan, Campeche, Mexico*, Middle American Research Institute Publication 43 (New Orleans: Tulane University).

1977b "An Hypothetical Outline of Coastal Maya Prehistory; 300 B.C.–A.D. 1200," in *Social Process in Maya Prehistory: Studies in Honor of Sir Eric Thompson*, ed. Norman Hammond, pp. 167–96 (London: Academic Press).

1977c "The Rise of the Northern Maya Chiefdoms: A Socioprocessual Analysis," in *The Origins of Maya Civilization*, ed. Richard E. W. Adams, pp. 101–32 (Albuquerque: University of New Mexico Press, School of American Research Advanced Seminar Series).

1978 "Archaeological Pottery of the Yucatan-Campeche Coast," in *Studies in the Archaeology of Coastal Yucatan and Campeche*, Middle American Research Institute Publication 46: 69–146 (New Orleans: Tulane University).

1979a "Ceramics, Culture History, and the Puuc Tradition: Some Alternative Possibilities," in *The Puuc: New Perspectives*, ed. Lawrence Mills, pp. 18–35. Scholarly Studies in the Liberal Arts 1 (Pella, Iowa: Central College).

1979b   "The 1977 Central College Symposium on Puuc Archaeology: A Summary View," in *The Puuc: New Perspectives*, ed. Lawrence Mills, pp. 46–51. Scholarly Studies in the Liberal Arts 1 (Pella, Iowa: Central College).

1980   *The Archaeological Ceramics of Chinkultic, Chiapas, Mexico*, Papers of the New World Archaeological Foundation no. 43 (Provo: Brigham Young University).

1982a   "The Tancah Ceramic Situation: Cultural and Historical Insights from an Alternative Material Class," Appendix I, in *On the Edge of the Sea: Mural Painting at Tancah-Tulum, Quintana Roo, Mexico*, by Arthur G. Miller, pp. 105–18 (Washington, D.C.: Dumbarton Oaks).

1982b   "The Chronology of Public Ceremonialism at El Cenote Sagrado, Chichen Itza: A Reassessment," paper presented at the Forty-seventh Annual Meeting of the Society for American Archaeology, Minneapolis.

1985a   "The Postclassic Archaeology of the Western Gulf Coast: Some Initial Observations," in *The Lowland Maya Postclassic*, eds. Arlen F. Chase and Prudence M. Rice (Austin: University of Texas Press). In press.

1985b   "The Postclassic that Wasn't: The Thirteenth through Seventeenth Century Archaeology of Central Eastern Campeche, Mexico," in *The Lowland Maya Postclassic*, eds. Arlen F. Chase and Prudence M. Rice (Austin: University of Texas Press). In press.

n.d.   "The 1973 Rio Bec Cultural Ecology Project: Ceramic Evaluations and Notes." Manuscript in possession of the author.

BALL, JOSEPH W., AND JACK D. EATON
1972   "Marine Resources and the Prehistoric Lowland Maya: A Comment," *American Anthropologist* 74: 772–76.

BALL, JOSEPH W., AND IRWIN ROVNER
1972   "Protohistoric Putun Trade Patterns: Evidence from Two Graves at Atasta, Campeche, Mexico," *Katunob* 8 (2): 40–46 (Greeley: Department of Anthropology, University of Northern Colorado).

BALL, JOSEPH W., AND E. WYLLYS ANDREWS V
1975   "The Polychrome Pottery of Dzibilchaltun, Yucatan, Mexico: Typology and Archaeological Context," in *Archaeological Investigations on the Yucatan Peninsula*, pp. 227–47, Middle American Research Institute Publication 31 (New Orleans: Tulane University).

BARRERA RUBIO, ALFREDO
1973–74 "Evolución del Sacerdocio Maya en la Península de Yucatán,"

References

1976a   *Boletín de la Escuela de Ciencias Antropológicas de la Universidad de Yucatán* 1 (2): 6–20; 1 (3): 19–23; 1 (5) 16–20.

1976a   "La Pintura Mural de la Estructura 44 de Tancah, Quintana Roo," *Analte* 1: 25–40 (Merida: Escuela de Ciencias Antropológicas de la Universidad de Yucatán).

1976b   "Salvamento Arqueológico en Pisté, Yucatán," *Boletín de la Escuela de Ciencias Antropológicas de la Universidad de Yucatán* 4 (21): 34–43.

1977a   "Exploraciones Arqueológicas en Tulum, Quintana Roo," *Boletín de la Escuela de Ciencias Antropológicas de la Universidad de Yucatán* 4 (24) 23–63.

1977b   "Tulum: Economia Marino-Litoral y sus Implicaciones Sociales," *XV Mesa Redonda de la Sociedad Mexicana de Antropología* (Guanajuato 1977) 2: 237–45 (Mexico, D.F.).

1979   "Las Pinturas Murales del Area Maya de Norte," *Enciclopedia Yucatanense* 10: 189–222 (Mexico, D.F.).

1980a   "Mural Paintings of the Puuc Region in Yucatan," in *Third Palenque Round Table*, 1978, Part 2, ed. Merle Greene Robertson, pp. 173–82 (Austin: University of Texas Press).

1980b   "Patron de Asentamiento en el Area de Uxmal, Yucatan," *XVI Mesa Redonda de la Sociedad Mexicana de Antropología* (Saltillo 1979), 2: 389–98 (Mexico, D.F.).

1980c   "Tulum desde la Perspectiva del Materialismo Histórico," *Boletín de la Escuela de Ciencias Antropológicas de la Universidad de Yucatán* 8 (44): 27–54.

1982   "El Deterioro de los Edificios Mayas. El Caso de Sabacché, Yucatán," *Boletín de la Escuela de Ciencias Antropológicas de la Universidad de Yucatán* 9 (53): 54–60.

1983a   "La Conquista de Yucatán y la Fundación de Mérida," *Boletín de la Escuela de Ciencias Antropológicas de la Universidad de Yucatán* 10 (58): 9–21.

1983b   "Los Relieves Dinámico-narrativos de San Diego, Yucatán, México," *Mexicon* 5 (4): 63–68.

1985   "Littoral-Marine Economy at Tulum, Quintana Roo, Mexico," in *The Lowland Maya Postclassic*, eds. Arlen F. Chase and Prudence M. Rice (Austin: University of Texas Press). In press.

BARRERA VÁSQUEZ, ALFREDO

1948   *El Libro de los Libros de Chilam Balam* (Mexico City: Fondo de Cultura Económica).

1980   "Four Centuries of Archaeology in Yucatan: A Bibliographical Essay," in *Yucatan: A World Apart*, eds. Edward H. Moseley and Edward D. Terry, pp. 306–19 (University: University of Alabama Press).

1981   "La Arqueología en Yucatán: Pasado, Presente, y Futuro," in *Estudios Linguisticos. Obras Completas*, vol. 2, pp. 223–48 (Merida).

463

BARROLL, M. A.
1980   "Toward a General Theory of Imperialism," *Journal of Anthropological Research* 36 (2): 174–95.
BASTARRACHEA MANZANO, JUAN RAMÓN
1980   "El parentesco y sus implicaciones en la organización social de los mayas prehispánicos," *Enciclopedia Yucatenense* 11: 7–34 (Merida).
BECKER, MARSHALL J.
1973   "Archaeological Evidence for Occupational Specialization Among the Classic Period Maya at Tikal, Guatemala," *American Antiquity* 38: 396–406.
BECQUELIN, PIERRE
1979   "Tonina, a City-State of the Western Maya Periphery," paper presented at the International Congress of Americanists, Vancouver, B.C.
BENAVIDES CASTILLO, ANTONIO
1975a   "El Comercio Maya Prehispánico," *Boletín de la Escuela de Ciencias Antropológicas de la Universidad de Yucatán* 3 (14): 9–28.
1975b   "Los Animales Domesticos en el Norte del Area Maya," *Boletín de la Escuela de Ciencias Antropológicas de la Universidad de Yucatán* 2 (12): 2–13.
1976a   "El Sistema Prehispánico de Comunicaciones Terrestres en la Región de Cobá, Quintana Roo, y sus Implicaciones Sociales," M.A. thesis, Escuela Nacional de Antropología e Historia e Instituto Nacional de Antropología e Historia, Mexico, D.F.
1976b   "Tancah, Quintana Roo. Informe de Actividades, 1975," in *Investigaciones Arqueológicas en el Sureste*. Cuadernos de los Centros no 27: 99–108 (Mexico, D.F.: Instituto Nacional de Antropología e Historia).
1976c   "Xelha, Quintana Roo. Informe de Actividades, 1975," in *Investigaciones Arqueológicas en el Sureste*. Cuadernos de los Centros 27: 84–97 (Mexico, D.F.: Instituto Nacional de Antropología e Historia).
1977   "Los caminos prehispánicos de Cobá," *XV Mesa Redonda de la Sociedad Mexicana de Antropología* (Guanajuato 1977) 2: 215–25 (Mexico, D.F.).
1980a   "Cobá, Quintana Roo, Mexiko. Neue Archäologische Arbeiten," *Mexicon* 2 (1): 5–6.
1980b   "Ecab: una Provincia del Siglo XVI en Yucatán," *XVI Mesa Redonda de la Sociedad Mexicana de Antropología* (Saltillo 1979) 2: 219–26 (Mexico, D.F.).
1980c   "Las Clases Sociales entre los Mayas Antiquos," *Yucatán: Historia y Economía* 4 (20): 23–31.
1980d   "Las Rutas Internas de Yucatán: Problemas Teóricos y Prácticos," *XVI Mesa Redonda de la Sociedad Mexicana de Antropología* (Saltillo 1979) 2: 305–15 (Mexico, D.F.).

References

1981a   "Ecab: Panorama General de una Provincia del Siglo XVI en Yucatán," in *Memoria del Congreso Interno 1979*, pp. 29–37. Centro Regional del Sureste (Mexico, D.F.: Instituto Nacional de Antropología e Historia).

1981b   "La distribución del asentamiento prehispánico en Cobá, Quintana Roo. Observaciones Generales," in *Memoria del Congreso Interno 1979*, pp. 83–98. Centro Regional del Sureste (Mexico, D.F.: Instituto Nacional de Antropología e Historia).

1981c   "Investigaciones Arqueológicas en la Península de Yucatán," paper presented at the XVII Mesa Redonda de la Sociedad Mexicana de Antropología, San Cristóbal de las Casas, Chiapas, Mexico.

1981d   *Los Caminos de Cobá y sus Implicaciones Sociales* (Mexico, D.F.: Instituto Nacional de Antropología e Historia).

1981e   *Cobá. Una Ciudad Prehispánica de Quintana Roo: Guía Oficial* (Mexico, D.F.: Instituto Nacional de Antropología e Historia).

BENAVIDES CASTILLO, ANTONIO, AND ANTONIO P. ANDREWS

1979   *Ecab: Poblado y Provincia del Siglo XVI en Yucatán*. Cuadernos de los Centros Regionales. Centro Regional del Sureste (Mexico, D.F.: Instituto de Antropología e Historia).

BENAVIDES CASTILLO, ANTONIO, AND RAFAEL BURGOS V.

1982   "Xkokoh y Nakaskat, dos sitios del Puuc," *Boletín de la Escuela de Ciencias Antropológicas de la Universidad de Yucatán* 10 (57): 27–30.

BENAVIDES CASTILLO, ANTONIO, AND ABEL MORALES L.

1979   "Los monumentos mayas de Yaxché-Xlabpak a un siglo de su descubrimiento," Antropología e Historia, Epoca III, no. 27: 17–22 (Mexico, D.F.: Instituto Nacional de Antropología e Historia).

BENAVIDES CASTILLO, ANTONIO, AND FERNANDO ROBLES C.

1976   "Cobá: sus Sacbeob y Dzib Mul," *Boletin del INAH*, 2 (15): 55–61 (Mexico, D.F.: Instituto Nacional de Antropología e Historia).

BENAVIDES CASTILLO, ANTONIO, JAIME GARDUÑO A.,
MARGARITA ROSALES DE B., AND FERNANDO ROBLES C.

1976   *Cobá: un Sitio Maya en Quintana Roo*. Cuadernos de los Centros Regionales 26. Centro Regional del Sureste (Mexico, D.F.: Instituto Nacional de Antropología e Historia).

BERLIN, HEINRICH

1953   *Archaeological Reconnaissance in Tabasco*, Carnegie Institution of Washington Current Reports 7 (Washington, D.C.).

1956   *Late Pottery Horizons of Tabasco, Mexico*, Carnegie Institution of Washington Publication 606, Contribution no. 59 (Washington, D.C.).

BEYER, HERMANN

1934   "The Relation of the Synodical Month and Eclipses to the Maya Correlation Problem," in *Studies in Middle America*, pp. 301–19. Middle American Research Institute, Publications 5 (New Orleans: Tulane University).

BINFORD, LEWIS R.
1983   *Working at Archaeology* (New York: Academic Press).
BINFORD, MICHAEL
1983   "Paleolimnology of the Peten Lake District, Guatemala. I. Erosion and Deposition of Inorganic Sediment as Inferred from Granulometry," *Hydrobiologia* 103: 199–203.
BLANTON, RICHARD, AND GARY FEINMAN
1984   "The Mesoamerican World System," *American Anthropologist* 86 (3): 673–82.
BLOCH, MARC
1974   *Feudal Society, Vol. 1: The Growth of Ties of Dependence*, trans. L. A. Manyon (Chicago: University of Chicago Press).
BOLLES, JOHN S.
1977   *Las Monjas: A Major Pre-Mexican Architectural Complex at Chichén Itzá* (Norman: University of Oklahoma Press).
BOVE, FREDERICK J.
1981   "Trend Surface Analysis and the Lowland Classic Maya Collapse," *American Antiquity* 46 (1): 93–112.
BRAINERD, G. W.
1941   "Fine Orange Pottery in Yucatan," *Revista Mexicana de Estudios Antropológicos* 5: 163–83.
1953   "On the Design of the Fine Orange Pottery Found at Chichen Itza, Yucatan," *Huastecos, Totonacos, y sus vecinos, Revista Mexicana de Estudios Antropológicos* 13: 463–73.
1958   *The Archaeological Ceramics of Yucatan*, University of California Anthropological Records, vol. 19 (Berkeley and Los Angeles: University of California Press).
BRAY, WARWICK
1977   "Maya Metalwork and its External Connections," in *Social Process in Maya Prehistory: Studies in Honor of Sir Eric Thompson*, ed. Norman Hammond, pp. 365–404 (New York: Academic Press).
BRICKER, HARVEY M., AND VICTORIA R. BRICKER
1983   "Classic Maya Prediction of Solar Eclipses," *Current Anthropology* 24: 1–24.
BRINTON, DANIEL G.
1881   "Notes on the Codex Troano, and Maya Chronology," *American Naturalist* 15: 719–24.
1882   *The Maya Chronicles*, Brinton's Library of Aboriginal American Literature 1 (Philadelphia).
BRONITSKY, GORDON
1978   "Postclassic Maya Plainware Ceramics: Measures of Cultural Homogeneity," in *Papers on the Economy and Architecture of the Ancient Maya*, ed. Raymond W. Sidrys, pp. 142–54. Institute of Archaeology Monograph 8 (Los Angeles: University of California).
BROTHERSTON, GORDON
1979   "Continuity in Maya Writing: New Readings of Two Passages in

the Book of Chilam Balam of Chumayel," in *Maya Archaeology and Ethnohistory*, eds. Norman Hammond and Gordon R. Willey, pp. 241–58 (Austin: University of Texas Press).

BROWN, KENNETH L.

1977   "The Valley of Guatemala: A Highland Port of Trade," in *Teotihuacan and Kaminaljuyu: A Study in Prehistoric Cultural Contact*, eds. William T. Sanders and Joseph W. Michels, pp. 205–396. Monograph Series in Kaminaljuyu (University Park: Pennsylvania State University Press).

BRUMFIEL, ELIZABETH M.

1981   "The Economics of Power: Tribute Distribution and the Aztec State," paper presented in a Symposium entitled "New Models for the Political Economy of Pre-Columbian Polities," Eightieth Annual Meeting of the American Anthropological Association, Los Angeles.

n.d.   "Tribute Allocation and the Organization of Rural Labor in the Aztec State," in *Pathways to Power: New Approaches to New World Political Economy*, eds. P. Netherley and D. Freidel.

BULLARD, WILLIAM R., JR.

1952   "Residential Property Walls at Mayapan," Carnegie Institution of Washington, Department of Archaeology, *Current Reports* 1 (3): 36–44.

1954   "Boundary Walls and House Lots at Mayapan," in Carnegie Institution of Washington, Department of Archaeology, *Current Reports* 1 (13): 234–53 (Washington, D.C.).

1961   "Archaeological Investigations of the Maya Ruins of Topoxte," in *American Philosophical Society Yearbook 1960*, pp. 551–54 (Philadelphia).

1970   "Topoxte: A Postclassic Maya Site in Peten, Guatemala," *Monographs and Papers in Maya Archaeology*, ed. W. R. Bullard, pp. 245–309. Papers of the Peabody Museum, vol. 61 (Cambridge, Mass.: Harvard University).

1973   "Postclassic Culture in Central Peten and Adjacent British Honduras," in *The Classic Maya Collapse*, ed. T. Patrick Culbert, pp. 221–42 (Albuquerque: University of New Mexico Press, School of American Research Advanced Seminar Series).

CARMACK, ROBERT M.

1981   *The Quiche Mayas of Utatlan* (Norman: University of Oklahoma Press).

CHAMBERLAIN, ROBERT S.

1948   *The Conquest and Colonization of Yucatan, 1517–1550*, Carnegie Institution of Washington Publication 582 (Washington, D.C.)

CHAPMAN, ANNE M.

1957   "Port of Trade Enclaves in Aztec and Maya Civilizations," in *Trade and Market in the Early Empires: Economies in History and The-*

ory, eds. Karl Polanyi, Conrad M. Arensberg, and Harry W. Pearson, pp. 114–53 (Glencoe, Ill.: Free Press).

CHARLTON, THOMAS H.

1968 "Post-conquest Aztec Ceramics: Implications for Archaeological Interpretation," *Florida Anthropologist* 21: 96–101.

1978 "Teotihuacan, Tepeapulco, and Obsidian Exploitation," *Science* 200: 1227–36.

CHASE, ARLEN F.

1976 "Topoxte and Tayasal: Ethnohistory in Archaeology," *American Antiquity* 41: 154–67.

1978 "The 11.3.0.0.0 Correlation, the Books of Chilam Balam, and Yucatecan Culture History." Unpublished manuscript in possession of the author.

1979 "Regional Development in the Tayasal-Paxcaman Zone, El Pete, Guatemala: A Preliminary Statement," *Ceramica de Cultura Maya* 11: 86–119 (Philadelphia: Temple University).

1980 "Major Find from Maya Era Unearthed," *The New Belize* 10 (8): 2–3.

1982 "Con Manos Arriba: Tayasal and Archaeology," *American Antiquity* 47: 167–71.

1983 "A Contextual Consideration of the Tayasal-Paxcaman Zone, El Peten, Guatemala," Ph.D. diss., University of Pennsylvania.

1985 "Postclassic Peten Interaction Spheres: The View from Tayasal," in *The Lowland Maya Postclassic*, eds. Arlen Chase and Prudence Rice (Austin: University of Texas Press). In press.

n.d. "Contextual Implications of Pictorial Vases from Tayasal, Peten," in *Cuarta Mesa Redonda de Palenque*, vol. 5, ed. Elizabeth Benson (Austin: University of Texas Press). In press.

CHASE, ARLEN F., AND DIANE Z. CHASE

1981 "Archaeological Investigations at Hohmul and Santa Rita, Belize: 1979–1980," *Mexicon* 3 (3): 42–44.

CHASE, ARLEN F., AND PRUDENCE M. RICE

1985 *The Lowland Maya Postclassic: Questions and Answers* (Austin:
(eds.) University of Texas Press). In press.

CHASE, DIANE Z.

1981 "The Maya Postclassic at Santa Rita Corozal," *Archaeology* 34 (1): 25–33.

1982a "Temporal and Spatial Variability in Postclassic Northern Belize," Ph.D. diss., University of Pennsylvania.

1982b "The Ikilik Ceramic Complex at Hogmul, Northern Belize," *Cerámica de Cultura Maya* 12: 71–81 (Philadelphia: Temple University).

1985 "Ganned But Not Forgotten: Late Postclassic Archaeology and Ritual at Santa Rita Corozal, Belize," in *The Lowland Maya Postclassic*, eds. Arlen Chase and Prudence Rice (Austin: University of Texas Press). In press.

References

CHASE, DIANE Z., AND ARLEN F. CHASE
1980   "New Finds at Santa Rita Show Corozal Site to be Thriving Maya
         Center," *Brukdown: The Magazine of Belize* 8: 18–21.
1982   "Yucatec Influence in Terminal Classic Northern Belize," *American Antiquity* 47: 596–614.
CHASE, DIANE Z., AND NORMAN HAMMOND
1982   Excavation of Nohmul Structure 20. *Mexicon* 4 (1): 7–12. Berlin.
CIUDAD REAL, ANTONIO DE
1872   "Relación Breve y Verdadera de Algunas Cosas de las Muchas que
         Sucedieron al Padre Fray Alonso Ponce en las Provincias de la
         Nueva Espana," in *Colección de Documentos Inéditos para la
         Historia de España*, vols. 57–58 (Madrid).
CLOSS, MICHAEL P.
1976   "New Information on the European Discovery of Yucatan and the
         Correlation of the Maya and Christian Calendars," *American Antiquity* 41: 192–95.
COE, MICHAEL D.
1956   "The Funerary Temple Among the Classic Maya," *Southwestern
         Journal of Anthropology* 12: 387–94.
1965   "A Model of Ancient Community Structure in the Maya Lowlands," *Southwestern Journal of Anthropology* 21: 97–114.
1977   "Olmec and Maya: A Study in Relationships," in *The Origins of
         Maya Civilization*, ed. Richard E. W. Adams, pp. 183–97 (Albuquerque: University of New Mexico Press, School of American
         Research Advanced Seminar Series).
1981   "Religion and the Rise of Mesoamerican States," in *The Transition
         to Statehood in the New World*, eds. Grant D. Jones and Robert
         R. Kautz, pp. 157–71 (Cambridge: Cambridge University Press).
COE, WILLIAM R.
1965a   "Tikal, Guatemala, and Emergent Maya Civilization," *Science*
         147: 1401–19.
1965b   "Tikal: Ten Years of Study of a Maya Ruin in the Lowlands of
         Guatemala," *Expedition* 8 (1): 5–56.
1967   *Tikal, A Handbook of the Ancient Maya Ruins* (Philadelphia: University Museum, University of Pennsylvania).
COE, WILLIAM R., AND VIVIAN L. BROMAN
1958   "Excavations in the Stela 23 Group," *Museum Monographs, University of Pennsylvania, Tikal Reports*, no. 2.
COGGINS, CLEMENCY C.
1975   "Painting and Drawing Styles at Tikal: An Historical and Iconographic Reconstruction," Ph.D. diss., Harvard University.
1979   "A New Order and the Role of the Calendar: Some Characteristics
         of the Middle Classic Period at Tikal," in *Maya Archaeology and
         Ethnohistory*, eds. Norman Hammond and Gordon R. Willey,
         pp. 38–51 (Austin: University of Texas Press).
1983   *The Stucco Decoration and Architectural Assemblage of Structure*

1-Sub, Dzibilchaltun, Yucatan, Mexico. Middle American Research Institute Publication no. 49 (New Orleans: Tulane University Program of Research on the Yucatan Peninsula, National Geographic Society).

1984   "Catalog," in *Cenote of Sacrifice: Maya Treasures from the Sacred Well at Chichen Itza,* ed. Clemency Chase Coggins and Orrin C. Shane III (Austin: University of Texas Press).

COHODAS, MARVIN

1974   "The Great Ball Court at Chichen Itza, Yucatan, Mexico," Ph.D. diss., Columbia University.

1978   "Diverse Architectural Styles and the Ball Game Cult: The Late Middle Classic Period in Yucatan," in *Middle Classic Mesoamerica: A.D. 400–700,* ed. Esther Pasztory, pp. 86–107 (New York: Columbia University Press).

1982   "Architecture of the Warrior Cult at Chichen Itza: symbolic configurations and astronomical orientations," paper presented at the Symposium on the Northern Maya Lowlands: New Data, Syntheses, and Problems, Universidad Nacional Autónoma de México, Mexico, D.F.

COLLEA, BETH

1981   "The Postclassic in Belize," manuscript, Seminar in Middle American Archaeology, Tozzer Library, Peabody Museum (Cambridge, Mass.: Harvard University).

CONNOR, JUDITH G.

1975   "Ceramics and Artifacts," in *A Study of Changing Pre-Columbian Commercial Systems. The 1972–1973 Seasons at Cozumel, Mexico,* eds. Jeremy A. Sabloff and William L. Rathje, pp. 114–35. Peabody Museum Monographs 3 (Cambridge, Mass.: Harvard University).

CORTÉS, HERNÁN

1963   *Cartas de Relación de la Conquista de México* (Mexico, D.F.: Editorial Porrua).

CORTÉS DE BRASDEFER, FERNANDO

1981a   "La Extensión de Cobá," paper presented at the XVII Mesa Redonda de la sociedad Mexicana de Antropología, San Cristobal de las Casas, Chiapas, Mexico.

1981b   "El Templo del Señor Thompson," *Boletín de la Escuela de Ciencias Antropológicas de la Universidad de Yucatán* 8–9 (48–49): 51–61.

1981c   "La Zona Habitacional de Cobá," paper presented at the XVII Mesa Redonda de la Sociedad Mexicana der Antropología, San Cristobal de las Casas, Chiapas, Mexico.

1981d   "Hallazgos Recientes en Cobá, Quintana Roo," *Boletín de la Escuela de Ciencias Antropológicas de la Universidad de Yucatán* 9 (50–51): 52–59.

References

COTTIER, JOHN W.
1982 "The Dzibilchaltun Survey: Consideration of the Test-Pitting Evidence," Ph.D. diss., University of Missouri, Columbia.

COWGILL, GEORGE L.
1963 "Postclassic Period Culture in the Vicinity of Flores, Peten, Guatemala," Ph.D. diss., Harvard University.

1964 "The End of Classic Maya Culture: a review of recent evidence," *Southwestern Journal of Anthropology*, 20 (2): 145–59.

1979 "Teotihuacan, internal militaristic competition, and the fall of the Classic Maya," in *Maya Archaeology and Ethnohistory*, eds. Norman Hammond and Gordon R. Willey (Austin: University of Texas Press).

CRAINE, EUGENE R., AND REGINALD C. REINDORF
1979 *The Codex Perez and the Book of Chilam Balam of Mani* (Norman: University of Oklahoma Press).

CRANE, CATHY
n.d. "Late Preclassic Maya Agriculture, Wild Plant Utilization, and Land Use Practices at Cerros," in *Investigations at Cerros, Belize: An Interim Report*, eds. R. A. Robertson and D. A. Freidel (Dallas: Institute for the Study of Earth and Man and Department of Anthropology, Southern Methodist University, forthcoming).

CULBERT, T. PATRICK
1973a "The Maya Downfall at Tikal," in *The Classic Maya Collapse*, ed. T. Patrick Culbert, pp. 63–92 (Albuquerque: University of New Mexico Press, School of American Research Advanced Seminar Series).

1973b *The Classic Maya Collapse* (Albuquerque: University of New Mex-
(ed.) ico Press, School of American Research Advanced Seminar Series).

in press "The Collapse of Classic Maya Civilization," paper prepared for the School of American Research Seminar on the Collapse of Ancient Civilization, February 1982, Santa Fe.

DALTON, GEORGE
1975 "Karl Polanyi's Analysis of Long-Distance Trade and His Wider Paradigm," in *Ancient Civilization and Trade*, eds. Jeremy A. Sabloff and C. C. Lamberg-Karlovsky, pp. 63–132 (Albuquerque: University of New Mexico, School of American Research Advanced Seminar Series).

DAMON, P. E., C. W. FERGUSON, A. LONG, AND E. I. WALLICK
1974 "Dendrochronologic Calibration of the Radiocarbon Time Scale," *American Antiquity* 39: 350–66.

DAVOUST, MICHEL
1977 *Etude Epigraphique 2: Les Chefs Mayas de Chichén Itzá et les Glyphs de Filiation* (Angers, France).

1980 "Les Premiers Chefs Mayas de Chichén Itzá," *Mexicon* 2 (2): 25–29.

DEEVEY, EDWARD S.
1978 "Holocene Forests and Maya Disturbance Near Quexil Lake, Peten, Guatemala," *Polskie Archivum Hydrobiologii* 25: 117–29.
1984 "Stress, Strain, and Stability of Lacustrine Ecosystems," in *Lake Sediments and Environmental History*, eds. E. Y. Hayworth and J. W. G. Lund (Leicester: Leicester University Press).

DEEVEY, EDWARD S., AND DON RICE
1980 "Colluviación y retención de nutrimentos en el distrito lacustre del Peten, Central, Guatemala," *Biotica* 5: 129–44.

DEEVEY, EDWARD S., MARK BRENNER, AND MICHAEL BINFORD
1983 "Paleolimnology of the Peten Lake District, Guatemala. III. Late Plesitocene and Gamblian Environments of the Maya Area," *Hydrobiologia* 103: 211–16.

DEEVEY, EDWARD S., L. J. GRALENSKI, AND V. HOFFREN
1959 "Yale Natural Radiocarbon Measurements IV," *American Journal of Science Radiocarbon Supplement* 1: 144–72.

DEEVEY, EDWARD S., DON RICE, PRUDENCE RICE, HAGUE H. VAUGHAN, MARK BRENNER, AND MICHAEL S. FLANNERY
1979 "Maya Urbanism: Impact on a Tropical Karst Environment," *Science* 206: 298–306.

DRENNAN, ROBERT
1984 "Long-Distance Movement of Goods in Prehispanic Mesoamerica: Its Importance in the Complex Societies of the Formative and Classic," *American Antiquity* 49: 27–43.

EATON, JACK D.
1974a "Shell Celts from Coastan Yucatan, Mexico," *Bulletin of the Texas Archaeological Society* 45: 197–208.
1974b "Chicanna: An Elite Center in the Rio Bec Region," in *Archaeological Investigations on the Yucatan Peninsula*, Middle American Research Institute Publication 31 (New Orleans: Tulane University).
1976 "Ancient Fishing Technology on the Gulf Coast of Yucatan, Mexico," *Bulletin of the Texas Archaeological Society* 47: 231–243.
1978 "Archaeological Survey of the Yucatan-Campeche Coast," in *Studies in the Archaeology of Coastal Yucatan and Campeche, Mexico*, Middle American Research Institute Publication 46 (New Orleans: Tulane University).

EBRIGHT, R. H.
1981 "Mayapan, Yucatan, Mexico, the Archaeology and the Ethnohistory," manuscript, Seminar in Middle American Archaeology, Tozzer Library, Peabody Museum (Cambridge, Mass.: Harvard University).

References

EDIGER, DONALD
1971   *The Well of Sacrifice* (Garden City, N.Y.: Doubleday).
EDMONSON, MUNRO S.
1976   "The Mayan Calendar Reform of 11.16.0.0.0," *Current Anthropology* 17: 713–17.
1978   *See* 1979.
1979   "Some Postclassic Questions about the Classic Maya," in *Tercera Mesa Redonda de Palenque*, vol. IV, eds. Merle Greene Robertson and D. C. Jeffers, pp. 9–18 (Chiapas, Mexico: Precolumbian Art Research Center; and Herald Printers, Monterey, Calif.).
1982   *The Ancient Future of the Itza: The Book of Chilam Balam of Tizimin* (Austin: University of Texas Press).
EDWARDS, CLINTON R.
1976   "Nautical Technology and Maritime Routes in Mesoamerica," *Atti del XL Congressi Internazionale degli Americanisti* (Rome 1972) IV: 199–202 (Genova, Tilgher).
ERASMUS, CHARLES J.
1968   "Thoughts on Upward Collapse: An Essay on Explanation in Anthropology," *Southwestern Journal of Anthropology* 24: 170–94.
ESCALONA RAMOS, ALBERTO
1940   *Cronología y Astronomía Maya-Méxica (con un anexo de historias indígenas* (Mexico).
1946   "Algunas Ruinas Prehispánicas en Quintana Roo," *Boletín de la Sociedad Mexicana de Geografía y Estadística* 61: 513–628.
EWING, M. ROBERT
1972   "A History of the Archaeological Activity at Chichen-Itza, Yucatan, Mexico," Ph.D. diss., Kent State University.
FARRISS, NANCY M.
1978   "Nucleation vs. Dispersal: The Dynamics of Population Movement in Colonial Yucatan," *Hispanic American Historical Review* 58: 187–216
n.d.   "The Colonial Maya of Yucatan," manuscript on file with the author.
FARRISS, NANCY M., AND ARTHUR G. MILLER
1974   "Maritime Culture Contact of the Maya: Underwater Surveys and Test Excavations in Quintana Roo, Mexico," *International Journal of Nautical Archaeology and Underwater Exploration* 6 (2): 141–51.
FARRISS, NANCY M., ARTHUR G. MILLER, AND ARLEN F. CHASE
1975   "Late Maya Mural Paintings from Quintana Roo, Mexico," *Journal of Field Archaeology* 2: 5–10.
FELDMAN, LAWRENCE H.
1972   "Moluscos Mayas: Especies y Orígenes," *Estudios de Cultura Maya* 8: 117–38.

473

FERNÁNDEZ DE OVIEDO Y VALDÉZ, GONZALO
1851–55 *Historia General y Natural de las Indias, Islas y Tierra Firme del Mar Océano*, 4 vols., Amador de los Ríos (Madrid: Real Academia de la Historia).

FETTWEIS-VIENOT, MARTINE
1976 "Algunos Sitios con Pintura Mural de la Costa Oriental de Quintana Roo," in *Investigaciones Arqueológicas en el Sureste*, Cuadernos de los Centros 27: 125–50 (Mexico, D.F.: Instituto Nacional de Antropología e Historia).
1980 "Las Pinturas Murales de Cobá: Período Postclásico," *Boletín de la Escuela de Ciencias Antropológicas de la Universidad de Yucatán* 7 (40): 2–50.
1981 "Les peintures murales postclassiques de Quintana Roo, Mexique," 2 vols., Ph.D. diss., E.H.E.S.S., Paris.

FLANNERY, KENT V.
1982 *Maya Subsistence: Studies in Memory of Dennis E. Puleston* (New
(ed.) York: Academic Press).

FLETCHER, LARAINE A.
1978 "Sociocultural Implications of the Linear Features at Coba, Quintana Roo, Mexico," Ph.D. diss., State University of New York, Stony Brook.

FOGEL, HEIDY
1981 "Cozumel," manuscript, Seminar in Middle American Archaeology, Tozzer Library, Peabody Museum (Cambridge, Mass.: Harvard University).

FOLAN, WILLIAM J.
1972 "Kululkán y un Culto Fálico en Chichén-Itzá, Yucatán, Mexico," *Estudios de Cultura Maya* 8: 77–82.
1977 "El Sacbé Cobá-Ixil: Un Camino Maya del Pasado," *Nueva Antropología* 2 (6): 30–42 (Mexico, D.F.).
1978a "Algunos Ejemplos Arquelógicos de Piedras de Sacrificio en Cobá, Q. Roo," *Boletín de la Escuela de Ciencias Antropológicas de la Universidad de Yucatán* 6 (31): 10–14.
1978b "Coba, Quintana Roo, Mexico: An Analysis of a Prehispanic and Contemporary Source of Sascab," *American Antiquity* 43: 79–85.
1980 "Chichén Itzá, el Cenote Sagrado y Xibalbá: una nueva visión," *Boletín de la Escuela de Ciencias Antropológicas de la Universidad de Yucatán* 8 (44): 70–76.

FOLAN, WILLIAM J., LARAINE A. FLETCHER, AND ELLEN R. KINTZ
1979 "Fruit, Fiber, Bark and Resin: Social Organization of a Maya Urban Center, *Science* 204: 679–701.

FOLAN, WILLIAM J., E. R. KINTZ AND L. A. FLETCHER
1983 *Coba: A Classic Maya Metropolis* (New York: Academic Press).

References

FOLAN, WILLIAM J., ELLEN R. KINTZ, LARAINE A. FLETCHER, AND BURMA H. HYDE
1982   "An Examination of Settlement Patterns at Coba, Quintana Roo, Mexico, and Tikal, Guatemala: A Reply to Arnold and Ford," *American Antiquity* 47: 430–36.

FOLAN, WILLIAM J., AND GEORGE E. STUART
1977   "El Proyecto Cartográfico Arqueológico de Cobá, Q. Roo: Informes Interinos Números 1, 2 y 3," *Boletín de la Escuela de Ciencias Antropológicas de la Universidad de Yucatán* 4 (22–23): 15–71.

FONCERRADA DE MOLINA, MARTA
1980   "Mural Painting in Cacaxtla and Teotihuacan Cosmopolitism," in *Third Palenque Round Table, 1978,* vol. V, part 2, ed. Merle Greene Robertson, pp. 183–98 (Austin: University of Texas Press).

FORD, ANABEL
1981   "Conditions for the Evolution of Complex Societies: Rise of the Central Lowland Maya," Ph.D. diss., University of California at Santa Barbara.

FOX, JOHN W.
1980   "Lowland to Highland Mexicanization Processes in Southern Mesoamerica," *American Antiquity* 45 (1): 43–54.
1981   "The Late Postclassic Eastern Frontier of Mesoamerica: Cultural Innovation Along the Periphery," *Current Anthropology* 22: 321–46.

FREIDEL, DAVID A.
1975   "The Ix Chel Shrine and Other Temples of Talking Idols," in *A Study of Changing Pre-Columbian Commercial Systems: The 1972–1973 Seasons at Cozumel, Mexico,* eds. Jeremy A. Sabloff and William L. Rathje, pp. 107–13. Peabody Museum Monographs no. 3 (Cambridge, Mass.: Harvard University).
1976   "Late Postclassic Settlement Patterns on Cozumel Island, Quintana Roo, Mexico," Ph.D. diss., Department of Anthropology, Harvard University.
1978   "Maritime Adaptation and the Rise of Maya Civilization: The View from Cerros, Belize," in *Prehistoric Coastal Adaptations: The Economy and Ecology of Maritime Middle America,* eds. Barbara L. Stark and Barbara Voorhies, pp. 239–65 (New York: Academic Press).
1981a   "Continuity and Disjunction: Late Postclassic Settlement Patterns in Northern Yucatan," in *Lowland Maya Settlement Patterns,* ed. Wendy Ashmore, pp. 311–32 (Albuquerque: University of New Mexico Press, School of American Research Advanced Seminar Series).
1981b   "The Political Economics of Residential Dispersion Among the Lowland Maya," in *Lowland Maya Settlement Patterns,* ed. Wendy

Ashmore, pp. 371–82 (Albuquerque: University of New Mexico Press, School of American Research Advanced Seminar Series).

1982   "Civilization as State of Mind: The Cultural Evolution of the Lowland Maya," in *The Transition to Statehood in the New World*, eds. Grant D. Jones and Robert R. Kautz, pp. 188–227 (Cambridge: Cambridge University Press).

1983a   "Political Systems in Lowland Yucatan: Dynamics and Structure in Maya Settlement," in *Prehistoric Settlement Patterns: Essays in Honor of Gordon R. Willey*, eds. Evon Z. Vogt and Richard M. Leventhal, pp. 375–86 (Albuquerque: University of New Mexico Press, and Peabody Museum, Harvard University).

1983b   "Lowland Maya Political Economy: Historical and Archaeological Perspectives in Light of Intensive Agriculture," in *Spaniards and Indians in Southeastern Mesoamerica: Essays on the History of Ethnic Relations*, eds. Robert Wasserstrom and Murdo J. Macleod, pp. 40–63 (Lincoln: University of Nebraska Press).

n.d.   "Maya Warfare: An Example of Peer Polity Interaction," in *Peer Polity Interaction*, eds. A. C. Renfrew and J. F. Cherry (Cambridge: Cambridge University Press, forthcoming).

FREIDEL, DAVID A., AND MAYNARD B. CLIFF

1978   "Energy Investment in Late Postclassic Maya Masonry Religious Structures," in *Papers on the Economy and Architecture of the Ancient Maya*, ed. Raymond V. Sidrys, pp. 184–208. Institute of Archaeology Monograph 8 (Los Angeles: University of California).

FREIDEL, DAVID A., AND RICHARD M. LEVENTHAL

1975   "The Settlement Survey," in *A Study of Changing Pre-Columbian Commercial Systems. The 1972–1973 Seasons at Cozumel, Mexico*, eds. Jeremy A. Sabloff and William L. Rathje, pp. 60–76. Peabody Museum Monographs, no. 3 (Cambridge, Mass.: Harvard University).

FREIDEL, DAVID A., AND VERNON L. SCARBOROUGH

1982   "Subsistence, Trade, and Development of the Coastal Maya," in *Maya Subsistence: Studies in Memory of Dennis E. Puleston*, ed. Kent V. Flannery, pp. 131–55 (New York: Academic Press).

FREIDEL, DAVID A., AND LINDA SCHELE

1982   "Symbol and Power: A History of the Lowland Maya Cosmogram," part 2, paper delivered at the Princeton Conference on the Beginnings of Maya Iconography, October.

FRY, R. E.

1969   "Ceramics and Settlement in the Periphery of Tikal, Guatemala," Ph.D. diss., Department of Anthropology, University of Arizona.

GALLARETA NEGRÓN, TOMÁS

1979   "Arqueología de Siete Ciudades Muertas de la Peninsula," *Enciclopedia Yucatanense* 10: 223–59 (Merida, Yucatan, Mexico, D.F.).

1981   "Proyecto Cobá: Extensión y Análisis Preliminar del Asentamiento

References

Prehispánico," *Boletín de la Escuela de Ciencias Antropológicas de la Universidad de Yucatán* 9 (50–51): 60–76.

GALLARETA NEGRÓN, TOMÁS, AND JAMES CALLAGHAN

1981 "Proyecto arqueológico de conservación de la ciudad de Mérida, Yucatán," *Memoria del Congreso Interno* 1979: 145–52.

GANN, T[OMAS W. F.]

1900 "Mounds in Northern Honduras" *Nineteenth Annual Report, 1897– 1898, Bureau of American Ethnology*, part 2, pp. 655–92 (Washington, D.C.: Smithsonian Institution).

1901 *See* 1900.

1911 "Explorations Carried on in British Honduras during 1908–9," *University of Liverpool Annals of Archaeology and Anthropology* 4: 72–87.

1914–16 "Report on Some Excavations in British Honduras," *University of Liverpool Annals of Archaeology and Anthropology* 7: 28–42.

1918 *The Maya Indians of Southern Yucatan and Northern British Honduras*, Bureau of American Ethnology Bulletin 64 (Washington, D.C.: Smithsonian Institution).

GARDUÑO ARGUETA, JAIME

1979a "El muestreo en forma de cruz en Cobá," *Boletín de la Escuela de Ciencias Antropológicas de la Universidad de Yucatán* 7 (38): 29–43.

1979b "Introducción al Patrón de Asentamiento del Sitio de Cobá, Quintana Roo," M.A. thesis, Escuela Nacional de Antropología e Historia, Mexico, D.F.

GARZA TARAZONA DE GONZÁLEZ, SILVIA, AND EDWARD B. KURJACK

1977 "El proyecto Atlas Arqueológico de Yucatán," *XV Mesa Redonda de la Sociedad Mexicana de Antropología* (Guanajuateo 1977) 2: 163–72 (Mexico, D.F.).

1980 *Atlas Arqueológico del Estado de Yucatan*, 2 vols. (Mexico, D.F.: Instituto Nacional de Antropología e Historia).

1981a "El Medio Ambiente y los Asentamientos Mayas en Época Prehispánica," *Memoria del Congreso Interno* 1979: 17–28, Centro Regional del Sureste (Mexico, D.F.: Instituto Nacional de Antropología e Historia).

1981b "Organización territorial de los antiguos mayas peninsulares," paper presented at the XVII Mesa Redonda de la Sociedad Mexicana de Antropología, San Cristobal de las Casas, Chiapas, Mexico.

GENET, JEAN

1934 Letter, *Maya Research* 1: 136.

GESELOWITZ, M. N.

1981 "Chichen Itza," manuscript, Seminar in Middle American Archaeology, Tozzer Library, Peabody Museum (Cambridge, Mass.: Harvard University).

GIFFORD, JAMES C.
1976 *Prehistoric Pottery Analysis and the Ceramics of Barton Ramie in the Belize Valley*, Peabody Museum Memoirs, vol. 18 (Cambridge, Mass.: Harvard University).

GONZÁLEZ DE LA MATA, ROCÍO
1981 "Xamanhá—un puerto prehispánico en la costa de Quintana Roo," paper presented at XVII Mesa Redonda de la Sociedad Mexicana de Antropología, San Cristobal de las Casas, Chiapas, Mexico.
1982 "Proyecto de salvamento arqueológico de Punta Piedra, Quintana Roo," unpublished manuscript on file at the Centro Regional del Sureste (Merida, Yucatan, Mexico).

GONZÁLES DE LA MATA, ROCÍO, AND ELIA DEL CARMEN TREJO ALVARADO
1981 "Playa del Carmen: Excavaciones en la Costa Oriental de Quintana Roo. Temporada 1978," *Memoria del Congreso Interno 1979*, pp. 123–38. Centro Regional del Sureste (Mexico, D.F.: Instituto Nacional de Antropología e Historia).

GONZALES FERNÁNDEZ, BÁLTAZAR
1975 "Cobá, Proyecto Arqueológico," *Boletín de la Escuela de Ciencias Antropológicas de la Universidad de Yucatán* 2 (12): 14–19.
1981 "Depósitos Subterráneos en Uxmal, Yucatán," *Memoria del Congreso Interno 1979*, pp 203–210. Centro Regional del Sureste (Mexico, D.F.: Instituto Nacional de Antropología e Historia).

GONZÁLES LICÓN, ERNESTO
1983 "Salvamento de los terrenos del Centro Regional del Sureste del I.N.A.H.," *Boletín de la Escuela de Ciencias Antropológicas de la Universidad de Yucatán* 10 (58): 23–26.

GOODMAN, J. T.
1905 "Maya Dates," *American Anthropologist* 7: 642–47.

GORDON, GEORGE B.
1913 *The Book of Chilam Balam of Chumayel*, Museum Anthropological Publications, vol. 5 (Philadelphia: University of Pennsylvania).

GRAHAM, ELIZABETH A.
1983 "The Highlands of the Lowlands: Environment and Archaeology in the Stann Creek District, Belize," Ph.D. diss., Cambridge University.

GRAHAM, ELIZABETH, GRANT D. JONES, AND ROBERT R. KAUTZ
1985 "Archaeology and Ethnohistory on a Spanish Colonial Frontier: An Interim Report on the Macal-Tipu Project in Western Belize," in *The Lowland Maya Postclassic*, ed. Arlen F. Chase and Prudence M. Rice (Austin: University of Texas Press). In press.

GRAHAM, J. A.
1972 *The Hieroglyphic Inscriptions and Monumental Art of Altar de Sacrificios*, Papers of the Peabody Museum, vol. 64, no. 2 (Cambridge, Mass.: Harvard University).
1973 "Aspects of Non-Classic Presences in the Inscriptions and Sculp-

tural Art of Seibal," in *The Classic Maya Collapse*, ed. T. Patrick Culbert, pp. 207–19 (Albuquerque: University of New Mexico Press, School of American Research Advanced Seminar Series).

1979 "Maya, Olmecs, and Izapans at Abaj Takalik," *Actes du XLII Congrès Internacional des Americanistes* (Paris 1976) 8: 179–88.

GREGORY, DAVID A.

1975 "San Gervasio," in *A Study of Changing Pre-Columbian Commercial Systems. The 1972–1973 Seasons at Cozumel, Mexico*, eds. Jeremy A. Sabloff and William L. Rathje, pp. 88–106, Monographs of the Peabody Museum, no. 3 (Cambridge, Mass.: Harvard University).

GUILLEMIN, J. F.

1977 "Urbanism and Hierarchy at Iximche," in *Social Process in Maya Prehistory*, ed. Norman Hammond, pp. 228–64 (London: Academic Press).

GUTHE, C[ARL E.]

1921 "Report of Dr. Carl E. Guthe," in *Carnegie Institution of Washington Yearbook* 20: 364–68 (Washington, D.C.).

1922 "Report on the Excavations at Tayasal," in *Carnegie Institution of Washington Yearbook* 21: 318–19 (Washington, D.C.).

HAMBLIN, NANCY L.

1980 "Animal Utilization by the Cozumel Maya: Interpretation through Faunal Analysis," Ph.D. diss., University of Arizona.

1981 "The Magic Toads of Cozumel," *Mexicon* 3 (1): 10–14.

HAMBLIN, NANCY L., AND AMADEO M. REA

1979 "La avifauna arqueológica de Cozumel," *Boletín de la Escuela de Ciencias Antropológicas de la Universidad de Yucatán* 7 (37): 21–49.

HAMMOND, NORMAN

1974 "Preclassic to Postclassic in Northern Belize," *Antiquity* 48: 177–80.

1975 *Lubaantun, A Classic Maya Realm*, Peabody Museum Monographs, no. 2 (Cambridge, Mass.: Harvard University).

1976 "Maya Obsidian Trade in Southern Belize," in *Maya Lithic Studies: Papers from the 1976 Belize Field Symposium*, eds. Thomas R. Hester and Norman Hammond, pp. 71–81. Center for Archaeological Research Special Report no. 4 (San Antonio: University of Texas).

1977 "Ex Oriente Lux: A View from Belize," in *The Origins of Maya Civilization*, ed. Richard E. W. Adams, pp. 45–76 (Albuquerque: University of New Mexico Press, School of American Research Advanced Seminar Series).

1978 "Cacao and Cobaneros: An Overland Trade Route Between the Maya Highlands and Lowlands," in *Mesoamerican Communication Routes and Cultural Contacts*, eds. T. A. Lee, Jr., and C. Navarrete, pp. 19–25. Papers of the New World Archaeological Foundation, no. 40, Provo, Utah.

1982   *Ancient Maya Civilization* (New Brunswick: Rutgers University Press).

1985   *Nohmul: A Prehistoric Maya Community in Belize. Excavations 1973–1983.* BAR International Series 250 (Oxford: B.A.R.).

HAMMOND, NORMAN, AND WENDY ASHMORE

1981   "Lowland Maya Settlement: Geographical and Chronological Frameworks," in *Lowland Maya Settlement Patterns,* ed. Wendy Ashmore, pp. 19–36 (Albuquerque: University of New Mexico Press, School of American Research Advanced Seminar Series).

HAMMOND, NORMAN, DUNCAN PRING, RICHARD WILK, SARA DONAGHEY, FRANK P. SAUL, ELIZABETH S. WING, ARLENE V. MILLER, AND LAWRENCE H. FELDMAN

1979   "The Earliest Lowland Maya? Definition of the Swasey Phase," *American Antiquity* 44: 92–110.

HARRISON, PETER D.

1974   "Archaeology in Southwestern Quintana Roo: Interim Report of the Uaymil Survey Project," paper presented at the XLI Congreso Internacional de Americanistas, Mexico, D.F.

1979   "The Lobil Postclassic Phase in the Southern Interior of the Yucatan Peninsula," in *Maya Archaeology and Ethnohistory,* eds. Norman Hammond and Gordon R. Willey, pp. 189–207 (Austin: University of Texas Press).

1980   "The Organization of Lowland Maya Culture History: Space and Diversity," paper presented at the Fourth Palenque Round Table, Merle Greene Robertson, organizer. To be published in *Cuarta Mesa Redonda de Palenque,* vol. 5, ed. Elizabeth Benson (Austin: University of Texas Press). In press.

1981   "Some Aspects of Preconquest Settlement in Southern Quintana Roo, Mexico," in *Lowland Maya Settlement Patterns,* ed. Wendy Ashmore, pp. 259–87 (Albuquerque: University of New Mexico Press, School of American Research Advanced Seminar Series).

1982   "Subsistence and Society in Eastern Yucatan," in *Maya Subsistence: Studies in Memory of Dennis E. Puleston,* ed. Kent V. Flannery, pp. 119–30 (New York: Academic Press).

HARRISON, PETER D., AND B. L. TURNER II

1978   *Pre-Hispanic Maya Agriculture* (Albuquerque: University of New
(eds.)   Mexico Press).

HARTIG, HELGA-MARIA

1979   "Datiertes Lintel in Playa del Carmen," *Mexicon* 1 (1): 5–6.

HAVILAND, WILLIAM A.

1968   "Ancient Lowland Maya Social Organization," in *Archaeological Studies in Middle America,* Middle American Research Institute Publication no. 26, pp. 93–117 (New Orleans: Tulane University).

1972   "Family Size, Prehistoric Population Estimates, and the Ancient Maya," *American Antiquity* 37 (1): 135–39.

References

1973a   "Marriage and the Family among the Maya of Cozumel Island, 1570," *Estudios de Cultura Maya* 8: 217–26.

1973b   "Rules of Descent in Sixteenth Century Yucatan," *Estudios de Cultura Maya* 9: 135–50.

HEIGHWAY, CAROLYN, IRIS BARRY, ELIZABETH GRAHAM, DUNCAN PRING, AND NORMAN HAMMOND

1975   "Excavations in the Platform 137 Group, Nohmul," in *Archaeology in Northern Belize: British Museum–Cambridge University Corozal Project 1974–75 Interim Report*, ed. Norman Hammond, pp. 15–72 (Centre of Latin American Studies, University of Cambridge).

HELLMUTH, N. M.

1972   "Excavations begin at Maya Site in Guatemala," *Archaeology* 25: 148–49.

1974   Maps of the Topoxte Islands, unpublished data, FLAAR, Guatemala City.

HELMS, MARY W.

1979   *Ancient Panama: Chiefs in Search of Power* (Austin: University of Texas Press).

HENIGE, DAVID P.

1974   *The Chronology of Oral Tradition: Quest for a Chimera* (Oxford: Clarendon Press).

HESTER, THOMAS R.

1979   *The Colha Project, 1979: A Collection of Interim Papers*, Center
(ed.)   for Archaeological Research (San Antonio: University of Texas).

1980   "The 1980 Season at Colha, Belize: An Overview," in *The Colha Project Second Season, 1980 Interim Report*, eds. Hester et al., pp. 1–14. Article prepared with the collaboration of G. Ligabue, H. J. Shafer, J. D. Eaton, and R. E. W. Adams (San Antonio: University of Texas Center for Archaeological Research and Centro Studi e Ricerche Ligabue, Venezia).

HESTER, THOMAS R., JACK D. EATON, AND HARRY J. SHAFER

(eds.)

1980   *The Colha Project, Second Season, 1980 Interim Report* (San Antonio: University of Texas Center for Archaeological Research and Centro Studi e Ricerche Ligabue, Venezia).

HIRTH, KENNETH G.

1978   "Interregional Trade and the Formation of Prehistoric Gateway Communities," *American Antiquity* 43: 35–45.

ICHON, ALAIN, M. F. FAUVET-BERTHELOT, C. PLOCIENIAK, ET AL.

1980   *Archéologie de sauvetage dans la vallée du Rio Chixoy, no. 2 Cauinal* (Paris: Institut d'Ethnologie).

ICHON, ALAIN, AND RITA GRIGNON

1981   *Archéologie de sauvetage dans la vallée du Rio Chixoy, no. 3 El Jocote* (Paris: Institut d'Ethnologie).

JAECKEL, PAUL
1981   "The Western Maya Lowlands," manuscript, Seminar in Middle
         American Archaeology, Tozzer Library, Peabody Museum (Cam-
         bridge, Mass.: Harvard University).
JAKEMAN, M. WELLS
1945   *The Origins and History of the Mayas* (Los Angeles: Research
         Publishing).
1946   "The Identity of the Itzas," *American Antiquity* 12: 127–30.
1947   *The Ancient Middle-American Calendar System: Its Origin and
         Development*. Brigham Young University Publications in Archae-
         ology and Early History 1 (Provo).
JIMÉNEZ MORENO, WIGBERTO
1941   "Tula y los Toltecas según las fuentes históricas," *Revista Mexi-
         cano de Estudios Antropológicos* 5: 79–83.
JOHNSON, JAY K.
1985   "Postclassic Maya Site Structure at Topoxte, El Peten, Guate-
         mala," in *The Lowland Maya Postclassic*, eds. Arlen Chase and
         Prudence Rice (Austin: University of Texas Press). In press.
JONES, CHRISTOPHER
1969   "The Twin-Pyramid Group Pattern: A Classic Maya Architectural
         Assemblage at Tikal, Guatemala," Ph.D. diss., University of
         Pennsylvania (Ann Arbor: University Microfilms).
1975   "A Painted Capstone from the Maya Area," *Contributions of the
         University of California Archaeological Research Facility* 27: 83–
         110 (Berkeley).
1979   "Tikal as a Trading Center: Why it Rose and Fell," paper presented
         at the Forty-third International Congress of Americanists (Van-
         couver).
JONES, CHRISTOPHER, AND ROBERT J. SHARER
1980   "Archaeological Investigations in the Site-Core of Quirigua," *Ex-
         pedition* 23 (1): 11–20.
JONES, CHRISTOPHER, WENDY ASHMORE, AND ROBERT J.
SHARER
n.d.   "The Quirigua Project: 1977 Season," Quirigua Reports III, Mu-
         seum Monographs, University Museum (Philadelphia: University
         Museum, University of Pennsylvania). In press.
JONES, GRANT D.
1982   "Agriculture and Trade in the Colonial Period Southern Maya
         Lowlands," in *Maya Subsistence: Studies in Memory of Dennis
         E. Puleston*, ed. Kent V. Flannery, pp. 275–93 (New York: Aca-
         demic Press).
1983   "The Last Maya Frontiers of Colonial Yucatan," in *Spaniards and
         Indians in Southeastern Mesoamerica: Essays on the History of
         Ethnic Relations*, eds. Murdo J. Macleod and Robert Wasser-
         strom, pp. 64–91 (Lincoln: University of Nebraska Press).
JONES, G[RANT] D., AND R. KAUTZ
1981   "Archaeology and Ethnohistory on a Spanish Colonial Frontier,"

paper presented at the symposium on Arqueología Historica en el area Maya, XVII Mesa Redonda de la Sociedad Mexicana de Antropología, San Cristobal, Chiapas, Mexico.

JONES, GRANT D., DON S. RICE, AND PRUDENCE M. RICE
1981   "The Location of Tayasal: A Reconsideration in Light of Peten Maya Ethnohistory and Archaeology," *American Antiquity* 46: 530–47.

JUSTESON, JOHN S.
1978   "Maya Scribal Practice in the Classic Period: A Test-Case of an Explanatory Approach to the Study of Writing Systems," Ph.D. diss., Stanford University.

KAUTZ, ROBERT R.
1985   "Postclassic Population, Settlement and Production: Archaeological and Ethnohistoric Perspectives of Tipu,"in *The Lowland Maya Postclassic*, eds. Arlen F. Chase and Prudence Rice (Austin: University of Texas Press).

KELLEY, DAVID H.
1968   "Kakupacal and the Itzas," *Estudios de Cultura Maya* 7: 255–68.
1976   *Deciphering the Maya Script* (Austin: University of Texas Press).
1982   "Notes on Puuc Inscriptions and History," supplement to *The Puuc: New Perspectives*, ed. Lawrence Mills. Scholarly Studies in the Liberal Arts 1 (Pella, Iowa: Central College).
1983   "The Maya Calendar Correlation Problem," in *Civilization in the Ancient Americas: Essays in Honor of Gordon R. Willey*, eds. Richard M. Leventhal and Alan L. Kolata, pp. 157–208 (Albuquerque: University of New Mexico Press and Peabody Museum, Harvard University).
1984   "The Toltec Empire in Yucatan," *Quarterly Review of Archaeology* 5 (1): 12–13.

KINTZ, ELLEN R.
1978   "The Social Organization of a Classic Maya City: Coba, Quintana Roo, Mexico," Ph.D. diss., State University of New York, Stony Brook.

KIRCHOFF, PAUL
1950   "The League of Mayapan and Its Thirteen Calendars: An Historical Geographical Interpretation," abstract of a paper presented to the Viking Fund Supper Conference for Anthropologists.

KONIECZNA, BARBARA, AND PABLO MAYER GUALA
1976   "Uxmal, Yucatán. Informe de la Temporada 1973–1974," in *Investigaciones Arqueológicas en el Sureste*, Cuadernos de los Centros no. 27: 1–18 (Mexico, D.F.: Instituto Nacional de Antropología e Historia).

KOWALSKI, JEFFREY K.
1980   "A Historical Interpretation of the Inscriptions at Uxmal," paper presented at the Fourth Mesa Redonda of Palenque, Chiapas, Mexico.

1981   "The House of the Governor, a Maya Palace at Uxmal, Yucatan, Mexico," Ph.D. diss., Yale University.

KUBLER, GEORGE
1975   *The Art and Architecture of Ancient America: The Mexican, Maya, and Andean Peoples*, 2nd edition (Harmondsworth, England: Penguin Books).
1976   "Mythological Dates at Palenque and the Ring Numbers in the Dresden Codex," in *The Art, Iconography and Dynastic History of Palenque*, Proceedings of the Segunda Mesa Redonda de Palenque, part 3, pp. 225–30 (Pebble Beach, Calif.: Robert Louis Stevenson School).

KUBLER, GEORGE
1980   "Eclecticism at Cacaxtla," in *Third Palenque Round Table, 1978*, vol. 5, part 2, ed. Merle Greene Robertson, pp. 163–72 (Austin: University of Texas Press).

KULP, J. LAURENCE, HERBERT W. FEELY, AND LANSING E. TRYON
1951   "Lamont Natural Radiocarbon Measurements, I," *Science* 114: 565–68.

KURJACK, EDWARD B.
1974   *Prehistoric Lowland Maya Community and Social Organization: A Case Study at Dzibilchaltun, Yucatan, Mexico*, Middle American Research Institute Publication 38, (New Orleans: Tulane University).
1975   "Geografía Politica de los Antiquos Mayas en el NW. de Yucatán, Mexico," *Boletín de la Escuela de Ciencias Antropológicas de la Universidad de Yucatán* 3 (13): 2–8.
1977   See 1979a.
1978   "The Distribution of Vaulted Architecture at Dzibilchaltun, Yucatan, Mexico," *Estudios de Cultura Maya* 10: 91–101.
1979a   *Introduction to the Map of the Ruins of Dzibilchaltun, Yucatan, Mexico*, Middle American Research Institute Publication 47 (New Orleans: Tulane University).
1979b   "Sacbeob: parentesco y el desarollo del estado maya," *XV Mesa Redonda de la Sociedad Mexicana de Antropología* (Guanajuato 1977) 1: 217–30 (Mexico, D.F.).

KURJACK, EDWARD B., AND E. WYLLYS ANDREWS V
1976   "Early Boundary Maintenance in Northwest Yucatan, Mexico," *American Antiquity* 41: 318–25.

KURJACK, EDWARD B., AND SILVIA GARZA T. DE GONZÁLEZ
1981a   "Pre-Colombian Community Form and Distribution in the Northern Maya Area," in *Lowland Maya Settlement Patterns*, ed. Wendy Ashmore, pp. 287–309 (Albuquerque: University of New Mexico Press, School of American Research Advanced Seminar Series).
1981b   "Una vision de la geografía humana en la región serrana de Yucatán," in *Memoria del Congreso Interno 1979*, pp. 39–54. Centro

References

Regional del Sureste (Mexico, D.F.: Instituto Nacional de Antropología e Historia).

KURJACK, EDWARD B., SILVIA GARZA T. DE GONZÁLEZ, AND JERRY LUCAS
1979 "Archaeological Settlement Patterns and Modern Geography in the Hill Region of Yucatan," in *The Puuc: New Perspectives*, ed. Lawrence Mills, pp. 36–45. Scholarly Studies in the Liberal Arts 1 (Pella, Iowa, Central College).

LAMB, WELDON
1980 "The Sun, Moon and Venus at Uxmal," *American Antiquity* 45: 79–86.

LAMBERT, JOHN D. H., AND J. THOR ARNASON
1982 "Ramon and Maya Ruins: An Ecological, not an Economic, Relation," *Science* 216: 298–99.

LANGE, FREDERICK W.
1971 "Marine Resources: A Viable Subsistence Alternative for the Prehistoric Lowland Maya," *American Anthropologist* 73: 619–39.

LEHMANN, WALTER
1910 "Ergebnisse einer Forschungsreise in Mittelamerika und Mexiko, 1907–1909," *Zeitschrift für Ethnologie* 42: 687–749 (Berlin).

LEVENTHAL, RICHARD M.
1974 "Cozumel: A Functional Analysis of Structures," B.A. thesis, Harvard University.

LIBBY W. F.
1954 "Chicago Radiocarbon Dates V," *Science* 120: 733–42.

LINCOLN, CHARLES E.
1980 "A Preliminary Assessment of Izamal, Yucatan, Mexico," B.A. thesis, Tulane University.
1982 "The 'Total Overlap' Model of Chichen Itza as a Terminal Classic Maya Site: A Discussion of Monumental Sculpture," paper presented at a Symposium on the Northern Maya Lowlands: New Data, Syntheses, and Problems, organizers Paul Gendrop and George F. Andrews, Universidad Nacional Autónoma de México, Mexico, D.F.
1983 "The 'Toltec' at Chichen Itza," paper presented at the Annual Meeting of the American Anthropological Association, Chicago.

LINCOLN, CHARLES E., AND PATRICIA K. ANDERSON
n.d. "Report on the 1983 Field Season at Chichen Itza, Yucatan: Mapping, Reconnaissance, and Overview of Settlement Patterns," Department of Anthropology, Harvard University. In preparation.

LIZANA, BERNARDO DE
1633 *Historia de Yucatán. Devocionario de Nuestra Señora de Izmal y conquista espiritual* (Mexico, D.F. Museo Nacional de México, 2nd edition, 1893).

LONG, AUSTIN, AND BRUCE RIPPETEAU
1974 "Testing Contemporaneity and Averaging Radiocarbon Dates," *American Antiquity* 39: 205–15.

485

LONG, RICHARD C. E.
1931   "The Correlation of Maya and Christian Chronology," *Journal of the Royal Anthropological Institute* 61: 407–12 (London).
LONGYEAR, JOHN M., III
1952   *Copan Ceramics: A Study of Southeastern Maya Pottery*, Carnegie Institution of Washington Publication no. 597 (Washington, D.C.).
LÓPEZ DE COGOLLUDO, D.
1867–68   *Historia de Yucatan*, 3rd edition, 2 vols (Merida).
LÓPEZ DE GÓMARA, FRANCISCO
1552   *Historia General de las Indias . . . y Conquista de México y de la Nueva España, Zaragazo*, various editions. Portions reprinted in *Serie de Cronistas* 1 (Nicaragua).
LOTHROP, SAMUEL K.
1924   *Tulum. An Archaeological Study of the East Coast of Yucatan*, Carnegie Institution of Washington Publication no. 335 (Washington, D.C.).
1952   *Metals from the Cenote of Sacrifice, Chichen Itza, Yucatan*, Memoirs of the Peabody Museum of Archaeology and Ethnology, vol. 10, no. 2 (Cambridge, Mass.: Harvard University).
LUNA E., PILAR
1976   "Un proyecto de arqueología subacuática en Quintana Roo," in *Investigaciones Arqueológicas en el Sureste*, Cuadernos de los Centros 27: 109–24 (Mexico, D.F.: Instituto Nacional de Antropología e Historia).
MACKIE, EUAN W.
1961   "New Light on the End of Classic Maya Culture at Benque Viejo, British Honduras," *American Antiquity* 27: 216–24.
MACNEISH, RICHARD S.
1978   *The Science of Archaeology?* (North Scituate, Mass.: Duxbury Press).
MALDONADO CÁRDENAS, RUBÉN
1977   "La pintura maya en el Clásico y Postclásico," XV *Mesa Redonda de la Sociedad Mexicana de Antropología* (Guanajuato 1977) 2: 179–87 (Mexico).
1979a   "Izamal-Aké, Cansahcab-Ucí, Sistemas Prehispánicos del Norte de Yucatán," *Boletín de la Escuela de Ciencias Antropológicas de la Universidad de Yucatán* 6 (36): 33–34.
1979b   "Los sacbeob de Izamal-Aké y Ucí-Cansahcab en el noroeste de Yucatán," *Antropología e Historia* 27: 23–29 (Mexico, D.F.: Instituto Nacional de Antropología e Historia).
1979c   "Ofrenda del Juego de Pelota de Uxmal," *Novedades de Yucatán*, April 29 (Merida).
1981a   "Implementos de molienda en Ucanhá, un sitio maya del norte de Yucatán," paper presented at the XVII Mesa Redonda de la Sociedad Mexicana de Antropología, San Cristobal de las Casas, Chiapas, Mexico.
1981b   "Intervención de Restauración en el Juego de Pelota de Uxmal, Yucatán," *Memoria del Congreso Interno 1979*: 233–43, Centro

References

Regional del Sureste (Mexico, D.F.: Instituto Nacional de Antropología e Historia).

n.d.   "Dos ofrendas encontradas en el Juego de Pelota, Uxmal," unpublished report on file at the Centro Regional del Sureste (Merida).

MALDONADO CÁRDENAS, RUBÉN, AND BEATRIZ REPETTO TIO

1981   "Ruinas de Aké, un sitio con presencia en el pasado y presente," paper presented at the XVII Mesa Redonda de la Sociedad Mexicana de Antropología, San Cristobal de las Casas, Chiapas, Mexico.

MARCUS, JOYCE

1976   *Emblem and State in the Classic Maya Lowlands* (Washington, D.C.: Dumbarton Oaks).

1982   "The Plant World of the Sixteenth- and Seventeenth-Century Lowland Maya," in *Maya Subsistence: Studies in Memory of Dennis E. Puleston*, ed. Kent V. Flannery, pp. 239–73 (New York: Academic Press).

1983   "Lowland Maya Archaeology at the Crossroads," *American Antiquity* 48: 454–88.

MÁRQUEZ DE GONZÁLES, LOURDES

n.d.   "Dos tumbas en Chichén Itzá: estudio osteológico," manuscript.

MÁRQUEZ DE GONZÁLEZ, LOURDES, AND RICK HARRINGTON

1981   "Spongy Hyperostosis and Cribra Orbitalia in a Maya Subadult Temple," *Paleopathology Newsletter* 35: 12–13 (Detroit, Mich.: Paleopathology Association).

MÁRQUEZ DE GONZÁLEZ, LOURDES, AND TERESA MIRANDA

1981   "Estudios de la variabilidad física de las poblaciones desaparecidas de la península de Yucatán," paper presented at the XVII Mesa Redonda de la Sociedad Mexicana de Antropología, San Cristobal de las Casas, Chiapas, Mexico.

MÁRQUEZ DE GONZÁLEZ, LOURDES, AND PEDRO J. SCHMIDT

1981   Condiciones de salud de una muestra infantil del clásico tardío en Chichen Itza," paper presented at the XVII Mesa Redonda de la Sociedad Mexicana de Antropología, San Cristobal de las Casas, Chiapas, Mexico.

MÁRQUEZ MORFÍN, LOURDES (ed.)

1982   "Playa del Carmen: Una Población de la Costa Oriental en el Postclasico [Un estudio osteológico]," *Colección Científica* 119, Centro Regional del Sureste, Seccion de Antropología Física (Mexico, D.F.: Instituto Nacional de Antropología e Historia).

MARTÍNEZ HERNÁNDEZ, JUAN

1926   *Crónicas Mayas: Crónica de Yaxkukul* (Merida).

MATHENY, RAY T.

1970   *The Ceramics of Aguacatal, Campeche, Mexico*, Papers of the New World Archaeological Foundation no. 27 (Provo: Brigham Young University).

1980   *El Mirador, Peten, Guatemala: An Interim Report*, Papers of the (ed.) New World Archaeological Foundation no. 45 (Provo: Brigham Young University).

MAYER, KARL H.

1982a "Die Skulpturen von Santa Bárbara in Yucatán, Mexiko," *Das Altertum* 28 (3): 215–26 (Berlin).

1982b "Esculturas de Yaxhóm, Yucatán, México," *Boletín de la Escuela de Ciencias Antropológicas de la Universidad de Yucatán* 10 (57): 31–32.

1983a "Gewolgedecksteine mit dekor der Maya-Kultur," *Archiv für Völkerkunde* 37, Museum für Völkerkunde im Selbstverlag.

1983b "Maya-Wandmalerein in Einem Bauwerk von Tancah," *Antike Welt* 14: 30–35.

1983c "Mayaforshung. Entdeckung von Wandmalerein in Xelhá," *I.C. Nachrichten* no. 43/44: 19–20 (Hallein, Austria: Institutum Canarium).

1983d "Steinskulpturen aus Mulultsekal, Yucatán, México," *Ethnologia Americana* 19 (4): 1085–86.

MAYER, KARL H., ROCÍO GONZÁLEZ DE LA MATA, AND ELIA DEL CARMEN TREJO ALVARADO

1979 "Ausgrabungen in Playa del Carmen, Quintana Roo, Mexico: Vorläufiger Beright, *Mexicon* 1 (1): 4–5.

MAYER GUALA, PABLO M.

1977 "Can Cún: Informe Preliminar," *XV Mesa Redonda de la Sociedad Mexicana de Antropología* (Guanajuato 1977) 2: 207–13 (Mexico).

1978 *Can Cún. Guía Oficial* (Mexico, D.F.: Instituto Nacional de Antropología e Historia).

1981 "Interpretaciones preliminares de la cerámica de Cancún," paper presented at the XVII Mesa Redonda de la Sociedad Mexicana de Antropología, San Cristobal de las Casas, Chiapas, Mexico.

MEANS, P. A.

1917 *History of the Spanish Conquest of Yucatan and of the Itzas*, Papers of the Peabody Museum of Archaeology and Ethnology no. 7, Cambridge, Mass.: Harvard University).

MILLER, ARTHUR G.

1972 "The Iconography of the Painting in the Temple of the Diving God, Tulum, Quintana Roo, A Tentative Hypothesis," in *XII Mesa Redonda de la Sociedad Mexicana de Antropología*, pp. 329–33 (Mexico, D.F.).

1973a "Archaeological Investigations of the Quintana Roo Mural Project: A Preliminary Report of the 1973 Season," *Contributions of the University of California Archaeological Research Facility* 18: 137–48 (Berkeley).

1973b "The Mural Painting in Structure 12 at Tancah and in Structure 5 in Tulum, Quintana Roo, Mexico: Implications of Their Style and Iconography," *Atti del XL Congresso Internazionale degli Americanisti* (Roma-Genova 1972) 1: 465–71 (Genova: Tilgher).

1974a "The Iconography of the Painting in the Temple of the Diving

God, Tulum, Quintana Roo, Mexico: The Twisted Cords," in *Mesoamerican Archaeology: New Approaches*, ed. Norman Hammond, pp. 167–86 (Austin: University of Texas Press).

1974b   "West and East in Maya Thought: Death and Rebirth at Palenque and Tulum," *Primera Mesa Redonda de Palenque*, part 2, ed. Merle Green Robertson, pp. 45–49 (Pebble Beach, Calif.: The Robert Louis Stevenson School).

1975   "Archaeological Investigations at Tulum and Tancah, Quintana Roo, Mexico: A Progress Report of the 1974 Season," *Contributions of the University of California Archaeological Research Facility* 27: 10–16 (Berkeley).

1977a   " 'Captains of the Itzá': Unpublished Mural Evidence from Chichén Itzá," in *Social Process in Maya Prehistory: Studies in Honour of Sir Eric Thompson*, ed. Norman Hammond, pp. 197–225 (London: Academic Press).

1977b   "The Maya and the Sea: Trade and Cult at Tancah and Tulum, Quintana Roo, Mexico," in *The Sea in the Pre-Columbian World*, ed. Elizabeth Benson, pp. 96–138 (Washington, D.C.: Dumbarton Oaks).

1978   "Capitanes del Itzá: Evidencia Mural Inédita de Chichén Itzá," *Estudios de Cultura Maya* 11: 121–53.

1979   " 'The Little Descent': Manifest Destiny from the East," *Actes du XLII Congrès International des Américanistes* 8: 221–36 (Paris, 1976).

1981   "The Quintana Roo Mural Project," *National Geographic Society Research Reports* 13: 443–57 (Washington, D.C.).

1982   *On the Edge of the Sea: Mural Painting at Tancah-Tulum, Quintana Roo, Mexico* (Washington, D.C.: Dumbarton Oaks).

1984   "Stylistic Implications of Quirigua Sculpture," in *Quirigua Reports II*, University Museum Monographs (Philadelphia).

MILLER, ARTHUR G., AND NANCY M. FARRISS

1979   "Religious Syncretism in Colonial Yucatan: The Archaeological and Ethnohistorical Evidence from Tancah, Quintana Roo," in *Maya Archaeology and Ethnohistory*, eds. Norman Hammond and Gordon R. Willey, pp. 223–40 (Austin: University of Texas Press).

MILLER, MARY ELLEN

1980   See 1981.

1981   "The Murals of Bonamak, Chiapas, Mexico," Ph.D. diss., Yale University.

MILLET CAMARA, LUIS

1981   "Los Canales de la Costa de Campeche y su Relación con la Industria del Palo de Tinte," paper presented at the XVII Mesa Redonda de la Sociedad Mexicana de Antropología, San Cristobal de las Casas, Chiapas, Mexico.

MILLON, RENE F.

1955   "When Money Grew on Trees: A Study of Cacao in Ancient Mesoamerica," Ph.D. diss., Columbia University.

1973   *Urbanization at Teotihuacan, Mexico. Volume One, The Teoti-*
(ed.)   *huacan Map, Part One: Text* (Austin: University of Texas Press).
1974   "The Study of Urbanism at Teotihuacan, Mexico," in *Meso-*
          american Archaeology: New Approaches, ed. Norman Hammond,
          pp. 335– 62 (Austin: University of Texas Press).
1981   "Teotihuacan: City, State, and Civilization," in *Supplement to*
          the Handbook of Middle American Indians 1, eds. Victoria R.
          Bricker and Jeremy A. Sabloff, pp. 198–243 (Austin: University
          of Texas Press).

MILLS, LAWRENCE
1979   *The Puuc: New Perspectives*, Scholarly Studies in the Liberal Arts
(ed.)   1 (Pella, Iowa: Central College).

MOLINA MONTES, AUGUSTO
1982   "Archaeological Buildings: Restoration or Misrepresentation," in
          Falsifications and Misreconstructions of Pre-columbian Art, ed.
          Elizabeth H. Boone, pp. 125–41 (Washington, D.C.: Dumbarton
          Oaks).

MONTOLIU, MARIA
1978   "Algunos aspectos del venado en la religión de los mayas de Yu-
          catán," *Estudios de Cultura Maya* 10: 149–72.

MORLEY, SYLVANUS G.
1910   "The Correlation of Maya and Christian Chronology," *American*
          Journal of Archaeology, 2nd Series, 14: 193–204.
1911   "The Historical Value of the Books of Chilam Balam," *American*
          Journal of Archaeology, 2nd Series 15: 195–214.
1913   "Archaeological Research at the Ruins of Chichen Itza, Yucatan,"
          in *Reports upon the present condition and future needs of the science*
          of anthropology, by W. H. R. Rivers, A. E. Jenks, and S. G.
          Morley, pp. 61–91. Carnegie Institution of Washington Publica-
          tion 200 (Washington, D.C.).
1920   "Appendix II: The Correlation of Maya and Christian Chronol-
          ogy," in *The Inscriptions at Copan*, Carnegie Institution of Wash-
          ington Publication 219, pp. 465–535 (Washington, D.C.).
1931   "Report of the Chichen Itza Project," in *Division of Historical*
          Research, by A. V. Kidder, pp. 104–108; Carnegie Institution of
          Washington Year Book 30: 101– 65 (Washington, D.C.).
1935   "Inscriptions at the Caracol," appendix to *The Caracol at Chichen*
          Itza, Yucatan, Mexico, by Karl Ruppert, pp. 276–93. Carnegie
          Institution of Washington Publication 454 (Washington, D.C.).
1937–38   *The Inscriptions of Peten*, Carnegie Institution of Washington Pub-
          lication 437 (Washington, D.C.).
1946   *The Ancient Maya* (Palo Alto: Stanford University Press).
1970   "The Stela Platform at Uxmal, Yucatan," edited with notes by H.
          E. D. Pollock, in *Archaeological Studies in Middle America*, pp.
          151–80. Middle American Research Institute Publication 26 (New
          Orleans: Tulane University).

References

MORRIS, CRAIG
1972   "State Settlements in Tawantinsuyu: A Strategy of Compulsory Urbanism," in *Contemporary Archaeology*, ed. Mark Leone, pp. 393–401 (Carbondale: Southern Illinois University Press).
MORRIS, EARL H., JEAN CHARLOT, AND ANN AXTELL MORRIS
1931   *The Temple of the Warriors at Chichen Itza, Yucatan*, 2 vols. Carnegie Institution of Washington Publication 406 (Washington, D.C.).
NAVARRETE, CARLOS
1974   "Material cerámico de la Cueva de Xelhá, Quintana Roo," *Notas Antropológicas* 1 (8): 53–57 (Mexico, D.F.: Universidad Nacional Autónoma de México).
NAVARRETE, CARLOS, J. M. CON URIBE, AND A. MARTÍNEZ MURIEL
1979   *Observaciones arqueológicas en Cobá, Quintana Roo* (Mexico: Universidad Nacional Autónoma de México).
NELSON, FRED W.
1980   "Rutas de intercambio en la península de Yucatán en las diferentes épocas arqueológicas según la evidencia de la obsidiana," in *XVI Mesa Redonda de la Sociedad Mexicana de Antropología* (Saltillo 1979) 1: 349–55 (Mexico, D.F.).
NELSON, FRED W., KIRK K. NIELSEN, NOLAN F. MANGELSON, MAX W. HILL, AND RAY T. MATHENY
1977   "Preliminary Studies of the Trace Element Composition of Obsidian Artifacts from Northern Campeche, Mexico," *American Antiquity* 42 (2): 209–25.
NELSON, FRED W., DAVID A. PHILLIPS, AND ALFREDO BARRERA RUBIO
1983   "Trace Element Analysis of Obsidian Artifacts from the Northern Maya Lowlands," in *Investigations at Edzna, Campeche, Mexico*. vol. 1, part 1: *The Hydraulic System*, by Ray T. Matheny, D. L. Gurr, D. W. Forsyth, and F. R. Hauck, pp. 204–19. Papers of the New World Archaeological Foundation no. 46 (Provo: Brigham Young University).
NETTING, ROBERT McC.
1977   "Maya Subsistence: Mythologies, Analogies, Possibilities," in *The Origins of Maya Civilization*, ed. Richard E. W. Adams, pp. 229–333 (Albuquerque: University of New Mexico Press, School of American Research Advanced Seminar Series).
1982   "Some Home Truths on Household Size and Wealth," *American Behavioral Scientist* 25 (6): 641–62.
NICHOLSON, HENRY B.
1960   "The Mixteca-Puebla Concept in Mesoamerican Archaeology: A Re-examination," in *Men and Cultures*, ed. Anthony F. C. Wallace, pp. 612–18. (Philadelphia: University of Pennsylvania).
1975   "Middle American Ethnohistory: An Overview," in *Handbook of*

Middle American Indians, vol. 15, ed. R. Wauchope, pp. 487–504 (Austin: University of Texas Press).

NIGH, RONALD B.
1981   "Review of *Pre-Hispanic Maya Agriculture*, eds. Peter D. Harrison and B. L. Turner II," *American Antiquity* 46: 707–09.

OCHOA, LORENZO, AND LUIS CASASOLA
1978   "Los Cambios del Patrón de Asentamiento en el Área del Asumacinta," in *Estudios Preliminares Sobre los Mayas de las Tierras Bajas Noroccidentales*, ed. Lorenzo Ochoa, pp. 19–43 (Mexico, D.F.: Universidad Nacional Autónoma de México).

OGDEN J. G., III
1977   "The Use and Abuse of Radiocarbon Dating," in *Amerinds and Their Paleoenvironments in Northeastern North America*, eds. W. Newman and B. Salwen, pp. 167–73 (New York: New York Academy of Sciences).

OVIEDO Y VALDES, G. F. DE
1851–55   *Historia general y natural de las Indias, islas y tierra firme de mar oceano*, 4 vols. (Madrid: Real Academia de la Historia).

PAGDEN, A. R. (trans. and ed.)
1971   *Hernán Cortés: Letters from Mexico* (New York: Orion/Grossman).

PARDI, R., AND L. MARCUS
1977   "Non-Counting Errors in C-14 Dating," in *Amerinds and Their Paleoenvironments in Northeastern North America*, eds. W. Newman and B. Salwen, pp. 174–80 (New York: New York Academy of Sciences).

PARRY, JAMES
1981   "Dawn Comes to Zama: The Postclassic in Quintana Roo, Mexico," manuscript, Seminar in Middle American Archaeology, Tozzer Library, Peabody Museum (Cambridge, Mass.: Harvard University).

PARSONS, LEE A.
1969a   *Bilboa, Guatemala: An Archaeological Study of the Pacific Coast Cotzumalhuapa Region*, vol. 2, Milwaukee Public Museum Publications in Anthropology 12.

1969b   "The Pacific Coast Cotzumalhuapa Region and Middle American Culture History," in *Thirty-eighth International Congress of Americanists* 1: 197–201 (Stüttgart-Munich).

PATCH, ROBERT
1977   "El Mercado Urbano y la Economía Campesina en el Siglo XVIII," *Boletín de la Escuela de Ciencias Antropológicas de la Universidad de Yucatán* 5 (27): 52–66.

PAXTON, MERIDETH
1982a   "Los frescos de Tulum, Quintana Roo: algunos fotos de Samuel K. Lothrop," *Boletín de la Escuela de Ciencias Antropológicas de la Universidad de Yucatán* 9 (53): 50–53.

References

1982b   "The Tulum Frescoes: Some Early Photographs," *Mexicon* 4 (1): 4–7.

PENDERGAST, D. M.

1964   "Excavaciones en la Cueva Eduardo Quiroz, Distrito Cayo, Honduras Britanica," *Estudios de Cultura Maya* 4: 119–39.

1967   "Occupación post-clásica en Altun Ha, Hunduras Britanica," *Revista Mexicana de Estudios Antropológicos* 21: 213–24.

1969   *The Prehistory of Actun Balam, British Honduras*, Royal Ontario Museum, Art and Archaeology, Occasional Paper 16 (Toronto: Royal Ontario Museum).

1970   *A. H. Anderson's Excavations at Rio Frio Cave E, British Honduras (Belize)*, Royal Ontario Museum, Art and Archaeology, Occasional Paper 20 (Toronto: Royal Ontario Museum).

1974   *Excavations at Actun Polbilche, Belize*, Royal Ontario Museum, Archaeology Monograph 1 (Toronto: Royal Ontario Museum).

1975   "The Church in the Jungle," *Rotunda* 8: 32–40.

1977   "Royal Ontario Museum Excavation: Finds at Lamanai, Belize," *Archaeology* 30: 129–31.

1979   *Excavations at Altun H, Belize, 1964–1970*, vol. 1 (Toronto: Royal Ontario Museum).

1980   "Lamanai 1980: As Easy as Picking Up Quicksilver with a Fork," *Royal Ontario Museum Archaeological Newsletter*, n.s., no. 180 (Toronto: Royal Ontario Museum).

1981a   "Lamanai, Belize: Summary of Excavation Results, 1974–1980," *Journal of Field Archaeology* 8 (1): 29–53.

1981b   "The 1980 Excavations at Lamanai, Belize," *Mexicon* 2 (6): 96–99.

1981c   "Lamanai, Belize: 1981 Excavations," *Mexicon* 3 (4): 62–63.

1982a   *Excavations at Altun Ha, Belize, 1964–1970*, vol. 2 (Toronto: Royal Ontario Museum).

1982b   "Ancient Maya Mercury," *Science* 217: 533–35.

1982c   "Lamanai 1980: Ottawa, Stella Dallas and the Woodlice," *Royal Ontario Museum Archaeological Newsletter*, n.s., no. 203 (Toronto: Royal Ontario Museum).

1982d   "Lamanai 1982 (II): Headaches in Ottawa as Stella Remains Dateless," *Royal Ontario Museum Archaeological Newsletter*, n.s., no. 208 (Toronto: Royal Ontario Museum).

PENICHE RIVERO, PIEDAD, AND WILLIAM J. FOLAN

1978   "Cobá, Quintana Roo, México: Reporte sobre una Metrópoli Maya del Noreste," *Boletín de la Escuela de Ciencias Antropológicas de la Universidad de Yucatán* 5 (30): 48–74.

PÉREZ ÁLVAREZ, CARLOS, AND FERNANDO ROBLES C.

1981   "Xelha: un puerto maya prehispánico en el Caribe," paper presented at the XVII Mesa Redonda de la Sociedad Mexicana de Antropología, San Cristobal de las Casas, Chiapas, Mexico.

PHILLIPS, DAVID A., JR.
1978   "Additional Notes on the Fishing Technology of the Yucatan Pen-
            insula, Mexico," *Bulletin of the Texas Archaeological Society* 49:
            349–53.
1979a   "Material Culture and Trade of the Postclassic Maya," Ph.D. diss.,
            University of Arizona.
1979b   "Pesas de Pesca de Cozumel, Quintana Roo," *Boletín de la Escuela
            de Ciencias Antropológicas de la Universidad de Yucatán* 6 (36):
            2–18.
PIÑA CHÁN, ROMÁN
1970   *Informa Preliminar de la Reciente Exploración del Cenote Sagrado
            de Chichén Itzá*, Serie Investigaciones no. 24 (Mexico, D.F.: In-
            stituto Nacional de Antropología e Historia).
1978   "Commerce in the Yucatan Peninsula: The Conquest and Colo-
            nial Period," in *Mesoamerican Communication Routes and Cul-
            ture Contacts*, eds. Thomas A. Lee, Jr., and Carlos Navarrete,
            pp. 37–48. Papers of the New World Archaeological Foundation
            no. 40 (Provo: Brigham Young University).
POHL, MARY
1981   "Ritual Continuity and Transformation in Mesoamerica: Recon-
            struction of the Ancient Maya *Cuch* Ritual," *American Antiquity*
            46: 513–29.
1983   "Maya Ritual Faunas: Vertebrate Remains from Burials, Caches,
            Caves, and Cenotes in the Maya Lowlands," in *Civilization in
            the Ancient Americas: Essays in Honor of Gordon R. Willey*, eds.
            Richard M. Leventhal and Alan R. Kolata, pp. 55–103 (Albu-
            querque: University of New Mexico Press, and Peabody Museum,
            Harvard University).
POHL, MARY, AND LAWRENCE H. FELDMAN
1982   "The Traditional Role of Women and Animals in Lowland Maya
            Economy," in *Maya Subsistence: Studies in Memory of Dennis
            E. Puleston*, ed. Kent V. Flannery, pp. 295–311 (New York: Ac-
            ademic Press).
POLANYI, KARL
1971   *Primitive, Archaic, and Modern Economies: Essays of Karl Polanyi*,
            ed. George Dalton (Boston: Beacon Press).
1975   "Traders and Trade," in *Ancient Civilization and Trade*, eds.
            Jeremy A. Sabloff and C. C. Lamberg-Karlovsky, pp. 133–54
            (Albuquerque: University of New Mexico Press, School of Amer-
            ican Research Advanced Seminar Series).
POLANYI, KARL, CONRAD M. ARENSBERG, AND HARRY W.
PEARSON
1957   *Trade and Market in the Early Empires* (Glencoe, Ill.: Free Press).
POLLOCK, H[ARRY] E. D.
1936   *Round Structures of Aboriginal Middle America*, Carnegie Insti-
            tution of Washington, Publication 471 (Washington, D.C.).

References

1952   "Department of Archaeology," Carnegie Institution of Washington, *Year Book* 51: 235–43 (Washington, D.C.).

1962   "Introduction," in *Mayapan, Yucatan, Mexico*, by H. E. D. Pollock, Ralph L. Roys, Tatiana Proskouriakoff, and A. Ledyard Smith. Carnegie Institution of Washington Publication 619 (Washington, D.C.).

1965   "Architecture of the Maya Lowlands," in *Handbook of Middle American Indians*, vol. 2, pp. 378–440, eds. Robert Wauchope and Gordon R. Willey (Austin: University of Texas Press).

1980   *The Puuc: An Architectural Survey of the Hill Country of Yucatan and Northern Campeche, Mexico*, Memoirs of the Peabody Museum, vol. 19 (Cambridge, Mass.: Harvard University).

POLLOCK, H. E. D., RALPH L. ROYS, TATIANA
PROSKOURIAKOFF, AND A. LEDYARD SMITH
1962   *Mayapan, Yucatan, Mexico*, Carnegie Institution of Washington Publication 619 (Washington, D.C.).

PORTER WEAVER, MURIEL
1972   *The Aztecs, Maya, and Their Predecessors: Archaeology of Mesoamerica* (New York: Seminar Press).

POTTER, DAVID F.
1977   *Maya Architecture of the Central Yucatan Peninsula, Mexico*, Middle American Research Institute Publication 44 (New Orleans: Tulane University).

PRICE, BARBARA J.
1974   "The Burden of the *Cargo*: Ethnographical Models and Archaeological Inference," in *Mesoamerican Archaeology: New Approaches*, ed. Norman Hammond, pp. 445–65 (Austin: University of Texas Press).

1977   "Shifts in Production and Organization: A Cluster-Interaction Model," *Current Anthropology* 18: 209–33.

1978   "Commerce and Cultural Process in Mesoamerica," in *Mesoamerican Communication Routes and Cultural Contacts*, eds. Thomas A. Lee, Jr., and Carlos Navarrete, pp. 231–45. Papers of the New World Archaeological Foundation no. 40 (Provo: Brigham Young University).

PRING, DUNCAN
1975   "The Ceramic Sequence in Northern Belize," in *Archaeology in Northern Belize, British Museum–Cambridge University Corozal Project 1974–1975 Interim Report*, ed. Norman Hammond, pp. 190–211 (Cambridge University Centre of Latin American Studies).

1976a   "The Preclassic Ceramics of Northern Belize," Ph.D. diss., University of London.

1976b   "Outline of the Northern Belize Ceramic Sequence," *Ceramica de Cultura Maya* 9: 11–51.

PROSKOURIAKOFF, TATIANA

1950   A *Study of Classic Maya Sculpture*, Carnegie Institution of Washington publication 593 (Washington, D.C.).

1951   "Some Non-Classic Traits in the Sculpture of Yucatan," in *The Civilizations of Ancient America. Selected Papers of the 29th International Congress of Americanists*, ed. Sol Tax, pp. 108–18 (Chicago: University of Chicago Press).

1955   "The Death of a Civilization," *Scientific American* 192 (5): 82–88.

1960   "Historical Implications of a Pattern of Dates at Piedras Negras, Guatemala," *American Antiquity* 25: 454–75.

1962   "Civic and Religious Structures of Mayapan," in *Mayapan, Yucatan, Mexico*, by H. E. D. Pollock, Ralph L. Roys, Tatiana Proskouriakoff, and A. Ledyard Smith, pp. 87–163. Carnegie Institution of Washington Publication 619 (Washington, D.C.).

1964   "Historical Data in the Inscriptions of Yaxchilan. Part II," *Estudios Cultura Maya* 4: 177–201.

1970   "On Two Inscriptions at Chichen Itza," in *Monographs and Papers in Maya Archaeology*, ed. William R. Bullard, Jr., pp. 457–67. Papers of the Peabody Museum, vol. 61 (Cambridge, Mass.: Harvard University).

1974   *Jades from the Cenote of Sacrifice, Chichen Itza, Yucatan*, Memoirs of the Peabody Museum vol. 10, no. 1 (Cambridge, Mass.: Harvard University).

PULESTON, DENNIS E.

1968   "*Brosimum alicastrum* as a Subsistence Alternative for the Classic Maya of the Central Southern Lowlands," M.A. thesis, University of Pennsylvania.

1979   "An Epistemological Pathology and the Collapse, or Why the Maya Kept the Short Count," in *Maya Archaeology and Ethnohistory*, eds. N. Hammond and G. R. Willey, pp. 63–71 (Austin: University of Texas Press).

1982   "The Role of Ramon in Maya Subsistence," Appendix 2 in *Maya Subsistence; Studies in Memory of Dennis E. Puleston*, ed. Kent V. Flannery, pp. 353–66 (New York: Academic Press).

QUIRARTE, JACINTO

1977   "Early Art Styles of Mesoamerica and Early Classic Maya Art," in *The Origins of Maya Civilization*, ed. Richard E. W. Adams, pp. 249–83. (Albuquerque: University of New Mexico Press, School of American Research Advanced Seminar Series).

RAMOS RODRÍGUEZ, ROSA MARÍA

1978   "Algunos observaciones sobre los enterramientos humanos en el sitio 'El Rey' (Can Cun)," *Anales de Antropología* 15: 251–65 (Mexico, D.F.: Universidad Nacional Autónoma de México).

References

RAMOS RODRÍGUEZ, ROSA MARÍA, E. VARGAS PACHECO, AND
M. GUILLERMO ESPINOSA
1980   "Arqueología, antropología física y matemáticas: estudio de la pob-
            lación prehispánica de Cancún," in Simposio. Quintana Roo:
            Problemática y Perspectivas (Cancun, Q. R., 1980) Memorias,
            pp. 161–71 (Mexico, D.F.: Centro de Investigaciones de Quintana
            Roo and Universidad Nacional Autónoma de México).
RANDS, ROBERT L.
1954   "Artistic Connections between the Chichen Itza Toltec and the
            Classic Maya," American Antiquity 19: 281–82.
1967a   "Ceramic Technology and Trade in the Palenque Region, Mex-
            ico," in American Historical Anthropology, Essays in Honor of
            Leslie Spier, eds. Charles L. Riley and Walter W. Taylor, pp. 135–
            51 (Carbondale: Southern Illinois University Press).
1967b   "Cerámica de la Región de Palenque, México," Estudios de Cul-
            tura Maya 6: 111–47.
1973a   "The Classic Collapse in the Southern Maya Lowlands: Chro-
            nology," in The Classic Maya Collapse, ed. T. Patrick Culbert,
            pp. 43–62 (Albuquerque: University of New Mexico Press, School
            of American Research Advanced Seminar Series).
1973b   "The Classic Maya Collapse: Usumacinta Zone and the North-
            western Periphery," in The Classic Maya Collapse, ed. T. Patrick
            Culbert, pp. 165–205 (Albuquerque: University of New Mexico
            Press, School of American Research Advanced Seminar Series).
1979   "Comparative Data from the Palenque Zone on Maya Civiliza-
            tion," Actes du XLII Congrès International des Américanistes (Paris,
            1976) 8: 135–45 (Paris: Société des Américanistes).
RANDS, ROBERT L., AND RONALD L. BISHOP
1982   "Exchange and Localized Distribution of Maya Fine Orange–Fine
            Gray Ceramics," paper presented at the Forty-seventh Meeting of
            the Society for American Archaeology, Minneapolis, Minn.
RANDS, ROBERT, RONALD L. BISHOP, AND JEREMY A.
SABLOFF
1982   "Maya Fine Paste Ceramics: An Archaeological Perspective," in
            Analyses of Fine Paste Ceramics, ed. Jeremy A. Sabloff. Memoirs
            of the Peabody Museum of Archaeology and Ethnology, vol. 15,
            no. 2 (Cambridge: Harvard University).
RATHJE, WILLIAM L.
1971   "The Origin and Development of Lowland Classic Maya Civili-
            zation," American Antiquity 36: 275–85.
1975   "The Last Tango in Mayapan: A Tentative Trajectory of Produc-
            tion-Distribution Systems," in Ancient Civilization and Trade.
            eds. Jeremy A. Sabloff and C. C. Lamberg-Karlovsky, pp. 409–
            48 (Albuquerque: University of New Mexico Press, School of
            American Research Advanced Seminar Series).

RATHJE, WILLIAM L., AND DAVID A. PHILLIPS, JR.
1975   "The Ruins of Buena Vista," in A *Study of Changing Pre-Colum-
        bian Commercial Systems. The 1972–1973 Seasons at Cozumel,
        Mexico*, eds. Jeremy A. Sabloff and William L. Rathje, pp. 77–
        87. Monographs of the Peabody Museum, no. 3 (Cambridge,
        Mass.: Harvard University).
RATHJE, WILLIAM L., AND JEREMY A. SABLOFF
1973   "Ancient Maya Commercial Systems: A Research Design for the
        Island of Cozumel, Mexico," *World Archaeology* 5 (2): 221–31.
1975   "Theoretical Background: General Models and Questions," in
        A *Study of Changing Pre-Columbian Commercial Systems. The
        1972–1973 Seasons at Cozumel, Mexico*, eds. Jeremy A. Sabloff
        and William L. Rathje. Monographs of the Peabody Museum,
        no. 3 (Cambridge, Mass.: Harvard University).
1978   "A Model of Ports-of-Trade," *Estudios de Cultura Maya* 10: 81–
        90.
REINA, R. E.
1962   "The Ritual of the Skull of Peten, Guatemala," *Expedition* 4 (4):
        26–36.
REINA, R. E., AND R. M. HILL II
1978   *The Traditional Pottery of Guatemala*. Austin: University of Texas
        Press.
RELACIONES DE YUCATAN
1898–1900"Relaciones de Yucatán, in *Colleción de documentos inéditos re-
        lativos al descubrimiento, conquista y organización de las antiguas
        posesiones españoles de ultramar*, 2nd series, vols. 11 and 13 (I,
        II) (Madrid).
REPETTO-TIO, BEATRIZ
1979a   "Desarollo Militar de los Mayas Prehispánicos," B.A. thesis, Univ-
        ersidad de Yucatán, Merida.
1979b   "La organización militar de los mayas del postclásico," *Revista de
        la Universidad de Yucatán* 11 (121): 44–50.
1980   "El concepto de la fortificación y su aplicación en las tierras bajas
        de la zona maya," *Yucatán: Historia y Economía* 4 (22): 26–42.
RICE, DON S.
1974   *The Archaeology of British Honduras: A Review and Synthesis*,
        Katunob, Occasional Publications in Mesoamerican Anthropol-
        ogy, no. 6 (Greeley, Colo.: Museum of Anthropology, University
        of Northern Colorado).
1976   "The Historical Ecology of Lakes Yaxha and Sacnab, El Peten,
        Guatemala," Ph.D. diss., Pennsylvania State University.
1978   "Population growth and subsistence alternatives in a tropical la-
        custrine environment," in *Prehispanic Maya Agriculture*, eds. Pe-
        ter D. Harrison and B. L. Turner II, pp. 35–61 (Albuquerque:
        University of New Mexico Press).
1981   "Zacpeten: A Postclassic Center in Central Peten, Guatemala,"

498

paper presented at the Forty-sixth Annual Meeting of the Society for American Archaeology, San Diego.

RICE, DON S., AND PRUDENCE M. RICE
1979   "Preliminary Report, Proyecto Lacustre, First Field Season, 1979," manuscript prepared for the National Science Foundation.
1980a   "The Northeast Peten Revisited," *American Antiquity* 45: 432–54.
1980b   "Proyecto Lacustre, Second Preliminary Report, Second Season, 1980," manuscript prepared for the National Science Foundation.
1981   "Muralla de Leon: A Lowland Maya Fortification," *Journal of Field Archaeology* 8: 271–88.
1984a   "Collapse to Contact: Postclassic Archaeology of the Peten Maya," *Archaeology* 36: 45–51.
1984b   "Lessons from the Maya," *Latin American Research Review* 19 (3): 7–34.

RICE, PRUDENCE M.
1979   "Ceramic and Nonceramic Artifacts of Lakes Yaxha-Sacnab, El Peten, Guatemala. Part I. The Ceramics. Section B, Postclassic Pottery from Topoxte," *Cerámica de Cultura Maya* 11: 1–85 (Philadelphia: Temple University).
1980   "Peten Postclassic Pottery Production and Exchange: A View from Macanche," in *Models and Methods in Regional Exchange*, ed. R. Fry, pp. 67–82. Occasional Papers of the Society for American Archaeology 1.
1982   "Some Reflections on Change in a Pottery-producing System," paper presented at the symposium on Multidimensional Approaches to the Study of Ancient Ceramics, Lhee, The Netherlands.
1983   "Serpents and Styles in Peten Postclassic Pottery," *American Anthropologist* 85: 866–80.
1984a   "The Ceramics of Negroman-Tipu: A Preliminary Overview," paper presented at the Annual Meeting of the Northeastern Anthropological Association, Hartford, Connecticut.
1984b   "Obsidian Procurement in the Central Peten Lakes Region, Guatemala," *Journal of Field Archaeology* 11: 181–94.
n.d.a   "Macanche Island, El Peten, Guatemala: Excavations, Pottery, and Artifacts," manuscript on file with the author.
n.d.b   "Economic Change in the Lowland Maya Late Classic," in *Production, Exchange, and Complex Societies*, ed. Elizabeth Brumfiel and Timothy Earle (Cambridge: Cambridge University Press). In preparation.

RICE, PRUDENCE M., AND DON S. RICE
1985   "Topoxte, Macanche, and the Central Peten Postclassic," in *The Lowland Maya Postclassic*, eds. Arlen F. Chase and Prudence M. Rice (Austin: University of Texas Press). In press.

RIVERA DORADO, M.
1975   "Exploraciones arqueológicas en Guatemala, 1973," *International Congress of Americanists* 1: 542–550 (Mexico).

ROBERTSON, DONALD
1970   "The Tulum Murals: The International Style of the Late Post-classic," *Thirty-eighth International Congress of Americanists* (Stüttgart and Munich 1968) *Acta* 2: 77–88 (Munich).

ROBLES CASTELLANOS, J. FERNANDO
1976   "Ixil, centro agricola de Cobá," *Boletín de la Escuela de Ciencias Antropológicas de la Universidad de Yucatán* 4 (20): 13–43.
1977   "Evidence for Late Classic Political Units Among the Maya: The Sacbes of Northern Yucatan," paper presented to the Forty-second Annual Meeting of the Society for American Archaeology, New Orleans.
1980   "La Secuencia Cerámica de la Región de Cobá, Quintana Roo," M.A. thesis, Escuela Nacional de Antropología e Historia and Instituto Nacional de Antropología e Historia, Mexico, D.F.
1981a   "La secuencia cerámica preliminar de El Meco, Quintana Roo," in *Memoria del Congreso Interno 1979*, pp. 153–78, Centro Regional del Sureste (Mexico, D.F: Secretaría de Educación Pública).
1981b   "Xelha: un proyecto de investigación," *Memoria del Congreso Interno 1979*, pp. 101–21, Centro Regional del Sureste (Mexico, D.F.: Instituto Nacional de Antropología e Historia).
1981c   *Informe Anual del Proyecto Arqueológico de Cozumel 1980* (Mexico: Fideicomiso Caleta de Xelha y del Caribe).

ROVNER, IRWIN
1974   "Implications of the Lithic Analysis at Becan," in *Archaeological Investigations on the Yucatan Peninsula*, pp. 128–32. Middle American Research Institute Publication 31 (New Orleans: Tulane University).
1975a   "The Cyclical Rise and Fall of Maya Lithic Trade Spheres," paper presented at the Fortieth Annual Meeting of the Society for American Archaeology, Montreal.
1975b   "Lithic Sequences from the Maya Lowlands," Ph.D. diss., University of Wisconsin, Madison.
1978   "Evidence for a Secondary Obsidian Workshop at Mayapan, Yucatan," in *Archaeological Studies of Mesoamerican Obsidian*, ed. Thomas R. Hester, pp. 125–30. Ballena Press Studies in Mesoamerican art, Archaeology and Ethnohistory, no. 3 (Socorro, N.M.: Ballena Press).
1981   "Patrones Anómalos de la Importación de Obsidiana en el Centro de las Tierras Bajas Mayas," paper presented at the I.N.A.H. symposium La Obsidiana en Mesoamerica, Pachuca.

ROYS, LAWRENCE
1933   "The Maya Correlation Problem Today," *American Anthropologist* 35: 403–17.

ROYS, LAWRENCE, AND EDWIN M. SHOOK
1966   *Preliminary Report on the Ruins of Ake, Yucatan,* Society for American Archaeology Memoir 20 (*American Antiquity* 31 [3], Part 2).

ROYS, RALPH L.
1933   *The Book of Chilam Balam of Chumayel,* Carnegie Institution of Washington Publication 438 (Washington, D.C.)

1939   *The Titles of Ebtun,* Carnegie Institution of Washington Publication 505 (Washington, D.C.)

1943   *The Indian Background of Colonial Yucatan,* Carnegie Institution of Washington Publication 548 (Washington, D.C.). (Reprinted 1967, Norman: University of Oklahoma Press).

1954   *The Maya Katun Prophesies of the Books of Chilam Balam,* Carnegie Institution of Washington Publication 606, Contribution 57 (Washington, D.C.).

1957   *The Political Geography of the Yucatan Maya,* Carnegie Institution of Washington Publication 613 (Washington, D.C.).

1960   "The Maya Katun Prophecies of the Books of Chilam Balam," in *Contributions to Anthropology and History,* series 1, vol. 12 (57), pp. 1–60. Carnegie Institution of Washington Publication 606 (Washington, D.C.).

1962   "Literary Sources for the History of Mayapan," in *Mayapan, Yucatan, Mexico,* by H. E. D. Pollock, Ralph L. Roys, Tatiana Proskouriakoff, and A. Ledyard Smith, pp. 24–86. Carnegie Institution of Washington Publication 619 (Washington, D.C.).

1965   "Lowland Maya Native Society at Spanish Contact," in *Handbook of Middle American Indians* 3, eds. Robert Wauchope and Gordon R. Willey, pp. 659–78 (Austin: University of Texas Press).

1966   "Native Empires in Yucatan: The Maya-Toltec Empire," *Revista Mexicana de Estudios Antropológicos* 20: 153–77.

1967   *The Book of Chilam Balam of Chumayel* (Norman: University of Oklahoma Press).

1972   *The Indian Background of Colonial Yucatan,* reprint of Carnegie Institution of Washington Publication 548 (1943) (Norman: University of Oklahoma Press).

RUPPERT, KARL
1931   "The Temple of the Well Panels, Chichen Itza," Carnegie Institution of Washington Publication 403, Contribution 3 (Washington, D.C.).

1935   *The Caracol at Chichen Itza, Yucatan, Mexico,* Carnegie Institution of Washington Publication 454 (Washington, D.C.).

1950   "Gallery-patio Type Structures at Chichen Itza," in *For the Dean,*

Essays in Anthropology in Honor of Byron S. Cummings, eds. Erik K. Reed and Dale S. King, pp. 249–58 (Tucson and Santa Fe: Hohokam Museums Associations and the Southwestern Monuments Association).

1952   *Chichen Itza: Architectural Notes and Plans*, Carnegie Institution of Washington Publication 595 (Washington, D.C.).

RUPPERT, K., AND A. L. SMITH

1957   *House types in the Environs of Mayapan and at Uxmal, Kabah, Sayil, Chichen Itza, and Chacchob*, Carnegie Institution of Washington Current Reports, no. 39 (Washington, D.C.).

RUPPERT, KARL, J. ERIC THOMPSON, AND TATIANA PROSKOURIAKOFF

1955   *Bonampak, Chiapas, Mexico*, Carnegie Institution of Washington Publication 602 (Washington, D.C.).

RUZ LHUILLIER, ALBERTO

1969   *La Costa de Campeche en los Tiempos Prehispánicos: Prospección Cerámica y Bosquejo Histórico*, Serie Investigaciones 18 (Mexico, D.F.: Instituto Nacional de Antropología e Historia).

SABLOFF, JEREMY A.

1970   "Type descriptions of the Fine Paste Ceramics of the Bayal Boca Complex, Seibal, Peten, Guatemala," in *Monographs and Papers in Maya Archaeology*, ed. William R. Bulland, pp. 357–404. Papers of the Peabody Museum of Archaeology and Ethnology, vol. 61 (Cambridge, Mass.: Harvard University).

1971   "Review of *Maya History and Religion*, by J. E. S. Thompson," *American Anthropologist* 73: 311–36.

1973   "Continuity and Disruption During Terminal Late Classic Times at Seibal: Ceramic and Other Evidence," in *The Classic Maya Collapse*, ed. T. Patrick Culbert, pp. 107–31 (Albuquerque: University of New Mexico Press, School of American Research Advanced Seminar Series).

1975   *Excavations at Seibal: Ceramics*, Memoirs of the Peabody Museum of Archaeology and Ethnology, vol. 13(2) (Cambridge, Mass.: Harvard University).

1977   "Old Myths, New Myths: The Role of Sea Traders in the Development of Ancient Maya Civilization," in *The Sea in the Pre-Columbian World*, ed. Elizabeth P. Benson, pp. 67–88 (Washington, D.C.: Dumbarton Oaks).

1983   "Classic Maya Settlement Pattern Studies: Past Problems, Future Prospects," in *Prehistoric Settlement Patterns: Essays in Honor of Gordon R. Willey*, eds. Evon Z. Vogt and Richard M. Leventhal, pp. 413–22 (Albuquerque: University of New Mexico Press, and Peabody Museum, Harvard University).

1985   "New Directions in Archaeological Methodology: Some Implications for Mesoamerican Archaeology," in *La Antropología de Mesoamerica y el Norte de México: Una Puesta al Día*, eds. Jaime

References

Litvak King and Antonio Pompa y Pompa (Mexico, D.F.: Sociedad Mexicana de Antropología). In press.

SABLOFF, JEREMY A., RONALD L. BISHOP, GARMAN HARBOTTLE, ROBERT L. RANDS, AND EDWARD V. SAYRE
1982   *Analyses of Fine Paste Ceramics*, Memoirs of the Peabody Museum of Archaeology and Ethnology, vol. 15(2) (Cambridge, Mass.: Harvard University).

SABLOFF, JEREMY A., AND DAVID A. FREIDEL
1975   "A Model of a Pre-Columbian Trading Center," in *Ancient Civilization and Trade*, eds. Jeremy A. Sabloff and C. C. Lamberg-Karlovsky, pp. 369–405 (Albuquerque: University of New Mexico Press, School of American Research Advanced Seminar Series).

SABLOFF, JEREMY A., AND WILLIAM L. RATHJE
1973   "A Study of Changing Precolumbian Commercial Patterns on the Island of Cozumel, Mexico," *Atti del XL Congresso Internazionale degli Americanisti* (Roma-Genova, 1972) 1: 455–63 (Genova: Tilgher).
1975a   "The Rise of a Maya Merchant Class," *Scientific American* 233 (4): 72–82.
1975b   *A Study of Changing Pre-Columbian Commercial Systems. The 1972–1973 Seasons at Cozumel, Mexico*, Monographs of the Peabody Museum no. 3 (Cambridge, Mass.: Harvard University).
1980   "Archaeological Research on the Island of Cozumel, Mexico," *National Geographic Society Research Reports* 12: 595–99 (Washington, D.C.: National Geographic Society).

SABLOFF, JEREMY A., WILLIAM L. RATHJE, DAVID A. FREIDEL, JUDITH G. CONNOR, AND PAULA L. W. SABLOFF
1974   "Trade and Power in Postclassic Yucatan: Initial Observations," in *Mesoamerican Archaeology: New Approaches*, ed. Norman Hammond, pp. 397–416 (Austin: University of Texas Press).

SABLOFF, JEREMY A., AND GORDON R. WILLEY
1967   "The Collapse of Maya Civilization in the Southern Lowlands: A Consideration of History and Process," *Southwestern Journal of Anthropology* 23: 311–36.

SÁENZ, CÉSAR A.
1972   "Exploraciones y restauraciones en Uxmal (1970–1971)," *Boletín del Instituto Nacional de Antropología e Historia*, época 2, 2: 31–40 (Mexico, D.F.).
1975a   "Exploraciones y reconstrucciones en la Gran Pirámide de Uxmal, Yucatán," *Boletín del Instituto Nacional de Antropología e Historia* época 2, 12: 39–44 (Mexico, D.F.).
1975b   "Cerámica de Uxmal, Yucatán," *Anales del Instituto Nacional de Antropología e Historia*, época 7, 5: 171–86 (Mexico, D.F.).

SANDERS, WILLIAM T.
1955   "An Archaeological Reconnaissance of Northern Quintana Roo,"

Carnegie Institution of Washington Current Reports 24 (2): 179–219 (Washington, D.C.).

1956   "The Central Mexican Symbiotic Region," in *Prehistoric Settlement Patterns in the New World*, ed. Gordon R. Willey, pp. 115–27. Viking Fund Publications in Anthropology no. 23 (New York).

1960   *Prehistoric Ceramics and Settlement Patterns in Quintana Roo, Mexico*, Contributions to American Anthropology and History, vol. 12, no. 60, Carnegie Institution of Washington Publication 606 (Washington, D.C.).

1973   "The Cultural Ecology of the Lowland Maya: A Reevaluation," in *The Classic Maya Collapse*, ed. T. Patrick Culbert, pp. 325–65 (Albuquerque: University of New Mexico Press, School of American Research Advanced Seminar Series).

1977   "Environmental Heterogeneity and the Evolution of Lowland Maya Civilization," in *The Origins of Maya Civilization*, ed. Richard E. W. Adams, pp. 287–97 (Albuquerque: University of New Mexico Press, School of American Research Advanced Seminar Series).

1981   "Classic Maya Settlement Patterns and Ethnographic Analogy," in *Lowland Maya Settlement Patterns*, ed. Wendy Ashmore, pp. 351–69 (Albuquerque: University of New Mexico Press, School of American Research Advanced Seminar Series).

SANDERS, WILLIAM T., JEFFREY R. PARSONS, AND ROBERT S. SANTLEY

1979   *The Basin of Mexico: Ecological Processes in the Evolution of a Civilization* (New York: Academic Press).

SANDERS, WILLIAM T., AND BARBARA J. PRICE

1968   *Mesoamerica: The Evolution of a Civilization* (New York: Random House).

SATTERTHWAITE, LINTON

1956   "Radiocarbon Dates and the Maya Correlation Problem," *American Antiquity* 21: 416–19.

1958   *The Problem of Abnormal Stela Placements at Tikal and Elsewhere*, Tikal Reports 3, University Museum Monographs (Philadelphia).

1965   "Calendrics of the Maya Lowlands," in *Handbook of Middle American Indians*, vol. 3, eds. Robert Wauchope and Gordon R. Willey, pp. 603–31 (Austin: University of Texas Press).

1971   "The Form, Dating and Probable Use of Landa's Christian-Maya Year Table," *Revista Española de Antropología Americana* 6: 9–44 (Universidad de Madrid: Departamento de Antropología y Etnología de America).

SATTERTHWAITE, LINTON, AND WILLIAM R. COE

1968   "The Maya-Christian Calendrical Correlation and the Archaeology of the Peten," in *XXXVII Congreso Internacional de Americanistas: Actas y Memorias* (Buenos Aires, 1966) 3: 3–21.

References

SATTERTHWAITE, LINTON, AND ELIZABETH K. RALPH
1960   "New Radiocarbon Dates and the Maya Correlation Problem,"
        American Antiquity 26: 165–84.
SAUL, FRANK P.
1982   "The Human Skeletal Remains from Tancah, Mexico," Appendix
        II in *On the Edge of the Sea: Mural Painting at Tancah-Tulum,
        Quintana Roo, Mexico*, by Arthur G. Miller, pp. 115–28.
SCARBOROUGH, VERNON L.
1980   "The Settlement System in the Late Preclassic Maya Community:
        Cerros, Northern Belize," Ph.D. diss., Southern Methodist Uni-
        versity.
1983   "A Preclassic Maya Water System," *American Antiquity* 48: 720–
        44.
SCHELE, LINDA
1976   "Accession Iconography of Chan-Bahlum in the Group of the
        Cross at Palenque," in *The Art, Iconography and Dynastic History
        of Palenque, Part III*, pp. 9–34, Proceedings of the Segunda Mesa
        Redonda at Palenque (Pebble Beach, California: The Robert Louis
        Stevenson School).
SCHIFFER, MICHAEL B.
1976   *Behavioral Archaeology* (New York: Academic Press).
SCHMIDT, PETER J.
1981a   "Chichén Itzá: apuntes para el estudio del patrón de asenta-
        miento," *Memoria del Congreso Interno 1979*, pp. 55–70, Centro
        Regional del Sureste (Mexico, D.F.: Instituto Nacional de Antro-
        pología e Historia).
1981b   "La producción agrícola prehistórica de los mayas," *Yucatán: His-
        toria y Economía* 4 —23): 38–54 (Merida).
SCHOLES, F[RANCE] V., AND R[ALPH] L. ROYS
1948   The Maya Chontal Indians of Acalan-Tixchel: A Contribution to
(1968) the History and Ethnography of the Yucatan Peninsula, Carnegie
        Institution of Washington Publication 560 (Washington, D.C.).
        (Reprinted 1968). Norman: University of Oklahoma Press.
SCHOLES, F[RANCE] V., AND J. E. S. THOMPSON
1977   "The Francisco Perez *Probanza* of 1654–1656 and the *Matricula*
        of Tipu (Belize)," in *Anthropology and History in Yucatan*, ed.
        G. Jones, pp. 43–68 (Austin: University of Texas Press).
SELER, EDUARD
1909   "Die Ruinen von Chichen Itza in Yucatan," in *Proceedings of the
        Sixteenth International Congress of Americanists* (Vienna, 1908),
        pp. 151–239; *Gesamelte Abhandlungen* 5: 197–288 (Graz, Aus-
        tria).
1915   *Gesamelte Abhandlungen zur Amerikanischen Sprach un Alter-
        thumskunde*, vol. 5 (reprinted in 1961 by Akademische Druck U.
        Verlaganstalt, Graz, Austria).

SHARER, ROBERT J.
1980   "The Quirigua Project, 1974–1979," *Expedition* 23 (1): 5–10.
1982   "Did the Maya Collapse? A New World Perspective on the Demise of Harappan Civilization," in *Harappan Civilization: A Contemporary Perspective,* ed. G. A. Possehl (Oxford and IBH: American Institute of Indian Studies).

SHARER, ROBERT J., AND WENDY ASHMORE
1979   *Fundamentals of Archaeology* (Menlo Park, California: Benjamin/ Cummings).

SHARER, ROBERT J., AND ARLEN F. CHASE
1976   "New Town Ceramic Complex," in *Prehistoric Pottery Analysis and the Ceramics of Barton Ramie in the Belize Valley,* Memoirs of the Peabody Museum, vol. 18, pp. 288–315 (Cambridge, Mass.: Harvard University).

SHARP, ROSEMARY
1973   "Architecture as Inter-Elite Communication in Pre-Conquest Veracruz, Oaxaca and Yucatan," paper delivered at the Thirty-seventh Annual Meeting of the Society for American Archaeology, San Francisco.
1978   "Architecture as Interelite Communication in Preconquest Oaxaca, Veracruz, and Yucatan," in *Middle Classic Mesoamerica: A.D. 400–700,* ed. Esther Pasztory, pp.158–71 (New York: Columbia University Press).
1981   *Chacs and Chiefs: The Iconology of Mosaic Stone Sculpture in Pre-Conquest Yucatan, Mexico,* Studies in Pre-Columbian Art and Archaeology, no. 24 (Washington, D.C.: Dumbarton Oaks).

SHEPARD, ANNA O.
1948   *Plumbate—A Mesoamerican Trade Ware,* Carnegie Institution of Washington Publication 573 (Washington, D.C.).

SHUMAN, MALCOLM K.
1977   "Archaeology and Ethnohistory: The Case of the Lowland Maya," *Ethnohistory* 24 (1): 1–18.

SIDRYS, RAYMOND V.
1976   "Mesoamerica: An Archaeological Analysis of a Low-Energy Civilization," Ph.D. diss., University of California, Los Angeles.

SIEMENS, ALBERT
1982   "Prehistoric Agricultural Use of the Wetlands of Northern Belize," in *Maya Subsistence: Studies in Memory of Dennis E. Puleston,* ed. K. V. Flannery, pp. 205–25 (New York: Academic Press).

SIERRA SOSA, THELMA, AND FERNANDO ROBLES CASTELLANOS
1981   "Investigaciones arqueológicas en San Gervasio, Isla de Cozumel," paper presented at the XVII Mesa Redonda de la Sociedad Mexicana de Antropología, San Cristobal de las Casas, Chiapas, Mexico.

References

SIMMONS, MICHAEL P., AND GERALD F. BREM
1979   "The Analysis and Distribution of Volcanic Ash-Tempered Pottery in the Lowland Maya Area," *American Antiquity* 44: 79–91.
SIMPSON, LESLEY B. (trans. and ed.)
1966   *Cortés: The Life of the Conqueror by His Secretary Francisco López de Gómara* (Berkeley: University of California Press).
SIRCAR, KANIKA
1982   "The House as Symbol of Identity," paper presented at the Eighty-first Annual Meeting of the American Anthropological Association, Washington, D.C.
SMITH, A. LEDYARD
1950   *Uaxactun, Guatemala, Excavations of 1931–1937*, Carnegie Institution of Washington Publication 588 (Washington, D.C.).
1962   "Residential and Associated Structures at Mayapan," in *Mayapan, Yucatan, Mexico*, by H. E. D. Pollock, Ralph L. Roys, Tatiana Proskouriakoff, and A. Ledyard Smith, pp. 165–319. Carnegie Institution of Washington Publication 619 (Washington, D.C.).
1972   *Excavations at Altar de Sacrificios: Architecture, Settlement, Burials, and Caches*, Papers of the Peabody Museum, vol. 62, no. 2 (Cambridge, Mass.: Harvard University).
SMITH, ROBERT E.
1955   *Ceramic Sequence at Uaxactun, Guatemala*, Middle American Research Institute Publication 20 (New Orleans: Tulane University).
1958   "The Place of Fine Orange Pottery in Mesoamerican Archaeology," *American Antiquity* 24: 151–60.
1971   *The Pottery of Mayapan, Including Studies of Ceramic Material from Uxmal, Kabah, and Chichen Itza*, Papers of the Peabody Museum of Archaeology and Ethnology, vol. 66 (Cambridge, Mass.: Harvard University).
SMITH, ROBERT E., AND JAMES C. GIFFORD
1965   "Pottery of the Maya Lowlands," in *Handbook of Middle American Indians*, vol. 2, eds. Robert Wauchope and Gordon R. Willey, pp. 498–534 (Austin: University of Texas Press).
1966   "Maya Ceramic Varieties, Types, and Wares at Uaxactun: Supplement to 'Ceramic Sequence at Uaxactun, Guatemala'," in *Middle American Research Institute Publication 28*, pp. 125–74 (New Orleans: Tulane University).
SPINDEN, HERBERT J.
1924   *The Reduction of Mayan Dates*, Papers of the Peabody Musuem of American Archaeology and Ethnology, vol. 6, no. 4 (Cambridge, Mass.: Harvard University).
1928   *Ancient Civilizations of Mexico and Central America*, American Museum of Natural History Handbook Series no. 3, 3rd edition. (New York). (Originally published in 1917.)

1930   "Maya Dates and What They Reveal," *Brooklyn [New York] Institute of Arts and Science* 4 (1).

STEPHENS, JOHN L.
1843   *Incidents of Travel in Yucatan*, 2 vols. (New York: Harper and Bros.).

STEWART, T. DALE
1974   "Human Skeletal Remains from Dzibilchaltun, Yucatan, Mexico," in *Archaeological Investigations on the Yucatan Peninsula*, pp. 199–225. Middle American Research Institute Publication no. 31 (New Orleans: Tulane University).

STRECKER, MATTHIAS
1976a   "Felsbilder Yucatans," *Ethnologia Americana* 13 Jahrgang Heft 2, Nr. 74: 708–11 (Dusseldorf).
1976b   "Pinturas rupestres de la Cueva de Loltún, Oxkutzcab, Yucatán," *Boletín del Instituto Nacional de Antropología e Historia*, época 2, 18: 3–8 (Mexico, D.F.).
1979   *Rock Art of East Mexico and Central America: An Annotated Bibliography*, Institute of Archaeology Monograph X (Los Angeles: University of California).
1981   "Exploraciones Arqueológicas de Teobert Maler en Cuevas Yucatecas," *Boletín de la Escuela de Ciencias Antropológicas de la Universidad de Yucatán* 8–9 (48–49): 20–31.

STROMSVIK, GUSTAV
1937   "Notes on the Metates from Calakmul, Campeche, and from the Mercado, Chichen Itza, Yucatan," Contribution 16, *Carnegie Institution of Washington Publication 456* (Washington, D.C.).

STUART, GEORGE E.
1975   "Riddle of the Glyphs," *National Geographic* 148 (6): 768–91.
1981   "Maya Art Treasures Discovered in Cave," *National Geographic*, 160 (2): 221–35.

STUART, GEORGE E., JOHN C. SCHEFFLER, EDWARD B. KURJACK, AND JOHN W. COTTIER
1979   *Map of the Ruins of Dzibilchaltun, Yucatan, Mexico*, Middle American Research Institute Publication no. 47 (New Orleans: Tulane University).

STUCKENRATH, ROBERT, JR.
1977   "Radiocarbon: Some Notes from Merlin's Diary," in *Amerinds and Their Paleoenvironments in Northeastern North America*, eds. W. Newman and B. Salwen (New York: New York Academy of Sciences).

STUCKENRATH, ROBERT, JR., WILLIAM R. COE, AND ELIZABETH K. RALPH
1966   "University of Pennsylvania Radiocarbon Dates IX," *Radiocarbon* 8: 348–85.

TASCHEK, JENNIFER T.
1981   "The Non-Ceramic, Non-Chipped Stone Artifacts from Dzibil-

chaltun, Yucatan, Mexico," Ph.D. diss., University of Wisconsin, Madison.

n.d.   *The Artifacts of Dzibilchaltun, Yucatan, Mexico: Shell, Polished Stone, Bone, Wood and Ceramics*, Middle American Research Institute Publication no. 50 (New Orleans: Tulane University). In press.

TEEPLE, JOHN E.

1930   "Maya Astronomy," in *Contributions to American Archaeology* no. 2, Carnegie Institution of Washington Publicaton 403: 29–115 (Washington, D.C.).

THOMAS, CYRUS

1881a   "An Attempt to Reconcile the Differences Between Authorities in Reference to the Maya Calendar and Certain Dates; Also to Determine the Age of the Manuscript Troano," *American Naturalist* 15: 767–72.

1881b   "The Manuscript Troano," *American Naturalist* 15: 625–41.

1882   A *Study of the Manuscript Troano*, Contributions to North American Ethnology, vol. 5 (Washington, D.C.: U.S. Department of the Interior).

1886   "Discoveries in the Mexican and Maya Codices," *American Antiquarian* 8: 69–76.

THOMAS, PRENTICE M., JR.

1981   *Prehistoric Maya Settlement Patterns at Becan, Campeche, Mexico*, Middle American Research Institute Publication no. 45 (New Orleans: Tulane University).

THOMPSON, EDWARD H., AND J. ERIC S. THOMPSON

1938   "The High Priest's Grave, Chichen Itza, Yucatan, Mexico," *Field Museum of Natural History Publication 412*, pp. 1–64. (Reprinted in 1968 by Kraus Reprint, New York.)

THOMPSON, J. ERIC S.

1927   "A Correlation of the Mayan and European Calendars," *Field Museum of Natural History Publication 241*, pp. 1–22 (Chicago, Field Museum).

1932   "A Maya Calendar from the Atlas Vera Paz, Guatemala," *American Anthropologist* 34: 449–54.

1935   "Maya Chronology: The Correlation Question," in *Contributions to American Archaeology* no. 14, Carnegie Institution Publication 456, pp. 51–104 (Washington, D.C.).

1937   "A New Method of Deciphering Yucatecan Dates with Special Reference to Chichen Itza," in *Contributions to American Archaeology* 22, Carnegie Institution of Washington Publication no. 483, pp. 177–97 (Washington, D.C.).

1939   *Excavation at San Jose, British Honduras*, Carnegie Institution of Washington Publication no. 506 (Washington, D.C.).

1940   *Late Ceramic Horizons at Benque Viejo, British Honduras*, Car-

509

negie Institution of Washington Contributions to American Anthropology and History no. 35 (Washington, D.C.).

1941a   "Dating of Certain Inscriptions of Non-Maya Origin," *Theoretical Approaches to Problems* no. 1, Carnegie Institution of Washington, Division of Historical Research (Cambridge, Mass.).

1941b   "A Coordination of the History of Chichen Itza with Ceramic Sequences in Central Mexico," *Revista Mexicana de Estudios Antropológicos* 5: 97–111.

1942   "Representations of Tezcatlipoca at Chichen Itza," *Notes on Middle American Archaeology and Ethnology* no. 12, Carnegie Institution of Washington, Department of Archaeology (Cambridge, Mass.).

1945   "A Survey of the Northern Maya Area," *American Antiquity* 11: 2–24.

1946   "Review of *The Origins and History of the Mayas; in Three Parts: Part I: Introductory Investigations*, by M. Wells Jakeman," *American Antiquity* 11: 205–6.

1950   *Maya Hieroglyphic Writing: Introduction*, Carnegie Institution of Washington Publication 589 (Washington, D.C.).

1951   "The Itza of Tayasal, Peten," in *Homenaje al Doctor Alfonso Caso*, pp. 389–400 (Mexico, D.F.: Imprenta Nuevo Mundo).

1953   "A Stela at San Lorenzo, Southeastern Campeche," *Notes on Middle American Archaeology and Ethnology*, no. 115, Carnegie Institution of Washington, Department of Archaeology (Cambridge, Mass.).

1959   "Review of *Chichen Itza and its Cenote of Sacrifice*, by Alfred M. Tozzer," *American Journal of Archaeology* 63: 119–20.

1970   *Maya History and Religion* (Norman: University of Oklahoma Press).

1972   *The Maya of Belize: Historical Chapters Since Columbus* (Belize: Benex Press).

1973   "The Painted Capstone at Sacnicte, Yucatan, and Two Others at Uxmal," *Indiana* 1: 59–63 (Berlin).

1977   "The Hieroglyphic Texts of Las Monjas and Their Bearing on Building Activities," in *Las Monjas: A Major Pre-Mexican Architectural Complex at Chichen Itza*, by John S. Bolles, pp. 262–67 (Norman: University of Oklahoma Press).

THOMPSON, J. ERIC S., H. E. D. POLLOCK, AND JEAN CHARLOT

1932   *A Preliminary Study of the Ruins of Coba, Quintana Roo, Mexico*, Carnegie Institution of Washington Publication 424 (Washington, D.C.).

THOMPSON, PHILIP C.

1978   "Tekanto in the Eighteenth Century," Ph.D. diss., Tulane University.

TIO, A.
1972   "Historia del Descubrimiento de la Florida y Beimeni o Yucatan,"
        Boletín de la Academia Puertoriquena de la Historia 2 (8).
TOURTELLOT III, GAIR
1970   "The Peripheries of Seibal: An Interim Report," in Monographs
        and Papers in Maya Archaeology, ed. William R. Bullard, pp.
        405–19. Papers of the Peabody Museum, vol. 61 (Cambridge,
        Mass.: Harvard University).
1982   "Ancient Maya Settlement at Seibal, Peten, Guatemala: Peripheral
        Survey and Excavation," Ph.D. diss., Harvard University.
1983   "An Assessment of Classic Maya Household Composition," in
        Prehistoric Settlement Patterns, Essays in Honor of Gordon R.
        Willey, eds. Evon Z. Vogt and Richard M. Leventhal, pp. 35–54
        (Albuquerque: University of New Mexico Press, and Peabody Mu-
        seum, Harvard University).
TOURTELLOT III, GAIR, AND JEREMY A. SABLOFF
1972   "Exchange Systems Among the Ancient Maya," American Antiq-
        uity 37: 126–35.
TOZZER, ALFRED M.
1913   "A Spanish Manuscript Letter on the Lacandones in the Archives
        of the Indies in Seville," Eighteenth International Congress of
        Americanists (London, 1912), Acta 2: 496–509.
1930   "Maya and Toltec Figures at Chichen Itza," in Twenty-third In-
        ternational Congress of Americanists (New York, 1928), Acta, pp.
        155–64.
1941   Landa's Relación de las Cosas de Yucatán, Papers of the Peabody
(ed.   Museum of Archaeology and Ethnology, vol. 18 (Cambridge,
and   Mass.: Harvard University).
trans.)
1957   Chichen Itza and Its Cenote of Sacrifice: A Comparative Study of
        Contemporaneous Maya and Toltec, Memoirs of the Peabody Mu-
        seum, vols. 11 and 12 (Cambridge, Mass.: Harvard University).
TREJO ALVARADO, ELIA DEL CARMEN
1981   "El Meco: un asentamiento de la costa norte de Quintana Roo,"
        paper presented at the XVII Mesa Redonda de la Sociedad Mex-
        icana de Antropología, San Cristobal de las Casas, Chiapas, Mex-
        ico.
TSCHOPIK, HARRY, JR.
1950   "An Andean Ceramic Tradition in Historical Perspective," Amer-
        ican Antiquity 15: 196–218.
TURNER II, B. L.
1974   "Prehistoric Intensive Agriculture in the Mayan Lowlands," Sci-
        ence 185: 118–24.
1983   "Comparison of Agrotechnologies in the Basin of Mexico and
        Central Maya Lowlands: Formative to the Classic Maya Collapse,"

in *Mesoamerica: Interdisciplinary Approaches*, ed. Arthur G. Miller, pp. 13–47 (Washington, D.C.: Dumbarton Oaks).

TURNER II, B. L., AND PETER D. HARRISON
1981   "Prehistoric Raised-Field Agriculture in the Maya Lowlands: Pull-trouser Swamp, Northern Belize," *Science* 213: 399–405.

VAILLANT, GEORGE C.
1927   "The Chronological Significance of Maya Ceramics," Ph.D. diss., Harvard University.
1935   "Chronology and Stratigraphy in the Maya Area," *Maya Research* 2: 119–43.
1938   "A Correlation of Archaeological and Historical Sequences in the Valley of Mexico," *American Anthropologist* 40: 535–73.

VALENTINI, PHILIPP J. J.
1880   "The Katunes of Maya History," *Proceedings of the American Antiquarian Society* 74: 45–102.

VALÉSQUEZ VALADEZ, RICARDO
1976   "Informe de las exploraciones arqueológicas y trabajos de mantenimiento en la zona de Tulum, Quintana Roo, 1975," in *Investigaciones Arqueologicas en el Sureste*, Cuadernos de los Centros 27: 19–83 (Mexico, D.F.: Instituto Nacional de Antropología e Historia).

VARGAS PACHECO, ERNESTO
1978   "Los Asentamientos Prehispanicos y la Arquitectura en la Isla Can Cún, Quintana Roo," *Estudios de Cultura Maya* 11: 95–112.

VILLAGUTIERRE SOTO-MAYOR, JUAN DE
1933   *Historia de la Conquista de la Provincia de el Itza* (Guatemala: Biblioteca Guatemala). (First edition, Madrid, 1701.)

VLCEK, DAVID T.
1978   "Muros de delimitación residencial en Chunchucmil," *Boletín de la Escuela de Ciencias Antropológicas de la Universidad de Yucatán* 5 (28): 55–64.

VLCEK, DAVID T., SILVIA GARZA T. DE GONZÁLEZ, AND EDWARD B. KURJACK
1978   "Contemporary Farming and Ancient Maya Settlements: Some Disconcerting Evidence," in *Pre-Hispanic Maya Agriculture*, eds. Peter D. Harrison and B. L. Turner II, pp. 211–23 (Albuquerque: University of New Mexico Press).

VOKES, ARTHUR
1977   "Shelling Out: The Role of Mollusks in a Postclassic Maya Economy," paper presented at the Forty-second Annual Meeting of the Society for American Archaeology, New Orleans.
1978   "They Don't Make Them Like They Used To," paper presented at the Forty-third Annual Meeting of the Society for American Archaeology, Tucson.

WAUCHOPE, ROBERT
1947   "An Approach to the Maya Correlation Problem Through Gua-

temala Highland Archaeology and Native Annals," *American Antiquity* 13: 59–66.

1948   *Excavations at Zacualpa, Guatemala*, Middle American Research Institute Publication 14 (New Orleans: Tulane University).

1954   "Implications of Radiocarbon Dates from Middle and South America," *Middle American Research Records* 2 (2): 17–40, Middle American Research Institute Publication 18 (New Orleans: Tulane University).

1968   *Activities of the Middle American Research Institute, 1957–1967*, Middle American Research Institute, Miscellaneous Series 12 (New Orleans: Tulane University).

1970   "Protohistoric Pottery of the Guatemala Highlands," in *Monographs and Papers in Maya Archaeology*, ed. William R. Bullard, pp. 89–244. Papers of the Peabody Museum, vol. 61 (Cambridge, Mass.: Harvard University).

1975   *Zacualpa, El Quiche, Guatemala: An Ancient Provincial Center of the Highland Maya*, Middle American Research Institute Publication 39 (New Orleans: Tulane University).

WEBB, MALCOLM C.

1973   "The Peten Maya Decline Viewed in the Perspective of State Formation," in *The Classic Maya Collapse*, ed. T. Patrick Culbert, pp. 367–404 (Albuquerque: University of New Mexico Press, School of American Research Advanced Seminar Series).

WEBSTER, DAVID L.

1976a   *Defensive Earthworks at Becan, Campeche, Mexico: Implications for Maya Warfare*, Middle American Research Institute Publication 41 (New Orleans: Tulane University).

1976b   "Lowland Maya Fortifications," *Proceedings of the American Philosophical Society* 120: 361–71.

1977   "Warfare and the Evolution of Maya Civilization," in *The Origins of Maya Civilization*, ed. Richard E. W. Adams, pp. 335–72 (Albuquerque: University of New Mexico Press, School of American Research Advanced Seminar Series).

1978   "Three Walled Sites of the Northern Maya Lowlands," *Journal of Field Archaeology* 5: 375–90.

1979   "Cuca, Chacchob, Dzonot Ake—Three Walled Northern Maya Centers," *Occasional Papers in Anthropology* no. 11 (University Park: Department of Anthropology, Pennsylvania State University).

WEIDIE, A. E.

1974 (ed.)   *Field Seminar on Water and Carbonate Rocks of the Yucatan Peninsula, Mexico* (New Orleans: New Orleans Geological Society).

WEITZEL, ROBERT B.

1930   "Maya Chronological Systems," *American Journal of Archaeology* 34: 182–89.

1931a   "Uxmal Inscriptions," *American Journal of Archaeology* 35: 53–56.

1931b   "The Books of Chilam Balam as Tradition," *American Journal of Archaeology* 35: 319–23.

WILK, RICHARD R., AND WILLIAM L. RATHJE

1982   "Household Archaeology," *American Behavioral Scientist* 25 (6): 617–40.

WILLEY, GORDON R.

1956   *Prehistoric Settlement Patterns in the New World*, Viking Fund
(ed.)   Publications in Anthropology no. 23 (New York: Wenner-Gren Foundation for Anthropological Research).

1965   "Artifacts," in *Prehistoric Maya Settlements in the Belize Valley*, by Gordon R. Willey, William R. Bullard, Jr., John B. Glass, and James C. Gifford, pp. 391–522. Papers of the Peabody Museum, vol. 54 (Cambridge, Mass.: Harvard University).

1973a   "Certain Aspects of the Late Classic to Postclassic Periods in the Belize Valley," in *The Classic Maya Collapse*, ed. T. Patrick Culbert, pp. 93–106 (Albuquerque: University of New Mexico Press, School of American Research Advanced Seminar Series).

1973b   *The Altar de Sacrificios Excavations: General Summary and Conclusions*, Papers of the Peabody Museum, vol. 64, no. 3 (Cambridge, Mass.: Harvard University).

1974   "The Classic Maya Hiatus: A Rehearsal for the Collapse?," in *Mesoamerican Archaeology: New Approaches*, ed. Norman Hammond, pp. 417–31 (Austin: University of Texas Press).

1977   "The Rise of Classic Maya Civilization: A Pasion Valley Perspective," in *The Origins of Maya Civilization*, ed. Richard E. W. Adams, pp. 133–57 (Albuquerque: University of New Mexico Press, School of American Research Advanced Seminar Series).

1978   *Excavations at Seibal, Department of Peten, Guatemala: Artifacts*, Memoirs of the Peabody Museum, vol. 14, no. 1 (Cambridge, Mass.: Harvard University).

1979   "Highland Culture Contacts in the Lowland Maya Area: An Introductory Commentary," *Actes du XLII Congrès International des Americanistes* (Paris, 1976) 8: 213–20 (Paris: Société des Americanistes).

1981   "Maya Lowland Settlement Patterns: A Summary Review," in *Lowland Maya Settlement Patterns*, ed. Wendy Ashmore, pp. 385–415 (Albuquerque: University of New Mexico Press, School of American Research Advanced Seminar Series).

1982   "Maya Archeology," *Science* 215: 260–67.

1984   "Changing Conceptions of Lowland Maya Culture History," *Journal of Anthropological Research* 40: 41–59.

WILLEY, GORDON R., AND RICHARD M. LEVENTHAL

1979   "Prehistoric Settlement at Copan," in *Maya Archaeology and*

Ethnohistory, eds. Norman Hammond and Gordon R. Willey, pp. 75–102 (Austin: University of Texas Press).

WILLEY, GORDON R., AND DMITRI B. SHIMKIN
1973   "The Maya Collapse: A Summary View," in *The Classic Maya Collapse*, ed. T. Patrick Culbert, pp. 457–501 (Albuquerque: University of New Mexico Press, School of American Research Advanced Seminar Series).

WILLEY, GORDON R., AND A. LEDYARD SMITH
1967   "Seibal 1966: Third Preliminary Report," manuscript on file at the Peabody Museum, Harvard University.

WILLEY, GORDON R., RICHARD M. LEVENTHAL, AND WILLIAM L. FASH, JR.
1978   "Maya Settlement in the Copan Valley," *Archaeology* 31 (4): 32–44.

WILLEY, GORDON R., WILLIAM R. BULLARD, JR., JOHN B. GLASS, AND JAMES C. GIFFORD
1965   *Prehistoric Maya Settlements in the Belize Valley*, Papers of the Peabody Museum, vol. 54 (Cambridge, Mass.: Harvard University).

WILLEY, GORDON R., A. LEDYARD SMITH, GAIR TOURTELLOT III, AND IAN GRAHAM
1975   *Excavations at Seibal, Department of Peten, Guatemala: Introduction: The Site and Its Setting*, Memoirs of the Peabody Museum, vol. 13, no. 1 (Cambridge, Mass.: Harvard University).

WING, ELIZABETH S., AND DAVID STEADMAN
1980   "Vertebrate Faunal Remains from Dzibilchaltun," Appendix to *Excavations at Dzibilchaltun, Yucatan, Mexico*, by E. Wyllys Andrews IV and E. Wyllys Andrews V, pp. 326–31. Middle American Research Institute Publication 48 (New Orleans: Tulane University).

WONDERLEY, A. W.
1981   *Late Postclassic Excavations at Naco, Honduras*, Latin American Studies Program Dissertation Series 86 (Ithaca: Cornell University).

WREN, LINNEA, AND PETER SCHMIDT
1984   "A New Sculpture from the Great Ball Court at Chichen Itza," paper presented at the Annual Meeting of the Society for American Archaeology, Portland, Oregon.

Index

Abascal, R. P., 426
Adams, Richard E. W., 23, 24, 56, 281, 282, 292, 349, 372, 400, 410, 411, 413; for ceramics, 170, 173, 332; for chronology, 104, 119, 120,135
Adams, W. Y., 290
agriculture, 28, 74, 410–12
aguada, 264
ah cuch cab, 351, 364
Allen, William L., 353
Altar de Sacrificios, 24, 44, 83, 135, 335
Altun Ha, 23, 35, 224–27, 335
Andrews, Anthony P., 30, 54, 58, 62, 63, 64, 71, 72, 91, 149, 190, 440, 450; for architecture, 67, 93, 202, 371; for ceramics, 171, 172, 173, 175, 182; for economics, 74, 75, 83, 87, 89; for trade, 203
Andrews IV, E. Wyllys, 13, 30, 58, 63, 64, 72, 73, 74, 76, 89, 169, 381, 391, 392, 421, 424, 439, 442, 447; for architecture, 67, 93, 202, 371; for ceramics, 165, 171, 177; for Chichen Itza, 59, 142, 145,

184, 436, 452; for chronology, 65–67, 82, 102, 103, 104, 112, 114, 141, 144; for Dzibilchaltun, 29, 39, 148
Andrews V, E. Wyllys, 57, 58, 141, 144, 150, 391, 396, 411, 420, 439, 447; for ceramics, 85, 165, 171, 172, 177, 182; for chronology, 65–67, 85, 103, 104, 117, 141, 144, 149; for Dzibilchaltun, 29, 39, 148, 422, 424, 428; for regionalism, 437, 440, 442, 444
Andrews, George, 58, 67
Andrews, Joann M., 394
architecture: building activity reviewed by zone, 19, 22–30; coastal shrines, 218; comparisons, 38, 304, 305, 311–15, 333, 342, 423, 435; foreign, 202–6, 370; pure or traditional, 145, 151–55, 160–64, 188, 190; range structures, 152, 270; religious shrine, 367; research reviewed, 58, 59, 62, 67; social elements, 153–55, 160, 188, 331, 332, 339, 354, 367, 370–72; spatial and temporal distribution, 316–30;

517

519

Index